BATTLE REPORT

BATTLE REPORT

PEARL HARBOR TO CORAL SEA

Prepared from Official Sources by

Commander Walter Karig, USNR

and

Lieutenant Welbourn Kelley, USNR

PUBLISHED FOR THE COUNCIL ON BOOKS IN WARTIME BY

FARRAR & RINEHART, INC. • 1944

New York • Toronto

This book has been manufactured in accordance with paper conservation orders of the War Production Board.

The illustrations for this book were selected and edited by Commander E. John Long, USNR, assisted by C. Earl Cooley, Sp(P) 1/c, USNR. Charts and maps were drawn especially by George Sixta, Sp(P) 1/c, USNR. All pictures are Official United States Navy Photographs unless otherwise designated.

Notes on the Background and Writing of this Book

WHEN the authors of this book were directed by Secretary of the Navy Frank Knox to begin its preparation, a few months before his death, the instructions were brief and to the point.

"Tell the story of the Navy's part in this war," he said. "Particularly those early days, when the Japs were having things their own way, and when we had to examine every scrap of information with a microscope for fear it would be helpful to the enemy. Admiral King has agreed that it is now possible to release much of the information which, up to now, we have had to hold back. Tell the whole story, in a nontechnical, readable form, the good and the bad."

With those instructions, the authors selected for the first volume the period treated within these pages—a period that is nearly all defeat, but defeat in a manner of which every United States citizen can well be proud: The story of officers and men who fought with all the weapons they had, who continued to fight against overwhelming odds as often as the enemy challenged, and as often took the initiative themselves. Succeeding volumes are projected to cover the Navy's war in the Atlantic, and Pacific operations from the Coral Sea onward.

Before a line of this present volume was written the authors decided (and they hope wisely) to tell their story with complete objectivity, eschewing personal opinions, and confining themselves to the simple description of *what happened to the Navy's men and ships and planes and bases.* Thus there was avoided any discussion of strategy and tactics, any analysis or evaluation of battle plans, logistics or international diplomacy. Even when viewed from the standpoint of time and fuller knowledge, aspects of battle differ in the eyes of each new beholder. For instance, historians still find themselves unable to name with unanimity the winner of the Battle of Jutland.

This, then, is a simple book, told with all the honesty and integrity with which its authors have been endowed.

Professional writers on naval operations in this war will naturally want to know how much factual material was removed when the manuscript received its final review for security. The answer is a very happy one: Very little was deleted, and that little left the narrative unimpaired. As commissioned officers, the authors have some knowledge of the technical information which the enemy would like to know—technical details of armor, armament and other equipment. The authors decided in the beginning to leave out such details, not only in the interest of security but because such technical details were irrelevant to a nontechnical work. Otherwise they set themselves to tell the story in full. Professional writers on naval subjects, after viewing the information contained herein, should find it easy to understand how little has been unsaid, either by omission or by deletion from the final manuscript. Just as the authors accept full responsibility for all that has been left out of this book, they likewise are responsible for all that it contains, and the manner of its presentation. (Every author tends to find one particular incident of more interest than another, and to give more space to that which interests him; and most authors, in the effort to achieve dramatic unity, select only those incidents which seem to demand inclusion in the formation of a rounded and entire picture. Without this process of selectivity, the result is often a mere catalogue of names, places and events—a school of history writing, however, which also has its admirers.)

Once having decided upon the method of presentation, the authors then proceeded to the task of gathering their material. Fortunately, either one or both of the authors were able to interview actual participants in every battle or engagement described. The interviews were supplemented from several sources of information: by recorded interviews on file in the Navy Department Office of Records and Library; by first-person accounts turned in by participants in battles and engagements; by reports and official data too numerous to itemize; by personal recollections written or dictated by naval personnel and forwarded to the authors from many parts of the globe; and by a small amount of previously published material.

Where published material was used, credits will be found in footnotes to the text. So little of the material contained herein has been previously published, however, that it has been found unnecessary to include a bibliography. No list of official sources is included because these sources come within a restricted category during wartime.

Many persons have helped in the preparation of this book, either by providing information, or access to information, or by giving helpful advice. Many of them are mentioned in the text as participants in action, and so are not mentioned here again. A number of others—and some of them were particularly helpful—specifically asked that they receive no credit. Their help is gratefully, if anonymously, acknowledged.

Much information and assistance was provided by the attachés in Washington of the Navies of the United Nations: the British Admiralty, the Royal Netherlands Navy, the Royal Australian Navy, the Royal New Zealand Navy, and the Chinese Navy.

Among naval personnel who should be mentioned as having assisted this work in their official capacities are Mr. Eugene Duffield, special assistant to the Secretary of the Navy; Captain Dudley W. Knox, USN (Ret.), of the Office of Naval Records and Library, himself an historian of considerable note and Commander P. T. Wright, USN (Ret.), assistant to Captain Knox; the officers in Captain Knox's office, particularly Lieutenant George Porter, USNR; Mrs. Jane F. Blakeney, civilian employee of the Marine Corps; the Misses Helene and Estelle Philibert of the Reference Section, Navy Department, Office of Public Relations; Commander William C. Chambliss, USNR, whose help was so extensive that at times he almost became a collaborator; and Captain John S. Phillips, USN, a source of guidance and practical advice.

Especial thanks are saved to the last for two persons widely separated in the naval hierarchy.

One is a petty officer in the WAVES, Yeoman Second Class Elvina Joan Sudol, who served as amanuensis, office manager, typist, copyist, occasional reseacher, final authority on spelling—and who is a fine example of the young women who are now serving in blue.

The other is Admiral Harry E. Yarnell USN (Ret.), whose help, friendship and advice will be remembered and cherished long after this war is over, and when the authors once again will subscribe themselves simply as

WALTER KARIG
WELBOURN KELLEY

Washington, D. C.
9 September 1944

Table of Contents

List of Illustrations

MAPS

PHOTOGRAPHS

Photographs appear in four sections. General classification headings are as follows:

PART ONE

And Then There Was War

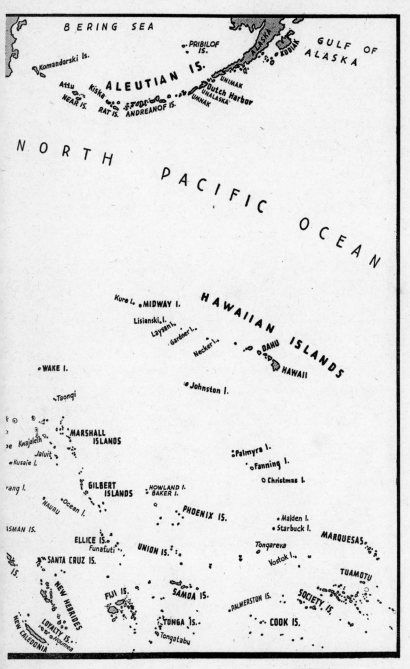

FIGURE I

Chapter One

O N the last day of peace in the Pacific, on December 6, 1941, Japan's Navy was already stronger than the combined Pacific fleets of the nations she was to make her adversaries.

By noon of December 7, Pearl Harbor time, Japan was without dispute the ruler of that greatest of oceans, at least temporarily. It was a mastery that Tojo's Samurai hoped would be permanently extended to all seas. Actually, Japan's domination of the Pacific lasted less than six months.

The Imperial Japanese Fleet was in reality smaller than the combined sea power of the United States, but Japan's was concentrated whereas that of the United States had to be divided between two oceans. In the Atlantic, Germany's aggressive submarine invasion of all the Atlantic waters had reached the stage of undeclared war in the sinking of the American destroyer USS REUBEN JAMES on October 31, the torpedoing of the USS KEARNY and the Navy tanker SALINAS a fortnight earlier. German submarines were attacking American vessels without warning. It was necessary to provide our shipping with the protection of our warships, or else abjectly surrender the western Atlantic to the Fascists' challenge.

Thus, of the 216 major combat surface craft of the United States Navy—battleships, aircraft carriers, cruisers, and destroyers—114 were on the Atlantic side of the continent. The 102 others were ranged over the Pacific from the Philippines to the coast of South America, about two-thirds of them being berthed in Pearl Harbor, Oahu Island, Territory of Hawaii, on the morning of "this day that will live in infamy."

Against these 102 and the approximately 50 combat surface craft of the Netherlands and the nations of the British Commonwealth, Japan had at least 180 fighting ships, probably more. To the initial advantage of numerical superiority, Japan added the priceless ingredients of tactical position and surprise attack.

5

Japan was, therefore, gambling with loaded dice in a game whose rules were written in Tokyo, when she interrupted the negotiations of her peace-proclaiming ambassadors with the epochal treachery at Pearl Harbor.

A goodly part of Japan's total striking power was employed in that assault, although the only contact was with the enemy's pygmy submarines. There were two powerful task forces sent against Pearl Harbor, the major elements of one lurking just over the horizon from its companion fleet to overwhelm any American attempt to engage the invaders.

The United States, too, had two task forces at sea, and Japanese espionage had so informed Tokyo. One task force was returning from Midway and the other one was bound there from Wake, with the whole chain of the Hawaiian Islands between them and the invaders. The American task forces aggregated two carriers, six heavy cruisers, and fourteen destroyers. Berthed in Pearl Harbor were eight of the nine battleships of the United States Pacific Fleet, nine cruisers, and a third of the fleet's destroyers. One battleship, COLORADO, was in overhaul at the Bremerton Navy Yard, and the third of the Pacific carriers also was in a mainland harbor, scrubbing down after an overhaul.

Two heavy cruisers of the United States Pacific Fleet, INDIANAPOLIS and MINNEAPOLIS, were on patrol south of the islands; two, PENSACOLA and LOUISVILLE, were Manila-bound with convoys of troopships, all of which were diverted in time. One light cruiser, BOISE, had recently arrived in Philippine waters with a convoy, where HOUSTON and MARBLE-HEAD were already stationed with 13 destroyers to form the Asiatic fleet. Three other light cruisers, RICHMOND, CONCORD and TRENTON, were prowling the southeastern Pacific.

In the Atlantic were eight battleships, four carriers, five heavy cruisers and eight light cruisers, and between 80 and 90 destroyers. That was the size and the disposition of the United States fleet on the eve of Pearl Harbor.

One of the ships at Pearl was the destroyer USS WARD . . .

2

USS WARD was slightly on the decrepit side, but she was Lieutenant William Woodward Outerbridge's first command, and he was proud of her.

Outerbridge had been executive officer of USS CUMMINGS, one of the more modern destroyers, when he was promoted to the command of the WARD, which was named for Commander James Harmon Ward, first naval officer killed in the War Between the States. The WARD was a product of the 1918 construction frenzy, an obsolescent four-piper which had been launched in the world's record time of seventeen and a half days after her keel was laid in the Mare Island Navy Yard on May 15 in that "last year of the war." She had been catalogued as over-age since July 24, 1934, and although the destroyer had been reconditioned a year or so before, her designed top speed of 30-plus knots would cause her to get lost in the wake of the newer tin cans. Her 4-inch 50-caliber guns were antiques beside the dual-purpose 5-inch 38's of later destroyers, and they could not be elevated sufficiently to serve as antiaircraft weapons.

But still she was a fighting ship. Most important, she was *his* ship, and as his first command the name WARD would echo fondly in his memory all the rest of his life. (In this respect it could be pointed out that a certain other officer might have felt it to be a personal blow when, in 1937, the Japanese coolly bombed and sank the old Yangtze River gunboat PANAY. An older PANAY, the gunboat's predecessor in Asiatic waters, had been Ensign Chester W. Nimitz's first command, back in 1907; and Admiral Chester W. Nimitz, as Commander in Chief Pacific Fleet, later found himself in an excellent position from which to exact revenge for the insult to what to him was a proud and fondly remembered name.)

And so Outerbridge proudly took the WARD to sea. The date was December 5, 1941.

There were reasons, too, for Outerbridge to consider his ship a better than average assignment. Her station was not in the bleak North Atlantic, where for some time an undeclared war had been carried into American waters by German submarines. The WARD's job was to patrol the sea lanes converging on Pearl Harbor. This meant shore leave after each three days at sea, with the opportunity to see family and friends; and this, of course, was a welcome change from the constant cramped routine Outerbridge had known on the CUMMINGS.

"It felt pretty good to be able to see a newspaper once in a while," Outerbridge recalls, "or to take in a movie."

For instance, on this coming Sunday night of December 7, after the

WARD was berthed again in Pearl Harbor, Outerbridge recalls he had thought of going to the Waikiki Theater in Honolulu to see *A Yank In the R.A.F.* That is, if he didn't decide to take in *The Great Dictator* at the Princess. Or, maybe, he would just relax from the strain of his first command by reading the newspapers.

To a professional Navy man, each day brought news of utmost interest. Was there going to be war with Japan? The Honolulu *Star-Bulletin,* of the date on which Outerbridge stood out to sea on his own bridge, proclaimed in an 8-column front page headline: "Japan Parries Open U. S. Break," and the story read:

> TOKYO, Dec. 5 (AP)—A Japanese government spokesman expressed the belief today that the United States and Japan will "continue with sincerity to find a common formula for a peaceful solution in the Pacific." . . .

The spokesman declared himself grieved that Secretary Hull appeared "to allege that we are following a policy of force and conquest in establishing a military despotism."

But there was other news not so cheering. In Singapore, all military and naval leaves had been canceled. Clark Lee, Associated Press correspondent in Manila, cabled that President Manuel Quezon urged all "nonessential civilians" to leave "danger zones."

3

That month of December had just begun when HMS PRINCE OF WALES and REPULSE steamed up the straits of Johore to Singapore with the white ensign of Britain at their mastheads. From the harbors of the Netherlands East Indies, Queen Wilhelmina's submarines and destroyers quietly left to inspect the waters between Java, Sumatra, Borneo, and the Celebes.

At sea, near the end of this first week of December, was the carrier USS LEXINGTON, accompanied by three cruisers and five destroyers, on a combined search and battle problem which took them to the south and westward. Rear Admiral John Henry Newton was in command of the force, and his flag was in the heavy cruiser USS CHICAGO, one of the NORTHAMPTON class. Among the other ships in the task force was USS

DRAYTON, a destroyer of the MAHAN class known to the fleet as the "Blue Beetle" because of her peculiar (and experimental) color. Captain of DRAYTON was Lieutenant Commander Laurence A. Abercrombie, USN, of the Academy class of '21, "Abe" to everybody until a few months later when Admiral Halsey gave him the more resounding sobriquet of the "one-man scourge of the Pacific."

Far to the westward, USS ENTERPRISE, the only other carrier active in the Pacific, was delivering a dozen Marine fighter pilots in Grumman Wildcats to Wake Island. As the flagship, as well as the burden-bearer, of a task force which included three cruisers and nine destroyers, the ENTERPRISE flew at her stubby mainmast the three-starred bunting of Vice-Admiral William F. Halsey, Jr., known variously (and mostly behind his back) as "Bull" Halsey, "Stud" Halsey, and simply as the "Old Man."

According to the subsequent Roberts report, the Japanese, through their espionage, had a very good idea where all these ships were heading, and when they were due to return.

USS SARATOGA was in San Diego for repairs, the third carrier in the Pacific unless you count the venerable seaplane tender LANGLEY, the Navy's first carrier, based in Philippine waters. Operating off the Atlantic coast were the flat-tops WASP, YORKTOWN, and RANGER. The HORNET was on her shakedown, which was to be abruptly terminated. That was the United States fleet aircraft carrier total in December, 1941—six and the newly commissioned HORNET.

Special mention is made of carriers here because no ship of this type was sunk or damaged in the Pearl Harbor raid, and these ships later were to become the spearhead of our attacks on much stronger enemy forces.

4

The twelve Marine pilots on the ENTERPRISE wondered what it was all about. They had received such short notice of their departure that some had reported on board with no more than the clothes they stood in.

The Navy had determined that the Marines' mission was to be a secret. With the war scare steadily mounting in the Far East, the Commander in Chief Pacific Fleet (according to the subsequent Roberts Report) had already ordered instant attack upon any alien submarine found in the Oahu operational area.

So the scout pilots aboard the ENTERPRISE were ordered to keep a sharp lookout for any strange planes or ships which might be operating to observe and report on the carrier's mission.

Not until the second day at sea from Pearl Harbor did the entire ship know that the ENTERPRISE was headed for Wake, and that the Marine aviators were to be left there to reinforce that tiny American outpost against possible attack in the future.

The days thereafter were very busy, and likewise the nights, as the entire officer and enlisted personnel of Fighting Six taught Marine Major Paul A. Putnam's fliers the intricacies of the F4F, then new to the naval service and almost totally strange to the Marines. Much was to be heard of this fighter plane, the Grumman 'Wildcat', in the bloody months to come. Much was to be heard of the "Big E," and of Fighting Six whose commanding officer, Lieutenant Commander Clarence W. Mc-Clusky, USN, was to be decorated for his conspicuous part in turning back the Japanese at Midway. And much more was to be heard, much sooner, of Major Putnam and all the Marines on Wake Island.

Also aboard the ENTERPRISE was a junior-grade lieutenant, a "jay-gee" in the Navy's clipped nomenclature, who had been designated to keep an unofficial history of VF-6, "Fighting Six." This was to be a record of wardroom cribbage and acey-deucey tournaments, and such matters of moment, including the legendary appetite of one certain pilot, the public progress of another's love affairs, and the foibles of all.

But History is no respecter of persons, even of those persons who are sometimes unwittingly called upon to write history:

Tuesday, December 1, 1941: Crossed international date-line. Bound for Wake Island. No such day as December 1. It is now December 2. Everybody up on the flight deck after sunset. When the ship is dark a beautiful moonlight night seems even more beautiful. At least, an awful lot of hard-boiled blue jackets think so, tonight.

And:

Wednesday, December 3, 1941: The group commander took the Marines into Wake Island. All landed okay. Now let's get the hell out

*of here before they leave us. (Later) Vogt says he saw a large fleet at the
end of his scouting leg, but it was hazy and his tanks were low, so he
isn't sure. Some imagination!*

Because this incident has been magnified and variously interpreted in
the press, in magazine articles and books, here are the facts:

Vogt—Ensign John H. L. Vogt, Jr., USN—may have seen something afloat, but it was not a Japanese fleet on its way to Pearl Harbor,
or in all probability, Japanese warships bound anywhere on a mission of
attack. The enemy's approach was on an entirely different course. Had
conditions permitted an investigation, and even verification, of Vogt's
report, the results would not have averted the attack on Pearl Harbor, or
Hong Kong or Kota Bharu.

But the ENTERPRISE was on a secret mission, under radio silence, and
with strict orders not to be discovered, so there was nothing her captain
or the Admiral could do about Vogt's report.

It must stand as one of the grim coincidences of war that Vogt took
off from the ENTERPRISE for Ford Island at dawn on December 7 and
flew into a swarm of the Japanese planes attacking Pearl Harbor. He
was shot down, and killed.

5

Honolulu had gone to bed on the night of December 6, 1941, discussing President Roosevelt's last-minute appeal to Emperor Hirohito
himself to avert war.

There was discussion, too, of the lead editorial in the *Star-Bulletin* that
night. "Still In The Planning Stage" was the headline of the editor's
comment on the detailed recommendations for a mobilization day which
Governor Poindexter's advisory committee had just handed him.

(On page 1, the headlines said that there was a "New Peace Effort
Urged in Tokyo—Joint Commission to Iron Out Deadlock With U.S.
Proposed." And another: "Jap Press Asks For War." On page 10, the
spokesman for a group of United States Senators inspecting the Caribbean defenses told an AP reporter that "the United States Navy can defeat the Japanese Navy any place, any time." The advertising columns
were dedicated to Christmas. Hollister's drugstores had a $1.95 "Aloha
Box—It's Different," and Tung Chun Tong at 473 North King St. an-

nounced the opening of a complete retail holiday liquor department. Patton's suggested more practical gifts, alarm clocks and typewriters. . . .)

But the M-day editorial was grim, and talked about war homeside. The recommendations of the governor's advisory committee were not enough, said the editorial, which continued:

"With this action, there is given the bland impression that administration of the provisions of the [Territorial Mobilization] act could, if necessary, be undertaken within 24 hours. But, on examination, this proves to be rather an optimistic comment. . . ."

As it turned out, the "bland impression" was not overoptimistic by more than an hour or so; for, in just about 24 hours after the editorial had been set in type, martial law had been declared and M-day had come to Honolulu.

6

The WARD was standing in for Pearl Harbor that night of December 6, having completed her first patrol under Lieutenant Outerbridge's command. After a check to make sure that all stations were manned and everything aboard shipshape, the new skipper turned in at around 2400—midnight.[1] There was no sea cabin on the WARD, so Outerbridge slept in the charthouse, just aft of the bridge. His bed was a wire bunk which could be easily stowed. There were, of course, comparatively good quarters below, but when a ship is at sea her captain is never far from the bridge.

Of course when the captain is asleep or resting he can be called at any time by the officer of the deck, whose duty it is to notify his superior at any hour of significant changes in the weather, deviations from the established course or speed, the sighting of shore points or ships, or anything else of however mild importance to the ship's mission.

Outerbridge recalls that he felt the usual nervousness of a young officer not yet wholly accustomed to his first full command, and so he dozed fitfully in the cramped wire cot atop the chartroom table. He was the only "regular Navy" officer aboard, of the Academy class of '27. All others of the ship's company and crew were Naval Reservists, prac-

[1] On shipboard time is measured from 0100, or 1:00 A.M., straight through to 2400. Thus 1200 is meridian, or noon; 1300 is 1:00 P.M., 1500 is 3:00 P.M., and so on.

tically all from the 47th Reserve division of St. Paul, Minnesota. But that did not worry the skipper. "They were a good bunch—they were all 4.0 boys," he said later. Four-point-o is Navy parlance for perfection.

The WARD was operating on only two of her four boilers, standard practice for the kind of work she was doing—cutting three-mile figure 8's by steaming up one side and drifting down the other with the tide. With half her power cut out, WARD had a top speed of 20 knots but she was not making that much when Outerbridge hazily heard, in his half-sleep, the shuffle of feet on deck plates as the men on the morning watch came up to relieve the midwatch.

The midwatch was not relieved at the stroke of eight bells that morning.

Two minutes before 0400 Ensign L. F. Platt, USNR, notified Outerbridge that a blinker signal had been received from the minesweeper CONDOR, informing WARD that she had detected a suspicious object in the darkness to the westward of her sweep area, and that she believed it to have been a submarine.

Outerbridge immediately ordered the ship to general quarters.

The gong sounded its summons. The ship sprang to life.

When general quarters is sounded aboard a ship it demands instant action from all, bar none except the helpless in sick bay. Gun crews race for the deck and ammunition handlers tumble below to magazines and hoists. Watertight doors clang shut and are dogged down. Damage control parties spring to their stations. First-aid equipment is broken out and placed at strategic points about the ship where it might be needed. Every man has a job to do—fast. For a minute or two all is apparently frenzy. Then comes quiet, as every man stands at his station awaiting orders.

Lieutenant H. T. Doughty, USNR, the executive officer, reached the bridge from his quarters below while the alarm was still sounding.

"What's up, Captain?"

Outerbridge told him, as he rang for all the speed WARD's two boilers would provide and as he conned the ship in the direction CONDOR had given.

The WARD searched for nearly an hour, combing a wide pattern and with all topside hands on lookout. No sound contact was made, no suspicious craft or object was sighted. Then she returned and spoke CONDOR again, this time by voice radio over the TBS (talk-between-ships) circuit. As intercepted and logged by a naval radio station on Oahu, the dialogue went:

WARD: What was the approximate distance and course of the submarine you sighted?

CONDOR: The course was about what we were steering at the time, 020 magnetic and about 1,000 yards from the entrance.

WARD: Do you have any additional information on the sub?

CONDOR: No additional information.

WARD: When was the last time approximately that you saw the submarine?

CONDOR: Approximately 0350 and he was apparently heading for the entrance.

"If the CONDOR people saw anything, it isn't out here now," Outerbridge concluded. "Secure from quarters, Mr. Doughty. Set condition two and keep a sharp lookout."

The bosun passed the word to secure, and the ship relaxed. Those men not on watch straggled back to their sleeping quarters and hit the sack. Doughty returned to his bunk, and Outerbridge to his cot in the charthouse. Ensign Platt turned over the deck to Lieutenant (jg) O. W. Goepner, USNR, a young Chicagoan who had entered the service via the naval ROTC unit at Northwestern University. He was also gunnery officer of the destroyer.

At 0637, Outerbridge was again awakened, this time by Goepner shouting: "Come on the bridge, Captain! Come on the bridge!"

Outerbridge grumbled sleepily, as he swung his feet to the floor. But what Goepner had to say caused the destroyer captain to cancel his comment on overzealous young Reserve officers. He grabbed his spectacles and Japanese kimono. On the bridge in the next instant he followed Goepner's excited directions: off the port bow was the target ship ANTARES, towing her cumbersome raft to Pearl Harbor, and between ship and raft was a smaller object which had no right to be there.

"We've been watching it, sir, and we think it's moving," Goepner said. He hurriedly explained that the object had been first sighted to port as WARD and ANTARES came abreast, and that he had ordered the destroyer's course reversed to bring it to closer view.

"Go to general quarters," instantly ordered Outerbridge. "Go to general quarters—and bear a hand!"

One look at the suspicious object, and he knew that it was a submarine conning tower; he knew, too, it was unlike any submarine's silhouette with which he was familiar. And, with that, ANTARES blinker-messaged her suspicion that she was being followed.

Later Outerbridge admitted to an awful moment when it occurred to him that the submarine might just possibly be one of our own; that if he attacked and sank it he would be sending some of his own brothers-in-arms to death. Whatever his thoughts, they caused no delay in his actions. He had his orders. He acted upon them.

Outerbridge rang up full speed and ordered the helmsman to come hard right and to head for the submarine.

"Load all guns and stand by to commence firing."

Over the battle circuit came the word: "Number one gun manned and ready, sir . . . Number two gun manned and ready . . ."

"Stand by to drop depth charges," ordered Outerbridge, and he told Goepner to fire when ready.

The WARD's new course was plotted just barely to miss collision with the submarine. As the destroyer bore down upon the target a Navy PBY, returning from long-range patrol, circled overhead and dropped a smoke bomb to help mark the submarine's location. In the confusion of the next few hours, the plane was first understood to have sunk a submarine. It was now about 0645, with a murky dawn rising behind the destroyer.

(From the far-distant ENTERPRISE, *the carrier's winged brood was taking off for Ford Island; from Japan's unseen and unsuspected carriers, the torpedo bombers were also roaring into the sky. Somewhere the fringe of the American flight intercepted the invader's course. Back on the* ENTERPRISE *listeners heard the voice of Ensign Manuel Gonzalez, USNR, of Bombing Squadron Six, come over the radio: "Don't shoot! This is an American plane." That was the last that was heard of Gonzalez.)*

The WARD was now within a hundred yards of the submarine.

"Commence firing," said Goepner, and number 1 gun in the bow of the destroyer loosed the first shot in the war of the Pacific!

The shell screamed over the target by inches and ricocheted into the sea. And now it was obvious that the submarine was truly a mystery ship, a pygmy whose conning tower presented only a sharpshooter's target.

Number 3 gun opened up from the waist of the ship. The WARD's range finders did not operate under 600 yards, so the gun was on the pointer fire, like a squirrel rifle, with a point-blank range of 75 yards.

The gun spoke and its detonation was echoed in a yell as the projectile was seen to strike the conning tower. As the WARD's stern crossed the bow of the diving submarine, Outerbridge ordered: "Drop depth charges!"

Chief Torpedoman W. C. Maskzawitz was at his station on the fantail, adjusting the pistols on the depth charges so that the explosions would meet the submarine at the stages of its estimated descent.

There were four short blasts of the ship's whistle, and with each blast an ashcan rolled off the stern into the submarine's path. The pattern was perfect.

"I let go the first charge just as the sub started under," Maskzawitz said later. "The second charge was already in the water when the first one exploded. I think the sub waded directly into our first charge."

There was no doubt in the mind of anyone topside that the submarine had been struck and sunk. Outerbridge marked the time—0651—and sent a message to Pearl Harbor:

"We have dropped depth charges on sub operating in defensive area."

Outerbridge thought that perhaps this was inadequate notification of a most extraordinary event, so the first message was followed in two minutes by a second:

WE HAVE ATTACKED FIRED UPON AND DROPPED DEPTH CHARGES UPON SUBMARINE OPERATING IN DEFENSIVE AREA.

He waited for a few minutes and then queried the naval radio station to be sure his message had been received and understood. The operator at Bishop's Point acknowledged receipt.

When some of the secrecy guarding the Navy's files may be relaxed after the war, historians can read the eyewitness reports of this engagement submitted by every officer and man in a position to view it. Most terse of them all is Seaman 2/c William Fenton's, the young Reservist who pointed No. 3 gun:

"Was standing 4-8 watch when general alarm sounded. I manned gun 3, my station, saw submarine conning tower, got word to fire when on. Got on target and fired. We shot at their port side. Submarine went down just after it passed our stern, then depth charges were dropped."

One of the fullest statements is that of Seaman 1/c H. F. Gearin, who was quartermaster when, as he described it, "the ANTARES stood out over the horizon from the southwest. She had a tow with about 300 feet of line out. At 0640 the helmsman, H. E. Raenbig, Seaman 2/c, called my attention to a black object almost midway between the ANTARES and her tow. I immediately took a look at it and reported it to the officer-of-the-deck. The ANTARES at this time was almost broad on our port beam. Her tow was broad on our port bow. She was about a mile distant . . ."

Raenbig, the first man to sight the enemy, had a view of the ensuing action so good that he could see the gleam of glass in the periscope. In his report he tells of seeing a hole appear in the conning tower after No. 3 gun spoke. Russell H. Knapp, boatswain's mate second class and gun captain, said that "it looked to me as if our shot hit at the base of the moving object, but I am not sure that the shell exploded, although there was a loud report at the time."

The depositions independently taken from every officer and man in a position to view the engagement agreed that the first shot was a near miss, that the second penetrated the conning tower at the water line. From captured specimens it was later learned that the two-man subs had no hatch between conning tower and hull. A hit meant a kill. It was to a mortally wounded submarine that Chief Maskzawitz's depth charges gave the coup de grâce a full hour before the enemy's descent in force on Pearl Harbor.

7

The WARD's work was by no means over. Now that the submarine had been sunk, the destroyer began a methodical search of the restricted area. Caught in the level rays of sunrise, a fishing craft was sighted where it should not have been—a motor-driven sampan out of Honolulu which put on all speed as WARD charged down upon it. But the sampan quickly abandoned hopeless flight and hove to, wallowing in the water as the destroyer surged alongside. Three Japanese came to the rail, two with their hands in the air and one waving a white flag. The prize taken by WARD was turned over to a Coast Guard cutter that had joined the pursuit, and WARD proceeded with her task of combing the harbor entrance, dropping depth charges on every suspicious echo her sonic apparatus raised.

"I suppose we killed a lot of innocent fish," Outerbridge now remarks, "but there is a chance—a chance—that we got one other submarine."

The Coast Guard cutter, with the sampan in tow, was heading into the harbor mouth when WARD's lookouts passed the word of an extraordinary number of airplanes over Pearl. With that, pillars of black smoke rose up inland, and, seconds later, the reverberations of tremendous explosions boomed across the water. War maneuvers of the past few months had been realistic enough, but they had not reached these fantastic proportions.

Then an airplane screeched out of a dive, and Outerbridge saw a black, cylindrical object hurtle from it in an arc toward the cutter and its captive. The bomb fell astern of the sampan, its explosion demolishing a skiff that was in tow, but what WARD's men were looking at were the vermilion disks on the plane's wings.

"I knew then," Outerbridge says mildly, "that all hell had broken loose."

8

"—all hell had broken loose."

None aboard the WARD that morning had time to shape fine phrases for posterity. None pondered that they had delivered the first blow, in anticipation of an attack in the instant of its launching. They were too busy keeping alive.

Where Oahu's green and blue and chocolate slopes had shown color against a rising sun, the torpedo bombers of Japan now were raising a towering pall of flame-shot sooty smoke.

Under the pall lay the greater part of the United States Pacific Fleet, how badly wounded none could see—least of all the attackers who survived to report. Under it, too, in the growing company of the dead, lay Ensign John H. L. Vogt, Jr., USN.

With other members of Scouting Eight, Vogt had taken off from ENTERPRISE that morning at about the time Japanese aviators were secretly soaring aloft from their own flat-tops to the northwestward. The carrier was about 200 miles off Pearl, having been held up several hours by rough weather, when she began discharging her planes. Eleven of them were shot down over Pearl Harbor; nine pilots and their gunners were lost.

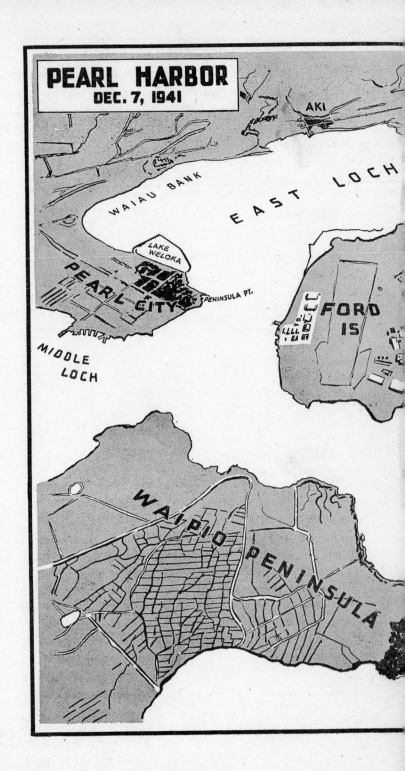

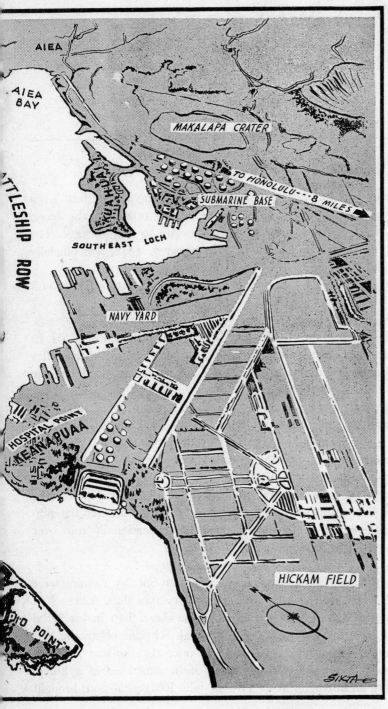

FIGURE 2

Chapter Two

THE setup at Pearl Harbor that Sunday morning was perfect. Even the weather seemed to have been made to order for the secret drama whose tragic prologue had already begun to play offstage. The weather at Pearl Harbor on Sunday, December 7, 1941, was officially logged by the Navy as:

"Averaging partly cloudy, with clouds mostly over the mountains . . ."

This was not unusual.

The island of Oahu is characterized by mountain ranges at its eastern and western edges, with Honolulu and Pearl Harbor in the valley between. For the greater part of the year the prevailing winds are the northeast trades. These winds are deflected upward by the peaks of the Koolau Range to the eastward, forming banks of cumulus around the pinnacles, and bringing rain to the windward slopes. Usually when there is rain in the hills, Honolulu and Pearl Harbor are bathed in sunshine.

But December is one of the so-called rainy months. During these very rare periods the wind occasionally shifts to northward, blowing down through the valley as well as against the northern slopes of the hills. When this occurs there are still banks of cumulus over the pinnacles, but there are also scattered clouds and occasionally rain over Honolulu and Pearl Harbor.

" . . . Cloud base at 3,500 feet, visibility good . . ."

Flying conditions in the Pearl Harbor area that Sunday morning were not too bad. There were at least three civilian airplanes aloft. A Honolulu attorney named Roy Vitousek went up for a dawn hop in his aerial put-put. He soon found himself flying through echelons of strange and sinister aircraft, but he did not realize at once that he was flying in formation with history. He landed safely if in something of a hurry. Cornelia Fort, an instructor at the civilian John Rodgers airport, brought

22

her student to earth through a crazy traffic of diving planes and hurtling bombs, and ran to shelter paced by a splatter of bullets. A man was killed on the field as she landed.

Jimmy Duncan, member of the *Hui Lele* Flying Club, was up taking a lesson in advanced flying from Tommy Pomerlin, an Inter-Island Airways pilot. Tracer bullets pursued them all over southern Oahu when they innocently flew into the battle. The Japanese, however, were only brushing away a sparrow that had blundered into the flock of birds of prey. Duncan and Pomerlin also landed safely, at John Rodgers field.

" . . . *Wind north, 10 knots* . . ."

There was a north wind of 10 knots over Pearl Harbor that Sunday morning; and fighter, bomber, and torpedo planes bearing the symbol of the Rising Sun came riding down this wind. The invading planes were screened by the cumulus banks over the mountains until they were ready to split up and make predetermined approaches on their targets from several points of the compass. In speaking of the weather conditions on that morning a naval officer later remarked, "There were just enough scattered clouds over Pearl to give protection to the Japs and cause confusion to our antiaircraft."

At Pearl Harbor that Sunday morning, at least as far as the weather was concerned, the setup was perfect—*for the Japanese.*

2

At 0430 on the morning of December 7 a Japanese two-man submarine was inside Pearl Harbor just off Hospital Point.

From the log of this submarine, subsequently beached outside Pearl Harbor and recovered intact, it is not difficult to reconstruct its survey of the harbor, leg by leg. Thus the commander of the sub noted that he swung his tiny battery-driven craft to starboard on a course of 60 degrees, sailing past the Navy Yard, and incorrectly noting on his chart that the battleships PENNSYLVANIA and ARIZONA were tied up alongside Ten Ten Dock. (The ships he saw actually were the cruiser HELENA and the minelayer OGLALA.) Peering through his periscope to the left, he logged a number of ships tied up along Battleship Row on the south side of Ford Island, which is roughly in the center of Pearl Harbor. There was not much light to go by, and he could not identify the first ship in the line of those at berth, the oiler NEOSHO. But he roughed this ship in on

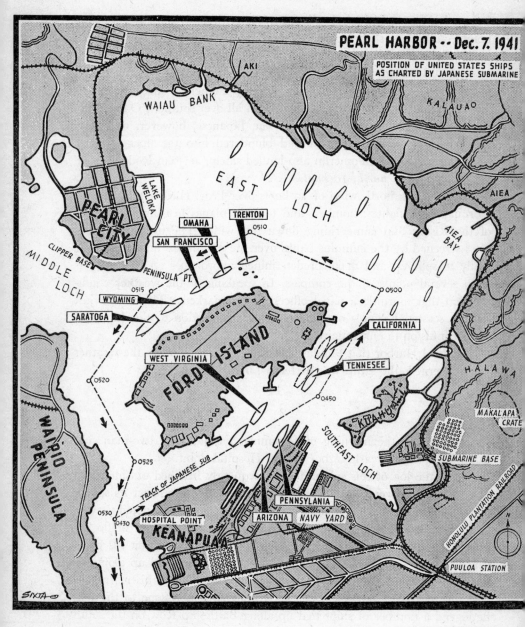

FIGURE 3

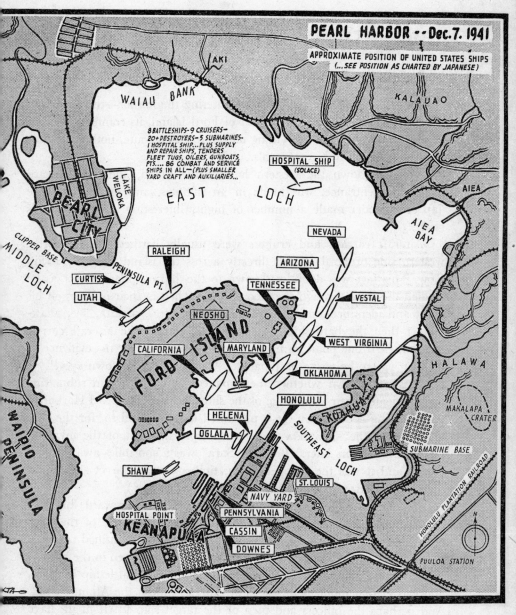

PEARL HARBOR -- Dec. 7, 1941

APPROXIMATE POSITION OF UNITED STATES SHIPS
(... SEE POSITION AS CHARTED BY JAPANESE)

8 BATTLESHIPS-9 CRUISERS-
20+ DESTROYERS-5 SUBMARINES-
1 HOSPITAL SHIP...PLUS SUPPLY
AND REPAIR SHIPS, TENDERS
FLEET TUGS, OILERS, GUNBOATS
PT'S.... 86 COMBAT AND SERVICE
SHIPS IN ALL—(PLUS SMALLER
YARD CRAFT AND AUXILIARIES...

FIGURE 4

his chart, and he then successively located, at least to his own satisfaction, WEST VIRGINIA, TENNESSEE and CALIFORNIA, all battleships.

At 0450, after taking a bearing on Kuahua Island, he veered to port on a 30-degree course for a five-minute run, thence steering 295 degrees for another ten minutes.

Thus at 0510—40 minutes after entering the harbor—the small Jap sub had negotiated the eastern half of Ford Island, its commander writing his observations of everything encountered en route, noting the time of each turn in Arabic numerals.

The run down the western half of the island, and back toward the harbor entrance, was made in 20 minutes, and on this run the Jap commander made a number of highly interesting notations on his chart.

Aircraft carriers and cruisers were usually berthed on the north-western side of Ford Island, directly across the island from Battleship Row. This fact was doubtless known to the Jap commander, for as he studied the ships through the gloom, he sketched in their outlines on his chart and identified them as the cruisers TRENTON, OMAHA, SAN FRAN-CISCO; then the battleship WYOMING and, finally, the aircraft carrier SARATOGA. At one point on his chart, and as if to bolster the evidence of his own vision, he wrote in Japanese, "I saw it with my own eyes!"

It is not known whether the Japanese in the two-man submarine communicated their knowledge of the ships based inside Pearl Harbor to their waiting countrymen. It is presumed that they did so, for the ship identified as the SARATOGA became an especial target of the invading planes a few hours later. (But the "Sara" was 2,000 miles away in San Diego, and it was the stripped-down, timber-covered target ship UTAH that capsized from the torpedoes meant for a carrier.)

However, the Japanese should have received no reward for their daring higher than an E for honest effort. Although some of the ships named were actually in the harbor, not one ship was identified correctly at its proper berth. Some of the ships named were not even in the harbor. For example, WYOMING had been demilitarized as a battleship in 1932, and was at that moment in use as a training ship on the Atlantic coast. And perhaps the officers and men of the target ship UTAH might have been flattered at having the old ship mistaken for a mighty aircraft carrier—but not if they had been told in advance of the price they and UTAH would have to pay for this flattery.

In laying and executing their plans, the Japanese attackers depended on no single source of information. It is known now that their knowledge of the ships inside Pearl Harbor was gained also from observers other than the underwater prowler. There is no doubt, however, that the Japs in the two-man submarine that morning had put forth their best effort.

But another Jap two-man submarine was still inside the inner harbor, and this one never again was to come out.

3

On all ships and stations of the United States Navy morning colors are displayed at 0800. With a dozen ships in a single harbor an observer can note that the national ensign on each ship will begin to flutter aloft at almost exactly the same time.

The reason for this smart concert of action is that, at exactly 0755, on order from the Senior Officer Present, there is hoisted the bunting known in the international flag code as Prep. (A white square in a solid field of blue.) Prep stands for the letter P. On a naval vessel Prep can have several meanings, but, hoisted at 0755, it means that morning colors will rise in exactly five minutes.

The signal tower at Pearl Harbor was atop the Navy Yard water tank to the north and east of the harbor entrance. On the morning of December 7 the signalmen in the tower had already broken Prep out of the bag and had bent it on its halyard. There was still a minute to go before 0755.

From their lofty eminence these signalmen could look down upon all the ships of the Pacific Fleet moored there in the harbor beneath them. Eight of these ships were battleships. Nine were cruisers, more than a score were destroyers, and five were submarines. The hospital ship SOLACE was out there at anchor. And there were supply ships, repair ships, tenders, fleet tugs, oilers, gunboats, PTs—ships of many varieties. There were 86 combatant and service ships of the Pacific Fleet in all, not counting smaller yard craft and auxiliaries. Missing were the ships of the two carrier task forces at sea and the few vessels on duty outside the harbor.

Nearest the signal tower was the battleship PENNSYLVANIA, flagship of the Pacific Fleet. She was in Drydock No. 1. In this dock with her, resting side by side, were the destroyers CASSIN and DOWNES. To the left of this drydock was YFD2, Floating Drydock No. 2, and in this drydock was the destroyer SHAW. Alongside of Ten Ten Dock was USS HELENA, with the minelayer OGLALA moored outboard of this light cruiser. The light cruiser HONOLULU was in one of the yard berths to the northeast of HELENA, along with other cruisers.

As the signalmen looked out of their tower, though, Battleship Row on the south side of Ford Island presented the most formidable appearance, as it always did when heavy units of the fleet were in. At about the center of the southern edge, CALIFORNIA lay at her berth; then NEOSHO at the gasoline dock, and farther to the northeast OKLAHOMA and MARYLAND, with MARYLAND inboard between OKLAHOMA and the island. Next were WEST VIRGINIA—known as the "Weevie" to her men—and TENNESSEE, with TENNESSEE inboard. The next pair in line were ARIZONA and the repair ship VESTAL, with VESTAL outboard. At the end of the line, in a northeasterly direction from the signal tower, was NEVADA.

Ford Island of course was just what one would expect of a naval air station, with its rows of hangars, its runways, its fuel tanks, its administration buildings, its ferry landing, its bachelor officer quarters, and its enlisted barracks.

Moored on the north side of the island were the light cruiser RALEIGH and, squat and ugly in its demilitarized state, the target ship UTAH.

A petty officer in the signal tower looked at his watch. He was paying no particular attention to the mounting drone of plane engines that was beginning to fill the air. After all, seven Navy patrol planes were up on the Dawn Alert, and doubtless the Army had several planes up from nearby Hickam Field . . . . Sure enough, his watch said 0755.

"Execute," said the petty officer, meaning that the men at the signal racks should hoist Prep.

Opinions differ as to whether Prep actually was hoisted that morning.[1] The immediate interval after the order was given in the tower was spent in a frenzied telephone call to the headquarters of the Commander in Chief Pacific Fleet. For at that instant the Japanese planes hurtled down upon Pearl Harbor.

4

The Japanese planes struck first at the naval air station at Kaneohe Bay, a base for heavy flying boats on the east coast of Oahu, and half the

[1] The signal tower log shows that it was raised on schedule.

breadth of the island from Pearl Harbor. This was at about 7:50 A.M. Some of these planes continued on across Oahu to Ewa (pronounced Evva) Plantation to westward and wrecked the Marine air base. Bellows Field and Wheeler Field, Army airdromes, were bombed. The invaders struck at Pearl Harbor and the Army's adjacent Hickam Field a few minutes before eight o'clock.

Nobody kept an exact play-by-play account of the Japanese attack on Pearl Harbor. No official scorekeeper was posted. No officer or man detailed himself to act as a recorder of what went on. The urgency of the moment centered upon fighting the attackers. The record of the battle is the summation of the stories of hundreds and the statements of officers, dictated while the harbor still bubbled with air escaping from the hulls of sunken ships.

Even when a battle is known to be impending, and has been prepared for, there are likely to be at least minor discrepancies in the reports of several participants in an identical action. All historians are aware of this fact. And it should not be surprising that some observers at Pearl Harbor that Sunday morning—particularly some untrained lay observers who were not averse to being quoted—reported that the Japanese used multi-engine bombing planes and that they used Messerschmitt fighters bearing the swastika brand. It should not be too surprising that both statements, among others, were wholly contrary to the facts.

On February 15, 1942, a complete report on the Pearl Harbor raid was submitted to Secretary of the Navy Frank Knox (who had immediately flown to Hawaii to see the damage for himself) and to Admiral Ernest J. King, newly designated Commander in Chief United States Fleet and shortly later also to become Chief of Naval Operations.

The report pointed out that there were conflicting statements in the individual accounts of the commanding officers of the ships present, particularly variations of time, although there was complete agreement on all major events. It had been especially difficult to determine the exact number of enemy aircraft of the several types employed. For example, some Japanese planes which had completed bombing runs on Kaneohe, the Army's Wheeler Field, Ewa or other points continued on to Pearl Harbor to carry out strafing attacks. Horizontal bombers in some cases undoubtedly made several approaches before releasing their last bombs. Dive bombers made repeated attacks, at first bombing and machine-gunning, and then simply strafing when bombs had been expended.

Light bombers sometimes were mistaken for fighters. While one surface vessel was engaged in repelling a heavy dive-bombing attack, other ships in the harbor were fighting off torpedo planes or high-level bombers; and, on a number of occasions, a ship or group of ships was under attack by all three types at once.

To facilitate understanding of the attack, it should be remembered that the primary objectives of the Japanese were *the heavy ships, and the planes in the Oahu area.* Most damage to light ships or industrial facilities was incidental. (Evidence indicates, however, that a few Japanese aviators wantonly strafed, and in fewer cases bombed, groups of civilians, automobiles, residential areas, and other nonmilitary targets.)

It should be noted, too, that the Japanese showed a remarkable ability to deviate from orders to take advantage of a tactical situation. For instance, when a ship got clear of her berth and headed toward the sea, hoping to gain freedom for evasive action, Japanese planes in the area concentrated on her, in an effort to sink the vessel in the channel, to bottle up the other ships. Thus, at the very outset, the invaders themselves helpfully corrected any misconception which pictured the Japanese fighting man as a myopic automaton, noted principally for buckteeth and an inability to think for himself.

Every commanding officer who survived is willing to concede that the Japanese executed their plan of attack that morning with utmost mastery. And no veteran of Pearl Harbor, whether officer or enlisted man, remembers the Japanese attack chiefly because of some Japanese mistake.

Total absence of observers posted to do nothing but observe, coupled with the fact that there was at all times more going on than the human mind could easily grasp, makes any detailed description of the Japanese attack difficult to follow. To clarify this maze of action, the description of the attack has been arbitrarily divided into five phases as follows:

Phase   I——7:55-8:25 A.M. Combined torpedo plane and dive bomber attack.

Phase   II——8:25-8:40 A.M. Comparative lull.

Phase III——8:40-9:15 A.M. Horizontal bomber attack.

Phase IV——9:15-9:45 A.M. Dive bomber attacks.

Phase   V——9:45 A.M. Waning of attack and completion of raid.

Despite this arbitrary division for the purpose of simplification, it will be seen that parts of one phase will overlap into another; and while the total of Japanese planes probably did not exceed 105, some of these planes probably made two separate attacks.

For the sake of simplification and a more accurate understanding, the Japanese efforts will be described here first and in their actual sequence. On the American ships below, the battle to fight off the attack began almost with the dropping of the first enemy bomb, but, again in the interest of simplification, this will be separately related.

PHASE I

(7:55-8:25 A.M. Combined torpedo plane and dive bomber attacks.)

The first Japanese planes in the Pearl Harbor area struck at the naval air base on Ford Island and simultaneously at Hickam Field, the Army air base bordering to the southeast of the naval reservation.

An estimated 18 dive bombers were directed at Hickam, spreading destruction among the orderly rows of Army aircraft, parked in plain view on the field and under heavy guard against possible sabotage. The Japanese, before they had finished, did a thorough job in removing this field as a useful base for an air threat against their own forces. Approximately nine dive bombers struck at the smaller Ford Island from out of the northeast, bombing and strafing the station, barracks, and planes at that base. The Japanese destruction at Ford Island was as thorough as at Hickam.

With the dropping of the first bomb on the naval air station the commander of Patrol Wing Two at 0758 broadcast to all ships present: "Air raid, Pearl Harbor! This is no drill! This is no drill!" A similar message from the Commander in Chief Pacific Fleet followed almost immediately. Shocked listeners intercepted the broadcast on the mainland and relayed it to Washington.

Bare seconds after the Japanese appeared over the airfields, enemy torpedo planes and dive bombers swung in from several sectors to concentrate their attack on the heavy ships moored at Pearl Harbor. High-level bombers appeared overhead almost simultaneously.

Torpedo planes constituted the major threat of Phase I, although they were at all times effectively assisted by dive bombers. From the beginning of the raid, it was apparent that the torpedo pilots had been assigned definite targets among the heavy ships. And as an evidence of the long and careful planning that had gone into the raid, the Japanese used torpedoes particularly adapted to the shallow waters of Pearl Harbor. Remnants of these torpedoes were salvaged, and they were found to be fitted out with specially contrived wooden fins which prevented them from sinking too deeply when first dropped from their planes. It was also found that the exploders had been specially designed to operate after a short run, to make them effective in the narrow reaches of Pearl Harbor. There were many similar evidences that the Japanese had thoroughly rehearsed their attack, and had planned for it in every detail.

Of the four separate torpedo plane attacks in Phase I, as distinguished by direction of attack, the heaviest blow was struck by 12 planes which swooped out of the clouds and made a low and fast run from the southeast. These planes launched their torpedoes from very short distances at the heavy ships tied up in Battleship Row. All the outboard battleships [1] were hit by one or more torpedoes, and the Japanese torpedoes at that time bore bigger and more powerful warheads than those used by any other of the world's navies. Simultaneously the ships' decks were sprayed with machine-gun fire from the attacking planes.

Three other torpedo planes swept in from the southwest to confuse the antiaircraft crews, aiming their torpedoes at CALIFORNIA, OKLAHOMA, and WEST VIRGINIA.

A third attack was made by a single plane from the west, which discharged its torpedo at the two ships tied up together alongside Ten Ten Dock. Perhaps this plane was acting on information from a two-man submarine which had penetrated the harbor, and which had marked this dock as the location of USS PENNSYLVANIA, flagship of the Pacific Fleet. It is true that PENNSYLVANIA often used this dock, but she was at present in drydock, and the space at this time was occupied by the cruiser HELENA, with the minelayer OGLALA moored outboard. The Japanese torpedo passed underneath OGLALA and exploded against the side of HELENA. The blast caved in the side plates of OGLALA. She capsized

---

[1] Some criticism was voiced of the fact that the battleships were tied up "two-by-two," thereby presumably affording a better target. It should be noted that only the battleships moored outboard were torpedoed, those being berthed inboard in each case receiving less damage. The inboard ships were the first to be repaired and again made ready for battle.

against the dock an hour later, having been quickly towed from beside the wounded HELENA.

The fourth and final wave of torpedo planes in Phase I consisted of five planes. This flight came in from the northwest but split up to attack the ships moored on the north side of Ford Island. The cruiser RALEIGH shuddered under the impact of a torpedo blast, and the target ship UTAH quickly got two in succession. If the Japanese were under the impression that UTAH was the aircraft carrier SARATOGA, as they probably were, they must have been surprised at the ease with which she turned turtle after only two torpedoes. But here again the Japanese showed their ability to deviate from orders to capitalize on a situation. Other torpedo planes, with obvious instructions to attack SARATOGA, very handily selected different targets when they saw that what they thought was the carrier had been put out of action.

It is estimated that 21 torpedo planes took part in the attacks during Phase I.

While these four torpedo attacks were taking place, Japanese dive bombers were making eight separate strikes, these planes plummeting through the clouds from several different points of the compass. And high-altitude horizontal bombers also were busy as will be seen.

Immediately after the attack on Ford Island, and coincidental with the first torpedo plane attack, five dive bombers approached from east-southeast and aimed their explosives at the big ships in Battleship Row. Their aim was good. In fact, one Japanese pilot realized the dive bomber's dream when his bomb went down one of ARIZONA's stacks. (Few ships of the United States Navy at that time had been protected against this type of freak attack.) The ARIZONA's forward boilers and magazine blew sky high. Oil from her tanks ignited and covered the water around the ship with flames, endangering the nearby TENNESSEE.

Smoke from this fire, and from a later fire on CALIFORNIA, not only hindered the aim of the American antiaircraft crews; it prevented Japanese photo reconnaissance from determining the damage to the American ships below. Proof of this immediately became available when pictures taken from the Navy's own planes during the attack were rushed to the darkroom and developed. And this fact alone determined the Navy's policy in withholding full details of the damage for some time after the raid.

By that reticence the Navy was not concealing calamitous damage.

It told the public more than the Japanese themselves knew for certain. All that was concealed was the good news that most of the damage could be repaired, but to proclaim that good news might have been an invitation to the enemy to come again before Pearl Harbor was ready to meet him.

Of the remaining six attacks by dive bombers, each quickly following the other, two groups totaling five planes attacked from the northwest, two planes attacking the aircraft tender CURTISS and other ships moored in Middle Loch, and three planes aiming at UTAH and the cruiser RALEIGH on the north side of Ford Island; two planes came in from the west, one diving at PENNSYLVANIA and the other at the destroyer SHAW in Floating Drydock No. 2; three more planes immediately dived from the southwest, again hitting at PENNSYLVANIA and SHAW and also at HELENA and OGLALA; four planes from the southeast concentrated on Battleship Row, scoring on CALIFORNIA, WEST VIRGINIA, and TENNESSEE. Two dive bombers flew in from the north and attacked the destroyers and ships of the train moored in that section of the harbor in the concluding maneuver of Phase I. These last planes did no damage; the American antiaircraft fire was now very heavy, despite the damage which had been done to the ships below, and the bombers missed.

It is estimated that 30 dive bombers participated in the opening attack. But, and in addition to the torpedo planes already mentioned, some 15 high-level horizontal bombers were busy at the same time.

Six of these high-level bombing planes were in the first attack group. They appeared from due south and bombed objectives while crossing over the Navy Yard docks, but saved the major portion of their load for the big vessels in Battleship Row. After completely passing over the harbor, this flight wheeled to the right and reversed its course at approximately 12,000 feet. On the return trip, one or more planes dropped bombs on SHAW.

A group of five planes flew in from the southwest, and another group of five planes simultaneously approached from the northwest, bombing the Navy Yard docks and UTAH and CALIFORNIA.

The Japanese launched their attack in total surprise. And although the fight put up by the Americans on the ships below will be described later, it should be noted here that American guns were firing before the first of the invading planes had cleared the scene of the attack. (At least one enlisted crew at a ready gun, after a few unprintable comments, opened up without orders and before its ship had been called to battle stations.) Two of the Japanese planes in the first wave were shot down and others were damaged.

PHASE II

(8:25-8:40 A.M. Comparative lull in attacks.)

This part of the attack is designated as a "lull" only because it covers a slacking, temporarily, of the sustained onslaught. The attacks during this period were sporadic and lacked the co-ordination of the three types of planes which distinguished the beginning of the raid. In fact, no torpedo planes at all were observed during the period, and the attacks by dive bombers were a continuation, on a lesser scale, of Phase I.

Three dive bombers veered in from the southeast over the submarine base at 8:25, directing their principal efforts at the battleships OKLA-HOMA, MARYLAND, and NEVADA, but also machine-gunning HONOLULU and other ships in the nearby Navy Yard berths.

Three more planes from the southeast split up and dive-bombed HONOLULU, HELENA and OGLALA, and PENNSYLVANIA and the two destroyers in Drydock No. 1.

A third attack of three planes came in from the southwest, again hitting PENNSYLVANIA, but also aiming bombs at SHAW in Floating Drydock No. 2.

A fourth attack came from the northwest, but the three dive bombers in this flight seemed unable to hit any of the ships anchored in the northwestern section of the harbor. The antiaircraft fire from below had by now become intense, despite the damage that had been done to the ships.

The remaining dive bomber attack in this phase was made by three planes from the northeast and was aimed at ships in that section of the harbor. But again the bombs exploded harmlessly in the water.

An estimated 15 dive bombers took part in the attacks during this phase, but some of them probably had already been counted among the 30 planes of this type active in the opening assault. In addition, three flights of horizontal bombers made attacks in this so-called lull period, but these overlapped into Phase III and are described there.

But, during the second stage, the American ships had more to contend with than air attack alone. It was during this period that a two-man sub inside the harbor came up for a look and to launch a torpedo. Guns aboard half a dozen vessels opened as the stubby conning tower broached, and the gunfire alone would have sunk the submarine in five minutes. She was not allowed to stay afloat that long. The sub had surfaced almost under the bows of the destroyer MONAGHAN, which immediately rammed her, sent her to the bottom of the harbor, and then neatly decorated her grave with depth charges.

Later, this combat casualty to Japan's fleet during the actual attack was raised, forming the smallest part of the most gigantic naval salvage operation the world has ever known. The battered, silt-clogged vessel, its crew of two still inside, was to have a most interesting and unusual ending.

PHASE III

(8:40-9:15 A.M. Horizontal bomber attacks.)

After the comparative breathing spell of 15 minutes during Phase II the Japanese now came back strong with attacks by high-level bombers. These planes crossed and recrossed their targets from several directions, occasionally holding their bomb loads and turning back for a better aim on the ships below.

Six of them, approaching from almost due south, crossed over the ships moored in the Navy Yard berths, flew over Battleship Row and then over the destroyers moored in the northern section of the harbor. These planes then returned over the same course, concentrating their attack on the battleships TENNESSEE and WEST VIRGINIA.

Another group of nine bombers crossed from southwest to northwest over OGLALA and HELENA, again striking at TENNESSEE and WEST VIRGINIA.

A third group, also from the southwest, split into two three-plane sections before dropping their bombs. One section crossed over SHAW and let go its bombs at CASSIN and DOWNES, berthed in Drydock No. 1 with PENNSYLVANIA. The other section devoted itself to the vessels in Battleship Row. Here again a freakish hit caused much damage, when a 15-inch armor-piercing shell fitted with fins for use as an aerial bomb penetrated to CALIFORNIA's second deck where a large part of the ship's company was assembled. Many were killed in the blast, and a raging fire swept between-decks.

Two groups of bombers came in from the east. Six planes were in the first group and three in the second. Their main targets were the vessels in Battleship Row but they also dropped bombs on HELENA and OGLALA and the smaller ships in Middle Loch.

Approximately 30 horizontal bombers engaged in this phase, including nine which also participated in the opening of the attack. In addition, a total of 18 dive bombers were active.

A group of six dive bombers from the southeast again bombed the big ships in Battleship Row. Three dive bombers from the southwest split up, aiming effectively at Floating Drydock No. 2 and at Drydock No. 1, starting fires on SHAW and severely damaging CASSIN and DOWNES.

There were three other dive bomber attacks during this phase, each attack by a group of three planes, and with the major targets TENNESSEE and WEST VIRGINIA.

It was at this time that USS NEVADA got away from her berth and stood down the channel. Immediately every Japanese plane in the vicinity jumped NEVADA, and she grounded temporarily near YFD2, the floating drydock holding SHAW. The NEVADA took all the punishment the Japanese could hand out. Her bridge and forestructure were a pillar of flame, but her guns were blazing back at the enemy, and they did not falter.

At about the time NEVADA left her berth near Ford Island, approximately 8:40 A.M., the repair ship VESTAL managed to clear the burning ARIZONA and moved to the northward. And, shortly thereafter, yard tugs began to move the listing OGLALA away from HELENA. The OGLALA was secured in her new berth at about 9:00 A.M., but her damage had been too great. Shortly thereafter she began slowly to heel over at the dock. Her men continued to fire until their tilted guns could no longer be brought to bear.

PHASE IV

(9:15-9:45 A.M. Dive bomber attacks.)

The reappearance of dive bombers overlapped by perhaps ten minutes the attacks by horizontal bombers. Some of these dive bombers may have participated in the first attack, because they dropped no bombs but raked decks and docks with machine-gun fire.

Two groups of dive bombers came in from the southeast. They swooped low, spraying streams of lead and tracers at Battleship Row and at the ships and facilities in the Navy Yard to the southward. Another group of dive bombers came in from the southwest, firing at the installations on the southern end of Ford Island, at SHAW, and at CASSIN and DOWNES in Drydock No. 1. Still another three-plane group dived from the west, attacking SHAW and Battleship Row. From the north and from the east came two more flights of three, to dive upon the burning goliaths with spitting machine guns.

Two groups came out of the northwest. One group again bombed and strafed Ford Island and the ships in Middle Loch. The other group, also of three planes, attacked the cruiser RALEIGH and the destroyers and other ships moored north of Ford Island. Another three-plane group swooped out of the north, upon the ships in that section of the harbor.

An estimated total of 27 dive bombers participated during the fourth phase of attack. It was also during this period that VESTAL, to keep from sinking, weighed anchor and deliberately grounded opposite the northeast end of Ford Island.

PHASE V
(9:45 A.M. and after. Waning of attacks and end of raid.)

All enemy aircraft had retired by 9:45 A.M. There was considerable antiaircraft fire after this time, and three to four of our own planes coming in from ENTERPRISE were shot down because they were thought to be enemy.

During this period NEVADA managed to pull clear of the mud in which she had grounded near Floating Drydock No. 2; and at 10:45 this battleship was deliberately grounded on Waipo Peninsula, near the western side of the channel entrance. This skillfully executed maneuver prevented her sinking and blocking the channel entrance.

There were numerous sortie movements by various ships during the attack and immediately thereafter. But by noon, and with the exception of destroyer antisubmarine patrols, ship activity within Pearl Harbor terminated.

Chapter Three

TO facilitate understanding of those two crowded hours aboard the ships in Pearl Harbor, the device is again employed of making an arbitrary division of events which actually happened simultaneously.

At times more than twenty ships were under attack at once—ships of several types and many classes. The story of how they met the attack, how they survived, or how they succumbed can better be told and more easily understood if related by categories; because the ships of each classification have different functions, different powers of resistance, and varying degrees of vulnerability. Too, at Pearl Harbor, they had different kinds of attraction for the enemy, whose plan was to destroy the ships of greatest range and fire power to prevent interference with Japan's advance in Asia and the Western Pacific.

Most of the damage was committed in the first few minutes of the raid. It must be remembered that all that follows happened almost at once and in such magnitude of violence that no one witness could see and report it all. And it should also be remembered that while Japan's aircraft were pouring destruction upon Pearl Harbor the ships and planes and troops of Dai Nippon were leaping at Hong Kong, at the Philippines and Wake and Guam, and at Malaya.

Categorically, then, this chapter relates the happenings at the naval air stations at Kaneohe and Ford Island, where the Japanese bombs fell first by scant seconds; then to the story of the ships, the auxiliaries, the destroyers, the cruisers, and the battleships, in that order.

2

The PBY flying boat which participated with the WARD in sinking the Japanese two-man submarine outside Pearl Harbor at once radioed a report of this action to Commander Patrol Wing One at Kaneohe, Commander Knefler McGinnis, USN.

"Evidence seemed conclusive that this submarine had been destroyed," declared Commander McGinnis. "When the message was received it seemed so impossible, that the first reaction was that it was a case of mistaken identity, since some of our own submarines were due to enter that morning. While we were investigating to insure that the information concerning our own submarines was in the hands of patrolling aircraft, about nine enemy fighters circled at low altitude over Kaneohe and attacked with machine guns the control tower located on the hill and the four patrol planes moored in the bay."

Several small boats were in the water near the four seaplanes, as these aircraft were being serviced for the day. The men in these small boats were machine-gunned by the Japanese without mercy. Commander McGinnis continues:

"This was followed by an attack on the planes on the ramp. This attack lasted for some fifteen minutes. The very first plane attacked was the wing commander's OS2U-1 on the landing mat. At the time a chief petty officer was turning over the propeller by hand and it was apparently thought to be a fighter preparing to take off. This plane was thoroughly riddled. After the first wave there was a few minutes' lull and then another attack by an estimated six to nine fighters. All attacks were directed at planes on the ground, in the water, and at the hangar."

The Japanese, in the very beginning, were trying to make sure that they would meet no opposition in the air. And, at Kaneohe, they were almost completely successful. Every one of 34 planes at the air station at the time of the first attack was put out of commission, although some were later to be salvaged and repaired. The only planes to escape were the three patrol planes in the air on the Dawn Alert; and one of these, a lumbering flying boat, landed badly shot up in aerial combat.

"At the very beginning of the first attack," said Commander McGinnis, "there was immediate action on the part of personnel to get machine guns in action against the attacking planes. The conduct of all personnel throughout the entire attack was magnificent; in fact, too much so. Had they not, with no protection, deliberately set themselves up with machine guns right in line with the drop of attacking and strafing planes we would have lost less men. It was, however, due to this reckless resistance that two enemy planes were destroyed and six or more were sent away with heavy gas leaks."

Two of the Japanese planes in the first wave were pinked by that hastily organized fire from below. They fled, streaming gasoline from their tanks, one of them smoking. It is almost certain that neither returned to its carrier. Those of the defenders without guns labored to save the planes which were not damaged in the first attack, and to check the flames on those which had been set afire. Every man in an exposed position became a target for Japanese gunners.

One of these human targets was 32-year-old Aviation Chief Ordnanceman John W. Finn, of Los Angeles, later commissioned ensign in the line of the regular Navy and subsequently promoted.

As the first Japanese plane came over, Finn grabbed up a loaded machine gun and raced to mount it on an instruction stand, completely disregarding the fact that the stand was on an exposed ramp, near several parked planes.

Machine guns on roaring Japanese planes were spitting at Finn before he could finish mounting his gun. He paid no attention to the hot slugs tearing at him.

And Finn's own gun immediately made answer. As an official citation later put it: "Although painfully wounded many times, he continued to man his gun and to return the enemy fire vigorously and with telling effect throughout the enemy strafing and bombing attack, and with complete disregard for his own personal safety. It was only by specific orders that he was persuaded to leave his post to seek medical attention. Following first aid treatment, although obviously suffering much pain and moving with great difficulty, he returned to the squadron area and actively supervised the rearming of returning planes. His extraordinary heroism and conduct in this action are considered to be in accord with the highest traditions of the Naval Service."

Accompanying the citation was the Congressional Medal of Honor.

"Reckless resistance" was not enough, however, to prevent the attacking Japanese from giving Kaneohe a thorough blasting. Planes were burning on the beach and in the water. The hangars and buildings were smashed by bombs.

The aviation facilities on Ford Island, in the middle of Pearl Harbor, were next on the Japanese list—next by seconds.

The senior officer of the naval air station at Pearl Harbor, Rear

Admiral P. N. L. Bellinger, USN, arrived while the first attack was under way. The scene that met his eyes was not a pleasant one. Black smoke and flames were boiling upward from exploding ammunition and fuel stores in bombed hangars. Twisted wreckage that had once been planes was burning on the field. And there was a steady series of blasts from bombs and torpedoes that were now finding their marks on ships in the harbor.

Admiral Bellinger's first thought was to get planes in the air to fight off the Japs. But to prevent just this the enemy had been very thorough. At the end of the first wave of attacking planes, only three naval aircraft were capable of taking the air. This was due in some cases to blocked or blasted runways, but many of the American planes had been damaged or destroyed. Although unable to take to the air, the men below were fighting back.

"Fire was opened . . . from machine guns mounted in planes on the ground, or removed from planes to extemporized mountings with greater arcs of fire," Admiral Bellinger stated. "All communications . . . were knocked out of commission. Immediate steps were taken to restore communications. Communications personnel proceeded to repair the radio antennae during the height of the attack."

Tremendous efforts were made to repair damaged planes and get them into the air. Thirteen dive bombers from the ENTERPRISE landed on the field, not without considerable resistance from friendly gun crews below, and these planes were immediately sent out again. Eighteen dive bombers had started from the carrier.

One of these planes was piloted by Lieutenant C. D. Dickinson, USN. Dickinson shot down one Japanese plane over Pearl Harbor but was himself shot down. He parachuted to safety, hitchhiked to the naval air station, and took up another plane without telling anyone there of his recent experience.

Dickinson came out of his experiences unhurt; others were not so fortunate, and not all of these were victims of the Japanese. It is now believed that as many as ten Navy planes might have been shot down or forced to crash by antiaircraft fire from Army and Navy guns on ships or at shore stations on Oahu. Other American planes were hit by their own antiaircraft fire but managed to land safely. And at least one Navy surface ship was unsuccessfully bombarded at sea outside Pearl Harbor by land-based American artillery.

It would perhaps be easy, many months afterward, to criticize this obvious confusion. But, at the time, it was understandable even to those few American aviators who unfortunately became the targets for American guns.

"The suddenness and magnitude of the enemy attack caused such a stunning effect upon ground and ship personnel," reported Commander H. L. ("Cy") Young, commander of USS ENTERPRISE air group, "that all aircraft were fired upon, regardless of their being friendly. I was under fire all the way across Oahu and until my wheels touched the ground."

There were 301 naval planes of all types in the Oahu area at the beginning of the raid. This total included 54 noncombat planes, and 99 planes unable to fly because they were in storage as replacements, stripped down for shipping, or undergoing overhaul. There were, then, 148 serviceable combat naval planes in Oahu. When the raid was over, only 52 planes were capable of flight, 16 of them being noncombat types.

Planes and equipment could be repaired or replaced almost overnight, and were. But with some of the men it was different. These were the men for whom the first day of war was the last day of life.

3

Almost twoscore of the vessels in Pearl Harbor when the raid began could be entered under the classification of auxiliary ships, but the ships picked for mention in this account are those selected by the Japanese attackers themselves.

For example, there were several minelayers in the harbor that morning, but only the minelayer OGLALA, formerly a passenger boat of the Fall River Line, was sunk. There were also several seaplane tenders in the harbor, but only the CURTISS was damaged, by bombs and by a Japanese plane which crashed on her deck. This same process of selectivity is used in the description of action aboard destroyers and cruisers, but it was not necessary in the case of battleships: every battleship in the harbor was damaged by bombs or torpedoes and at least temporarily placed out of action.

One of the best descriptions of the raid to come from all the officers and enlisted men who participated was dictated, just three hours after the attack began, by the flag officer stationed aboard the OGLALA, Rear Admiral William R. Furlong, USN, commander of minecraft in the Pacific Fleet. Admiral Furlong's narrative is stamped with the unstudied vividness of having been written while his flagship was still settling in the mud at the bottom of Pearl Harbor.

This officer's role in the complete story of Pearl Harbor was to go far beyond the narration of events. On Christmas Day of 1941 Admiral Furlong was ordered to duty as commandant of the Pearl Harbor Navy Yard. As such, he was to have charge of the salvage job ahead.

"At about 0800 this morning, Sunday, December 7, 1941," Admiral Furlong dictated to his yeoman, three hours after the time noted, "I was on the deck of my flagship and saw the first enemy bomb fall on the seaward end of Ford Island close to the water. This one did not hit the planes parked there. Another fell immediately afterwards in the same vicinity and caused fires near the water. U.S. planes were on the ground nearby and later flames flared up from the structures at the south end of the island. The next bombs fell alongside or on board the seven battleships moored on the east side of Ford Island.

"Japanese planes flew within fifty and one hundred feet of the water and dropped three torpedoes or mines in the channel on a line between OGLALA and the seaward end of Ford Island. A torpedo hit OGLALA and HELENA, which were moored abreast at Ten Ten Dock with OGLALA outboard of HELENA. Fire was opened by OGLALA and HELENA anti-aircraft battery.

"I at once signalled Commander-in-Chief that these three objects mentioned above which had just been dropped might be mines because they were dropped in the middle of channel. They could have been torpedoes or mines because no plume went up from them; whereas plumes over one hundred feet high went up from bombs that hit close alongside of battleships.

"I then hailed two small contractor tugs, which were working with dredges across the channel from OGLALA, to give assistance to haul OGLALA aft of the HELENA in order that HELENA could sortie. I obtained submersible pumps from the HELENA but then discovered that there was no power in the OGLALA because of the hit which flooded the fireroom, and she could not use her pumps.

"One Japanese plane was shot down over the harbor and came down in flames to seaward of Ford Island but probably on land. There was no trouble distinguishing Japanese planes because the red Sun painted on the side showed plainly.

"Meanwhile planes were strafing as well as bombing. Planes kept coming for quite some time, making it difficult to estimate numbers. I saw four battleships hit with bombs and fires broke out. I saw one battleship turn over. There were six to ten enemy planes visible at any one time over the harbor.

"The NEVADA got underway and passed out of channel near where I had seen the three mines or torpedoes fall. When she arrived in this vicinity her bow apparently hove up as if she had passed over a mine and about a minute later two bombs fell, one of which hit her starboard topside throwing up flame and smoke, and the other missed close along the port side, throwing up a plume of water.

"During all this, as these dive bombers flew within five hundred to a thousand feet of the OGLALA, we were given an excellent opportunity to fire our anti-aircraft battery and did so for over an hour, the HELENA firing over us.

"The OGLALA was got astern of the HELENA with help of tugs mentioned, and was hauled and pushed into the pier and secured with many wires and manila lines. As all compartments were closed below she settled slowly.

"At this time I ordered the two tugs which were assisting the OGLALA to go to the assistance of the NEVADA, which was then in the channel between the floating dry-dock and seaward end of Ford Island.

"On the second attack I saw a bomb drop which hit the forward part of the PENNSYLVANIA or in the dry-dock ahead of the PENNSYLVANIA. Two destroyers of Destroyer Division FIVE were in the dock ahead of the PENNSYLVANIA, and flames went up from them.

"Another Japanese plane was hit and fell in flames seaward of 1010 dock, possibly falling near the entrance of the channel. It went down in a streak of flame as did the first one mentioned. Of the two planes that I saw shot down in this part of the harbor one was in flames after passing over the battleships from north to south about 2,000 feet altitude; the other plane shot down flew over the harbor at about 2,000 feet in the same general direction but closer to 1010 dock and pier, and was engaged by vessels on this side of the harbor. Guns operable by hand proved particularly advantageous, especially where power was knocked out of the steaming firerooms by torpedoes.

"Following the bombing of the PENNSYLVANIA, I saw a bomb fall near or on the destroyer SHAW in the floating dry-dock. This destroyer was later in flames.

"Meanwhile the OGLALA had taken a list of about 40 degrees. The wire lines to the dock parted and her port upper deck rail was so far under that she might sink suddenly at any moment. I ordered all hands to abandon the ship shortly after 9:00 A.M., the only ones remaining being the guns' crews and myself. The OGLALA kept up the anti-aircraft fire until the ship's list was at such an angle that the men on the machine guns were sliding off the deck and the angle was too steep to longer stick on the deck and serve the 3″ gun. During this last period the Japanese planes were strafing us, not bombing. As the ship was about to turn over, I ordered the guns' crews to leave the ship, and left with them. The machine guns were slid off the top of deckhouse to the pier as the ship went over and were set up on the pier.

"The guns' crews manned their battle stations promptly and stood to their guns during bombing and strafing as if at target practice, keeping up a continuous fire at enemy planes during the bombing and strafing. The signal force manned their bridge stations and sent signals during the action; one to sortie and one to the NEVADA warning her of mines, during which time the bridge was struck by machine gun bullets. The men on the fires when the fireroom was flooding very promptly turned off the oil fires and no one suffered oil burns. . . .

"Above dictated at 11:00 A.M. William R. Furlong."

Admiral Furlong's praise for the Navy enlisted man under fire was repeated without exception by every commanding officer who turned in a report.

In the Navy's system of fitness reports, the highest praise a junior officer can receive is for his commander to mark a check opposite the statement "Particularly desire to have him serve under me in time of war." This was paraphrased by Commander Cassin Young, USN, skipper of the repair ship VESTAL, in the statement he made immediately after the raid. "The conduct of all officers and enlisted personnel was of such a high order," he wrote, "that I would especially desire to have them with me in future engagements."

The VESTAL was moored alongside ARIZONA, in Battleship Row, when the attack began. This was a hot spot, for ARIZONA seemed to be a particular target of the Japanese dive bombers and torpedo planes. Indeed, the two 15-inch armor-piercing bombs which struck VESTAL might well have been intended for the larger vessel moored alongside.

The first of these bombs smashed through the starboard side of the VESTAL'S forecastle and penetrated three decks before it exploded in a metal storeroom, starting fires, which made it necessary to flood the forward magazine. The second bomb hit the main deck aft and passed downward through the ship, exploding underneath, causing the ship to flood in its after compartments and to lose several feet of buoyancy at the stern.

When the ARIZONA blew up, the water around the VESTAL became covered with seething, blazing fuel oil. With the help of a tug the repair ship was maneuvered away from this danger and, to prevent her sinking, was deliberately grounded.

But in citing his officers and men, Commander Young neglected to include any word of his own participation in the action. In paragraph 5 of his battle narrative there are these words: "At about 0805 opened fire with the 3″ anti-aircraft gun and machine guns. After firing three rounds, 3″ anti-aircraft gun breech jammed; breech was cleared and one additional round was fired when blast from ARIZONA magazine cleared gun station killing one man. Machine guns continued firing on planes until they withdrew."

What Commander Young did not report was that he had himself taken charge of the 3-inch gun and was among those on the gun station "cleared" by the ARIZONA blast. Stunned by the blast as he was blown over the VESTAL'S side, he revived when he fell into the water. Young swam back to his ship through the burning oil, clambered up its side, and again took command.

Commander Young became one of the four recipients of the Congressional Medal of Honor who survived the Pearl Harbor attack, eleven others being designated for posthumous awards. He had been promoted to captain and was skipper of the heavy cruiser SAN FRANCISCO when, eleven months later in the battle which decided possession of Guadalcanal, Captain Young lost his life.

Burning oil from the stricken ARIZONA was a minor danger compared to the potential hazard contained in the fleet oiler NEOSHO. This ship was berthed at the Ford Island fuel dock in Battleship Row, near MARYLAND and OKLAHOMA, unloading aviation gasoline. She earned distinction as the first ship to get under way at Pearl Harbor.

In the jumbled confusion that followed the beginning of the raid, NEOSHO's skipper, Commander John Spinning Phillips, USN, received no immediate orders. But he did not need any—he knew what to do, as attested in a subsequent citation accompanying a Navy Cross.

He knew that his ship blocked the fairway for MARYLAND and OKLAHOMA, in case they were able to sortie. So Commander Phillips ordered the mooring lines slipped, but in the confusion no dock crew was available to cast off ashore.

"Chop those lines," ordered Commander Phillips, and his men fell to with axes, and cut the heavy manila cables at the bollards.

By the time the NEOSHO could get under way OKLAHOMA had capsized, and the oiler barely cleared the battleship's exposed stern. As the NEOSHO drew abreast of Battleship Row, two Japanese torpedo planes came in on a glide that was aimed for the big ships beyond. The NEOSHO's antiaircraft fire was so hot that these planes decided to change course in radical evasive action without dropping their deadly fish. And all the way across the harbor to a place of safety, NEOSHO shot at every enemy plane in range of her guns. At least one Japanese plane took a solid hit, and crashed.

One of three bombers was pulling out of a dive over the naval air station when the guns of the seaplane tender CURTISS caught it full on. News reports immediately after the raid declared that the pilot of this plane deliberately crashed onto the deck of the CURTISS, which was moored at the north end of Ford Island. Although Japanese suicide crashes are known to have occurred in later engagements, it is highly unlikely that such was the case in this instance because "it began to stream smoke and flame, and before it hit the ship it was coming apart like a jigsaw puzzle," as one witness described it.

The hurtling aircraft struck a seaplane crane on the starboard side of the main deck aft, near No. 3 gun. The crash sprayed CURTISS's decks with burning gasoline and started fires so menacing that No. 3 gun had to be temporarily abandoned.

After an initial strafing, by the first Japanese planes to come over at the beginning of the battle, CURTISS was unsuccessfully attacked by dive bombers. Then the two-man submarine broached the surface some 700 yards off the ship's starboard quarter and was taken under fire. Following the crash of the Japanese plane on her deck, the tender became the target of a determined attack by dive bombers. One bomb hit the stern mooring buoy. Another fell short, while another dropped over. A fourth aerial bomb hit the ship on the starboard side of the boat deck and ripped through to the main deck level before it exploded. This blast killed some 20 men and injured another 50, at the same time causing heavy damage and raging fires. While this was going on, tight-lipped CURTISS gunners were shooting down three of the attacking planes.

As the armor-piercing bomb knifed through the seaplane tender's upper works it made a shambles of the electronic equipment in the radio room, trapping two enlisted men under radio transmitters. The bomb then passed through the movie projection booth below, setting fire to the films stored there. Choking fumes from the burning film almost suffocated two other radio men, R. E. Jones and J. G. Raines, as they strove to rescue their trapped shipmates. Finally they released one, D. B. Orwick, RM2/c. Time and time again, as long as Jones and Raines could stand, they went back into the gas-filled radio room in an effort to save the other man, trapped and dying, but without success. They were among the officers and men cited for decoration by the commanding officer, Captain H. S. Kendall, USN, who later became the first naval aviator to bear the title of commodore when that rank was revived.

Some of the CURTISS's 33 wounded men were transferred to the Navy Hospital and the hospital ship SOLACE while the raid was going on.

Patients aboard the SOLACE begged to be allowed to return to their ships to help in the fight. Those who were not too ill were allowed to go, and the medical staff immediately opened emergency facilities for casualties. Six doctors from ships not under attack and one civilian doctor of the U.S. Public Health Service made their way by boat to the SOLACE to help out with the anticipated rush of wounded.

This rush began some twenty minutes after the raid opened, most of the casualties being brought to the hospital ship by her own motor launches which had been put over the side for this purpose. The commanding officer of the SOLACE, Captain Benjamin Perlman, USN, reported that his boat crews and stretcher parties "boarded the burning ARIZONA, while its crew was abandoning ship, and rescued the burned and injured casualties found on its deck, some very close to the flames."

In addition to several trips to the ARIZONA, these motor launches braved what were literally seas of flame to make numerous trips to the stricken WEST VIRGINIA. In speaking of one boat crew, Captain Perlman said: "On its fourth trip, having on board the WEST VIRGINIA executive officer, it picked up some men in the water and transferred them to a gig. Shortly thereafter, when many men had jumped into the water after an explosion on board [the WEST VIRGINIA], the boat picked up over three dozen. The surface was covered with flames. Ley, F. C., F2/c, USNR, the boat engineer, jumped into the water to rescue an ensign. Saccavino, J. W., S1/c, USNR, the coxswain, had to get into the water to quench his own smoldering jumper. With this boatload delivered to the SOLACE, and a quick change of clothes for the boat crew, the boat took Carpenter M. G. Bowman, USN, and a salvage party to the OKLAHOMA where it remained until about midnight."

The reason for the salvage party having to stay so long at the capsized OKLAHOMA was because more than 30 men were trapped in her overturned hull, and cutting through the plates of a battleship is no easy job.

Nor was it a simple task to cut through the hull of the demilitarized UTAH, the target ship which also capsized, and the final vessel for consideration in this present category of auxiliary ships.

The UTAH had recently returned from serving as a target for aerial bombardment, giving the Navy's aviators practice in attacking a moving ship. All her larger caliber guns were covered with steel houses. Her machine guns were dismounted and stowed below-decks in storerooms. The entire flat deck surface had been covered with two layers of 6″ by 12″ timbers, and this fact no doubt helped the Japanese in their belief that the 33-year-old veteran was the aircraft carrier SARATOGA.

Actually, the UTAH lasted just 11 minutes after the first Japanese supertorpedo exploded against her unarmored side plates. The senior surviving officer aboard the ship was Lieutenant Commander S. S. Isquith, USN, and he later reported that the first torpedo was felt at 0801. The UTAH immediately took a heavy list to port.

A second torpedo shock was felt a minute or so after the first and it became obvious that the ship would not remain upright. Word was passed for "all hands to lay up on deck and prepare to abandon ship." The severe list of the ship was now causing the heavy timbers on deck to slide about, and many men were injured or killed when pinned beneath them.

By 0805 the ship had listed to about 40 degrees. Lights were still on. No report had been received from the dynamo room, so word was again passed: "All hands on deck and abandon ship over starboard side." The crew commenced getting over the side as the ship continued to list.

Attacking planes were now flying low and machine-gunning the men climbing over the side and swimming away from the capsizing ship.

There was a reason why no report had been received from the dynamo room. One man, Fireman 2/c John B. Vaessen, USNR, was still down there at his post, seeing to it that the lights were kept burning on the ship. And one man was still at his post in the fireroom, too, seeing to it that all his shipmates got out safely. And whereas Vaessen was just a youngster, Chief Water Tender Peter Tomich, a native of Austria, was a Navy veteran with five four-year hashmarks on his sleeve. His hashmarks were gold, meaning that there was not a bad mark on his 20-year record.

"Although realizing that the ship was capsizing as a result of enemy bombing and torpedoing," said an official citation of Tomich, "he remained at his post in the engineering plant of the USS UTAH until he saw that all boilers were secured and all fireroom personnel had left their stations, and by so doing he lost his own life."

Chief Water Tender Peter Tomich, USN, became one of some 15 officers and men of the Navy at Pearl Harbor to be awarded the Congressional Medal of Honor.

While Tomich stood at his post, and with young Vaessen still in the dynamo room, the UTAH was slowly turning over. At about 0812, the last mooring lines parted and the ship capsized, keel above water.

The Japanese planes strafing the men in the water and those in the ship's·boats began to machine-gun those who had reached the comparative safety of Ford Island. Fortunately, a trench had recently been dug ashore as part of a PWA project, in which the survivors found shelter. A young hospital apprentice of the Naval Reserve, Jean Kerns, HA 1/c, had managed to hang on to a first-aid kit while abandoning ship, and Commander G. H. Larson, USN, of the Medical Corps, began to treat the wounded.

"While in the trenches," Lieutenant Commander Isquith declared, "knocking was heard on the ship's hull. At this time planes were still strafing and dropping bombs. I called for a volunteer crew to return to the UTAH to investigate the knocking."

Two warrant officers, Chief Motor Machinist Terrance MacSelwiney and Machinist S. A. Szymanski, immediately stepped forward, with two seamen whose names were not obtained at the time. They got a boat and returned to the ship. Clambering over its hull, they finally located the knocking within, and their own knocks were immediately answered. Inside was Fireman John Vaessen.

Vaessen had been on duty at the electrical controls in the bowels of the ship when the UTAH was hit, said Lieutenant Commander Isquith, and "when the voltage commenced dropping he cut out power forward and then aft, in an effort to maintain lights in the ship. Finally the lights dimmed and went out and he, then being unable to escape to the deck, proceeded to the dynamo room, entered the starboard dynamo workshop, opened the manhole to a compartment and climbed up to the ship's bottom, taking his wrench and flashlight with him." Vaessen had used his wrench to tap out his call for help.

MacSelwiney and Szymanski obtained a cutting tool from USS RALEIGH, and soon the trapped seaman was ashore, stooping with his shipmates in the PWA trench as the strafing Japanese planes spattered bullets about them. And Vaessen, along with Lieutenant Commander Isquith, was among the recipients of the Navy Cross for actions that day which were described as "above and beyond the call of duty."

But six of the UTAH's officers and 52 of her men had answered their final call to quarters.

4

Immediately after the raid on Pearl Harbor the Navy Department announced that three destroyers, CASSIN, DOWNES, and SHAW, had been lost. As it later turned out, not one of these vessels was to be stricken from the active list, although each was severely damaged.

Indeed, had not these three ships been immobilized in drydock it is probable that they would have escaped with as little damage as the other destroyers in the harbor. Every ship of this class capable of getting under way joined the sortie out to sea to take up the hunt for the enemy's fleet or to carry out other assigned tasks.

Aboard one destroyer, USS AYLWIN, a 26-year-old ensign of the Naval Reserve named Stanley Caplan found himself the senior officer and automatically in command when the attack came. Caplan was a native of Elmira, New York, and he had studied at the University of Michigan for a career in civil life as a chemist. He had been at sea just eight months.

But Caplan knew what to do. The men raced to general quarters and stood at their guns. Below, the "black gang" crowded on steam. The

PLATE I—(*upper*) Shortly after Admiral Ernest J. King, USN, was appointed Commander in Chief United States Fleet—"COMINCH"—he was also designated Chief of Naval Operations. Here, March 26, 1942, he is sworn in by the Judge Advocate General, Rear Admiral Walter B. Woodson, USN, as the Secretary of the Navy, the late Frank Knox, looks on. (*lower*) The new Commander in Chief Pacific Fleet, Admiral Chester W. Nimitz, USN, former Chief of the Bureau of Navigation, took over his duties at the end of December, 1941. Admiral Nimitz here describes operations to the press at his headquarters in Pearl Harbor. At his left is Captain L. J. Wiltse, USN, Assistant Chief of Staff.

PLATE II—(*upper*) They fired the first shot of the Pacific war! Number Three gun crew of the USS WARD, which spotted a submarine outside Pearl Harbor early on the morning of December 7, 1941, and sank it. Crew members: R. H. Knapp, C. W. Fenton, R. B. Nolde, A. A. Domagall, D. W. Gruening, J. A. Peick, H. P. Flanagan, E. J. Bukret, K. D. J. Lasch. *Inset:* Lieut. Comdr. W. W. Outerbridge, USN, Commanding Officer, USS WARD. (*lower*) Japanese two-man submarine washed up on the beach near Kaneohe Naval Air Station, Oahu. The sub's skipper was captured.

PLATE III—(*upper*) An amateurish example of Japanese leaflet propaganda. The Japanese inscription says, "Hear! The voice of the moment of death. Wake up, you fools." (*lower*) Flags found in a Japanese midget submarine. Left: apparently personal flag of commanding officer. Upper right: Japanese naval ensign. The crude U.S. flag was probably intended to confuse observers in case the submarine had been spotted en route to Hawaii.

PLATE IV—(*upper left*) This Japanese propaganda photograph was captioned: "The moment at which the Hawaii surprise attack force is about to take off from the carrier. . . . On the faces of those who go forth to conquer and those who send them off there floats only that beautiful smile which transcends death . . ." The photograph was made aboard a Japanese carrier. (*lower left*) "Our Sea Eagles' determined attack had already opened, and a column of water from a direct torpedo hit on a MARYLAND class is rising. On the surface of the water concentric waves are traced by the direct torpedo hits, while murky crude oil flows out. The three bright white streaks between the waves are the torpedo tracks. In the distance the conflagration at the Hickam Field hangars is seen." Caption from Japanese aerial photograph sent to neutral countries for propaganda purposes.

PLATE V—(*above*) Japanese chart of Pearl Harbor found in captured Japanese midget submarine. (See FIGS. 3 and 4, pp. 24-25.)

PLATE VI—(*upper left*) The USS SHAW, hit by an aerial bomb, explodes. (*lower left*) The wreckage-strewn ramp of the Naval Air Station on Ford Island. Explosion in the background is the USS ARIZONA blowing up.

PLATE VII—(*upper*) One of the most daring feats of "Pearl Harbor Day" was the successful evacuation of the USS NEOSHO, a Navy tanker loaded with 90,000 barrels of oil and gasoline. At the height of the attack, Captain John S. Phillips, USN, backed his 18,000-ton craft between the USS CALIFORNIA (center) and the overturned USS OKLAHOMA, and made his way to safety. The NEOSHO was later sunk in the Battle of the Coral Sea. (*lower*) Bunting and drapes help to conceal an improvised anti-aircraft station set up after the attack began.

PLATE VIII—(*upper*) Ten Ten Dock, with the minesweeper USS oglala capsized, and the USS shaw burning in the background. The cruiser (left) is the USS helena, later sunk in the Solomons. The oglala was moored to the helena as the attack began. A Jap aerial torpedo passed under her and exploded against the helena. Although the cruiser was not badly damaged, concussion opened the seams of the oglala, which was pulled away before sinking. (*lower*) Remains of a Japanese Zero plane can be seen on the deck of the seaplane tender USS curtiss. The plane was shot down by anti-aircraft fire.

PLATE IX—Two destroyers in drydock, USS DOWNES (left) and USS CASSIN (right) were battered by aerial bomb hits. USS PENNSYLVANIA, 33,100-ton flagship of the Pacific Fleet, suffered minor damage, but was soon out with the Fleet. Machinery and other fittings of the two destroyers were transferred to new hulls and the ships were never stricken from the active list.

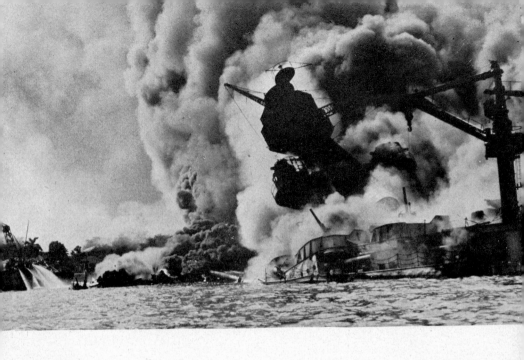

PLATE X—(*upper*) USS ARIZONA burns furiously after a Japanese aerial bomb, by a freak of chance, went down her stack and exploded in the powder magazine. (*lower*) Dense smoke from burning ships almost obscures "Battleship Row"—one of the reasons why Secretary Knox delayed giving the public a complete report of Pearl Harbor damage. In the foreground, crew members leave the listing USS CALIFORNIA.

PLATE XI—(*upper*) A panorama of Pearl Harbor during the second phase of the attack reveals a lively barrage of ack-ack thrown up against the enemy when the Navy's gunners were able to get to their weapons. (*lower*) A Navy launch crew rescues a seaman (center) about to be engulfed by flaming oil. This stage-like backdrop for disaster shows the USS WEST VIRGINIA burning in the foreground, and the USS TENNESSEE beyond.

PLATE XII—(*upper left*) Burning and settled on the bottom, the USS ARIZONA still defiantly shows its colors, hoisted as the attack began. *Inset:* Rear Admiral Isaac C. Kidd, USN, who died at his post of duty, first U.S. Naval officer of flag rank to give his life in World War II. (*lower left*) USS NEVADA, after an exciting attempt to put to sea, is finally beached off Hospital Point. She was the only battleship able to get under way during the attack. Her wounds were not serious and since rejoining the fleet she has seen much action, including support of D-Day landings off Normandy.

PLATE XIII—(*above*) Naval aircraft wrecked in the first phases of the Japanese sneak attack on Ford Island were soon stripped of their guns, which were mounted on improvised stands. In the background is one of the new hangars—riddled by Japanese strafing—and the wreckage of many planes.

PLATE XIV—(*upper left*) Working frantically, skilled mechanics drill holes in the thick plates of the OKLAHOMA to release seamen trapped when the battleship capsized a few minutes after the first Jap aerial torpedoes struck. In the background the MARYLAND, which suffered minor damage. (*lower left*) Christmas letters salvaged from the USS OKLAHOMA.

PLATE XV—(*upper*) The Japs mistook the USS UTAH, a decommissioned target ship, for the SARATOGA, because she was berthed where the aircraft carrier (then at sea) usually tied up. They wasted many bombs on a hulk which the Navy does not think valuable enough to salvage. The UTAH will become part of a new dock along Ford Island. (*lower*) One of the 2,117 U.S. Naval dead during the Jap attack on Pearl Harbor washes in on the tide.

PLATE XVI—(*upper*) While the attack rages, a U.S. cruiser sets out in search of the treacherous enemy. The USS PHOENIX, like its mythical namesake, seems to be rising from ashes as the greatest naval war in history begins. (*lower*) Everything that floats sets out in search of the Japanese fleet. Here the fast minesweeper USS CHANDLER, a converted destroyer, leaves Pearl Harbor on December 7, 1941.

AYLWIN's gunners claimed three planes shot down in the harbor, and the ship was already prepared to stand out to sea when her division was ordered to sortie. The AYLWIN, in fact, was among the first vessels to leave the harbor.

One immediate effect of the Japanese raid had been to snarl up traffic on all roads leading to the naval base, which is why the AYLWIN's skipper, Lieutenant Commander R. H. Rodgers, USN, could not reach the destroyer berths from his home before the ship had put to sea. He boarded another destroyer and assisted in its operations for the next two days. And in his narrative of the action, Lieutenant Commander Rodgers declared: "The conduct of Ensign S. Caplan, USNR, . . . in taking command for 33 hours during war operations of the severest kind, is considered outstanding."

Of the three destroyers most severely damaged—and they were the only three ships of this class to be put out of action even temporarily—SHAW was first to be hit.

The SHAW was in Floating Drydock No. 2, which was moored off the yard piers nearest the harbor entrance. Also in YFD No. 2 was the small harbor tug SOTOYOMO. Fortunately, much of the personnel of these vessels was ashore, since both were completely immobilized by overhaul and repair.

Three Japanese aerial bombs of about 300 pounds each struck the SHAW. The first two passed through several topside platforms and decks and exploded in the crew's mess on the main deck. The third bomb crashed through the bridge area and exploded in the pantry of the officers' wardroom. These explosions, coming very close together, ruptured an oil storage tank and blasted flaming oil throughout the forward part of the ship. The forward magazine went off with a roar, and the ship's back was broken just ahead of the No. 1 stack. Oil from this wreckage set the SOTOYOMO on fire, and she was severely damaged.

Meanwhile, YFD No. 2 also was taking a beating. Five bombs hit this floating drydock; the structure was set afire and its watertight compartments were holed by more than 150 shell fragments. The YFD-2 settled into the shallow water of the harbor at a 15-degree list, coming to rest with one side of the drydock and the SHAW's upper works still above the surface.

The attack had been under way for approximately an hour before the invading planes directed serious attention to CASSIN and DOWNES, in

Drydock No. 1. The withering curtain of fire maintained by the battleship PENNSYLVANIA, flagship of the Pacific Fleet, in drydock astern of the two destroyers, stood off wave after wave of enemy planes until a final concentration of bombers broke through.

Because of extensive repairs and overhaul, the PENNSYLVANIA—Captain C. M. Cooke, Jr., USN, commanding—had been excused from antiaircraft drills. Nevertheless, her men were at the ready machine guns and among the first to open fire. The PENNSYLVANIA expended considerably more than 50,000 rounds of 50-caliber ammunition during the attack. With this machine-gun barrage, and the fire from her other antiaircraft armament, she is credited with breaking up at least one attack by more than a dozen torpedo planes on Battleship Row. Her gunners claimed two Japanese planes definitely shot down, with four probables.

The first bomb to hit either of the destroyers berthed with the PENNSYLVANIA in drydock was a 100-pound incendiary that struck the DOWNES near the port deck-edge aft. It passed through the ship and exploded on the drydock underneath. The side of the ship at this point was riddled, and the oil from ruptured tanks began to burn under both destroyers. A second incendiary struck between the two ships forward, causing the fire to spread.

A third bomb exploded in the charthouse of the DOWNES, causing considerable damage to the bridge.

Both ships were now ablaze from stem to stern; and the intensity of the fires in the DOWNES, particularly, caused such heat that the oil in her bunkers reached the flash point and exploded with further extensive damage. The torpedoes on the deck were armed with live warheads. Some of these warheads melted off without exploding, but at least·two went off with a mighty roar, sending flames more than 100 feet high, and showering that section of the harbor with metal fragments. A portion of a torpedo tube weighing nearly a thousand pounds was blown onto the PENNSYLVANIA's forecastle, and the battleship's entire bow was pockmarked by fragments.

Efforts to fight the fires aboard CASSIN and DOWNES were hampered because both destroyers were being supplied with steam, electricity, and water by the Navy Yard, as was the PENNSYLVANIA, and these facilities were disrupted by the attack.

Both destroyers had to be abandoned, but their officers and men refused to leave the dockside. They managed to get water on several hoses and brought them to bear on the burning ships, falling flat behind any available cover when the explosions aboard the ships became too heavy.

During one of these explosions, a five-inch shell fragment struck the neck of Lieutenant (jg) J. D. Parker, USN, of the DOWNES. Parker continued to fight the fire, but his blouse was soon a gory mess, and those about him thought he was near collapse. The skipper of the CASSIN, Lieutenant Commander D. F. J. Shea, USN, stopped a small truck and directed the injured man to ride to the hospital. "Within a short time he was back," Lieutenant Commander Shea officially reported, "minus his coat and with his head bandaged, rejoining the fire fighting forces. I believe his hospital corpsman fixed him on the spot."

The final paragraph of the report turned in by the commanding officer of the DOWNES, Lieutenant Commander W. R. Thayer, USN, sums up the story in pride and pathos:

"The ship was lost, but the commanding officer has naught but praise for the officers and men of the crew who fought her under such unfortunate circumstances. They did their utmost to inflict damage on the enemy, working against almost insurmountable odds. They did all in their power to save the ship from fire. They showed that they were real shipmates with a concern for each other's safety. They were loyal and determined. Their primary concern during the engagement was to get the guns in action, and their biggest regret was that they couldn't meet the enemy in a fair fight at sea. I am proud to have commanded the USS DOWNES."

After the drydock had been flooded, and the fires were under control, there was ample reason for the belief (and the official Navy Department announcement) that the two destroyers must be counted lost. The hulls of both ships were wrinkled by extreme heat. They had been battered and riddled by bombs from the air and explosions aboard. The CASSIN had slipped her blocks and capsized against the DOWNES in a crazy mess of twisted metal. The picture was one of utter destruction.

Yet CASSIN and the DOWNES still had a lot of fight left in them, and their story had not reached its end.

5

Of the nine cruisers listed as in the area of the Japanese attack, only seven actually were in the harbor. Two others were out on assigned patrol but were in the Pearl Harbor operational area. Of the three cruisers bombed or torpedoed, one was USS HONOLULU, completed in June of 1938.

The HONOLULU was berthed at the Navy Yard piers to the north and east of Ten Ten Dock. This berth was less exposed to the Japanese attack than were some of the other mooring spaces. In addition, the HONOLULU was not in a direct line with the heavy ships which were the principal targets for the Japanese, and consequently suffered the least damage of the three.

Although the HONOLULU was strafed on several occasions by low-flying planes, her worst damage came from a 500-pound bomb which did not strike the ship at all. This bomb pierced a concrete section of the pier, continued downward on a slant in the general direction of the ship, and exploded in the water near the ship's side. The force of this blast caused only a slight buckling of the cruiser's side plates, but it blew open a sea valve and this caused a number of compartments to be flooded. This resulted in impairment of the ship's electrical system, particularly that connected with armament and fire control.

The HONOLULU's wounds were slight, however, compared to those sustained by the two other cruisers, and all permanent repairs were completed and she had put to sea in little more than a month.

The story of USS RALEIGH was a different one. She was moored to the north of Ford Island near the UTAH, and it is probable that the Japanese mistook the cruiser for a battleship.

"About 0755 on the morning of December 7, 1941," Captain R. B. Simons, USN, begins his narrative of the action, "I was in my cabin drinking a cup of coffee when I heard and felt a dull explosion in the ship. Looking out my airport I saw the water boiling amidships. I started up to the bridge and was met by Lieutenant Taylor who reported that the Japanese were attacking the Fleet. All hands were called to general quarters."

Within minutes the RALEIGH was firing with every antiaircraft gun she had, but the dull explosion heard by Captain Simons had been a Japanese torpedo which struck near No. 2 fireroom and caused extensive flooding. The ship began to heel to port immediately. She was in imminent danger of capsizing. A damage control party under Ensign H. S. Cohn, USNR, and Carpenter R. C. Tellin, USN, directed a counter-flooding operation which arrested the list just in time. But it seemed that the RALEIGH still had little chance to remain upright.

Captain Simons immediately ordered all topside weights jettisoned in an effort to keep the ship from turning over.

The ship's power had been knocked out, so the RALEIGH's two planes were hoisted over the side by hand, and taxied into Ford Island to report for further duty there. The warheads were removed from the ship's torpedoes, and the torpedoes were then directed ashore under their own power. They beached on Ford Island, where they were later recovered.

The topside weight of the ship was still too great. The torpedo tubes were thrown over the side. So were the airplane catapults. Then followed the steel cargo boom, all life rafts, boats, stanchions, boat skids—everything that was removable and movable by hand was jettisoned in an effort to save the ship. In addition, another cruiser nearby sent pontoon rafts alongside and these were secured to the ship with steel hawsers, thereby acting as stabilizing outriggers. A number of heavy wire and manila hawsers also were run to the nearby dock to help keep the ship upright. All these labors were performed under almost incessant machine-gun fire from the Japanese airplanes.

An hour after the beginning of the raid it was felt that the RALEIGH was out of danger provided she did not sustain further major damage. But the Japanese had not finished. Shortly after nine o'clock the Japanese centered a determined dive-bombing attack on the cruiser. The RALEIGH's antiaircraft fire was so hot that some of these planes veered off wildly and wasted their bombs in aimless drops. One bomb fell true, however. This probably was a 15-inch or 16-inch gun projectile which had been fitted with fins as an armor-piercing aerial bomb. It struck the RALEIGH on the port side aft, went through several decks, came out through the side of the ship and exploded nearly fifty feet away. Fortunately no personnel was in line of this projectile's course through the ship, and the explosion did little further to endanger the ship's precarious stability.

The ship's gunners claimed to have shot down five Japanese planes during the attack. Nevertheless, the RALEIGH herself had been badly hurt; although she soon sailed again for the United States under her own power, some six months were to pass before she was fully ready to put to sea in search of vengeance.

And about the same amount of damage was suffered by the light cruiser HELENA, moored alongside Ten Ten Dock with the minelayer OGLALA tied outboard. The Japanese were more determined in the number and intensity of their attacks on the HELENA, perhaps because they believed her to be the battleship PENNSYLVANIA. On his chart, the skipper of the two-man Japanese sub in the harbor had so identified the ship. This was an understandable error: the HELENA was at the berth usually occupied by the larger ship, and the berth would have been so occupied on this occasion had not the PENNSYLVANIA been in drydock. Less understandable, however, was the Japanese identification of the OGLALA as the ARIZONA.

The HELENA's lookout spotted the first Japanese plane to fly into the area. As the ship's log put it: "The Officer of the Deck was promptly notified by C. A. Flood, Signalman First Class, on watch on the signal bridge. This man has had recent duty on the Asiatic Station, and identified the character of the planes immediately."

The Officer of the Deck, Ensign W. W. Jones, USN, sounded the general alarm. Then he passed word over the ship's bullhorn: "Japanese planes bombing Ford Island. Man all battle stations. Break out service ammunition."

As the HELENA's men were racing for their stations, a torpedo plane swooped low over the southern tip of Ford Island. At 500 yards the plane dropped its fish. The torpedo passed underneath the shallow-draft OGLALA and hit the cruiser at the turn of the bilge, the blast also caving in the OGLALA's side.

The explosion bounced the 10,000-ton cruiser as if she had been a rubber ball. Sheets of flame ran through the passageways of several decks. Many of the ship's officers and men were in these passageways on the way to their battle stations, and the casualty toll was heavy.

As on the RALEIGH, the HELENA's power was knocked out; but the ship's emergency diesel generator was not damaged, and the power was resumed within two minutes after the blast, allowing free operation of the guns.

A typical example of the discipline aboard the ship occurred when the torpedo blast ruptured a fuel tank aft of the steaming boiler in the forward boiler room. As the power failed, this room was plunged into darkness, but the men knew that if the leaking fuel rose high enough to get into the boilers the result would be a tremendous fire or explosion, probably both.

This situation was described by the commanding officer, Captain R. H. English, USN, later killed in a Pacific plane crash after having attained flag rank. The boiler-room personnel did not know what was happening topside, said Captain English, "but proceeded to put to right a distorted situation in the dark, with guns firing, bombs exploding, water pouring through a bulkhead, and super-heater alarms and horns blowing due to a short circuit. With all this they continued their work of securing, and water was up to their chests before they abandoned."

Topside, the men at the guns were doing their best to save the ship. Near misses were exploding all around them, and men were falling as shrapnel riddled the upper works. On more than one occasion the gunners forced dive bomber and torpedo groups to alter course and ruin their aim, and they shot down or assisted in shooting down seven enemy planes. On one of these occasions an enlisted man, captain of a five-inch gun, shouted for the nearby OGLALA's officers to clear their bridge, as he wished to fire across it at an approaching torpedo plane. The officers cleared, among them Rear Admiral Furlong, and the gunfire forced the torpedo plane to change course. In fact, Captain English pointed out that all major damage to the ships in the harbor occurred in the first few minutes of the attack, before the forces below could organize the full effectiveness of their fire.

Like the RALEIGH, the HELENA was shortly able to proceed to the West Coast under her own steam for final repairs. But the HELENA had suffered a much heavier personnel loss, for she counted 31 dead and more than 70 injured.

All the cruisers not damaged or immobilized by overhaul joined the destroyers in the sortie in search of the enemy fleet.

The cruiser ST. LOUIS was moored near the HONOLULU when the raid began. She raised full steam and stood down the harbor as quickly as possible.

Near the outer channel entrance, where the waters are closely confined, a two-man Jap submarine was sighted and fire was immediately opened. The submarine returned the attack with one torpedo, possibly two, and the ST. LOUIS had to take violent evasive action to escape being hit.

"The ship was proceeding at about 20 knots at this time," said Captain G. A. Rood, USN, "and experienced difficulty in dodging the submarine, keeping off the reef, and in avoiding two minesweepers and their sweep. However, it managed to clear, and stood on out to sea at 25 knots speed, and zig-zagging."

The torpedo, or torpedoes, missed the ST. LOUIS and exploded against a nearby reef. The ship is believed by some observers to have hit the submarine, possibly sinking it. But in referring to the manner in which the ST. LOUIS hightailed it for open water, one junior officer always remarked: "Hell, we didn't have a bone in our teeth—we were foaming at the mouth."

6

With the PENNSYLVANIA in drydock, the seven other battleships in Pearl Harbor were moored in Battleship Row, along the southern edge of Ford Island. All these ships were damaged in the early part of the attack, most of them by the first wave of planes. Four of the battleships were moored together, two-by-two; and only the two ships moored inboard, MARYLAND and TENNESSEE, escaped being torpedoed. All the battleships were hit by one or more bombs with the exception of the OKLAHOMA, which took four torpedoes before it capsized.

The only battleship which got under way during the raid was USS NEVADA, a 29,000-ton vessel with 14-inch guns which had three months to go before being classed as over-age. She was 25 years old.

The NEVADA was moored at the northerly end of Battleship Row. As the first invading planes came over, her four ready machine guns, two forward and two aft, opened fire at once, and were shortly joined by the ship's 5-inch antiaircraft and broadside batteries.

On the larger ships of war of the United States Navy a portion of the antiaircraft armament is manned by the ship's Marine Corps detail. There is always competition between the Navy gun crews and the "Gyrenes," and this rivalry results in a general raising of the marksmanship level.

Master Gunnery Sergeant Charles E. Douglas, USMC, had charge of the NEVADA's forward machine guns which assisted in shooting down a Japanese plane in the first wave that came over, one of five planes claimed by the ship during the attack. Then a flight of torpedo planes swept in, low and fast. The NEVADA's port broadside 5-inch guns connected with a bull's-eye on one of these torpedo planes. It is possible that the projectile actually hit the plane's torpedo, for it struck with a blinding flash in which the enemy plane seemed to disintegrate.

Undeterred, one Japanese plane kept coming, and its torpedo caught the NEVADA near the port bow, blowing a hole in the side of the ship which caused the vessel to go down several feet by the head. Almost at the same time a bomb hit the quarterdeck, causing heavy personnel casualties.

Then the ARIZONA blew up, and the water around the NEVADA was covered with flaming oil.

The senior officer aboard the NEVADA at the beginning of the raid, and during most of the attack, was a Naval Reservist, Lieutenant Commander Francis J. Thomas. Thomas decided at once that he would have a better chance of saving the NEVADA if he could get her to open water where he could maneuver. He asked the engine room about getting under way.

"The engine room said it would take half an hour," Thomas reported, "but I told them we had better get going right now. We cast off the lines, backed the engines and the bow started moving out. We cleared the burning ARIZONA and a repair ship [the VESTAL] about forty feet away. Our gun crews shielded the ammunition with their own bodies as we moved past the blazing ARIZONA. As we squared off down the channel the Japs began dive-bombing."

The manner in which the NEVADA "cast off the lines" did not occur in quite so casual a way as that indicated in the reserved language of Lieutenant Commander Thomas. The first bomb, which struck the forecastle, caused intense fires on the forward part of the ship. Master Sergeant Douglas and his gun crew were threatened by the flames, but they refused to leave station. One of their guns was knocked out by the bomb; they kept the other in action.

When Thomas gave the order to cast off, no handling crew was on the quay. This detail was taken in hand by Chief Boatswain Edwin Joseph Hill, a warrant officer rounding out his 29th year in the Navy. As the lines were cast off, the battleship began to drift away from the quay with the tide. Hill plunged into the water, swam to the ship and clambered aboard. Later, while on the forecastle attempting to let go the anchors, after the ship had grounded, Hill was blown over the side and killed by bombs exploding in the water about him. He was one of the two men aboard the NEVADA awarded the Congressional Medal of Honor.

As the NEVADA passed the capsizing OKLAHOMA, already listing so far that the crews of her deck guns were being washed away from their stations, those of the OKLAHOMA's men who could stood up and cheered as the more fortunate NEVADA slowly sailed by in the direction of the harbor entrance.

But the Japanese became aware at once of the NEVADA's intentions, and they saw this as a golden opportunity to sink the ship in the channel, thereby bottling up the entire harbor. Every Japanese dive bomber in the vicinity immediately centered on the NEVADA; bomb after bomb exploded in the water as the Japanese planes streamed down the sky to within a few hundred feet of the battleship's decks, before finding their bull's-eye.

In all, the NEVADA was hit by six bombs, causing extensive flooding and severe structural damage.

One of these bombs exploded near the forward antiaircraft fire director, causing serious injuries to Ensign J. K. Taussig, Jr., USN. More than a year previously, Rear Admiral J. K. Taussig, Sr., USN, had been bitterly criticized for his sharp warning to the nation to expect a Japanese attack in the Pacific.

Ensign Taussig was ordered to leave his station for medical aid. He refused to do so, continuing to direct the 5-inch fire at the attacking planes, from his station high up in the foremast. Despite a spreading fire in the vicinity, Pharmacist's Mate 1/c Ned Bigelow Curtis climbed up to offer Ensign Taussig first aid. Taussig told the enlisted man to leave him, to attend to others who were more seriously wounded; that it was his intention to remain at his post. Curtis saw at once that the young officer was seriously injured. Disregarding orders, he supervised Taussig's removal from the fire control director. By this time, however, normal descent from the foremast was blocked by fire, so Curtis improvised a stretcher and lowered Taussig to the boat deck by hand lines.

That Ensign Taussig's injuries had indeed been serious was to be proved by the many months he spent in naval hospitals. Curtis's judgment and initiative in disregarding orders were signalized later when the Navy Cross was pinned on him.

Many acts of self-sacrifice and heroism were performed that morning on the NEVADA, as on every ship, on every shore station. Machinist Donald K. Ross was to receive the Congressional Medal of Honor for saving the lives of shipmates caught in the NEVADA's forward dynamo room. On two of his trips, Ross himself lost consciousness and had to be rescued and resuscitated. Each time he insisted upon returning to his duties.

There was Coxswain Louis George Gombasy, who helped Boatswain Hill cast off the NEVADA's lines. Gombasy was himself wounded, but he helped to care for others whose injuries were a little worse than his own, and he fought the NEVADA's fires until the last one had been brought under control.

And there was Chief Shipfitter George D. Etcell, a veteran of more than 20 years, who was ordered to go below to determine whether a forward magazine had been flooded. One part of his journey carried him through creeping fires in the interior of the ship. Another·time he was up to his waist in hot oil and water. He carried out his mission, and when he returned he was carrying an unconscious shipmate who had been overcome by smoke; the man would have died but for Etcell.

In the port antiaircraft battery the men at the guns observed that the officer in charge, Ensign T. H. Taylor, USN, was having trouble with his hearing. Then they saw thin trickles of blood coursing from each of his ears. Captain F. W. Scanland, USN, subsequently reported that Taylor had been "under fire from strafing attacks, bomb explosions in the immediate vicinity, and serious fires that exploded one ready box of ammunition in the battery, wounded by fragments, burned, shell-shocked, and completely deafened due to broken eardrums." But he continued to direct his battery.

Hundreds of like examples of loyalty and of bravery went unrecognized, unrecorded, unrewarded. Those cited here from the Navy's records are representative of a far more numerous company, illustrations of how men respond to the unpredictable emergencies of battle.

When it was all over, the NEVADA had lost 3 of her officers and 47 men. But the ship was to live to fight again. Upon orders from the yard signal tower, the ship was moved by tugs from the position where she first grounded, near the PENNSYLVANIA's drydock, and carefully run aground in the shallow across from Hospital Point. She gradually settled in the water as she flooded through three holes in her side.

Southwestward along Battleship Row from the NEVADA's mooring place, at the other extremity of the line, in fact, was USS CALIFORNIA, a 32,600-ton battleship with 14-inch guns, commissioned in 1921. The flag of Vice-Admiral W. S. Pye, USN, flew at the CALIFORNIA's mainmast, signifying her as the flagship of Commander Battle Force, United States Pacific Fleet.

"I was sitting in my cabin a little before 0800, when the general alarm sounded," declared Captain H. C. Train, USN, chief of staff to Admiral Pye. "My first thought was that the alarm had been set off by accident. I put on my blouse and cap, hurried on deck, and started rapidly toward the bridge.

"Some time en route between the quarterdeck and the bridge I felt the shock of something hitting the ship, and saw a low-flying plane flash over the ship from port to starboard."

The "shock of something hitting the ship" which Captain Train felt was the almost simultaneous explosion of two Japanese torpedoes and the blast of a near miss close aboard on the port side. Almost at once the CALIFORNIA took an 8-degree list and began to settle.

The complete surprise and the severity of the Japanese attack was the main reason why the CALIFORNIA settled to the bottom. This was true also of the other ships which were later to be listed as sunk at their berths in the shallow waters of the harbor. Very wisely for their plans, the Japanese delivered their heaviest blows at the very outset of the attack. Thus ships were holed by torpedoes and armor-piercing bombs before they could be brought to a complete state of readiness. Later in the war many United States ships were to take worse poundings than most of those received at Pearl Harbor. But in these later actions ships were at battle stations—they were able to maintain watertight integrity, and to move under their own power even with an entire section of the ship shot away, as was the case with the NEW ORLEANS in the Battle of Tassafaronga. At Pearl Harbor there was no time to make the ships ready to withstand attack.

This was particularly true of the CALIFORNIA. The ship was loaded almost to maximum with a supply of fuel oil. Torpedo and bomb blasts ruptured her fuel tanks, flooding an entire lower deck with oil.

Fires sprang up intermittently in various sections of the ship, filling the inner spaces with noxious fumes and gases. The CALIFORNIA's medical officer, Commander J. D. Jewell, USN, was severely burned when a sheet of flame swept through his battle dressing station. He did not leave his post, and continued to treat the burned and wounded men as they were brought to him.

The ship's ready guns went into action almost with the very beginning of the raid. Power was soon lost in the ship, however, and ammunition had to be passed up to the guns by hand.

Three of the CALIFORNIA's personnel were posthumously awarded the Congressional Medal of Honor for their efforts to keep the guns going during the attack. One of those who lost his life in this effort was Machinist's Mate 1/c Robert R. Scott, USN, whose station was at an air-compressing machine supplying the 5-inch guns from below-decks. One of the torpedo blasts crashed through Scott's compartment, and oil and water began to spew in through the ugly hole. The other men on this detail evacuated the compartment, but Scott refused to go.

"This is my station," he yelled up through the hatch. "I'll stay here and give them air as long as the guns are going."

The steel door was slammed shut against the waters threatening the entire ship; slammed shut, too, on the life of Robert Scott, who kept the guns supplied with the jets of air that cleared the barrels after each round fired until the flood extinguished the machines and the life of the man who served them.

Warrant Radio Electrician Thomas James Reeves, a Navy veteran of more than 20 years, formed a party of ammunition passers and plunged into a burning passageway. As members of his party were overcome he assisted them to safety. Finally, only Reeves was left, and he worked until he slipped into unconsciousness at his station. It was there he died.

Another ammunition detail was formed by three young Naval Reserve ensigns, Herbert Charpiot Jones, I. W. Jeffrey, and W. F. Cage. They were working at an ammunition hoist near a magazine when a Japanese bomb penetrated the upper works and exploded in their vicinity. All three were hurt, but Ensign Jones's wounds were mortal.

"Leave me alone," the dying man protested, when the others tried despite their own hurts to remove him. "I'm done for. Get out of here, before the magazines go off."

As it happened, the CALIFORNIA's magazines did not go off. But the ship was in enough trouble. The erupting oil had now ringed the entire vessel in flame, there was no power on the guns, and there seemed little likelihood that the ship could be saved.

An order was passed to abandon ship, and some of the officers and men were able to leave through the burning waters. They immediately manned fire-fighting equipment stored on Ford Island and returned to battle the flames on their ship. Within a short time, the abandon-ship order was canceled, and topside gun stations continued to blaze away at the attacking Japanese planes.

The CALIFORNIA remained afloat for three days, but the water continued to flood into the ship until she finally rested on the soft mud of the bottom, with only her upper works exposed. None of the ship's people felt that more could have been done to save the CALIFORNIA; nearly a hundred of these officers and men were cited for commendation by Captain J. W. Bunkley, a number of those cited being among the 6 officers and 92 men who lost their lives.

Like the NEVADA, the CALIFORNIA would live to fight again. With the exception of the ARIZONA and the OKLAHOMA, this was equally true of every other ship damaged in the raid.

Of the five remaining battleships on which the action is yet to be described, three were the flagships of admirals, and one of these flag officers was to lose his life. USS MARYLAND was the flagship of the Commander Battleships, Battle Force; the ARIZONA flew the two-starred bunting of Commander Battleship Division One, Battle Force, and the TENNESSEE was the flagship of Commander Battleship Division Two.

Looking northward along Battleship Row from the CALIFORNIA's mooring place at the end of the line, OKLAHOMA and MARYLAND were paired, with MARYLAND moored inboard nearest Ford Island; WEST VIRGINIA and TENNESSEE were tied up together, with the TENNESSEE inboard, and ARIZONA was berthed inboard of the repair ship VESTAL until the VESTAL was towed to safety after ARIZONA blew up.

Again with the exception of the ARIZONA, the ships berthed inboard sustained much less damage and suffered many fewer casualties than the ships with which they were paired. The nearness of Ford Island prevented the Japanese from launching torpedoes from that direction, while the outboard vessels stopped the torpedoes launched in the harbor. Thus, although neither MARYLAND nor TENNESSEE was hit by one of these missiles, OKLAHOMA was staggered by four while WEST VIRGINIA was blasted by six. That the ARIZONA was torpedoed, even though moored inboard, is perhaps explained by the fact that one or more of the deadly explosives passed completely underneath the VESTAL's shallow draft and detonated against the battleship's much deeper keel.

Of the pair of battleships nearest the CALIFORNIA, the doom of the

OKLAHOMA, a 29,000-ton ship commissioned in 1916, was sealed in the first minutes of the attack. As on the other capital ships which were the targets for the first wave of planes, there was no time in which to close all doors and hatches and seal all compartments against damage.

Four Japanese torpedoes hit the OKLAHOMA on her port side and exploded at intervals not longer than 15 seconds. The ship at once began to list to port. Most of the men below were trapped. Some 400 bodies were still in the ship when it was refloated by salvage operations months later.

Executive officer of the OKLAHOMA, and also senior officer aboard during the attack, was Commander J. L. Kenworthy, USN. As he raced for the bridge, Commander Kenworthy found the going very hard because of the fuel oil which had been blasted up through the tilted weather decks by the torpedo explosions. He saw at once that the ship was going to roll over. His first efforts were to clear the ship of the men below. Then he ordered the ship abandoned over the high starboard side, with the men walking along the ship's side and across its bottom as the OKLAHOMA turned over.

"When it became impossible to remain on the tilted starboard side longer," said Commander Kenworthy, "I walked up the ship's side over the blister ledge and up over the bottom. The ship settled with the starboard side of the bottom above water, and a portion of the keel and starboard propeller shaft were clear."

The OKLAHOMA had rotated through an arc approximately 150 degrees; that portion of the ship kept above the surface was supported by the ship's masts, thrust into the mud of the harbor bottom.

Shortly after the ship came to rest, tappings from within were heard along her hull. Workmen from the Navy Yard and bluejackets immediately began desperate efforts to rescue the trapped men. The work was pushed all night and until the following afternoon, stopping only when no more signals were heard. Thirty-two men were saved through holes cut into the capsized hull.

The entire crew of one of the aged battleship's 14-inch gun turrets were trapped inside as the ship capsized. The door of the turret was finally pried open by the men, the air inside preventing the water from completely filling the interior. Ensign Francis Charles Flaherty, USNR, the turret officer, called for a volunteer to stand by him in helping the others to escape. Seaman 1/c James Richard Ward responded first, and he and Ensign Flaherty held flashlights, fixing the direction of the door, while the other men dived out and swam to the surface. Flaherty and Ward were the only two men who failed to escape from the turret; they were posthumously awarded the Congressional Medal of Honor.

Another of the OKLAHOMA's company deliberately gave to others his own opportunity to survive, Lieutenant (jg) Aloysius Herman Schmitt (ChC) USN. Chaplain Schmitt was in his quarters on the starboard side of the ship, near the crew's messing space, when the OKLAHOMA began to heel over. He was vesting himself for 0800 Sunday Mass, and he had a handsomely bound breviary in a hip pocket.

Several men, unable to find an exit as the ship rolled, entered Chaplain Schmitt's stateroom, which they knew to contain a porthole. The chaplain helped them out through the opening. Then he himself started through, men standing on the now-horizontal side of the turning ship tugging at his arms and shoulders. Although not a large man (as was erroneously reported in news dispatches at the time) Chaplain Schmitt's progress through the porthole was stopped when the breviary in his pocket caught on the coaming. He backed into the ship, removed the prayerbook, and was about to make another attempt to escape when several other enlisted men climbed into the room. The padre insisted that these men push through the porthole ahead of him. As the last one climbed through, Chaplain Schmitt's porthole rolled beneath the surface, and water gushed in with the force of a high-pressure fire main. He did not escape.

It was a most fantastic series of adventures that befell a member of the OKLAHOMA's Marine Corps detail, Gunnery Sergeant Thomas Edgar Hailey, 25-year-old native of St. Joseph, Missouri. Hailey was asleep in the Marine Quarters on the OKLAHOMA's third deck when the call to general quarters fetched him up standing.

As he sprang out of his bunk, clad only in summer underwear, Hailey felt the thud of the first torpedo exploding against the hull. He sprinted topside for his station—he was captain of No. 10 broadside 5-inch gun. Before he could reach his post the ship had begun to turn over. Hailey plunged into the harbor, thrashing wildly to push back the oil that spewed from the stricken ship. Some 30 feet away was the MARYLAND, and Hailey swarmed up a line that was hanging over that ship's side. Then he helped pull aboard several of his shipmates who likewise had taken to the water. This task accomplished, Hailey spied an antiaircraft gun not fully manned. He rallied some of his dripping, oil-blackened shipmates from the OKLAHOMA and the gun went into fast action.

But not for long: a Japanese bomb exploded on the MARYLAND's quarterdeck, dispersing the gun crew, and then smoke and flames from the blast on the nearby ARIZONA made the position untenable.

Once again the young ˙Marine sergeant plunged into the water; this time he had to fight flaming oil. After swimming a few yards, Hailey's feet touched something. It was a suction pipe about four feet under the surface, and connected ashore with a harbor dredge. Hailey walked the pipe like a tightrope artist until he stepped ashore on Ford Island. He at once reported to the air station, just as a call sounded for volunteers to undertake a dangerous mission.

Hailey stepped forward in his oil-soaked underwear, to be told that an aviator was about to take up an unarmed observation plane, and the pilot needed a rear-seat passenger who was also an expert rifleman. Hailey replied that he fitted the qualifications. He was handed a parachute and a Springfield rifle, and the plane took off. During a flight of five hours the plane had trouble with its gas tanks and almost crashed at sea. Fortunately for Hailey and the naval aviator, it encountered no Japs at shooting range.

Meanwhile, nearly a hundred of the OKLAHOMA's people had manned guns on the nearby MARYLAND. Some of the officers and men boarded the MARYLAND by using one of the OKLAHOMA's broadside guns as a precarious gangplank, before the ship tilted so far that this route had to be abandoned. Others, like Hailey, had climbed aboard, or had been rescued, from the water.

The MARYLAND, a 31,500-ton vessel commissioned in 1921, was one of the two 16-inch-gun battleships stationed at Pearl Harbor, the other being WEST VIRGINIA. The other big-gun battleships of the United States Fleet were in the Atlantic or on the West Coast.

The first person aboard the MARYLAND to fire at the attacking planes was Seaman 1/c Leslie Vernon Short, a 22-year-old enlistee from Garden City, Kansas. Short was working hard to become a machine gunner. He spent every spare minute as close to the deadly mechanism as he could get. He did not know much about the gun's intricacies, but he knew how to make it shoot. Captain D. C. Godwin, USN, the MARY-

LAND's commander, was so impressed by Short's initiative in firing without orders, and before the ship was called to general quarters, that he later directed the young seaman to write a report of his actions.

"After breakfast on Sunday morning," wrote Short in compliance, "I came to Group 'A' Machine Gun Station to write some letters home and address some Christmas cards. Suddenly I noticed planes diving on the Naval Air Station nearby. At first I thought they were our planes in mock diving attack, but when I saw smoke and flames rise from a building I looked closer and saw that they were not American planes. I broke out ammunition nearby, loaded my machine gun, and opened fire on two torpedo planes coming in from the east which had just dropped two torpedoes. Flames and smoke burst from the first plane I aimed at, and it veered off to the left, falling toward the hospital. I think I also hit the second plane, which I aimed at immediately after shooting at the first one, but by then I was so busy that I cannot say for sure."

Although the MARYLAND was hit by two bombs, one of which blew a hole in the side of the ship and caused her to settle several feet by the bow, her damage was not sufficient to keep her long out of action from the standpoint of permanent repairs. In addition, her casualty list included only 2 officers and 2 men as compared to a toll of 20 officers and 395 men lost on the OKLAHOMA.

Of the next two battleships in the line, the WEST VIRGINIA earned the unhappy distinction of having been hit by a greater weight of enemy explosive than any other ship in the harbor, and this statement is not altered by the fact that the nearby ARIZONA was completely destroyed. The "Weevie," as she was affectionately known to her officers and men, was hit by two heavy bombs in addition to six torpedoes, and many near misses exploded along her sides. Her loss of life included 2 officers and 103 men; and one of those who died was the ship's commanding officer, Captain Mervyn Sharp Bennion, USN.

Like the CALIFORNIA, the WEST VIRGINIA had to be temporarily abandoned because of fires. Her men later returned, those who were physically able to do so, and fought the flames until they were under control. By that time, the proud WEST VIRGINIA—one of the Navy's more modern battleships despite her 18 years in service—was resting on the shallow bottom of the harbor.

One of the Weevie's officers not aboard at the beginning of the attack was Ensign H. W. Sears, USNR, who was ashore on authorized leave. By the time Sears got to the harbor, the Weevie was enveloped in flames. Since no boat was handy to take him to his own ship, Sears went aboard the light cruiser PHOENIX, then about to get under way to stand out to sea.

Sears' specialty was gunnery. He reported to the skipper of the PHOENIX and asked if the cruiser captain could use another turret officer. The skipper, completely occupied by the effort to save his ship, replied that all his turrets and guns were fully manned. By this time the PHOENIX was under way and had drawn abreast of the burning WEST VIRGINIA.

"Aye, aye, sir," said Ensign Sears, the reply prescribed by naval custom and usage. But Sears' subsequent actions were not in the book.

He saluted smartly, did an about-turn, walked to the rail and plunged over the side. He swam through oil and water to his own ship, boarded the accommodation ladder, and joined the rescue and fire-fighting parties on the Weevie's decks, where he stayed until ordered to abandon ship. While perhaps more spectacular than some others, Sears' actions furnish a yardstick by which to measure the conduct of all the Weevie's officers and men, including a certain Negro mess attendant second class named Doris Miller.

But the WEST VIRGINIA'S story is perhaps best told by piecing the statements of the surviving officers. The senior survivor was the Weevie's exec, Commander R. H. Hillenkoetter, USN, who was in his cabin just commencing to dress when, at 0755 the word was passed, "Away fire and rescue party." Thirty seconds later general quarters was sounded just as the Marine orderly rushed into the commander's cabin to report the Japanese attack. As Commander Hillenkoetter headed for the ladder he felt the jar of the first torpedoes and by the time he had reached the quarterdeck the ship was listing rapidly to port.

Commander Hillenkoetter went to his battle station aft—as executive officer, it was his duty to post himself in a section of the ship far away from the captain's bridge, thereby minimizing the danger that both captain and executive officer might be killed by a single hit. By the time Commander Hillenkoetter reached his battle station, much of the dangerous list had been taken off by prompt action on the part of Lieutenant C. V. Rickett, USN, who rushed below with a party of enlisted men and counterflooded the ship.

Next senior to the executive officer was Lieutenant Commander John S. Harper, USN, the ship's first lieutenant and damage-control officer.

Harper went at once to his assigned position in Central Station, the communication and control center in the very core of the ship. From this post he directed repair parties until rising water forced its evacuation. The only escape from Central, with all hatches closed, was through an armored tube leading up to the bridge. Through this, Commander Harper directed all hands except the telephone talker to evacuate. The commander and a second-class yeoman named Rogers stayed below until the water in the compartment was six feet deep in the tilted port side of the room. Then they, too, wriggled up the narrow escape tube.

The WEST VIRGINIA's navigator, Lieutenant Commander T. T. Beattie, USN, accompanied Captain Bennion to the bridge when general quarters was sounded.

"The Captain and I went to the conning tower, our battle stations," reported Lieutenant Commander Beattie, "and at this time dive-bombing attacks started to take place. Numerous explosions were felt throughout the ship. Upon testing our communications with Central Station and to the guns we found they were disrupted. I suggested to the Captain that as long as no communications were in the battle conning tower that we leave there and attempt to establish messenger communication and try to save the ship. We went out on the starboard side of the bridge, discussing what to do. During all this time extremely heavy bombing and strafing attacks occurred. The ship was constantly shaken by bomb hits.

"The Captain doubled up with a groan and stated that he had been wounded. I saw that he had been hit in the stomach, probably by a large piece of shrapnel, and was very seriously wounded. He then sank to the deck, and I loosened his collar. I then sent a messenger for a pharmacist's mate to assist the Captain."

But Lieutenant Commander Beattie's first duty was to his ship, rather than to any officer or man aboard. With this fact in mind, it is understandable, when "the ARIZONA's forward magazines blew up with a tremendous explosion and large sheets of flame shot skyward, and I began to wonder about our own magazines and whether they were being flooded," that the navigator posted a man with the Captain and went down to the forecastle.

On the forecastle, Beattie found the ship's communications officer, Lieutenant Commander D. C. Johnson, USN, directing the transfer of wounded men to rescue boats. Beattie took charge of this work, and also began to direct the parties fighting fires on the deck. He asked Johnson to go to the bridge, to assist the Captain.

Lieutenant Commander Johnson relates: "I proceeded to the signal bridge where I found Captain Bennion lying on a cot in full uniform, wounded. I had brought a colored mess attendant with me, a very powerfully-built individual, having in mind that he might pick the Captain up and carry him below. . . ."

The "powerfully-built individual" was Doris Miller.

But Captain Bennion was past all help, and he knew it. He had been wounded by a large fragment from a 15-inch aerial projectile which struck a main turret of the nearby TENNESSEE. The Captain's only interest was the manner in which his ship was being fought; he demanded to be told about the progress of the fire-fighting parties, instead of answering questions about his own condition, and he seemed to cheer up when told that every antiaircraft battery on the ship was in action.

"The Captain's abdomen was cut by a fragment of bomb, about three or four inches, with part of his intestines protruding," reported Lieutenant (jg) F. H. White, USNR. . . . "The Captain did not want to be moved, but he was carefully carried to shelter abaft the conning tower where Leak, Chief Pharmacist's Mate, administered first aid."

Then while other officers and men were rigging up a stretcher, in the hope of lowering the captain to safety, Lieutenant White and Mess Attendant Doris Miller sprang to the machine guns forward of the conning tower as dive bombers attacked the ship. The Negro messman had not been trained as a machine gunner, but he was a keen observer who had watched many a machine-gun drill. In the interest of a legend already in existence, it would be pleasant to be able to report that Miller shot down one or more planes. A careful search of the records, including eyewitness reports of all those present, fails to bring forth either a contradiction or a substantiation in fact. Nevertheless, Doris Miller, M. Att. 2/c, later to be reported missing in the sinking of the small aircraft carrier LISCOMBE BAY, merited to the fullest the Navy Cross which he so proudly wore.

Captain Bennion lived only a few minutes after the beginning of the dive-bombing attack. As fires leapt up toward the bridge all ordinary methods of exit were cut off. The only means of leaving the bridge was by swinging hand over hand along a fire hose secured to a crane, then

climbing down the crane to the deck. For the time being, the body of
Captain Bennion had to be left on his bridge.

Sunday afternoon was well along before all fires on the WEST VIR-
GINIA were finally brought under control. The ship rested on the bottom,
her list causing the port side of the main deck to be covered with water.
The wreckage of the ship's topside presented such a shambles that those
who saw her immediately after the battle doubted that she ever again
would sail. In this they were to be proved wrong.

But even after the Weevie was sunk, a tragic drama was secretly
unfolding in a watertight compartment deep within her. When the WEST
VIRGINIA was finally raised, a mute record chalked on a bulkhead showed
that three of her trapped men lived until the day before Christmas
Eve.

As has been noted, the inboard TENNESSEE sustained considerably
less attack damage than the WEST VIRGINIA. The TENNESSEE, a 32,000-
ton battleship completed in 1920, was struck by two 15-inch armor-
piercing bombs, each of which landed on one of the ship's main turrets.
A fragment from one of these bombs is believed to have killed Captain
Bennion. The other blew out its base plug and its detonating charge
burned out on the deck without exploding.

But the TENNESSEE, although her fighting ability was not seriously
impaired, was temporarily immobilized as much as if she had been sent
to the bottom. As the WEST VIRGINIA settled into the water, she wedged
the TENNESSEE against a concrete quay. Captain Charles E. Reordan,
USN, discovered this when he made an effort to remove his ship to
safety. The TENNESSEE's propellers were churning the water, but she
was not moving. In fact, a part of the concrete quay later had to be
blasted away before the ship could be extricated.

But the fact that the ship's propellers were turning probably saved
her from considerably more damage than she actually suffered. As the
ARIZONA blew up, a few yards astern, the water about the TENNESSEE
was covered with flaming oil. This created so much heat at the vessel's
stern that the after officers' quarters were ravaged by flames, and other
fires in the interior of the ship were constantly breaking out. Then Captain Reordan noted that the wash of the TENNESSEE's propellers drove
the burning oil away, so he kept them turning. Thus the TENNESSEE's
engines, for 24 hours after the attack, were running at full speed ahead
without the battleship budging an inch.

Captain Reordan was ashore, and on the sick list, when the attack began. He returned to his ship at once.

"Thirty-six hours later," said the TENNESSEE's commander, "I left my bridge a well man. I had rushed aboard in my civilian clothes, which we always wore when we went on the beach. I had been on the bridge for several hours before I realized that I had been fighting the ship while wearing a straw hat."

Casualties on the TENNESSEE, as on PENNSYLVANIA and MARYLAND, were comparatively light, her losses totaling only five men.

On the ARIZONA there was a different and sadder story. Her personnel loss was by far the heaviest of all the ships in the harbor. Of the ship's Marine Corps complement of 87 men only 13 escaped, although the Marines were stationed topside where escape was possible. The ARIZONA's musicians were assigned, on the ship's Battle Bill, to action stations below-decks, where they served as ammunition passers—aboard a combat ship of the United States Navy there are no noncombatants once battle has been joined. When the ARIZONA's forward magazine exploded, the twenty members of the ship's band, and their musician first class leader, were among those killed.

The ARIZONA was hit by the first torpedo planes and dive bombers the Japanese sent into the attack. One and possibly two torpedoes passed completely underneath the VESTAL and struck the big battleship slightly forward of amidships. One bomb struck the forecastle. Another exploded on a face plate on No. 4 turret aft. Still another ripped through the bridge and detonated on the boat deck. And then it was that one of the attacking Japanese pilots realized the dive bomber's dream. His bomb dropped exactly into the ARIZONA's stack, exploding in the boilers and setting off the vast amount of powder stored in the forward magazine.

The ship's bow seemed to leap out of the water, and her weather decks cracked open as fire and debris shot skyward. Plumes of oil and water showered topside, and fires immediately enveloped the forward part of the ship. The fate of the ARIZONA, a 32,600-ton battleship within less than nine months of being declared over-age, was sealed in the first five minutes of the attack. The magazine blast broke the ship's back and she rapidly settled in the water.

And in the explosion of the magazine, or in the explosion of the bomb that hit the bridge, the ARIZONA lost her skipper and the rear admiral for whom she served as a flagship.

The senior officer to survive the attack was the first lieutenant and damage-control officer, Lieutenant Commander Samuel Glenn Fuqua, USN, who called the ship to general quarters as soon as the first enemy planes were sighted. Then he headed for his battle station.

"As I was running forward on the starboard side of the quarterdeck," he declared, "I was apparently knocked out by the blast of a bomb. . . . When I came to and got up off the deck the ship was a mass of flames amidships on the boat deck, and the deck aft was partly awash. The anti-aircraft battery and machine guns apparently were still firing at this time. Some of the ARIZONA's boats had pulled clear of the oil and were lying off the stern."

Lieutenant Commander Fuqua suspected that he was the senior officer still alive, and thus in command. It was up to him to see that the guns continued to fire as long as possible. It was his responsibility to fight the fires and to attempt to save the burned and wounded—that the ARIZONA was lost was already becoming obvious. The citation which accompanied his Congressional Medal of Honor pointed out that his courage and coolness were an inspiration that resulted in the saving of many lives. But the story is better in his own words, although told with considerably more restraint:

"At this time I attempted, with the assistance of the crews of No. 3 and No. 4 turrets, to put out the fire which was coming from the boat deck, and which had extended to the quarterdeck. There was no pressure on the fire mains. However, about 14 CO_2's were obtained that were stowed on the port side, and held the flames back from the quarterdeck in order to pick up wounded who were running down the boat deck out of the flames. I placed about 70 wounded and injured in the boats, which had been picked up off the deck aft, and landed them at the Ford Island landing. This was completed about 0900 or 0930. Not knowing whether the Captain or the Admiral had ever reached the bridge, I had the Captain's hatch opened up, immediately after I came to, and sent Ensign G. B. Lenning, USNR, and Ensign J. D. Miller, USN, down to search the Captain's and Admiral's cabins to see if they were there. By that time the Captain's cabin and Admiral's cabin were about waist deep in water. A search of the two cabins revealed that the Admiral and Captain were not there. Knowing that they were on board I assumed that they had proceeded to the bridge.

"About 0900, seeing that all guns of the anti-aircraft and secondary battery were out of action and that the ship could not possibly be saved, I ordered all hands to abandon ship."

The commanding officer of the ARIZONA was Captain Franklin Van Valkenburgh, USN; and the ARIZONA was the flagship of Rear Admiral Isaac Campbell Kidd, USN, commander of Battleship Division One. Both were posthumously awarded the Medal of Honor. The exact manner in which these two officers lost their lives perhaps will never be known. It is known that Captain Van Valkenburgh was one of the first persons to reach the bridge of his ship after the call to battle stations. And observers retained a vivid picture of Admiral Kidd, in the first heat of the action, helping to serve an undermanned machine gun. Presumably, they were killed in the opening minutes of the attack.

All told, the ARIZONA lost 47 officers and 1,057 men. Some hundreds of the bodies were never removed from the sunken hulk of the ship.

Two new ships were to carry on the names of the commanding officers who lost their lives. One of these ships was the destroyer VAN VALKEN-BURGH.

The other, also a speedy, hard-hitting destroyer, taking the name of the first United States naval officer of flag rank to be killed in action, was proudly christened—USS KIDD.

Chapter Four

A ND so, by noon of December 7, 1941, the United States Navy's base at Pearl Harbor lay hidden, crippled, under a heavy blanket of the smoke of war.

Since this is first and last a narrative of men and ships and planes in combat, no attempt is made to assign the causes of the war or to relate the steps by which the war approached actuality. Once a battle begins, the answers to such questions are of little immediate interest to the men who are fighting and dying.

Secretary of the Navy Frank Knox[1] spent that Sunday morning at the State Department, conferring with Secretary of State Hull and Secretary of War Stimson on the critical situation between this country and Japan; two other callers waiting to see the Secretary of State were the Japanese ambassador, Admiral Kichisaburo Nomura, one-eyed, ramrod stiff, and tall for a Japanese; and Hirohito's special "peace envoy," Saburo Kurusu.

As the conference ended Secretary Knox returned to his office in the Navy Department, a jerry-built, sprawling structure between 17th and 19th streets on Constitution Avenue. It was perhaps an unconscious commentary on the United States' national view of world affairs that, while such governmental departments as Commerce, Labor, and Justice were housed in ornate granite structures, State was crowded into a gingerbready Victorian antique while War and Navy were assigned to quarters hastily slapped together as "temporary" buildings during World War I.

Knox went at once to his office on the second floor of the building, overlooking Constitution Avenue and with a view up 18th Street. His

[1] Secretary Knox personally initiated the preparation of this series on the participation of the Navy in World War II, of which this is the first volume. He was keenly interested in the progress of the work, although he had seen none of it before he died. The last interview before his brief illness and untimely death on April 28, 1944, was granted to the authors. In this interview he recalled his actions and reactions on the day of the Pearl Harbor raid. The substance of the interview is here set down.

lunchtime had passed and he was about to order some food, but this intention was never carried out—in fact, not until he was snatching a hasty snack that night did he remember that he had missed his midday meal entirely.

As he sat at his desk his outer door burst open. Admiral Harold R. Stark, USN, Chief of Naval Operations, strode quickly to the Secretary's desk with a dispatch.

It read: FROM CINCPAC TO ALL SHIPS HAWAII AREA: AIR RAID ON PEARL HARBOR. THIS IS NO DRILL.

The message had been intercepted by the Navy Radio Station at Mare Island Navy Yard, San Francisco, and forwarded via urgent communication. Secretary Knox immediately picked up his White House telephone. The time was 1:47 P.M., EST.

President Roosevelt was found at luncheon in the Oval Room with Harry Hopkins.

"I don't remember the President's exact words," said Secretary Knox. "He was astonished, of course. I think he expressed disbelief. Anyway, I read the dispatch to him."

President Roosevelt then told the Secretary to place the entire Navy on a full war basis at once. He directed the Navy Secretary to obtain all possible details of the attack immediately.

Knox already had put through an urgent telephone call to Pearl Harbor. As he ended his conversation with the President he was connected with Rear Admiral C. C. Bloch, USN, Commandant Fourteenth Naval District, and former Commander in Chief Pacific Fleet.

"Bloch was cool as a cucumber. He told me of the damage as it was then believed to exist. As he talked, he could look through a window and see smoke and flames from the ships still burning in the harbor. Our undamaged ships and planes were searching for the Japs. It was expected that the enemy might return, either with continued aerial attacks or with an invasion force."

After this telephone conversation Knox rushed to the White House for an extraordinary meeting of the President's Cabinet, at which was discussed the war message the President was to deliver before Congress, and to the nation, on the following day.

Secretary Knox joined other members of the Cabinet in the House of Representatives on December 8, 1941. President Roosevelt asked Congress for a declaration of war on Japan. Mrs. Knox and Mrs. Frank

E. Beatty, wife of the Secretary's naval aide, sat in the gallery to listen to the President.

After the Secretary left the Capitol, Mrs. Knox noted that her husband appeared to have been greatly moved by the President's words. There was silence in the car for several blocks.

"I must know exactly what happened at Pearl Harbor," said Knox. "I want all the details. I'm going out there."

There was immediate agreement from Mrs. Knox.

Accompanied by Captain Beatty and two trusted advisers, Lieutenant Commander Edward A. Hayes, USNR, and Special Assistant Joseph W. Powell, the Secretary took off the following day in his own plane. They were grounded that night in Texas but reached San Diego by noon on Wednesday.

Preparations had been made very hastily. Knox and his party were assigned to a large flying boat, a PB2Y, which had already been heavily loaded with plasma, antitoxin, and other supplies vitally needed for the Pearl Harbor wounded. The pilot, Lieutenant Commander S. M. Pickering, USN, wanted to remove some of this load. Knox asked the aviator if he thought it possible to take off without removing any of the precious cargo. The pilot agreed to try. Finally the flying boat cleared the water sluggishly after having taxied for "what seemed like miles." The take-off was made at about dark that day, with a record load for the plane's type.

As the plane neared Kaneohe Bay Naval Air Station there was a constant interchange between the pilot and the station by radio. The Pearl Harbor area was still wary of an attempted return by the Japanese attackers.

"Kaneohe Bay gave us strict instructions as to how we were to come in for the landing," said Secretary Knox. "We were told the direction and altitude of approach. They told us they would have the guns on us. We were warned that if we deviated in the slightest from the instructions given us we would be fired upon. After getting these instructions from the copilot, each of us was given a parachute and a life preserver. 'What's this for?' I asked. The copilot shrugged his shoulders and said, 'Well, you never know what will happen in a war. There's never been a war yet in which somebody didn't make a mistake.' We all laughed at that. We put on the life preservers and parachutes.

"The air station at Kaneohe seemed to have been completely

devastated. Many planes had been shot to pieces or burned. The barracks and station facilities had been bombed and strafed. They had just buried their own dead the day before. They also buried an enemy pilot, a Japanese naval officer, and they gave him full military honors. . . . Looking at the destruction, I felt that if this was what they had done to a mere air station, Pearl Harbor would be a lot worse. In this respect I was gratefully surprised, although the damage at Pearl Harbor was certainly bad enough.

"Some of the damaged ships in Pearl Harbor were still smoking when I got there, although the worst fire—the one on the ARIZONA—had already been brought under control. They had buried some 600 men killed in the raid just before my arrival.

"I was taken by ferry across to the Naval Air Station on Ford Island. The destruction there was thorough and complete. Then I went to see the men in the hospital, on Hospital Point. That was the hardest part of my entire trip. I saw hundreds of wounded, and burned, and more hundreds suffering from shock. The worst cases, though, were the men who had been burned. Some of them were charred or blistered beyond recognition.

"The sight of those men made me angry as I had never been in my life. It made me realize what a big job lay ahead of us, and that we had to finish the job all the way, all along the line."

Upon returning to Washington, Secretary Knox immediately reported to the White House. "I told the President that the details of the disaster, in human terms, were worse than we had feared, but that the long-term damage was a lot less. It was clear that most of the ships could be repaired and made even better than new. We had a lot of new equipment coming along; new types of antiaircraft guns and other equipment, and the overhaul and repair gave us a chance to put these deadly new improvements on the ships."

Even so, in his official announcement of the damage, Secretary Knox painted a picture darker than actuality. The exact facts became known only with the fuller knowledge of detailed and expert study. They were not to be revealed, for it was important to keep the truth from the enemy until the resurrected ships returned to battle.

To help him prepare his report, Secretary Knox called upon Commander Leland P. Lovette, USN, commander of Destroyer Division Five which included CASSIN, DOWNES, and SHAW. Lovette, one of the Navy's better known officer-authors, had just completed a monumental history to be called *The Naval Officer in American Diplomacy*. He had notified his publishers that the manuscript would shortly be on its way, the culmination of five years of writing and research.

"My quarters were in the CASSIN," said Commander Lovette. "All I saved was my sword, which I had had since my days at the Academy. I've still got three sea chests full of source material stored out at Pearl, and maybe someday . . ."

Even though Secretary Knox's report on ship damage was to prove pessimistic, the raid on Pearl Harbor made the Japanese temporarily supreme in the Pacific; the supremacy was more temporary than the enemy planned.

2

Like the men on the ships at Pearl Harbor, the men on the Navy's ships at sea were completely surprised by the Japanese attack.

One of the ships in the LEXINGTON task force, two days south and west of Pearl Harbor, was USS FLUSSER, a 1936 two-stack destroyer with five 5-inch mounts and twelve torpedo tubes in three quads.

Skipper of the FLUSSER was Lieutenant Commander W. G. ("Slim") Beecher, Jr., of the Annapolis class of '25. Beecher had been in old 4-pipers for a year and a half, and he had been in command of this newer-type ship just four days. He was having breakfast in his cabin when an excited radioman rushed in with the dispatch.

"That was at 7:58 that Sunday morning," he said. "In no time at all the news was all over the ship. Some members of the crew off watch turned on their long-wave radios. They were getting Japanese stations. The Japanese claimed they had sunk the entire Pacific Fleet. I assumed that Japanese subs would be on the prowl, and they might pick up a regenerated circuit from the radios. I ordered them shut off."

The LEXINGTON and her task force immediately went in Condition Zed,[1] with all battle stations manned and all watertight doors and hatches secured. A dispatch came through from Pearl Harbor: INTERCEPT AND DESTROY ENEMY. BELIEVED RETREATING ON A COURSE BETWEEN PEARL AND JALUIT. INTERCEPT AND DESTROY. An intercepting course was set, and speed was increased.

[1] Maximum condition of readiness for attack or defense aboard ship.

"The first plane of the Dawn Patrol hit the deck of 'Old Lady Lex' and crashed over the side," Beecher recalled. "The FLUSSER was on plane guard, and we managed to rescue the plane's radioman. The pilot was lost. Coming on top of the war news, this didn't make us feel any better."

Beecher feared, even as he broke formation to save the aviator, that his action might merit a court martial, or at least an official reprimand. Instead he was officially commended and thus was inaugurated the Navy's practice in this war of exerting every effort to rescue downed aviators, even though it meant hazardous penetration of enemy-held waters. This practice was to pay rich dividends, not only in men saved but in pilot morale. Contrarily, the Japanese, to whom life is cheap, were content to consider a man downed as a man lost.

No Japanese were sighted by the LEXINGTON task force. As the FLUSSER's skipper was junior, she was detached from the group and ordered to run back into Pearl, carrying as passengers a group of Army and Marine Corps generals who had been with the force as observers. The FLUSSER also took on all the fleet mail that was to go back in— even the coming of war was not allowed to hold up the mail—and the ship made port on Friday the 12th.

Those aboard the FLUSSER still had few details of the attack, beyond the skeleton reports received in code. Meanwhile, the Japanese radio had made all sorts of wild claims, including the statement that Pearl Harbor had been wiped off the map.

"I didn't know whether my wife and kids were still alive," said Beecher. "It was a tough five days."

They were also "tough days" for the wives and kin waiting in Pearl Harbor for their men at sea.

Mrs. Beecher, for instance, heard on her radio a Japanese broadcast in which the enemy claimed to have sunk the FLUSSER, as well as the LEXINGTON and all the other ships in the task force. "That didn't help my morale any," she said, "although I tried to tell myself it wasn't so. It seemed like years before I saw Slim. Finally, on Friday I got word that he was in Pearl Harbor. I saw him for an hour. He looked awful— I don't believe he'd had more than a few hours' sleep since Sunday."

Almost as bad, said Mrs. Beecher, was the uncertainty about everything, particularly on that Sunday and Sunday night of the war's beginning. A breakdown in the plant of the Honolulu *Advertiser* had prevented the Sunday paper being printed; telephone circuits were jammed by complaining subscribers and this hampered the transmission of the alarm that Pearl Harbor was under attack. As the word was passed from mouth to mouth rumor inevitably was grafted to the sufficiently bad news. There were reports that the Japanese had landed, and were coming with an invasion force. On Sunday night all Honolulu was blacked out. In their house out by Diamond Head, Mrs. Beecher and the two children, Skippy, 13, and Lee, 8, waited for the unknown.

"About eight o'clock that night we thought our time had come. A bomb hit right out in front—at least, it sounded like a bomb. My knees were shaking and my stomach wouldn't behave as I went to peep out the square glass opening in the front door. It was hard to see anything in the darkness—the darkness literally hurt my eyes. Gradually I made out a faint glow, and then I was sure it was a bomb. Then I heard voices, and from the conversation I found out what had happened. Two cars and an Army truck, all traveling without lights, and all in a hurry, had had a collision. An ambulance came, but I don't believe anyone was badly hurt.

"It seemed that we sat in the dark for years. There wasn't anything we could do, so we decided we might as well go to bed. The children and I all slept upstairs.

"The children finally went to sleep. I lay there, listening, listening for something on the radio, listening to noises outside—palm trees brushing against the house were no help—listening to the silence. Finally I got up, sat in the window seat, and looked out. The moon was coming up, and relieving that awful darkness. Then I saw a most beautiful sight— plane after plane, flying low, right past the house, with running lights brilliant against the night. Our planes, coming in from the mainland! They were the prettiest things I've ever seen, coming in through the clouds and moonlight. I guess I felt better after that. I went back to bed and slept."

3

When the Japanese paid their surprise visit to Oahu every person under attack became a combatant, regardless of whether or not that person was entitled to wear a uniform.

The telephone supervisor at the naval air station at Kaneohe, Alice

Beckley Spencer, was not ordinarily on duty on Sunday. Like many others, she at first thought the attack was a strange and very realistic kind of practice maneuver. Then she saw planes burning, men dying, and buildings going up in smoke. Miss Spencer went to her post in the air station, in a building that was constantly being machine-gunned and more than once was the target for bombs. An enlisted man was operating the switchboard.

"I'll take over," said Miss Spencer.

The enlisted man streaked for his gun station, near the seaplane ramps. Miss Spencer was commended in a letter from the President of the United States.

Verva N. Jones, chief telephone operator at the Pearl Harbor Navy Yard, was cited by the Yard Commandant for staying at her post for more than 24 hours, including the entire period of the Japanese attack.

Another civilian commended was the wife of a naval officer. The home of Lieutenant Commander W. D. Chandler, of the Navy's Civil Engineer Corps, was near the ship berths in the Navy Yard. Mrs. Chandler, with her husband's assistance, turned this home into a field hospital, treating burned and wounded as they were rescued from the ships. More than a hundred casualties were given first aid at this hastily organized center alone.

But Henry R. Danner, a machinist working in the Navy Yard, achieved distinction of a different kind. Danner became, as far as is known, the first civilian in Navy history to become part of a combat gun crew on shipboard.

Danner was working near the PENNSYLVANIA's drydock when the attack began, and he noticed that men were needed on one of the immobilized battleship's antiaircraft guns. He walked up the gangplank and offered his services. He was soon handling ammunition like a veteran. During one dive-bombing attack a heavy object fell on Danner's foot. Three of his toes were mashed, and he was in intense pain. He refused to leave his post; and for five days he insisted on working on urgent repair jobs in the yard. He stopped only when he was no longer able to stand on his feet.

The day laborers in the yard, many of them of mixed Oriental parentage, turned to without exception and volunteered their services. They were used to fight fires, in clearing bomb damage obstructing roadways, in belting machine-gun ammunition, and in other capacities as they were needed. After the battle, all were asked by their foreman, as a result of a yard directive, to turn in an account of their actions and observations.

One of those who reported was Isaac Lum, employed in the Navy Yard woodworking shop.

"On Sunday morning, December 7, 1941," wrote Lum, "when I just about started to work in the Mill Shop, suddenly I heard canons roar, at first I thought it was just routine practice of navy, then some one from the wood working shop said that it was war. I did take it hard at first, I thought was just joking or something like that. Then suddenly I saw a plane flew about the old mill shop bearing a red circle, they told me it was the Japanese plane. At this very minute I then realize what danger we are in, mostly all the mill men working went to· the beneath the lumber pile to seek safety. I stood by in the mill behind a pile of wood to safety there. Then about 15 minutes passed. Frank Hart our supervisor came and told the boys to go the munition· warehouse I quickly got on my feet and started to go the munition warehouse. On the way I saw a lot of marines at the munition warehouse, shooting at enemy air plane, then I saw a Japanese plane burst into flame, and it was out of control then a Marine came and told a few boys and I to help carry munition boxes to another part of the warehouse. Then the sergeant in charge taught us how to fill bullets to the magazine case of a automatic rifle. We quickly caught on how it is done, and started to fill them. While filling the magazines we heard guns, cannons and planes making a lot of noise outside. It was about 2 o'clock a Marine brought some food. We all ate turkey sandwiches and a cup of coffee for our lunch. Later we continued to fill magazines cases until there was no magazine case left. Then I started to go back to my shop to help my mechanic in feeding two by six inches lumber in to the sticker machine until our work is through."

The noncombatant ships at Pearl Harbor also turned in a good account of themselves. Commercial yard tugs were used to move the repair ship VESTAL from the ARIZONA's side. They also assisted in beaching the battered NEVADA, after her run down the harbor. Perhaps the prize of all these noncombatant craft was a Navy barge, the YG-17.

The YG-17 was a 110-foot flatboat of 170 tons and about 25 feet in the beam. She had no guns or armor of any kind, but she was self-propelled and she had pumps aboard. Despite her lack of fighting qualities, her skipper, Chief Boatswain L. M. Jahnsen, was rather proud of her this pride was not diminished by the fact that, in the Navy, the symbol YG is the designation of a yard garbage scow, or "honey-barge."

Jahnsen was on his morning garbage rounds in the harbor, collecting refuse from the various ships, when the first Japanese planes came over. As the WEST VIRGINIA began to burn he headed his lumbering craft into an area covered with smoke and burning oil. He ordered his men to man their single fire hose. Bombs were exploding in the water all about him. Overheated ammunition was going off on the WEST VIRGINIA'S deck. Telltale spurts of water raced about his barge as enemy planes flew low and strafed.

In the Navy, the person who is placed in charge of a ship is that ship's captain, whether he be a commissioned officer or an enlisted man. He is solely responsible for the ship's conduct until officially relieved of responsibility.

Jahnsen was fully aware of his responsibility. Although a YG has no quarterdeck, he stood and fought his garbage scow as if she had been the flagship of the Pacific Fleet.

4

Captain Reynolds Hayden, of the Navy Medical Corps, was in the dining room of his quarters on Hospital Point. He was finishing breakfast, also a little annoyed that the Honolulu *Advertiser* had not been delivered as usual that Sunday morning. Captain Hayden liked to have a look at the morning paper before beginning his usual rounds as commanding officer of the hospital.

As he looked out his window toward the harbor entrance he noted that an unusual number of planes seemed to be in the air. But of course both the Army and the Navy had lately stepped up maneuvers of all kinds. There was the sound of heavy explosions, too. Doubtless the construction crews were working a Sunday shift—they had been blasting near the hospital for several days. At this moment 13-year-old Billy, the captain's son, came running into the room.

"They're Jap planes," shouted Billy. "They're Jap planes!"

Ten minutes later Captain Hayden had ample proof of this report. A blazing enemy bomber spiraled out of the air and headed on a deadstick glide directly toward the front of the main hospital building. At the last moment it swerved crazily, caromed off a corner of the laboratory and crashed into the side of the chief petty officer's quarters, destroying them.

The hospital went to general quarters as if it had been a combat ship at sea. Battle stations were manned in the receiving rooms, the ward dressing rooms, and the operating suites. One of the patients already in the hospital was a doctor on the hospital staff, Lieutenant Commander Herman A. Gross (MC), USN, who had undergone a major operation just three days before. Dr. Gross insisted on being allowed to leave his bed so that he could assist in treating casualties. He worked steadily for three days, at the end of which time he again became a patient. He had collapsed at a wounded man's bedside.

The patients began to stream into the hospital shortly after the raid began, some on stretchers, some in ambulances or private automobiles, some limping along as best they could. The hospital at Pearl Harbor operated on a 24-hour shift, with the doctors working in relays, for the next ten days.

Many medical lessons were learned as the number of casualties rose into the hundreds. Doctors noted at once that men who wore undershirts in the vicinity of bomb explosions suffered flash burns only on exposed arms, shoulders, and heads. Those who did not wear undershirts were burned on the back and chest as well. Now all men in exposed battle stations wear head-to-toe covering. And the comparatively new sulfa drugs were given their first trial on an extensive scale.

"Much had been written on this subject," Captain Hayden reported, "but our experience, gained through necessity, completely demonstrated that the free local use of sulfanilamide powder in wounds permits us safely to select the best time to operate on these patients. Cases too numerous to mention proved this point. . . . Massive, lacerated wounds, sometimes complicated by severe compound fractures, and which had received only the barest essentials of preliminary surgery plus sulfanilamide powder freely in the wound, were operated upon the second and third day after injury with excellent results."

Patients suffering from burns were treated by spraying burned surfaces with one or more of several solutions. "Because of the great number of burn cases, it was necessary to use anything that was available which could be converted into a spray. Ordinary Flit guns were emptied, sterilized, immediately refilled with medicated spray, and used to spray patients."

Pearl Harbor's supply of dried blood plasma began to run out. The liquid plasma banks of Honolulu hospitals were levied upon. Several hundred civilians immediately volunteered and gave blood.

Nearly all patients were suffering in greater or less degree from shock. Casualties showing clinical evidence of only minor wounds died from this cause. "The great importance of prompt treatment for battle shock was impressed upon us all," Captain Hayden reported. "It takes precedence over all other treatment except control of hemorrhage."

A special group of doctors and nurses was assigned to administer shock treatment immediately upon entrance to the hospital. Generally, each patient was given a hypodermic injection of morphine sulphate, followed by tetanus antitoxin.

A good example of the mental reaction of a patient suffering from battle shock was furnished by a young officer from the WEST VIRGINIA, who turned in an account of his actions immediately after the attack, and while still under medical treatment. This officer had been knocked unconscious by a blast below-decks, but managed to make his way topside.

"I grabbed someone," he reported, "and told everyone to haul somebody out the starboard hatch on the quarterdeck just aft of the break of the deck. Then, again, I remember nothing until I was under the overhang of turret two, my turret. My head ached terrifically, I could not breathe and all my extremities tingled as if they had been asleep and were just being wakened. Finding out from my CTC, Crawford, that no one was in Control, I started for that station with the starboard AA guns firing in my face, it seemed to me. That was the first time I realized the AA guns were firing. I ran into Lieut. Ricketts on the boat deck by number three AA gun and asked him if he needed men. He said, 'Yes, on the AA ammunition supply.' I noticed several AA officers on the battery and it was functioning wonderfully. I got back under the overhang of the turret, but the hatches were closed. I passed out in the exertion of opening the right tail hatch, but was able to tell Crawford to get men on the AA ammunition train. How long I lay there trying to breathe I do not know until Crawford returned, told me that the ammunition train was flooded, that all boat deck ammunition was exhausted and that the Captain had ordered, 'Abandon Ship.' I made sure that my turret was evacuated, then remember hitting the water from the forecastle. I tried to swim but was too weak. Glover, E. R., FM2/c and Bircher, H. C.,

S1/c of my division held me up and dumped me into a life raft. The next I definitely remember I was on Ford Island at the dispensary."

Although this officer's name is not given here, it is of interest to know that he made a complete recovery, and that he was to meet the Japanese on several subsequent occasions, each time in engagements which took place in waters successively nearer the Japanese homeland.

5

Perhaps someday a meticulous historian will be able to establish the name of the United States naval vessel first to fire as the invaders flew over. So far, a close examination of all available evidence fails to bring forth this information, although many ships in all honesty put forth their claims for this honor.

For example, USS TUCKER, a destroyer:

"The start of the air raid on Pearl Harbor on December 7, 1941," declared Lieutenant Commander W. R. Terrell, USN, in his narrative, "was first seen on this vessel by Bowe, Walter E., GM2/c, USN, who immediately manned the after 50 caliber machine guns of this vessel. Almost simultaneously (at 0757) the quartermaster on watch, Burns, Robert, S1/c, USN, on the bridge sounded the general alarm. Before the general alarm started ringing Bowe was firing one of the after machine guns. It is believed from numerous reports and comments by personnel of this and other ships that Bowe fired the first shot fired by the American forces in Pearl Harbor. . . ."

But, as has been noted, several other ships put forth similar claims with equal honesty.

The fact is, though, that the TUCKER was alert, as were the other ships in the harbor. All ships had ammunition at their ready guns, a minimum of two 50-caliber guns and in most cases two 5-inch dual-purpose guns. The exceptions were a few vessels whose guns had been removed as part of overhaul, and these ships supplied ammunition and crews to other ships. Shore leave in Honolulu had been limited to chief petty officers and petty officers first class. Eighty-five per cent of the destroyer crews were aboard their vessels when the first bomb was dropped. This ratio jumps to 95 per cent aboard the cruisers, and to 98 per cent aboard battleships.

Shore leave for officers had not been restricted as much, but the commanding officers of five of the eight battleships were aboard their ships. The other three had properly designated officers to serve in their stead during their absence. The skippers of eight out of nine of the cruisers were aboard when the attack began.

The captain and the executive officer of the destroyer HENLEY happened to be ashore when the raid began, and their efforts to get back aboard their ship imparted a somewhat Hollywood flavor to an otherwise grim affair. The HENLEY had already put to sea when these two officers, Lieutenant Commander Robert Hall Smith, USN, and Lieutenant H. G. Corey, USN, managed to struggle through the disorganized traffic to Pearl Harbor. They immediately boarded the destroyer-minelayer TREVER, just getting under way to sortie from the harbor.

There were submarine contacts outside the harbor, so there could be no stopping at sea to transfer passengers. Instead, the HENLEY cranked on speed and took position ahead of the TREVER. Then a life raft was streamed from HENLEY's fantail, the two officers jumped aboard, and were pulled alongside their own ship.

Through a freak accident, incidentally, the HENLEY's officers and men were at battle stations as the first Japanese planes appeared, and before any warning of the air raid had been given. Aboard this ship it was customary to call the crew to muster at 0755 each morning by sounding the gas alarm, a slow and regular tapping of a gong. One member of the gangway watch was not long out of boot camp, however, and through an error he sounded the gong for general quarters. The HENLEY's men hit the deck and raced for their stations. As a result, the HENLEY was also among the claimants for the honor of first ship to fire at the Japanese planes.

But the destroyers BAGLEY and BLUE were equally convinced, individually, that each had fired the first shot. So were the officers and men of the cruisers HELENA and RALEIGH. So were the skippers of several PT boats. And so on at considerable length.

If there is difficulty in naming the first ship to fire, however, the same drawbacks have not been encountered in the effort to isolate the first encounter between individuals of the opposing forces.

As the destroyer-minelayer MONTGOMERY was making ready to stand out of the harbor word was received by her captain, Lieutenant Commander R. A. Guthrie, USN, that one of the Japanese planes which had been shot down was still afloat near the Pearl City docks. The Japanese pilot and rear gunner, according to this report, were swimming around the capsized plane.

The MONTGOMERY'S motor whaleboat was lowered over the side and sent to investigate. Sure enough, one wing of the shattered bomber was still above the surface, its crimson Rising Sun lifting and falling defiantly on the harbor swells. The rear gunner had disappeared, presumably a victim of drowning, but the pilot was still afloat, treading water near his partly submerged plane.

As the MONTGOMERY'S boat came alongside, the Japanese aviator was ordered to surrender and come aboard. He refused. The order was repeated several times, and with pantomimed gestures, in the event that the pilot did not understand. The only reaction from the Japanese was a stony glare. Thereupon the boat was maneuvered closer so that the swimmer could be hauled aboard by force. Shouting in Japanese, the aviator jerked a pistol from a holster beneath his flight jacket.

The enemy pilot was given no opportunity to use his weapon. He was shot by the coxswain of the boat, Seaman 1/c D. F. Calkins, and his body sank from sight.

6

After the last fire had been put out, and the smoke had blown away, the Navy began a summing up of the action. The appraisal of Japanese plane losses was distinctly on the conservative side. It was realized that in most cases when a Japanese plane was seen to fall, more than one ship had fired at it. Thus, generous allowance was made for duplication of claims. The total, with all evaluations completed, was 28 Japanese planes shot down.

While small, this included only those Japanese aircraft actually seen to crash by several witnesses. It did not include a number of planes which were leaking gasoline or streaming smoke or flames when they left the scene, nor did it include planes probably forced to crash at sea by damage or lack of fuel.

In addition, the Navy counted three of the Japanese two-man submarines destroyed.

One of these was sunk by the WARD outside the harbor.

Another was depth-bombed, and it later beached itself on a reef near Bellows Field, southeast of Kaneohe Bay. Like all the submarines of this particular type, this craft was supposedly manned by an officer pilot and one enlisted man. Only the officer came ashore and surrendered. The enlisted man was never seen.

SubLieutenant Sakamaki, of the Japanese Naval Academy Class of 1940, was one officer at least who showed no desire to die for his emperor, by his own hand if necessary. Sakamaki swam ashore and surrendered. His submarine was later studied by the experts at Pearl Harbor, and subsequently was brought to the United States for exhibit during War Bond drives.

The third two-man submarine was the one rammed by the MONAGHAN and hit by the guns of the CURTISS and possibly others. This craft was later fished from the bottom of the harbor and found to have been badly damaged. A new landside pier was being built at the submarine base in the southeastern section of Pearl Harbor. Material was needed to make a fill-in, and the silt-filled submarine hulk was of no further use.

A military funeral was held over the submarine. Then the battered Japanese undersea boat, with its crew of two still inside, was dropped into the excavation and covered over, forming a part of the permanent installation of the Naval Base which she so vainly tried to attack.

7

In an attack lasting one hour and fifty minutes the Japanese had brought a major disaster to the United States Pacific Fleet. Had the Japanese decided to follow up their attack with a fleet invasion they would have found not one battleship capable of opposing them. And yet all but one of those ships rose from their presumed graves in one of the most extensive salvage operations the world has ever known.

The ARIZONA was sunk at her berth, burned and blasted in two.

The OKLAHOMA capsized, and was resting with her twisted superstructure on the bottom of the harbor.

The WEST VIRGINIA had settled into the shallow water at her berth.

The CALIFORNIA was sunk at her berth.

· The NEVADA was run aground to prevent sinking.

The old UTAH was sunk, bottom up.

The PENNSYLVANIA, MARYLAND, and TENNESSEE were damaged by bombs.

The destroyers CASSIN and DOWNES were twisted by fire and the SHAW had her bow blown off. (An earlier SHAW had her bow cut off in the English Channel by the AQUITANIA during World War I. But like her namesake at Pearl Harbor, she was repaired.)

Other vessels damaged but not sunk, although in some cases seriously flooded, were the light cruisers HELENA, HONOLULU, and RALEIGH, the seaplane tender CURTISS and the repair ship VESTAL.

This, on the face of it, was an impressive toll. Headlines were black, and a nation was in mourning. Some spokesmen within the nation were willing to report, doubtless in all sincerity, that the damage was worse than the public (or the Japanese) had been told. Perhaps this was fortunate—there is the possibility that the Japanese were led to believe that they had destroyed as many ships as they claimed in their official communiques, and thus were surprised when they later met these ships in action.

But the heavy cruisers SAN FRANCISCO, NEW ORLEANS, and MINNEAPOLIS were in Pearl Harbor on the day of the raid. Not one was damaged. Three light cruisers—DETROIT, PHOENIX, and ST. LOUIS—also escaped damage.

Three of the damaged battleships were at sea in less than two weeks.

The three light cruisers which were damaged left Pearl Harbor by the end of January.

In its official announcement the Navy admitted the loss of the battleship ARIZONA, the target ship UTAH, the destroyers CASSIN, DOWNES, and SHAW, and the minelayer OGLALA. It did not include the antique OKLAHOMA, which could have been repaired and refitted, except for the decision to divert the labor and materials to new ships.

Only the ARIZONA, then, was destroyed in the Battle of Pearl Harbor. The UTAH was recovered, as was the OGLALA. The machinery and fittings and parts of the hulls of CASSIN and DOWNES were reworked into vessels as good as any in their class, and these ships were never stricken from the active list. The destroyer SHAW, wearing a stubby false bow, made her own way to a West Coast yard for the repairs that made her better than new.

United States seapower in the Pacific had been dealt a staggering blow though not a crippling one. And the Japanese must have been disappointed. No United States aircraft carrier had been damaged by bomb or bullet; and not only were all intact and in fighting trim, but they were soon to be joined by new ones of both the fleet type and the converted ships of the LONG ISLAND class.

Casualties on ships alone totaled 1,763 officers and men. This figure, as recorded immediately after the battle, was raised to 2,638 by losses ashore. But this was death alone. Many officers and men were injured. Many died, days and weeks later. Some recovered and were able to fight again; others went home with their pensions and their scars, and the right to place after their names the naval symbol (Ret.).

Three of the damaged battleships took several months to repair, but they rejoined the fleet with vastly improved protection and much greater offensive power.

When the repaired battleships went back into action it is probable that they were not recognized by the enemy as the ships the Japanese had so often boasted that they had "destroyed to pieces": the repaired battleships went back with new contours and sometimes completely new silhouettes, but always they went back better than new.

The damage had to be repaired. Obviously there was no question of restoring the ships to their original condition. The rehabilitation was performed according to improvements in design and equipment developed since even the newest of the battered ships had been launched. But when the repairs were completed, the fleet was stronger by added protection, firepower, and operating efficiency than if the Japanese had been stopped before they reached Pearl Harbor and we had gone to war with the ships undamaged but archaic.

One of the officers engaged in the salvage work at Pearl Harbor was Captain Homer N. Wallin, USN—and there were many who earned distinction in this field. Six months after Pearl Harbor, Captain Wallin made a complete accounting of the accomplishments up to that time.

"The salvage work thus far completed at Pearl Harbor," said the concluding paragraph of his lengthy report, "has been successful well beyond the most optimistic anticipations. The work has been carried on as a co-operative endeavor to which many persons have contributed their support, their ideas, and their effort. The various important steps taken and the decisions made have usually followed a meeting of the minds of several persons. I am pleased to make grateful acknowledgment of this fact, and to express the conviction that this important work has throughout been directed and controlled by the One Mind which governs all things well."

When Captain Wallin made this report the Pacific Fleet was stronger than it had been on the day the first bombs fell.

On the day after the attack, the Navy stepped up its plans to finish the big job ahead "all the way, all along the line." The building of aircraft carriers and combat planes was multiplied many times over; and the construction of some of the mightiest battleships ever designed was given a top A-1-A priority.

As it turned out, the first six months in the Pacific were to be the hardest.

Chapter Five

SOMEWHERE, at what was five minutes before 8 A.M. Honolulu time, a Japanese master timepiece pointed the moment toward which Japan had planned and built for years. The bombs that fell on Pearl Harbor were echoed by explosions in Hong Kong, China; in Singora, Thailand; and in Kota Bharu on the Thai-Malayan border.

In simultaneous attack, the Japanese struck at the perimeter of a vast arc extending from Pearl Harbor to the Gulf of Siam. On the western wing of that arc the task forces were augmented by scores of troop transports from which tens of thousands of trained soldiers, veterans of the long China campaign, swarmed ashore in the first stride of a march calculated to push Japan's frontiers to include all East and South Asia.

The Japanese also were striking in other areas of the Pacific. Before 1941 had ended, Japanese naval units had been detected in the Aleutians. Japanese surface vessels or undersea craft had made nuisance raids on Johnston, Palmyra, and far to the southward, on Tutuila, Samoa. Japanese submarines were on battle patrol in the Eastern Pacific between the Hawaiians and the west coast of the United States: in December a dozen merchant ships were shelled or torpedoed, and some of them were sunk.

Pearl Harbor, to General Tojo, was but an incident in a day from which all time would hereafter be calculated in Dai Nippon.

How long the Japanese had been preparing the war in the Pacific is a question which only time and the victory of the United Nations can answer. Certainly the simultaneous attacks on the morning of December 7/8, 1941, were the execution of plans long in preparation, minute in blueprint attention to detail. Fleets and armies cannot be deployed over millions of square miles on the decision of a moment nor yet of a month. Preparations must have been under way even when Secretary of the Navy

97

Frank Knox first expressed his fear, in January, 1941, that the Japanese might attempt a coup by surprise and treachery.

Whenever the preparations were begun, it must now be realized that Japan's plans for ultimate world conquest were decades old. Fifty years earlier Viscount Tani laid down the tenet that "Japan must with patience wait for the time of confusion in Europe to gain its objectives." In 1915, Count Shigenobu Okuma, the Premier of Japan, predicted that "in the middle of the twentieth century Japan will meet Europe on the plains of Asia and wrest from her the mastery of the world." And that was said by the head of a government allied with Britain, France, and Russia in a war against militarism! Nobody paid attention to what Tani counseled and Okuma predicted: nobody, that is, except the Japanese, who take themselves very seriously.

Therefore, Pearl Harbor and all the other barriers westward from there opposed Japan's ambition. There were, however, other islands representing not America's might but America's sovereignty in the Pacific, and upon these, too, Japan pounced.

The Japanese immediately struck at Midway Island, a part of the Hawaiian chain, 1,100 miles from Pearl Harbor. They struck at Wake Island, a thousand miles west of Midway. They struck at Guam, 1,300 miles from Wake; and they struck at the Philippines, some 1,500 miles southward from Tokyo. Of all the Pacific territory under United States protection the Japanese most wanted the Philippines; and in all these places save one the American flag was foredoomed to be dipped and removed in favor of the white and crimson banner of the Rising Sun.

The one exception was Midway. . . .

2

Darkness came to Midway that night at about 2000, or 8 P.M., after a half hour's twilight. But the moon rode high, and soon after nightfall the Midway group, composed of Sand and Eastern islands, became bathed in a moonglow that would have done credit to a tropical travel poster. To many a Marine, waiting tensely at his gun, the ethereal beauty of the scene evoked the appreciative comment: "God—we stand out like a sore thumb!"

The description turned in by Lieutenant Colonel Harold D. Shannon, USMC, is most specific on the subject.

"There was a bright moon. All the new construction glistened in the moonlight. . . . The reflection of the moon on the white buildings, window glass, and on the black-and-white squares of the water tower must have been visible for miles at sea. The sand looked like snow and the breakers on the reef clearly outlined the island area. It was an ideal night for such an attack. Since the attack, steps have been taken to repaint and camouflage . . ." And so on.

Since Midway in time is two hours behind Pearl Harbor, the island had been awaiting Japanese attack since the first radio warning from Hawaii that morning, at about 0630 Midway time. At twilight all ships present and all island facilities had been darkened. Buoys and navigational lights had been screened or extinguished. There had not been time to paint out the black-and-white squares on the water tank, so useful in ordinary times as an aviation beacon. The Marines were at their battle stations. All other persons on the islands, such as construction workers, had been dispersed to places of safety.

At 2130 the waiting was over.

Lookouts in the communication tower spotted orange flashes to seaward southwest of the island, out of range of the shore guns. There was a mighty splash in the lagoon, and towers of smoke and water shot skyward as the shells from the distant Japanese ships exploded.

A quick wink of orange to the southwestward proclaimed another salvo on its way. This time fire had been raised, and the shells burst on the beach and near the defense establishments on the islands, clear indication of good spotting. A third flash of orange, and the salvo was on. The shells skimmed over the dunes and onto the hangar. The hangar began to blaze brightly, making a perfect target of every object in the vicinity.

Then it became clear why the spotting had been so accurate. Two Japanese ships were seen closing in at high speed, their guns suddenly blazing as they came. The leading ship was clearly a destroyer. The trailing ship was a light cruiser or one of the heavy destroyer-leaders that are so similar in appearance to some types of Japanese light cruisers. From the sidelines they had observed, and corrected, the first salvos from the distant task force.

On the shore of Sand Island a searchlight stabbed the moonglow and lighted up the destroyer, the Japanese battle flag at her main truck. Simultaneously, shore batteries went into action. The engagement was brief for the simple reason that the Japanese "poured on the coal" and got out of there. But they did some damage before they escaped.

Salvos from the trailing ship blasted the searchlight out of existence. Several buildings were hit by shellfire.

One Japanese salvo crashed into the command post of First Lieutenant George H. Cannon, USMC, commander of a battery. Lieutenant Cannon was riddled by shrapnel. Both his legs were broken and his pelvis was crushed. He was bleeding profusely but he refused to leave his post. It was there he died from loss of blood; and he became the first United States Marine of World War II to be awarded the Congressional Medal of Honor.

Cannon's battery did not stop firing at the retreating Japanese ships. This was attributable in good part to the work of Corporal Harold R. Hazelwood. The blast that killed Cannon wrecked the command post switchboard, and it also shattered Corporal Hazelwood's left leg, but Hazelwood quickly repaired the switchboard and re-established communication with the guns, before allowing himself to be carried away.

Corporal Dale L. Peters was checking communications in the hangar tower when that building was hit by the third Japanese salvo. The blast blew him through a window onto the hangar roof. Shocked and dazed, he clambered back into the tower and attempted to go below to help fight the fires. By mistake, Peters opened the wrong hatch, and in the smoke and flames he fell 14 feet upon a group of men working below. They revived him, whereupon he joined them in the urgent task of removing large aerial bombs from the burning hangar. Both Peters and Hazelwood received the Navy Cross.

The retiring Japanese did not get away without damage to themselves, however. The destroyer in the lead was hit three times and the trailing cruiser at least twice. Both ships were raked by heavy machine-gun fire, and inevitably many of their personnel topside were killed or injured. Both ships retired at their best speed.

Midway was not to become a serious target of Japanese attack until half a year had passed. This delay is one of the major mysteries of Japanese strategy. If the Japanese wanted to take Midway they would have found the island's defenses at their weakest in the first few days or weeks after Pearl Harbor. It would have been a costly venture but not an impossible one, nor even extravagant.

And Japan did want to take Midway. That was proved early in June of 1942 when a large-scale attack was launched, and Japan suffered one of the worst defeats in modern naval history.

3

Wake Island is a coral atoll shaped like a U, with the open end pointed northwest. The island of Peale, site of the Pan American Airways station and hotel, is an extension of the upper arm of the U, while Wilkes Island is in a somewhat similar position at the lower, or southern, prong. The channel between Wilkes and Wake is a narrow tiderace inlet, the only ship entrance to the lagoon through the outer coral barrier which circles the entire island group.

The Marine and naval personnel, numbering less than 400, were quartered on the southern arm of the U on December 8 (December 7 on the eastward side of the international date line). Also on this section of the island were the newly completed landing strip, the command posts, plane revetments, and other units of the military installation. At the end of the upper arm of the U was the camp occupied by some 1,200 civilian construction workers, complete with barracks, messhalls, company store, outdoor movies and other recreational facilities.

Prior to 1941—and with the exception of the Pan American development begun in 1935—Wake had been designated by the United States government as a bird sanctuary. And birds there were on Wake, by the tens of thousands—amorous Japanese lovebirds, fiercely thievish pirate birds, fluttery little canaries from an imported strain—and the gooney bird. While of undoubted interest to ornithologists, the gooney birds were mostly a nuisance to the defenders of Wake. They were underfoot at every turn. They flew into aerials and antennae, to their own and the equipment's disaster. A pilot in landing or taking off could count on hitting from one to half a dozen of the birds, always with the chance of breaking a windshield or knocking a propeller out of alignment. They had a nerve-racking habit of soaring in formation, wings motionless, causing air spotters to turn in many a false alarm.

Then there were the Wake Island rats—large, slow-moving sticky creatures with opera-bouffé whiskers—which seemed to take a perverse delight in clambering over the hunched-up human occupants of foxholes during visits by the Japanese.

And visits from the Japanese at once became a common and regular occurrence.

In *Last Man Off Wake Island*, a book written with Cecil Garnes, Colonel Walter L. J. Bayler, USMC, has given a detailed and graphic account of how war came to Wake, and of the fight put up by the defenders until his departure some 36 hours before the island was overrun by Japanese. Colonel Bayler arrived on Wake just as December was beginning, detailed on special temporary duty to supervise the installation of radio and electronic equipment as a part of the island's belated defenses. Also a passenger on the seaplane tender WRIGHT was Commander Winfield Scott ("Spiv") Cunningham, USN, to take over command of all Wake's naval activity. They were greeted on the island by Major James Patrick Sinnot Devereux, USMC, commander of Wake's ground forces. On Thursday, December 4, Major Paul Putnam flew in from the ENTERPRISE with his 12 Grumman fighter planes, known officially as Marfitron 211, Marine Fighting Squadron 211.

Until the very welcome arrival of Marfitron 211, Wake had had no planes at all except for an occasional Navy flying boat and, of course, the regular stopover of the Pan American Clippers.

Sunday, December 7, was a quiet day on Wake—that night most of the pilots and ground crew went over to the civilian construction camp for a free movie show. Of course, when it was Sunday on Wake the Pearl Harbor calendar said Saturday. Monday on Wake, though, was different.

"I had my usual excellent breakfast at the messhall the following Monday morning," said Colonel Bayler in his narrative of Wake's last days. "It was still early, only about 7 o'clock, when I left the building and set a leisurely course for my tent. I looked ahead and saw Jimmy Devereux standing on the wooden platform in front of his quarters. He was staring at a sheet of paper he was holding; at the sound of my footsteps he turned his head and motioned me to join him.

" 'Morning, Walt,' he said. He showed me the paper, which I now saw was a decoded radiogram, and added in a quiet conversational tone: 'I've just had this message to say the Japs attacked Pearl Harbor this morning.'

"My mouth opened. It stayed open, but no sound issued from it. Before I could get out even so much as a gasp the imperturbable Devereux went on calmly:

" 'Of course it may be just another false alarm, so I have requested verification. If it comes through, I'll let everyone know immediately.' "

The verification came through, and Major Devereux "let everyone know" by ordering all Wake to battle stations.

From this time until the day he left, Colonel Bayler kept a battle diary of events on Wake, a document now in the archives of the Navy Department. Although millions of words have been written about Wake's gallantly heartbreaking defense, there could be no better summary of the action than the bare-bones entries of Colonel Bayler's journal.

Dec. 8, 7 a.m.–11:58 a.m. . . . .*Received word bombing Oahu. General quarters station. 24 Jap bombers on a northern course hit airdrome in close column of division "V's" from 3,000 feet. 100-pound fragmentation bombs and simultaneous strafing. Casualties 25 dead, 7 wounded, 7 airplanes burned, destroyed.*

Dec. 9, 11:45 a.m. . . . .*27 Japs. Bombed hospital, Camp No. 2. Killed several patients, 3 dead. Got one Jap plane.*

Dec. 10, 10:45 a.m. . . . .*27 Jap bombers. No casualties.*

Dec. 11, 5 a.m. . . . .*Landing attempt by 12 Jap ships, including light cruisers, destroyers, gunboats, 2 troop or supply ships. Jap casualties: 1 light cruiser, 2 destroyers, 1 gunboat, 2 bombers.*
NOTE.—That Japs closed in to 4,700 yards before 5- and 3-inch guns opened up at point blank range.

Dec. 12 . . . .*27 Jap planes bombed Peale and Wake from 22,000 feet. No casualties.*

Dec. 13 . . . .*All quiet.*

Dec. 14 . . . .*32 Jap planes hit airdrome. Two killed, 1 plane down (own destroyed by bombs).*

Dec. 15, 11 a.m. . . . .*Dawn raid by 3 four-engine seaplanes. 27 Jap bombers. Shot down 2 Japs.*

Dec. 16, 5:45 p.m. . . . .*41 Jap bombers hit Camp 2 and airdrome. Jap four-motor plane raid. One Jap shot down.*

Dec. 17 . . . .*32 Jap bombers at 1317 hit Camp 1, Peale Island, Diesel oil supply, mess hall, and pumps of evaporators, Camp 1.*

Dec. 18, 11:40 a.m. ....*One Jap high rec. plane (2 engines) (photo?).*

Dec. 19, 10:30 a.m. ....*Jap bombers hit airport and camp.*

Dec. 20 ....*All quiet—first day of bad weather.*

After the first bombing raid only four of the Grumman F4F-3 fighter planes were left. Then two of these were lost as the hopelessly outnumbered Marine aviators went up on mission after mission. Occasionally only one plane was able to take off. But the Marine ground crews performed wonders. As an official Navy announcement put it: "At one time only one serviceable plane was left to Major Putnam's squadron, but the mechanics and ground crews evidently made an additional plane, or even planes out of the wreckage of the remainder." As the skipper of Marfitron 211 himself described it in the last message he is known to have written—brought out by Colonel Bayler: "Parts and assemblies have been traded back and forth so that no airplane can be identified. Engines have been traded from plane to plane, have been junked, stripped, rebuilt, and all but created."

The Marine gun crews performed equally prodigious tasks. Major Devereux took it for granted that as the Japanese bombers came over each day, after their 700-mile trips from the Marshalls, they took pictures of the defense installations below. Therefore there was no rest for the men on the guns. After standing at their posts all day they labored far into the night, setting up their antiaircraft armament in new positions so that they would not be blasted as the Japs aimed for the old locations on their next visit over.

The 1,200 civilian construction workers presented a problem after the first bombs fell, but not the kind of problem that might logically have been expected from men untrained in the ways of war. On the day after the first raid, Colonel Bayler had to explain, patiently and at some length, why these workers could not be enlisted in the Marine Corps. The line of applicants outside the tent was long, but he finally succeeded. "I personally talked to one hundred and eighty-six of the men," said Colonel Bayler. "By this time the others began to get the idea."

There was of course little likelihood that Wake would be captured, he explained to the men. But in that unlikely event, there would be no way for the workmen to prove that they were, indeed, bona fide members of the Corps. They would have no protection under the Geneva Convention for prisoners of war, and after capture would immediately be shot out of hand as snipers or guerrillas. As civilians—in that remote possibility of capture—they would be accorded certain privileges of care and comfort accorded by all civilized nations to captured noncombatants.

Few Americans at that time, Colonel Bayler among them, had any accurate idea of the things that could happen to prisoners of the Japanese. (If Bayler could have projected himself into the future eighteen months he could have heard the horrifying details from one of his classmates of Annapolis '27, Commander Melvyn H. McCoy, USN, leader of the first party of Americans to escape from a Japanese military prison in the Philippines. But such a tale of inhumanity probably would have been hard to believe, then.)

Nevertheless, the Marines had to keep an eagle eye on the construction workers to prevent them from joining the fight willy-nilly. "We couldn't put down a rifle or pistol," said Colonel Bayler, "without one of the workmen trying to snatch it up and make off with it. They wanted to help in the fight."

But the civilian workers did help in many legitimate ways. They supplied the Marine fighters with food. They built bombproof dugouts near the landing strip, although they were not able to devise means of keeping out the ubiquitous Wake Island rats. They brought water to the fighting men, and they helped with the wounded as needed.

By December 20, Wake Island had settled down to a harried and unpleasant existence which, nevertheless, was beginning to seem normal. The Japs were expected to come over and drop their bombs at about the same time every day. Of course, the Japs sometimes varied this schedule by sending over night bombers. There was the constant sharp lookout for a landing attempt from the sea: after the first attempt, in which the Japs lost a cruiser, two destroyers and a gunboat, there were many Marines who hoped the Japs would try it again. There was the usual plane patrol above the island, made up of all the planes able to fly; too often this patrol consisted of one lone patched-up Grumman fighter.

All in all, things were beginning to settle down. Wake had its chin out and its fists ready—after the routing of the Jap invasion attempt on the 14th, Major Devereux had replied to Pearl's query as to what was needed with his famous message: "Send us more Japs." That was the way the Marines felt about the situation at the time.

And so on December 20, when a Navy flying boat made a call at the island, it was decided that Colonel Bayler should return to Midway, as specified in the original orders which sent him to Wake on temporary additional duty. The 1,100-mile air trip was uneventful, but Colonel Bayler had been on Midway only a few hours before he learned that he had left Wake just ahead of the Japanese landing.

"The news of the fall of Wake Island was a staggering blow to me," he wrote. "I was almost dazed when confirmation was received of what at first seemed a fantastic, incredible rumor. Official reports from the Navy Department set all doubts at rest; Wake had definitely fallen. Remained for me the question: What the hell *happened?*

"The answer in general was obvious. The defense force had been simply overwhelmed by superior power in every quarter; on land, on sea and in the air. Only the details of the disaster were lacking, as they still are and probably will be till the veil is lifted at the end of the war.

"The last two dispatches from the island command to Pearl Harbor were received in the closing minutes of the fifteen-day siege. They show the final phase of the Battle of Wake was reached at a little after five o'clock on the afternoon of December 22, Wake Island time. Only thirty-six hours after I had looked back from Murphy's seaplane and told myself all would be well with Wake.

"The first of those last two dispatches reported the enemy had effected a landing on the island, and added magnificently: 'The issue is in doubt.' One of two men wrote those words, Devereux or Cunningham, and from what I know of each, I believe it was Spiv Cunningham. The phrase is more typical of him than of Jimmy Devereux.

"I could imagine Spiv taking up his pencil, frowning a little, wondering just what to write, while Captain Wilson waited for the text he was to transmit. The enemy was on the island. Okay, but perched in the small trees or snugged down in the sand were a lot of sharp-shooting Marines still able to squeeze a trigger. Spiv's brow must have cleared as he remembered them and wrote firmly: 'The issue is in doubt.'

"We know from earlier reports that the Japs, on the last day, sent over an enormous number of heavy planes which subjected the whole island to an incessant, merciless bombing. They were out to hit everything they could see, and everything they thought might be hidden, and most especially that battery of deadly 5-inch cannon which had blasted their ships so effectively on the eleventh. After that experience I would not have expected them to use surface craft again till they were sure they had silenced every gun and gunner on Peacock Point.

"But apparently they chose to do it the hard way. The second and last dispatch revealed that at least some part of the battery came through the bombing intact. The report said more ships and a transport were moving in, and ended with the statement that two enemy destroyers had been disabled.

"I read those closing words and had to swallow hard. As simply as could be, yet as eloquently as if the entire dictionary had been used, they told the story of how Wake Island had gone down with colors flying and guns shooting to the last."

President Roosevelt issued a unit citation for the defenders of the island, soon to learn for themselves the grim details of life in a Japanese prison camp. And, but for the fortunes of war, aid might have reached Wake in time, and Wake's defenders might have been evacuated or reinforced so that the island could hold out, although this latter possibility is doubtful.

A naval task force was on the way to Wake even as the Japanese invasion fleet approached. Reconnaissance made it obvious that the risk to the Navy's already weakened strength was too great, and there were other gambles in the Pacific in which the odds were not stacked so heavily on the Japanese side. One of the vessels in the task force which made the futile sweep toward Wake was a ship sometimes affectionately called by her men the "Sara Maru"—the aircraft carrier SARATOGA, only recently undocked from a West Coast overhaul. Within a fortnight after the futile Wake rescue attempt the SARATOGA got a Japanese tin fish in her side and the damage was considerable. No announcement was made of the torpedoing, for this would have been telling the Japanese that the Navy's already weakened forces had staggered under another blow. And precious days and weeks were to pass before the "Sara" could again be sent against the enemy in an effort to stop his Pacific rampage.

4

COMMUNIQUE NO. 5   *DECEMBER 13, 1941*

The Navy Department announced that it is unable to communicate with Guam either by radio or cable. The capture of the island is probable. A small force of less than 400 naval personnel and 155 Marines were sta-

tioned on Guam. According to the latest reports from Guam, the island had been bombed repeatedly and Japanese troops had landed at several points on the island. . . . The above is based on reports until 9 a.m. today.

Actually, the government headquarters of the island, at Agaña, had been invested by the Japanese early on the morning of the 10th, Guam time, although there was scattered resistance in the interior until December 22.

As in the case of Wake, efforts to strengthen the defenses of Guam were delayed until too late, despite Japan's provocative fortification of two technically demilitarized islands less than a hundred miles away.

On a clear day, an observer standing on Mount Tenjo could see the Japanese base of Rota in the Mariana Islands. Some 30 miles beyond Rota to the northward was Saipan, sometimes called "Japan's second Truk." Literally, the Navy and Marine Corps personnel on Guam were "under the guns." Japanese reconnaissance planes had mapped and photographed the island down to the last inch.

"I wasn't surprised at the Japanese attack," said Ensign Leona Jackson, of the Navy Nurse Corps, one of those captured by the Japanese when the island fell. "And I think for many of the people there it didn't come as a surprise. The situation had been tense, and the governor had sent the families from the island several weeks before. When the first bombs began to fall I think our first reaction was one of relief that we didn't have the women and children there on the island."

Those "first bombs" began to fall shortly after eight o'clock on the morning of the 8th—December 7th on the other side of the international date line—when nine Japanese bombers soared over and attacked the defense facilities of Apra Harbor. The island station ship, the PENGUIN, was badly damaged and was scuttled by her own men.

There was no doubt in the mind of anybody about the extent of Guam's ability to defend itself, from the governor, Captain George J. McMillin, USN, on down. About all Guam could do was wait for the Japanese to come and take it.

There was another air raid on the afternoon of the first day, and on the following day the Japanese made three aerial attacks. On the third of these forays the enemy bombers swooped low and strafed indiscriminately. As Captain McMillin said in his last message: "Last attack on Agaña.

Civilians machine-gunned in streets. Two native wards of hospital and hospital compound machine-gunned. Building in which Japanese nationals are confined bombed."

The first landings by the Japanese were accomplished at 3:30 on the morning of the 10th, Guam time. The bluejackets and Marines fought every step of the way as the invaders aimed their drive at Agaña, the island's principal village. The defenders were hopelessly outnumbered and many were captured or killed.

"The firing ceased about dawn," said Nurse Jackson. "I think the bitterest moment of my life came at sunrise when, standing in the door of the hospital library, I saw the Rising Sun ascend the flagpole where the day before the Stars and Stripes had proudly flown.

"The Japanese appeared in the hospital compound about 8:30. They used the hospital as a headquarters at first. They thought that if the Americans came over to retaliate they wouldn't fire on the hospital, and that was the reason they used it."

Japanese troops ran riot throughout Agaña, and the Japanese officers made no effort to control their men until they had finished with their looting. A Japanese Navy captain stalked into the nurses' quarters, seated himself, and asked if the nurses had had any news about the war. The nurses would not give him the satisfaction of learning that they had had radio reports of the attack on Pearl Harbor, so they replied in the negative.

"So sorry to tell you," said the Japanese naval officer—"all your fleet sunk. All your ships on bottom. No more."

Captain McMillin was questioned endlessly and, from the Americans' viewpoint, stupidly. He was asked to tell the name of the commander of the United States Asiatic Fleet, what position General MacArthur held in the Philippines, what he thought of the Japanese tactics in the landing, and so on to no apparent conclusions.

Shortly after the arrival of the Japanese in Agaña the military and civilian casualties began to arrive at the hospital. The Japanese had taken over most of the hospital facilities, leaving one ward for the use of the Americans and natives.

"It was probably the most amazing ward I'll ever see," Nurse Jackson declared. "We had war casualties there, and native men, women and children; we even had a Caesarean section by way of variety."

Bodies of Marines and bluejackets killed in defending the island were brought to the hospital morgue. "Some of the men who had surrendered had been required to strip off all their clothing except their shorts, had been searched, evidently had been required to kneel at the feet of the Japanese, and had been bayoneted in the back. That was typical. Any of the natives that got in their way had been bayoneted without regard to their age or their sex. Conditions for some days were chaotic."

The common attitude of the Japanese conquerors was one of pride in their own victory and arrogance toward those they had defeated. They made clear their belief that the United States had been forever defeated in the Pacific, and their treatment of American prisoners indicated their conviction that they themselves would never have to look forward to a day of reckoning.

The five Navy nurses on the island maintained a calm exterior for the benefit of their patients, but they admitted to themselves that they would not be surprised at any moment to find themselves lined up before a firing squad or worse. And they thought, indeed, that such treatment was beginning one steaming hot day soon after the Japanese investiture. All the American officers were lined up and marched up the hill off Agaña Square toward the Officers' Club. A short time later there was the sound of firing. The nurses were sure, then, that the worst had come.

But an hour later the Americans were marched down the hill again, tired and sweaty but unharmed. The nurses soon found out what it was all about, from actual demonstration.

"We were informed that all the Navy nurses and any of the native nurses who could be spared were to report to the Japanese," Nurse Jackson relates. "We reported, and assembled in the plaza. We found that we had been marched out to become impressed by Japan's armed might. I tried to determine whether the Japanese were running the same equipment around and around or if they really had that much equipment on the island. At that time one Jap looked just like another to me and I couldn't tell the difference. They had, however, considerable anti-aircraft equipment on the island. They had a full troop of cavalry, brought over from Rota—what in the world they thought they were going to do with cavalry on Guam I don't know, but they had them there. After this review we were taken up the hill to the Officers' Club where the Japanese proceeded to demonstrate some of their military tactics, their machine guns and their flame-throwers, and their tactics in taking a position—that sort of thing. I don't think any of us was awfully impressed, though naturally we didn't make any comments."

The American prisoners were kept on Guam until January 15, when they were packed aboard a merchant ship, the ARGENTINA MARU, and taken to Japan. The prisoners had not been allowed to take any extra clothing with them—they were assured by the Japanese that they were going south—and they landed in Japan shivering in the frigid temperature of winter.

On the whole, however, the five Navy nurses received treatment that was not too bad, although the Japs were surly and short-tempered immediately after the Doolittle raid. The nurses were repatriated on the first trip of the SS GRIPSHOLM, after a captivity of a little longer than six months. American military prisoners captured in the Philippines were to tell a different story—those who lived to talk about it.

5

War's advent in the Pacific was marked everywhere by a certain pattern despite the great distances between points at which the news was received. There was everywhere—at Midway, Wake, Guam, the Philippines, and on ships at sea—first the shock of learning of the attack on Pearl Harbor. Then came the reaction of just enough incredulity to demand verification, even as preparations were rushed to resist the enemy to the limit of the inadequate forces available. Shock and surprise, however, seemed to decrease in direct proportion to the distance between United States forces and Japan.

For instance, in the Japanese-flanked Philippines, Admiral Thomas C. Hart, USN, was awakened at 0300 on the morning of Monday, December 8, by a telephone call from Marine Lieutenant Colonel William T. Clement, who had the night duty in Pacific Fleet Headquarters, Manila.

"Admiral Hart speaking," said the admiral as he picked up the telephone at his bedside.

"Clement, sir."

"Yes, Clement."

"A very important dispatch has come in, sir. Most important. I'll be over with it in three minutes, and I wanted to be sure you'd be awake," Clement reported.

"I'll be awake, Clement. Come right up with it."

That was all. But Admiral Hart had an idea—perhaps it was more of a foreboding—as to what the dispatch might contain. He doused some cold water on his face and called his chief of staff, Rear Admiral William R. Purnell, USN, whose quarters were a few doors down the hall from Hart's own modest two-room suite in the Manila Hotel. And with the arrival of Lieutenant Colonel Clement, Admiral Hart learned that his foreboding had been more than correct. It was a shock, yes; but no surprise. The Japanese had finally struck.

Other Americans, farther westward, also received an unexpected awakening that night, and a far ruder awakening it was.

Anchored off the Bund at Shanghai was the 370-ton United States gunboat WAKE, with the British gunboat PETREL nearby. The American gunboats OAHU and LUZON had already been withdrawn from Shanghai, and the TUTUILA had been taken far up the river where she later passed into the hands of the Chinese and was renamed MEI YAUN. The gunboat MINDANAO left Hong Kong in the first days of December and arrived in Manila on the day after war began.

Only the WAKE remained to fly the American flag in Chinese waters, and the WAKE had been left only as a means of maintaining radio contact. The ship had been stripped, and was now manned by a pickup crew of Americans in Shanghai several of whom had formerly served in the Navy. Results were not too happy.

Shortly after 0300 on the morning of the 8th—December 7 West Longitude—two destroyers steamed purposefully into view and hove to alongside the American and British patrol craft. The destroyers had the flaring bows and sloping, inverted-Y stacks that marked them as Nipponese. If any further identification were needed it was provided immediately by a megaphone-amplified voice which demanded unconditional surrender of the British and American ships in the name of the Emperor of Japan.

The British reply was prompt. The PETREL opened fire at once. The much heavier armament on one Japanese destroyer responded, one salvo proving resistance by the British to be hopeless. The ship was scuttled by her own crew. The skipper of the American ship had seen fit to sleep ashore that night, and although the WAKE had been wired for demolition there was no time for the charges to be set off. The sleepy Americans awoke to find their tiny craft swarming with armed Japanese seamen, who had formed boarding parties before their destroyer had lost way. Most of the Americans simply dived over the side and swam to a nearby ship, although some were captured on board.

The Japanese captured the WAKE intact. She was rearmed and commissioned in the Japanese Navy as the TATARU, named after a bay on the west coast of the Japanese main island, all to the accompaniment of a fanfaronade which could not have been much more brassy if the tiny gunboat had been a battleship of the IOWA class. "Witness the exalted might of His Imperial Majesty's Japanese Fleet," said the propaganda in effect, "capable of capturing a mighty American warcraft without the enemy being able to fire a shot." The WAKE was, in fact, considerably smaller than some of the vessels used for taking tourists on a rubberneck circuit of Manhattan Island.

The Japanese Navy loosed a similarly stentorian propaganda barrage with the attack on Hong Kong, the British crown colony at the mouth of the Canton River, which capitulated on Christmas Day, 1941. This propaganda magnified many times the size and number of the British fleet units based on that city. Actually—and according to official records of the British Admiralty—only eight light auxiliary craft and a few motor torpedo boats were in the port when the Japanese began their siege of Hong Kong; and of this puny force only the torpedo boats could have been classed as modern warcraft.

In magnification of their claims of defeating a British fleet, the Japanese trumpeted far and wide that, in capturing Hong Kong, they had killed His Excellency Admiral Chin Chek, chief of the Chinese mission assigned to assist in the defense of the British stronghold and something of a colorful figure in the Orient. (In some Japanese propaganda versions Admiral Chin had surrendered himself.)

The real story of this claim, however, was far different when told by Chinese naval officials and backed up by British Admiralty records.

The Japanese did make a determined effort to capture the Chinese admiral, and the British were determined upon his escape, for Chin's prestige in the Orient was great. When it became evident that Hong Kong would fall, Admiral Chin and members of his mission were placed aboard a Royal Navy launch for transfer to a motor torpedo boat. The Japanese spotted the launch and opened fire with machine guns. The launch went down, and Admiral Chin and his party began to swim for the waiting torpedo boats. The distance was too great and the Japanese opposition was too heavy—by this time all of Telegraph Bay was under Japanese guns. "He nevertheless managed to swim to a small island," says a British Admiralty report, "where the MTB's picked him up, ran the gauntlet of heavy shelling, eluded a Japanese destroyer, and eventually landed the party on the Chinese mainland, whence they made their way through the Japanese lines into the area held by the Chinese Regular Forces."

Despite Japan's propaganda claims, Admiral Chin had suffered only two mishaps: while in the motor launch a machine-gun slug passed through one of his wrists, and while swimming in the water he suffered the loss of a leg—artificial.

6

From all available reports it would appear that, after the initial raids, a submarine of the Royal Netherlands Navy was the first Allied fleet unit to take successful offensive action in returning the attack of the Japanese invaders.

In fact, Queen Wilhelmina's government-in-exile did not wait for Netherlands territory to be invaded before declaring war on Japan—the Netherlanders knew only too well that, of all the Japanese coveted, the riches of Java, Sumatra, Borneo, Celebes, and the other islands of the Malay Barrier were the richest prize. Therefore, a few hours after the first bombs fell on Hong Kong, Kota Bharu and Pearl Harbor, the Netherlands declared war, actually before the formal declarations were concluded by the United States and the United Kingdom.

"You know how Germany, in the same manner that Japan now emulates in Asia, attacked many countries in Europe, one after the other," said Queen Wilhelmina in her proclamation of war on December 8. "Japan, motivated by the same spirit of aggression and the same disregard for law, follows in the footsteps of her Axis partner. . . . The Kingdom of the Netherlands considers itself in a state of war with Japan because the aggression, that seeks to put out of action one by one the countries which desire peace, can only be halted through a strong coalition." And, after calling on the courage and resolution of all her subjects, and invoking the aid and understanding of a just God, the Netherlands sovereign made the ringing declaration that, since "our cause is righteous and our conscience clear, we accept the challenge, together with our powerful Allies."

The notification of the declaration of war came to Lieutenant Commander A. J. Bussemaker, RNN, as he was piloting his submarine on a patrol of the Gulf of Thailand in the waters between the southern tip of Indo-China and the Malay Peninsula. Commander Bussemaker was already nursing a grudge against the Japanese; on the night before, while cruising on the surface, he had been forced to crash-dive by two pointedly unfriendly Japanese destroyers which bore down on him out of the darkness. Now he had his war orders.

As darkness drew on, a few hours after Queen Wilhelmina's broadcast, the Dutch skipper sighted a large Japanese transport, headed southward and jammed to the guards with Nipponese troops. Commander Bussemaker changed course in pursuit. The going for the submarine soon became rugged, for the transport headed into the shallow waters of Patani Roads, a bay on the border between Thailand and the Federated Malay States. The undersea craft was literally slithering over the mud bottom of the bay in pursuit as it cruised at periscope depth, so Commander Bussemaker had to take a chance on being sighted: he ordered down periscope, blew his Kingstons and set his bow planes for hard rise. But even on the surface the deeper-draft submarine had trouble keeping the enemy transport in sight.

All this was forgotten, however, when the transport rounded the hook of Patani Roads and nosed up to her berth. The enemy vessel had led the Dutch submarine into a nest of three other invasion transports, all loaded with troops, ready to begin the march on Singapore.

Bussemaker fired his bow tubes and then, after a tight turn, let fly with his stern. There were six hits on the nest of transports, and all four were burning or sinking as the Dutch submarine got out at top speed. Once in blue water Bussemaker filed his report—the last report, as it turned out, he was ever to make. The next that was heard from the Netherlands submarine was when a naked, bleeding Hollander dazedly stumbled ashore on the east coast of Malaya. Into the muzzle of an Australian sentry's raised rifle he gasped his identity. He had been on the bridge of the submarine when it struck a mine. He had been in the water for thirty-five hours. He—Quartermaster Cornelius de Wolf—was the only survivor of the first Allied fleet unit to draw Japanese blood in World War II.

7

The first victory by a United States Navy vessel over a Japanese Fleet unit on the high seas occurred some two weeks after the submarine action in Patani Roads. USS DRAYTON, a destroyer, was serving in the screen of the LEXINGTON task force near Midway when the Japanese first struck. The DRAYTON, also known as the "Blue Beetle" because of a peculiar experimental color she at one time wore, then went on a decoy mission as a detached portion of the force which set out on the thwarted effort to relieve Wake. By December 21 the ship was back at Pearl, her officers and men goggle-eyed at the destruction that met their eyes, but cheered by the extensive work of repair and salvage which was already under way.

Families of Army and Navy personnel were being sent to the States from the Hawaii area. The skipper of the DRAYTON, Lieutenant Commander L. A. ("Abe") Abercrombie, USN, had been for many months without leave in the States, and he hoped that the DRAYTON would be given the job of escorting some of the homebound ships. This was not to be. The DRAYTON was given time only for refueling and taking on provisions. Then Abercrombie got orders to convoy a job lot of four ships southward to Palmyra and Christmas islands—two old 4-piper destroyers turned into fast transports, a surveying ship, and an inter-island steamer.

Shortly before three o'clock on the afternoon of December 24, Abercrombie was on the bridge with Commander George C. Kriner, USN, commodore of the destroyer division of which the DRAYTON ordinarily formed a part. A young soundman named Farrell came rushing out of the box which contained the sound gear. What followed is best told in the words of Abercrombie himself.[1]

" 'Captain, do you see anything on the port bow, bearing 120 true?' he demanded excitedly.

"I picked up my binoculars. 'Not a thing.'

[1] As contained in *My Life to the Destroyers*, by Captain L. A. Abercrombie, USN, with Fletcher Pratt; published September, 1944, by Henry Holt & Co., New York. Captain Abercrombie, incidentally, was the first surface ship commander in World War II to be awarded three Navy Crosses.

PLATE XVII—(*upper*) Attacked by a Japanese bomber in a Honolulu residential district, three civilians were killed in this shrapnel-riddled car on December 7, 1941. Heads of two of the victims can be seen in the car's front seat. (*lower*) The enemy did not get away unscathed. A Japanese Zero fighter, one of those brought down by U.S. gunners, lies a crumpled heap of wreckage near a busy Hawaiian highway.

PLATE XVIII—(*upper*) This *was* the enemy! The charred corpse of a Japanese flier is brought up from the bottom of Pearl Harbor where he crashed with his burning plane. (*lower*) Despite the treacherous attack without declaration of war, a Japanese lieutenant who crashed near Kaneohe Bay, Hawaii, is buried with the honors customarily given an officer.

PLATE XIX—(*upper*) The flag for which they gave their lives decorates the coffins of our gallant dead, Kaneohe Naval Air Station, Hawaii. (*lower*) Members of the Roberts Board investigating the Pearl Harbor disaster join a group of native Hawaiians in paying homage to those killed on December 7, 1941. Included in the group of dignitaries (left) are Associate Justice Owen J. Roberts, Admiral William H. Standley, USN, and Brig. Gen. Frank McCoy, USA.

PLATE XX—(*upper*) Last pre-war photographs of Wake Island, taken in November, 1941, show Marine and civil workers feverishly unloading supplies and strengthening this outpost. *Insets:* (left) Major James P. S. Devereux, USMC, taken prisoner when the Japs overwhelmed the gallant defending garrison, December, 1941, and (right) Colonel W. L. J. Bayler, USMC, famous "last man off Wake Island" before its capture. (*lower*) Floats support a gasoline line carrying fuel to tanks ashore, Wake Island, November, 1941.

PLATE XXI—(*upper*) USS DRAYTON, nemesis of Jap submarines and one of the destroyers that bore the brunt of the early fighting that followed Pearl Harbor. *Inset:* Lieutenant Commander Laurence A. Abercrombie, USN, Commanding Officer. (*lower*) Pearl Harbor saw many new names added to the Navy's hero list. A typical group received medals aboard a carrier on May 27, 1942. Left to right: Lieut. Comdr. C. W. Wilkins; Lieut. Comdr. W. S. Weeder; Lieut. Comdr. W. L. Anderson; Lieut. Comdr. C. W. McCluskey; Lieut. R. W. Mehle; Lieut. (jg) N. J. Kleiss; Lieut. (jg) C. J. Dobson; and Doris Miller, MAtt 1/c.

PLATE XXII—(*upper*) The smoke of battle had hardly cleared away before the enormous job of salvage and repair began. The destroyer SHAW, despite the terrific damage done by an aerial bomb (PLATE VI) was soon afloat again. After temporary repairs at Pearl Harbor Navy Yard she left for the mainland, February 8, 1942. (*lower*) A stubby bow was fashioned for the SHAW by Navy Yard workers. It was fitted on in drydock, replacing the bow, bridge, and turrets blasted away by the attack—a miracle of faith and ingenuity.

PLATE XXIII—(*upper*) The stricken CALIFORNIA sank into the Pearl Harbor mud until her main deck was awash. A cofferdam had to be built around the outline of her deck and the water pumped out. At the left is a work barge. (*lower*) The CALIFORNIA, afloat again, enters a dry-dock, counter-balanced against capsizing by tons of sandbags.

PLATE XXIV—Some of the ships that carried the brunt of the early Pacific fighting—*Left row, top to bottom:* USS ENTERPRISE, carrier; USS HONOLULU, USS TRENTON and USS CHICAGO, cruisers. *Right row, top to bottom:* USS SARATOGA, carrier; USS RALEIGH, USS DETROIT and USS OMAHA, cruisers.

PLATE XXV—They held the line in the days of the "bow and arrow" Navy, following the Pearl Harbor attack. *Left row, top to bottom:* USS CONCORD and USS NEW ORLEANS, cruisers; USS TUCKER, destroyer; USS ANTARES, cargo ship. *Right row, top to bottom:* USS RICHMOND, cruiser; USS TREVER and USS MONAGHAN, destroyers; and USS SOLACE, hospital ship.

PLATE XXVI—(*upper left*) Many ingenious devices were used to speed salvage, clear valuable wharfage. The OGLALA (PLATE VIII) was righted by big submarine salvage pontoons, or YSPs. Flooded and sunk, the YSP is secured by chains extending around the hull. Air is then pumped into the YSPs, which rise and roll the sunken vessel enough to permit other salvage methods to operate. (*lower left*) USS WEST VIRGINIA, victim of both bombs and fire, triumphantly glides into drydock at Pearl Harbor.

PLATE XXVII—(*above*) Aground opposite Hospital Point, the USS NEVADA, known as the "Cheerup Ship," lived up to its name by being one of the first of the Pearl Harbor casualties to go back into action.

PLATE XXVIII—(*upper*) Most difficult of all Pearl Harbor salvage jobs was the righting of the OKLAHOMA, which rested upside down for months before special gear could be rigged to turn her over. Divers are about to enter an air lock before descending into the murky depths of the ship to close openings. (*lower*) Cables were first stretched from her starboard side over wooden A frames to Ford Island.

PLATE XXIX—(*upper*) A multiple system of cables and electric motors ashore gradually pulled the 29,000-ton hulk over, exposing superstructure encrusted with barnacles and other marine growth. (*lower*) Several acres of land were cleared on Ford Island to provide space for the pulley system and motors. Perfect coordination of operations was needed at all times.

PLATE XXX—(*upper left*) Like a scene from *Gulliver's Travels*, this aerial view of OKLA-
HOMA salvage shows the stricken ship almost half righted. The risky work of cutting away loose
gear is about to begin. The great hull had no buoyancy. After she was rolled over, a cofferdam
had to be built around the low stern section and holes had to be patched before pumping could
begin. (*lower left*) Assistant Secretary of the Navy, Ralph A. Bard (left) inspects the work. On
the still slanting main deck of the OKLAHOMA stand (left to right) Rear Admiral W. R. Furlong,
USN, Commandant, Pearl Harbor Navy Yard; Commander F. H. Whitaker; Captain E. P.
Forrestel, USN; Mr. Jack Graham, Vice President of Pacific Bridge Company, salvage contrac-
tors; and Commander S. S. Isquith, USN.

PLATE XXXI—(*above*) Triumph of patience, precision, and engineering skill—the USS
OKLAHOMA floats again! As she leaves the Pearl Harbor drydock a huge patch along her star-
board side reveals where Japanese aerial torpedoes ripped open a third of her 583-foot length.
Her future undetermined, the OKLAHOMA has remained at a Pearl Harbor anchorage.

PLATE XXXII—(*upper*) Stripped of her cage masts, and bristling with new anti-aircraft weapons, the USS CALIFORNIA puts to sea, a stronger and better fighting unit than she was before December 7. (*lower*) The USS NEVADA stands out from Pearl Harbor with scout planes on her turrets and guns ready for action. She was one of the many ships which the Japs claimed they "destroyed to pieces" in the Pearl Harbor sneak attack.

" 'Well, sir, it must be a sub then, 'cause I have a good sound contact.'

"I turned to the officer of the deck, who happened to be Ensign Simmons, the former cadet from the Merchant Marine who was our sound officer. 'Send all hands to battle stations.'

"Dutch Kriner sent an emergency submarine contact signal to the convoy; they snapped smoke from their funnels and bore out sharp to starboard at their best speed, which was about 10 knots for the inter-island steamer, as the sirens shrieked all over the ship. Of course we had to have one of those incidents that showed how much we were still amateurs in war. Just as Bing Mitchell reported all stations manned and ready someone below got excited and pulled the sound gear switch. Farrell's instrument went dead.

" 'Contact lost!' he shouted through the door.

" 'Just another big fish,' said Mitchell, but before he had finished saying it they got the switch closed again and Farrell yelled:

" 'Contact regained, zero-thirty true.'

"This was close quarters. 'She's inside our turning circle,' said Bing.

" 'Full right rudder,' I ordered the helmsman, and to Farrell, 'Hold your contact!'

"Maybe I did the wrong thing; some of those people who figure things out on the manoeuvre board told me afterward that I did, but that sub was so close in on our left that we couldn't turn into its track, so I went round the other way, hoping to pick him up. It was a marvel that we made it, but with the help of Farrell and some wonderful work by the helmsmen we did.

" 'Contact good, sir,' shouted Farrell as I gave an order to steady her on a course north, then 'Contact closing rapidly.'

"It was a sub, all right, a fat, happy sub, running submerged merely because it was daylight, heading for Pearl, probably expecting nothing so little as to find American ships on the way.

" 'Range closing.'

"Simmons had his stop watch out. 'Stand by to attack with depth charges,' I ordered. 'All engines ahead full.'

"Simmons punched his stop watch. 'Stand by to drop!' I said. 'Now,' said Simmons, bringing down the arm he had lifted.

" 'Drop one!' I said, and as Shelly, the torpedo officer, repeated it the Chief Torpedoman swung the lever. . . . 'Drop two! Drop three!'

"At that speed the shock of a depth charge makes you feel as though the whole world were being violently shaken from side to side, and down in the engine room their feet go to sleep. A shout went up from the whole ship as I leaned around the signal rack to look at our wake. In the center of the boiling water where our depth charges had fallen oil was welling to the surface with fragments of debris in the middle of it.

"I shouted for the rudder to be put hard left and we charged back into the slick, dropping three more depth charges. More oil came up; we swung out the sound gear range again, and Farrell shouted that he had picked her up, now turned and headed southwestward from the point where we had hit her. He was a wonder to do it with all that racket in the gear and well deserved the special letter of commendation from the admiral that he got along with his promotion later.

"Bing Mitchell said, 'She'll probably go deep, Captain. Better give her a deep barrage.' The Commodore had rushed to the wing of the bridge with me, his nose lifted like that of a bird dog to catch the odor of the slick as we ran through it. 'Get a rag, get a rag,' he was shouting. 'Get me a line and some rag, we'll bring up a sample of that oil.' He was the only one to remember that frequent reports of depth charging submarines had come in before and that what looked like an oil slick was all too often merely debris [1] from the depth charges themselves.

"As we swung toward the slick for the third time he lowered the rag triumphantly from his nose, not noticing that it was one of his best towels, picked up in the excitement. 'Diesel all right,' he said, and we were over the slick again, with Farrell shouting, 'Lost sound contact!'

"Drop one, drop two, drop three again and we came full left.

"Before we had completed the turn I heard another shout. 'Look, a submarine!' It was, too; the bow of an enormous submarine, fully 50 feet of it, pushing up through the water slowly at a steep 70 degree angle, dripping oil, the net cutter at the bow looking like a set of teeth and the diving planes at its side showing the characteristic Jap shape. 'Commence firing!' I yelled.

"Nothing happened. Everybody simply stood there popeyed with a mouth full of teeth, looking at the monster as though it were a movie. 'Commence firing!' I shouted again, and then ran out into the wings of

---

[1] When a depth charge explodes it gives off an oily exudation which was sometimes mistaken, particularly in the early days of the war, for diesel oil from a wounded submarine.

the bridge to yell at the top of my lungs to Dewey, to the gunnery officer, 'For God's sake, why don't you commence firing?'

"I heard him yell in return to his talker but never heard what he said because at the same moment all the .50s seemed to open up at once. They went right in, stitching a row of holes along that bow, but I don't know whether they had any real share in it. Even as they were hitting her the sub tilted majestically to the vertical, then slid backwards and down with gathering speed.

"We completed our turn, rushed past the spot, and just for luck I dropped four more charges into it. Oil boiled out of that pit of sea, spreading and spreading till it covered a circle a mile in diameter, and from beneath it came the shock of an explosion, heavier and deeper than our own depth charges. The last barrage must have set off something within the sub itself. . . .

"We were under a strict rule of radio silence, but the Commodore felt the way I did about it, that our position placed us in 'proximity' to Pearl, where the rule was off, especially for such a message, so we told them about our victory.

" 'Well done. Get another,' the Admiral radioed back, without a word about our breaking radio silence, and we knew it was all right."

The DRAYTON's victim was not the first Japanese submarine to be engaged by American warships in the Eastern Pacific, but, discounting the two-man submersibles destroyed at Pearl Harbor, it was the first verified kill of the war. Other ships' skippers and crews may have, as they unshakingly believe, destroyed enemy submarines before the DRAYTON's victory, but so meticulous are the Navy's standards of accounting enemy losses that, unless the actual destruction is witnessed, credit is given for a "probable" only. The rule applies as well to enemy ships torpedoed by our submarines. Thus neither the Navy nor the public is self-deluded about the attrition of the enemy's naval or maritime strength.

And coming on Christmas Eve, as it did, the news of even a minor victory was a welcome ray of light on a holiday scene otherwise shrouded in deepest gloom.

PART TWO

Rape of An Empire

Chapter Six

O F all the Pacific territory under the protection of the United States the Japanese most wanted the Philippines. . . .

From the Japanese standpoint, the prize doubtless was well worth the taking, no matter what the ultimate cost might turn out to be. There were many reasons why Japan might covet the Philippines. Once Japan had fully embarked upon her campaign of expansion through aggression, however—the campaign long planned under the grandiose title of the Co-Prosperity Sphere in Greater East Asia—the subjugation of the Philippines transcended a desire for empire and became a military necessity.

The islands lay in long parallel to the Japanese seaways to those treasure lands of the Western and Southwestern Pacific which Tokyo had marked out for conquest. Additionally, American forces in the Philippines were to the Japanese military a grave potential threat to the coast of South China, already invaded and blockaded by the Japanese in their undeclared war on Asia, and to the Japanese island stronghold of Formosa, itself the fruit of earlier Japanese aggression.

From the standpoint of geopolitics, the Philippines menaced Japan's ambitions in Asia because they were a living symbol of the ability of a free republic in the Western Hemisphere to co-operate in the establishment and maintenance of an Asiatic democracy. That was the negation of all Japan's polemics that democracies were decadent, and that the Occidentals were a predatory gang.

True, the way had not always been smooth between the United States and the Philippines. But progress had been steady and, down through the years, friendship between the two peoples had flourished alongside the growth of mutual respect. Partly owing to the aid and encouragement of the United States, but certainly owing to the initiative and enterprise of her own people, the Philippine Islands were benefiting to an increasing degree from the technical and cultural progress of the leading nations of the world. The average urban Filipino, for instance, could look at his standard of living and make a favorable comparison with the lot of a similar individual in almost any other section of the globe. This was more than true when such a comparison was made with the lands and peoples immediately about him.

But lest too much emphasis be placed on modern convenience and material comfort, it should also be recorded that of all Asiatic peoples the Filipinos had an educational system equaled only by the Japanese themselves. There were eight universities in Manila alone. The University of Santo Tomas, founded in 1611, was as proud of its modern curriculum as it was of its great age. But, whereas the Spanish sovereignty had established universities for the relatively few, United States administration of the islands had introduced universal free public schools of which the Filipinos had taken eager advantage. In the field of religion, Roman Catholic and Moslem and the Protestant minority were achieving a world's example of harmony.

All aspects of the Philippine Commonwealth, then, combined to expose the rapacious falsity of Japan's "Co-Prosperity" program. Even with the departure of the Americans, a progressive, independent Philippine state would menace Japan's ambitions. In perfecting their plans for the Greater New Order in East Asia the Japanese decided, as subsequent events made amply clear, that the glory of Nippon was to be maintained by profit to Nippon, profit exacted from enslaved peoples exploiting their own lands for the benefit of economic shoguns and military daimios in Tokyo.

It would never do, obviously, for the free, enlightened, and prosperous Philippines to remain in plain view of the conquered peoples—or of the regimented Japanese masses. With such an example before them, the millions would be hard to keep convinced of the advantages of slavery.

Taking all facts into account, then, the course must have seemed clear to the world planners in Tokyo. Wholly aside from the considerable military value of the islands, the Philippines obviously would have to be placed high on the priority list of territories to be assaulted and absorbed.

2

The city of Manila gets its name from a native phrase meaning "place by the river of flowers." Events were to rob Manila of any association with the poetic and the beautiful.

At the headquarters of the United States Navy in Manila there was no exact knowledge that the Japanese were about to launch an attack on the American flag. Despite this lack of exact knowledge, however, there was no corresponding lack of planning for such an eventuality; and in the formation of these plans Admiral Thomas C. Hart was awaiting the secret arrival in Manila of an important visitor from Singapore.

The time was shortly before noon; the day and date, Friday, December 5, 1941.

The possibility of war with Japan was not a matter of recent consideration. In January of that year, almost 12 months before, Admiral Hart had ordered the wives and families of naval personnel evacuated from the Philippines and China. The order was obeyed, of course, although not without argument in some family councils and not without tears and perhaps petulance from some of the younger Navy wives. (This evacuation order subsequently gave rise to a one-of-my-best-friends-heard-it story which, although apocryphal, might have come from the pen of a latter-day de Maupassant: On reaching the States one romantic young wife craftily divorced her husband, so she would not be subject to naval authority, and then defiantly journeyed back to the Philippines so that she could be near him—only to be caught in Manila by the coming of war, and interned by the Japs after her beloved though divorced husband had successfully fought his ship to the safety of Allied waters.)

To the moment that the homebound ship cast off from Pier Seven the women were demanding an answer to a rhetorical question with the querulous refrain: "Why do we have to go home when the Army wives are staying?" That the young wives' question was rhetorical, however, was proved some three months later when the Army also ordered the wives and families of its personnel removed from the Philippines.

"I was convinced, finally, in June of 1941," said Admiral Hart later, "that Japan intended to go to war. There were a number of reasons for this conviction, among them the fact that American credits to Japan were being frozen, and that the Japanese were having trouble paying cash for oil purchased in the Netherlands East Indies."

Admiral Hart was equally convinced that, in the event of war, the line-up would be Japan versus a combination of the United States, Great Britain, and the Netherlands—for reasons economic as well as military and diplomatic, the Japanese would find it extremely difficult to attack one of these powers without involving the other two. Consequently, and with the authority of Secretary of the Navy Frank Knox, he had been having discussions with representatives of the British and Netherlands navies exploring possible joint action in resisting a Japanese onslaught.

"These discussions had to be conducted in utmost secrecy," said Admiral Hart. "It soon became clear to me that to maintain adequate and safe communications, as well as personal contact with the British and Dutch, I would have to set up a command post ashore. With much regret, I determined to remove my flag from the HOUSTON to a head-quarters in Manila."

The task of finding suitable quarters ashore turned out to be not so difficult as might have been expected. The one building which seemed to meet all the requirements—in fact, the only privately owned structure fronting on Manila Bay—was the big new Marsman Building, completed in 1940, and just one of the many fabulous interests of J. H. Marsman [1] throughout the Far East.

Office space in the Marsman Building was in great demand because of such modern features as air conditioning, accessibility to harbor shipping, and, perhaps, because the building's penthouse contained the swanky and select Transportation Club. The structure was completely tenanted, but this again presented no problem to the Navy. The third floor of the building facing Manila Bay was occupied by the Cardinal Life Insurance Company, a Marsman enterprise; the president of this company was a former naval officer, Mr. Frank J. Courtney, of the Annapolis class of '18, and later to return to active duty as a lieutenant commander. Courtney also was a director of the company that owned the building and, on behalf of the Marsman interests, he notified Admiral Purnell that as much of the quarters of the Cardinal Life Insurance Company as Admiral Hart required could be made available to the Navy at once. The offer was accepted.

Admiral Hart's offices were in the northwest corner of the building. From the windows he could look out over Manila Bay to the naval base at Cavite, and beyond that into the blue haze which shrouded Corregidor in the distance. From the windows, and roof too, visual signals could be exchanged with ships in the bay. The admiral's living quarters were in

---

[1] Against the advice of Admiral Hart and his chief of staff, Admiral Purnell, Marsman made a flying trip to Hong Kong a few days before the outbreak of war. He was accompanied by Richard C. Wilson, chief of the Manila office of the United Press. Both were interned by the Japanese after the fall of Hong Kong. Wilson was repatriated on the GRIPSHOLM and Marsman escaped.

the new wing of the sprawling, Spanish-style Manila Hotel, owned and operated by the commonwealth, whose handsome terrace and outdoor swimming pool President Quezon had ordered patterned after the Shoreham Hotel in Washington.

As Admiral Hart looked out his office windows it was easy for him to distinguish the new wing of the hotel from the old: the huge sliding windows of the old wing were made of paper-thin, opaque seashells in wooden frames, kept open in the daytime and making a mosquito bar mandatory equipment in every room; the new wing was completely air-conditioned and the windows were always kept closed. (All Manila was familiar with the fact that when the admiral's cap was hanging in his hotel window he was "at home" to members of his staff and other interested callers.) In building the new wing of the hotel, President Quezon had ordered the architects to include a roomy and well-appointed penthouse for his own personal use. The chief executive of the Philippines had never occupied the penthouse, however; upon completion it had been offered for the use of, and accepted by, General Douglas MacArthur, when the former United States Army chief of staff took over the direction of the Philippine defense preparations.

All in all, the Manila Hotel was a focal point for Manila's more conservative social and semi-state activities. It was the residence of many high United States and commonwealth officials, and visiting foreign dignitaries invariably made it their temporary home. All the "regulars" had their own tables in the hotel pavilion, where there was an excellent cuisine and music by two orchestras. Time had been when President Quezon had a ringside table, as had General MacArthur, but with the evacuation of the womenfolk austerity set in. Until the end of 1939 a table adjoining General MacArthur's was always reserved for a very popular young couple known to almost everybody as Ike and Mamie— Lieutenant Colonel and Mrs. Dwight D. Eisenhower. The lessening of purely social activity was in direct proportion to the growing tenseness of international relations in the Far East.

Tense indeed was the feeling on that fifth day of December, 1941.

Admiral Hart noted the time and rang for his flag secretary, Lieutenant Commander A. S. McDill, USN, an officer who could call himself a native Filipino because his public-health-surgeon father and mother were in the Philippines at his birth. "Get a position check on the plane from Singapore," the admiral ordered. With the information in hand, the admiral ordered his barge brought alongside his private dock, adjoining President Quezon's in the lagoon.

At Cavite, Admiral Hart was piped ashore just as a heavy seaplane with British markings taxied across the protected waters to the landing ramp. A rather short, ruddy-faced figure stepped from the plane; and presently Admiral Hart had shaken hands with, and returned the salute of Admiral Sir Tom Phillips, of the Royal Navy.

There were the usual civilities beginning with a hearty welcome, and the polite interchange ordained by custom: the trip from British home waters had been uneventful, and with only the conventional fueling stops; the weather had been mostly favorable; the flight up from Singapore along the coast of Borneo had been most interesting but without particular incident; yes, it was indeed true that the arrival of two powerful ships should exert a quieting influence on the present turmoil in the Far East. And it was easy to tell from Admiral Sir Tom Phillips's conversation that his ships were his first and foremost interest.

"REPULSE is a good ship, Admiral," said the British flag officer warmly, "but my flagship—you must see her! In fact, my own invitation is backed up by my entire staff: we hope that conditions in the near future will be such that you can soon pay a visit aboard HMS PRINCE OF WALES."

3

Admiral Phillips was given quarters at the Cavite Naval Base, where a heavy guard and a security patrol of wartime rigidity was already in force, and where it was hoped his presence would not become known. Conversations on the general Asiatic naval situation began that night. After a few hours out for sleep, they were continued into the late afternoon of the next day. Participating with Admiral Hart and his chief of staff, Rear Admiral William R. Purnell, on the American side of the discussion were Rear Admiral Francis W. Rockwell, USN, Commandant of the Sixteenth Naval District, and, as often as he wished to join, General MacArthur.

There was general agreement among the conferees that the Far East situation was more serious than it had been at any time in the recent hot-and-cold past—that this seriousness was no secret to seasoned Asiatic skippers was indicated by the 40 merchant ships which had altered course to run for the supposed safety of Manila Harbor, where they were now lined up at anchor behind the breakwater. British, Dutch, and United States reconnaissance showed unusual movement of Japanese war and merchant shipping along the east coast of China. These reports were all available on the conference table, in a room lined with detail charts of all areas considered to be in possible danger. In addition, Captain Frank D. Wagner, USN, commander of Patrol Wing Ten, was brought in to tell of the observations of his naval aviators in their long-range PBYs. Excerpts from a report subsequently turned in by Captain Wagner give an indication of the scope of Patwing Ten's work:

"By the latter part of November, the international situation had become such that Patrol Wing Ten was ordered by Admiral Hart to start extensive patrols. The seaplane tender PRESTON and her planes were in the Gulf of Davao, and her planes patrolled the eastern approaches to the Celebes Sea. The HERON with four light planes was at the southeastern tip of Palawan Island, covering the western approaches to the Celebes Sea. The Dutch were patrolling along the northern edge of the Netherlands East Indies, covering the territory contiguous to us, while the rest of our planes from Manila searched the area to the west of us as far as the coast of Indo-China, to the northwest to Hainan, and to the north to Formosa. . . .

"Up to 2 December our planes had sighted nothing alarming. On 2 December 20 Japanese merchant ships, including transports, were found in Camranh Bay, on the lower southeast coast of French Indo-China. On 3 December there were 50 Japanese ships, including destroyers and cruisers, in Camranh Bay. On 4 December there were none."

Violent weather had imposed a cessation of reconnaissance over Camranh Bay, said Captain Wagner. Patrols were to be resumed as soon as possible, but it was most likely that the first reports on the whereabouts of the Japanese armada would come from British planes out of Singapore, across the Gulf of Siam from Camranh, and much nearer than the Patwing Ten bases in the Philippines. Or the reports might come from British or Dutch planes on the west coast of Borneo, also nearer to the last-reported location of the suspicious Japanese concentration of shipping.

Meanwhile, reported Captain Wagner, there was an ominous development from another quarter.

"Beginning yesterday," he said in effect, although his exact words were not recorded at the time, "our planes from Manila have been meeting Japanese planes patrolling in the vicinity of the northwest coastline of Luzon. As the planes approach, each has its guns manned. Neither side has fired a shot, but they are keeping a wary eye on each other, and avoiding each. other like stiff-legged dogs." [1]

The disappearance of the Japanese fleet off the coast of Indo-China of course came in for much discussion and speculation by the conferees. But Admiral Phillips also had some specific requests—the immediate purpose, in fact, of his flying trip to Manila. He had brought with him from home waters, he pointed out, only four destroyers, HMS ELECTRA, ENCOUNTER, JUPITER, and EXPRESS. In addition, there were in the Far East the destroyers HMAS VAMPIRE and HMS TENEDOS, but they were assigned on detached missions and it was doubtful if he could count on them as part of the screen for PRINCE OF WALES and REPULSE. Phillips needed, he said emphatically, at least four American destroyers before he could set out with confidence on a patrol of Asiatic waters, because Britain had become very short on this type of craft.

Admiral Hart agreed with the reasonableness of Admiral Phillips's request, but there were a number of difficulties in the way of its fulfillment. First of all, Admiral Hart felt that he had none too many ships for his own purposes. Then there were the diplomatic angles to be considered: there was no military alliance in effect between the United States and Britain. Glancing at his chart of ship movements, Admiral Hart noted that by coincidence the destroyer tender BLACK HAWK and four destroyers happened to be visiting at Balikpapan, while four destroyers and the cruiser MARBLEHEAD were fueling at Tarakan, both oil ports on the east coast of Dutch Borneo. But Admiral Phillips's request would require quite a bit of consideration. Britain was at war with Germany, of course. There was little likelihood of encountering German battle craft in Asiatic or Indian waters. And there was nothing in international law that prevented United States ships from making an indoctrinational cruise with vessels of a friendly power, in nonbelligerent waters.

The conference was brought to an abrupt halt at 1800 on the afternoon of December 6. The weather had lifted over the Gulf of Siam.

[1] Although not recorded at the time, as indicated above, these words were taken from a narrative by Captain Wagner, later to become, as a rear admiral, Assistant Deputy Chief of Naval Operations (Air).

Reconnaissance planes reported that the missing Japanese armada had now been sighted in the vicinity of latitude 8 degrees north, longitude 104 degrees east. The ships were on a westerly heading. If this course were maintained the destination could only be the Malay Peninsula, either Thailand or the Federated States under British protectorate. The British interpretation relayed to Admiral Phillips was a thrust at the narrow neck of Thailand, beyond which lay the Bay of Bengal. If this was another Japanese bluff it was being conducted in the most realistic manner imaginable. In any case it demanded action.

"I should be at sea," said Admiral Phillips. "I've got to get back to Singapore."

Admiral Hart asked whether the British flag officer's pilot had been trained for night flying in Asiatic waters, at the same time offering him the use of any of the Navy's PBYs. Admiral Phillips made a hurried inquiry. Yes, his pilot felt capable of making the 1,300-mile night hop to Singapore, and was ready to take off at once. Secret dispatches ordered PRINCE OF WALES and REPULSE made ready for sea, their officers and men recalled from shore leave wherever they happened to be.

As Admiral Phillips prepared to board his plane, Admiral Hart bade him farewell. In later recounting his impressions of the British flag officer Admiral Hart said, "I liked Phillips very much. He was most realistic about the situation at Singapore and in the Far East in case of attack. I felt that I could depend on him—that he would be a good man to work with. He was a seaman and an officer of the finest type."

As Phillips shook hands with Admiral Hart the American naval officer said, "About those four destroyers—they should already be at sea. I immediately ordered them and the BLACK HAWK to proceed toward Batavia for supplies and recreation." There was a possibility that the destroyers would reach Singapore within 48 hours.

The four United States destroyers did not leave Balikpapan that night as ordered because Dutch naval authorities felt, probably with justification, that the antisubmarine booms should not be opened until daylight: there had been reports of strange submarines in the northeast Borneo area. But even if the ships had cleared Balikpapan that night they might have arrived in Singapore too late.

The British battleships sailed at 1730 on the afternoon of the 8th. The United States destroyers arrived at Singapore barely in time to take on fuel and go out again in search of survivors from HMS REPULSE and HMS PRINCE OF WALES.

Admiral Sir Tom Spencer Vaughan Phillips, RN, KCB, CB, was not among the survivors. "A gallant seaman and gentleman," Admiral Hart says. "His project of getting one or both of his heavy ships into the Japanese transports was the only chance of defeating the invasion of Malaya and preserving Singapore."

4

Admiral Hart was not surprised at the coming of war. He was surprised at the manner of the war's coming, and surprised that the Japs struck first by air at Pearl Harbor rather than at the Philippines.

When Lieutenant Colonel Clement arrived at Admiral Hart's room in the Manila Hotel the Marine officer handed over the dispatch announcing the Pearl Harbor attack.

"Are you sure this is authentic?"

"Yes, Admiral. It was sent in Morse in the clear, not in code. It was repeated twice. It was received by one of our senior operators. He recognized and identified the sending technique of the operator at Pearl."

"Have you notified General MacArthur?"

"That has been done, sir."

Admiral Hart then ordered his chief of staff, Admiral Purnell, to go at once to Asiatic Fleet headquarters and set previously planned and rehearsed battle tactics in motion. "I'll be over as soon as I can get on some clothes," he said.

He realized as he gave the order that the forces at his command were pitifully weak to be thrown against the ships and submarines and planes of one of the world's great naval powers. He realized that the resounding official designation of "United States Asiatic Fleet" applied to a handful of ships which the Japanese could assess as a small task force—it was no larger than the support which the Japanese provided their assault transports in the wake of fleets more powerful.

Aside from his former flagship, the HOUSTON, commanded by Captain Albert H. Rooks, USN, he had two light cruisers, the MARBLEHEAD, Captain Arthur G. Robinson, USN, and the BOISE, Captain Stephen E. Robinson, USN (until the later part of January, when he was relieved by Captain Edward J. "Mike" Moran, USN). Of heavy ships that was all.

To support the cruisers there were 13 over-age destroyers of the 1917-18 class. These ships were designated as Desdron 29—Destroyer Squadron 29—commanded by Captain Herbert V. Wiley, USN, whose flag was in USS PAUL JONES, commanded by Lieutenant Commander John J. Hourihan, USN. Desdron 29 was in turn broken up into Destroyer Division 57, with Commander Edwin M. Crouch, USN, as commodore; Destroyer Division 58, Commander Thomas H. Binford, USN, as commodore; and Destroyer Division 50, Commander Paul H. Talbot, USN, as commodore. The ships and commanding officers of these divisions were as follows:

Desdiv 57

WHIPPLE, Lieutenant Commander Eugene S. Karpe, USN
ALDEN, Lieutenant Commander Lewis E. Coley, USN
JOHN D. EDWARDS, Commander Henry E. Eccles, USN
EDSALL, Lieutenant Joshua J. Nix, USN

Desdiv 58

STEWART, Lieutenant Commander Harold P. Smith, USN
PARROTT, Lieutenant Commander Edward N. Parker, USN (On January 28, Parker became commodore of Desdiv 50, and Lieutenant John N. Hughes, USN, became skipper of PARROTT)
BULMER, Commander Leon J. Manees, USN (Lieutenant David A. Harris, USN, after January 28)
BARKER, Commander Louis J. McGlone, USN

Desdiv 50

PEARY, Commander Harry H. Keith, USN (until wounded on December 10 in the bombing of Cavite, and relieved by Commander John M. Bermingham, USN)
POPE, Lieutenant Commander Welford C. Blinn, USN
FORD, Lieutenant Commander Jacob E. Cooper, USN
PILLSBURY, Lieutenant Commander Harold C. Pound, USN

Also attached to Desdron 29 was the tender BLACK HAWK, Commander George L. Harriss, USN.

Submarines of the Asiatic Fleet had been gradually increased over the past few months until now there were 29 of them. They were tended by the CANOPUS, Commander Earl L. Sackett, USN; HOLLAND, Captain

Joseph W. Gregory, USN; otus, Commander Joel Newsom, USN. A submarine rescue vessel, PIGEON, Lieutenant Commander Richard E. Hawes (later Lieutenant Commander Frank A. Davis, USN), also was attached to this group. The submarines were organized as follows:

Submarine Division 21

SALMON, Lieutenant Commander Eugene B. McKinney, USN
SEAL, Lieutenant Commander Kenneth C. Hurd, USN
SKIPJACK, Lieutenant Commander Charles L. Freeman, USN
SARGO, Lieutenant Commander Tyrrell D. Jacobs, USN
SAURY, Lieutenant Commander John L. Burnside, USN
SPEARFISH, Lieutenant Roland F. Pryce, USN

Submarine Division 22

SNAPPER, Lieutenant Commander Hamilton L. Stone, USN
STINGRAY, Lieutenant Commander Raymond S. Lamb, USN
STURGEON, Lieutenant Commander William L. Wright, USN
SCULPIN, Lieutenant Commander Lucius H. Chappell, USN
SAILFISH, Lieutenant Commander Morton C. Mumma, Jr., USN
SWORDFISH, Lieutenant Commander Chester C. Smith, USN

Submarine Division 201

S-36, Lieutenant Commander John R. McKnight, Jr., USN
S-37, Lieutenant James C. Dempsey, USN
S-38, Lieutenant Wreford G. Chapple, USN
S-39, Lieutenant James W. Coe, USN
S-40, Lieutenant Nicholas Lucker, Jr., USN
S-41, Lieutenant Commander George M. Holley, USN

Submarine Division 202

SEADRAGON, Lieutenant Commander William E. Ferrall, USN
SEALION, Lieutenant Commander Richard G. Voge, USN
SEARAVEN, Lieutenant Commander Theodore G. Aylward, USN
SEAWOLF, Lieutenant Commander Frederick B. Warder, USN

Submarine Division 203

PERCH, Lieutenant Commander David A. Hurt, USN
PICKEREL, Lieutenant Commander Barton E. Bacon, USN

PORPOISE, Lieutenant Commander Joseph A. Callaghan, USN
PIKE, Lieutenant Commander William A. New, USN
SHARK, Lieutenant Commander Louis Shane, Jr., USN
TARPON, Lieutenant Commander Lewis Wallace, USN
PERMIT, Lieutenant Commander Adrian M. Hurst, USN

As already mentioned, there were the 30 PBYs of Patrol Wing Ten. These planes, as well as other lighter aircraft, were tended by LANGLEY, Captain Felix B. Stump, USN (until relieved by Commander Robert P. McConnell, USN); CHILDS, Commander John L. Pratt, USN; WILLIAM B. PRESTON, Lieutenant Commander Etheridge Grant, USN; and HERON, Lieutenant William L. Kabler, USN.

There were the old seagoing gunboats TULSA, Lieutenant Commander Tillet S. Daniel, USN, and ASHEVILLE, of which Captain Kenneth M. Hoeffel, USN, was in command until he was relieved in December by Lieutenant Commander Jacob W. Britt, USN. Captain Hoeffel then became commander of the Inshore Patrol, and he was the senior naval officer captured by the Japanese when Corregidor fell some five months later as the culmination of a series of events to be described in more detail elsewhere in this narrative.[1] The river gunboats LUZON, Lieutenant Commander George M. Brooke, USN, and OAHU, Lieutenant Commander Douglas E. Smith, USN, had been brought back from Shanghai, as has been noted. The MINDANAO, Commander Alan R. McCracken, USN, was now one day from Manila on the way back from Hong Kong, where the ill-fated WAKE had been stripped and left. The ISABEL, Lieutenant John W. Payne, Jr., USN, was a former yacht converted into a 20-knot gunboat.

Finally, there were the usual auxiliaries: the oilers PECOS, Commander Elmer P. Abernethy, USN, and TRINITY, Commander William Hibbs, USN; several minesweepers of the bird class—BITTERN, Lieutenant Thomas G. Warfield, USN; FINCH, Lieutenant Commander Thurlow W. Davison, USN; LARK, Lieutenant Commander Hugh P. Thomason, USN; QUAIL, Lieutenant Commander John H. Morrill, USN; TANAGER, Lieutenant Commander Egbert A. Roth, USN; WHIP-POORWILL, Lieutenant Commander Charles A. Ferriter, USN; and a tug, NAPA, Lieutenant Nathaniel M. Dial, USN.

And there were, of course, the six motor torpedo boats of PT Squad-

[1] See Part IV.

ron Three which had arrived in September under command of Lieutenant John D. Bulkeley, USN, and which were to have a spectacular and well-publicized history.

For obvious strategic reasons these ships were not all in Manila Bay or the Manila area. After hurriedly mounting additional machine guns at Cavite at the beginning of December, HOUSTON had been ordered south to Iloilo and was now at that central Philippine port awaiting developments. With the outbreak of war, Admiral William A. Glassford flew to Iloilo at once and hoisted his flag on the only United States heavy cruiser in Asiatic waters. He had reached Manila from command of the Yangtze River Patrol just one week before. The BOISE had arrived at Manila with an Army convoy on December 4, had been refueled and sailed at once for Cebu, in the center of the Philippine archipelago.

The MARBLEHEAD and four destroyers had been sent to Tarakan, Borneo, with instructions to delay in that area, and the BLACK HAWK and four destroyers had gone to Balikpapan, Borneo, with similar orders.

Two destroyers, PEARY and PILLSBURY, were in drydock at Cavite as the result of a collision in October, their repairs almost completed, and the submarines SEALION and SEADRAGON were in for overhaul. Three other destroyers were patrolling in the Manila-Subic Bay area.

Patwing Ten's PBYs were carefully dispersed against the possibility that a surprise attack might find them in a single concentration. In addition to the planes stationed in Davao and at the approaches to the Celebes Sea, one squadron of PBYs was based on Sangley Point, near Cavite, where a new seaplane base was under construction, and other detachments were at Olongapo, in Subic Bay, and at Los Banos on the inland Luzon lake called Laguna de Bay. The three submarine tenders CANOPUS, OTUS, and HOLLAND were all in the Manila area, as were the submarines.[1]

---

[1] That little will be told in this volume about the exploits of United States submarines perhaps can best be explained by quoting a statement contained in a narrative of the Java Sea campaign prepared in the Navy Department and available only to authorized personnel. "This narrative has done considerably less than justice to our submarines," says the document. "It has not been practicable to trace their individual movements and successes. But the courage and skill with which they were handled enabled them to inflict probably greater damage on the enemy than any other element of our forces." Actually, the U.S. naval high command found itself in the somewhat anomalous position of waging a successful war against German submarines in the Atlantic while United States submarines were tremendously successful in the Pacific, and consequently forced to remain ultrasecretive about both. To announce details of

Those were the ships, the submarines, and the planes available in the Far East to send against the Japanese invader. From published sources it would appear that for each one of the Asiatic Fleet's three cruisers the Japanese had four battleships. For each of the 13 over-age destroyers the Japanese had approximately three heavy or light cruisers. And the Japanese had at least nine aircraft carriers, destroyers and submarines by scores, and planes by hundreds, not to mention the advantage of short supply lines and secretly prepared bases.

In describing the days immediately before the outbreak of war Admiral Hart liked to use a homely parable. "It was like living near a neighbor who was big and burly and who you knew held a deadly grudge against you. You could see him building up his muscles and training himself to a fine edge for a fight. You were not allowed to do anything about it, yet you knew that sooner or later he was going to spring out of the darkness and slug you when you weren't looking. You knew that he would kill you if he could, but because you were peaceable and law-abiding you couldn't do much about it."

Nobody knew better than Admiral Hart the American weaknesses in the Far East. When the war finally began, he said, it was like using bare fists against a vicious gangster armed with a tommy gun.

5

For reasons that are still obscure, the Japanese did not at once attack Manila or the defense installations of Luzon, therefore presumably giving Army and Navy forces in that area, particularly aviation, ample time to prepare a defense or to take the offensive if they so desired. The Japs struck first at the southern island of Mindanao, and doubtless with good reason they attempted to knock out the Navy's air strength in that area at the very outset.

"We entered the war with a group of pilots I considered the best in the world," said Captain Wagner proudly of the men who flew the long-range PBYs. "They were used to operating in the Far East. They had

---

success against the Germans would supply valuable information to the Japanese for use against our own submarines. To describe the successes of our undersea war against Japan was to give Germany instructions in its submarine campaign against American troop and supply ships. Consequently, information about the heroic deeds of the "silent service" doubtless will remain in the most restricted category until the end of the war.

been on neutrality patrol so long that they were adept at identifying
various types of merchant ships. They knew our own fleet and they knew
what the enemy ships should look like. They were skilled navigators,
used to flying in bad weather day or night.

"At 3:15 on the morning of December 8 . . . we immediately
loaded bombs on all planes and dispatched them to their preassigned war
operating bases. . . . By dawn, all the planes were on patrol or at their
wartime locations."

Two of these planes were on "wartime location" in the Gulf of Davao
before dawn. A third plane was out on patrol, and the plan was for the
two reserve planes to go in as an attack force if the scout plane sighted
enemy activity. Just at dawn a force of Japanese dive bombers came over,
aiming for the two planes on the water and the seaplane tender PRESTON.
By violent maneuvers the PRESTON managed to dodge the bombs aimed
at her, shooting down at least one enemy attacker as she did so. But the
two PBYs on the water were sunk. "In this attack," said Captain Wagner,
"our very best bomber, Ensign Robert G. Tills, was killed." [1]

That the Japanese attack was well-planned was proved by the arrival
of four Japanese destroyers in the Gulf of Davao simultaneously with
the attack from the air. Fortunately the PRESTON spotted the enemy warships first, and managed to slip out and find a new hiding place without
being sighted. Her two planes which had been destroyed were immediately replaced.

But the invaders had not overlooked their main objective, despite
their obscure delay in launching their attack upon it.

Shortly before noon on December 8 the Japanese directed a heavy
force of fighters, bombers, and dive bombers in attacks against all the
Army airfields in the vicinity of Manila. Damage was very heavy. As one
observer put it: "This attack put out of action on the first day of the war
about two-thirds of our Army's fighter strength and over one-half of
our Army bomber strength. It was a most disappointing blow." This
estimate of Army air loss, while unofficial, is borne out in a general way
in a statement released by General George C. Marshall, Chief of Staff,
U.S. Army, on September 8, 1943: "The enemy led off with systematic
bombing of airfields and key points in Luzon which resulted in the
destruction of a large number of our planes due to limited dispersal

[1] Asiatic Fleet officials believe that Ensign Robert G. Tills, USN, of Manitowoc,
Wisconsin, was the first American killed in the Japanese attack on the Philippines.

fields and lack of sufficient radar warning equipment, antiaircraft guns, and other matériel."

The Navy's PBYs were to find their patrols extremely hazardous without fighter protection—later in the war a PBY pilot is said to have radioed back to base: "Have sighted enemy planes—please notify next of kin." Under an interservice agreement of some ten years' standing, military aviation was divided into land-based for Army and seaborne or carrier-based for Navy; and the use of a weak carrier force in the confined waters of the Philippine Archipelago would have been an invitation to disaster.

That the cumbersome and sturdy PBYs were good for more than reconnaissance, however, was proved almost at once. "On the second day of the war," said Captain Wagner, "an ex-football star on the Naval Academy team, Lieutenant Al Gray, sighted a suspicious-looking vessel. Although we had been instructed to wage unrestricted war, Gray was a bit too polite. He flew by the unidentified vessel to find out who she was. She did not answer challenges, she showed no flag, her name was unreadable. Gray made a second pass along the ship and fired a machine gun across her bow. He came back a third time. This time the Japanese flag went up and she opened up on Gray at close range. His plane was badly shot up, but not brought down. He reported the incident in such annoyed language that we sent out three other planes to bomb the Japanese."

The three attack planes which went out could not locate a Japanese-flag ship. They did find a vessel which, although she wore the flag of an Axis-overrun country, could not identify herself properly and acted in a highly suspicious manner. The three PBYs promptly dropped bombs, but observed only near misses.

Captain Wagner telephoned Admiral Hart's office to report this incident and to tell of other air activity.

"What's going on to the northeast of Luzon?" Admiral Hart asked at once.

"I told him," said Captain Wagner, "that patrol planes had dropped bombs but had observed only near misses."

"Apparently they got better than near misses. There is a ship out there now calling for help in plain Japanese."

Chapter Seven

WEDNESDAY, December 10, was to become known as a black day for United Nations forces in the Far East.

On that day HMS REPULSE and HMS PRINCE OF WALES went down northwest of the Anambas Islands, off Kuantan, Malaya. On that day Cavite Navy Yard was almost completely destroyed by Japanese air attack. On that day enemy assault forces landed at three points on the island of Luzon. These disasters were in no wise mitigated nor offset by the fact that the Navy's PBYs made a heavy bombing attack on Japanese warships on that date, and that later on the same day the gallant Captain Colin Kelly, in an attack on Japanese forces farther to the north, was credited by the Army with having sunk a Japanese battleship of the 29,000-ton class.[1]

Any one of these calamities would have been classed as a major catastrophe. But in the light of the dire need for heavy warships in the later campaigns to the southward, perhaps the loss of the two British vessels was the most serious of the lot. . . .

2

Attack from the air was no new experience to HMS PRINCE OF WALES. In fact, she had experienced just about everything in the book of naval warfare in her short and equally exciting lifetime—she had been commissioned on January 18, 1941, as the newest and most powerful battleship in the British Fleet.

The PRINCE OF WALES's first spectacular action occurred when she was part of the British forces which sent Germany's mighty BISMARCK to the bottom after the German battleship had sunk HMS HOOD with a

---

[1] In *AAF*, official handbook of the Army Air Forces, this claim is amended to "hits" on the battleship.

lucky shot in that battle cruiser's magazine. In August she literally became a "ship of state" when she journeyed to Placentia Bay, Newfoundland, with Prime Minister Winston Churchill occupying her flag quarters. In Placentia Bay PRINCE OF WALES made rendezvous with the heavy cruiser USS AUGUSTA, with President Franklin D. Roosevelt aboard; and as the two ships rode together, under a heavy guard of surface, undersea and air protection, there were visits back and forth between the two warcraft as weighty problems of international consequence were discussed and decided.[1]

After returning the Prime Minister to England, the big British battleship saw action in the Mediterranean on the way to Malta, enduring fierce attacks by the vaunted aviators of the Luftwaffe.

On October 20, 1941, and then in home waters, the ship received an order to take on an unusual amount of ammunition and supplies. Rumor aboard had the ship headed for almost every section of the globe; and the rumors really began to get warm when, after an October 25 departure, it became known that the first port of call was to be Freetown, Sierra Leone. At this West African port the heat was intense, but this discomfort was somewhat mitigated by the fact that most of the junior officers were allowed to go ashore for a swim off Lumley Beach, while others amused themselves by tossing coins for the native divers who clustered about the ship on bumboats. The trip from Freetown to Cape Town, at the southern tip of Africa, was as smooth as a yachting cruise in sheltered waters, and the ship dropped its hook in beautiful Table Bay, with the grandeur of Table Mountain beyond.

In heading for Colombo, Ceylon, the ship swung wide to touch at Mauritius, thereby giving Vichy Madagascar a clear berth, and at Colombo she was joined by HMS REPULSE, already in Indian waters. Both ships and their escorts steamed up the Straits of Johore to anchorage in the naval base at Singapore, arriving late on the afternoon of Tuesday, December 2.[2]

As has been noted, Admiral Sir Tom Phillips flew at once to Manila

[1] For a fuller report of the meeting in Placentia Bay see Volume II of this series, projected for 1945 publication under the auspices of the Council on Books in Wartime, and dealing with the activities of the United States Navy in the Atlantic in World War II.

[2] An interesting personal account of this voyage, as well as the action in which REPULSE and PRINCE OF WALES were lost, is contained in the January, 1944, issue of *Blackwood's Magazine,* published in Edinburgh: "One Year of Life. The story of HMS PRINCE OF WALES," by Alan and Gordon Franklin.

to confer with Admiral Hart, returning when word was received that the Japanese armada was moving westward in the Gulf of Siam. On December 8 the Japanese struck at Kota Bharu and Singora. The attack met with considerable success, and the Royal Air Force had to abandon its forward air bases in that area. Other airfields were put out of action by Japanese air attack. In an effort to prevent new landings at Singora, PRINCE OF WALES and REPULSE were constituted as "Force Z," with destroyers ELECTRA, EXPRESS, TENEDOS, and HMS VAMPIRE. It was decided that these ships should put out on the hazardous attempt to pinch off the Japanese assault forces in surprise raids and lightning attacks, especially on the enemy transports.

The PRINCE OF WALES and REPULSE were the first capital ships in World War II to be sunk by air power alone, while under way and in a state of readiness at sea; and the action in which they figured was seized upon by special pleaders in the United States as evidence of the superiority of one military arm over another. One partisan group criticized the RAF for not supplying air cover. Another countered with the claim that the mighty battleships had scorned air protection, preferring to rely on the firepower of their own guns. Neither of these claims was wholly justified. Perhaps a more temperate statement was one made by Admiral Hart: "Any ship versus plane controversy is just plain silly. Amphibious warfare is primarily a matter of ships *and* planes. The ships and planes must be handled and fought together, and that can be successfully done only if all the personnel is continuously trained together, understands each other's problems and speaks each other's language."

Because there was a controversy about the action, however, it was decided to go back to original sources for the account contained in this narrative. The following report, therefore, is one which was officially forwarded to the authors by the British Admiralty, and as extracted from confidential Admiralty files:

"Force Z left harbour at 1735 on 8th December. It consisted of His Majesty's Ships PRINCE OF WALES, REPULSE, ELECTRA, EXPRESS, VAMPIRE and TENEDOS.

"The C. in C. decided to carry out the attack at dawn on 10th December, provided he was not seen by reconnaissance aircraft during the 9th. Weather conditions were favourable for evasion, with an overcast sky and low cloud, but between 1700 and 1830 on the 9th the sky cleared, and three Japanese reconnaissance aircraft were sighted from the PRINCE OF WALES.

"The C. in C. had not asked for fighter protection over the landing areas which he proposed to attack. He knew that it would have been very difficult to provide, as the army had need of every available fighter and the protection which could have been given would have been on a small scale only and at long range from the aircraft bases.

"As soon as he knew that his force had been sighted, he decided that the risk of attacking Singora was no longer justified. His ships would be expected, the Japanese would have had time to organize air attack on a large scale, and the targets might already have been withdrawn. Therefore, as soon as night fell and the reconnaissance aircraft were shaken off, he ordered Force Z to turn south again and return to Singapore.

"At about midnight, however, he received a report of enemy landings at Kuantan—far south of any previously known landing. Kuantan was not far off his return track to Singapore; it was an important military position and a landing there would seriously threaten all our forces in the peninsula. C. in C. had no reason to suppose that the enemy would expect Force Z (which had last been reported steering to the northward towards Singora) to be in the area of Kuantan by daylight. At about one o'clock on the 10th, therefore, C. in C. ordered his force to alter course towards Kuantan with the intention of smashing the new landing.

"The force arrived off Kuantan at 0800 on the 10th. No enemy forces were sighted and it was clear that the report had been untrue.

"One hour before reaching Kuantan, Force Z had passed at extreme range what appeared to be one small ship in company with a number of barges or junks. Finding Kuantan all quiet, C. in C. decided to go back and investigate these barges. It was while he was on his way to do this that the first air attack developed at 1118.

"The first degree of A.A. readiness had already been ordered. TENEDOS had been detached and ordered back to Singapore as she was short of fuel. A signal from her reported that she had sighted large formations of enemy aircraft and was being bombed. The first aircraft sighted by Force Z consisted of nine twin-engined bombers flying at about 12,000 feet, which attacked HMS REPULSE and straddled her with a salvo of bombs. This attack was ineffective, although it achieved one hit on the REPULSE which did no serious damage.

"At 1141, however, nine torpedo bombers approached HMS PRINCE OF WALES from the port side. Their attack, made in waves of two or three in line abreast, was pressed home in spite of heavy gunfire. One aircraft was shot down. The PRINCE OF WALES managed to avoid all torpedoes except one. This one hit her abreast P 4 turret.

"At 1156 and 1158 two attacks were made on REPULSE by formations of torpedo carrying aircraft and high level bombers. The REPULSE avoided all the torpedoes and was not hit by the bombs. The PRINCE OF WALES helped to engage the enemy with those of her guns which were not out of action.

"At 1220 another torpedo attack developed on the starboard side of the PRINCE OF WALES, which was hit three times; the REPULSE received one hit.

"Three minutes later nine more torpedo bombers attacked. The REPULSE, already listing heavily to port, was hit four times. She shot down two aircraft just before she heeled over and sank very quickly at 1233.

"At 1246 another wave of aircraft appeared. These were high level bombers. The PRINCE OF WALES at this time was making practically no way, and was indeed almost a sitting target. The bombers scored one direct hit and numerous near misses may have caused further damage. The PRINCE OF WALES, however, continued to fight with her two remaining 5.25 guns.

"The Captain decided to disembark first the wounded and then those that were not required to fight on the ship. The destroyer HMS EXPRESS closed the PRINCE OF WALES and came alongside her starboard quarter. She stayed alongside until the very last moment, when at 1320 the PRINCE OF WALES heeled over sharply, turned turtle and sank.

"While the EXPRESS and the ELECTRA were picking up survivors, some of our fighter aircraft appeared upon the scene and drove off another wave of Japanese bombers. These fighters had been ordered to the scene as soon as the report of the air attack was received in Singapore. The first to arrive was piloted by Flight Lieutenant Vigors, who subsequently addressed the following letter to Commander-in-Chief, Far Eastern Fleet. It provides what perhaps is the only ray of light in the whole of that dark and disastrous day:

"Sir,

"I had the privilege to be the first aircraft to reach the crews of the PRINCE OF WALES and the REPULSE after they had been sunk. I say the privilege, for during the next hour, while I flew around low over them, I witnessed a show of that indomitable spirit for which the Royal Navy is famous. I have seen show of spirit in this war over Dunkirk, during the Battle of Britain, and in the London night raids, but never before have I seen anything comparable with what I saw yesterday. . . . Even to an eye so inexperienced as mine it was obvious that the destroyers were going to take hours to pick up those hundreds of men clinging to bits of wreckage and swimming around in filthy, oily water. Above all this, the threat of another bombing and machine-gunning attack was imminent. Every one of those men must have realized that. Yet as I flew around every man waved and put his thumb up as I flew over him. After an hour, lack of petrol forced me to leave, but during that hour I had seen many men in dire danger waving, cheering and joking as if they were holiday-makers at Brighton, joking at a low flying aircraft.

"It shook me, for here was something above human nature; I take off my hat to them, for in them I saw the spirit which wins wars."

The loss of personnel on the two ships was far less than might have been expected. The three remaining destroyers were loaded to the last inch of deck and cabin space with oil-soaked, shell-shocked, wounded and exhausted survivors. Out of a total complement of 170 officers and 2,755 men, 130 officers and 2,200 men were saved.

The significance of the loss of REPULSE and PRINCE OF WALES loomed very large in the mind of the senior United Nations naval officer in Asiatic waters. "It meant," said Admiral Hart, "that we entered the war in the Far East under a very grave handicap. We knew from the beginning that we might have to make a fighting retreat, but now the odds against us would be bigger as we tried to hamper and delay the enemy. To oppose a large and well-balanced Japanese fleet we now had a small handful of vessels whose numbers did not include a single capital ship. And we knew, then, that not only could we get little surface-ship assistance from the westward, but such also was the case from the eastward, incidental to the effect of the attack on Pearl Harbor."

In short, the United Nations forces would have to fight it out with what they had, an inferior force further handicapped because the Japanese controlled the air. The danger was not so great from aerial attack, in the opinion of the United Nations command, as from the enemy's ability to keep our ships under continual aerial surveillance while their own were almost immune from observation.

So the defenders did the best they could, both to resist the Japanese advance and to prevent the enemy from destroying helpless noncombatant craft. To the latter end, the seaplane tender LANGLEY and the oilers TRINITY and PECOS were sent southward from the Philippines as soon as their cargoes could be unloaded. They managed to escape to safety, although there was a tense moment in crossing the Sulu Sea. Against the evening afterglow, lookouts on the three vessels sighted the top-hamper of two Japanese warships, believed to be a light cruiser and a destroyer. Luck was with the American vessels, which were sailing on the dark side of the horizon, and they were not sighted.

The following afternoon the United States cruisers HOUSTON and BOISE glimpsed the identical evidence, but they and their destroyer escort were seen by the Japanese, who turned and ran. The cruisers pursued, but lost the enemy's trail in the darkness. The uncompleted chase was almost as good as a victory, however, because for ten days thereafter no Japanese warships appeared in the Sulu Sea or the Macassar Strait, enabling a larger detachment of naval auxiliaries and the forty-odd deep-sea merchantmen to escape from Philippine waters without molestation. Perhaps the Japanese did not believe that they had forces adequate to engage HOUSTON, BOISE and their two destroyers.

3

A bombing attack on the naval installations at Cavite was just a matter of time—the amount of time necessary, as it turned out, for the Japanese to make certain that their bombers would not be too seriously hampered by Army fighter planes. On the third day of the war it came. "On the early afternoon of December 10th," said a narrative of the event prepared by the Navy Department, "Japanese bombers destroyed the navy yard at Cavite. More than 50 two-engine bombers came over and dropped their bombs from above the range of the nine Navy 3-inch anti-aircraft guns which were supposed to protect the station. There was no fighter opposition, and the bombing was leisurely and accurate. Practically the entire establishment was destroyed."

Admiral Hart had a good view of the bombing from the windows of his office overlooking Manila Bay. "The Jap bombers took their time that day," he said. "They came over in V formation. If they were not completely satisfied with their aim they held their bombs and kept making runs until they were satisfied. Our gunners did their best, but they were effective only on those few Japanese planes which came down within range."

The skipper of one of the bird-class minesweepers, kept at Manila to sweep the ship channels, has turned in one of the better accounts of the Japanese attack on Cavite.[1] Lieutenant Commander C. A. Ferriter, USN, had come in from a channel sweep on the 10th and had fueled and provisioned his ship to the limit.

"After lunch I was in a horizontal position on my bunk," Ferriter reported, "looking at the overhead and wondering whether it would hold up very well or not. A heavy weight falling on the deck or an explosion occurring there might cause the overhead to fall on the bunk. This would be inconvenient. The dead air space between the overhead and the deck would then be removed and the cabin would be most uncomfortable in the tropic heat. While lying there a messenger came in. He said, 'A large enemy force of planes is reported to be approaching from the direction of Manila!' I got up and went to the bridge."

Ferriter sounded general quarters and then ordered "heave around" so as to head his ship in the general direction of Manila, with plenty of water for maneuvers in case of air attack. Submarines began to get out of the danger area at top speed, leaving their mooring places at buoys or alongside tenders, and submerging as soon as they cleared the breakwater. Then the Japs began to come in.

"An attack was started on our starboard side, toward Nichols Field, an Army airport. We shot at a number of planes in that direction. Two planes were hit and crashed. We were shooting at them but so were a lot of other people. Every once in a while a submarine would show his conning tower, so we would not run over them. They became quite a nuisance. It seemed that we annoyed some sub or other every time we turned. After we neared the breakwater we turned and headed toward San Nicholas Shoal. Bombs were dropped on Manila Harbor among the merchant ships. Only one was hit. The attack on the Navy Yard was now in progress. We kept up a fire on low-flying fighters and dive bombers

---

[1] In U.S. Naval Institute *Proceedings*, November, 1942: "The Captain of the 'Whip'—Pearl Harbor to Australia," by Lieutenant Commander C. A. Ferriter, USN.

coming out from attacks on the Navy Yard. One came very near to us. He came up on our port quarter. The after machine guns fired at him. Some light colored smoke came out of his fuselage. He tried some kind of a maneuver. He banked his plane and put a burst of machine gun bullets about 50 feet ahead of the ship. We put on full left rudder and went from 'Ahead' to 'Full Astern' in an effort to let him get ahead of the 'Whip.' He crossed close aboard ahead of us and fell into the water about a thousand yards away from us. He sank immediately.

"Cavite Navy Yard was a mass of flame. We headed for the navy yard to see if we could help, and to see if our ship's boat was still there. The boat had been left in Canacao Bay to reduce the splinter hazard. We left one man in the boat, the boat engineer. He was armed with a Springfield rifle. As we approached Sangley Point Buoy we passed the QUAIL. The QUAIL turned and followed the 'Whip' to the navy yard. We passed the TANAGER off the Sangley Point Buoy. The QUAIL and TANAGER had been moored together at a pier in the navy yard at the start of the raid. The QUAIL's engineering plant had been in operation. The QUAIL took the TANAGER out of the yard. They separated near the Sangley Point Buoy. The TANAGER anchored and completed preparations to get under way.

"About this time the ISABEL reported over the radio telephone that she was in communication with the navy yard. I asked her to have the navy yard tell me where they needed us most. The navy yard never answered. We saw the yard signal station. It was flying a distress signal. I said, 'Boy! she isn't lying! She is in distress if anything ever was!' It was difficult to decide where to go. The PIGEON was playing her hoses on some barges that were burning at the end of Guadeloupe Pier. I made out a destroyer at the small pier between Machina Wharf and Guadeloupe Pier.

"I sent the PIGEON a signal: 'The "Whip" is going in and take out that destroyer.' We went in between Guadeloupe Pier and Machina Wharf. It was a mess. It was the PEARY. The ship had many little fires all over her. She had been strafed and had been struck by bomb fragments and debris. The war heads and torpedo air flasks in the torpedo overhaul shop on Machina Wharf next to her were exploding. The air was filled with clouds of debris. A small motorboat under the command of an Ensign, a young reserve officer, attached to Inshore Patrol, assisted in the efforts to take out the PEARY. The heat and explosions made ship handling difficult. The pressure would be on one side and then on the other. The Ensign tried to take lines from the 'Whip' to the PEARY without success as we made our approach. We put our bow against her stern. We made fast with a 6-inch line. We backed and parted the line. The heat of a falling fragment might have caused the line to part. We tried it again. Again the line parted. It became more difficult to keep in position for backing out. The wind and the current kept working to put the 'Whip' broadside to the end of the pier. This was bad. Guadeloupe Pier and Machina Wharf each extended a good distance beyond this little pier. We went quite far up on her port quarter. This was the side away from the pier. I sent a man over to the PEARY to make sure that she had no mooring lines to the pier. The 'Whip's' man reported when the lines were clear. We backed and she came away.

"We backed clear of the dock. There was shoal water not far from the piers. We went alongside the PEARY. This was more easily done than jackknifing her. The 'Whip' went between the PEARY and the burning barges off Guadeloupe Pier. We had all of our hoses going all of the time. Once in a while we played the water on the bridge to cool that place off. The men on deck were kept cool by hosing them down when it became too hot.

"Our boat was near by and my messboy was in it. The three others ashore on duty never returned. They joined the Naval Battalion on Corregidor.[1] My boy was returning to the ship at the time of the attack. He made his way through the burning navy yard to Puerta del Mar Wharf and found our boat there. The engineer had stayed near the landing during the attack. He brought some Pharmacist's Mates and Hospital Corpsmen from the navy yard. The dispensary had been burned. . . .

"We put our Damage Control party aboard the PEARY as soon as she came clear to the pier. She had no power and was helpless. The Damage Control party with the aid of the PEARY's crew put out the fires and cleared away the wreckage. The Pharmacist's Mate and a working party tended the wounded and removed the bodies of the casualties to the 'Whip.' Our boat took the wounded to the hospital in Canacao. . . .

"The Inshore Patrol Headquarters went up in a blaze of glory, as did the Commandancia.

"A large number of persons had been killed by the fire in the navy

[1] See Part IV.

yard. The buildings were ignited so quickly that many inside found it impossible to escape. The navy yard had given leave to all workers who desired to move their families that day and prepare them for the bombings which were expected. Many workmen were outside the yard for that reason. Many also escaped due to the attack having its inception during the noon hour. The fire did not get to the Ammunition Depot, although it was surrounded on three sides by fire. . . .

"The scene was one which brought to mind an old-time description of Hell. The navy yard was ablaze. Fuel tanks at Nichols Field were burning. A ship was on fire in Manila Harbor."

While the "Whip" was hauling the PEARY to safety PIGEON was performing an equally successful rescue job on the submarine SEADRAGON. The SEADRAGON and SEALION were docked together for repairs, and the latter submarine was completely destroyed by two direct hits. One merchant vessel was hit and sunk in the harbor—observers considered it a miracle that more were not hit and sunk—and in addition the minesweeper BITTERN was so badly damaged that she had to be scuttled. The destruction of the Cavite Navy Yard was of major importance, of course, but the damage to shipping was amazingly light.

With the destruction of Cavite, the naval forces had to fall back upon such accommodations as could be extemporized along the Manila waterfront, and when General MacArthur declared Manila an open city to prevent further destruction of nonmilitary targets, things continued to go from bad to worse. The supplementary naval base facilities authorized at Mariveles Bay had only been under construction a few months; they were useless.

So, with only the weakest antiaircraft protection, and with almost no supporting fighter aircraft, it became obvious to Admiral Hart that surface ships could no longer remain in, or operate near, the Manila Bay area, without great danger from enemy aircraft. The Japanese had complete control of the air, as the Navy's gallant but clumsy PBYs were soon to learn.

Admiral Hart ordered the remaining naval vessels in the harbor to move southward to safer waters. The submarines were to stay as long as they could, so the submarine tender CANOPUS was detailed to remain in the Manila area to tend them. On December 11 Admiral Hart called a conference of all merchant shipowners, agents, and masters. The ships, he said, would be as safe under way as if they remained in harbor, and perhaps much safer. He advised that they leave at once, offering to provide an escort of all his destroyers but two. With that escort, and accompanied by the submarine tenders HOLLAND and OTUS and lesser auxiliaries, over 200,000 tons of merchant shipping escaped without damage.

Among the naval vessels which made the trip to the Malay Barrier was the minesweeper WHIPPOORWILL, later to take part in much of the Java Sea campaign. The WHIP in fact was at Soerabaja when that Allied base was bombed by Japanese airmen for the first time on February 3, 1942. Lieutenant Commander Ferriter managed to get ashore that night to view the bomb damage and confusion. Hearing that several United States news correspondents were in Soerabaja it occurred to him that Stateside newspapers might carry stories of the air attack, and he was afraid his family would be worried for his safety. "I called home over the telephone that evening," he said. "It was a long talk. It was from Soerabaja, Java, to Kittery, Maine."

4

COMMUNIQUE NO. 3   *DECEMBER 11, 1941*

The Navy Department announced that Admiral Thomas C. Hart, U. S. Navy, Commander in Chief, United States Asiatic Fleet, has reported that Navy patrol planes scored hits on a Japanese battleship of the KONGO *class off the coast of Luzon. The ship was badly damaged. . . .*

The action which resulted in this Washington communique was set in motion shortly before 0900 Manila time on December 10, December 9 in Washington. To understand it more fully, however, it is necessary to look briefly at the general plan for defense in effect in Asiatic waters, especially as applied to naval aircraft. Patwing Ten, for instance, contained two squadrons of PBYs: VP 102, commanded by Lieutenant Commander E. T. Neale, USN, and VP 101, commanded by Lieutenant Commander J. V. Peterson, USN, later to succeed Captain Wagner as skipper.

"The general plan in case of war," reported Lieutenant Commander Peterson, "as understood by myself and various other commanding officers of the unit was as follows: First and foremost the Wing must be dispersed in lakes, swamps, coves, bays or any other place where dispersal facilities were available. Second, we were to search and attack from advance bases when we could make use of those bases. Third, we were to retire with the Asiatic Fleet, searching and scouting for the Fleet, and making bombing flights or torpedo attacks as opportunity afforded itself. Finally, we were to take advantage of all hideout areas and gasoline supplies which were liberally dispersed throughout the Philippine Islands in various coves, tenders and towns."

Lieutenant C. A. Keller, USN, was about 300 miles west of Manila over the South China Sea when he spotted a Japanese task force consisting of two battleships of the KONGO class, two heavy cruisers and four big destroyers.[1] The Japanese ships opened up with their antiaircraft. They also launched seaplanes from their catapults. Keller hightailed it for cloud cover and hung grimly on.

As soon as it was sighted the Japanese task force increased speed to about 25 knots. Realizing that he would find it difficult to keep a running plot of position, Keller reported what he had seen and then began to send out MOs on his radio. This is simply the repetition of the letters M and O; other planes in the air locate the transmitting plane by taking frequent bearings on their radio compasses.

Lieutenant Commander Peterson was at Los Banos with five PBYs as a striking force. He was ordered to attack the enemy ships and he took off at once.

"We 'homed' on Keller's MO signals," he reported, "and at about 1130 we sighted the enemy fleet. They were zigzagging at about 23 to 24 knots in a generally northwesterly direction; the sea was fairly rough and there were two layers of overcast. There was a solid overcast at 16,000 feet.

"I waited until the two layers overlapped—that is, there was a clear area over the task force—and then made a bombing run on the largest battleship, which I believe was the KONGO. The Japs sent up a terrific anti-aircraft fire as soon as we started our bombing run. We were knocked about a good bit by the AA bursts. Sometimes there were hundreds of bursts around us. Some seemed to be as big as shade trees, and others were smaller. The fire was fairly accurate but usually above and behind us. It was difficult to make the bombing run, but we had an excel-

---

[1] The complement of this force has varied in reports by different observers. The above listing was based on a report by Lieutenant Commander Peterson who, as will be noted, became a target for the Japanese ships.

lent bomber who stuck to his job and made what I consider a very good run on the KONGO. . . .

"Our bombs hit all around the stern of the battleship and three or four of them made direct hits on the target, on the after section of the stern. I did my best to observe the damage done, and as far as I can make out we probably damaged her rudders and propellers. I base this on the fact that she turned sharply through 360 degrees, then slowed down on a sort of wavering course and eventually stopped still. The rest of the task force ran off and left her."

On the flight back to base Peterson sent radio reports of the action but, as he learned later, the reports were never received by the radio station at Cavite. As he approached the Manila Bay area he saw the reason for this. Cavite was a tall pillar of black smoke with fire and explosions at its base, and with swarms of Japanese planes leisurely and methodically going about the business of destruction. Several of these Japanese planes detached themselves and set out after the PBYs as the big flying boats came in low over the water. Fortunately the PBYs found cloud cover, and they reached their base safely. Other patrol planes were immediately loaded with torpedoes and sent out to get the KONGO, and these were not so lucky. Of a three-plane attack group, two were shot down by the Japanese. The third had used up nearly all its fuel in evading Japanese fighters when it reached the area in which the crippled enemy battleship was expected to be sighted. Darkness was closing in when, after a brief search, the pilot observed that he had just enough gasoline to get back to his base. The KONGO was not found. No claim was made that the ship had been sunk.

While the Japanese aviators were bombing Cavite, other enemy assault forces were landing at Aparri on the north coast of Luzon and at Vigan on the northwest coast. A third landing was made at Legaspi by way of Albay Gulf to the southward a day or so later. And the Japanese lost no time in setting up airfields, thereby vastly increasing the range and efficiency of the planes which formerly had attacked Luzon from bases on Formosa.

The Japanese troop landings were executed with an efficiency that denoted long study and much training. Knowing that they had only our submarines to fear, the Japanese guarded their large transports extremely well against submarine attack. In the main, however, the thousands of Nipponese troops that swarmed ashore in the Philippines were carried thence by hordes of shallow-draft vessels, drawn from Japan's huge deep-sea fishing fleet. Such craft presented an almost impossible target to the American submarines; when they were hit and sunk, the loss to the invaders in men, supplies and shipping was of small consequence. Nevertheless, in that first month of the war the American submarines began the long, slow process of weakening the enemy by attrition, which in two years made the Japanese problem of supplying their far-flung troops a desperate one.

As further evidence of Japanese planning, the invasion was carried out at that season when the weather is thickest in the latitudes straddling the equator, and in the dark of the moon. Fog and darkness and extravagant antisubmarine defenses were combined by the Japanese to land their armies successfully, and when any of those ingredients were missing, they still had other tricks up their kimono sleeves, as on December 12 when Patwing Ten suffered its most disastrous single loss of the war.

Reports were received that a large force of Japanese ships was moving down the coast toward Lingayen Gulf. Seven Catalinas were based at Olongapo, and the senior naval aviator ordered them to search and attack. The sky was clear, visibility was unlimited. The PBYs searched far at sea for several hours and found nothing—the report had been false.

Lack of fuel finally forced the American planes to return. They had no sooner taxied up to their base at Olongapo than Japanese fighters swooped out of the sky. Two of these enemy planes were shot down, but the seven PBYs were destroyed on the water.

"By this time," said Captain Wagner, "the air over Manila was continually occupied by the Japanese. With the enemy in complete control, it was apparent that we could not long remain in this area. Admiral Hart told me to move south. Of the twenty-eight planes we started with I had seventeen remaining, eleven of which could fly. The remaining six had gasoline tanks, hulls and wings full of holes from fighter machine guns and from ships' anti-aircraft guns.

"The eleven PBYs that were fit to fly took off at the first crack of dawn on December 15th and proceeded to Lake Lanao on the Island of Mindanao. We had our first flying accident there when one of the planes struck a rock in the course of taxiing to a fuel cache. In the meantime the tenders LANGLEY, PRESTON and HERON were moving further to the south into the Netherlands East Indies."

Captain Wagner himself went south on the seaplane tender CHILDS, taking on fuel at Cebu and continuing across the Celebes Sea to Menado.

"Upon arrival at Menado we sighted a strange three-engine airplane in the distance and challenged him. He responded with the correct answer, then flew close alongside the CHILDS. It was one of our Dutch friends. We exchanged greetings and he hauled off into the distance, came back, waved at us again, then disappeared.

"As the ship continued moving slowly to where she was to anchor, we were electrified when a chief petty officer standing alongside me said, 'Here comes that four-engined Dutchman again.' I yelled, 'Four-engined! Commence firing!' I heard the gun crews yell, 'She's dropping bombs,' and of course our guns opened up forthwith."

The big Jap flying boat was hit and went off smoking, and the bombs missed the CHILDS. But the incident had taught officers and men a lesson. "The mistake was understandable," said Captain Wagner, "as from a distance the three-engined Dornier and the four-engined Kawanishi did not look unlike. But that, I believe, was the last time the CHILDS ever trusted another airplane."

Of the planes left in the Manila area four were soon put back into condition to fly. These planes were used for scouting and transportation for high Army and Navy officers. On the night of December 24, a PBY piloted by Lieutenant Harmon Utter, USN, and Lieutenant (jg) T. F. Pollock, USNR, was to fly a load of passengers southward. Among these passengers was Major General Lewis H. Brereton, who chose Army service after graduating from the Naval Academy in 1911, and who later was to become one of the top commanders of the Army Air Force. The PBY was "on the step" and doing about 40 knots across the inky harbor when a small boat loomed up dead ahead. Lieutenant Utter kicked hard rudder and the plane did a violent water loop, losing its port wing float as it did so. The passengers were transferred to another plane while mechanics were put to work to replace the float. "The mechs did their very best," said Lieutenant Pollock, "because we knew that the next night we were to fly Admiral Hart to Java." This trip, however, was not to be made.

Before dawn the next morning the repaired PBY was flown to its hiding place in Laguna de Bay and camouflaged with leaves and water plants. Utter, Pollock and the members of the crew decided to take a bath and put on clean uniforms before flying back to Manila to pick up their commander in chief.

"There was a natural warm spring near our plane anchorage," said Lieutenant Pollock. "We scooped out a hole in the sand and most of the crew took the opportunity for a warm bath. Utter and I were aboard the plane, finishing our change to clean clothes, when we looked out the rear hatch and saw our doom. He said, 'Here they come—let's get going.' Our plane was so situated that only one gun could be brought to bear, and due to the high altitude of the two attacking bombers its fire would have been ineffective. So we went swimming instead."

As each Jap plane made a strafing pass, Utter and Pollock would dive and stay under as long as their breath held out. Occasionally they came up in the middle of a burst and found vicious water splashes all about them. Soon their plane was riddled with machine-gun slugs, its gasoline burning, and its bombs and ammunition exploding. Another plane anchored nearby fared somewhat better in that it was in such a position that its guns could be brought to bear.

"We saw the waist gun fire and then the bow gun would fire," said Pollock. "After it was all over we found that the guns had been fired by one man, Rollin D. Foster, AMM2/c, now a prisoner of the Japanese. He would run from one gun to the other as the Japs came over. In between times, he found time to put out several fires in the plane."

The one fire Foster could not overcome destroyed the second plane. With no air transportation available, Admiral Hart perforce delayed his departure, but not for long. From the beginning he had determined to remain on Luzon as long as his submarines were operating from Manila. Now that most of his fleet was already in the south, and it was evident that the submarines would soon have to follow, he decided to go directly to the Netherlands East Indies rather than move into Corregidor, as Admiral Rockwell had done on the 21st.

Manila Bay was now being bombed daily, and without opposition. Submarines were finding it necessary to lie on the bottom during daylight hours, conducting their base activities during darkness. This meant that submarine crews, accustomed to such routine while at sea, now had no time for rest. Those submarines at sea, therefore, were ordered to go south to the Malay Barrier when their patrols were completed. And on Christmas Day Admiral Hart, himself a seasoned submariner, left Manila

on the SHARK. The destroyers PEARY and PILLSBURY were ordered by
Admiral Rockwell to follow on the 27th, and on December 31 the last of
the submarines headed southward, taking the submarine staff and as
much material as possible. Japanese troops under General Homma
marched into Manila two days later.

Rear Admiral Rockwell remained on Corregidor as the senior naval
officer in the unified command set up under General MacArthur. There
were left in the Manila area, mainly at Corregidor and Mariveles, the
submarine tender CANOPUS, the minesweepers PIGEON, FINCH, TANAGER,
and QUAIL, the gunboats MINDANAO, LUZON, and OAHU, and a few tugs
and ex-yachts.

Of all the ships and submarines which sailed southward, one of the
destroyers was to have a voyage long to be remembered.

5

The destroyer PEARY had a narrow escape on the day after Christmas
when squadrons of Japanese bombers flew over Cavite and attempted to
send her to the bottom, along with the PILLSBURY. Luck was temporarily
with the two ships, which had already earned reputations for ill fortune.
Neither of the ships suffered a direct hit, although the PEARY was slightly
damaged by shrapnel splinters from some of the 45 bombs which the
Japanese aimed at her. After this experience, Rear Admiral Rockwell
gave permission for the two ships to attempt to escape to the southward.
It was decided that they would not sail in company, as the greatest danger
was expected from Japanese aircraft, and there was less chance of discovery for single ships.

Sailing the night of the 26th, the PEARY arrived the next morning at
Campomanes Bay on the southwest bulge of the island of Negros, one of
more than two thousand large and small isles in the Philippine Archipelago. Japanese planes were known to be in the area, so as soon as the
ship was tied up along the shore her crew was set to work with green paint
and palm fronds in an artful effort to hide her from enemy eyes. This
work, when completed, received the admiration of both officers and men,
including the skipper, Lieutenant Commander John M. Bermingham,
USN, who had taken over after Commander Harry H. Keith was
wounded during the bombing of Cavite on December 10.

The officers and men of the PEARY were still admiring their handiwork when five Japanese bombers zoomed past, headed north. The Japanese probably did not sight the ship, but the PEARY decided to take no chances. The ship was moved southward to nearby Asia Bay, and again the camouflage artists were put to work. With the coming of nightfall the destroyer shook off her greenery, upped anchor, and cranked on 25 knots on a heading that would take her through Pilas Straits, between the western arm of Mindanao and the northern tip of the Sulu Archipelago. She held this speed all night, although it ate up fuel at great rate, and by morning she was well out in the Celebes Sea. The PEARY's officers and men began to feel better—it began to look now as if the ship would get through to safety.

The PEARY's luck was not good, then or later.

At 0810 a lookout sighted a Japanese bomber which appeared to be getting set for a bombing run on the ship. The PEARY manned her guns and took evasive action, and the enemy bomber moved into the sun. From that position it appeared all set to shadow the ship for the rest of the day. This was very bad, for the PEARY had a report from a reconnaissance plane which said that a Japanese submarine and cruiser were working off the northern coast of Borneo. The Jap bomber probably at this moment was on his radio, calling in his friends for the kill. The PEARY worked up to top speed and headed for Menado, on the northeast tip of the Celebes. At the same time she radioed that she was being followed by an enemy plane. She could raise no answer on her radio. The Jap plane hung on, just out of range of the guns, and the fact of its presence was to mean disaster.

But then the destroyer's luck seemed to change for the better. Early in the afternoon lookouts on the ship sighted two of Patwing Ten's PBYs off in the distance. The ship frantically flashed recognition signals at the PBYs. There was no answer, although those on the ship were certain that the American patrol planes had spotted them. The PBYs flew on and vanished into the distance. And of course the Japanese shadow plane grimly hung on, still out of antiaircraft range.

A short time later three more Japanese bombers hove into view. It was obvious that they meant business. The planes attacked individually, with the first Japanese shadow bomber still holding its place in the sun, each plane dropping two 500-pounders on each run. The PEARY maneuvered violently and successfully, firing every gun that would bear as the Japanese planes came within range. All except the shadowing bomber had made two runs each when a torpedo plane suddenly appeared low on the port bow. At about 500 yards it dropped two torpedoes and banked sharply, the red balls gleaming on its wings. The PEARY's starboard engine was reversed, the ship swung sharply around, and the grim white tracks of the torpedoes shot past dead ahead. A few seconds later another torpedo plane came in on the port quarter—two more torpedoes. This time the skipper gave the ship full right rudder and the destroyer heeled over to answer the helm. The two torpedoes passed close aboard on the starboard side, about ten yards away. "They were so close," said an enlisted man topside, "that I could have reached in the spud locker and hit them with a Murphy."

Meanwhile the fourth bomber, the first to sight the PEARY, had come out of the sun and timed its bombing run to coincide with the second torpedo attack. The PEARY, by now almost at a standstill, called for emergency full ahead. The engines strained at their blocks and the bombs fell harmlessly a hundred feet astern. Both bombers and torpedo planes had done their best to strafe the ship as they ended their runs, but the PEARY's gunfire was so effective that the Japanese pilots changed their minds and swerved before they were well within range. The result was that, at the end of a two-hour attack, the ship had suffered little battle damage beyond a few holes in her stacks.

The PEARY's complement uncrossed their fingers and began to congratulate each other as the last enemy plane faded into the distance. As darkness was now approaching it seemed unlikely that the Japanese would make any attack until after nightfall, when their flares would come in handy. Therefore it was decided not to go into Menado for shelter but to run on through Banka Strait into Molucca Passage. In passing Menado at 1743 the signal searchlight was used to ask if the strait was mined. There was no answer. The PEARY by now was used to taking chances, so she decided to take another one.

The strait had just been negotiated in safety when the lookouts sang out again. Three planes were making an approach in bombing position. But this could not be—or could it? The planes were a twin-engine type which looked remarkably like Lockheed Hudsons. The observers on the PEARY could have sworn that they *were* Lockheed Hudsons, yet they were headed for the PEARY in a grim and purposeful manner. In addition to the fact that the planes appeared to be of an Allied make, they also wore the markings of the Royal Air Force. This was very bad, indeed.

Again there were frantic recognition flashes, and again there was no answer, although some of those on the ship thought one pilot waved in greeting. This obviously was a mistaken notion, for the planes began to come in for a glide bombing attack.

The PEARY opened fire and swung hard to starboard, so that the first bomb fell wide on the port beam. The ship had turned so sharply, however, that a machine gunner on deck fell over the side. He was last seen swimming, in his life jacket, toward a small island nearby. Each of the attacking planes made two attacks, dropping a 250-pound shrapnel bomb on each run. The PEARY succeeded in avoiding all but the last, which was a close miss. This bomb exploded ten yards off the port propeller guard. Shrapnel spattered against the ship's side like hail on a greenhouse. Fragments pierced the hull and entered the steering engine room aft—destroyermen are rather proud of the fact that the three-eighth inch thickness of their ships' hulls is only "strong enough to keep out some of the air and most of the water." Several steam pipes were ruptured and the main steering lines were severed. Other fragments killed a machine gunner on the fire control platform and set fire to a 4-inch cartridge. G. A. Fryman, fire controlman third class, seized this cartridge with his bare hands and heaved it over the side just before it exploded.

The Lockheed Hudsons also had attempted to strafe the ship, but again without doing much damage.

The PEARY's prolonged maneuvering at high speed had reduced fuel to a dangerously low level, and there was also a shortage of feed water for the ship's boilers. In addition, the starboard engine's Kingsbury thrust had been damaged and was overheating. Consequently, it was .decided to put in at Maitara Island, near Ternate, where supplies were obtained and repairs effected. On the 30th the ship was able to get under way on the port engine, and on the 31st she arrived at Ambon, her officers and men utterly exhausted but glad to be alive. As the PEARY's people went ashore they were still puzzling over the fact that they had been attacked by friendly planes. They soon had the answer. The Japanese shadow plane, they were to learn, was the key to the puzzle.

Several of Patwing Ten's PBY scouts were now based at Ambon, which is southwest of Ceram in the Banda Sea. At this base there was a detachment of Royal Australian Air Force aviators who were using American-made Lockheed Hudsons. These latter pilots, it developed, were in the process of celebrating a considerable victory when the PEARY's people stumbled wearily ashore. It seemed that the Aussies had attacked a Japanese warship—it was probably a light cruiser—and had damaged it heavily, perhaps sending it to the bottom. Instant suspicion flared in the minds of the PEARY's weary crew. And just where, they pointedly inquired, did this great victory take place? Just what was the position, they wanted to know, of the Japanese light cruiser which the Aussie pilots had attacked? That was easy, said the genial RAAF aviators. The ship had been attacked off Kema in the Molucca Passage.

Then the PEARY's people knew, and they lost no time in vociferously announcing to all and sundry that the so-called Japanese light cruiser had been none other than USS PEARY, listed in *Ships' Data U.S. Naval Vessels* as DD 226. Furthermore, certain persons in the immediate vicinity would do well to prepare to defend themselves from immediate mayhem.

Explanations were immediately forthcoming. The two PBYs seen before either bombing attack had spotted the PEARY right enough, but— they had first spotted the shadowing enemy bomber which appeared to be keeping a protective station on the supposedly enemy ship. The PBYs had considered attacking the ship themselves, but they had decided that the setup looked too much like an enemy decoy, with other planes waiting in the clouds or out of sight. So they had reported a Japanese force of one ship—the PEARY's silhouette could have been confused with a Japanese light cruiser—with a Japanese plane on guard. The Australian pilots had acted accordingly!

"Our only consolation," said an officer of the PEARY later, "was that the bomber pilots on our side were a hell of a lot better than the Japanese."

But the PEARY was not so lucky in another encounter. She was bombed and sunk in the big Japanese raid on Port Darwin, Australia, just two and a half months later.

6

The adventures of the PEARY in turn brought action to another vessel of the meager handful that composed the Asiatic Fleet. This was USS HERON, an 840-ton minesweeper of the bird class which had been converted for use as a seaplane tender.

The HERON had set up a base on Ambon when word came through that the PEARY was in need of help after the bombing she received in

Molucca Passage. The HERON set out with oil and engine replacements on December 29. She expected to rendezvous with the damaged destroyer at Ternate, on the east shore of Molucca Passage, on December 30.

"The rendezvous was to be made at night," said Lieutenant William L. Kabler, USN, skipper of the HERON, "inasmuch as Japanese bomber planes had been rather active in that section. We arrived off Ternate but were unable to negotiate the pass to the inner harbor because of the darkness. At about the time we were anchoring at the entrance to the southern pass the PEARY was leaving by the northern pass. When we got word that the PEARY had gone we then set out ourselves to return to Ambon.

"The next morning—the morning of the 31st—we had just crossed the Equator at about 127 degrees east longitude when we sighted two of our own planes out on patrol. They gave us the word that the PEARY had cleared safely and was on her way.

"At about 0930 another plane was sighted, coming in on approximately the same course as the two patrol planes we had seen earlier. Inasmuch as that was the correct approach bearing the plane was not at once identified as enemy. The plane immediately came in on a bombing run, but by this time we had opened fire with every gun on the ship. Apparently enough of our machine gun bullets hit her to discourage a bomb drop on the first run."

The Japanese bomber was determined, however, and twice bombs were dropped on the twisting and turning HERON. Each time the bombs fell clear.

"At about that time a rain squall was observed to the southwest," said Lieutenant Kabler. "We ran for the rain squall, made it safely, and were sure that we had lost the enemy plane."

But that was not true. Some two hours later the weather cleared, and Kabler saw that the Japanese plane, a flying boat, was sitting on the water on the HERON's starboard beam, patiently waiting, and just out of range of the ship's guns. The plane then took off and lazily circled the HERON for almost four hours, and the HERON's people knew that they were being shadowed for a very unpleasant purpose. The purpose became clear at about 1430 when other planes were sighted on the horizon, headed in the ship's direction.

"There was a saying among the Asiatic Fleet then," said Kabler, "that any time you sighted more than one plane you wouldn't have to identify them—you could be sure they belonged to the enemy." Certainly in this case he was correct.

The reinforcements consisted of two sections of three four-engined Kawanishi 97 patrol planes. About three o'clock one of the sections broke off and came in on a horizontal bombing attack. The first pass was not to their liking, so they swung around and came upwind on a second attack. Altogether, this section made three bombing attacks and in each case the ship was adroitly maneuvered to avoid the bombs.

Then the second section of four-engine patrol planes came in on a bombing attack and on their first run the HERON drew first blood by hitting one of the planes with a 3-inch shell. The plane started smoking, dropped out of formation, and then retired north. The two remaining planes made one more pass and in both cases the HERON was able to outmaneuver the falling bombs.

"About this time additional reinforcements were sighted consisting of five twin-engine land-based bombers and three more four-engine patrol bombers," Kabler relates. "The five twin-engine bombers then made a pass over the ship and, apparently not liking the run, did not release any bombs, but proceeded down wind and came back for another up wind run. On this up wind run they dropped a stick of bombs. It was impossible to maneuver the ship to avoid the entire stick and one of the bombs hit directly on the top of the mainmast and approximately three others hit just off the port bow. This attack damaged the ship considerably. Pieces of shrapnel from the bomb hit on the mainmast cut all the stays to the boat.booms and injured most of the gun crew of the machine guns there. The near misses off the port bow set the paint locker in the forward storeroom on fire, damaged the port three-inch gun and killed one of the lookouts and injured all the gun crew on the port three-inch gun and all the gun crews on the port machine guns.

"The next attack was by the three four-engine patrol planes and they came in in a torpedo angle, one plane coming on the starboard bow, one on the port bow, and one on the port quarter. Their timing was bad, so that the ship was turned to meet each torpedo as it was released. In that way all three torpedoes were avoided. However, the three planes came on in after releasing their torpedoes and strafed the ship. In strafing the ship they did considerable damage, but with the one remaining three-inch gun we were able to shoot down one of the planes.

"Altogether, in the bombs that hit, and in the strafing attack, we had approximately twenty-six casualties which was almost 50% of the crew. The crew escaped from the plane that was shot down while it was burning on the water, and seeing the crew in the water, we turned the ship back to try to pick them up. We stopped the ship and threw them life lines. They all refused the life lines and, since we were in submarine waters, it was not advisable to remain there for much time, so we proceeded on our course. However, we made sure before leaving that all the planes had departed from the area and it was then too dark for the Japs to have been rescued. During the night we were able to get the fires out, to pump out the forward hold, bring the ship back to an even keel, and repair the three-inch gun so that on our arrival back at Ambon we could report that the ship was again ready to tend the planes."

Subsequently, Kabler was to see more action in Asiatic and Australian waters. When he finally returned to the States on leave even his closest friends found it difficult to get him to talk about the action in which he saw his men killed and wounded aboard the HERON. In his battle narrative, of which the above is a sample, his description was unemotional and reserved. The official Navy communique on the action was equally reserved in tone, but it probably gave a few more details. Communique No. 24, on January 5, 1942, said:

"The USS HERON, a small seaplane tender, while engaged in action with enemy planes over a period of 7 hours sustained one direct bomb hit and 3 very near misses. The HERON was attacked by a total of 10 four-engined flying boats and 5 twin-engined landplane bombers. Forty-six 100-pound bombs were dropped by the enemy planes and 3 torpedoes were launched at her sides. Due to very skillful handling, the ship most courageously fought against overwhelming odds, and destroyed one four-engined flying boat, badly damaged at least one other and probably more. The ship though receiving damage from one bomb that found its mark managed to reach port safely. The Commander in Chief of the Asiatic Fleet, Thomas C. Hart, in accordance with an order of the Secretary of the Navy has awarded the Navy Cross to the Commanding Officer, Lt. William Leverette Kabler, and recommended that he be advanced immediately to the rank of lieutenant commander. . . ."

As far as is known, this was the first and only time in the history of the Navy that an officer's promotion was announced in a war communique.

Chapter Eight

BY THE end of December, 1941, the Asiatic Fleet had been forced southward in a fighting retreat from the Philippines. The few small craft which remained there assisted in the defense of Bataan and Corregidor. The submarine tender CANOPUS continued to do double duty for the Army and the Navy in spite of bombings in which she was hit; one of the gunboats assisted in blasting out a dangerous enemy force which landed behind the Army's lines on Bataan; and the PT boats performed extremely valuable service in spite of constantly increasing difficulties of fuel and repairs.[1] The submarines continued patrols in Philippine waters and beyond, but there could no longer be any major naval activity in the north.

The Army's stubborn defense of Bataan, conducted with a heartbreaking gallantry, occupied considerable numbers of the enemy for several months, but it could not prevent the Japanese from establishing bases in the Philippines for further conquest. Even before the end of December the Japanese were preparing bases at Davao on Mindanao and at Jolo in the Sulu Archipelago for their next attacks. On December 27 Patrol Wing Ten sent six PBYs north to attack shipping at Jolo, but Japanese fighters intercepted them and shot down four. Many members of the plane crews were saved, and lived to fight again. The Japanese tide was rolling on, with only an eddy about Bataan, which still stood stoutly against it. The American submarines were now being forced to extend their patrols farther to the south in their attacks on enemy communications. And after getting off to a slow start the subs now were doing better. On January 7 SEAWOLF came into Soerabaja after having sunk four Japanese ships off Hainan, thus equaling the contemporary record of the most successful Dutch submarines. And the American subs continued to get better as they went along, as the Japanese were to learn as

[1] See Part IV.

they scratched ship after ship from their list of war and merchant craft.

Meanwhile the Navy was reorganizing in the south. The Navy and War Departments, correctly judging that the Malay Barrier might not remain secure, chose Port Darwin in Australia for development as a major base, and the fleet auxiliaries were sent there. But for the Navy's purposes, Port Darwin was not to prove a success. Its existing facilities were poor, its situation exposed, and it was too far away for effective operations north and west of Java. Therefore the operational command was set up at Soerabaja.

A command post for the southern task force was already established in space supplied by the Dutch, a comfortable house in the western section of Soerabaja. Admiral Glassford remained in the HOUSTON in command of the task force and Admiral Purnell, chief of staff, exercised a de facto fleet command until Admiral Hart arrived on January 1, 1942. Facilities at Soerabaja were good except for radio, and the fleet staff personnel did well in remedying this deficiency by rigging up apparatus from parts obtained from a variety of sources. In all, the Asiatic Fleet used the Dutch basing facilities on Java to good advantage.

The Dutch Naval Command was in Batavia and Vice-Admiral Conrad E. L. Helfrich, of the Royal Netherlands Navy, urged Admiral Hart to join him there. However, with the prospective main fleet base at Port Darwin and with a large proportion of its ships engaged in conveying Army ships through Torres Strait, the American center of gravity was in the east, and Soerabaja was better suited to current needs. Meanwhile it was learned that the British Far Eastern Command had left Singapore. While Admiral Sir Geoffrey Layton, RN, and most of his staff were at Colombo awaiting reinforcements, a secondary command post was to be established in Batavia.

All these arrangements were overshadowed, however, by the question of a unified command. On January 10 General Sir Archibald Percival Wavell arrived to take over the Supreme Command, for which he chose the title of ABDACOM, a cipher for American-British-Dutch-Australian Command. His staff organization was as follows:

Intendant General (and Deputy ABDACOM): Lieutenant General
   George H. Brett, USA
Chief of Staff: Major General Sir Henry R. Pownall
Intelligence: Colonel Leonard F. Field (British)

Navy Operational Command: Admiral Thomas C. Hart, USN
  (ABDAFLOAT)
Chief of Staff: Rear Admiral Arthur F. E. Palliser, RN
Air Operational Command: Air Chief Marshal Sir Richard E. C.
  Peirse, RAF (ABDAIR)
Army Operational Command: Lieutenant General Hein ter Poorten,
  Netherlands East Indies Army (ABDARM)
Chief of Staff: Major General Sir Ian S. Playfair

The next week or so was spent in organization of the new command.
Consequently, Admiral Hart was engaged in Batavia most of the time
after January 9 and could visit the American operational base at Soerabaja only briefly. General Wavell formally took command on January 15
and three days later established his headquarters at a mountain resort
hotel at Lembang, 10 miles north of Bandoeng. The site was chosen
because it permitted dispersal and (it was hoped) offered some security
from air attack. Its remoteness from the sea was a handicap for the naval
command, but Admiral Hart agreed to join it in the interest of unity.
Communications were far from adequate and remained so in spite of
hard work for their improvement. To keep in touch with American
operations at Soerabaja Admiral Hart established at Lembang an American communication unit, which proved of tremendous value for several
purposes.

The machinery of a unified command was thus established, but the
obstacles to its smooth working were tremendous. ABDACOM had a
complicated command, involving four Army, four Navy, and six Air
organizations. Consequently, there was a great deal to do in organizing
and equipping a GHQ, which naturally required time. In the face of a
relentlessly advancing enemy there was, of course, no time for establishing a conventional organization, and so a condition was never reached
wherein the function of command could operate smoothly, with efficient
communication, swift distribution of information and directives. There
was, too, the difference in language, always a handicap, even in such
small ways as the inability of American officers to read Dutch charts and
sailing instructions, which were greatly superior to U. S. charts for
Netherlands East Indies waters (but not better than Japanese charts of
the same area).

The actual solution was that in fact each nation in effect retained control of its own forces. Throughout January actual operation of the Asiatic

Fleet was in the eastern end of the theater and generally separate from the British and Dutch. The working arrangement was that the Dutch covered the line of communications to Singapore, over which the British squadron directly escorted the shipping. The sincere desire—and desperate necessity—for co-operation made this system work, but it was not a unified command in the strict sense.[1]

The attention of the Supreme Command was focused on Malaya and Burma, where things were going badly. General Wavell was for some time absent from Lembang to visit Singapore and a second time to visit Rangoon, better than a thousand miles to the northwest. The British naval interest was chiefly in convoying troops to Singapore, in which the Dutch assisted. This work was necessary, but it diverted cruisers and destroyers from a possible creation of a striking force which might have

[1] That this pioneer attempt to achieve a unity of command was followed by more successful efforts under more favorable conditions is attested in statements subsequently made by General George C. Marshall, Chief of Staff U.S. Army, and Admiral Ernest J. King, USN, Commander in Chief United States Fleet and Chief of Naval Operations.

General Marshall, in his report of September 8, 1943: "During this first [Washington] meeting between the British and American military authorities, which terminated January 14, 1942, steps were taken to insure unified direction of the war effort in the Far East to meet the rapidly spreading attacks of the Japanese in that area. General Sir Archibald Wavell, Commander in Chief in India, who was in Chungking, China, at the time with Major General (now Lieutenant General) George H. Brett of the United States Army, was designated Supreme Commander for American, British, Dutch and Australian forces, with General Brett as his deputy, and although the strong, carefully prepared tide of the Japanese advance overran the Philippines, the Netherlands East Indies, the Malay Peninsula, and Burma, the co-operative results obtained in this desperate emergency by the creation of a united command established a firm basis for future combined operations."

Admiral King in his report of March 1, 1944: "In February, 1942, the President established an agency known as the U.S. Chiefs of Staff (frequently called the 'Joint Chiefs of Staff'), whose function it is to exercise strategic control of our armed forces in the war. The members of the U.S. Chiefs of Staff are the Chief of Staff to the Commander in Chief of the United States Army and Navy; the Chief of Staff U.S. Army, the Commander in Chief, United States Fleet and Chief of Naval Operations; and the Commanding General, Army Air Forces.

"By effective co-ordination of strategic plans and their execution the U.S. Chiefs of Staff have in effect operated the Army and Navy as one national military force. Furthermore, by continuous exchange of information of all kinds, including that relating to operating techniques, new weapons, and strategic and tactical problems, the two services have been able to derive the maximum benefit not only from each other, but from all other agencies whose activities have a direct bearing on the conduct of the war. . . .

"The principle of unity of command as it exists within our own forces, by agreement with the British Chiefs of Staff, is extended to situations where forces of more than one nation are engaged in the same operation. The operations in the Mediterranean theater illustrate that arrangement, which has worked well."

been used to break up Japanese amphibious expeditions advancing from other directions. The Dutch were interested in convoying their own merchant shipping, which, of course, was carrying cargoes for the use of all, but at the same time the Netherlanders worked for the formation of a striking force. The hard truth was evident at once: there simply was not enough of anything to go around.

The news that the Japanese, operating from Davao and Jolo, had taken Tarakan, Borneo, and Menado in Celebes, on January 11, served as a reminder to the Supreme Command that while one prong of the Japanese advance was threatening Singapore there was another equally dangerous to the east. This second spearhead, if not stopped, would pierce the shore of Australia, already decided upon as a base for future American operations.

Japanese tactics were now becoming clear. The invaders depended heavily upon sea-air power. After building up a force at one captured base, their planes proceeded to overcome Allied air opposition (when there was any) at the next point of attack. The bombing softened up the coastal defenses. Sometimes this was done by seaplanes, sometimes by carrier planes, or, if the distance was not too great, by land-based planes; but in almost every instance the aircraft operated under command of the Japanese Navy. Closely following the aerial attack came the warships to blast a beachhead for the troops aboard the crowded little transports next in the line of attack. The transports were largely shore-hugging shallow-draft vessels, coastal steamers and trawlers, strongly screened against submarines. If one was hit, or even a dozen, the loss in men, material and transport was small. As soon as the Japanese were in control of the new area, they repaired the airfield and set about gathering force for the next advance.

These amphibious sea-air tactics—"triphibious" was the word Prime Minister Churchill later used—were well-adapted to the geography of the Dutch East Indies. In the millions of square miles of the East Indies there was, outside Java and Sumatra, only about 50 miles of railroad, and few roads. It was necessary for the Japanese to seize only a few coastal points to control, by sea and air, everything in their vicinity. The Japanese had learned the method only too well in their seizure of the coast of China. And since the Japanese maintained the initiative it was simple for them to build up a local sea and air superiority for each move, with warships, planes, assault transports, and landing forces always

moving smoothly forward under a unified, naval-directed command.

In one sense, Japanese naval air power was decisive.[1] It was thus
Japan's unopposed air power which had virtually driven the Asiatic
Fleet—with no comparable air power of its own—from the Manila Bay
bases two weeks before Japanese ground forces entered the city on January 2. It later made Soerabaja and Port Darwin untenable in the same
manner. It was this sea-air power which dogged Allied ships on passage
and on occasion pounded Allied striking forces before they could approach their objectives. The only really successful surface engagements
were fought at night, or when for some reason of weather Japanese
planes could not be present. Japanese planes provided excellent intelligence of Allied movements and often denied Allied forces information
concerning their own surface operations. Admiral Hart was keenly aware
of this and worked hard for closer co-operation of Allied air and naval
forces, but it was never possible to plan an operation with air support.

To oppose Japanese sea-air power ABDAIR had a handful of
bombers based on Java, and a few fighters. These planes fought gallantly
and well—as long as they lasted. The greatest weakness was in fighters,
of which there were never enough adequately to protect fleet bases. The
Navy relied heavily on Captain Wagner's Patrol Wing Ten, which, flying
highly vulnerable PBYs, did magnificent work. But they led a hunted
existence, dodging into clouds to escape Jap fighters while on mission,
moving from place to place to escape destruction on the water to which
they had to return for rest and repair and fuel. Only the mobility of the
tenders—tough little ships like HERON—made the continued operation
of the cumbersome PBYs possible at all.

2

At the beginning of the second week in January, 1942, Admiral Hart
assembled his meager forces south of Borneo and the Celebes, minus such
vital units as the HOUSTON, and the British and Dutch cruisers of which
most were engaged in convoy duty aimed at preventing the capture of the
Malay Peninsula and its supposedly impregnable bastion of Singapore.
Admiral Hart's problem, then, was to use his few ships in such a manner
that they would do the most harm to the Japanese and the most good to

[1] See Admiral Hart's statement on sea-air power, p. 142.

the Allied cause. Judged by any standard, the problem was not an easy one.

To understand the strategic situation better, it must be realized that the Japanese invasion roughly centered on a single major objective—the capture, occupation, and exploitation of all the rich area of the Malay Barrier and the South China Sea. The size of the stake can be judged by the fact that this area produced nearly all the world's quinine; nine-tenths of the world's rubber; one-half of the world's tin and tungsten; petroleum sufficient for all Japan's needs and surpluses of rice, cotton, teas, spices, hemp, and tropical hardwoods. Taking into consideration the item that all these riches were to be produced by slave labor, this was indeed a worth-while piece of swag.

The Japanese method of achieving their objective was basically simple. One spear of the invasion, the western, was aimed down the east coast of China at the heart of Malaya and Sumatra, taking in French Indo-China and the west coast of Borneo on its flanks. The central invasion prong was to thrust down the east coast of Borneo, impaling Celebes, and striking at the central Netherlands East Indies. The eastern tine of the trident was directed against New Guinea, New Britain, and the Solomons. If all three were successfully driven home, the Japanese forces could then reach out for Burma and India to the west and the equatorial island bridge to the Americas on the west, rendering useless the sites already earmarked as bases from which the Navy intended to fight its way back into conquered areas: Efate in the New Hebrides group, Noumea in New Caledonia, and even Tongatabu in the faraway Tongas.

ABDAFLOAT obviously did not have enough ships to fight off both central and eastern thrusts—nor enough, in strict truth, to fight even one of them. In addition, the Japanese western column had moved so fast that the British already were beginning to talk of withdrawing their army all the way to Singapore. Therefore, the correct procedure seemed to be to attempt to accomplish, now, those objectives which would react with greatest advantage to the Navy's operations in the future—the Navy that even then was being built and trained.

On the central thrust the Japanese had completed occupation of Tarakan, the Borneo oil port whose fabulous wells were so pure that their product could be used without refining. Japanese assault forces in both Tarakan and Menado, in the Celebes, now seemed to be preparing for a new drive at Kendari. Kendari, on the southeast peninsula of the Celebes, was of no particular importance in itself. It was an export point for rattan and varnish resins, and a center for skilled Chinese workers in jewels and precious metals. But Kendari was less than 400 miles from Ambon to the eastward, an Allied seaplane and naval base on the path to New Guinea, and less than 700 miles from Soerabaja itself.

Admiral Hart computed that the Japanese would make their next move through either Macassar or Molucca straits, or possibly both. His submarines were stationed accordingly. A Japanese invasion fleet was reported to be gathering at Kema, near Menado, so it was decided to hit this concentration in a night torpedo attack. The striking force was to be made up of destroyers, with the cruiser MARBLEHEAD in support. This attack did not come off.

The Allied ships had made the greater part of the difficult run to Kema when the submarines PIKE and PERMIT, scouting ahead, reported no enemy force present, and the Allied ships were withdrawn. A few days later SEAWOLF poked up her periscope off this port and saw that the Japanese had finally arrived. The enemy was in such force that SEAWOLF could not attack, nor could the submarines stationed to intercept the Japanese as they swept down upon Kendari do more than annoy the enemy advance with the cheap toll of two steamers.

Both American and Dutch submarines had been stationed in Macassar Strait. On the 20th Dutch aviators reported a large Japanese convoy headed southward toward the important oil port of Balikpapan—between them, Tarakan and Balikpapan produced nearly two million tons of crude oil a year. That night PORPOISE and PICKEREL were stationed in Macassar Strait between North Watcher and Mangkalihat, with STURGEON in reserve. The SPEARFISH, SAURY, and S-40 were detailed off Balikpapan. The submarines had to exercise great care in the daytime, because Japanese planes were operating in the area.

On January 22 PORPOISE and PICKEREL reported that the enemy force was moving south. The STURGEON was playing in the backfield to the southward, and she had just intercepted this message when her sound gear picked up the steady and growing whine of a multiple-screw ship. Sounds indicated that the ship was either a carrier or a cruiser. The STURGEON got set. She did not have long to wait, and soon two of her torpedoes had exploded against the enemy vessel's hull.

The STURGEON could not observe the results because of darkness and enemy countermeasures, but her people were confident that the enemy ship had been sunk. Their confidence must have been mixed with a certain amount of exuberance. The sub's skipper, Lieutenant Commander William H. ("Bull") Wright, USN, sent the simple but completely explanatory dispatch: "STURGEON no longer virgin." And that STURGEON had altered her status in a worthy cause—that she may have sunk or damaged an aircraft carrier—was given some substantiation the following day when the area was observed to be completely free of enemy aircraft.

Meanwhile, ABDAFLOAT and staff had completed plans for a torpedo attack on the Macassar convoy similar to the abortive attempt off Kema, chiefly under direction of Rear Admiral William R. Purnell, USN. In its beginning, the Macassar attempt ran into even worse luck. The torpedo attack was to be made by the four destroyers of Desdiv 59, the JOHN D. FORD, POPE, PARROTT, and PAUL JONES, supported by the BOISE and the MARBLEHEAD. Admiral Glassford, whose flag was in BOISE, commanded the expedition with Commander Paul H. Talbot, USN, as commodore of the four destroyers, on FORD.

The shabby, overworked destroyers fueled from the MARBLEHEAD in Koepang Bay, Timor, and headed north. They were not in too good trim. The FORD, for example, had been two years without overhaul.

Then the bad luck started.

On the way through Sape Strait, between Soembawa and Komodo islands, the BOISE suddenly bucked and shuddered as her garboard strakes hit the jagged point of an uncharted pinnacle-rock. Her bottom was laid open along the keel, and it was obvious at once that she was not in condition to enter an engagement. Admiral Glassford transferred his flag to the MARBLEHEAD. The BOISE limped to port on the south coast of Java, thence on to India for repairs, and thus out of the Java Sea Campaign. (The BOISE's "bad luck" possibly saved her from sharing the fate of the HOUSTON; certainly it saved her for later glory in the Solomons Campaign.) Next MARBLEHEAD's value was diminished by a turbine casualty which reduced her speed to 15 knots.

Even with BOISE and MARBLEHEAD to back them up with all their strength, the destroyers had known that they would face a Japanese force superior to their own. Now, with BOISE out and MARBLEHEAD limping, they wondered what the orders would be. And the destroyers were glad when the word from CINCAF [1] was passed: Go on in there, and fight!

[1] CINCAF—Commander in Chief Asiatic Fleet.

3

The Strait of Macassar is a semisheltered seaway between Borneo and Celebes. It is about 450 miles long and from 60 to 250 miles wide. Unlike the larger Banda Sea to the southeastward, with depths of 25,000 feet, Macassar's soundings jump from 9,000 feet at one point to another a cable's length away which is only slightly damp at low tide. As an official Netherlands government gazetteer puts it: "The depth of the Strait varies widely, rendering navigation at some points impossible."

Dutch planes and Patwing Ten had been dogging the Japanese invasion fleet as it felt its way down the strait for Balikpapan. On the afternoon of January 23 the Dutch aircraft darted in on an attack on the enemy fleet, claiming hits with small bombs on two cruisers, four transports, and a destroyer. But, said furtive messages from Patwing Ten, there were still at least 13 destroyers, four cruisers, and five or more armed transports left for the four old American destroyers of Desdiv 59 to polish off.

Commander Talbot ordered a speed and course that would bring his ships off the southeastern· entrance of the straits, at Hoek Mandar, by nightfall. Heavy north swells were running, and since the ships were making 25 knots the seas were breaking green over bow and bridge, smashing windows and buckling spray shields. The gunnery and torpedo complements fidgeted nervously; soon their lives would depend on the efficiency of gun and torpedo mechanisms which all that brine was doing no good at all.

During the afternoon Commander Talbot issued his orders for the action: "Initial weapon will be torps. Transports chief objective. Cruisers as required to accomplish mission. Launch torps at close range if unsighted by enemy. Each tube set for normal spread torps. Fire single shots if size of target warrants. . . . Will try to avoid action en route. . . . Attack independently when targets located if necessary. When all torps fired, close with all guns. Use initiative and determination."

Course was set directly for Mandar Bay, Celebes, in the hope of deceiving Japanese reconnaissance planes which were expected; but, probably owing to the work of the STURGEON, the only plane sighted was one of the faithful American PBYs. An hour after sunset Desdiv 59 changed course to the northwest, passing Cape Mandar abeam to star-

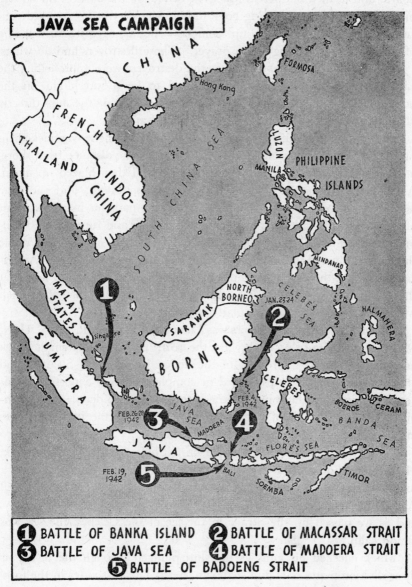

JAVA SEA CAMPAIGN

① BATTLE OF BANKA ISLAND ② BATTLE OF MACASSAR STRAIT
③ BATTLE OF JAVA SEA ④ BATTLE OF MADOERA STRAIT
⑤ BATTLE OF BADOENG STRAIT

FIGURE 5

board, and headed out across Macassar Strait toward Borneo. Speed was increased to 27 knots, causing POPE to hoist signals which expressed concern over her ability to keep up. Somehow she managed it. Airmen sing of coming in on "a wing and a prayer." Those destroyers had no wings.

A little after 2200 Java time, as the destroyers were approaching the Little Paternoster Group, what appeared to be a searchlight on the horizon was sighted ahead. Course was changed to bring the ships directly off Balikpapan, with estimated time of arrival at 0300.

At 2357, as the ships approached Balikpapan, a light was picked up far ahead. This light seemed to be in the water some distance from shore, and observers noted that it flickered, flared, and then blazed up again. A second reflection was observed on Balikpapan itself, and then the destroyers realized that the Dutch bombardiers had put in an excellent afternoon's work with their small missiles: smoke and fumes from burning oil caused an odorous haze that had penetrated 20 miles to sea. While the haze hampered visibility, it also screened the approach of the American ships from the enemy. And the gunnery officers were glad to note that the sea had now abated considerably, giving promise that their men would be able to work on dry platforms.

One of these gunnery officers was Lieutenant William P. Mack, USN, who was in the lead ship of the line, the JOHN D. FORD. Lieutenant Mack has written a vivid impression of the action in Macassar Strait;[1] and although each of the ships turned in complete reports, a portion of his account is included here in preference to others more detailed and technical. His narrative is of added interest because of the insight it gives into the reactions of an individual under fire.

"I've always wondered how a person felt before battle," wrote Mack. "I still don't know. I fell asleep, or as near to sleep as you can get on a four-stacker that is making 27 knots in a rough sea. When the General Alarm awakened me at 11:00 P.M. the sea had calmed considerably, and as we passed up the Straits in the lee of the Celebes, the sea was almost calm."

Mack checked his guns as the ship plunged through the night, its three division mates only dim shadows astern. Then a spotter in the foretop sighted the first of the lights mentioned. As these lights were passed they were made out as burning hulks of Japanese ships which had fallen

---

[1] U.S. Naval Institute *Proceedings*, "Macassar Merry-go-Round," Lieutenant William P. Mack, USN, May, 1943.

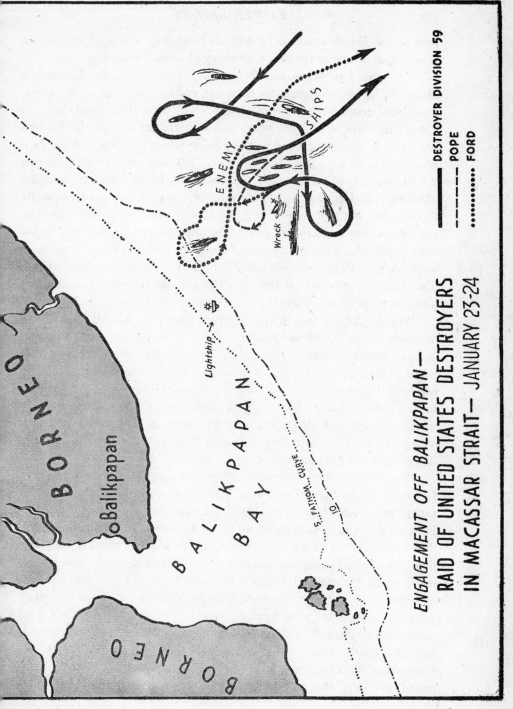

ENGAGEMENT OFF BALIKPAPAN—
RAID OF UNITED STATES DESTROYERS
IN MACASSAR STRAIT— JANUARY 23-24

FIGURE 6

prey to the Dutch aviators. In half an hour they had been left astern, "burning as a monument to the accuracy of some bombardier."

"At 2:00 A.M. we came abreast of Balikpapan," said Lieutenant Mack. "The loom of gigantic fires was visible. The Dutch, we knew, were busy destroying everything burnable to deny it to the Japs. . . . Using these fires as beacons, we turned west and set a course to the area just north of Balikpapan and its mine fields, where we suspected the Japs would land. At 2:45 A.M. I saw my first Japanese ship. I can't describe the feeling it gave me. I could remember the hours I'd spent studying silhouettes of Japanese warships. Suddenly, here was one, a silhouette all right, but not a picture—a big, black, ugly ship. We passed it so close and so fast that neither of us could take any action. Our plan was to fire our torpedoes as long as they lasted and then, and only then, to open up with our guns. That way we could conceal our presence as long as possible. Consequently, we couldn't fire our guns at this ship, and couldn't train our torpedo tubes fast enough to bear on him.

"We didn't have long to wait for more game. A whole division of Jap destroyers burst out of the gloom and oil smoke on our port bow and steamed rapidly across in front of us and off into the darkness to starboard. Again we kept quiet and attempted to avoid them. Our objective was something far more important, the troop-and-supply-laden transports farther inshore. I don't know why these destroyers didn't see us. Possibly several of their own destroyers were patrolling in the vicinity and they mistook us for their own forces. Maybe that was why the first ship we sighted had not fired on us.

"Suddenly we found ourselves right in the midst of the Jap transports. Down on the bridge I could hear Captain Cooper saying 'action port, action port,' and Lieutenant Slaughter readying the torpedo battery. Back aft the tube mounts swung to follow his director. 'Fire one,' he said. 'Fire one' repeated his telephone talker. Then came the peculiar combination of a muffled explosion, a whine, a swish, and a splash, that follows the firing of a torpedo. I watched the torpedo come to the surface once and then dive again as it steadied on its run. Astern, the POPE, PAUL JONES, and PARROTT were carefully picking targets and firing. We fired our second torpedo. So did the ships astern. My talker was calmly counting off seconds as our first torpedo ran toward its target. 'Mark,' he shouted, as the time came for it to hit. Seconds passed. Nothing happened. We knew our first had missed. Then came a blinding, ear-shattering explosion. One of our torpedoes had hit. The explosion of a torpedo at night at close range is an awe-inspiring sight. The blast is terrific, blinding; then comes the concussion wave, which leaves you gasping for breath. It is seconds before your dazed eyes can see anything at all.

"Close on the heels of the first close-range hit came other hits. The crippled ships began to list and sink. We reversed course and ran through the convoy again, firing torpedoes on both sides as transports loomed out of the dark. By now there were only three of us, the PAUL JONES having lost us as we came around the last turn. At one time I could count five sinking ships. A third time we reversed course and ran through the demoralized convoy. Once we had to veer to port to avoid a sinking transport. The water was covered with swimming Japs. Our wash over-turned several lifeboats loaded with Japs. Other ships looked as if they were covered with flies. Jap soldiers were clambering down their sides in panic. It was becoming difficult to keep from firing at transports that had already been torpedoed. Again we turned for another run through the convoy. So far I believed the Japs had not discovered that we were in their midst, attributing the torpedoes to submarines and believing we were their own destroyers.

"Down on the bridge I heard 'Fire ten.' Just two torpedoes left. Now only the POPE was left astern of us. We fired our last two torpedoes at a group of three transports. Now I knew the stage was mine. Many a time I had fired at target rafts, but this was the real thing. 'Commence firing' rang in my earphones. I was ready, but how different this was from peacetime firings! I could still remember the sonorous arguments of the publications I had studied at the Naval Academy over the relative effectiveness of searchlights and star shells. I didn't use either, nor did we use any of the complicated fire-control apparatus installed. This was draw shooting at its best. As targets loomed out of the dark at ranges of 500 to 1,500 yards we trained on and let go a salvo or two, sights set at their lower limits, using the illumination furnished by burning ships. Finally we sighted a transport far enough away to let us get in three salvos before we had passed it. The projectile explosions were tremendous. Deck plates and debris flew in all directions. When we last saw her she was on end, slipping slowly under. . . . A transport began firing at us. I turned my guns on her, but before we could silence her a shell had hit us aft. Flames grew and spread around the area. Over the telephones I could hear a torpedoman describing the damage—'four men wounded, the after deck-house wrecked, ammunition burning.' Thirty seconds later the burning ammunition had been thrown over the side, the wounded men cared for, and the gun crew was firing again.

"By now the POPE had also lost us, and we were fighting alone. One more transport we mauled badly, then there was nothing left to shoot at. On the bridge I heard our Division Commander give the order to withdraw. Back aft the blowers began to whine even louder as the Chief Engineer squeezed the last ounce of speed out of the old boat. Later I learned we were making almost 32 knots, faster than the FORD had gone since her trials. In the east the sky was growing uncomfortably bright. Astern of us the sky was also bright, but from the fires of burning ships.

"For almost 30 minutes we ran south before dawn came. All hands strained their eyes astern for signs of pursuit that we thought inevitable. We could see none. The only ships in sight were three familiar shapes on the port bow that we knew to be the PARROT, PAUL JONES, and POPE. Proudly they fell in astern of us, and we sped south together. Down on the bridge a flag hoist whipped out smartly. 'Well done,' it said."

Three signal flags fluttered from the halyards—Yoke-William-Xray —but "well done" was the most fulsome praise in the Navy's lexicon.

The entire action had taken place within an area of only four or five miles radius, with its center about four or five miles northeast of Balik-papan Lightship. The four destroyers had performed the almost incredible feat of steaming back and forth through a considerably superior enemy force for more than an hour. Surprise of course was the major element of success. The plan of using only torpedoes as long as they lasted probably prevented the Japanese from realizing what was happening for the first half hour. From the enemy's reactions it was evident that he thought he was being attacked by submarines, and that the American destroyers were units of his own force, scurrying about on the hunt for the attacking subs. When the Japanese finally realized what was happening they had the choice of withholding their fire or hitting their own ships, for the Americans were having a field day plump in the middle of their convoy. Some of the Jap destroyers did fire torpedoes, and it is quite possible that they helped to run up the Americans' score.

The American and Dutch submarines in the vicinity had been warned to keep clear of the attack area. One doughty Dutch submariner, however, must have concluded that the show would be too good to miss. He

PLATE XXXIII—Headquarters of the Commander in Chief Asiatic Fleet at the outbreak of war was on the third floor of this new air-conditioned office building in Manila, Philippine Islands. *Upper right:* Admiral Thomas C. Hart, USN, Commander in Chief U. S. Asiatic Fleet. *Lower right:* Rear Admiral William R. Purnell, USN, Chief of Staff, Commander in Chief U. S. Asiatic Fleet.

Rear Admiral Francis W. Rockwell, USN (center), and members of his staff confer near a sandbag trench of his headquarters at Cavite, near Manila, December 17, 1941. Left to right: Lieut. Comdr. Frank J. Granfield; Admiral Rockwell; and Lieut. Malcolm Champlin, USNR. Admiral Rockwell was Commandant of the Sixteenth Naval District (Philippine Islands). He was evacuated by submarine.

PLATE XXXIV—(*upper*) Typical of the small bases held by the Army and Navy in the Far East was Olongapo, on the west coast of Luzon, north of Manila Bay. This aerial view shows the Navy Yard (right), shops (center), and living quarters (left). (*lower*) A palm-shaded walk borders the officers' quarters, Olongapo Naval Station.

PLATE XXXV—(*right*) Two views showing the damage done by Japanese aerial attacks during December, 1941, at Cavite Naval Station, near Manila. In order to remove all records, supplies and equipment possible to Bataan and Corregidor, Cavite was evacuated before the enemy entered the city.

PLATE XXXVI—(*upper*) The USS HOUSTON, heavy cruiser, which fought against overwhelming odds in battles around the Java Sea. On the night of February 28, 1942, the HOUSTON was engaged by Japanese ships off St. Nicholas Point, Java, about midnight. Nothing has been heard from her since. *Inset:* Captain Albert H. Rooks, USN, Commanding Officer of the USS HOUSTON, officially listed as dead. (*lower*) Secretary of the Navy Frank Knox congratulates Rear Admiral William A. Glassford, Jr., USN, for exceptionally meritorious services. As Vice Admiral, he commanded U.S. Naval Forces, Southwest Pacific, later taking charge, on February 7, 1942, of the crumbling remnants of the Asiatic Fleet.

PLATE XXXVII—Some of the heroes of the USS MARBLEHEAD. *Upper left:* Captain A. G. Robinson, USN, Commanding Officer. *Upper right:* Commander William B. Goggins, USN, Executive Officer. *Lower left:* Lieutenant Thomas C. Ryan (MC), USN, the junior doctor, gets a hair cut on deck after the barber shop had been bombed out below. *Lower right:* Commander Nicholas B. Van Bergen, USN (with white cap), Gunnery Officer and later Executive Officer of the cruiser, chats with other officers of the MARBLEHEAD.

PLATE XXXVIII—(*upper*) On February 4, 1942, seven Jap bombers approached the USS
MARBLEHEAD as the American cruiser rendezvoused with other Allied ships to make a run up
Macassar Strait. It was here the MARBLEHEAD's luck trickled out. Two bombs from these planes
landed directly on the ship and a third missed so closely that the blast blew a hole in the
cruiser's bottom. (*lower*) A Dutch destroyer, of the WITTE DE WITH class, which formed part of
the screening force for the Allied squadron in the Java Sea.

PLATE XXXIX—(upper) The MARBLEHEAD heels over at high speed and escapes a hit. Swirling wake indicates that the cruiser has adopted evasive action to escape Jap bombs. The battle was not one-sided, however, because the cruiser's anti-aircraft batteries scored a hit on one Jap plane's bomb rack and the plane disintegrated in mid-air. (lower) A stick of Japanese aerial bombs brackets one of the screening force ships accompanying the MARBLEHEAD and HOUSTON in the opening phase of the Java Sea Campaign, which lasted from February 3 to 28, 1942.

PLATE XL—(*upper*) A close-up view of the spot where one of the Jap bombs hit the MARBLEHEAD. It ripped through the side of a motor launch and penetrated the steel deck before exploding. (*lower*) Entry hole made by the Japanese bomb on the steel deck of the cruiser MARBLEHEAD. The bomb exploded as it entered the main deck below, bowed the upper deck about a foot, starting seams and rivets.

PLATE XLI—(*upper*) A wounded seaman has a cup of coffee on the deck of the MARBLE-HEAD shortly after the Japanese aerial attack was driven off. There were 70 or 80 casualties as a result of two bomb hits. Several were fatal. The ship's Executive Officer, Commander William B. Goggins, USN, was among those seriously burned. (*lower*) The ship's cooks carry on in the MARBLEHEAD's wrecked Ward Room pantry. Note the steam line broken overhead. The downward force of the blasts demolished the sick bay and fragments penetrated fuel tanks. The main engines were not damaged, however, and the cruiser was still able to do 25 knots.

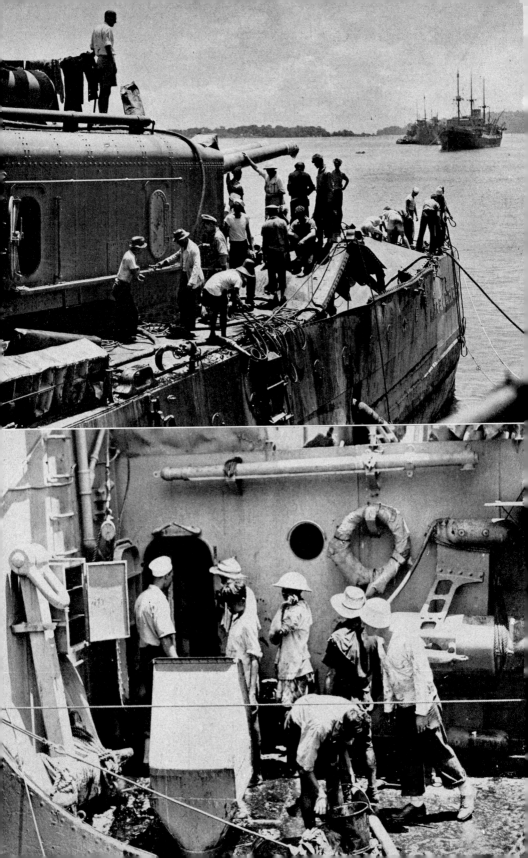

PLATE XLII—(*upper left*) The MARBLEHEAD limps back to Tjilatjap, Java. The stern of the 19-year-old cruiser was buckled when the second bomb landed near the fan-tail during the action of February 4. (*lower left*) Working against time and approaching Japanese forces, Javanese natives help the crew of the MARBLEHEAD to clean up some of the damage done by enemy bombs and fire. The MARBLEHEAD finally was patched up enough to return to New York via Capetown, South Africa.

PLATE XLIII—(*upper*) Carefully the MARBLEHEAD's wounded are placed aboard a hospital train at Tjilatjap, Java. It was from this picture that a scene in the motion picture *The Story of Dr. Wassell* was reproduced. The ship in the background is the USS HOUSTON. This is probably the last photograph of the HOUSTON, because she was lost in action a few days later. (*lower*) Lieutenant Commander Corydon McAlmont Wassell (MC), USNR, who received the Navy Cross for his faithful services to the MARBLEHEAD wounded in Java.

PLATE XLIV—(*upper left*) In the feverish haste to repair the USS STEWART at Soerabaja, before the advancing Japanese could reach the base, the destroyer was placed in the drydock improperly. The vessel rolled off her blocks and damaged both herself and the drydock. Before she could be righted, Japanese naval bombers came over and demolished both the STEWART and drydock. (*lower left*) Like Pearl Harbor in miniature were the smoke and explosions caused by Japanese bombings at Soerabaja, Dutch naval base in Java.

PLATE XLV—(*upper*) Soerabaja's docks and waterfront were piled high with broken and burning ships after the Japanese bombing raids of February, 1942. (*lower*) Shipyards suffered heavily in the Japanese bombing raids at Soerabaja.

PLATE XLVI—A few of the ships and a type of plane that made history in the early months of Pacific fighting. *Left row, top to bottom:* USS BOISE, cruiser; USS PECOS, oiler; USS HERON, small seaplane tender; USS BLACK HAWK, destroyer tender. *Right row, top to bottom:* USS LANGLEY, seaplane tender; USS STURGEON, submarine; and PBY, Consolidated patrol bombing plane.

PLATE XLVII—These "Cans" and their sister destroyers, of World War I vintage, held the Japs at bay longer than anyone thought possible. *Left row, top to bottom:* USS PEARY, USS ALDEN, and USS EDSALL. *Right row, top to bottom:* USS BARKER, USS FORD, USS PAUL JONES, and USS PARROTT.

UNITED STATES SHIP HOUSTON Thursday 1 January , 19
             (Day) (Date) (Month)

NE DESCRIPTION -9½   REMARKS CONFIDENTIA

00 to 04

Steaming on true course one zero eight,
Enroute Port Darwin to Torres Strait.
The standard compass reads one two three
(the degaussing increases the error you see).
ALDEN, WHIPPLE, and EDSALL; destroyers lean,
About us form an inner sound screen.
Seven, six, three, and two are the boilers we need
For fifteen knots, which is standard speed.
To keep from sinking (and that's no joke)
Material is in condition "Yoke".
The guns in condition of readiness TWO,
Are waiting to sink any ship named Maru.
While all is as dark as the ace of spades,
As a means of protection from enemy raids.

        H.S Hamlin Jr.
       H.S. HAMLIN Jr.
       Lieut(jg), U.S. Navy.

4 to 08 Steaming as before. 0500 Lighted fires under boilers Nos. 1, 4, 5, and
 0525 Let fires die under boilers Nos. 1 and 8. 0537 Exercised at general
uarters: set material condition "Zed".

PLATE XLVIII—(*upper*) The last log of the USS HOUSTON. An age-old tradition requires that the first entry on the new year must be written in rhyme. Lieut. (jg) H. S. Hamlin, the author, is reported a prisoner of war. (*lower*) USS HOLLAND, pioneer submarine tender, and her brood of undersea boats. The HOLLAND saw much action in the Philippines and the Netherlands East Indies.

popped up in the very thick of things, and hung around until, as the commanding officer put it, "I saw that my friends were doing very well."

The Dutch sub commander's curiosity provided the report that the four destroyers' tally that night was thirteen enemy ships. The Americans were more conservative—in the frenzied action of the melee accurate observation was most difficult—and they were officially credited with only six kills, one of these being a Jap destroyer which blew up, his destruction clearly visible in the glare of other burning ships. The Dutch sub commander did all right on his own hook, too; the next morning as he was leaving the area he waylaid a Jap cruiser and torpedoed it at such close range that the submarine itself was damaged and forced to lie on the bottom all day.

The action did not end with the destroyer raid. Japanese ships in the area were given a rough touching up on January 25 and 28, and again on February 2, by U.S. Army Flying Fortresses which made several kills. In all, the Dutch estimated that the Japanese lost more than thirty ships in the Macassar Strait, many of them to their own Netherlands airmen.

None of these blows was enough, however, to prevent the Japanese from sweeping down in force to occupy the burned-out port of Balikpapan, although they were stalled there for some time. The four American destroyers could only console themselves with the knowledge that they had been completely and enjoyably successful in the first American naval engagement in Asiatic waters since the Battle of Manila Bay.

4

On January 21 the Japanese began a series of bombing attacks on points in northeastern New Guinea and in the Bismarck Archipelago, heralding the feared extension of the invasion toward the Australian-American life line. They followed these by landings at Kavieng in New Ireland and at Rabaul in New Britain, where Australian airmen bombed their ships three times within a week.

On the west coast of Borneo they advanced overland from Sarawak, which they had controlled since early January. On January 29 they took Pemangkat, and within a few days, Pontianak. At the same time planes operating from Samarinda and Balikpapan began to bomb Bandjermasin on the southeast coast of Borneo. These movements threatened to bring the invaders opposite Java and southeastern Sumatra.

Admiral Hart did not have the force to strike at these expeditions as effectively as in Macassar Strait; the Japanese advance might have been slowed sufficiently to permit help to arrive from the United States if such had been the case. But the Japanese tide rolled on. The MARBLEHEAD required repairs to her turbine. The destroyers were beginning to show the effects of having been almost constantly overexerted at sea since the beginning of the war. Many of their torpedo tubes were empty and no more torpedoes were readily to be had. All of our submarines had been running patrols that stretched the limits of man's endurance; and often, when the subs crept wearily into port for a badly needed rest, a new emergency required their turning to sea at once.

The Dutch ships were in better condition, but, acting on information which later proved inaccurate, Admiral Helfrich had sent his fleet northwest into Karimata Channel, between Borneo and Sumatra. Consequently, it was not available to strengthen the striking force in the east at this crucial time.

The British were concentrating their attention and naval forces in the west, where the situation was critical. In Burma they were holding the line of the Salween River, but in the south, Moulmein, anchor of their right flank, was seriously threatened. The last reinforcements were being thrown into Singapore "under a hail of bombs running clear down to Banka Strait" and at the cost of EMPRESS OF JAPAN sunk, DUCHESS OF BEDFORD and USS WAKEFIELD damaged. By the end of January ABDA-COM decided to withdraw the British troops in Malaya to Singapore Island, and he again left Lembang to visit the great base. While General Wavell believed that Singapore might hold out indefinitely, it had become useless as a naval base. The Royal Navy was closing its dockyard— a bitter blow. ABDACOM's decision meant too that the RAF was forced to move from Singapore and to base its operations on Sumatra. But already the northern and eastern ports of Sumatra were too dangerous for merchant shipping and vessels had been sunk at Padang on the west coast and at Emmahaven just below. The Japs were steadily closing the jaws of their vise.

In the face of these difficulties, Admiral Hart's choice of action was at best highly restricted. He felt that the enemy force which had again gathered in Macassar Strait and which again offered "some attractive targets" should be the next objective. Submarines were placed to protect Bandjermasin and Macassar, while repairs on the MARBLEHEAD and the destroyers were rushed to completion for another raid up the straits. But as the patched-up attack force worked northward on the afternoon of February 1, it was sighted and shadowed by a Japanese plane. That night there was bright moonlight and it was prudently decided not to attack a superior force (as air reconnaissance had reported it to be) after the element of surprise had obviously been lost, and without American air cover. The lesson of REPULSE and PRINCE OF WALES was not forgotten.

It was known that the Japanese had been building up a force at Kendari and Staring Bay on the southeast coast of Celebes. While Allied forces were occupied in Macassar Strait, this force moved in the Molucca Sea. On February 1 they bombed Laha airfield on Ceram and subsequently occupied it. On the same day a large convoy, reported to consist of 10 transports, 10 destroyers, and 6 cruisers, approached Amboina, chief Dutch stronghold on the eastern flank of the Indies. The Dutch and Australian air force there had been sadly whittled down during previous raids, and within two or three days the island was in the possession of the Japanese.

The foreseen difficulty in repairing and servicing his ships convinced Admiral Hart that Port Darwin was too far removed from the scene of operations. Moreover, it had proved unsuitable as a base in other respects and was now within the range of the Japanese bombers. On January 29 the fleet auxiliaries were ordered to move westward to Netherlands East Indies harbors. The ships sailed on February 3 and HOLLAND and OTUS arrived belatedly at Tjilatjap on the 10th, badly delayed by weather. On the same day that the auxiliaries left Darwin the Japanese, operating from their new bases, crossed the Java Sea to bomb Soerabaja and several other points in Java, as well as Timor, a large island within bombing range of the Australian mainland. It was the first of a series of raids that was to make Soerabaja first difficult, then untenable as a base. On the first raid most of the Dutch fighters were damaged or destroyed. The Navy planes escaped only because the tough little tenders, always on the move, enabled them always to be elsewhere than where the Japs expected to find them.

Japan now controlled all the northern approaches to the Indies and would soon be in a position to move directly against the islands of the Malay Barrier itself. It appeared that the bombing of Java and Timor marked the beginning of the "softening-up" process. The long-obvious need for a striking force capable of breaking up the next Japanese expedition was now more painfully insistent.

To attempt the creation of such a force Admiral Hart as ABDA-

FLOAT called a conference of Admiral Helfrich, Admiral Glassford, and the able Australian, Commodore John Collins. They met at Lembang on February 2. Dutch cruisers and destroyers and some British vessels had been released from the Singapore convoy, and had been thrown in with the American ships as one squadron. The conference had a double purpose—to establish command arrangements and to decide how and where to use the patchwork fleet to best advantage.

It was decided to put the Dutch rear admiral, Karel W. F. M. Doorman, in charge of the force that was to assemble east of Java as soon as possible. The LANGLEY was scurrying to Fremantle, Australia, for a load of Army P-40s desperately essential to the fight for Java. Admiral Hart realized that the tactical handling of the little fleet would present some difficulties, but there was no opportunity for joint training.

At long last there now seemed to be a possibility of forming a force capable of smashing the next Japanese expedition, even if it should be heavily protected. The promise was short-lived. In the operations ahead, the worst was yet to come.

Chapter Nine

ON February 3, 1942, the promise for naval accomplishment in action against the Japanese seemed brighter than at any time since the beginning of the war. In addition to the Dutch cruisers and destroyers (with British ships to be added later) there was now available for the first time in the formation of a striking force the hard-hitting heavy cruiser HOUSTON. Since the death of REPULSE and PRINCE OF WALES, and the departure of BOISE, HOUSTON was the strongest Allied ship in Asiatic waters.

There is an age-old naval tradition that the first entry in a ship's log on the first day of a new year must be written in rhyme; and, over the years, many a salt-weathered brow has become wrinkled and bedewed in carrying out this command of custom. The last log turned in by the cruiser HOUSTON was for the month of January, 1942, most of which (as has been noted) she spent on convoy duty. At 2400, on the night of December 31 the watch was relieved on the HOUSTON's bridge and a junior-grade lieutenant took over the tedious midwatch, from 2400 to 0400, at the beginning of the new year. He finished his trick and, in obeisance to tradition, wrote:

oo to 0400   *1 January, 1942*

> Steaming on true course one zero eight,
> Enroute Port Darwin to Torres Strait.
> The standard compass reads one two three
> (the degaussing increases the error you see).
> ALDEN, WHIPPLE, and EDSALL, destroyers lean,
> About us form an inner sound screen.
> Seven, six, three, and two are the boilers we need
> For fifteen knots, which is standard speed.
> To keep from sinking (and that's no joke)
> Material is in condition "Yoke."

The guns, in condition of readiness TWO,
Are waiting to sink any ship named Maru.
While all is dark as the ace of spades,
As a means of protection from enemy raids.

H. S. HAMLIN, JR.,
Lieut. (jg) U. S. Navy

Now, on February 3, 1942, HOUSTON was just a day away from a foretaste of her doom, and MARBLEHEAD was to share this foretaste with her. On February's last day, HOUSTON was to find herself in a situation in which nothing could be done "to keep from sinking (and that's no joke)."

2

With Admiral Doorman in command of the newly formed striking force, plans were now set in motion to launch a blow at the advancing enemy. Since February 1 air reconnaissance had reported a considerable enemy convoy still at Balikpapan. This force presumably would strike down Macassar Strait either at Bandjermasin on the east coast of Borneo or, across the strait, at Macassar on the southern arm of the Celebes. Possibly, the Japanese might hit both simultaneously. According to the lurking PBYs, the enemy concentration consisted of 3 cruisers, 10 destroyers, and 20 armed transports.

It was a force not too much for the Allied ships to take on—in fact, the engagement was eagerly anticipated, and with much confidence. Admiral Doorman's flag was in the Dutch cruiser DE RUYTER, with HOUSTON and MARBLEHEAD next in line, and followed by the small Dutch cruiser TROMP. As a screening force there were the four ships of Desdiv 58 and a division of three Dutch destroyers. The American destroyers were led by Commander Binford on STEWART, with EDWARDS, BARKER, and BULMER. The Dutch destroyers were commanded by Lieutenant Commander Krips on the VAN CHENT, with PIET HEIN and BANCKERT. The words of Admiral Doorman's directive were: "Enemy transports will be attacked and destroyed in a night attack."

The ships were assembled for the strike in Bounder Roads, Madoera Island, when, on the afternoon of February 3, flights of Japanese planes passed over on the way to bomb Soerabaja. The Japanese spotted the ships, but Admiral Doorman felt that he could cover enough distance during the night to nullify this information. The ships upped anchor and steamed away for an 0500 rendezvous off Meyndertsdroogte Light, from which they were to make the run up Macassar.

The rendezvous was carried out according to plan. The ships were zigzagging on an easterly course with a soft trailing breeze and a moderate following sea. The sky was partly overcast, but the mountains of Kangean Island stood as a dim sentinel 35 miles to the north, and from time to time the high peaks of Bali and Lombok appeared through the clouds to the south. At 0935 Admiral Doorman warned his ships by signal hoist that Japanese planes could be expected. The ships were just south of Kangean when, at 0949, the first enemy planes appeared. There were four or five formations of nine bombers each, with two or three planes flying alone.

As the ships scattered, the bomber groups separated to choose their targets. Their attack, which was to last all morning, was directed solely at the cruisers, with the destroyers in danger only when they accidentally maneuvered near a bomb hit as they strove to repel the planes. The HOUSTON, twisting and turning at top speed, successfully evaded all except the last bomb aimed in her direction. She had just maneuvered to thwart a group of planes when a single straggler came over and made a perfect drop. The bomb, falling on a slant, struck the leg of the mainmast and exploded on the main deck near the after turret. Fire somehow got into the turret and ignited the ready powder inside. There was a mighty blast. The turret was knocked out of commission, to remain that way for the remainder of the campaign. Worst of all, 48 men were instantly killed and 20 wounded.

The MARBLEHEAD fared no better. The first group of planes to approach the vessel held their bombs when the ship suddenly changed course at high speed. Back the bombers came, on their second try; the ship's antiaircraft fire scored on one Jap's bomb-rack and the plane disintegrated. Its eight companions dropped bombs which missed so closely that fragments rattled against the ship's sides and swept her decks, causing the men below to describe the sound as "like the ship scraping over a gravel shoal." One Japanese plane, apparently damaged by antiaircraft fire, spiraled downward in an apparent effort to crash on the MARBLEHEAD's deck. Machine-gun fire broke it into fragments and it splashed into the sea, 1,000 yards off the port bow.

Flight after flight of enemy planes dropped their bombs only to see the ship below them heel over and escape unhit. At 1026 a flight of seven single-engine planes came over. The skipper, Captain Arthur G. Robinson, USN, ordered full left rudder, but the MARBLEHEAD'S luck had trickled out: two bombs landed squarely on, and a third missed so close that its blast blew a hole in the cruiser's bottom.

One hit was in the forward section about 10 feet from the starboard side. It sheared the inboard side of the starboard motor launch, which probably started the bomb's fuse mechanism, so that after passing through the upper deck it exploded as it entered the main deck. The upward force of the explosion bowed the upper deck about a foot, starting seams and rivets. Laterally the blast spread destruction far and wide through that section of the ship (the wardroom and officers' country), and bent the forward uptakes. The downward force of the blast demolished the sick bay and fragments penetrated the top of the fuel tank below the hospital quarters. All electric, steam, and water lines (except the fire main) in the area were ruptured. Fires were started throughout the area.

The second bomb landed on the fantail, abaft the after twin mount and close to port. It passed through the main deck and exploded in the hand-steering room. The explosion lifted the main deck and blew a flap of it upward against the underside of the guns of the twin mount, which was put completely out of action. The chief petty officers' quarters and the adjacent crew's quarters were demolished. All steering gear and the hand-steering room were utterly disabled, and the rudder was jammed full left. Fuel tanks were ruptured and fires started. There were several ruptures in the sides of the vessel.

The "dished-in area" caused by the near-miss formed a great scoop which forced water into the ship at high pressure as she continued steaming. Moreover, the opening of seams and rivets started leaks in other forward sections, so that the peak tank was flooded, as were most of the compartments below the first platform deck and forward of frame 34.

The shock of the explosion gave the ship a sharp list to starboard and she settled by the head, so that her draft forward ultimately reached 30 feet. Fortunately, the main engines were not damaged, and when fire-rooms 1 and 2 had been secured because of ruptured uptakes she was still able to do 25 knots. Because of the jammed rudder the ship was steaming in a circle to port.

Several times TROMP approached MARBLEHEAD to take off survivors if it should become necessary. Fires were raging fore and aft. Damage-control crews and all unengaged men were busy fighting them or caring for the wounded. The executive officer had come to the bridge severely burned and his place had been taken by the gunnery officer. The damage-control officer supervised the fire fighting and efforts to free the rudder. By 1100 the fires were under control, but arcs from broken electric cables constantly started new ones in the oil-filled compartments. It was not till 1300 that the rudder angle was reduced to about 9 degrees left.

There were 70 or 80 casualties, several fatal and many serious, in addition to many minor injuries which did not take men out of action. The forward battle dressing station and collecting station had been destroyed and the amidship station was untenable, so that the wounded had to be carried aft to a makeshift station in the torpedo workshop. It was a precarious task on slanting decks made slippery with oil.

One of the MARBLEHEAD's casualties was the ship's executive officer, Commander William B. Goggins, USN, second in command to the captain. Commander Goggins's report of the action probably will come to rank with the best descriptions of all time of an individual in battle at sea. If anything, the quality of his narrative is enhanced by the fact that it was set down with no thought of ultimate publication in mind.

Commander Goggins was on the bridge when the enemy planes were sighted and, in accordance with previous orders from the captain, went below. As second in command, his post was distant from the captain's to minimize the risk of both being disabled at once.

"I went below and cruised the main deck to see that everything was all right, that people were properly stationed, that Zed [1] was set, and that people were lying down, those who did not have stations," Goggins relates. "I checked up particularly to see that the aviation gasoline tanks had been dumped. Had these caught fire, the entire stern of the ship would probably have been lost.

"It was unfortunate that I was wearing shorts at the time, as were several other officers. The crew was in dungarees for flash protection, but due to the heat a good many people either took off their top shirts or some of them even took off their undershirts, which was distinctly a bad idea.

"I recall going down the main deck on the starboard side, seeing everybody very cheerful and in good spirits, and I remember remarking to one of the men that the HERON had fought off a formation of Japa-

[1] Condition Zed: maximum preparation for battle.

nese bombers all day and that it looked as though we would be all right. The damage control parties were all at their stations and ready. I went forward on the port side and up to the wardroom.

"At this time the ship was maneuvering at high speed, the guns were firing, and our 3″ ammunition was being rapidly exhausted at the guns. An ammunition party from men on the 6″ battery and others was rapidly formed in the wardroom country and began bringing up ammunition from the forward 3″ magazine group and running it aft on the port side and up No. 2 hatch to the guns.

"During the attack, a wave of planes would come over and the battery would fire. As the planes got almost directly overhead, the .50 caliber would start firing and the resulting racket was tremendous, even down below in the wardroom where I was with the ammunition party. In this compartment were Ensign Coburn, Lieutenant Gluckman, the senior aviator; and myself. Just forward of us in the passageway where the ammunition was being whipped up was Lieutenant Goodhue.

"I do not recall how many attacks came over, but each time they came over there would be a salvo of bombs dropped and we were doing quite well, the Captain was avoiding the salvos, and everything looked pretty good to us down below. We could hear the cheers of the people on the deck when planes were shot down. I was to understand that three were shot down by our AA battery.

"I do not know exactly what time the bomb hit the ship. I remember that I was leaning against the edge of the wardroom table and watching the ammunition party and helping keep them in order. They were carrying boxes of four aft at double time. I remember just before we were hit, the gunner, Gunner Clendenin, dashed through the wardroom crying out, 'All gunner's mates on the AA batteries to set fuses,' and a number of these men departed. The gunner left them and I did not see him again.

"The first thing that I recall happening was that the ship was shaken, apparently by a hit astern and I just started to go forward and up the hatch to find out what the trouble was when the lights went out and there was a terrific explosion. My sensation was that the whole after end of the ship was coming right at me. I do not recall that the noise was particularly loud, but the shock was rather severe and I was struck by something, I don't know what it was, on the left hip, which afterwards I discovered to be black and blue.

"The wardroom was immediately full of a mass of wreckage. I could not see very well on account of the lights having all gone out. At this time I was standing about six feet from the forward door of the wardroom and I saw that I was almost completely surrounded by wreckage. Apparently I had not been hit, but I could feel an intense heat from the flash of the bomb. There is a product of combustion after the bomb had exploded of very hot gas and I was standing in this hot gas and I could feel myself burning. The heat was so intense that the bulkheads, the paint on the metal and the linoleum was sizzling and catching fire. Wherever this hot gas remains in contact and is not blown away it ignites anything that will burn. That means paint or anything else. My clothes did not catch fire, but I was severely burned.

"I did not see anybody around me. I did not see Coburn or Gluckman again. I did not see anyone that I recall except a signalman by the name of Murtch, who was between me and the wardroom door, the forward starboard door. The door was piled high with debris, but there was a small space above it through which we could climb. Murtch climbed through and I followed him and went up on deck.

"There was by this time a good fire burning in the wardroom and below steam was escaping from some pipes that had been cut. All the lights forward were out and the party which had been working on the ammunition apparently started up on deck, taking with them the wounded.

"I remember looking in my cabin at the top of the ladder and hearing someone in there groaning. Apparently there was a doctor or someone with him. He was lying on my transom,[1] but it was dark in there and I did not stop to see what the trouble was, but went out and up on the bridge to find out what the conditions were.

"I climbed up to the bridge and found that the Captain was all right, and the rudder indicator showed that the rudder was jammed full left, and he said he had no steering control. What had happened was that the bomb had hit in the sick bay and had cut off all intercommunications and ship control forward. The ship was circling as I recall at about 28 knots. The ships around us were keeping clear and were also circling and were firing at the planes overhead.

"I went down the ladder to the main deck and started aft to find out what the difficulty was with the steering. I could see a number of wounded, mostly burns, being taken aft, some of them were lying on the main deck.

[1] Transom: a leather-covered couch.

"The people who were on the damage control were already starting on the fire forward. I did not know what had happened aft. I went aft on the deck—someone asked me what was the matter with my neck and I then learned that a piece of shrapnel had clipped the back of my neck and that blood was running down my uniform. I did not know this until someone asked me, and I said, 'I'm all right,' but I could see that I had been pretty badly burned—I had second degree burns I found afterwards and my skin was burned and hanging in folds on my arms and legs. I had been burned in all areas not covered by my clothing.

"I went back on the main deck and I could see the hole of the bomb hit forward, and there was a lot of steam, smoke and flame coming up No. 1 hatch. I can recall this particularly because the flame and smoke was hot and burned me as I went by.

"The anti-aircraft battery was intact and was still firing and they were apparently doing all right.

"I went aft on the deck and started to find out what was going on. I climbed up to Battle Two to see if I could get communication with the steering gear. I got up there all right, there was no one there, and got to the voice tube and called down to the steering gear. Of course, the telephones were out of commission, sound power and otherwise, but there is a voice tube in Battle Two to hand steering and I tried to call down there. There was no answer and I afterwards learned that that was because the people down there had all been killed. A bomb had hit the stern just abaft the after twin and had penetrated down into the steering gear and wrecked it.

"I climbed down to Battle Two and went down the No. 3 hatch to find out if anything could be done about steering. I got down to the foot of the ladder and found Dr. Ryan there with his people dressing wounded as best they could. He started to put some tannic acid jelly on my leg, but it appeared to me that there were many others who needed it worse than I did, especially some who had some severe wounds from shrapnel and really required his attention.

"I went back and found that the fire party was starting down the escape hatch and was attempting to put out a large fire which was then burning in the after end of the ship in the chiefs' quarters. The bomb that hit down there had wounded a number of people, had killed some and had blown the whole chiefs' quarters forward into the after engineering compartment. I did not see this because it was impossible for me to get down there at the time. Having found that this damage would have to be corrected before anything could be done, I started forward again.

"Dr. Ryan stopped me and gave me two morphine pills—I did not want a shot because I did not want to be immobilized, but he gave me two pills which he said would help relieve the pain a little and he told me to hold them under my tongue, but by this time I had swallowed them and when I got up on deck my knees gave way under me, probably from the action of the morphine. I sat down on something by the loading machine for about a minute and then was able to get up and go forward again.

"The crew was taking care of the damage. The damage control people and others were already hard at work and it was with the greatest calmness and determination. I saw no one who was excited. I saw no one who was raising his voice or shouting. Our drills had stressed the necessity for silence during emergency drills of all kinds and they were carrying it out during the actual battle. Everywhere I saw men and officers who were proceeding to correct damage and to care for those who needed assistance.

"I went forward again and up to the bridge and reported what had happened aft as near as I could tell and at this time the senior medical officer, Dr. Wildebush, saw me and said that I would have to lie down, so I went down the ladder from the bridge one level to the conning tower, which was near enough to the bridge so that if I were needed I might be able to render some assistance.

"I was outside the conning tower when the forward damage control party from central station came up on deck. There had been a near miss close aboard on the port side right under the LC room, which had flooded that compartment and it was flooding central and other compartments adjacent thereto. The people in central tried to come up through the regular hatch, but were unable because of the fire burning over their heads. Accordingly they abandoned central through the leg of the tripod mast, which leads from there up into the chart house.

"This tube is large enough for easy transit, except it is now pretty well filled with voice tubes and wiring of one kind or another. Some people didn't think you could get up through there but they all did. The last one to leave was the ship's tailor, who was a member of the party, a man by the name of Delugh, who had been on the ship from the time it was commissioned in 1932. Delugh was a man who was rather fat and it was not thought that he could get through this escape hatch at all, so Delugh told everybody to go ahead of him so that if he got stuck he wouldn't trap anybody below. I saw them all outside the conning tower just before I entered it and Delugh managed to get up all right, although with some abrasions. They were all in good shape and immediately went about their business to correct damage. Lieutenant Blasdel, I recall particularly, was one who was up there in his party. I believe the damage control officer, Lieutenant Commander Drury, had already come up.

"I went into the conning tower and sat down and waited for developments. From time to time people would come through and inform me of the progress being made with the steering gear and with the control of the fire.

"My burns were beginning to become very painful and I trimmed off about two inches of my sleeves and trousers in order to keep them from rubbing on the burned areas. Murtch, the signalman, who had been in the wardroom with me, came down with a little can of gun grease and said that while it wasn't quite the thing to put on burns, at least it would keep the air off and wouldn't hurt, so I rubbed this grease over all my burns and pain stopped considerably and I was much more comfortable.

"I was in the conning tower from this time on until I was taken ashore in Tjilatjap.

"At this time the ship was steaming at about full speed, about 28 knots, with the rudder jammed hard left and listed over, with the Japs circling overhead trying to make another attack. I don't recall much about what happened, except that there was some shooting and we were not hit again."

3

Some time after noon the Japanese planes left. The MARBLEHEAD, steering with her engines, began working her way south toward Lombok Strait. Commander Goggins's duties were taken on by Commander Nicholas Van Bergen, USN, the gunnery officer, whose heroic efforts to organize the functions of shattered ship and shaken men are still being related. There was considerable doubt as to whether the ship could be kept afloat. All her pumps were working, but this was not enough: her officers and men harked back to the days when ships did not have

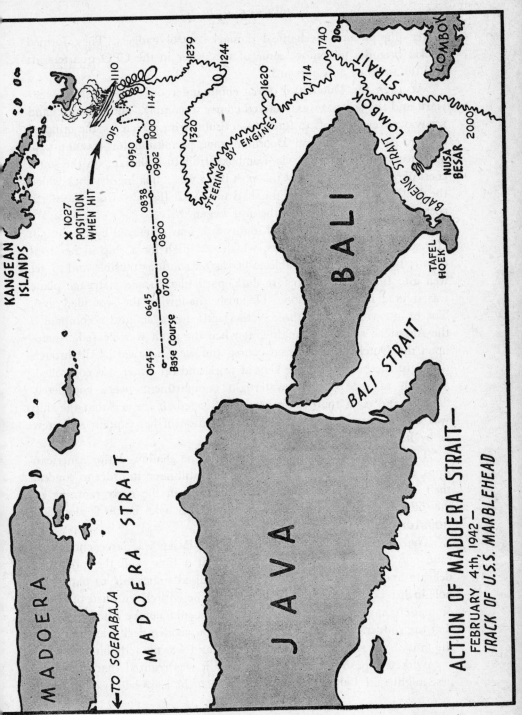

KANGEAN ISLANDS

× 1027 POSITION WHEN HIT

0545
0645
0700
0800
0838
0902
0900
0950
1000
1015
1110
1147
1239
1244

Base Course

TO SOERABAJA

MADOERA STRAIT

MADOERA

JAVA

BALI

BALI STRAIT

STEERING BY ENGINES

1620
1714
1740
1800

LOMBOK STRAIT

LOMBOK

BADOENG STRAIT

NUSA BESAR

2000

TAFEL HOEK

ACTION OF MADOERA STRAIT—
FEBRUARY 4th, 1942—
TRACK OF U.S.S. MARBLEHEAD

FIGURE 7

power pumps and mechanical damage-control gadgets. They formed bucket brigades to remove some of the water in the CPO quarters aft and the sick .bay area forward.

At 1225 the Dutch task force commander ordered the ships westward and the MARBLEHEAD altered course to comply. The EDWARDS and STEWART were told off to form an antisubmarine screen for the crippled cruiser. At 1415 Admiral Doorman gave permission for MARBLEHEAD and HOUSTON to proceed via Lombok Strait to Tjilatjap, on the south coast of Java, for repairs. At this port there was a floating drydock which the Dutch, with great foresight, had towed all the way from the north coast of Java shortly before the war began.

Again, MARBLEHEAD turned southward, now convoyed by Desdiv 58. Her speed was about 20 knots, which was high for a ship in her condition; but it seemed advisable to get as far south as possible and to get well into Lombok Strait before dark, particularly since a strange plane was sighted in the afternoon, obviously shadowing the wounded ship. The DE RUYTER and the three Netherlands destroyers also accompanied the American ships until midnight, when the strait was cleared, whereupon the Dutch ships reversed course and went westward. All through the night the bucket brigade kept at work and the water was controlled, although at the time 26 watertight compartments were completely flooded, and eight more were partially flooded. It seemed that the ship was kept afloat as much by the determination of her captain and crew as by her own buoyancy.

Through the morning of the 5th a plane shadowed the American ships, so that they held to a southerly course till noon in order to conceal their destination. They approached· Tjilatjap in the early morning of the 6th, and soon after noon MARBLEHEAD was berthed alongside HOUSTON.

The commercial floating drydock at Tjilatjap was large enough to raise only one end of the MARBLEHEAD at a time, and this proved a delicate and difficult task. The bow was raised sufficiently to patch the hole in her bottom, but the ship could not be entirely emptied of water or made completely watertight. The stern could not be lifted clear, so that the rudder could not be repaired, but a wooden deck was built over the fantail, the ship was cleared of debris and was made habitable.

Work was pushed day and night, for it was realized that the Japanese might raid Tjilatjap at any time. When the leaks had been patched so that the submersible pumps could cope with the water the ship put to sea. This was February 15. She was scarcely seaworthy, but it was thought that she would be safer at sea than in Tjilatjap.

The story of MARBLEHEAD's return to the United States via westward passage is one of the all-time great stories of the sea. In the 48 days which followed the action the ship steamed more than 9,000 miles, touching Trincomalee, Ceylon; Durban, Port Elizabeth, and Simons-town, South Africa. Almost half this distance was made without a rudder, and the remainder of the voyage was made with the rudder controlled from the steering engine room. But USS MARBLEHEAD had completed, and with credit, her stint in the Java Sea Campaign.

Some of her men were left behind, among them Commander Goggins, as well as some of the men from the HOUSTON. These were wounded so badly that they had to have medical care ashore, and at once. After the evacuation and fall of Java these men might have been left, helpless, to become prisoners of the Japanese. But that would have been reckoning without the devotion to duty and the tight-lipped determination of a single man—a lieutenant commander in the Navy Medical Corps Reserve, a middle-aged chain-smoking doctor from Arkansas with the somewhat resounding name of Corydon McAlmont Wassell.

The HOUSTON, although her after turret was demolished, was otherwise seaworthy and was still the most powerful ship available in the area. It was hoped that she could be sent home for repairs when the PHOENIX arrived, but meanwhile she was sent to escort troops from Darwin to Koepang, Timor, to aid in defending the airfield there. This field was of some importance not only because it partially covered the approach to Darwin, but because it could be used as a stop for the Army's fighter plane ferry. The Army had been flying P-40s from Darwin to Java via Timor, but the flight was too near the limit of their range. So many were lost that General Brereton finally had to halt the use of this route. It was this that made the LANGLEY's ferrying voyage important, and it was this voyage that was to cost the LANGLEY her life.

At Tjilatjap the HOUSTON buried her dead, sixty of them. The bomb that had destroyed the turret had been a big one, and the blast had twisted and cracked two steel beams—longitudinals—supporting the main deck.

Captain Albert H. Rooks, USN, commandeered some railroad rails and had his own mechanics use them to patch up the weakened girders.

"She's still quite a ship and doesn't have to get out of the campaign," Captain Rooks earnestly reported to ABDAFLOAT. "As against a Japanese heavy cruiser the disabled turret puts one strike against me before I come to bat, but she is still quite a fighting ship."

ABDAFLOAT was forced to agree, and so Captain Rooks took the HOUSTON out again to the war.

4

Instead of returning to Soerabaja, as was expected, Admiral Doorman took the Dutch contingent into Batavia; and, perhaps because of communications failures, Admiral Hart had no word of their whereabouts for nearly a day. During this time an enemy convoy was milling south of the Celebes and presenting a too inviting target to be regarded without suspicion. Admiral Hart ordered the ships returned to Tjilatjap and invited Admiral Doorman into a conference.

During the conference it was learned that a Japanese expedition was coming from the Molucca Sea around the southeast corner of Celebes near Bouton Island. Its destination was not clear, but it might have been heading for southeast Borneo, or even eastern Java. If the enemy attempted either of these moves a night attack would become necessary, and Admiral Doorman was ordered to make plans and get his fleet in readiness. But the enemy expedition moved only around the south of Celebes to take Macassar on the southwest coast, and there was no opportunity to strike.

This move now presented Allied forces with a dilemma. The Japanese were closing in on Java from both sides and there was scarcely the strength to stop either arm of the envelopment. In Burma the Japs took Martaban on the 11th, thus turning the flank of the Salween line and forcing the British to withdraw to the Bilin River, which offered a much less favorable line of defense. The Japanese were already on Singapore Island, and there were indications that they would not wait for its fall before moving on Sumatra or attacking Java from the northwest. On February 5 a large force was sighted in the Anambas Islands northeast of Singapore, and on the 7th a convoy was sighted near Banka Island, east of southern Sumatra.

While this danger appeared in the west, the situation on the east was no less threatening. The Japanese now controlled southern Celebes.

They were known to have built up an important base at Kendari and to have considerable air power based there. From that region they could attack Bali, Madoera, or eastern Java directly.

In which direction should the Allied striking force be turned? Where was the enemy likely to move first? Bad weather and ever-increasing aerial opposition interfered with reconnaissance at this critical juncture and so delayed this important decision. Meanwhile the Japanese were making good use of their positions, bombing Port Moresby, Koepang, and other cities. Soerabaja was bombed repeatedly, and Batavia received its initiation in aerial bombing on the 9th.

Then the Japanese surged forward almost simultaneously in the east and the west. On the 11th they converged on Bandjermasin, chief city of southeast Borneo; and two days later captured it. On the 14th, the day before Singapore surrendered, but when its fate was already sealed, they opened their attack on Palembang in southeast Sumatra. This region was a valuable prize indeed, as it produced more than half the oil of the Indies. The Dutch repulsed the first attack by paratroops, but the following day, while Singapore was falling in the north, the Japanese brought in their infantry, probably from the convoy which had been waiting in the Anambas Islands. The Dutch were overwhelmed and could only attempt ineffectually to fire their wells and tanks before the area passed to the enemy.

At the same time it was learned that another enemy convoy was on the move from Balikpapan.

As soon as the enemy's intention became clear, Admiral Doorman's little striking force had jumped off on February 13 to meet the threat to Palembang.

Although he did not have the American cruisers, Admiral Doorman's JAVA, DE RUYTER and the smaller TROMP had now been reinforced by the Australian light cruiser HOBART and the British heavy cruiser EXETER, one of the three warcraft which, although outgunned, stood to battle and forced the heavier German pocket battleship GRAF SPEE ignominiously to take her own life off Montevideo. There were six American and several British in addition to the three Dutch destroyers. As a result, Admiral Doorman was given a directive in which he was told that he should "consider the advisability of an attack by day as well as by night in view of the considerably increased power of his force."

Misfortune still dogged Doorman. On the way west the Dutch destroyer VAN GHENT ran hard aground and was lost. The BANCKERT was left behind to take off her people. The rest of the force reached the area northeast of Banka Island on the night of February 13-14, to find the Japanese already in Banka Strait in force and advancing up the river. On the 14th the Allied ships were bombed repeatedly. They escaped serious damage, although HOBART was straddled and two American destroyers, BARKER and BULMER, were shaken up and battered about by near misses.

Admiral Doorman concluded that to attempt to rush the strait would be a form of suicide, particularly with the Japanese in complete control of the skies. Bright moonlight precluded any surprise by night, and there seemed to be no point in remaining to be bombed again by day.

Once again Japanese sea-air power had called a heartbreaking turn. Once again, a project begun with high hope for accomplishment had suffered a sea-air change to despair.

5

On February 14, 1942, Admiral Thomas C. Hart, USN, gave up operational command of Allied naval forces in the Southwest Pacific and shortly returned to the United States, making part of the trip westward toward India aboard the old British cruiser DURHAM, badly in need of repairs. Statements widely circulated at the time declared that Admiral Hart was in ill-health, although no such official Navy Department statement was made, and the admiral's appearance belied them. He was acting on orders, deeply and regretfully aware that they required him to leave officers and men in Java, besides the 3,000 Navy and Marine personnel on Bataan and Corregidor.

Actually, the beginning of the end in Javanese waters was already in sight, although there were to be two weeks more of bitter-end battle against insurmountable odds, of weariness, of heartbreak—and of defeat.

Just ten days after Admiral Hart's departure ABDACOM, General Sir Archibald Percival Wavell, boarded an outward-bound British motor sloop, convoyed by an American destroyer, to set up new quarters in British India. In departing, General Wavell said: "I have received orders that in view of recent developments, command of the Allied forces in Java should be handed over to Dutch Commanders who, in fact, have actually been exercising it under my direction for some time. I hand over the command to them with confidence, knowing by experience their capabilities and skill in handling the forces at their disposal, and their unswerving resolution to do everything possible in the defense of Java."

Admiral Hart made no public statement at all, then or later. To friends of his own age and rank, back in the United States, he said: "I did the best I could with what I had, and under the conditions present. I was defeated. That's all there was to it."

The Naval Academy class of 1897 was perhaps one of the outstanding classes in the Academy's history. Of the 47 midshipmen who graduated that year several are responsible for achievements which properly are little known outside the naval service which they benefited. Others won reputations of wider note. One of these latter, Admiral William D. Leahy, was to become chief of staff to the President of the United States during the greatest of all wars. Another was Admiral Arthur J. Hepburn, who in 1938 headed a special board which strongly recommended strengthening of America's Pacific outposts—recommendations which, if they had been followed by the American people, might have been a strong argument against the Pacific Ocean ever becoming the setting for a great war. Still another was Admiral Harry E. Yarnell, Hart's predecessor as Commander in Chief Asiatic Fleet, and long a clear analyst—and forecaster—of the things that were to come in Oriental waters.[1]

And still another was Thomas C. Hart.

During a period when he had served as superintendent of the Naval Academy, Admiral Hart had often stressed to the young midshipmen a U.S. Navy axiom which says that the ability to command can be truly achieved only as a concomitant of the ability to carry out orders.

Some two weeks after the Netherlands East Indies Campaign had reached its bitter end in the Battle of the Java Sea, a fitting epitaph for this engagement, and all the other actions in that theater, was provided by a British naval leader, Admiral Sir William James, RN:

[1] In a letter dated October 19, 1941, seven weeks before Pearl Harbor, Admiral Yarnell wrote to one of the authors of this work, in reply to a telegram concerning a broadcast in which he strongly warned of Japanese imperialistic aims:
"My dear Kelley:
"Many thanks for your telegram, which has just arrived. Am glad you liked the broadcast. I enjoyed making it as I was able to say a few things I have wanted to get out of my system for some time.
"I hope we have strengthened our forces in the Far East. We have had 4½ years in which to do it . . .
"Hope all is going well with you in OPR . . ." etc.

"It was the most tremendous battle ever to take place against great odds. Always there were too few ships and too few of everything.

"The Dutch, British and American sailors fought to the last gun against impossible odds.

"Once we had to choose between guns and butter—we chose butter, but our enemies chose guns. Today we have to choose between ships and the shipwreck of everything we love."

The American people finally did choose ships, and all the other arms and armor in the overwhelming amounts necessary to the task in hand. But the choice had been made late, as no one knew better than Thomas C. Hart.

Chapter Ten

VICE-ADMIRAL CONRAD EMIL LAMBERT HELFRICH, Royal Netherlands Navy, was named by General Sir Archibald Percival Wavell as the new ABDAFLOAT. On the score of experience in the waters of the locality Admiral Helfrich was admirably suited for the post. After completing his training in 1907 at the naval school at Den Helder, in the Netherlands, he had served some twenty years in East Indies waters, and for more than a year had been CZM, commander in chief, of all Dutch naval forces in that area. He was known as a master of submarine strategy.

Rear Admiral Arthur F. E. Palliser, Royal Navy, continued to serve as ABDAFLOAT's chief of staff, as he had under Admiral Hart. Consequently, this left the United States with only one representative, Lieutenant General George H. Brett, USA, on the Allied High Command, with the ratio of this command now adding up to six British, two Dutch, and one American. The U.S. Navy was not represented on the High Command, although Admiral Glassford continued to serve as Commander U.S. Naval Forces Southwest Pacific, a post which he also had held under Admiral Hart.

The situation confronting the new ABDAFLOAT on February 14, 1942, was not only of the gravest character—there was, in addition, little likelihood that it would get better.

In rough outline the situation was this: The Japanese had leapfrogged Singapore to land on Sumatra, the island adjoining Java to the north and westward, and, with additional heavy Japanese forces on Malaya itself, Singapore was within a day of capitulation. To the northward Japanese forces were strongly entrenched on Borneo and the Celebes, and to the north and eastward the Japanese held Ambon and the Moluccas. The enemy forces on Sumatra could, and soon would, cross the Sunda Strait to invade Java from the west. The enemy forces to the north and east could, and soon would, pinch off the eastern end of Java and the other islands, including Bali, in the Sunda Chain extending eastward toward Australia.

Once these two movements were accomplished by the enemy the Allied ships would be trapped in the Java Sea; and all of Java—its 45,000,000 inhabitants made it the most densely populated land mass in the world—would be at the mercy of the invader.

The most pressing problem to confront ABDAFLOAT on February 14, then, was a move to prevent the remaining ships from being bottled up in the Java Sea, where they would be easy prey for the enemy's virtually unopposed air forces and hopelessly superior surface power. Soerabaja was being bombed daily, so there was no longer a question of using this port for any other than stealthy night visits by submarines, and as an occasional base for the ubiquitous PBYs. Since all the northern coastline of Java was equally vulnerable to Japanese land-based air power, it was decided to set up a base at Tjilatjap, on the south coast, although Admiral Glassford, among others, realized that this base itself could not long remain secure from Japanese attack.

Accordingly, much thought was given to new bases in Australia—out of range from any but Japanese carrier-based aircraft at the time, but not too far away for Allied surface ships to strike at the Japanese. Port Darwin had already been ruled out, although it was the nearest of all Australian ports. Little was known of the western coast of Australia. Adequate charts were not available except, just possibly, to those who had been receiving voluminous reports over past years from large and seemingly indolent fleets of Japanese "fishermen." The final decision was to base the American ships at Exmouth Gulf, midway down Australia's west coast and about 800 miles south of Bali.

Therefore the HOLLAND, on the 19th, was sent to Exmouth with two submarines which needed overhaul. The BLACK HAWK left the following day, accompanied by the destroyers BARKER and BULMER, which had been badly shaken up by the bombing near Banka Island. The tanker PECOS was held till the 25th in an effort to remove some of the oil from Tjilatjap, but the Dutch proprietors would not bring themselves to believe that Java could be lost and were unwilling to turn over petroleum from either Tjilatjap or Soerabaja until too late. To meet the shortage one Navy tanker was sent to Persia for oil, another to India, and still another was loaded in Australia and waited at Fremantle for orders.

But even if Port Darwin's lack of facilities had not ruled it out as a fleet base, it would have been no use to American vessels in the Southwest Pacific. The Japanese saw to this—and at once.

2

Shortly after midnight on the 15th a fast troop convoy left Port Darwin to reinforce the Allied garrison at Koepang, Timor, and to establish a base there. Aboard MAUNA LOA and MEIGS were Australian troops, while TULAGI and PORTMAR carried a U.S. infantry regiment. Admiral Glassford had provided HOUSTON and PEARY as escorts.

At about noon on the 15th lookouts on HOUSTON and PEARY sighted two four-engined seaplanes far in the distance, Japanese Kawanishi 97s. Both ships unlimbered their guns—HOUSTON had just put additional antiaircraft armament aboard—and the Japs were forced to stay high and at a distance. After an hour of shadowing the convoy the planes left, and the ships continued on their way.

The next day, however, was a different story. At 1113 a first attack wave of 27 Japanese heavy bombers came over, flying in formations of nine planes, and concentrating their attention on the HOUSTON. As the planes came over each dropped a single bomb. The HOUSTON was successful in evading these bombs, but the Japanese planes were equally successful in evading HOUSTON's guns.

A second wave of 44 planes, possibly from a Japanese aircraft carrier, then flew in from a new quarter and of these HOUSTON shot down seven for certain, and probably damaged others. The convoy had broken up, with every ship maneuvering at high speed and scattered over as large a target area as possible, but the MAUNA LOA received a glancing blow which sprang some of her seams and the other three transports developed leaks from near misses. All four were well-sprayed with shrapnel which left holes in decks and side platings. The number of bombs dropped may be gauged by the fact that PORTMAR reported that 23 bombs had landed within 200 feet, despite the fact that MEIGS had put down a smoke screen in an effort to protect her.

Though the enemy's attack had failed, the position of the convoy was obviously precarious. The presence of a Japanese carrier was likely, and Japanese warships were rumored to be lying in wait near Timor. Directions were received to return again to Darwin, and by the morning of the 18th the convoy had reached the port.

Limited facilities caused the PORTMAR and TULAGI to anchor in the harbor, while the MEIGS and MAUNA LOA proceeded to the dock so that, the troops might disembark. The HOUSTON and PEARY refueled at once and by the evening of the 18th had headed to the west. They had been ordered to join Admiral Doorman's striking force, which was preparing to defend Bali from invasion. A prolonged attack on an enemy submarine outside Darwin delayed the PEARY, however, and she was directed to return to port for refueling while the HOUSTON proceeded independently. This long fight with the enemy submarine was just another link in the PEARY's ill luck. As it turned out, it was the last link in the chain, for the PEARY was held in port another day by her fueling operations.

And on that day, February 19, the airport, warehouses, docks, and virtually every ship in Darwin Harbor were destroyed by severe air attack. A total of about 72 high-level bombers and 18 dive bombers were used. The city itself was strafed and set aflame, and so severe was the destruction that the evacuation of the entire area was ordered by nightfall.

At 0955 there appeared from the south 18 heavy bombers flying in horizontal rows of 4, with 2 planes bringing up the rear. Their size indicated that they were based on carriers. No warning of their approach was given, presumably because the attack came from an unexpected quarter. The docks were the first targets. By this time the MEIGS and MAUNA LOA had unloaded their troops and were anchored in the harbor, with equipment and ammunition still aboard. The British ships ZEALANDIA and NEPTUNA were at the dock, however, discharging ammunition; both vessels were hit. Shattering explosions shook the area as the NEPTUNA blew up and turned on her side. Hits scored on a Norwegian tanker, the BENJAMIN FRANKLIN, and another vessel caused loud and extensive detonations. Hits on the docks themselves started fires and scattered debris over a wide area. Though all the bombing was done at a high level it was accurate. Meeting practically no resistance, the planes could afford to take their time; while the dive bombers were attacking, the big bombers circled around without dropping bombs, waiting until their targets had been cleared.

The Darwin airport was next subjected to a severe bombing by a wave of high-level bombers. Two—perhaps four—American planes were able to take off and a P-40 shot down a dive bomber before succumbing to the hopeless odds. A survivor from the MAUNA LOA described the destruction at the airport as "like the battlefields of France; hangars, planes, and everything blown to bits, burnt holes all over the field." For over 24 hours fires burned from gas tanks and ammunition dumps.

Immediately following the first wave of high-level bombers came the dive bombers, painted a dull green in contrast to the bigger planes which were reported as "shining like silver, with a red sun and a burst of red and gold stripes." The single-engined dive bombers swung in on their individual targets at low angles of not more than 50 degrees. By this time many vessels were heading for the harbor entrance, some dragging anchor in their haste to escape. The BRITISH MOTORIST, a tanker which had swung away from the dock during the first attack, had now managed to back into the harbor, but she got no farther. The Japanese planes first concentrated on the transports and naval vessels, then leisurely attacked each merchantman in turn. For more than two hours harbor shipping and shore facilities endured almost continuous attacks, with the enemy wheeling and swooping in formations so deliberate and methodical as to remind observers of a target exercise.

The destroyer PEARY was hit five times by Japanese dive bombers. While trying to put a smoke screen around the Australian hospital ship MANUNDA, she was blasted on the fantail, removing the depth charge racks, propeller guards, and flooding the steering engine room. An incendiary bomb landed near the galley, while another went through the fireroom without exploding. The fourth bomb set off the forward ammunition magazines, while the last, an incendiary, exploded in the after engine room. Though the ship was damaged severely, her machine guns continued to blaze until the last enemy plane had departed. She sank stern first at about 1300, with a loss of all but 52 men of her crew of more than 100. One officer survived. The MANUNDA, which the PEARY had been protecting, also was hit by a bomb which failed to explode, and was strafed several times.

Of the four transports, MEIGS and MAUNA LOA were sunk, PORTMAR was beached, and TULAGI was badly damaged. The latter two vessels still had some troops aboard, and casualties were fortunately few—but there would be no reinforcements for Koepang, Timor.

The ADMIRAL HALSTEAD, an American cargo vessel loaded with 14,000 drums of high-test gasoline, had her plates sprung by near hits and was heavily strafed. In one of those inexplicable accidents of war, she did not catch fire and blow up. Another merchantman, the DON ISIDRO, was set afire and so badly burned that she was beached and abandoned near Melville Island. One of the ships which heard DON ISIDRO'S distress calls was FLORENCE D, a small interisland steamer with an Indonesian skipper. Before FLORENCE D had a chance to set out to assist DON ISIDRO, a flight of 27 Japanese dive bombers came over and she herself was placed under attack and sent to the bottom. This was a disaster out of proportion to the size of the vessel, as FLORENCE D was under charter at an exceptional price to run the Japanese blockade with munitions for the besieged defenders of the Philippines.

The attacking Japanese planes probably received a surprise, however, when they leisurely winged their way over the WILLIAM D. PRESTON, an old four-stacker destroyer which had been converted as a tender for the PBYs. As the raid began, the skipper of PRESTON, Lieutenant Commander Etheridge Grant, USN, was headed across the harbor toward his ship on a small boat. A Japanese bomb hit a munitions ship in the harbor and the resulting blast sent Grant's boat whirling in mid-air, and dropped it wrong side up. Grant managed to swim to a buoy and hang on.

As he watched his ship he probably felt a surge of pride. The PRESTON and PEARY had started down the harbor together. Now the PEARY had gone under, and the PRESTON was alone. And she was throwing up a hail of antiaircraft missiles far more intense than any ship of her class was supposed to fire. This might have puzzled the Japanese, but it was clear to Lieutenant Commander Grant, as he watched from his buoy.

In addition to the usual armament for a ship of her class the PRESTON had carefully set up on her afterdeck the guns which had been salvaged from the PBYs of Patwing Ten as, one by one, their life spans had reached their end under Japanese attack. The consequence was that the Japs, when they came in low over the ship for the kill, got considerably more than they had bargained for. They found themselves in a barrage which had been augmented by ten 50-caliber and seven 30-caliber machine guns, all fired by men with the deadly and intense bitterness that is motivated by personal grudge.

There was no denying, though, that the Japanese raid on Port Darwin had accomplished the Japanese purpose, completely. When the last enemy plane had left, the city was a disordered scene of smoke, fire, and confusion. By nightfall the roads leading outward were jammed with refugees in chaotic streams reminiscent of the evacuation of Paris in 1940—householders with families and belongings loaded into automobiles, wagons, and handcarts, others afoot with scant possessions on their backs, but all heading wearily toward a safety which no longer existed in their homes.

Port Darwin obviously would see no extensive use as a naval base for some time to come.

3

On the day the HOUSTON set out with her troop convoy on the ill-fated attempt to reinforce Timor, February 15, the Japanese turned their attention to Bali. This move had long been feared and expected.

At first, as was their custom, the Japanese began a softening-up process by air bombardment of Bali's strategic areas. Admiral Doorman ordered HOUSTON to return at once—which was the reason for the American cruiser's hasty and providential departure from Darwin in time to miss the attack on that port—but the ship could not reach Javanese waters in time for Doorman's purpose. This purpose was the Battle of Badoeng Strait, a narrow water between Bali and Lombok islands. (The engagement is popularly known as the Battle of Lombok Strait, and properly, since the Badoeng passage in the Lombok area is listed on few charts available to the average American.) Admiral Doorman was in something of a hurry, for the simple reason that he was being spurred on by the enemy: on the 17th the Japanese made an invasion leap that began in the lower Celebes and ended at dawn of the 18th on the shores of Bali itself.

The significance of this landing was very clear. The Japanese now controlled the airfield on the southeast coast of Bali. Consolidation of this position and use of its aviation facilities meant that the enemy could strike at Java at will, and that Tjilatjap and other southern Java ports might have to be abandoned. Admiral Doorman therefore decided on a night raid against the sea force used by the Japanese in their landing, the attack to be launched on the night of the 19th. Reconnaissance revealed that at least two cruisers and three transports were anchored in Badoeng Strait southeast of Bali—actual contact with this force was to reveal that it was far more powerful.

Admiral Doorman planned the attack in three waves. The Dutch cruisers DE RUYTER and JAVA were to come from Tjilatjap, accompanied by the Dutch PIET HEIN, a modern destroyer, and the two old American

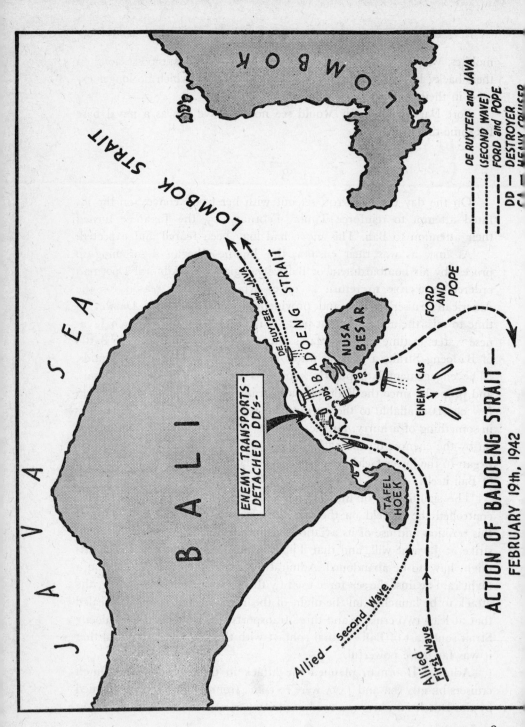

ACTION OF BADOENG STRAIT—
FEBRUARY 19th, 1942

DE RUYTER and JAVA
(SECOND WAVE)
FORD and POPE
DD — DESTROYER
CA — HEAVY CRUISER

LOMBOK

LOMBOK STRAIT

DE RUYTER and JAVA

BADOENG STRAIT

JAVA SEA

NUSA BESAR

DDS

ENEMY TRANSPORTS —
DETACHED DD's —

FORD AND POPE

ENEMY CAs

DDS

TAFEL HOEK

Allied — Second Wave

Allied
First Wave

FIGURE 8

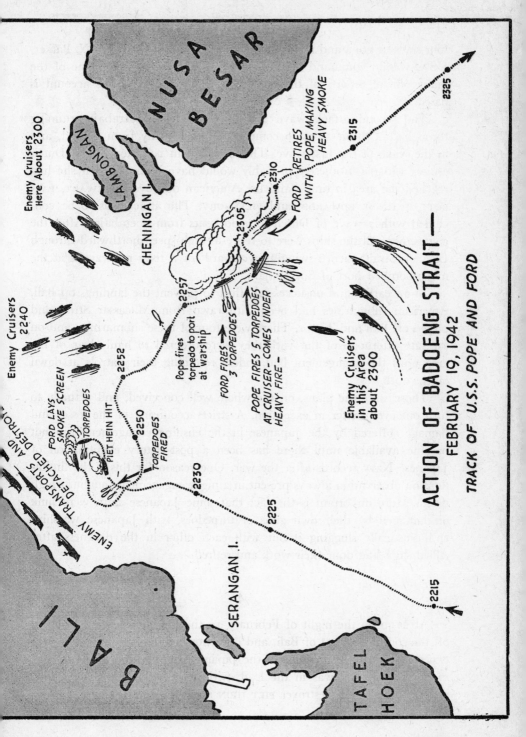

ACTION OF BADOENG STRAIT—
FEBRUARY 19, 1942
TRACK OF U.S.S. POPE AND FORD

NUSA BESAR

LEMBONGAN I.

CHENINGAN I.

Enemy Cruisers
Here About 2300

Enemy Cruisers
2240

FORD RETIRES
WITH POPE, MAKING
HEAVY SMOKE

2325

2315

2310

2305

2257

Pope fires torpedo to port
at warship

FORD FIRES
3 TORPEDOES

POPE FIRES 5 TORPEDOES
AT CRUISER-COMES UNDER
HEAVY FIRE—

Enemy Cruisers
in this Area
about 2300

2252

2250

PIET HEIN HIT

FORD LAYS
SMOKE SCREEN

TORPEDOES

TORPEDOES
FIRED

ENEMY TRANSPORTS AND DESTROYER

ENEMY TRANSPORTS AND DESTROYER DETACHED

2230

2225

SERANGAN I.

BALI

2215

TAFEL
HOEK

FIGURE 9

four-stackers POPE and FORD. Lieutenant Commander Edward N. Parker, USN, was in command of the latter two vessels, and his is one of the many official reports of the action on which the following account is based.

The second attack wave was to come from Soerabaja, running through Bali Strait so as to come up on the enemy from behind, and in the wake of the first wave. This detachment consisted of the Dutch cruiser TROMP—HOUSTON probably would have been added if she had reached the area in time—and the American destroyers STEWART, PARROTT, JOHN D. EDWARDS, and PILLSBURY. The attack was to be concluded with a wave of Dutch torpedo boats from Soerabaja. After the engagement all the ships were to retire at high speed northward through Lombok Strait, thence swinging westward for a risky rendezvous at the much-bombed port of Soerabaja.

In an earlier and unsuccessful effort to prevent the landings on Bali, American submarines had been withdrawn from Macassar Strait and posted off Bali and Timor. There were four of these submarines, and on the late afternoon of the 19th they were ordered to haul clear of the area until the engagement had ended, resuming their patrols at dawn on the 20th.

Those were the plans, on the whole well conceived, and actually to turn out even better in execution. A strict accounting of the losses and damage suffered by the Japanese in the ensuing engagement will not become available until there has been a post-victory examination of Japanese Navy records after the war. One reason for this is the limitations on observation always present in a night engagement fought at high speed. More important is the fact that some Japanese ships were sunk or damaged by their own guns or torpedoes, with Japanese warships enthusiastically slugging it out with each other in the darkness after Allied ships had done their work and retired.

4

At 2130 on the night of February 19 the first attack wave stood in off the southeast coast of Bali, and on a northeasterly heading that was expected to bring it in range of the Japanese ships within an hour. The cruiser DE RUYTER was in the lead, with JAVA following. Then came, in order, the Dutch destroyer PIET HEIN and the American four-stackers FORD and POPE.

The one flaw in the approach to action could be directly attributed to the skill of the Japanese naval command in the art of amphibious warfare, and Japanese skill in the use of weather and meteorological conditions as a weapon. There had been a brand-fresh moon on February 15, with luminescence at a minimum two nights later when the enemy began his sweep down from the Celebes. In addition, the Japanese had been fortunate enough to travel under a moderate weather front which had completely blotted out observation. Now, on the 19th, the moon was still only four days old, but although at 2130 it had slanted low into the westering sky, it now shone like a fine-ground scimitar, adding its light to that of a million stars reflected brightly in the water from the Balinese heavens. "We knew the Japs would hug the shadows of the shore," said an officer on FORD. "Out where we were, in all that light, we felt awfully naked—as when you dream that you suddenly find yourself out in a street without any clothes on. As we got closer we all tried to make ourselves sort of small."

Actually, the Dutch cruisers in the lead spotted the enemy before the Allied forces were themselves discovered. The DE RUYTER and JAVA had the arcs struck on their searchlights, but with shutters closed, when they sighted the shadowy loom of enemy ships to port and ahead. As the lights of the Dutch cruisers stabbed the darkness the JAVA opened fire. The DE RUYTER apparently did not fire a shot, presumably because her guns had been trained out to starboard while JAVA trained to port. The Japanese returned the fire at once, but they were fighting under a handicap. Their ships were disposed in such a manner as to bear on an opponent approaching from the north through Lombok Strait. So, although they had expected an attack, they had not been smart enough to guess the direction from which the attack would come. In the first return fire by the Japanese, however, JAVA took a hit on her stern, but with only slight damage; she continued to sweep forward at top speed.

The destroyers bringing up the rear now steamed head-on into a hornets' nest that had been very much stirred up. As the three little ships came within target range, PIET HEIN suddenly veered sharply to starboard and began to make black and white smoke. The FORD and POPE naturally turned to follow; and as they did so they saw that a large enemy vessel was now silhouetted at about 3,000 yards off the port beam, while what appeared to be an enemy cruiser was off the port bow. In turning to keep from running head-on into one enemy the Dutch destroyer in the lead now was bearing almost directly toward another.

The PIET HEIN opened with her guns, instead of with torpedoes, and this probably was a grave mistake. The FORD fired three torpedoes, and a blinding flash sent up a sulphurous doughnut of flame from the side of the enemy cruiser, believed to have been of the KATORI class. The cruiser had already opened fire, however, and now PIET HEIN herself was enveloped in flames and began to settle in the water. The POPE also had fired two torpedoes at the enemy cruiser, and the hit may have been scored by either of the two American destroyers.

Just about the time PIET HEIN was fatally struck, an enemy shell whistled through FORD's rigging, cutting the afterfalls of the ship's motor whaleboat. The boat thrashed about with the motion of the ship, and the FORD's men cut the forward falls and allowed the boat to drop over the side. The act of cutting away the boat, and another action to be observed later, provided the properties for what was to be another of those lucky accidents of war—particularly lucky for some thirty-odd survivors of the ill-fated PIET HEIN. That adventure will be related in its place.

With the Dutch destroyer gone, POPE and FORD now fired two torpedoes each at the enemy ship, believed to be a transport, on their port beam, without observing hits. Gunfire from port caused FORD to make smoke and head toward Bali, with POPE nipping at her heels, but not in too much of a hurry to fire in passing a torpedo that blasted an enemy destroyer.

At about 2300 an enemy searchlight suddenly lit up FORD and she immediately came under fire from a heavy cruiser 2,500 yards to starboard. The little destroyer was being smothered by a pattern of main and secondary battery near misses which literally picked her up and danced her from crest to crest across the waves. (No person aboard ship later was able to explain why he was still alive, or why at least one of his shipmates had not been seriously injured.) Both FORD and POPE replied to this attack by making a sharp right turn, and by illuminating their own battle lights. The FORD launched three of her torpedoes, and POPE fired five, at the same time opening up with her guns. In the melee it was impossible to tell whether the enemy cruiser had been hit; however, the enemy ceased fire and turned out his lights, so FORD and POPE did likewise and began to get out of there, retiring at high speed southeastward, and thence swinging back along the south coast of Java to Tjilatjap.

It was true that FORD and POPE had been ordered to retire through Lombok Strait to Soerabaja, but the two frail destroyers were practically without torpedoes (after the engagement, this sad truth applied also to most of the other Allied ships in the Java area) and they felt that they would not be able to fight their way through the heavy concentration of Japanese war vessels blocking the northward passage.

But as FORD and POPE looked backward over their shoulders, and along their own boiling wakes, they saw that the enemy was now testing out his vaunted naval superiority—on himself. Red gunflashes winked merrily in the distance as explosions reverberated across the night air. Several enemy destroyers in column were illuminated and two were seen to burst into flame as the retiring American spectators looked on, not without some enthusiasm. At least two enemy destroyers were believed sunk and another severely damaged in this interesting Japanese gun and torpedo exercise.[1]

With FORD and POPE headed for home, the second attack wave now began its run. The strategy for this attack was for the American destroyers STEWART, PARROTT, JOHN D. EDWARDS, and PILLSBURY to make a fast pass with torpedoes, with the Dutch cruiser TROMP to play in the backfield five miles astern, finishing off with her guns anything the torpedoes damaged or disabled. The ships of the second wave saw the searchlights and gunfire of the first wave, but their efforts to reach any of those ships by radio proved fruitless. Consequently, the four destroyers and the TROMP went in without exact knowledge of the Japanese dispositions; taking a range of such distance reduced the effectiveness of the destroyers' torpedoes.

At 0134—now February 20—STEWART in the lead sighted two enemy ships signaling off the port bow—possibly trying to explain why they had been firing on each other. The enemy vessels were now off Nusa Besar, on the Lombok side of the channel, hugging the shadows of the shore. The Allied ships, on the other hand, were brilliantly silhouetted in the clear starlight. Taking evasive action, and also to close the range, STEWART swung hard to starboard, with the other ships following, and

---

[1] Lest the account of this action give the impression that the Japanese have a monopoly on mistakes in night firing it should be pointed out that no navy participating in this war has been free from an occasional "improper identification of target." An American naval officer who participated in the later Solomons actions said, "In some of those night free-for-alls with the throttle tied down you first tried to hit your target; and then, after you hit, you prayed to God that you hadn't hurt a friend."

with STEWART and PARROTT simultaneously firing portside salvos of six torpedoes each. No hits were observed and the ships were ordered to hold their fire.

A few minutes later an enemy searchlight revealed a Japanese destroyer off the port quarter, and the American destroyers let go with both torpedoes and guns. A Japanese cruiser some 4,000 yards off the port bow, and closer to the Nusa Besar shore, now illuminated the STEWART, and the American column was soon heavily engaged. Fire from Japanese 8-inch batteries immediately bracketed the STEWART, which was firing back with everything she had, and at the same time attempting to throw off the enemy's aim by radical maneuvers. The STEWART, it turned out, was not quite so nimble as the little men in the turrets and fire control of the Japanese cruiser. An 8-inch shell caught STEWART square on, and the thin skin of the destroyer barely slowed the shell's progress as it whistled through the ship from side to side without exploding. If the Japanese had been using bombardment ammunition, instead of armor-piercing, STEWART might have met her end right there. Instead, she was given a few days' grace.

Meanwhile, the TROMP astern had now picked a Jap cruiser for herself, and the going between the two ships became heavy. This did not last long, however. An explosion suddenly flared up on the Japanese ship, and the cruiser simply disappeared in the resulting blast and smoke.

As the four destroyers continued northward they encountered one or more destroyers to port near Bali and three unidentified vessels to starboard. This was at about 0212. The PILLSBURY's guns scored four direct hits on the vessel to port, which she believes she sank. The three vessels to starboard were at a range of between 5,000 and 6,000 yards. The American destroyers swerved to take them under fire: STEWART released five torpedoes, PARROTT six, and J. D. EDWARDS "several." The answer to these salvos came with three blasts below the waterline on enemy ships, but the Japanese now had the Americans in a cross fire. The destroyers zigzagged radically and opened fire with their own guns. Two Japanese ships were seen to be burning and heavily smoking near the Nusa Besar shore, but these may have been ships previously hit by torpedoes. By this time TROMP had entered the Japanese range, and was returning the enemy's fire; but TROMP came out second best in this round, sustaining eight or ten hits and being damaged badly.

By 0225 the range was lengthening and all firing ceased, "a clear manifestation of God's grace," the captain of the PARROTT termed it, for his ship's steering control had jammed while maneuvering at 28 knots. This had caused her to swing hard toward the Bali shore. Emergency full speed astern was ordered, and this sudden maneuver threw overboard a chief petty officer. During the engagement he floated around in the warm tropic water, and luckily he reached the shore of Bali. There he joined some isolated Dutch soldiers, and together they made their way back to Java. The CPO rejoined his ship at Soerabaja.

The battle itself was over—the Dutch torpedo boats of the third wave made their scheduled run through the strait, but the results are not available. There were, however, several unhappy consequences, despite the fact that the engagement itself should clearly be scored as a success. The damage to TROMP was such that she was unable to participate in the subsequent Battle of the Java Sea, which was to begin within a week. And the TROMP ultimately was lost at Soerabaja as the Japanese flood inundated the island of Java. The American destroyer STEWART likewise went into Soerabaja for repairs, and was put into drydock. Owing to improper workmanship, the vessel rolled off her blocks and damaged both herself and the drydock. Before she could be righted for repairs Japanese naval bombers came over in great force and ended the life of STEWART forever.

The PIET HEIN also was lost, as has been noted, but there was a happier outcome for at least some of PIET HEIN's crew. It will be remembered that as PIET HEIN was sinking, the FORD was jettisoning her motor whaleboat. Before going into battle the gasoline tanks of these lifeboats are drained so as to minimize fire in case of a hit. The spare gasoline for the boats is carried in a drum on the destroyer's fantail, and this drum can be allowed to slide over the side simply by tripping a trigger.

By a freak of chance FORD's lifeboat landed right side up, and soon 13 survivors of PIET HEIN were pulling themselves aboard, meanwhile watching the battle that raged all about them. The first reaction of these survivors was to start the boat's engine and sail out of the danger area. But they soon found out that the boat's tanks had been drained.

By another freak of chance, POPE had tripped the trigger that jettisoned her gasoline, again to reduce the fire hazard aboard in case of a hit, at about the time the FORD's boat went over the side. As dawn began to lighten the sky on the morning of the 20th, the 13 PIET HEIN survivors in the dead lifeboat saw that they were drifting in company with a large metal drum. They frantically hauled it aboard, not daring to hope. One sniff of the fumes and they knew that the fates had been more than kind.

The boat's tanks were quickly filled and its engine started. Twenty other PIET HEIN survivors were floating in the area. These were picked up, and the boat made an uneventful run back to Java—carrying 33 men who, if they lived through the Java Campaign, probably never again would benefit from such a chain of fortunate circumstance.

5

The raid in Badoeng Strait had been successful from the standpoint of enemy ships sunk or damaged. But this did not alter the fact that the Japanese were now firmly planted in Bali as well as in Sumatra, with Java between like an egg in the jaws of a vise. It was generally believed in informed quarters that General Wavell had become convinced of the futility of further defense of Java, particularly in view of the virtual exhaustion of Allied fighter planes. On the 23rd he received orders from London to leave Java and set up his headquarters elsewhere at his discretion. This he proceeded to do, departing secretly with his staff on the 25th aboard the British sloop KEDAH, escorted for part of the way by the American destroyer PILLSBURY. General Wavell declared that he was confident of the ability and the determination of the Dutch in continuing to resist the Japanese, and to help in this resistance several thousand British Empire troops were left on the island. Dutch officers took over the defense of Java, with the co-ordinating command resting with Governor General Hubertus Van Mook.

The subsidiary command also threatened to collapse. It had been evident that the United States Army air force command would not remain longer than the British, and actually Major General Brereton had left three days ahead of General Wavell. It appeared too that the British Admiral Palliser intended to make his departure in General Wavell's party, but on the 24th he received orders from London to remain in Java as commander of the British naval forces. He was to withdraw these forces when, in his judgment, further resistance would be futile, and he was to use his influence to persuade the Dutch to withdraw their remaining naval forces in time to preserve them for future use. Palliser was retained as chief of staff by Admiral Helfrich.

Admiral Glassford received orders from Commander in Chief United

States Fleet to report for duty to Admiral Helfrich. This he did, and the latter expressed warmest gratitude to the Navy for "ever loyal" assistance.

But the American-British-Dutch-Australian Supreme Command had ceased to exist in Javanese waters, although the fighting ships and the fighting officers and men of this command were to remain for the bitter end.

Chapter Eleven

IN the early afternoon of February 27 the sleepy South Java town of Tjilatjap, the only deep-water port on Java's south-central coast, was foregoing its postprandial nap because of two items of unusual interest. Of the approximately 30,000 population, many of the thousand or less Europeans had skipped a dozen or so of the more than thirty courses often included in the incredible Indonesian meal which the Dutch call *rijsttafel,* a Gargantuan repast whose many sweets and sours and savories are dished up by a relay of native servitors.

The first item of interest was that the Japanese were finally moving on Java itself, sending down a large and well-protected convoy from the north. Admiral Doorman and his remaining handful of ships had gone out to check this report at battle range.

The second item of interest was the knowledge common to all Tjilatjap's inhabitants—more than a few of whom were doubtless in the pay of Tokyo—that help was finally on the way. Not much help, to be sure, but perhaps enough to force the Japanese invaders to turn back short of the shores of Java, and to break up the landing attempt which even now was on the way. The expected help was not strong enough to impose a permanent barrier against the attackers; but perhaps time might be gained in which help could be obtained from other quarters—although no one seemed to know quite where.

The expected help was in the shape of American fighter planes being brought in from Australia by two aircraft tenders, the American LANG-LEY, with 32 P-40Es assembled and on deck, and the British SEAWITCH, with 27 of the same kind of planes crated in her hold. Pilots and maintenance personnel also were aboard the ships. And while 59 fighter planes admittedly were not much to pit against the hordes of Japanese warships and naval planes in the Java area, particularly since 27 of them still had to be assembled, these 59 represented almost four times the number of planes then available and able to fly in defense of the island!

There was a reason why the expected arrival of the American planes was a matter of such public knowledge, knowledge which in all probability was in the hands of the Japanese.

The planes originally had been intended for Ceylon, in a convoy escorted by the United States light cruiser PHOENIX. One of Admiral Helfrich's first acts as commander in chief had been to order, on February 22, that LANGLEY and SEAWITCH be detached from the convoy as soon as it left Fremantle, Australia, and the planes brought to Java at top speed. The orders effecting this detachment had required considerable correspondence. In addition, the ports of Batavia and Soerabaja on the north coast of Java were now too hazardous for the planes to be unloaded at either. Tjilatjap was the only choice—and Tjilatjap's facilities for unloading were marked by their complete absence.

Lighters had to be provided to bring the cargo from deep-water anchorage to shore. Ramps had to be built for removing the planes from the lighters. A street through Tjilatjap had to be cleared so that the planes could be transported through the town to a level space in the outskirts—a meadow that was not a proper airfield at all but was now being put in shape for such use by native workmen. All in all, the fact that the planes were on the way was anybody's knowledge.

For some reason LANGLEY was detached ahead of SEAWITCH, and so she was the first to approach Java. She was still more than 100 miles to the southward of Tjilatjap when she was met by an old Dutch minesweeper and two Catalina flying boats of the Royal Netherlands Navy. The minesweeper was too slow, however, and so the American destroyers WHIPPLE and EDSALL were sent out to be the escort. A rendezvous with the destroyers was held on the morning of the 27th.

Commander Robert McConnell, USN, skipper of the LANGLEY, would have preferred to stay out at sea for the rest of the day and wait for the SEAWITCH before making a night entry into Tjilatjap, thereby possibly staying out of range of the Japanese air patrol. But the need for the fighter aircraft which LANGLEY carried was considered too urgent by the high command. Obediently the tender and her two escorts set a course for port.

The morning was fair, with only a few clouds that marched in

widely scattered formations at extreme altitude, pushed along by a gentle
northeast wind. Visibility was perfect—for the enemy.

That was realized at 0900, when an unidentified plane was sighted on
a heading that would bring it over the three ships. The LANGLEY's captain
immediately radioed a request for fighter support, a request which
Admiral Glassford was not able to fill for the simple reason that every
airplane capable of flying was in active use elsewhere.

There was no attack on the LANGLEY. The airplane's mission was
something else, a mission made plain two hours later when nine twin-
engined bombers approached at about 15,000 feet in answer to the lone
scout's information. As the bombers approached their release point,
LANGLEY swung hard right and the bombs exploded in the sea a hundred
feet off the port bow. On the second run the Japanese came over as
before, but this time they held their bombs while studying LANGLEY's evasion tactics. And as the nine planes made their third run, they waited
until LANGLEY had begun her turn. Then they also turned, and dropped
their bombs.

Seldom has a ship been hit more severely by a single salvo. Of the
nine bombs dropped, five were direct hits and three were damaging near
misses. The LANGLEY's parked aircraft were set on fire. The ship's fire
mains were disrupted and many blazes began to rage belowdecks. Water
was pouring into the hull forward and the ship took on a list of 10 degrees; but somehow she managed to retain power for a while and was
able to steer with her engines.

As a precautionary measure orders were given to prepare to abandon
ship. The order was misunderstood, and men began to jump overboard.
Others had been blown off the deck by the explosions, and the destroyers
were busy picking men out of the water.

Fortunately, the Japanese did not make another attack. Somehow
the fires were brought under control. Blasted and burning planes were
pushed over the side and over the fantail. All this effort was of no avail
in saving the LANGLEY, but it helped to save lives by restoring the men
to disciplined action. At 1332, then, the order was given to abandon ship
and all hands went over the side in orderly fashion to be picked up by the
destroyers. Only 11 of the tender's complement were missing. The
LANGLEY was sunk by nine 4-inch shells from the WHIPPLE, and thus the
Navy's first aircraft carrier—originally a collier and now a tender—
perished in honor.

But it was not the end of horror and suffering for the officers and men of LANGLEY. As WHIPPLE and EDSALL cleared the area at high speed they received orders to make for the lee of Christmas Island where they were to turn over the tender's survivors to the Navy tanker PECOS on her way to Ceylon for fuel. The destroyers were urgently needed elsewhere.

The rendezvous with PECOS was made on the morning of February 28, but Japanese planes came over before the transfer of LANGLEY's men could begin. Tanker and destroyers made for a rain squall nearby, in the protection of which the delivery of the survivors to PECOS was begun, and completed on the following morning, March 1. Thereupon the destroyers headed back for Java; the unattended PECOS pointed for Ceylon. Six hours later the PECOS's lookout sighted a Japanese plane of a carrier-borne type. Two hours after that, at 1245, three waves of enemy aircraft appeared, winging straight and true for the oiler.

In the next three hours the tanker was hit many times, and as often damaged by near misses. "Finally a bomb exploded near the ship forward on the port side," reported Commander Elmer P. Abernethy, USN, skipper of the tanker, "and the ship slowly settled forward and finally plunged bow first into the sea, leaving the stern poised in the air for an instant before finally sinking." That was at 1548.

An order to abandon ship had been given just prior to this time, and men went overboard with anything that would float. Additional Japanese planes now relieved the first attackers, and these newcomers proceeded to strafe the men floundering in the water.

When it had become apparent that PECOS was going to sink a distress signal was sent out. The radio had been jarred off frequency by explosions, but the operator aboard WHIPPLE happened to be fiddling with his tuning, and he picked up the call. The WHIPPLE reversed course and set out on the rescue, reaching the area at 2200, just two hours before midnight. As she arrived she was trailing cargo nets and lifelines, and the exhausted survivors of LANGLEY and PECOS began to clamber aboard. The destroyer had picked up 220 of the survivors, some of them rescued for the second time, when an enemy submarine poked up its periscope in the area. The WHIPPLE had no choice: after her depth charges failed to produce evidence of a kill she had to leave the scene.

Casualties were very heavy. Of some 700 men aboard both ships, only 220 were saved.

Meanwhile SEAWITCH had fared much better, although in the last

analysis she accomplished no more. The British tender arrived at Tjilatjap without incident on the morning of the 28th, and her planes were
taken ashore, still in their crates. But this is getting ahead of events.
For on the previous afternoon and night a major engagement had been
fought in the Java Sea in an unsuccessful attempt to prevent an enemy
landing. Exactly what happened to the crated P-40s put ashore from
SEAWITCH is not known. It is probable, however, that the gallant Dutch
defenders destroyed them in their crates before the Japanese landed
and took over the day after SEAWITCH made port.

2

From the moment of taking command, Admiral Helfrich had set
about his desperate task with energy and courage. But energy and
courage were not enough.

Beginning with the Japanese landing on Bali on the 18th, the enemy
had steadily stepped up his assault flood until by the 25th it was lapping
at the top of the dikes all along the Malay Barrier. On this latter date
the Japanese reinforced their Bali garrison, new landings were made on
Sumatra, and reconnaissance showed that Japanese invasion fleets were
approaching Java from several points in the north. February 25 also was
the date on which the Japanese made a landing on the island of Bawean,
and Bawean stood just 100 miles north of Soerabaja itself. The jaws of
the vise were closing.

Admiral Helfrich's desperate task obviously could be accomplished
only by a desperate effort. This was nothing less than the attempt to
sink or scatter the enemy's convoys before they could land upon and
invade Java. The Allied striking force, under Admiral Doorman, had
been patrolling the Java Sea since the 24th in an effort to engage the
enemy. Of this force, the ships which remained afloat and the men
who remained alive were to be at battle stations almost without letup
until early on the morning of the 28th, a period of more than 60 bitter
hours—60 hours preceded by days and weeks of catnaps snatched with
one ear open for general quarters and with makeshift meals wolfed on
watch or while waiting at the guns.

As for the striking force itself, Admiral Doorman went into the
Battle of the Java Sea with, literally, what was left. It was not enough, just
as energy and courage alone were not enough. Fuel supply was now

almost nonexistent, and Admiral Helfrich gave permission for five British ships to withdraw from the area on the 27th. These were the British light cruisers DRAGON and DANAE, the Australian HOBART, and the British destroyers TENEDOS and SCOUT. Unless their presence could have turned the scale of battle, which is doubtful, it is perhaps fortunate that they were not present to be caught in the final holocaust.

Of the original thirteen American destroyers only five were afloat or in fighting trim, and one of these had to fall out for repairs before the final battle began. As previously noted, the PEARY and STEWART had been sunk. The BARKER and BULMER had been badly shaken up in the bombing off Banka Island, and were en route to Australia with the tender BLACK HAWK. After the Bali raid, it had been necessary to withdraw PILLSBURY and PARROTT because of urgent need for overhaul. The EDSALL had dropped a depth charge at too slow a speed, with the result that she was leaking badly. The WHIPPLE had returned from her rescue of LANGLEY and PECOS survivors only to figure in a collision with a Dutch cruiser; she was now unfit for heavy duty. That left five of the old four-stackers; and that all were badly in need of repairs is pointed up by the fact that, as the ships started out for what was to be their last engagement in Java waters, POPE sprang a leak in her hot well that could only be repaired by a lengthy welding job. She had to risk the danger of air raids that was ever-present at Soerabaja.

And that left J. D. EDWARDS, ALDEN, FORD, and PAUL JONES. There was of course one other American ship available for the striking force. This was the HOUSTON, still able to fight although her after turret was out of commission as a result of the aerial bomb hit earlier in the month.

Admiral Doorman had his flag in the Dutch light cruiser DE RUYTER; and in addition to HOUSTON there were three other cruisers, the Dutch light JAVA, the British heavy EXETER, and the Australian light PERTH. These were supported by the Dutch destroyers KORTENAER and WITTE DE WITH, the British JUPITER, ELECTRA, and ENCOUNTER, and the quartet of old American four-stackers.

British, Dutch, and American submarines had been drawn in around the shores of Java and the outlying smaller islands; but the shallow waters of the area, and the fact that the Japanese hugged the shoreline, encouraged little hope that the submarines would be able to contribute more than information of enemy movements.

A minuscule force was not the only drawback, however. Doorman's little fleet was composed of ships of four nations which had had almost no opportunity for joint training or for working out common tactical methods. There was no opportunity at all to work out a plan of battle. Lack of a common method and language for communication was perhaps one of the greatest drawbacks. "There were no common flag signals or signal books available," said the commanding officer of one of the destroyers in his subsequent report, "nor were there any tactical plans save of a most rudimentary nature." This report pointed out that communications, inadequate to begin with, broke down completely during the battle. "Communications had to be carried on by flashing light in plain English, or by Dutch high-frequency radio to the HOUSTON, which relayed messages to the American destroyers." The work of Lieutenant Otto Kolb, of the Royal Netherlands Navy, a communications officer aboard the DE RUYTER, was highly commended by American observers; but there were still times when, owing to distance, darkness, or for other reasons, the four-stacker commanders had to fight "by guess and a gaze at the crystal ball."

Those, then, were the ships available, and some of the conditions they faced, when a large enemy assault convoy was located by reconnaissance on the afternoon of the 26th. Apparently the enemy had come through Macassar Strait and was on a southwesterly course near the Arends Islands, off the southeast coast of Borneo. The southwesterly heading suggested that a landing might be attempted at Toeban, on the north coast and slightly east of center of the long and narrow island of Java. Or the enemy might attempt to reinforce his troops on Bawean to the northward or make a landing on the larger island of Madoera, perched on Soerabaja's front doorstep. Admiral Doorman was informed that the enemy force consisted of 30 transports, two cruisers, and four destroyers; and while this information probably was correct of the force described, the Allied vessels were to find that many other Japanese warships were lurking in the Java Sea—ready and waiting.

On receiving this information of the enemy convoy, Admiral Helfrich ordered Doorman to proceed to sea, attack after dark, then retire toward Tandjong Priok near Java's western end. To these instructions was subsequently added: "You must continue attacks until the enemy is destroyed."

After requesting to be notified of any new reconnaissance reports that might be received at Admiral Helfrich's headquarters in Bandoeng,

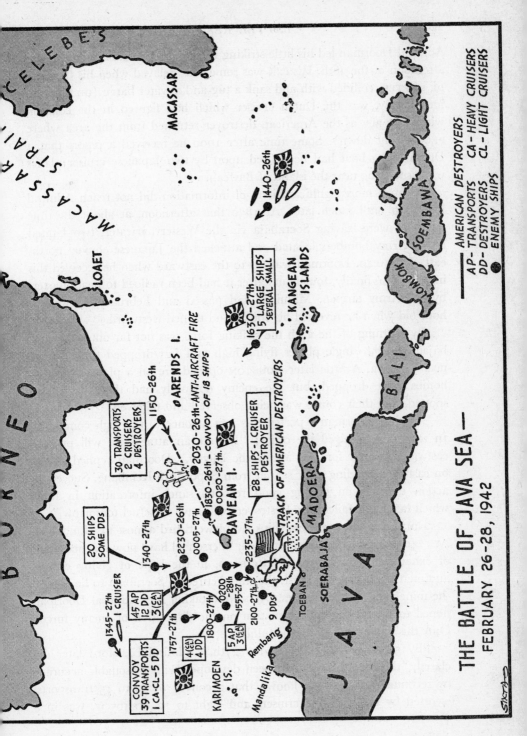

THE BATTLE OF JAVA SEA—
FEBRUARY 26-28, 1942

AMERICAN DESTROYERS   CA- HEAVY CRUISERS
AP- TRANSPORTS   CL- LIGHT CRUISERS
DD- DESTROYERS
● ENEMY SHIPS

CELEBES

MACASSAR

MACASSAR STRAIT

SOEMBAWA

LOMBOK

LOAET

KANGEAN ISLANDS

BALI

1440-26th

1630-27th
5 LARGE SHIPS
SEVERAL SMALL

ARENDS I.

2030-26th- ANTI-AIRCRAFT FIRE

1150-26th

BORNEO

30 TRANSPORTS
2 CRUISERS
4 DESTROYERS

1830-26th-CONVOY OF 18 SHIPS

0020-27th

2230-26th

0005-27th

BAWEAN I.

28 SHIPS-1 CRUISER
1 DESTROYER

20 SHIPS
SOME DDs

1340-27th

TRACK OF AMERICAN DESTROYERS

2235-27th

MADOERA

1345-27th
1 CRUISER

45 AP
12 DD
3 (CA)

1757-27th

1800-27th

4(CA)
4 DD

0200-28th

1555-27

5 AP
3 (CA)

2100-27th
9 DDS

SOERABAJA

TOEBAN

Rembang

Mandalika

KARIMOEN IS.

JAVA

FIGURE 10

Admiral Doorman led his little striking force out of Soerabaja on the late afternoon of the 26th. His exit was somewhat delayed when his flagship, DE RUYTER, collided with and sank a tug and a water barge (DE RUYTER, incidentally, was the Dutch cruiser which had figured in the collision with WHIPPLE as the American destroyer returned from the area where PECOS went down). Some time after 1900 he received a report that a Dutch flying boat had been fired upon by two Japanese cruiser planes while snooping near the island of Bawean.

A much more significant item of information did not reach Admiral Doorman until much later. At 1830 that afternoon, at about the time the ships were leaving Soerabaja via the Westervaarwater, two United States Army bombers located and attacked the Japanese convoy northeast of Bawean. Doorman was far to the eastward when he received this information, finally, four hours after it had been radioed to headquarters by the Army airmen. Midnight had passed and February 27 was an hour old when he reversed his course and turned westward.

By morning of the 27th the striking force was not far outside Soerabaja. At 0858 single planes flying high and fast dropped three bombs near JUPITER. A little later HOUSTON opened fire on a plane. No more bombs were dropped, but the enemy obviously had the Allied ships spotted, and their course was being observed and followed.

Admiral Doorman reported this fact at once to the high command. In return he received the order: "Despite air attack you will proceed eastward. Search for and attack the enemy." Doorman replied, "Was on eastward heading after search from Sapoedi to Rembang. Success of action depends on getting good reconnaissance information in time, which last night failed me. Destroyers will have to refuel tomorrow."

During the morning the ships swept westward almost to Mandalika. At 1240 Admiral Doorman reported, "Personnel have now reached point of exhaustion." In the early afternoon, in the hope of giving officers and men a much-needed rest, the ships retired to Soerabaja to lie behind the minefields. While the destroyers were taking fuel Admiral Doorman hoped to receive better information on the disposition of enemy forces. Only this latter hope was to be fulfilled.

"By 5 p.m., local time, on the 27th," Admiral Glassford later declared, "the enemy forces had been developed with reasonable accuracy by reconnaissance. It was known that a convoy of 39 to 45 transports, escorted by two or three cruisers and eight to 12 destroyers, was in a

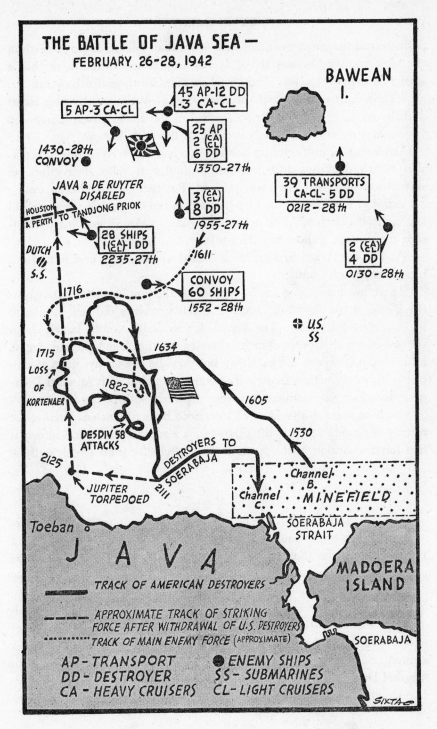

THE BATTLE OF JAVA SEA —
FEBRUARY 26-28, 1942

BAWEAN I.

45 AP-12 DD
-3 CA-CL

5 AP-3 CA-CL

25 AP
2 (CA)
(CL)
6 DD
1350-27th

1430-28th
CONVOY

39 TRANSPORTS
1 CA-CL- 5 DD
0212 - 28th

JAVA & DE RUYTER
DISABLED

HOUSTON
& PERTH   TO TANDJONG PRIOK

3 (CA)
(CL)
8 DD
1955-27th

DUTCH
S.S.

28 SHIPS
1 (CA)
(CL)-1 DD
2235-27th

2 (CA)
4 DD
0130-28th

1611

1716

CONVOY
60 SHIPS
1552 - 28th

⊕ U.S.
SS

1634

1715
LOSS
OF
KORTENAER

1822-

1605

1530

DESDIV 58
ATTACKS

2125

DESTROYERS TO
SOERABAJA

2111

Channel
B.

JUPITER
TORPEDOED

Channel C.   MINEFIELD

Toeban ○

SOERABAJA
STRAIT

J A V A

MADOERA
ISLAND

SOERABAJA

TRACK OF AMERICAN DESTROYERS

APPROXIMATE TRACK OF STRIKING
FORCE AFTER WITHDRAWAL OF U.S. DESTROYERS
TRACK OF MAIN ENEMY FORCE (APPROXIMATE)

AP - TRANSPORT   ● ENEMY SHIPS
DD - DESTROYER   SS - SUBMARINES
CA - HEAVY CRUISERS   CL - LIGHT CRUISERS

SIXTA

FIGURE 11

position approximately 20 miles west of Bawean Island, 60 miles north of
the west entrance to Soerabaja. It was established furthermore that a
strong covering force was then 35 to 40 miles southwest of Bawean. . . .

"Thus the two groups of the enemy, namely the convoy plus escort
and the covering force to the southward of the convoy, were fairly well
known and developed by early evening of the 27th."

Doorman was just entering Soerabaja when he received this information, his tired officers and men just beginning to relax their efforts to
stay awake and alert: rest was in sight. But there was to be no rest.

Admiral Doorman turned his flagship in the channel of the minefield
leading to the harbor. As he turned he signaled, "Am proceeding to intercept enemy unit. Follow me. Details later."

And so the Allied striking force turned in obedience and sortied out
for its last, fateful battle.

There are many gaps in the records of the ensuing action known as
the Battle of the Java Sea. Most of the larger ships did not survive to
make a detailed report. The knowledge available comes largely from
the American destroyers, which, alone of all the Allied ships engaged,
escaped. Their reports are excellent, but they did not always have a complete view of the action. Being out of communication with Admiral Doorman, the destroyer commanders were deprived both of the information
on which he was acting and of his intentions before he acted. Finally, the
destroyers were not present after 2100, or 9 P.M., that night, and information for this portion of the battle is derived chiefly from Dutch sources.

3

The Allied striking force stood out of Soerabaja at 1500 on the afternoon of the 27th on a northwest course and in a sea made choppy by a
15-knot wind from the east. Visibility was good, and this visibility was
put to good use by the enemy, whose planes at once began to shadow
the Allied ships.

At 1530 HOUSTON opened fire on planes nearly overhead, and all
the ships scattered. There was some overcast now, and the enemy planes
were above this and out of sight. This did not help the enemy's aim, for
a moment later several heavy bombs exploded fully 5,000 yards astern.
Admiral Doorman requested fighter protection but it could not be spared.
The Commander of Air Defense at Soerabaja required his eight remain-

ing Brewster Buffaloes to escort the four remaining dive bombers which were shortly to make an attack on Japanese sea forces.

The Allied cruisers were in column formation with DE RUYTER in the lead, followed by EXETER, HOUSTON, PERTH, and JAVA in that order. The ELECTRA was ahead of the column, with JUPITER to the starboard and ENCOUNTER to port of DE RUYTER. The four American destroyers were in column astern, with the two Dutch destroyers about 4,000 yards to port of EDWARDS. The Dutch destroyers were endeavoring to work up to the van of the formation, where they belonged, but boiler trouble limited KORTENAER to about 24 knots and they were having little success. The American destroyers were laboring under contradictory orders. Their assigned position was on the disengaged bow of the cruisers, but at the same time they were under orders not to pass ahead of the Dutch destroyers. As a matter of fact, the Americans too had little speed to spare; with their old machinery, leaky condensers, and fouled bottoms they had all they could do to keep up with the cruisers through the ensuing engagement.

At about 1600 the British destroyers sent contact reports, one of which mentioned two battleships. At 1611 the American destroyers sighted the enemy ships bearing between 315 and 340 degrees, which put them only a few points on their starboard bow. The ships went to general quarters and increased speed to 24 knots. Evidently they had run into the enemy's covering force, which was known to lie between them and the convoy.

The composition of the enemy force was not determined with complete accuracy, but it was known to be far superior, in both numbers and firepower, to the meager Allied force. The battle opened "at extreme range of visibility," and later smoke obscured the view, but it appears that the Allied force had to deal with from four to seven cruisers and two heavier ships described as battleships of either the KONGO or ISE class. Possibly these latter were in fact heavy cruisers. The other cruisers are variously described: There were two or three heavy cruisers of the NATI class, or possibly of the ATAGO class, which is quite similar. Most accounts agree that there were also present two or three light cruisers of the SENDAI class. Lieutenant Commander Lewis E. Coley of the ALDEN says that NATI class cruisers led the enemy line while some of the KAKO class brought up the rear, and remarks that "the latter must have suffered heavy damage." These were accompanied by 13 destroyers in two flotillas of either seven and six or eight and five ships, respectively. When first sighted these enemy cruisers were to the northwest, while the two heavy ships were considerably farther east. The latter gradually came in and closed the range all through the battle.

The enemy opened fire at 1616. The Allied cruisers changed course to about 290 degrees and replied a minute or two later, HOUSTON or EXETER first, followed shortly by DE RUYTER and PERTH. The range was approximately 30,000 yards, so it seems doubtful that the 5.9- and 6-inch guns of the light cruisers were effective in the early stages of the action. As enemy shells began to come near the Allied ships, JUPITER and ELECTRA, which had come under fire from a SENDAI class cruiser, left their exposed position for the disengaged side of their own cruisers. The JUPITER took a station abeam the main body, or about 800 yards on the port bow of the EDWARDS.

The opposing battle columns moved on roughly parallel courses in a westerly or northwesterly direction with the Japanese vessels somewhat ahead. From time to time the Allied cruisers turned either toward or away from the enemy, but it appears that in general the range diminished.

Japanese fire was good, and they had the advantage of a seaplane overhead to spot for them. Six- and eight-inch splashes appeared around the Allied cruisers. In this early stage the DE RUYTER and HOUSTON appeared to be bearing the brunt of the battle. At 1622 the first enemy salvo landed about 1,000 yards over DE RUYTER. At 1629 a salvo straddled that ship, as did a second salvo a minute later. In another minute she was hit, though not seriously. The splashes around the HOUSTON appeared to be from 6-inch shells, although the two hits she received during the battle were 8-inch. Shells were soon falling within a few yards of EXETER. Lieutenant Commander Jacob E. Cooper of the FORD remarks that about every fourth Japanese salvo was a straddle. The spread of the salvos was very small. Allied ships escaped serious damage only because, owing to the great range, the shells came down almost perpendicularly.

Meanwhile the American destroyers had worked up to a position about 3,000 yards on the disengaged quarter of the JAVA, which was last in the cruiser line. In order to avoid being pocketed along the Java shore they stayed as close to the cruiser column as they dared. They kept the splashes of the overs fired at the JAVA and HOUSTON about 1,000 yards on the starboard bow of the EDWARDS, leading the American destroyer column, but occasional ricochet shells came close. Several large splashes were seen on the port bow of the EDWARDS; these, according to Commander Henry E. Eccles, were "apparently from single gun salvos of a battleship."

Good as was the Japanese fire, the Allied cruisers were doing better. Admiral Helfrich remarks that the HOUSTON was firing five or six salvos a minute, while DE RUYTER also maintained a high rate of fire. In the early stages of the battle most of these shells were falling around two enemy cruisers, but one of the Allied 6-inch cruisers was sending up splashes around an enemy destroyer.

"At 1634 enemy gunfire appeared to decrease considerably," reported Lieutenant Commander Coley of ALDEN, "and at 1635, plainly visible from ALDEN's bridge, an explosion took place on the rear enemy cruiser (KAKO class) and a column of smoke about 300 feet high rose into the air." Lieutenant Commander Cooper of the FORD says that "during this time two columns of smoke were observed which appeared to be hits on the enemy by our main body."

It was perhaps to cover their crippled cruisers and force Admiral Doorman to open the range that the Japanese made a destroyer torpedo attack at 1634. Apparently it came from the direction of the enemy cruiser column now about 28,000 yards distant, bearing 325 degrees true. This attack was repulsed by gunfire, PERTH hitting and possibly sinking an enemy destroyer.

The battle seems to have continued for several minutes with the cruisers in parallel columns. At approximately 1645 Allied planes from Java attacked the enemy. The planes themselves could not be seen, but the geysers sent up by their bombs could be distinguished from the splashes of the shells from our cruisers. Sometime between 1645 and 1655 the JAVA was hit, and immediately afterward the Allied cruisers turned by simultaneous movements to the left. This falling away to the southwest may have been to open the range, as one-gun salvos from the battleships, if such they were, continued to fall close astern of the JAVA, but it seems more likely that the ships turned to avoid torpedoes launched on their starboard bow.

During the next half hour numerous torpedoes were seen. Some were undoubtedly launched by the enemy cruisers or destroyers, but it seems clear that the Allied force had come upon an enemy submarine group too. At 1650 JUPITER turned sharply to starboard across the bow of EDWARDS, signaling "torpedo," and a few minutes later a torpedo passed astern of EDWARDS, between her and FORD. At 1658 torpedoes and a periscope were reported on EDWARDS's port quarter. Two minutes later what Commander Eccles of JOHN D. EDWARDS described as a "huge geyser of water resembling a torpedo explosion" shot up in the same vicinity. With it went debris and "two large pieces of metal observed falling end over end." There were no surface ships near the spot, so it appeared that by some freak the enemy had hit one of his own submarines, with either a shell or a torpedo.

After holding a southwesterly course for only a few minutes, the Allied cruisers again re-formed their column on a course of about 290 degrees and renewed the action. Almost at once one of these cruisers scored a hit on the stern of the foremost Japanese cruiser. It was at about this time that the HOUSTON received an 8-inch hit in the engine room and slowed for a moment. The shell did not explode, however, and she was soon able to resume speed.

At about 1710 three additional enemy cruisers and several destroyers were seen over the horizon on the starboard bow. At about the same time the two enemy destroyer flotillas of the force made a torpedo attack. While Allied cruisers were maneuvering to avoid these torpedoes EXETER was hit in a boiler room by an 8-inch shell. It killed 14 men and cut out six of her eight boilers, reducing her speed first to about 20, then to about 15 knots. At about the same time—it is not clear whether it was just before or just after EXETER was hit—the Allied cruisers turned by individual movements to the south. As they turned, DE RUYTER lagged behind to close the enemy, whose cruisers had turned behind a smoke screen and were moving forward behind their attacking destroyers. The Allied cruisers opened a concentrated fire and the destroyers were driven back, but not before DE RUYTER had sunk one of them. Nevertheless, the waters were now literally aboil with enemy torpedoes.

From the FORD, now on a southerly course, a torpedo was seen on the port quarter, overtaking and converging on the destroyer at about a 20-degree angle. Skillful maneuvering avoided the danger. At about the same time EDWARDS put her rudder hard left to avoid a torpedo ahead, and several torpedoes surfaced in the vicinity of the destroyers. The Dutch KORTENAER, which was about 700 yards to starboard of EDWARDS, was caught in the starboard quarter at 1713 by a torpedo which came from behind. "There was a heavy, whitish explosion flinging debris 100 feet in the air," said the log of the JOHN D. EDWARDS. "She heeled way over and yawed 90° to the right. She poised momentarily and then turned turtle and folded up like a jackknife so that bow and stern came together. The stern end sank at once and the bow within 50 seconds of the original explosion. Men were blown high in the air and several jumped into the water or scrambled up her side as she heeled over. No survivors could be seen in the water." Later that night, however, the British destroyer ENCOUNTER picked up more than a hundred survivors while passing through the area.

It was apparently after the sinking of KORTENAER that EXETER slowed seriously and the formation fell into confusion. The enemy closed in from the north to take advantage of the situation. Commander Eccles of the EDWARDS remarks, "It appeared that the striking force had suffered heavy damage and that the enemy was pushing home an attack to drive us east."

4

The Allied confusion did not last long. While the destroyers laid smoke to cover the cruisers, Admiral Doorman re-formed his column. At 1726 he signaled all his ships to follow DE RUYTER, and the other cruisers, minus the crippled EXETER, fell in behind him. The PERTH, followed by ELECTRA and ENCOUNTER, delayed only long enough to dash between EXETER and the advancing enemy line to cover the crippled cruiser with smoke, after which they fell in behind the others. The EXETER started to withdraw slowly to the south. At this point there was another heavy explosion 2,000 yards on the EDWARDS's starboard bow. Several torpedo tracks were seen from WITTE DE WITH and a torpedo exploded to starboard, then another to port, as they finished their runs—even Japanese torpedoes commit suicide if their attack is a failure. The Dutch destroyer dropped several depth charges, indicating that submarines were in the vicinity.

The enemy, however, was pressing his advantage and was sending in his destroyers to finish off EXETER. Only the British destroyers were in a position to intercept them. About 1730 the DE RUYTER signaled "Counterattack." The ELECTRA entered the smoke to carry out the order. As she swung to starboard she met three enemy destroyers coming toward her through the smoke. All four destroyers opened fire. The ELECTRA scored four hits on one of the Japanese ships, but was herself badly hit in return. One shell entered her boiler room, while another demolished her steering engine. She stopped and lay dead in the water. The destroyer she had hit turned away and broke off the engagement, but the remaining two poured shell after shell into the British destroyer, coming so close that even their machine guns could be used. Many survivors of the ELECTRA were wounded in the water.

The JUPITER followed ELECTRA into the smoke. By the time she reached the spot where her sister ship had last been seen, the ELECTRA had disappeared and JUPITER found only two enemy destroyers, now apparently starting an attack on EXETER. The JUPITER opened fire and the two Japanese ships turned away and disappeared in the smoke and the failing light.

The EXETER, which had had her guns trained to port on the approaching NATI class cruisers, now turned them to starboard and opened fire on the SENDAI class cruiser which was supporting the destroyer attack. The Japanese ship promptly turned and ran into the smoke.

The WITTE DE WITH, which was ordered by Admiral Doorman to escort the EXETER to Soerabaja, now saw on her starboard quarter a Japanese destroyer engaging one of the British and opened fire. The Japanese ship shifted her fire from the British to the Dutch destroyer. In the brief exchange that followed, WITTE scored two hits before her opponent turned away. The WITTE was not hit, but she suffered extensive damage when one of her own depth charges accidentally fell overboard and exploded close astern.

The American destroyers apparently did not participate in this counterattack. At 1728 they had started laying a smoke screen to protect the other cruisers and probably were not in a position to meet this threat aimed at the EXETER.

Meanwhile Admiral Doorman had gathered his cruisers into column on a southeasterly course, then turned north toward the enemy to renew the engagement. As he was making this turn, his cruisers opened fire with their antiaircraft batteries and a stick of bombs fell 1,000 yards to port of the American destroyers. Five minutes later two more sticks fell near the ships without doing any damage. Furthermore, splashes from enemy 6-inch shells were drawing close and straddling just astern of the EDWARDS. Torpedo tracks were seen now and again.

But the Allied cruisers had emerged from the smoke and were again slinging shells at the enemy at a range of about 18,000 yards. "Their fire was particularly effective," said Lieutenant Commander Cooper of FORD, "as fire was seen on one of the enemy battleships and two fires noted on one of the enemy cruisers. These did not appear to have been brought under control as long as we could see them."

The DE RUYTER'S short-wave radio had been damaged and hand signal lamps were now the only means by which Admiral Doorman could communicate with his force. On board HOUSTON, too, the voice radio upon which the destroyers relied for communication had cut out.

At 1806 a signal came by flashing light from the DE RUYTER: "Counterattack." The American destroyers were preparing to carry out this order when Admiral Doorman signaled, "Cancel counterattack" and then "Make smoke." The destroyers again laid smoke to cover the retirement of EXETER and perhaps to cover the cruiser column. While they were thus engaged Admiral Doorman signaled, "Cover my retirement."

The reason for this order is not entirely clear, but it appears that Admiral Doorman was anxious to break off the engagement in order to go after his real objective, the enemy transports. It was now growing dark and visibility had decreased to about 15 miles, so that he might be able to slip into the convoy under cover of darkness.

When they received the order the four American destroyers were between the cruiser line and the enemy. To Commander Binford, as commodore of the four U.S. ships, a torpedo attack seemed the most effective means of covering the retirement. Breaking out of the smoke they had just laid, the destroyers saw the Japanese battle line some 22,000 yards distant on the starboard bow. They closed the range to 14,000 or 15,000 yards before firing their starboard torpedo broadside at 1822. The enemy cruisers attempted to stop them by gunfire, but their shells were falling about 800 yards short. As these first torpedoes hit the water there was a large explosion on an enemy ship, apparently the result of the cruisers' gunfire. The destroyers then turned by a column movement and fired their port topedoes at 1827. Lieutenant Commander Coley of the ALDEN remarks that at this time "the rear ship of the enemy column appeared to be on fire aft, and to have a fire in her high forward turret or superstructure."

The American destroyers' torpedo attack had been made at long range with the object of forcing the enemy to turn back. In this it was successful, for "immediately after our torpedo attack the two Japanese heavy cruisers turned by column movement to the north." Lieutenant Commander Coley remarks, "It is definitely considered that the EXETER was saved by this attack." It was too much to hope for a hit at the distance at which the torpedoes were fired, and yet at about 1830, approximately 10 minutes after the starboard broadside, a large explosion was seen in the Japanese battleline and it seemed very probable that a torpedo had found its mark.

At 1831 there was the signal from the DE RUYTER: "Follow me." The destroyers turned under cover of smoke, crossed under the stern of the cruiser column and took a position on their disengaged quarter on a course between east and northeast. Commander Binford reported to Admiral Helfrich that all his destroyers' torpedoes had been expended.

Within a few minutes the opening range and poor visibility forced an end to the cruiser gun action as the Allied force moved off on a northeasterly course. The destroyers trailed. "Darkness set in," reported the skipper of EDWARDS, "and we followed the main body endeavoring to regain station, and having not the slightest idea as to his [Doorman's] plans and still only a vague idea of what the enemy was doing."

The withdrawal of the enemy was at once reported to Admiral Helfrich by Admiral Doorman, who at the same time asked for further information as to the location of the enemy transports. This request indicates that he had not received the 1805 report. It is possible that it was again sent to him in reply, for he changed course to lead his ships to the northwest toward this last reported position of the convoy. But the men in the American destroyers could only guess his intention. One of the destroyer commanders reported that "There were no more signals and no one could tell what the next move would be. Attempts were made to communicate again with HOUSTON and DE RUYTER with no results."

If Admiral Doorman hoped to avoid the enemy cruisers in this thrust northwestward at the transports he was disappointed. Japanese planes followed his course with flares, thus eliminating any chance of a surprise attack, and the Allied ships made intermittent contact with enemy warships during the entire run. At 1902, while the force was on a course of 290 degrees, enemy ships, perhaps the ones which had just broken off the engagement, were observed on bearing 240 degrees.

Admiral Doorman pulled northward and again lost contact with the enemy for several minutes, but at about 1930 enemy planes dropped eight green parachute flares over the column, apparently to mark its position for their cruisers. Four ships now appeared on the port bow. It seems scarcely possible that this was the same group encountered a few minutes earlier. It may be that the previous contacts had been with a covering force while this last was possibly with a screening force close to the convoy. The DE RUYTER signaled, "Target to port." The Allied cruisers sent over a few star shells and opened fire. The engagement was brisk but lasted only a few minutes. Admiral Doorman's objective was the convoy and he was probably not anxious to re-engage enemy warships. When flashes in the enemy's direction indicated that the Japanese were firing torpedoes, his column turned away to the east and soon afterward a succession of small changes of course brought him again toward the south.

Why Admiral Doorman abandoned this attempt to reach the convoy is not clear. To the men on the American destroyers, struggling at full speed to keep their position, it appeared that he was retiring to Soerabaja. Actually his intention, as it subsequently appeared, was either to sweep westward along the north coast of Java to intercept an enemy landing or to attempt to get around the enemy covering force to the southward.

About the time the striking force turned back to the south, Rear Admiral Pieter Koenraad, Commandant of the Soerabaja Naval District, received a report from a United States Army bomber which had attacked the enemy convoy that evening at 1700. At that time there were 45 transports, 3 cruisers, and 12 destroyers on a westerly course 20 miles west of the Java Sea island of Bawean. This was approximately the same position in which they had been found at about 1350 that afternoon. The news was forwarded to Admiral Doorman, but presumably he was already well on his way south when he received it.

Enemy planes continued to follow the Allied ships—as indeed they did the rest of the night. At 2009, while on a southerly course, a single flare was dropped above them. One of the cruisers, probably HOUSTON, fired star shells, but nothing was to be seen. A few minutes later (at 2023) what appeared to be four enemy destroyers were observed on the port bow. It was thought that they fired torpedoes, so the Allied ships turned left to avoid them. Again at 2043 it was reported that torpedoes were fired, on the starboard bow this time, and course was altered to 175 degrees.

By 2100 the striking force was again near the coast of Java, between Soerabaja and Toeban. The American destroyers had not had opportunity to take on fuel the preceding afternoon, and their supply was now nearing exhaustion. After 24 hours of high-speed steaming they were experiencing increasing difficulty in keeping up with the cruisers. Commander Binford says, "Realizing that I had no more torpedoes and that further contact with the enemy would be useless, since my speed and gunpower were less than anything I would encounter . . . I retired to Soerabaja, which was about 50 miles away."

This retirement of Division 58 did not escape the notice of the enemy, for as the destroyers were entering the channel in the minefield a plane dropped a flare above them. While they were still in the channel orders came from Admiral Doorman to retire to Batavia and receive orders later for torpedo replacements. Commander Binford replied that it was impossible to get through to Batavia and that he was entering Soerabaja to fuel, after which he would proceed as directed. He never received another message from the commander of the striking force.

The POPE, which had completed repairs and had been standing outside the minefield waiting for an opportunity to join the striking force, was ordered to return to Soerabaja with the other destroyers. The EXETER and WITTE DE WITH were already there when the ships tied up at Holland Pier and started fueling. They left the pier and returned to the anchorage well before morning brought the daily air raid.

5

After the departure of the American destroyers the remaining ships of the striking force turned westward along the north coast of Java. They were in a single column led by ENCOUNTER, followed by DE RUYTER, PERTH, HOUSTON, JAVA, and JUPITER. They had been on this westerly course for about 20 minutes when at 2125 there was an underwater explosion on JUPITER's starboard side abreast her engine room and she flashed a signal to the JAVA: "JUPITER torpedoed."

A survivor describes the situation: "We had not blown up. We had not sunk. We had, in fact, just stopped, and the same oppressive silence of a ship in dock during the night watches descended on us." There was ample time for the launching of boats and rafts, but before the boats could return from the beach for a second load the destroyer heeled over to port and sank at about 0130. A detachment of the Dutch Army on guard along the coast came to the aid of the survivors.

Immediately after the loss of the JUPITER the striking force turned north. At 2217 it again passed the spot where the KORTENAER had gone down that afternoon, and survivors of the Dutch destroyer saw the cruisers foam past at high speed. The ENCOUNTER was ordered to stop, and picked up 113 men of the KORTENAER'S crew of 153. It was at first intended to take them to Batavia, but upon learning of a strong Japanese force to the west the captain returned to Soerabaja.

The cruisers of the striking force were now left without any destroyer protection whatever. This situation was aggravated by the fact that enemy planes continued to light the course with flares. But Admiral Doorman's orders were, "You must continue attacks until the enemy is destroyed," and he pressed on north with a grim determination to reach the enemy convoy.

It is doubtful if he ever knew how close he actually came to reaching it in his last magnificent attempt. The convoy had in fact remained in the area west or southwest of Bawean. At 1850 a PBY from Patwing Ten had taken off to shadow the convoy in the bright moonlight. At 2235 the PBY found the convoy southwest of Bawean. Twenty-eight ships were counted in two groups, escorted by a cruiser and a destroyer. At this moment Admiral Doorman was headed toward this very spot, but it is doubtful if he ever received the plane's report. It reached the commander of the naval forces at Soerabaja at 2352, after which it was sent on to the commander of the striking force; but by that time both DE RUYTER and JAVA were already beneath the waters of the Java Sea.

At 2315 the DE RUYTER signaled: "Target at port four points." In that direction were seen two cruisers, which opened fire from a distance of about 9,000 yards. The PERTH replied with two or three salvos which landed on one of the enemy cruisers for several hits. The Japanese thereupon fired star shells which exploded between the opposing battlelines, so that their ships could no longer be seen.

Shortly afterward DE RUYTER received a hit aft and turned to starboard away from the enemy, followed by the other cruisers. As JAVA, which had not been under enemy fire, turned to follow there was a tremendous explosion aft, evidently caused by a torpedo coming from port. Within a few seconds the whole after part of the ship was enveloped in flames.

The DE RUYTER had continued her turn onto a southeasterly course when, very soon after the JAVA, she too was caught by a torpedo. There was an extraordinarily heavy explosion following by fire. The PERTH, behind the flagship, swung sharply to the left to avoid a collision, while the HOUSTON turned out of column to starboard. The crew of the DE RUYTER assembled forward, as the after part of the ship up to the catapult was in flames. In a moment the 40-mm. ammunition began to explode, causing many casualties, and the ship had to be abandoned. She sank within a few minutes. For some time her foremast structure remained above the water, then a heavy explosion took the ship completely out of sight.

Of the entire striking force, only HOUSTON and PERTH now remained. They had expended most of their ammunition and were still followed by enemy aircraft. There seemed no possibility of reaching the enemy convoy, and at about 0100 on February 28 the two cruisers set course for Tandjong Priok in accordance with the original plan for retirement after the battle, making port shortly after noon of that day. On the way PERTH informed Dutch headquarters at Soerabaja of their destination and reported that DE RUYTER and JAVA had been disabled by heavy explosions at latitude 06° 00′ S., longitude 112° 00′ E. The Dutch hospital ship OP TEN NOORT was immediately dispatched toward the scene of their loss, but it is doubtful if she ever reached it. Radio contact with the ship was suddenly lost, but an observer in a plane later reported that he believed he had seen her in the custody of two Japanese destroyers, being escorted northward away from Java.

The hospital ship was not heard from again.

6

During the night of the 28th the Japanese made two landings on the north coast of Java. Aerial reconnaissance reported that the Japanese also were moving on the south coast of the island in two columns, one of which was convoyed by battleships. These facts were clear indication that there was no longer in Java a port usable as a base for surface forces. Rear Admiral Glassford had orders to retire to Australia when it became impossible to remain on the island. Rear Admiral Palliser had orders from the British Admiralty to withdraw when resistance would serve no further purpose. It appeared that the time had come.

On the morning of the 28th, Commander Binford had telephoned Admiral Glassford to advise him of "the vital necessity of leaving Soerabaja that day and no day later."

Admiral Helfrich would not concede defeat. The indomitable Dutchman planned to reassemble the remaining Allied forces at Tjilatjap (the approach of the Japanese on this port was not then known) and from there to continue fighting. Therefore the crippled British cruiser EXETER, still capable of making 16 knots, was ordered to the south Java port, to be accompanied by the British destroyer ENCOUNTER and the American destroyer POPE. The problem of the route the ships were to take was carefully considered, the course having to be determined by EXETER's deeper draft. After some discussion, Admiral Palliser decided that the British cruiser and the two destroyers should run north and east of Bawean, skirt the south coast of Borneo by daylight, and make a dash through Sunda Strait, between Java and Sumatra, that night.

Soon after leaving Soerabaja the cruiser and her two destroyers were discovered by an enemy reconnaissance plane, and the old story of the Java Sea was about to be retold. At about 1200 on March 1 they reported that three enemy cruisers were approaching. That was the last ever heard from the three ships.

The story of the American HOUSTON, the Australian PERTH, and the Dutch destroyer EVERTSEN—which had put in at Tandjong Priok after the Java Sea Battle had ended—was all too similar.

On the afternoon of the 28th, Admiral Glassford ordered Captain Albert H. Rooks, USN, to leave that night with HOUSTON for Tjilatjap, accompanied through Sunda Strait by PERTH and EVERTSEN. The two cruisers took on all the fuel that remained and sailed from Tandjong Priok some two hours before midnight. For some reason EVERTSEN did not sail until an hour later. At about midnight the Dutch destroyer reported a sea battle off St. Nicholas Point. Admiral Helfrich then sent orders to HOUSTON, PERTH, and EVERTSEN: "If any of addressees is engaged with enemy, others render assistance as possible." Some time later EVERTSEN reported that she had been intercepted by two enemy cruisers and had beached herself in a sinking condition on Seboekoe Island. Nothing further has been heard of the three ships, although some of HOUSTON's complement were known to have been taken prisoner by the Japanese and held for a time on the island.

There was, however, a different ending to the story of the escape attempt made by the American destroyers EDWARDS, ALDEN, FORD, and PAUL JONES, which were at Soerabaja when EXETER, POPE, and ENCOUNTER sailed off into the unknown.

Soerabaja was subjected to almost continuous air raids on the 28th.

None of the four destroyers was hit, however, and the American skippers began to make careful plans for their sortie to safety. The EDWARDS and ALDEN got under way at about 1700 and FORD and PAUL JONES some 30 minutes later. There was considerable evasive maneuvering to throw off air observers before the four ships met outside the harbor and formed up in column of EDWARDS, ALDEN, FORD, and PAUL JONES. The Dutch destroyer WITTE DE WITH had been unable to accompany the four-stackers as they departed, because of battle damage, and the WITTE was lost to the Japs.

After leaving the Soerabaja minefield in clear moonlight the American ships hugged the shore of Java as closely as they dared, with the navigation of Lieutenant William J. Giles, Jr., on EDWARDS, being credited with taking them safely through the difficult waters of Bali Strait. As the ships were emerging through the southern entrance of the strait, at about 0210, an enemy destroyer was seen some 8,000 yards on the port bow, obviously standing sentinel to keep any Allied ships from escaping. Shortly afterward dim flashing lights were seen to the southward and two more destroyers came up to join the first enemy ship. The Japanese vessels were clearly visible in the moonlight, but apparently they had not yet spotted the American ships in the darkness of the shore-line.

This was too good to last, for the American ships soon had to leave their protecting shadows and turn sharp east to round the outer tip of Blambangan Peninsula. The peninsula had just been cleared when the Japanese opened fire.

The American four-stackers immediately returned the fire, at the same time stepping up speed to 27 knots. Splashes were rising all around FORD, but the other ships were in no danger. The American ships had no torpedoes aboard, so torpedo flashes were simulated by dummy powder charges. Apparently the bluff was not entirely unsuccessful, for the Japanese began to widen the range by dropping astern. The four-stackers did not waste any time, for they suspected heavier Japanese units in the vicinity; they set a course for Australia, where they arrived some four days later.

As the log of one of the ships put it, "The voyage was without further incident."

Meanwhile, on the morning of March 1, even Admiral Helfrich probably had begun to realize that further resistance was, to put it mildly, without hope of accomplishment. At any rate, on the morning of the 1st he instructed Admiral Glassford to order his remaining ships to make for Australia.

Still at Tjilatjap were the destroyers PILLSBURY and PARROTT; the gunboats TULSA, ASHEVILLE, LANAKAI, and ISABEL, and the minesweepers WHIPPOORWILL and LARK. The destroyers WHIPPLE and EDSALL were operating south of Java and cleared for Australia from that direction. The light cruiser PHOENIX was en route for Java, having been released from convoy duty, and she was ordered to put about and reverse course. The submarine tender OTUS was on the way to Java from Ceylon, whence she had escorted the crippled MARBLEHEAD. Now all these vessels were ordered to make for Exmouth Gulf, Australia, this destination later being changed in some cases to Fremantle. The remaining British ships received similar orders.

Of the ships thus dispatched, the destroyers PILLSBURY and EDSALL, the gunboat ASHEVILLE, and a few of the smaller British craft have not since been heard from.

Late on the morning of March 1, after a conference with Governor General Van Mook, Admiral Helfrich advised Admiral Glassford and Admiral Palliser that the Allied Naval Command in the Netherlands East Indies was, as of that moment, no longer in existence.

Admiral Glassford and his staff finished up their affairs and left Bandoeng by automobile for Tjilatjap, from which port they proceeded, mostly by plane, to Australia.[1]

There now remained in Java waters only the American submarines, and the Japanese were to hear from these submarines more and more as time went on.

But the Japanese were to be given other reasons for remembering

---

[1] One civilian American who turned down a chance to leave Java with Admiral Glassford's party, and parties leaving subsequently, was Foreign Correspondent Daniel Witt Hancock, of the Associated Press. Hancock had served the Associated Press foreign staff in New York, London, Moscow, Istanbul, and New Delhi before going to Java to cover the Japanese invasion. While in Moscow, during the lean days two years earlier, Hancock had developed diabetes, and when last seen on Java (by United States Consul General Walter A. Foote, just before Foote's own departure) he had about a two months' supply of insulin. All efforts to learn of his fate through the State Department and other agencies subsequently failed. In the light of what is known of Japanese treatment of captives, it seems highly unlikely that, if captured, Hancock was furnished with the medicaments necessary to keep him alive. Until contrary evidence is received, he must be considered the first United States news correspondent lost after the attack on Pearl Harbor.

the Battle of the Java Sea. The loss of the HOUSTON, a very popular ship, was felt throughout the nation. In the city for which she was named more than a thousand young Americans volunteered to replace the HOUSTON's lost crew. These men were sworn into the Navy by Admiral Glassford on Memorial Day, 1942, in an impressive outdoor ceremony held at twilight on a downtown Houston street, and with a replica of the lost cruiser as a background. To a hushed and inspired audience, Mayor Neal Pickett read the following message from Franklin D. Roosevelt, whose presidential flag had flown on several happy peacetime voyages from HOUSTON's main truck:

"On this Memorial Day all America joins with you who are gathered in proud tribute to a great ship and a gallant company of American officers and men. That fighting ship and those fighting Americans shall live forever in our hearts. I knew that ship and loved her. Her officers and men were my friends. When ship and men went down, still fighting, they did not go down to defeat. They had helped remove at least two cruisers and probably other vessels from the active list of the enemy's ranks. The officers and men of the USS HOUSTON were privileged to prove once again that free Americans consider no price too high to pay in defense of their freedom. The officers and men of the USS HOUSTON drove a hard bargain. They sold their liberty and their lives most dearly.

"The spirit of these officers and men is still alive. That is being proved today in all Houston, in all Texas, in all America. Not one of us doubts that the thousand recruits sworn in today will carry on with the same determined spirit shown by the gallant men who have gone before them. Not one of us doubts that every true Texan and every true American will back up these new fighting men, and all our fighting men, with all our hearts and all our efforts.

"Our enemies have given us the chance to prove that there will be another USS HOUSTON, and yet another USS HOUSTON if that becomes necessary, and still another USS HOUSTON as long as American ideals are in jeopardy. Our enemies have given us the chance to prove that an attack on peace-loving but proud Americans is the very gravest of all mistakes.

"The officers and men of the USS HOUSTON have placed us all in their debt by winning a part of the victory which is our common goal. Reverently, and with all humility, we acknowledge this debt. To those officers and men, wherever they may be, we give our solemn pledge that the debt will be paid in full."

PART THREE

"Where Is The Navy!"

Chapter Twelve

THE Pacific is so vast an ocean that every land mass on earth, all the continents and all the islands, could be fitted into it and still leave a sizable sea.

But the Pacific is not a great waste of water. From Australia to South America there is a veritable steppingstone path of islands; and, beginning with the Hawaiian group, there is an ever-thickening company of archipelagoes and island chains southwestward to the East Indies' continents-in-miniature. Other echelons of islets stream out to meet Japan. All are lands still in the making; from the titanic forces of tides and earthquakes and volcanoes to the slow, minute toil of the coral polyps, the contours of uncounted isles and atolls and reefs are undergoing constant change. There are perverse currents and lonely coral heads to trap the mariner. The charts are few and unreliable.

So it was a theater ideal for the Japanese strategy; in fact, geography dictated the Japanese tactics. Following the radiating lines of the island chains and the Asiatic coast, the Japanese advanced in a series of jumps, a deadly game of leapfrog. These were tactics impossible to meet head-on. Japan had the initiative. Time and distance—which are to be reckoned as one in a war—were on Japan's side. So was the geography of the Pacific.

And all over the world rose the cry: "Where is the American Navy?"

It sounded jeeringly from the Tokyo radio. Tokyo knew where the United States Fleet was: wiped out, sunk, forever removed as a menace to Dai Nippon. Or, as a Japanese English-language propaganda broadcast put it, "destroyed to pieces." Tokyo said so, and all Japan believed it. So did many others.

The cry rose despairingly from the Philippines and from the crumbling United Nations forces in the East Indies, hoping without believing that a miraculously reconstituted fleet would come charging over the eastern horizon.

249

But Admiral Ernest J. King and Admiral Chester W. Nimitz had to be bitterly hard realists.

Admiral King became Commander in Chief United States Fleet on December 30, 1941. Admiral Nimitz, flying secretly from Washington to Pearl Harbor in mufti, became Commander in Chief Pacific Fleet on the following day, taking over from the ad interim CINCPAC, Vice-Admiral William S. Pye, USN.

Each knew, as he stepped into his unenviable command, that the primary necessity was not to stop the Japanese in their tracks on their southwesterly surge upon Malaya and the East Indies, but to prevent the enemy from spreading eastward through the equatorial archipelagoes and thus cutting off the sea roads between the United States and Australia. If that was the greatest danger to avert, the perils subsequent to Japanese expansion into the mid-Pacific would be scarcely less: the Americas isolated, the fleet confined, and the United States like a boxer driven into a corner.

From their mandated Marshall Islands, developed as a submarine base despite every international pledge, the Japanese had already pounced upon the neighboring British-governed Gilbert group to threaten Samoa, even then being strengthened by transport-loads of troops conveyed thither by two carrier task forces commanded by Vice Admiral William F. Halsey and Rear Admiral Frank J. Fletcher. Halsey's flag flew from USS ENTERPRISE, which was supported by three cruisers and six destroyers. Fletcher's flagship was the carrier YORKTOWN, attended by cruisers LOUISVILLE and ST. LOUIS, and four destroyers. Together, they comprised a large part of the effective fleet we had in the Pacific at the turn of the year.

It appeared to the high command that the time had come to break up Japanese plans for an eastward development, before the enemy could assemble forces too formidable for the meager, and hence doubly precious, American fleet to oppose.

January 9, 1942, was the day upon which Admiral Nimitz told Vice-Admiral Halsey what he had to do—sail up to the muzzle of the gun pointed at the American-Australian life line and blast that threat away. Halsey's orders were to raid the southern Marshall and northern Gilbert area, to block the enemy's harbors with the wreckage of the enemy's combatant ships, to destroy his aircraft and tenders, his fuel tanks, power and radio installations, storehouses, and radio apparatus. It was a large order.

Information concerning the area to be attacked was sketchy. A shuttle patrol of six Army bombers and six Navy patrol planes was established between Canton Island in the Phoenix group and Suva, in the Fiji Islands, on January 19. The patrol cut across the logical line of Japanese advance like the crossbar on an inverted T, and its purpose was not to keep the area to be attacked under surveillance—that was scarcely possible—but to watch for any premature Japanese sortie from the islands.

Plans for the raid called for the combined task forces to depart Samoa on January 25, and to proceed in a general north-northeasterly direction to the vicinity of Howland Island, about 1,000 miles distant and about 2,000 miles from the objective islands. There the ships were to refuel on January 28, sending the empty oiler PLATTE, Captain Ralph H. Henkle, USN, on to Pearl Harbor under escort of the destroyer CRAVEN, Lieutenant Commander Allen P. Calvert, USN. One other tanker, SABINE, Commander Houston L. Maples, USN, guarded by the destroyer MAHAN, Lieutenant Commander Roger W. Simpson, USN, was taken along part way. Theirs was to be the lonely and dangerous task of lagging far behind the combat ships, to refuel them for the last half of the homeward dash.

Few among the thousands of officers and men in that armada of twenty-one ships had ever heard a gun fired in anger. The pilots and gunners of the carriers' broods had never seen tracers stitch a flaming seam across their wings. The husky but untried football team of State Normal was going into its first game to stop the undefeated champions.

Seven island targets were set for the raid: Roi and Kwajalein in the Kwajalein atoll; Wotje, Jaluit and Mili, and Taroa in Maleolap atoll, all in the Jap-mandated Marshall group, and Makin, in the newly occupied Gilbert Islands. All were to be bombed from the air and, in addition, Wotje and Taroa were to be bombarded from the sea.

Logical division of the work, as a look at the chart will confirm, was for the stronger carrier task force to attack Roi, Kwajalein, Wotje, and Taroa-Maleolap, where the Japanese had been longest in preparation. Jaluit and Mili, on the outer fringe of the Marshalls, and the recently invested Makin, were therefore assigned to Rear Admiral Fletcher's ministrations.

Captain Elliott Buckmaster, USN, was skipper of Fletcher's flagship, YORKTOWN, which was flanked by the cruisers LOUISVILLE, Captain Elliott B. Nixon, USN, and ST. LOUIS, Captain George A. Rood, USN. The accompanying destroyers were the HUGHES, Lieutenant Commander Donald J. Ramsey, USN; SIMS, Lieutenant Commander Willford M.

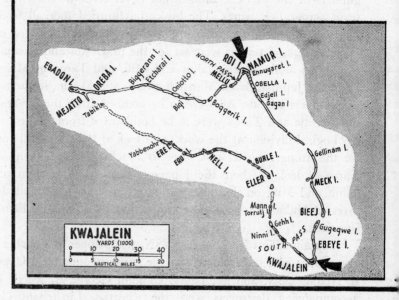

RAIDS ON
MARSHALL AND GILBERT
ISLANDS

MAR

ENIWETOK or
BROWN ATOLL

ADMIRAL HALSEY'S TASK—
...TO BLAST JAPANESE
THREATS POINTED AT THE
AMERICAN-AUSTRALIAN
LIFE-LINE......

UJELANG

JONARI & ONO IS.
EAST
FAYU I.   HALL IS.   C A R O L I N E

MINTO REEF

TRUK
IS.   OROLUK LAGOON
Nama I.   PAKIN or   SENYAVIN IS.
Losap Is.   PAGENEMA   PONAPE I.
ANT or ANDEMA   MOKIL IS.
Namoluk Is.   I.
Lukunor   NGATIK   PINGELAP IS.
Is.
NOMOI or
MORTLOCK IS.

I S L A N D S

NUKUORO

ROI I.   NAMUR I.
EBADON I.   OREBA I.   NORTH   MELLU   Ennugaret I.
Biggerann I.   PASS   OBELLA I.
Etcharai I.   Edjell I.
MEJATTO   Oniotto I.   Gagan I.
Tabikle   Bigi   Boggerik I.
Yabbenohr   Gellinam I.
ERE   NELL I.   BURLE I.
ERU   ELLER I.   MECK I.
Mann I.
Torrutj   BIEEJ I.
Gehh I.   Gugeqwe I.
Ninni I.   SOUTH   PASS   EBEYE I.
KWAJALEIN

KWAJALEIN
YARDS (1000)
0   10   20   30   40
0   5   10   15   20
NAUTICAL MILES

S H A L L I S

POKAAKKU ATOLL

ENTERPRISE
TALBOT (DD)
BLUE (DD)
McCALL (DD)

'AL SPRUANCE-TO WOTJE:
RTHAMPTON (CA)
T LAKE CITY (CA)
NLAP (DD)

BIKAR

BIKINI or
ESCHHOLTZ
ATOLL

RONGELAP

UTIRIK
TAKA

ADMIRAL HALSEY'S
TASK FORCE

RONGERIK
ATOLL

AILINGINAE ATOLL

Ailuk
Atoll

Mejit I.

ENTERPRISE

WOTHO
SCHANZ ATOLL

ROI

Likiep Atoll

Jemo

E or KATHERINE
ATOLL

KWAJALEIN
or MENSCHIKOV
ATOLL

WOTJE or
ROMANZOV ATOLL

LAE ATOLL

Lib or Lip I.

KWAJALEIN

ERIKUB
ATOLL

MALOELAP
ATOLL

AUR ATOLL

CHESTER (CA)
BALCH (DD)
MAURY (DD)

TO TAROA

NAMU
or MUSQUILLO ATOLL

AILINGLAPALAP
ELMORE or
ODIA ATOLL

MAJURO or
ARROWSMITH ATOLL

E or UALAN I.

ARNO ATOLL

JALUIT
or BONHAM
ATOLL

MILLE
or MULGRAVE ATOLL

Namorik
or Baring Atoll

YORKTOWN

ADMIRAL FLETCHER'S
TASK FORCE

KWAJALEIN.....
ERICAN LOSSES: *NONE—*
ANESE LOSSES:
BMARINES SUNK
GHT CRUISER DAMAGED
LERS BADLY DAMAGED
RGE SHIPS DAMAGED
NBOAT DAMAGED
EAMSHIP RENDERED USELESS
MALL TRANSPORTS SUNK
ORE-HOUSES, CANTONMENTS,
DIO, AND OTHER SHORE
STALLATIONS DAMAGED
DESTROYED...

Ebon or
Boston Atoll

MAKIN I.

G I L B E R T   I S.

Marakei

ABAIANG
TARAWA

Maiana

Kuria **ABEMAMA**
Aranuka

Nonouti

BERU

NAURU I.

TABITEUEA
Onotoa

Nukunau

OCEAN I.

ADMIRAL FLETCHER'S FORCE
YORKTOWN (CV)
LOUISVILLE (CA)
ST. LOUIS (CL)
HUGHES (DD)
SIMS (DD)
RUSSELL (DD)
WALKE (DD)

TASK FORCES DEPART.
FROM SAMOA, JAN. 25th
IN NORTHEASTERLY
DIRECTION FOR HOWLAND I.,
—THENCE TO MARSHALLS.

FIGURE 12

Hyman, USN; RUSSELL, Lieutenant Commander Glenn R. Hartwig, USN, and WALKE, Lieutenant Commander Thomas E. Fraser, USN. These seven vessels slanted away from the larger Halsey group, whose flagship ENTERPRISE was commanded by Captain George D. Murray, USN.

Halsey's force was subdivided to form two bombardment groups. Rear Admiral Raymond A. Spruance, with Wotje marked for his guns, had the cruisers NORTHAMPTON, Captain William D. Chandler, USN, and SALT LAKE CITY, Captain Ellis M. Zacharias, USN, his flag on the first-named. The destroyer DUNLAP, Lieutenant Commander Virginius R. Roane, USN, accompanied them. Captain Thomas M. Shock, skipper of the CHESTER, was to take the destroyers BALCH, Lieutenant Commander Charles R. Rend, USN, and MAURY, Lieutenant Commander Elmer D. Snare, USN, for the obliteration of Taroa. That left in attendance upon the ENTERPRISE the destroyers RALPH TALBOT, Commander Ralph Earle, Jr., USN; BLUE, Commander Harold N. Williams, USN, and MC CALL, Commander Frederick Moosbrugger, USN.

Abreast but invisible from each other, the two forces slid over the international date line and found themselves in tomorrow, but there was no festive initiation of novices into the Order of the Realm of the Golden Dragon. Another sort of initiation awaited them less than five degrees ahead.

2

Throughout the daylight hours of January 31—January 30 in the United States—Admiral Halsey's task force proceeded at reduced speed. Admiral Fletcher's ships had farther to go, and the plan was for both carriers to be in position so that their planes could strike their respective targets with unanimity at fifteen minutes before sunrise, February 1.

Just once Admiral Halsey had reason to fear that the surprise party he had arranged for the Nipponese might boomerang. An enemy plane passed the task force 35 miles astern. It was a clear, sunny day with no clouds under 18,000 feet, and the long wakes left by the task force on the calm sea trailed far behind. Perhaps the Japanese pilot was not looking; perhaps he did not believe what he saw. Anyhow, he did not deviate an inch from his set course, and the ships forged ahead into the welcome night.

All hands were called at 0300, when the ENTERPRISE was but 36 miles from Wotje. A full moon was still high in the west, and there was no wind to help lift the planes as the ENTERPRISE put on a surge of speed and the first group of 36 scout bombers took off, each burdened with one 500-pound bomb and two 100-pounders. After them came nine torpedo bombers, and an additional scout bomber, with the entire flight straightening out for Kwajalein atoll at 0630. Near the atoll the torpedo bombers separated from the flight to attack Kwajalein Island while the rest went on toward Roi on the opposite and northern end of the lagoon.

While the bombers were still assembling overhead, six fighter planes carrying a single 100-pound bomb apiece, whipped off the deck of the ENTERPRISE for Taroa-Maleolap. One crashed in the take-off, spinning into the sea before its pilot could free himself. Fast behind came another group of six, Wotje its goal.

No man there, in the air or aboard ship, knew what to expect. More was known about Tokyo itself than of the South Sea Islands. The pilots had only photostatic enlargements of clippings from old charts to help them identify their targets, which is why Roi Island was not recognized in the misty dawn by the 37 planes intent upon surprise and destruction. Twelve minutes' warning was thus accorded the Japanese, before the flight identified its target and the first division began its glide-bombing attack from an altitude of 14,000 feet in the face of antiaircraft fire and rising Japanese fighters.

The first American bomb to be dropped on Japanese territory was loosed by Commander Hallsted Hopping, who was killed a few seconds later when his plane ran into a vicious burst of antiaircraft fire as he swooped low to escape two enemy fighters.

The second division came in lower and faster under the flak and the fighters, and, hard behind it, the third. It was up to each man to pick his target, no one having knowledge of what the island contained, and the explosions, the gunfire, and the acrobatics of the Zeroes gave the bombers in the tail end of the procession little to choose. One American scout bomber cartwheeled into the hell of confusion below, riddled with flak. A Japanese fighter was erased in a red smear of flame. The attackers wheeled out to sea, with the enemy fighters in hot pursuit. Two more bombers plummeted, trailing a crape of black smoke, but two disintegrating Japanese planes went with them. A fourth American was last seen making a controlled but extremely fast downwind landing on the water about a mile north of the island.

In the midst of the hurly-burly of death and destruction, the bombers of Roi heard an appeal from the squadron over Kwajalein for help against enemy shipping. Air Group Commander Howard L. Young immediately detached the eighteen planes of Bombing Six, led by Lieutenant Commander William R. Hollingsworth, USN, from the flight and sent them to the opposite island of the long, amoeba-shaped atoll. Stock was taken of the damage done, and the·bombers headed back for the ENTERPRISE to report a clean sweep despite the bitter resistance of the Japanese.

Two big hangars on Roi had been destroyed with all they contained. An ammunition dump had blown up, to add its destruction to that of the American bombs, and a fuel depot was left in flames. The radio building was crushed beneath the tangled steel of its own antennae, and every other building in the base had been leveled.

Kwajalein, the harbor-island of the atoll, had been allotted to nine planes of the torpedo squadron, Air Group Commander Howard L. Young in command. Each plane carried three 500-pound bombs with delayed-action fuses, for use against the ships and naval shore facilities expected to be found.

But when the nine reached Kwajalein, on the calculated moment, they found such an array of shipping, and such a concentration of anti-aircraft fire too, that belief was automatic that they should have been at Roi and the 37 planes where the nine were. Fortunately, there were no enemy fighters in the air, or the slower, lightly protected American craft of Torpedo Six might have suffered casualties. As it was, they picked a row of nine cargo ships, two "sitting duck" four-engine planes and a cluster of buildings at the water's edge for their targets at two minutes before 7. Thirteen minutes later, having reported the rich pickings to be had at Kwajalein—carriers, they radioed, and submarines—they headed back for the ENTERPRISE lighter by seven tons of bombs distributed over shipping and shore.

Eight minutes after their departure, scout bombers from the battle at Roi roared over the startled Japanese. They picked targets and prepared to give the Nipponese their first taste of dive-bombing. Completely bewildered, the defenders raised an umbrella barrage of 3- to 5-inch shells with the fuses set for 1,000 feet. They aimed at nothing, putting all their faith into filling the air so heavily with shell fragments that the Americans would not come through—alive. In further evidence of Japanese panic was their wholesale and utterly useless firing of everything that would shoot.

The Americans were not in the least put out by the warmth of their welcome. They were a little disappointed that the two carriers reported by Torpedo Six were only big, lubberly merchantmen, but a ship was a ship, and down dived the bombers.

Choicest of the targets in the lagoon was a row of five submarines nuzzling like suckling pigs against a tanker, and a light cruiser bristling with dual-purpose antiaircraft guns.

By voice radio the targets were assigned. Two 500-pound bombs struck the cruiser; a third hit one of the submarines which went down so fast that it almost capsized the tender to which it was moored. A second submarine went in the opposite direction—blowing up in soaring fragments.

Having placed their high explosives to good advantage, the fliers threw in a lesson in machine-gunning, strafing the smaller vessels and the scurrying hordes on shore, and clearing the decks of an antiaircraft cruiser after planting the two 500-pound bombs in her superstructure.

Kwajalein had all of fifty minutes' rest before the third wave of ENTERPRISE fliers arrived—again nine torpedo bombers but armed on this trip with the deadly tin fish, Lieutenant Commander Lance E. Massey heading the pack.

The planes came in at 700 feet in a formation of right echelons of echelons, and they were met with everything the Japanese could throw into the air. The formation was broken up when the wounded Japanese cruiser was detected making a run for the pass through the reef. Three of the planes were ordered after the fugitive. The six others, zigzagging through the pom-pom shells and machine-gun fire, dropped their torpedoes and climbed fast.

The only material damage effected by the Japanese gunfire was— to the Japanese. Nonplused by the low-flying torpedo planes, the Japanese gunners thought of nothing but the immediate target and not what lay behind. Consequently, the first row of ships fired into the second row, and both fired into their own shore batteries which meanwhile were hulling the Japanese vessels continuously. Three of the returning planes contained bullet holes, of which their crews were tremendously proud.

The score for Kwajalein: inconsequential damage to a few planes, no injury to personnel, on the American side. On the Japanese side: two submarines sunk; one light cruiser hit by two 500-pound bombs and a torpedo; three large oilers badly damaged by 500-pound bombs and two sustaining torpedo hits; two cargo vessels damaged by 500-pound bombs, one of them beached; one gunboat damaged and beached; one large steamship of 20,000 tons rendered useless by three 500-pound bomb hits and a torpedo, and two smaller steamers, presumably transports, sunk. Of the damage ashore, the greatest was three bomb hits in a large compound composed of storehouses and cantonments.

And something new had been added to the conflict in the Orient— the American war whoop, modern style. Back on the ENTERPRISE the radio was kept tuned in to the planes over Kwajalein, whose pilots were keeping each other informed with such exchanges as: "Get out of my way, Joe, that big baby is mine" and "Watch out, that CL is making a sneak—go get him!" Then: "I got him! Oh, mamma! What a sock!" and "Yip-pee, right on the button!"

Maleolap is an arrow-shaped atoll a little south of east from Kwajalein, and Taroa is its main island, situated on what would be the right-hand barb of the arrowhead, which points at Wotje 125 miles away. Taroa was the destination of the five bomb-armed fighters whose sixth member was lost at the take-off.

What the quintet, led by Lieutenant Jim Gray, USN, saw as they came over Taroa was the nest prepared for Japan's long-range heavy bombers scheduled to blast the way to the Australia-American life line. Taroa, to the pilots' amazed eyes, compared favorably with their own Ford Island at Pearl Harbor, with two mile-long runways glistening white and unused, and a bevy of airplanes parked between the strips. Whatever its intended use, the field was an immediate menace to the ships of the task force.

The Americans attacked, with their puny 100-pounders, fighting off an enemy patrol which came buzzing in from the sea, Gray sending two of them down in flames. One enemy plane was destroyed on the ground, and many others that were hit escaped destruction only because the Americans lacked incendiary bullets. Those were meager days for our fighting men, but the five continued to rake parked planes, hangars, machine shops and barracks until they saw USS CHESTER steam into view at a quarter before 7, and the cruiser's four scout observation planes joined them. Shortly before 0715 the ENTERPRISE five, low in gasoline and with cartridge belts empty, turned over the war in that quarter to the warships. At 0715 the CHESTER and her destroyers opened fire. For twenty-five minutes the cruiser worked over the Japanese island, firing twenty-one salvos and silencing three shore batteries, one antiaircraft battery, knocking down a radio tower, and destroying an observation tower and a group of buildings. An oil dump was set ablaze, besides other fires of undetermined source. The bombardment lasted almost an hour. Fifty minutes after it was broken off, Taroa was subjected to the second of the three air attacks that it was to receive in all.

Nine of the planes which had hit Kwajalein, seven of the bombers and two of the scouts, were led out of the sun over the Japanese field by Lieutenant Commander William R. Hollingsworth, USN, and again the enemy was found with his guard down, obviously believing the raid completed. No enemy fighters were in the air to meet the bombers, and no antiaircraft fire interrupted the bombing run of the first section of three, which was directed against 25 Japanese aircraft dispersed around the hangars.

Seven of these, two of them large two-engine planes, went up in flames and debris as the first section's leader rippled his salvo of two 100-pound and one 500-pound bombs on the parking lot. The second plane's bombs hit a hangar that must have been filled with gasoline, because the resulting explosion seemed to claw at the bellies of the attackers. The third plane wiped out three enemy fighters on the ground and blasted the front of another hangar.

The second section's bombs fired an oil storage tank, a T-shaped barracks, and put out of commission an antiaircraft gun emplacement on the adjacent islet of Ollot. The third section did not have an undisturbed run over the field. Fighters were swarming up, and the machine-gun fire was heavy, but another hangar was hit and a runway plowed up.

On their way back to the ENTERPRISE the raiders passed another group of nine bombers being led in by Lieutenant "Dick" Best, USN. Of these, only eight were to come back because they flew into a disturbed hornets' nest. An umbrella barrage of antiaircraft fire had been raised over the field, and on its edges swarmed fighter planes which broke up the American formation and forced them into individual dogfights. Three of the Japanese were shot down to more than even the score for the American bomber lost, and despite the opposition the battered hangars and the surviving parked planes, the runways and barracks were squarely hit by more than three tons of bombs.

The morning's work at Taroa cost the Japanese two large hangars, a gasoline dump and a large oil tank, a radio station, a considerable but uncounted number of machine and repair shops, four gun batteries, eight fighter planes, five scout bombers and four twin-engined bombers. The tally includes what could be observed of the damage done by the warships' bombardment.

Wotje was the fourth island in Admiral Halsey's catalogue of the day's operations. It was to prove the most fully developed from the military standpoint.

Six fighters were sent out to look the ground over, and they were not doves. As Kwajalein had turned out to be, Wotje provided a deepwater anchorage served by sizable shore installations on which the Japanese had spent at least a decade of hard work. The job of the ENTERPRISE's fighters was to concentrate the enemy's attention upon the air while the surface ships came up to do the real business of demolition.

The first strafing attack upon the harbor and base was unopposed; then the startled Japs put up an umbrella barrage and sent a little group of fighters to intercept the Americans' return. The gunfire was badly co-ordinated, and the Japanese pilots, while performing all the acrobatics in the book and keeping their guns spouting, also managed to keep pretty well out of range of our aircraft. Four of the Japs spun out of the fight; it could not be verified that they were shot down, so they were not entered on the official score. And then, as the Sons of Heaven dug the dirt out of their eyes to watch the American planes streak for the sunrise, they were knocked off their feet and buried under rubble and earth as the first salvo from the NORTHAMPTON and SALT LAKE CITY landed fairly on the target.

Later in the day a group of eight scout bombers and nine torpedo planes were sent to Wotje to finish off anything the warships had missed. They found nothing to make the flight worth while, but bombed what little remained perpendicular.

So ended the aerial assault launched from the ENTERPRISE. American combat losses were five airplanes, one bomber and four scouts; one fighter was lost by accident at take-off. In all, six officers and five enlisted men were killed, two officers and two enlisted men wounded. Thirty-three airplanes were damaged. The American planes were demonstrated to be either slower than the Japanese or, if of comparable speed, far less maneuverable. But the Americans were better fliers, for with all their handicaps they shot down ten of the enemy, who lost, including aircraft destroyed on the ground, a total of 24 planes.

Taroa, site of the Japanese grand new airfield, was one of the two targets selected by Admiral Halsey for bombardment by surface craft; it was the cruiser CHESTER's assignment.

Feeling her way through the poorly charted waters, the CHESTER sighted Taroa dim on the starboard bow at ten minutes before 7. The recognition must have been mutual, for a few minutes later two enemy dive bombers roared out to meet the cruiser, but the Nipponese pilots apparently succumbed to an attack of buck fever. They dived too soon, and their bombs fell harmlessly into the sea.

From the cruiser's decks the ENTERPRISE's planes could be seen, highlighted by the horizon-topping rays of the rising sun, strafing the island. The CHESTER had launched her four scout-observation seaplanes, two to spot the ship's gunfire and two for reconnaissance, but the quartet was kept so occupied by Japanese fighters that the cruiser derived no benefit from her air support.

The CHESTER opened fire with the main battery at 0715, training her guns on the radio and observation towers at the island's northeast tip. Almost immediately a second, and again ineffectual, attack was made by Japanese dive bombers, and shore batteries opened up on the cruiser. Their aim was poor, but the range was good, so the CHESTER and her two destroyers turned away from the island and reversed course at the greater distance to pound the shore batteries. At least three were silenced, and the radio installation at the point of the island demolished, when eight twin-engine bombers were seen heading for the ship.

Captain Shock saw that a speedy retirement was in order, and at 0740 the CHESTER with a final salvo headed at top speed away from Taroa. The men at the main batteries were ordered to bear a hand with the antiaircraft guns, and for forty minutes the cruiser twisted and turned to avoid dive-bombing, strafing runs, and high-level attack from enemy aircraft. Forty minutes of successful evasive action, and then a more determined Japanese pilot bored in through the screen of antiaircraft fire to within 1,000 feet of the CHESTER's decks. The bomb missed, but so closely that spume from its underwater explosion rained upon the ship's machine gunners.

The Jap pulled out of his dive and immediately climbed for a second attempt. This time he succeeded. His bomb struck the ship close to the port catapult, exploding on impact and ripping a hole nine feet long and half as wide through the deckplates. Eight men were killed by the blast, and 34 wounded.

From clumps of cloud, the every-morning phenomenon of the South Seas, there now darted eight two-engine bombers which churned the seas around the cruiser with 500-pound missiles, some of which fell closer than 100 yards. It was the Japanese's last try at the CHESTER. The cruiser swung off to the north a few minutes after 9 o'clock, and at 1130, her four seaplanes again safely stowed aboard, the CHESTER and her destroyers turned toward the task force's rendezvous and the long journey home from battle.

On the instant that the CHESTER's first salvo was loosed against Taroa, 125 miles away, Admiral Spruance on the cruiser NORTHAMPTON spoke the order which sent his ships' batteries into action against Wotje, sturdiest of the Japanese outposts.

The NORTHAMPTON and SALT LAKE CITY, with the destroyer DUNLAP scouting ahead, launched their aircraft at 0620, forty minutes before sunrise. The thunderclap explosions of the catapults' propelling charges awoke unexpected life in the murky waters ahead. A crimson rocket suddenly arched into the sky, from a small Japanese patrol boat which had been lying, unseeing and unseen, two miles or so ahead. Having attempted to give warning to the shore watchers, the crew of the patrol boat now concentrated all their efforts on getting home fast from the black-bulking mysteries that had startled them into wakefulness. The DUNLAP went after her, in hot pursuit, but the water-hugging, fast little Jap presented an all but impossible target. The destroyer could only bring her bow gun to bear on the skittering fugitive.

The cruisers took up column formation, and went about their business, making landfall on the starboard bow at 0655, although Wotje's antiaircraft guns hammering away at the ENTERPRISE's planes had marked the target for minutes before it came into view. As the cruisers drew nearer, their topside men could see columns of black smoke rising from the island's silhouette—not bomb hits, it was soon made plain, but ships in the lagoon lighting off to make a run for it.

Considerable buffeting was being given the aerial spotters, who radioed the cruisers an initial report of "three ships and no shore batteries" as they ducked antiaircraft fire. It was erroneous information, which the Japanese themselves corrected shortly by opening up with five shore batteries from well-camouflaged positions. For a while the SALT LAKE CITY was dangerously close to the enemy's shell bursts, and once the NORTHAMPTON was straddled by a salvo, but the ships pulled out of the Japanese range to positions their own guns could still easily bridge. Not until the sun rose could the aerial spotters locate, by the shadows they cast, the all-but-perfectly camouflaged Japanese installations. And not until the sun rose could the DUNLAP get the Japanese patrol vessel squarely in her sights and blast that nuisance out of the water just as the boat was dashing for the lagoon's sheltering arms.

For an hour and thirty-seven minutes the two cruisers and the destroyer marched and countermarched past Wotje, firing at ranges from nearly 30,000 yards to less than 11,000 at the shore installations and over the island into the ships in the lagoon beyond. The Japanese vessels, auxiliaries or armed merchantmen, played a life-and-death game of hide-and-seek in the islands of the atoll. They would pop out to take a shot at the American ships, but our gunners were ready for them, and in the end Admiral Spruance's trio withdrew without a scratch, without a man lost, leaving behind seven or nine enemy ships sunk, one beached, and the only one afloat damaged and dead in the water. On shore, there was complete destruction. Two hangars, a cluster of fuel oil tanks, an aviation gasoline dump, all the warehouses, shops, and barracks were destroyed. All the coastal defense batteries had been blasted. The cleanup brigade of the ENTERPRISE aircraft found nothing to mop up.

Having launched her planes at dawn, the ENTERPRISE—the "Big E" in affectionate nickname—maneuvered in the vicinity of the Wotje atoll until the bombardment cruiser-destroyer units rejoined the carrier at high noon. And, shortly after that, the war was carried to the ENTERPRISE by vengeance-seeking Japanese bombers, evidently called in from the western atolls.

It had not been a dull day for those aboard the carrier before the bombers found her, of course. The returning planes, some of them perforated with machine-gun bullets, others torn by flak, brought stories of success; they were refueled, rearmed, and sent out again, or lowered for patching and mending. And some did not come back. Jimmy Gray, who had invented a homemade sort of bulletproofing for the cockpits of the fighters, proved the success of his device by counting fifteen pockmarks in the steel shield he had installed in his own plane.

Admiral Fletcher's YORKTOWN group, according to plans, was to find its way back to Pearl Harbor independently, so when the ENTERPRISE's planes were back aboard and her own complement of warships rejoined her, the formation turned toward home.

It was a little after half past one in the afternoon when five enemy bombers broke through the clouds on the carrier's starboard bow, in a shallow 20-degree glide attack. They were 3,500 yards away, at an altitude of 6,000 feet, when they came into view.

The ENTERPRISE and her escorts immediately put up a curtain of fire impressive in sound and appearance, but of scant effect. The gunners had not yet learned to lead a plane. The lessons learned on towed targets were forgotten in the excitement of shooting at a real enemy on a killing mission. Our fighters were prevented from closing with the bombers by the gunfire of their own fleet, and although the ENTERPRISE zigzagged until it seemed her plates would give, the Japanese bored steadily in.

Miraculously, the fifteen bombs that came tumbling down about the carrier all fell into the water. The nearest fell about 30 feet from the ship's port; fragments ripped 13 holes in a fuel line, and mangled the leg of George H. Smith, second-class boatswain's mate, who was manning a 50-caliber gun. Smith doggedly kept on firing until he was dragged from his place and rushed to the sick bay, where he died two hours later.

The five bombers passed over the ENTERPRISE at about 1,500 feet, when with dramatic suddenness the trailing plane fell out of formation, pivoted on a wingtip, and drove down hard upon the carrier's deck. Whatever it was that inspired the pilot—a suicide crash or complete contempt for the American gunnery—he dove down upon the zigzagging ENTERPRISE with all wing guns spitting.

Immediately the carrier's machine guns centered all fire upon the fanatic Jap, and still he came on. An aviation mechanic, Bruno Peter Gaida, leaped into the rear seat of one of the parked planes on deck, and turned the tail gun squarely upon the incoming bomber. Just as the Jap appeared to level off hard astern of the ENTERPRISE, Captain Murray swung the ship in a minutely calculated turn, and Gaida's gun bored into the bomber's nacelle.

With a ripping scream of disintegrating metal, the bomber cut across the carrier's stern, shearing the tail off the rearmost parked plane and ripping one of its own wings from the body against the No. 2 gun gallery. The bomber broke in two, drenching the bridge with gasoline, and fell into the sea.

The little fleet straightened course and had an hour's uninterrupted run when a twin-float seaplane with the sinister orange disks suddenly appeared out of the clouds. Again the Japanese intent was unfathomable. He was shot down by Lieutenant R. W. Mehle, USN, who was flying in the combat patrol.

Again there was calm and quiet, the shadow of the ships long on the bright blue water as the sun of an eventful day began to set. Then, coming up fast behind the fleet, two large enemy bombers were discovered at 14,000 feet. Keeping well out of range, the bombers maneuvered to get the sun at their backs, using cloud masses effectively for concealment, and then down they came upon the ENTERPRISE.

Lieutenant Commander C. W. McClusky, USN, skipper of Fighting Six, tried to intercept the bombers, but they left him behind. But he could see that the American gunfire was off and, what is more, by how much. "You're short," he radioed. "Now you're high 300 feet. You're on! You're on! You've got him!"

Trailing smoke and shedding fragments of wing cover, the mangled bomber kept right on in the wake of its companion. Both dropped two 500-pound bombs, far out on the carrier's starboard quarter, and then climbed desperately for the clouds.

And after them went McClusky, and Mehle, and Lieutenant (jg) J. G. Daniels, the acey-deucy champion of the ship. They concentrated on the unwounded bomber; it was obvious that the other one would never reach land.

The prey ducked into a great, billowing island of cumulus cloud, the fighters after him. On the ships' decks below, watchers could see the fighters buzz in and out of the cloud mass like angry bees, and on the radiophones the pilots could be overheard shouting directions to each other.

Then an excited yelp from McClusky. The br-r-r-rt of a machine-gun burst, and another, and clear and loud the exulting voice of the skipper of Fighting Six: "Bingo!"

Through the cloud little specks appeared to the watchers to rain into the sea, specks that actually were good-sized chunks of Jap bomber—and Japanese aviators. The sun went down. The planes were called in, and now it was full speed ahead for the rendezvous with the oilers. And then home.

3

Admiral Fletcher's task force found comparatively little of military value in the islands assigned to it, and reduced that little to nothing.

They also found an assortment of bad weather such as only the mis-named Pacific can brew. Eight planes were lost in the atmospheric tur-moil that rendered radio almost useless and buffeted the aircraft about as a kitten plays with a twist of paper. The crew of one plane was picked up by the supporting destroyers; three other aircraft were forced down so close to Jaluit Atoll that it is likely the crews survived and were made prisoner.

Jaluit, Mili, and Makin were the targets of the YORKTOWN force; the first two are the southernmost islands in the Marshall group, and Makin the northernmost in the adjacent Gilbert Islands. From a point about 70 miles due south of Mili, the YORKTOWN began to launch her aircraft at a few minutes before 5 o'clock on the morning of that same February 1, 1942.

Eleven torpedo bombers and 17 scout bombers, under the command of Commander Curtis S. Smiley, USN, took off first for Jaluit, 140 miles to the northwest, the prime target of the three. A few minutes later a group of nine scout bombers was launched against Makin, 127 miles distant, and, at 0600, five scout bombers took off for nearby Mili. The flights were calculated to bring each of the three atolls under attack simultaneously, so if Mili called on Jaluit for help, Jaluit would not be able to oblige.

There were large banks of cloud, thickening to the northwest, when the first planes took off. The lowering moon illumined the horizon enough for a good take-off as the Jaluit raiders roared off the flight deck and headed toward the storm clouds rushing down upon them. Before the flight could rendezvous for formation, however, the weather had thickened badly. There was lightning on all sides; the moon became obscured, and in ragged parade the 28 aircraft set their course for the target, flying at 115 knots a scant 500 feet above the unseen water.

Six of the planes lost in the operation were of that group. The story of Lieutenant Commander Robert G. Armstrong, USN, first man off the YORKTOWN, is representative of the experience of all who made the round trip.

After 70 minutes of flying, Armstrong figured that the section he was leading must be near the south tip of the atoll. The tops of the great thunderheads were showing pink from the sunrise, where they could be glimpsed through holes in the low overcast, and Armstrong decided to climb through the sagging gray ceiling to avoid detection. He pulled back on the stick and shot up through gruellike mist into a heavy "electrical disturbance," euphemistic technical language for continuous lightning, eccentric winds, and a downpour of rain. Two minutes of that was enough; Armstrong started down again, and when he broke out into the clear three minutes later he had five planes with him. But Jaluit was sighted only half a mile to the starboard, in a three-mile-wide patch of clear amidst the ranks of thunderstorms.

Armstrong headed his little flock in a climbing turn away from the atoll, and at 8,000 feet reversed the course to come in for the attack. He saw two other YORKTOWN planes 4,000 feet below, making for Jaluit, and he tried to call them into formation but the static so jammed the radio that no contact could be made. Fortunately, where ears and voice failed, eyes succeeded; the lonesome pair saw the five overhead, and fell in astern as the bombers charged down upon Jaluit.

And with that, the wind blew a gale out of the northeast and a thunderstorm pushed its mantle of cloud over the atoll. Armstrong's objective was the anchorage, and he had to lead his section on a veritable scavenger hunt through holes in the storm until the harbor was located, and one 8,000-ton ship—transport or large tender—fixed upon for the the target. With fogged windshields and telescope sights adding to the handicap, the fliers loosed their bombs. Armstrong thinks his bomb missed by 100 feet, but evaluation of marksmanship was made all but impossible by the weather. What counted was that the ship, which had steam up and was making a run for safety, was stopped by a bomb on her stern which apparently destroyed screws and steering apparatus. Another run over the ship scored two more hits, and she was left blazing amidships and forward, and going down by the stern.

The clusters of small interisland craft were then given a thorough machine-gunning, and Armstrong swept over little Kabbenbock Island from which a weak and erratic gunfire seemed to be rising. He saw nothing, even at low altitude, and kept on to Enybor Island which was supposed to have two landing fields. Enybor had been overrated; so had Emidji Island. Armstrong raked a half-built hangar and some smaller buildings with his 50-caliber, and hulled a small, 200-foot ship from fantail to forefoot with his machine guns.

He found that he was flying alone, so he circled a rainstorm, calling his missing planes to rejoin him. When, after five minutes, none appeared, Armstrong began a wider search, and, falling in with another section proceeding to the carrier, he joined that flight. Singly and in small groups, the 22 aircraft to complete the mission returned.

They had sunk one fair-sized ship and damaged another; numerous small craft had been sunk by machine-gun fire, the administration building, barracks, and breakwater at Jaluit village had been ruined. Bombs had been dropped near the airdrome workings on Enybor and seaplane facilities at Emidji, but with what results no one could see, or even guess. There had been no opposition from the air, and only inconsequential gunfire from the islands.

The nine scout bombers that visited Makin were almost rained out, too.

Through the scud and mist and sudden rain squalls, the section saw at least one target good enough for all hands to concentrate upon—an 8,000-ton seaplane tender with two four-engine bombers moored close by. Whatever other targets nature was concealing, this alone was good enough to pay off for the journey.

It took just seven minutes for the nine to put their 500-pound bombs in a 100-foot circle and to rake the tender and the seaplanes with their machine guns. The big floating bombers responded to these attentions by bursting into enveloping flames, and the last that was seen of the tender showed her to be capsizing ponderously.

The weather got in one final blow at the Makin raiders. One of the bombers was forced down near the end of the return to the YORKTOWN, but the crew was saved by destroyer action.

Mili was a washout. Five scout bombers found nothing on the atoll except a large, barnlike godown, or storehouse on stilts, a smaller building, and a water tower. Without interruption or opposition they bombed the structures, but rain and clouds prevented them from judging the effects. So they went home.

The YORKTOWN raiders quite obviously took the Japanese completely by surprise, although there was a mutuality of surprise because the bombers found so relatively little to destroy. Perhaps the Japanese felt themselves to be wholly secure and with nothing to fear, and were leisurely going about the business of fortifying the atolls convinced that the Tokyo reports of American impotence were true.

Tojo's little men made one attempt at retaliation. At midday, with the task force heading homeward, a four-engine bomber slanted out of the rain clouds for a run on the supporting destroyers. The airplane was of the Kawanishi type, a flying boat in imitation of the French Potez giant amphibians, and it was immediately attacked by planes of the YORKTOWN's combat patrol. The ships held their fire to give the fighters their chance, as the bomber leveled off and veered into a low-lying cloud for cover.

Hot in pursuit went Ensigns E. S. McCuskey and J. P. Adams for a game of blind man's buff with life the stakes. And again, as with the watchers on the ENTERPRISE that same afternoon, those aboard the YORKTOWN heard shrill yelps on the fighters' wave length, followed by a sudden rain of debris from the cloud as the Japanese bomber fell flaming into the sea.

The YORKTOWN group reached Pearl Harbor on February 6. The ENTERPRISE and her fleet of cruisers and destroyers had arrived the day before.

Although it was no part of Admiral Halsey's mission, one incalculable result of the Marshall-Gilbert raid was a tremendous surge in morale, not only for the Navy but for all the United States; not only for Americans, but for all the nations aligned with them in what had been—and still was, of course—a losing war thus far.

It was good news mixed with bad, however, for the forces beleaguered in the Philippines and the Allied fleet that was being pounded to pieces in the Netherlands East Indies. It was good to know that American warships were on the offensive. It was also grim notice that help was not coming to Manila Bay and Java Sea.

The mission had been a success. At insignificant cost of life and material, the twin-carrier fleet had destroyed an enemy naval base and naval air base on the threatening eastern perimeter; it had sunk some 73,000 tons of enemy ships, including two submarines and not counting a light cruiser which was certainly out of the war for many months; it had blasted two airfields, destroyed 35 Japanese aircraft, and in doing all that it had successfully completed a laboratory experiment that was to develop into a new kind of war at sea: the task force erected on the airplane carrier.

Here, in not-too-crude beginning, the United States Navy had countered, not with a defensive arrangement but with an offensive combination which utilized the best in aerial and surface combat power. It was an amalgam from which were to be molded fleets of a thousand planes or double the number, working in co-ordination with battleships, cruisers, destroyers, and a whole category of landing craft still unconceived, for the complete negation of Japan's conquests and the extinction of the predatory spirit that launched the war.

But on February 6, 1942, the Navy still seemed far from such attainment. It lacked ships, and planes, and men. The planes it had were not wholly adequate, either too slow or highly unmaneuverable, and they lacked self-sealing gasoline tanks, armor for the men, and the full firing-power they could carry. The attacks on the ships by Japanese aircraft had demonstrated American shooting to be woefully below necessary standards, the bitter fruit of years of economy.

But for all that, for all the deficiencies disclosed and all the work to be done to realize the potentialities revealed, it was a famous victory; and it was a victory badly needed.

Chapter Thirteen

I F THERE was one spot on the map, other than "home," for which
the men on the ENTERPRISE had particular interest, it was Wake
Island.

Wake was the first place in their minds and hearts whenever there
was talk of attacking the Japanese, because on the day that American
outpost surrendered, December 23, 1941, the ENTERPRISE was but a
day's journey away, with supplies and replacements for Wake. Every
man aboard had been taut with optimistic excitement at the prospect
of raising the siege of Wake, for the men of the Big E remembered well
that they had transported the last contingent of Marine fliers thither on
the very eve of war.

To drive the Japanese from Wake would have been not only to thwart
a most violently hated enemy in his attack on American territory. The
mission transcended even that. It was a mission of rescue for friends, for
shipmates, to bring succor to brave men who had eaten and slept and
prayed with the ENTERPRISE's company. And then, with all hands poised
to accomplish the rescue on that day late in December, they had had to
bear the bitter disappointment of seeing the task force reverse its course
in obedience to the signal to abandon the errand of liberation. Wake had
fallen before help could reach it.

When, therefore, Vice-Admiral Halsey was ordered on February 11
—six days after his triumphant return from the Marshall Islands raid—
to attack the Japanese invaders now entrenched on the island, no more
welcome assignment could have been received. The first plans called for
the twin-carrier group, the ENTERPRISE-YORKTOWN team, to attack Wake
and Eniwetok, the latter island standing as a northern sentinel guarding
the approaches to Japan's bastion of Truk.

The first group of the task force, that organized on Admiral Halsey's flagship, the Big E, left Pearl Harbor on February 14. It was substantially the same aggregation of ships which the admiral had led to the lee of Wotje two weeks before, with the cruiser CHESTER missing because of repairs and the oiler SABINE replacing the PLATTE.

It was the day before Singapore fell. Australia's doom was freely prophesied.

The second group, under Admiral Fletcher's immediate command, followed out of Pearl on the 16th. It, too, was a familiar company of ships in the main. The cruiser ASTORIA, Captain Francis W. Scanland, USN, had replaced the ST. LOUIS; the oiler SABINE's place was taken by the GUADALUPE, Commander Harry H. Thurber, USN, and the destroyer MAHAN was not with them. Two other destroyers had been added to the force: USS ANDERSON, Lieutenant Commander John K. B. Ginder, USN, and HAMMANN, Commander Arnold E. True, USN.

Plans were for the ENTERPRISE group to attack Wake, the YORKTOWN group to hit Eniwetok. But as Admiral Fletcher's ships put to sea, Admiral Halsey received orders to detach the YORKTOWN group, which was forthwith designated a task force in itself and sent southward on an important convoy mission. Admiral Halsey was ordered by CINCPAC to proceed with the attack on Wake. Eniwetok would have to be deferred. And nobody aboard the ENTERPRISE or her supporting ships had any feelings about the change in plan, so long as their own were not again disturbed.

Admiral Halsey issued his orders for the Wake operation on February 21, as the task force, which had ·been engaging in target practice and other setting-up exercises for battle, headed for the target in earnest. There was grumbling when the orders were heard to give the fliers the monopoly on killing Japs, but there was elation the following day aboard four ships when the admiral told off the two cruisers and the destroyers BALCH and MAURY to bombard the island and its north satellite Peale. Halsey's strategy was to have the bombardment group come in against Wake from the west, or Japan, side, and hence probably the least suspected quarter of attack.

Late in the afternoon of the 23rd, the four ships broke off from the task force and veered off to the west, Rear Admiral Raymond A. Spruance commanding and still flying his two-starred flag from the NORTHAMPTON. His orders were simple. He was to have his ships in position before sunrise, and at 10 minutes before daybreak to begin shooting. His signal to commence firing would be the first bursts on Wake from the carrier's bombers.

2

Halsey's luck with the weather did not quite hold, this trip.

From a point better than 100 miles north of Wake, the ENTERPRISE turned her shovel-nose into a foul, rain-soaked east wind and began launching her planes at 0517. And at once the scene on the ship's flight deck became a nightmarish fantasia of giant blue pinwheels. The dense humidity combined with the vapors and the electric-blue flame of the exhausts to form a halo of eerie light where each propellor whirled. Every pilot found himself peering at a solid, revolving disk of peacock-hued light spinning from the nose of his craft.

But there was an important date to be kept. The SBDs, the TBDs, and the F4Fs were ordered to roll, despite the weather; and raggedly, blindly, they roared down the deck, still appendages to a pinwheel of foxfire, even when airborne.

And then one of the SBDs wobbled as it streaked, cometlike, for the take-off. Its left wheel dropped off the deck to the catwalk, and the bomber somersaulted into the sea, over the port bow.

Aboard the ENTERPRISE the work of the minute had to proceed. She was streaking into the wind at 25 knots. Rescue was somebody else's mission. At the splash, the destroyers turned for the not unfamiliar work: Ensign N. D. Hodson, USNR, had crashed on take-off just three days before, and there had been more before that and all hands saved. But the heavily laden airplane went down through the water as if on a bombing dive. It carried the pilot, Lieutenant (jg) Perry Teaff, USNR, and his gunner, E. P. Jinks, RM3/c, down with it. Despite the proximity of the enemy, orders were given to the destroyer to turn on the searchlights to better the poor chances of rescuing the fliers, and thus it was that Teaff, badly injured, was seen to bob to the surface and his rescue effected. Jinks, however, was lost.

Meanwhile, the planes in the air were reporting difficulties in effecting a rendezvous, and the impossibility of achieving a formation. Admiral Halsey thereupon suspended flight operations for thirty minutes, so it was not until 0630, in a soupy gray dawn, that the attack group was finally in the air and headed for Wake. There were 36 bombers, each carrying one 500-pound and two 100-pound bombs, nine torpedo planes each carrying twelve 100-pound bombs, and an escort of six fighters.

They flew into clearing weather, with just enough clouds to provide much-needed concealment now that the sun was up and the enemy probably aware of the cruiser detachment. And indeed the enemy was fully aware of the surface bombardment group, for as the airplanes sighted Wake they saw the smoke and flames of the ships' shelling rising high. Commander Howard L. Young, USN, the air group's commander, ordered the prepared plan of operations canceled forthwith and led his planes in to unload their burdens upon the Japanese, the bombers diving and the torpedo planes making a horizontal attack.

To the Americans' surprise, no enemy aircraft arose to give battle, although Wake possessed the finest airfield between Hawaii and Japan. They decided not to leave it that way, for sure. Only slightly hampered by the weak and erratic antiaircraft fire from the batteries that had just been pounded by the big guns of the surface ships, the fliers did a fast but unhurried 40-minute job of destruction. When they had finished, they took a good, long look at the damage the bombs and the shellfire had accomplished, and found it to be satisfactory.

The enemy scored not one tally in revenge. The only life lost in the operation was that of Radioman Jinks at the take-off. One plane and its crew were lost in the attack, the 6-S-8, which was seen smoking badly but under control as it made a water landing near the reef. It is believed that the men were picked up and made prisoners by the Japanese. The pilot was Ensign Percy W. Forman, USNR, and with him was J. E. Winchester, AM2/c, and from all appearances it was the bitter misfortune of engine trouble rather than enemy action that forced their airplane down.

Before the fight ended, Lieutenant Commander McCluskey was again called upon, as he had been in the Marshall Islands action, to do something urgent about a four-engine Japanese aircraft. Ensign Delbert W. Halsey, USNR, having dropped his 500-pound bomb, was circumnavigating the islands looking for an adequate target for his two lighter missiles and meanwhile wasting no time by machine-gunning the enemy emplacements as he went. Suddenly he saw something in the sky where he knew no American plane should be, and with his second look he identified it as a four-motor Kawanishi which he was ill-equipped to tackle himself.

He spoke into his radiophone: "This is Halsey. This is Halsey. I got a Kawanishi five miles east of the island heading straight east and I can't catch him."

The Jap needed catching, indeed, because the cruiser-destroyer group was in sight; McCluskey, cruising at high altitude in his Wildcat, heard the alarm and dived down through the clouds. As if by calculation he broke into the clear almost on the tail of the Japanese, and with his machine guns McCluskey killed the enemy rear gunner and set the Kawanishi's two port engines on fire.

As he turned to climb, McCluskey's wingmen, Lieutenant Roger W. Mehle and Radio Electrician E. H. Bayers, bored in. The big Japanese aircraft exploded, so close to Mehle's plane that when his airplane was inspected aboard the ENTERPRISE a couple of hours later, a fragment of the Kawanishi was found embedded in the leading edge of one wing. It was clearly stamped with the date 1938.

So ended the aerial attack on Wake, but the aviators were to have one more brush with the enemy before returning to the carrier's deck. Ten miles east of Wake a group of the bombers making a rendezvous spotted a Japanese patrol boat, a craft some 100 feet in length, taking violent evasive action. The planes dove upon the vessel with their machine guns and the two or three unexpended light bombs left over from the raid, and while they were thus engaged their target disappeared from under their eyes in a mighty explosion which had the bombers momentarily puzzled until they saw the destroyer MAURY in the offing, her guns trailing sparks and fumes.

It was recorded that the fliers were most irate with the destroyer and so informed its personnel.

3

The NORTHAMPTON, SALT LAKE CITY, MAURY, and BALCH arrived at their appointed position west of Wake according to schedule, but wondering whether the surprise in which they were to participate had not been forestalled. Two hours before the bombardment was supposed to begin the air was filled with the high-pitched, monotonous drone of a Japanese reporting something of great moment over the radio. The likelihood was that the detachment had been spotted by a patrol craft, and that their arrival was being heralded. At that time the ships were only 37 miles from Wake, and Admiral Spruance decided to go ahead with the established plan.

But—there were no bombers over Wake to set the signal fires which Spruance had been told to expect. Instead, three Japanese reconnaissance planes appeared and, after some uncertain passes at the ship, dropped a splatter of light bombs in the neighborhood of the NORTHAMPTON and MAURY.

The cruisers launched their planes, SOC Seagulls, between 0710 and 0722, to provide eyes for the bombardment, six planes in all. At 0742, and 16,000 yards from the target, the guns began to lob a pattern of 8- and 5-inch shells into the irregular dome of mist that marked where the appendix-island of Peale lay. The bombardment lasted a little under half an hour, being broken off when the ENTERPRISE's dive bombers swarmed in. The shells set numerous fires, one towering conflagration marking the destruction of what must have been a large gasoline storage center. Some shore batteries were silenced, but not enough to satisfy Admiral Spruance. Apparently the lack of wholly satisfactory results was due to the type of ammunition with which the ships were provided, a paucity of bombardment shells and more armor-piercing projectiles than were needed in such an operation. But those were the Navy's leanest days; the ships did the best they could with what they had, and if it was hard work to shoot rabbits with a rifle, it was all the more satisfactory when one got a bag that way.

Between the dive-bombing and the high-level attacks on the island by the ENTERPRISE group, the cruiser's SOCs were permitted to enter the combat actively, and delivered eleven 100-pound bombs on a group of buildings and antiaircraft emplacements on the northwest tip of Wake. "Dropping our puny little bombs from our obsolete aircraft was more a gesture than anything else," one of the pilots later observed, but it was a more effective gesture than the one made by the Japanese in retaliation. The enemy sent up a fighter float-plane to attack the SOCs, and although the Japanese had more power, more speed, and more maneuverability than the Americans, he utilized them to keep out of range.

The bombardment completed, the four ships proceeded to the rendezvous point from which they were to rejoin the ENTERPRISE. It was during this maneuver that the MAURY injected herself into the fight between the patrol boat and the carrier's bombers, obliterating the target at 3,000 yards with a two-gun salvo. The destroyer stood by in an effort to rescue

PLATE XLIX—(*upper*) USS SARATOGA and USS LEXINGTON anchored off Diamond Head prior to the war. These two magnificent ships, converted from battle cruisers, spearheaded the task forces fighting in the lean days following Pearl Harbor. The LEXINGTON was lost in the Battle of the Coral Sea. (*lower*) Vice Admiral William F. Halsey, Jr., USN (center), Commander of U.S. Naval Forces in the Southwest Pacific, poses with members of one of his early staffs on a U.S. aircraft carrier. Left to right: Lieut. Col. J. P. Brown, USMC; Lieut. H. D. Moulton, USNR; Lieut. Comdr. S. E. Burroughs, Jr., USN; Capt. M. R. Browning, USN; Chief Signalman R. Gardner, USN; Lieut. Comdr. G. E. Griggs, USN; Vice Adm. Halsey; Capt. B. T. Holcomb, USMC; Lieut. Comdr. L. J. Dow, USN; Capt. B. Groesbeck (MC), USN; Chief Quartermaster H. G. Gibson, USN; Lieut. Comdr. W. H. Ashford, USN; Lieut. Comdr. B. B. Nichol, USN; Comdr. W. H. Duracher, USN; Chief Yeoman P. T. Hunt, USN; Chief Yeoman H. C. Carroll, USN; Chief Yeoman I. N. Bowman, USN.

PLATE L—(*left*) An SBD trio, typical of Navy carrier striking forces in the early Marshalls' raids, searches out the enemy from above the clouds. *Inset:* Lieut. Comdr. W. R. Hollingsworth, USN, Commanding Officer of Bombing Six, one of the squadrons attached to the USS ENTERPRISE.

(*right*) F4Fs, or Grumman fighter planes, in formation above the clouds. Such groups, from the USS YORKTOWN and the USS ENTERPRISE, hit powerful blows at the Marshalls and Gilberts, February 1-2, 1942. *Inset:* Lieut. J. S. Gray, Jr., USN, leader of an ENTERPRISE fighter division.

PLATE LI—U.S. cruisers and destroyers that pitted their skill and speed against the chance that the whole Jap Navy might be sent against them. *Left row, top to bottom:* USS PENSACOLA, USS ST. LOUIS, and USS LOUISVILLE, cruisers; and USS DUNLAP and USS SIMS, destroyers. *Right row, top to bottom:* USS MINNEAPOLIS, USS CHESTER and USS NORTHAMPTON, cruisers; USS MCCALL and USS AYLWIN, destroyers.

PLATE LII—(*upper left*) Propellers form weird white halos in the moisture-laden air as Navy fighters and bombers take off from the USS ENTERPRISE, February 24, 1942, for the attack on Wake Island. (*lower left*) A plane returning from a scouting mission drops a message (in circle) to the deck of its carrier during radio silence.

PLATE LIII—(*above, top*) First installment for Pearl Harbor! Navy scouting planes bring back a photographic record of the damage done to Japanese installations on Wotje, the Marshalls, during a combined carrier and cruiser raid, February 1, 1942. (*above, left*) Sometimes "general quarters," which means every man at his battle station, lasted for days. Coffee and sandwiches were served to the men at their posts. (*above, right*) In order that the public might get a firsthand report of the Pacific fighting, the Navy early accredited war correspondents to go out with the fleet. Here Joe James Custer, United Press (left), and Keith Wheeler, Chicago *Times* (right), talk things over with a Naval officer.

PLATE LIV—(*upper*) Tense faces aboard the ENTERPRISE watch a Jap plane plunge into the sea after missing their carrier by so narrow a margin that it clipped off the tail of the Douglas dive bomber (center) on the edge of the deck. (*lower*) Main batteries of the USS SALT LAKE CITY open up on Wake Island, February 24, 1942. *Inset:* Captain Ellis M. Zacharias, USN, Commanding Officer of the cruiser.

PLATE LV—(*upper right*) A Douglas torpedo bomber circles over Wake Island, waiting its turn to join the attack made by both surface ships and carrier planes. Smoke rises from burning installations. (*lower right*) Two famous Navy carrier pilots match notes over a plotting board. Lieut. Edward H. O'Hare, USN (left), subsequently reported missing in action, brought down six Jap planes in a single engagement near the Gilberts. Lieut. Comdr. J. S. Thach, USN (right), has accounted for twelve enemy planes.

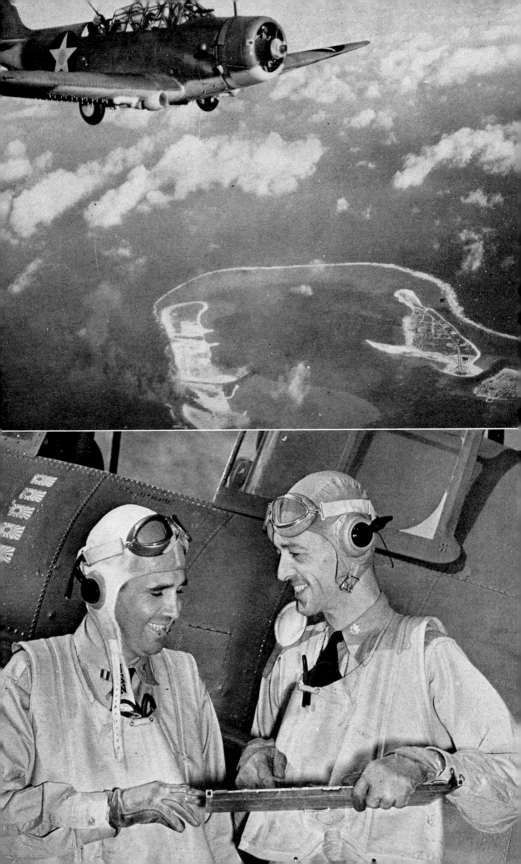

PLATE LVI—In April, 1942, the United Nations cheered the news that Tokyo and other Japanese cities had been bombed by Army Air Corps fliers. For a year the take-off place was known only as "Shangri-la." Then the story and these photographs were released. (*upper*) Lieut. Col. James H. Doolittle, USA, wires a Japanese medal to the fin of a 500-pound bomb. (*lower*) Insignia of one of the North American B-25 bombers aboard the USS HORNET.

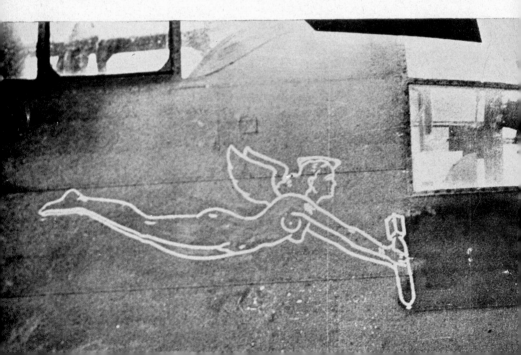

PLATE LVII—(*upper*) In a well-organized example of Army-Navy cooperation, a twin-engined B-25 takes off with a heavy load of gasoline and bombs, guided by the white lines on the carrier deck. (*lower*) "Off we go . . ." The words of the famous Army Air Corps song were never more appropriate than at this moment as a B-25 bomber lifts from the deck of the USS HORNET and heads west to give the Japanese their first taste of bombs dropping on home soil.

PLATE LVIII—(*upper*) Only a few days before the Japanese attack on Pearl Harbor, the Fourth Marines, evacuated from Shanghai, China, arrived in the Philippines aboard the *President Harrison*. The liner was later seized by the Japanese. (*lower*) Here part of the Fourth Marines disembarks at Olongapo, small U. S. Naval base north of Manila. They are still wearing peacetime uniforms.

PLATE LIX—(*upper*) On Bataan, Colonel Samuel Howard, USMC, awards Silver Star Medals to two Marine heroes: Pfc. Charles R. Greer, USMC, of Turtle Creek, Pennsylvania, and Pvt. Alexander Katchuck, USMC, of Sacramento, California. Col. Howard and Pvt. Katchuck are officially listed as missing in action. Pfc. Greer is listed as dead.

(*lower*) Lieut. Col. Curtis T. Beecher (left), Fourth Marines, and his runner, shown during fighting on Bataan peninsula, the Philippines. Col. Beecher is listed as a prisoner of war.

PLATE LX—(*upper*) The sub-tender USS CANOPUS, ordered to stay behind when most of the ships in Manila Bay were evacuated, not only took care of a submarine squadron but served as a machine shop and arsenal for our forces on Bataan. She was finally demolished to keep her from being used by the Japs. (*lower*) Around the shores of Bataan, marines and soldiers constructed emplacements for machine gunners and sharpshooters, resisting Japanese landing attempts for weeks. Companies of beached sailors also manned such defenses.

PLATE LXI—(*upper*) This barbed wire is part of the beach defenses along the shores of Bataan peninsula. From such crude barriers, the marksmanship of the soldiers, sailors and marines beat off attack after attack by Japanese landing parties. (*lower*) The men who held out on Corregidor never relaxed a moment. Here marines instruct Filipino soldiers in the use of a machine gun cartridge not familiar to them.

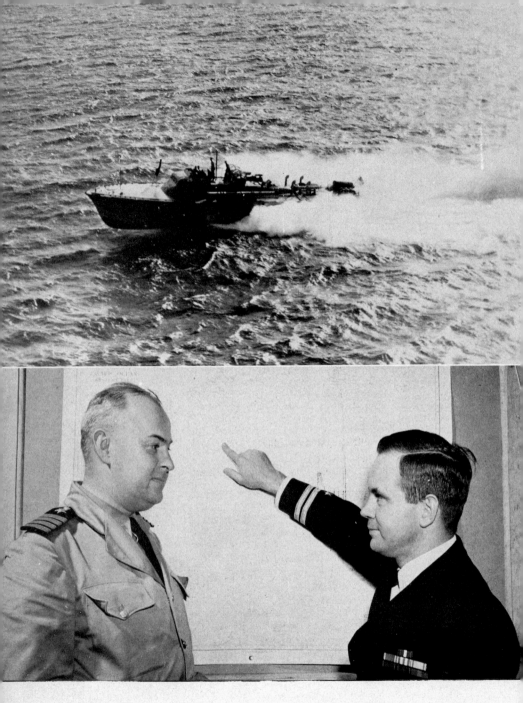

PLATE LXII (*upper*) A PT boat roars through the water. In night attacks around the Philippines the PTs sank and damaged warships and merchant craft to play a large part in disrupting enemy supplies and communications. (*lower*) Lieut. John D. Bulkeley, USN, Commanding Officer of the PT Boat Squadron that evacuated General MacArthur and his staff from the Philippines, points out to Captain Leland P. Lovette, USN, Navy Director of Public Relations, the scene of his mosquito boat operations against the Japanese.

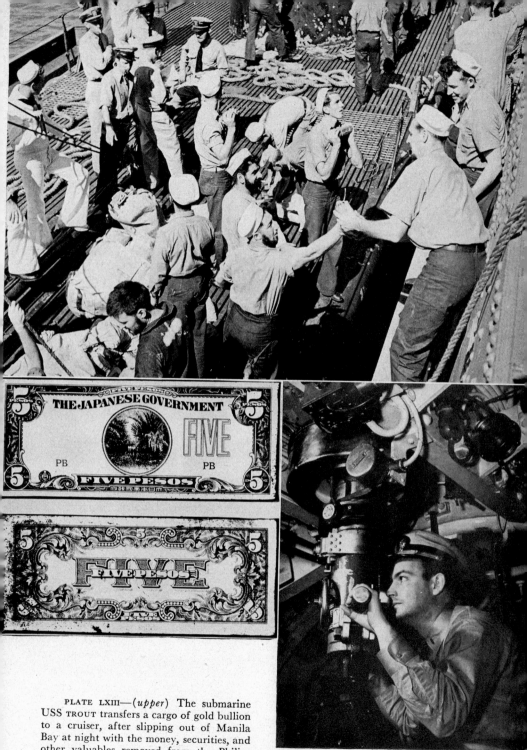

PLATE LXIII—(*upper*) The submarine USS TROUT transfers a cargo of gold bullion to a cruiser, after slipping out of Manila Bay at night with the money, securities, and other valuables removed from the Philippines just before the Japs moved in. (*lower left*) A 5-peso note printed by the Japanese for use in the Philippines, indicating that the enemy's plan for conquest had been long in preparation. (*lower right*) Typical of the alert officers and crewmen whose activities harassed both Japanese fighting and merchant ships is this submariner looking through the periscope of his underseas craft.

PLATE LXIV—(*upper*) This photograph was taken from the island fortress of Corregidor, looking across the narrow strait that separates the island from mountainous Bataan peninsula. The smokestack and masts of a sunken ship can be seen. (*lower*) Here in one picture are five elements of a Navy task force, the hard-hitting combination of sea-air power that was to revolutionize naval warfare. At right steams the carrier YORKTOWN, from which a plane (TBD, or Douglas Torpedo Bomber) has just taken off. In the distance is a destroyer of the SIMS class; in the center an oiler of the NEOSHO class. To the far left is a SALT LAKE CITY class cruiser. The YORKTOWN was lost in the Battle of Midway; the SIMS and NEOSHO in the Battle of the Coral Sea.

some of the surviving Japanese, as the disgusted ENTERPRISE bombers flew off.

As the MAURY was rigging her rescue apparatus, a Japanese seaplane (seeing the sky now free of opposition) came screaming down in a long dive on the destroyer from the overcast, and rocked the ship with a pair of close misses. The MAURY, her antiaircraft guns spewing, left the struggling Japanese sailors to the fate decreed them by their own compatriots.

As the quartet of bombardment ships fell into formation for withdrawal, another four-engine enemy airplane hove into view, cruising in long zigzags far out of range of the American guns. It was an annoyance; it meant that the antiaircraft guns had to be fully manned and on the alert while the Japanese shadower remained in sight. It meant some risk for the BALCH too, when that destroyer was sent off to sink a 400-ton enemy patrol boat and remained to rescue four survivors.

A request was radioed the ENTERPRISE, some 125 miles distant, to send a few fighter planes across to rid the cruisers of the menace. But all day the Japanese seaplane remained the only aircraft in the sky. At 1743, just before sunset, the enemy plane began to close the gap it had maintained all day between itself and the ships. All attention was centered on its approach, and fingers itched for triggers as machine gunners prepared to ward off any suicide dive.

The enemy bomber's spurt, however, was only a feint, a feint that tricked the inexperienced Americans into averting their attention from another quarter from which two large land-based bombers suddenly broke through the clouds. Before the guns could be swung to meet the surprise attack, the enemy planes let loose their bombs. They were overconfident, for each of the bombers cut loose both its big missiles at once. They were accurate, but not accurate enough. The cruisers spun on their stern-posts, and the bombs fell into the water—close, but not close enough to start a single rivet. With that, the three Japanese airplanes joined up in a fast getaway.

The ENTERPRISE had heard the appeal for help, and had responded, sending Lieutenant Mehle at the head of a trio of fighters—with Ensigns R. M. Rich and J. R. Daly, both USNR—to get rid of the "shadow." The trio spent nearly six hours in the air on that mission, encountering nothing but high winds and violent rain squalls and missing both the compatriot ships and the airplane that menaced them. The three returned only when their gasoline was nearly exhausted, and so closely did they figure their fuel limit that Daly's tanks went dry just as he was "in the groove" for the carrier's flight deck. He fought free of the sinking plane and was picked up by the RALPH TALBOT.

Mehle and Rich did not have 10 gallons between them when they landed. The ENTERPRISE was known as a lucky ship, and a happy one. That day, after a bad start, she shared her luck with the entire task force.

4

The raid was a success in every way. Apparently the attackers reached Wake as its captors were sitting back in relaxation after rehabilitating the island from the bombardment preceding its seizure, and while waiting for ships from Japan to bring it the airplanes and equipment which would make it the base of operations against the mid-Pacific.

And when the attackers left Wake, they left the survivors to tackle the whole job of rehabilitation all over again, while many a Japanese ship would have to run the gantlet of American submarines to replace the stores destroyed that day.

Between the bombarding ships and the aircraft, the score rolled up by the task force included:

Three four-engine aircraft destroyed

Two 400-500-ton patrol vessels sunk

Seven out of 10 large gasoline storage tanks destroyed

One fuel oil dump destroyed

One ammunition magazine blown up

Three magazines badly damaged

Two underground hangars destroyed

Four large buildings destroyed and six badly damaged

Two antiaircraft batteries destroyed

Twenty large craters on the east-west runway, rendering it useless for an indeterminate time, and the north end of the transverse runway made similarly useless

The Americans, on ship or in the air, had to pick their targets with care, for there probably were still some of their countrymen captive on Wake. It appeared that the contractor's camp on the northwest prong of the main island, where lived the men who had been completing Pan American Airways' tremendous project at Wake, had been converted into a prisoners' stockade. It was close to many desirable targets, a shore battery, antiaircraft gun emplacements, the power plant for the islands, fuel oil storage tanks, piers, and a new causeway connecting with Peale Island. All these desirable targets were left unmolested by the raiders, to avoid killing their compatriots if any were still there.

There were other achievements incidental to the battle. From the experience gained, it was determined that the ratio of fighters to other aircraft assigned to a carrier was too low, and that the complement of pilots in excess of planes had to be greatly increased to avoid disastrous overwork of the men who had to go into battle after flying patrols, and then fall to patrolling again. Other, and more technical, faults were revealed, both in the ships' gunnery and equipment and in the planes themselves. The raid on the Marshalls and Gilberts had been a laboratory test, whose results had been refined in the fiery retort of Wake. Much that had seemed perfect in theory, and acceptable after the test of simulated battle, proved wholly inadequate to actual warfare. From the detailed and unsparingly critical report of Admiral Halsey, the critiques of Admiral Spruance and Captain Zacharias and others in command, the Commander in Chief Pacific Fleet drew up recommendations which were to give the American forces that ascending advantage over the enemy by which domination of the ocean was eventually to be won.

But some hitherto unscheduled events were to delay Admiral Halsey's delivery of those reports to CINCPAC. As he was heading homeward, a message reached him directing him to pay another call on the Japanese while he was in the neighborhood—a call that would take him into the enemy's front yard.

The task force turned west again, and the word was passed with information on what the next target would be. And, as one unofficial chronicler recorded it aboard the ENTERPRISE: "Here's the latest. We're headed *west*. For Marcus Island this time! God be with us. Possibility of a surface scrap before that. *It's less than a thousand miles from TOKYO itself*. Well, we've been asking for it, and we have just the right admiral to give us what we want."

Chapter Fourteen

ROUGHLY 700 miles northwest of Wake and 975 miles from Japan, Marcus Island is a wedge-shaped morsel of land, five miles in circumference, whose rumored existence was verified by USS TUSCALOOSA in 1874. When Japan claimed it some years later, nobody objected. Nobody had yet heard of the radio, aviation was still a fantasy, and long-range weather prediction was based on such scientific data as the density of caterpillars' pelage and the migration of wild ducks.

Now, however, Marcus Island, or Minami Tori Shimu—Isle of the Southern Birds—as the Japanese (and only the Japanese) called it, was an important accessory to Japan's projected conquest of the Pacific. It contained an airfield and hangars; it was a weather-reporting station from whose calculations the Japanese could computed many days in advance what the atmospheric conditions would be at strategic points to the westward. And, of course, it housed a powerful radio station.

CINCPAC's orders to Admiral Halsey were received on the 25th. It was not wholly a surprise. When the original task force, including the YORKTOWN, left Pearl Harbor to raid Wake and Eniwetok, Marcus had been given as an alternative to the latter island at the discretion of the task force command.

Three days after reversing course, on February 28, Admiral Halsey took the ENTERPRISE, NORTHAMPTON, and SALT LAKE CITY off to visit Marcus, leaving the six destroyers to lag behind. The attack was set for the usual predawn hour on March 4, and the planes were launched according to plan 125 miles distant from the target. Air Group Commander Young again led the procession of 31 bombers and six fighters. The visiting cards consisted of 21,700 pounds of high explosive.

The planes were launched by moonlight, under a spotty overcast which thickened during the approach to the island. In those seas a dense mist usually shrouds most islands in the early morning, but not only did

Marcus stand out brilliantly in the cloud-filtered moonlight but there was a break in the overcast that brought the raiders a clear view of the target from nearly three miles in the air.

The Japanese were caught sleeping. Commander Young dropped the first bomb-load, and zoomed up into a cloud which immediately turned a sunset crimson. He had made a bull's-eye on a cluster of large tanks full of aviation gasoline. Four other planes dropped their bombs before the Japanese collected themselves sufficiently to man their antiaircraft guns.

Apparently the man on watch at the radio station was one of the first to awake and realize what was going on, because the fliers' earphones suddenly rang with the Japanese's high-pitched alarm to Tokyo. The cluster of buildings at the base of the radio transmitter towers was in the bombsight of Lieutenant J. D. Blitch, USN. He let go his bombs. The radio went suddenly silent. There was no more station from which to send a signal—if there was anyone left to send one.

Although the bombing started numerous fires, besides the fuel dump, the fliers dropped quantities of flares to help illumine the target in the expectation that enemy aircraft would rise to the attack. None was even seen on the ground, and such as might have been sheltered in the hangars were destroyed together with those buildings when the attacking planes swooped to within 2,000 feet of every visible target.

Antiaircraft fire, both 3-inch and heavy machine-gun, became intense as the raid reached its height. It prevented the bombers from making a survey sweep after dropping their missiles for an accurate evaluation of the damage they had wrought, but as they headed back to the ENTER-PRISE they could see two towering fires on the island from a distance of 30 miles. The "Isle of the Southern Birds" had been visited by birds of another plumage.

One airplane did not accompany the group on the return trip.

At 0705, just as Commander Young ordered the planes to assemble for the return, a voice came over the radiophone: "This is Dale. My plane is afire. I'm going to land east of the island, but I'm all right."

They saw him go down, trailing flame and black smoke. Lieutenant Richard H. Best, USN, followed the burning plane and circled the steaming eddy where it struck the sea. Then, out of the smoke bobbed the yellow self-inflating rubber boat with which each plane was equipped, and Best saw "Dale"—Lieutenant (jg) Hart Dale Hilton, USNR—and his gunner, Jack Leaming, AR3/c, hoist themselves into the rubber bubble.

As Best circled the little boat he was given a cheerful wave-off by Hilton and Leaming. Then they both lifted their hands high in the "thumbs up" signal. There was nothing to be done for them.

The loss was nearly doubled when Lieutenant J. S. Gray, Jr., USN, of the fighter escort lost contact with his fellows in the tumult of clouds between the island and the now eastward-steaming carrier force. Gray tried to pick up the flight on his radio. It had gone off frequency, and was as useless as none at all. Resorting to dead reckoning, Gray set out to find the carrier which was discreetly using rain squalls to hide in against the possibilities of enemy bombers, and so the pilot missed the ENTERPRISE completely.

But aboard the carrier there were several who had heard what they were sure was a searching Japanese airplane buzz past in the clouds, and when Gray failed to return with the rest of the Fighting Six unit—which reported no enemy aircraft at all at Marcus—an obvious conclusion was drawn.

Lieutenant John Baumeister, Jr., USN, electronics officer of the ENTERPRISE, did some quick calculations liberally spiced with hunch, and beamed a signal to where he figured Gray ought to be, on frequencies covering the range a possibly off-center radio should pick up. It was a man-made miracle that worked. Gray was brought home, landing with less than nine gallons of gasoline.

So ended another successful raid. Whatever the material damage to the Japanese installations, whatever setback to their plans for making the Pacific Ocean their own, the sheer audacity of smashing a Japanese outpost within easy bomber flight of Tokyo can be said to have given General Tojo something to ponder and even more to explain to underlings who believed his assurance that the United States, as a sea power, had been reduced to the level of Switzerland.

None of Admiral Halsey's smashing blows against the Japanese outposts in the Marshalls, Wake, and Marcus could be properly evaluated.

The results will not be measured exactly until the United States is in possession of the records of the Japanese high command, and has had time for its experts to study them. Perhaps the raids contributed much, and directly, to the enemy's resolve to strike westward directly against the United States, a resolve that resulted in the Japanese disaster in the

Battle of Midway. But these are events beyond the scope of this report, and should be saved for the historian equipped both with information now in the hands of the Japanese and with a perspective that will come only with the passing of time.

Chapter Fifteen

A NEW task force, under command of Vice Admiral Wilson Brown, USN, had been constructed around the carrier LEXINGTON, and had gone to sea in patrol of the Australian-American life line about the time that Admiral Halsey led his raiders into the Marshall and Gilbert islands.

The enemy was beginning to pile up in the islands of the Malay Barrier, Singapore fell on February 15, the Allied fleet in Netherlands East Indies waters was being pushed back as the vastly superior Japanese sea-air forces charged down through the many corridors of the archipelago. The Philippines were doomed, and the appeals from Australia had to be heeded not only to save an ally, but in the starkest appraisal of self-defense.

Admiral King's appraisal was that the enemy would gather his forces in the New Guinea-New Britain area where there were harbors to house the combined fleets of the world, and from there smother the tenuous defenses of the South Sea Islands to strike at the Hawaiians, the Canal Zone, or Australia unless the Japanese chose to leave that continent to wither with all its arteries of communication severed.

The necessity was plain. The Japanese had to be deterred from coordinating that plan, and so the LEXINGTON task force was ordered by COMINCH to proceed to the Southwest Pacific to operate under Vice Admiral Herbert F. Leary, USN, commander of Forces ANZAC. Additional naval forces were gathered under COMANZAC, together with Army aviation units. Early in February, then, the combatant vessels at Admiral Brown's disposal totaled 15 ships. They were, with their respective commanders:

Carrier (and flagship) LEXINGTON, Captain Frederick C. Sherman, USN

Four heavy cruisers:

MINNEAPOLIS, Captain Frank J. Lowry, USN
INDIANAPOLIS, Captain Edward W. Hanson, USN
PENSACOLA, Captain Frank L. Lowe, USN
SAN FRANCISCO, Captain Daniel J. Callaghan, USN

Ten destroyers:

CLARK, Commander Myron T. Richardson, USN
PATTERSON, Commander Frank R. Walker, USN
PHELPS, Lieutenant Commander Edward L. Beck, USN
DEWEY, Lieutenant Commander Charles F. Chillingworth, Jr., USN
MACDONOUGH, Lieutenant Commander John M. McIsaac, USN
HULL, Lieutenant Commander Richard F. Stout, USN
AYLWIN, Lieutenant Commander Robert H. Rodgers, USN
DALE, Lieutenant Commander Anthony L. Rorschach, USN
BAGLEY, Lieutenant Commander George A. Sinclair, USN
DRAYTON, Lieutenant Commander Laurence A. Abercrombie, USN

After taking up his station under COMANZAC and studying the situation, Admiral Brown conceived a plan for an attack on Rabaul, the magnificent harbor on the northeastern tip of New Britain which the Japanese were already using as a base and assembly point. Roughly, the plan was for the LEXINGTON's planes to hit Rabaul from the seaward, while heavy U.S. Army bombers of the Australian command came in from the south. If the air attack proved successful, the PENSACOLA, supported by the destroyers CLARK and BAGLEY, were to bombard the Japanese anchorage.

The risks were great. It meant penetrating waters none too well charted and in which Japanese warships were known to be operating, but in unknown numbers. Stopping the enemy's progress with the forces presently available was beyond hope. The best results in most optimistic preview would be to throw the Japanese off stride, force them to recast their plans, subtract from their strength by whatever ships and harbor installations could be destroyed. Though the risks were great, they were worth taking.

So Admiral Brown started northward, up into the Solomons area, past Bougainville and into the narrow strait between New Britain and New Ireland. The plan was to launch the aircraft four hours after midnight on February 21, at a position some 125 miles northeast of Rabaul.

The task force completed all but 225 miles of its hazardous journey with success. On the morning of the 20th a large patrol of enemy flying boats came over the horizon, head-on for the LEXINGTON and her escorts. There was no doubt at all that the task force had been detected for what it was, because the Japanese turned and hightailed back toward Rabaul without offering battle.

There was no time for disappointment, because the enemy came down upon the American ships forthwith. A six-plane combat patrol was circling the LEXINGTON when a four-engine enemy bomber was detected approaching the task force from the rear. Two of the six patrolling fighters were told off to intercept the bomber—and they did. It went down flaming from the guns of Lieutenant Commander John S. Thach, USN. Another bomber was then detected coming up high and fast to meet the task force, a four-engine flying boat. Lieutenant (jg) Onia B. Stanley, USNR, got that one. A third bomber, following the second, evidently thought the going a little too heavy. It turned and ran. That was not so good; the report that its crew would make could only pile up trouble for the LEXINGTON.

That trouble was not long in arriving.

It first took the shape of a big V of nine twin-engine bombers hurtling down from the direction of Rabaul. The LEXINGTON had twelve combat planes in the air at the time, a relief patrol of six having been sent aloft to relieve an equal number which had been in the air three hours. The tired, nerve-strained pilots of the relieved patrol, their planes running low in gasoline, straightened out to meet the Japanese.

Thach led the charge, and before the enemy could reach the bomb-release point five of the nine were down in flames. The four survivors then flew into a hailstorm of shell fire from the four ships, and in complete confusion they dropped their bombs 3,000 yards from the LEXINGTON and turned to flee in an every-man-for-himself maneuver which tangled them immediately with the American fighter planes. Out of that melee only one of the enemy bombers escaped.

One of the damaged bombers headed for the LEXINGTON on the ship's starboard beam with machine guns spouting. Whether it was intent upon a suicide dive to the carrier's deck—a Japanese doctrine which the facts do not support in perspective—the LEXINGTON's 1.1s and .50 calibers concentrated a cone of fire on the bomber and it crashed flaming just 75 yards astern.

While twisting about in evasive action the LEXINGTON launched 15 more planes, and took five aboard for gasoline and ammunition. All joined in the chase of the surviving bombers save two, and as the hunt headed for the horizon a second wave of nine Japanese bombers bore down upon the LEXINGTON.

The group commander must have shouted the Japanese equivalent of "Tally-ho" when he sighted the American ships defended by two lone fighters, even though these two immediately attacked. When the guns of one of the pair jammed, and the defenseless pilot had to break off the fight without completing one burst of machine-gun fire, the joy in the hearts of the Japanese probably was as great as the despair of the men on the ships which had now become waiting targets.

There was only one tiny wasp of a fighter between the nine bombers and the task force. And the pilot of that lone plane was Lieutenant Edward H. ("Butch") O'Hare.

The enemy formation was a V of Vs, a broad arrow of high-flying destruction, and O'Hare whizzed past them out of gunshot, pivoted on one wingtip, and came roaring back upon the bombers from the rear and on their right flank.

Admiral Brown and Captain Sherman were among those who witnessed what happened in the next few minutes. O'Hare's guns literally blasted the starboard motors out of the last two planes on the right. Then he ducked under the formation and turned his guns on the third plane of the V, which staggered out of formation. Two more began to smoke and shed fragments of wing covering, their crazy antics in trying to prevent destruction breaking up the rest of the formation.

Four of the flight of nine, however, had come through the one-man tornado and dropped their bombs haphazardly before turning back. The sky seemed to be filled with Japanese bombers in confused gyrations, with O'Hare coming back to bore into the disorganized covey again. One went down, and another, and a third.

The whole affray was over in four minutes. In that time O'Hare had shot down five enemy bombers and scored hits on three others. These three were destroyed when their flight carried them head-on into the LEXINGTON's planes returning from cleaning up the first wave of bombers. A fourth, attacked by Lieutenant Edward H. Allen, USN, with a scout bomber never designed for pursuit, escaped by the skin of his stabilizers —or what was left of it. The planes were evenly matched in speed; perhaps the American SBD had a slight edge. The Japanese did not want to fight, but poured on the coal to get away from his ponderous but dogged pursuer. Every time Allen crept up close enough for him or his gunner, RM1/c Bruce Rountree, to shoot at the fleeing *bakugeki,* the recoil of the guns slowed the SBD just enough to give the Japanese the advantage to forge ahead.

Allen had to give up the chase when his fuel ran low. It was too bad, for otherwise his score and Rountree's for the day would have been two enemy planes, a unique achievement for a bomber then. At that he earned the Navy Cross for his day's work.

Thach also received the Navy Cross for his leadership in dispersing and pursuing the enemy bombers, and his part in that memorable fight was cited again when he received the Distinguished Service Medal a few months later.

But nobody disputed that the honors of the day were Butch O'Hare's. Admiral Brown said that the LEXINGTON owed her life to him. O'Hare was brought to Washington, where the President hung the Medal of Honor upon him and presented him with a lieutenant commander's commission.

Stanley was given the Distinguished Flying Cross for getting his bomber, and there were many other awards for the work that was done to extricate the LEXINGTON from what more than once had appeared to be destruction.

The mission was a failure. The enemy could not, however, afford to let the United States Navy have many such failures, for it cost the Japanese two four-engine flying boats and 16 two-engine bombers, possibly 17, with all their crews.

The task force lost two planes and one pilot, Ensign John Woodrow Wilson, USNR, who was shot down by a Japanese tail gunner during the melee of the first attack on the LEXINGTON.

But much was learned by fliers and ships' companies in that postgraduate school of desperate conflict. Again the antiaircraft fire of our ships proved poor, very poor in some instances. The one enemy bomber brought down by antiaircraft fire was the bomber downed in the LEXINGTON's wake at tyro's range. It was a demonstration, if any was needed, that there is no economy in cutting down target practice.

The Japanese proceeded with their development of Rabaul, but in close adherence to the pattern they had initiated at the war's outset they did not pause in their operations to consolidate that gain. They engulfed

all of New Britain and New Ireland; they made a landing on Bougainville preparatory to the investiture of the Solomon Islands, and bombed
and bombed again the chief ports in Australian-British-Dutch-divided
New Guinea, the world's second largest island, whose dragon shape
appears on the chart just north of Australia.

New Guinea and its companion island Borneo were the last inhabited
places on earth whose interiors were still marked "unexplored" on the
maps. The travelers' tales of cannibals and head-hunters, of strange
beasts and prehistoric survivals, could be believed by the romantic or, at
worst, labeled "unproved" by the realists. But this much was certain:
whoever held Port Moresby on the southeast coast had the key to Australia, and whoever possessed Lae and Salamaua in the sharp angle of
Huon Gulf on the northeast coast had his foot in the door to all the
islands that stretch from Asia to South America between the equator and
the 10th south parallel.

The Japanese put their foot in that door on March 8. It would have
to be slammed and held, before the tedious work of severing that intrusive
limb could be started.

From the Commander in Chief United States Fleet, via Commander
in Chief of the Pacific, came orders to attack the Japanese. Decision as to
what objectives were to be attacked, and by what means, was left to
Admiral Brown, COMANZAC concurring.

It will be remembered that the USS YORKTOWN complement of Admiral
Halsey's task force had been detached and ordered south as it left Pearl
Harbor for the Wake-Marcus raid. That carrier, flagship of Rear Admiral
Fletcher, had now joined Admiral Brown's force together with its cruisers
ASTORIA and LOUISVILLE, and its six destroyers. Including the Australian
heavy cruiser HMAS AUSTRALIA, Captain H. P. Farncomb, RAN, Admiral Brown now had eight heavy cruisers, 14 destroyers, and two carriers
at his command. It was not quite a match, gun for gun, torpedo tube for
torpedo tube, bomb for bomb, for what the Japanese had in the area to
the north, augmented as that was with submarines and land-based heavy
bombing planes. What was more, Admiral Brown had no reserves to
call upon, if he got into serious trouble.

The situation demanded bold action, an incalculable surprise for the
enemy, with minimum risk to the United Nations' slender naval resources.

"Careful deliberation" marked the March 8 conference which determined the course of action, Admiral Brown wrote in his action
report.

Lae and Salamaua were to be attacked by the United States Navy—from the landward. Bold action—incalculable surprise—minimum risk (it was hoped).

The YORKTOWN's planes and the LEXINGTON's were to be launched from the Australian side of the island, hurdle the unsurveyed Owen Stanley Mountains, attack the Japanese from the rear as they looked seaward from the opposite shore for trouble.

March 10 was fixed as the day for the attack, the fleet to start north at once. At the last minute word was received that a convoy of troopships from the United States bound for New Caledonia would need protection, and Admiral Brown detached the RAN cruiser AUSTRALIA, the CHICAGO, ASTORIA, and LOUISVILLE with the destroyers ANDERSON, HAMMANN, HUGHES, and SIMS to act as a screen against a Japanese excursion from the south. Placed under command of Rear Admiral John Gregory Crace, RN, the cruiser-destroyer detachment was stationed off the Louisiade Islands which trail from New Guinea's long southeastern peninsula, to perform the double duty of intercepting any Japanese force which might debouch to attack the troop convoy or to attack the YORKTOWN-LEXINGTON force in the Gulf of Papua.

The task force had to enter waters inadequately charted to launch its planes for a flight over unmapped territory bisected by cloud-capped mountains. To many a man and officer occurred the thought that it would have been a lot easier on the nerves to sail boldly into Huon Gulf and shoot it out with the Japanese fleet.

To collect all the known data available, Commander Walton W. Smith, USN, of Admiral Brown's staff, flew to Townsville, Australia, and Commander William B. Ault of the LEXINGTON air group flew to Port Moresby, quickly to interview anybody who knew anything about the Gulf of Papua and the interior of New Guinea. Among the facts brought back to Admiral Brown was the information that there was a pass in the three-mile-high mountains with an altitude of only 7,500 feet, and that the gap was on an air line between Salamaua and a deep-water stretch of the Gulf of Papua less than 50 miles from shore. There was a footpath over the pass, and those who used it had declared the valley to be usually cloud-free between 0700 and 1100.

On that assertion from curious sources, Admiral Brown set course and speed in order to launch the carriers' aircraft at 0800 on March 10. And when the launching area was reached, and found to be as described, the admiral sent Commander Ault ahead of the bombers, torpedo planes, and fighters to find the pass and to fly figure eights about it, so that he could guide and advise the Jap-hunting squadrons.

The LEXINGTON sent up 18 SBD-3s of Scouting Two, 12 SBD-3s of Bombing Two, 13 TBD-1s of Torpedo Two, and eight F4F-3s of Fighting Three.

The YORKTOWN launched 17 SBD-3s of Bombing Five, 13 SBD-3s of Scouting Five, 12 TBD-1s of Torpedo Five, and 10 F4F-3s of Fighting Forty-two. Between them the planes carried 48 tons of bombs, ranging from 1,000-pounders to 30-pound antipersonnel missiles, and 13 torpedoes.

One hundred and three planes were in that formation, and the dozen fighters and nine bombers posted to fly patrol over the task force saw them go with envy.

There were two enemy cruisers and four destroyers in the Lae-Salamaua bight, protecting five transports and two cargo vessels as they unloaded, and the Japanese were caught flatfooted and off guard as the first bombers from the LEXINGTON poured through the mountain slot and dove upon the clustered ships.

And there was a surprise in store for the Navy pilots and bombardiers, too, when they saw another sizable enemy task force just coming over the horizon. It was 25 miles away, and the fliers were too busy to study its composition, but a cruiser and five destroyers put on speed when they saw there was trouble—and bad trouble—at Lae. Six transports and a seaplane tender of the 17,000-ton KAMOI class loafed behind.

The LEXINGTON group struck first, with the YORKTOWN squadrons coming in close behind or splitting off in sections to attack particular targets on the fringe of the area. It was after the first bombs were dropped that the dumfounded Japanese manned their antiaircraft guns on ships and on shore, and the first burst of that erratic fire killed Ensign Joseph Philip Johnson, USNR, and J. B. Jewell, RM3/c, his gunner, of Scouting Two. They were the only American casualties suffered in the entire operation. The only Japanese aircraft to rise against the Americans was a single-float biplane which Lieutenant Noel A. Gaylor, USN, shot down with little trouble, and another of the same type which fled smoking as three TBD rear-seat gunners turned their guns on it.

It was Port Darwin in reverse, with the Japanese on the receiving end this time and the Americans choosing their targets from the air. Without listing repetitious details, the bombers and torpedo planes that morning rolled up the following score against the Japanese:

They sank five transports and cargo ships of the seven in the bight, the light cruiser of the second convoy, and a destroyer which blew up when a bomb fell among its own depth charges;

A minelayer was left burning and low in the water, apparently sinking;

A 500-pound bomb hit one heavy cruiser, which evidently fired a magazine and caused a large explosion and a fierce fire;

A 1,000-bomb hit was scored on a second heavy cruiser, plus two close misses, which were believed to have left it in sinking condition.

Also listed as "seriously damaged and possibly sunk" were two destroyers and a gunboat.

The seaplane tender which tried to keep out of the fighting area was stopped dead in the water and left burning, and a second gunboat was badly damaged.

Most of the antiaircraft emplacements on shore were destroyed, the airfield pockmarked, and the military buildings around it shattered.

The planes headed for the attack at 0840, and the first bomb was dropped at 0922. By one minute past noon all the aircraft were back on their respective carriers except the lone casualty. The task force retired to rendezvous with its oilers NEOSHO and KASKASKIA and Admiral Crace's outer guard, whereafter they all returned to base without incident.

CINCPAC congratulated Admiral Brown on a raid "well planned and well executed." Aside from the bizarre fact that for the first time naval forces had been engaged with a 15,000-foot mountain range intervening, the battle contributed substantially to the initial processes of attrition which were, before another year, to make it difficult for the Japanese to service their far-flung and overextended forces. More immediately, if it did not dislodge the Japanese from New Guinea, the raid certainly checked the enemy plans to round the island's South Cape and occupy Port Moresby. And, of course, it again provided the pilots, bombardiers, and torpedomen with seasoning in battle for further profitable use in combats to come. Even their experience in mountainhopping was to be utilized in later operations, when the business of driving the Japanese back finally became feasible.

Chapter Sixteen

O N April 18, 1942, the people of the United States, sickened by the surrender of Bataan nine days before and aware by more than that portent that they were still on the losing side of the war, were galvanized by the news that Japan had been bombed.

Army fliers, led by Lieutenant Colonel James H. Doolittle, had come out of nowhere and laid a trail of bombs across the main island of Honshu from Tokyo to Kobe.

The story of that raid is well-known, because it has been told in the War Department's press release of April 20, 1943, and in *Thirty Seconds Over Tokyo,* the narrative of Captain Ted W. Lawson of the Army Air Forces, who lost a leg in the operation. Horror erased Allied exultation when the Japanese announced that some of the Army aviators captured had been executed by beheading. Of the 80 men who flew over Japan, one was killed, two are registered as missing, eight were taken prisoner, five were interned on Soviet territory and 64—many of them, like Captain Lawson, grievously wounded—eventually returned to the United States through China.

It was, of course, a joint Army-Navy operation in which the Navy's part heretofore has had to be largely kept secret. It was worked out with such secrecy that the volunteers chosen to make the flight did not know where they were bound until they were at sea aboard USS HORNET, the Navy's newest carrier. Nor did the HORNET's company, not even her captain, Marc A. Mitscher, USN, know why the carrier was laboring under the curious deck-load of 16 Army B-25 medium bombers.

True, when the HORNET returned from her abbreviated shakedown cruise to the Caribbean in early February of 1942, the crew was disappointed to find its hopes for shore leave postponed while the carrier put out to sea again with two of the ponderous-looking Army aircraft aboard, which Navy pilots flew off the deck as if simply to demonstrate that it could be done. Rear Admiral D. B. Duncan, USN, represented Admiral King at the experimental take-off. With that, the carrier returned to port and presently joined a troop convoy bound for the Pacific.

The bluejackets and the "airedales"—men who work directly with the planes—gossiped as to HORNET's destination. Of course, she was bound for the fabulous South Sea Islands, where Japanese warships were so thick you couldn't miss and it wouldn't be long before the HORNET's spanking new bombers and torpedo planes had whittled the enemy down to size. But when the carrier turned north and lay off the California coast for three weeks while relays of Navy pilots flew out from shore to practice landings and take-offs, the gloom between-decks was profound.

"We're nothing but an asterisk schoolship," was the word that was passed. "These guys on the Big E and the Lex and the Yorkie, they have all the luck."

Then the HORNET moved north again, to put into San Francisco Bay and to be tied up to a dock at Alameda. Again there was no shore leave.

On the evening of the carrier's arrival a flight of Army B-25s came over the ship, and landed on a field near the harbor. Lieutenant John F. Sutherland, USN, one of the HORNET's pilots, remembers the bombers' arrival. He and a group of his fellows watched the B-25s land, and remarked at the unusual technique displayed.

"Aren't they coming in slow?"

"Yeah, looks as if they've been having a little Navy indoctrination."

And to the Navy men's surprise, when they greeted the Army pilots, that was the exact truth.

For a month the Army men had been practicing under the expert tutelage of Lieutenant Henry L. Miller, USN, in Florida. Day after day they had taken lessons in landing slowly and with the shortest roll possible; then they had more lessons on taking off in as short a space as possible, after a run so abbreviated that none would have deemed it possible.

And when they had reached what the Army pilots believed to be the minimum for take-off, they were taken to a field on which an oblong had been staked out "no bigger than my back yard," and they had to practice landing well within those narrower confines, and taking off at 60 miles an hour with full loads. The normal take-off speed for a B-25 is 90 miles an hour, after a run three times longer than Miller allowed.

Between times they were coached in hedgehopping, flying fast and low. And at all times they were preached secrecy—secrecy—secrecy. They were not even allowed to guess how their unusual training was to be utilized.

So here they were at last, aboard the HORNET, their big planes being hoisted to the carrier's cleared decks where they were lashed down aft, the wings of the outer row projecting abovewater over the ship's side. The Army men had even been drilled by Lieutenant Miller in the courtesies of the sea, to salute the quarterdeck and the officer of the deck, and the proper (though usually mumbled) formula to be spoken in boarding or leaving a ship.

The day after the planes were secured aboard, the HORNET put to sea. Outside the harbor she made rendezvous with her escort, which included the heavy cruiser VINCENNES, Captain Frederick L. Riefkohl, USN, and the light cruiser NASHVILLE, Captain Francis S. Craven, USN. Then Captain Mitscher opened his sealed orders, and shortly afterward the agony of speculation which gripped every man on board was dispelled. Over the loud-speaker system trilled the summons of the boatswain's pipe, followed by the time-old introductory sentence so familiar to Navy men:

"Now hear this—"

What all hands heard was Captain Mitscher describing the ship's mission. "There could be no greater one." The HORNET was to take Colonel Doolittle across the Pacific to within a few hundred miles of Japan's coast, and there launch them for an attack on Tokyo.

Cheers rolled across the sea to the escorting ships, and were echoed back from the other vessels in the task force as Captain Mitscher's message was relayed by winking lights.

About the time that the cheers were frightening the gulls trailing the HORNET, a veteran in the art of disturbing the Japanese put out from Pearl Harbor.

The ENTERPRISE, having spruced up and drawn replacements after the Wake-Marcus raid, headed north. She took up a patrol station about 400 miles north of Wake and began steaming in circles while her tropics-seasoned company and crew shivered, and her pilots flew through low-lying clouds as they boned up on their gunnery.

"Cold as all Alaska," one of the fliers noted on Sunday, April 12, in the sparse record to which personal journals are limited in wartime. "Only God and the admiral know what we are up here for. We're probably going to bomb Japan itself."

The next day the Big E's pilot-diarist flew over to investigate a strange carrier coming up over the horizon. Recognition signals were exchanged as the pilot's eyes popped at what he saw on the HORNET's deck. The conjecture he exchanged with his companions was that some land base was being reinforced by an Army bomber unit, but then somebody asked, "What land base?"

There was no answer to that; but the correct answer for the HORNET's strange load, and the ENTERPRISE's contribution to the mission, was not long in coming. The two task forces merged, ENTERPRISE providing the air screen for both carriers because the HORNET was as helpless as a honey-barge, except for her guns.

It was an impressive fleet that headed for Japan through enemy waters. There were the two carriers, the cruisers NORTHAMPTON, SALT LAKE CITY, VINCENNES, and NASHVILLE, under Rear Admiral Spruance. Captain R. L. Conelly again commanded the destroyers from the BALCH, now skippered by Lieutenant Commander Harold H. Tiemroth. They were the BENHAM, Lieutenant Commander Joseph M. Worthington; ELLET, Lieutenant Commander Francis H. Gardner; FANNING, Commander William R. Cook, Jr.; GRAYSON, Commander Thomas M. Stokes; GWIN, Commander John M. Higgins; MEREDITH, Lieutenant Commander Harry E. Hubbard, and MONSSEN, Commander Roland N. Smoot, all USN. The vital nurse-ships, revictualers of the force, were the oilers CIMARRON, Commander Russel M. Ihrig, and SABINE, Commander Houston L. Maples.

Vice Admiral Halsey, of course, was in charge of the whole.

It was the admiral's job to get the HORNET as close to the Japanese coast as safety would permit, and, as soon as the Army planes were launched, to get all his ships out again. The United States Fleet was still heavily outnumbered by the Japanese, and it had to be divided between two oceans at that.

All went well, until the day before what was to have been the last day of the Navy's job.

3

On the HORNET the Army pilots were still going to school. Lieutenant Miller was aboard to give his pupils post-graduate lectures and to answer questions. And they had a new professor, Lieutenant Commander Stephen

Jurika, USN, who had spent years in Japan as a naval student and on the staff of the naval attaché in Tokyo.

Every obtainable kind of map and chart of Japan, its chief cities, and of the China landing area had been assembled for the Army men, and from them Commander Jurika lectured the class on landmarks and targets. Betweentimes the Army men were given lessons in celestial navigation, the use of the octant, and the way of the sea with a man.

Not all the time was spent in work, of course. Lieutenant Sutherland remembers that "on the way across there was lots of nice liaison between the Army and the Navy, involving the Army's famous old game of poker.

"There was one amusing incident. The admiral came in and looked over the shoulder of one Army second lieutenant, very proud of himself with a cigar stuck in one corner of his mouth. The admiral said, 'How are you doing?' or something to that effect, and this young kid looking up but without recognizing who it was, said 'Okay, Joe, wanna take a hand?' "

4

April 18 dawned gray and gusty, with a heavy sea. The task force was then about 700 miles east of Inubee Saki Light, on a line with Tokyo Bay, when the VINCENNES reported a Japanese patrol ship only ten miles away directly on the course of the expedition. Admiral Halsey ordered a sharp turn to escape detection, on the chance that that misfortune had not already occurred. The ENTERPRISE's planes were launched, and they were not long aloft before they reported the sea dotted with similar patrol boats, 100-foot deep-sea fishing vessels obviously well equipped with radio.

There was no doubt, then, that the task force had been sighted by the Japanese. Still the ENTERPRISE plugged ahead on Tokyo's beam, Admiral Halsey ordering any patrol boats encountered to be destroyed. By bomb and shellfire, three were sent down, one of the trio however charging at the array of American vessels like a spaniel attacking a wolf pack before a flock of 6-inch shells from the NASHVILLE obliterated it. Four survivors were picked up from the vessels destroyed.

Between the ENTERPRISE and the HORNET passed lively conversation in blinker signals. The plan for the Tokyo raid had to be canceled or radically altered. Originally it had called for Colonel Doolittle to take off that night with a load of incendiaries, to blaze a trail of flame across Japan for the 15 bombers to follow in the dawn. Now that the force had been discovered, the timetable had to be pushed ahead.

On the HORNET the colonel ran down from the bridge to the ready room where his pilots waited anxiously.

"Come on, fellows," he said. "Let's go."

He was to be the first one off. Navy mechanics gave the B-25s a final check, topped off the gasoline tanks and loaded extra cans of fuel on each plane. The HORNET was pitching in the heavy sea, taking green water over the bow. And now the bluejackets and handlers were writing picturesque messages to Tojo on the bombs. A cluster of Japanese decorations was tied to one by the colonel and the carrier's skipper, as the bombers warmed up.

It was bad enough weather to make any take-off precarious, but the Army pilots had learned their lessons well. Colonel Doolittle's departure was a model for the rest. As each B-25 roared down the abbreviated flight deck in obedience to signals which would send the plane over the bow just as it rose to meet a wave, its outboard wingtip extended over the ship's side. One Army pilot, striving for perfection, took off at such a sharp angle that his bomber "rose right up by the island like an elevator." It swooped down, clear of the ship, to within inches of the water, rose again, and "went over the horizon something on the order of a kangaroo."

The departure cost the HORNET one casualty. An aviation machinist's mate was pitched into a whirling propeller and lost an arm.

As soon as the last bomber had been launched, the entire task force reversed course and headed eastward at high speed, its part in the initiation of Tokyo into the horrors it had brought to Pearl Harbor completed. There were some indications that Japanese bombers were searching for the task force, proof that the patrol boats had warned Japan there was trouble abroad. More such small craft were encountered as the ships headed away from the launching point, Pilots Mehle and Hoyle of the ENTERPRISE each getting one of them.

There was, then, a minimum of risk and ample cause for Admiral Halsey to break the strict rule of radio silence at sea. From the antennae of the ENTERPRISE pulsed the message:

TO COL DOOLITTLE AND HIS GALLANT COMMAND GOOD LUCK AND GOD BLESS YOU—HALSEY.

PART FOUR

Philippine Farewell

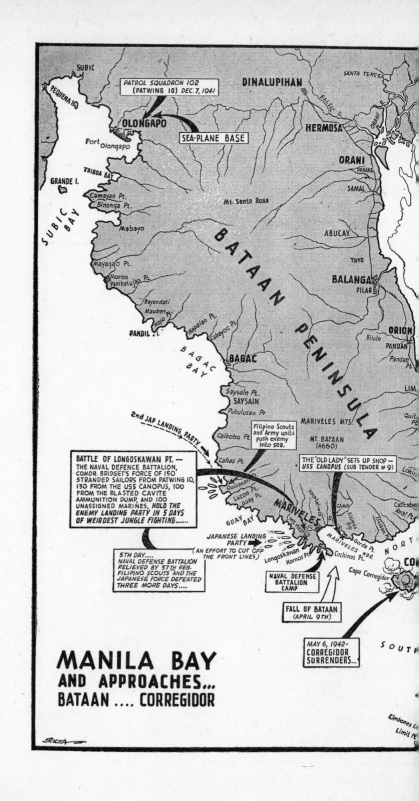

PATROL SQUADRON 102
(PATWING 10) DEC. 7, 1941

DINALUPIHAN

SANTA TERESA

SUBIC

PEQUENA I.

OLONGAPO

SEA-PLANE BASE

Port Olongapo

HERMOSA

TRIBOA BAY

ORANI

PARANG

GRANDE I.

Camayan Pt.
Binanga Pt.

SAMAL

Mt. Santa Rosa

B A T A A N

ABUCAY

S U B I C   B A Y

Mabayo

Mayagao Pt.
Moron
Panibatujan Pt.

TUYO

BALANGA

PILAR

Bayandati
Mauban
Papo
Mapalan Pt.
Caboyoc Pt.

PANDIL I.

P E N I N S U L A

BAGAC BAY

BAGAC

Bilulo

ORION

PANDAN

Pandan Pt.

Saysain Pt.
SAYSAIN
Pubulusan Pt.

MARIVELES MTS.

LIM

Quit

2nd JAP LANDING PARTY

Csibobo Pt.

Filipino Scouts
and Army units
push enemy
into sea.

MT. BATAAN
(4660)

THE "OLD LADY" SETS UP SHOP—
USS CANOPUS (SUB TENDER # 9)

Lokir

Cañas Pt.

BATTLE OF LONGOSKAWAN PT. —
THE NAVAL DEFENCE BATTALION,
COMDR. BRIDGET'S FORCE OF 150
STRANDED SAILORS FROM PATWING 10,
130 FROM THE USS CANOPUS, 100
FROM THE BLASTED CAVITE
AMMUNITION DUMP, AND 100
UNASSIGNED MARINES, *HOLD THE
ENEMY LANDING PARTY IN 5 DAYS
OF WEIRDEST JUNGLE FIGHTING......*

Quinauan
Luzon Pt.
guay Pt.

MARIVELES

CAMP

Cabcabe
Real Pt.

GUAY BAY

MARIVELES N.B.R.

Gorda Pt.

NORT

5TH DAY....
NAVAL DEFENSE BATTALION
RELIEVED BY 57TH REG.
FILIPINO SCOUTS AND THE
JAPANESE FORCE DEFEATED
THREE MORE DAYS....

JAPANESE LANDING
PARTY—
(AN EFFORT TO CUT OFF
THE FRONT LINES)

Longoskawan
Hornos Pt.

Cochinos Pt.

NAVAL DEFENSE
BATTALION
CAMP

Cape Corregidor

CO

FALL OF BATAAN
(APRIL 9TH)

MAY 6, 1942-
CORREGIDOR
SURRENDERS...

SOUTH

MANILA BAY
AND APPROACHES...
BATAAN .... CORREGIDOR

Limbones I.
Limit P

SIXTA

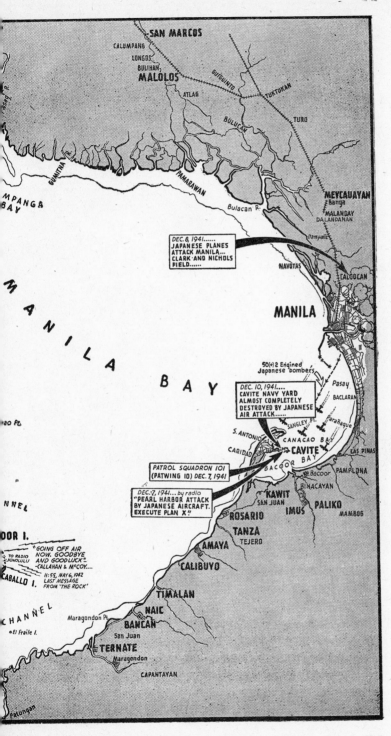

FIGURE 13

Chapter Seventeen

AFTER the forced retirement of the American warships from the Philippines in late December of 1941 the defense of Bataan and Corregidor perforce had to be shouldered in its entirety by the ground troops, aided by the pitiably few patched-up planes which managed to survive the repeated Japanese assaults from the skies. The gallant American and Philippine defenders—more than 60,000 of them—finally had to lay down their arms in surrender, after a bitter and stubborn resistance against hunger, disease, and an overpowering enemy; but in doing so they added new glory and new luster to the proud name of the United States Army.

In the sad and defeat-ridden days that followed the Japanese attack, the Army's superb tactical use of inspired courage and human gallantry, in attempting to accomplish the impossible, perhaps served to remind Americans at home that the traditions in their school history books might have a basis in fact, after all.

Through December, January, and February the Army in the Philippines held the swarming Japanese at bay, and thereby contributed toward slowing the Japanese timetable. But, by March, many Americans-at-home began to suspect that the end would not be pleasant, hoping they were wrong as they eagerly waited for fresh news: the Army had beaten off a Japanese counterattack on Bataan; General MacArthur's forces had swept to new gains; the Army was retreating on Bataan; the Army had dug in for a last stand on Corregidor.

The fact was little noted at the time, or later, that the United States Navy also was at Bataan and Corregidor. The fact was so little noted, for instance, that when a Navy announcement casually mentioned that a detachment of Marines was aiding in the defense of the besieged Manila area, the press of the country bombarded the Navy Department in Washington with hopeful queries as to whether reinforcements had been landed. The answer of course was in the negative—the Marines had been there all the time, conducting themselves as Marines always had. More than 3,500 Navy and Marine Corps personnel were among the defense forces—and all of them in there fighting.

In perspective, perhaps the Navy's accomplishments during those last days in the Philippines should be scaled to the size of its forces present, and thus might deserve only a footnote on the Army's honor roll. It should be noted also that not all the Navy's activities went unheralded at the time: Lieutenant Bulkeley's swashbuckling, hip-shooting PT boats, equally handy at knocking over Jap ships or aiding in the rescue of General MacArthur and President Quezon, captured the imagination of an entire nation. There were other instances.

But, and again in all propriety, communique writers and press correspondents could spare little time from massive engagements to chronicle the background and activities of the Naval Defense Battalion on Bataan —a strange and wonderful collection of sailors-turned-footsloggers whose weird and completely unorthodox jungle fighting perhaps kept the Japs from cutting the peninsula in two, an accomplishment which probably should be entered on the record as one good reason why Bataan did not fall days or weeks earlier.

And little was told, then or later, of the handful of ships left behind to wait for the end—such ships as the USS CANOPUS, a lumbering and supposedly highly vulnerable submarine tender lovingly known to her men as the "Old Lady."

The "Old Lady" was at Bataan and Corregidor, too.

2

The CANOPUS was a bastard ship which, somewhat like the Army's mule, was "without pride of ancestry or hope of posterity." Or was the latter part of that statement true, that part about "hope of posterity"? The United States Navy hates to see a good ship die, and it would be surprising indeed if the Navy in this case were to allow death to remain permanent. But that, of course, was no concern of the moment.

And certainly the first part of the statement was incontrovertible. The CANOPUS was a product of that final frenzy of merchant shipbuilding which was spawned of the war conditions in 1919. Built for the Shipping

Board, she was turned over to the Grace Line, which decided that she should fare forth into the sea lanes of the world under the name of SANTA LEONORA. Then the Navy took her over in 1921. Probably no specific thought was given to a new name—she was to be converted into a submarine tender, and there had been few forerunners of her class in the naval service. The historical section of *Ships' Data, U.S. Naval Vessels* lists her simply as: "Submarine Tender No. 9—CANOPUS—named for the star of the same name—the first vessel so called."

Nearly all ships are given a personal pet name by their officers and men: the battleship ARKANSAS thus became the "Arkie"; to her men, the ill-fated REUBEN JAMES was always the "Rube"; the unlucky ATLANTA was proudly called the "Mighty A"; and the walloping new SOUTH DAKOTA was christened belowdecks, with becoming delicacy, simply as the "Big Bastard" (and certainly not as "Battleship X").

With her complete lack of tradition, the CANOPUS could have fared far worse in the matter of nicknames. Only a seer with access to the vagaries of a bluejacket's mind could say why she was not immediately dubbed "USS CAN OPENER," thereafter to be called, for short, the "Can." But no. She was called the "Old Lady." The name was spoken with pride and reverence, sentiments mixed with a certain amount of truculence when used in the presence of crewmen from bigger and better ships of the same class.

Bigger and better ships—there was the rub. The submarine tender HOLLAND fell into this class, for instance, and HOLLAND was immediately ordered to escape southward. Such comparatively slow auxiliary ships as OTUS, LANGLEY, and TRINITY likewise were given their escape orders and got out before the invading Japs arrived. That left only the minesweepers PIGEON, TANAGER, FINCH, and QUAIL; the gunboats MINDANAO, LUZON, and OAHU, and a few ex-yachts, tugs, and yard garbage scows. And the CANOPUS.[1]

The Old Lady was to stay behind and tend her brood of subs as long as possible; and when this brood was tied up about her she lay there fat and happy, looking like nothing more than a dozing sow and her nuzzling pigs. Actually, the CANOPUS's hold was jammed with supply bunkers, forges, and machine shops in myriad variety. Her artificers worked with equal skill on the hairspring of a chronometer or a 10-ton hunk of diesel engine from the belly of a sub. These artificers could do

[1] See page 157.

other things too, as the men on Bataan were to learn—feverish wounded in Bataan's field hospitals were to see real, honest-to-God cakes of ice, coaxed out of strange contraptions by the men of CANOPUS and the ground crews of Patwing Ten.

Soon, however, CANOPUS'S reason for being, the tending of her subs, became a furtive affair carried on in strictest blackout under the cloak of night, with the submarines sinking below the surface of Manila Bay to hide from the Japanese bombers during daylight. Then, on Christmas Eve, the Japanese found enough leisure to turn serious attention to the sub tender, tied up alongside the building in which Captain John Wilkes, USN, housed his submarine headquarters.

The building itself was hit and badly damaged, and fragments rained on CANOPUS'S decks and banged against her sides. Admiral Rockwell, who had moved his headquarters to Corregidor, so as to be available to General MacArthur, immediately ordered the Old Lady to hunt up a safer anchorage. In Manila itself the Army was burning and destroying all strategic supplies and materials which it could not take with it into Bataan. And that night CANOPUS set out on her last journey with her 400 officers and men, her way lighted by towering flames as Manila, "Place by the River of Flowers," was being evacuated and left to await a triumphal entry by the Japanese.

The Old Lady's skipper, Commander E. L. Sackett, USN, says: "We decided to set up shop again in Mariveles Bay, on the southern tip of Bataan Peninsula. Some of our submarines were still with us, but now we had no source from which our supplies could be replenished, and it was obvious that the best we could hope to do would be to equip this last group for war patrol, and then 'turn in our suits' as far as submarines were concerned."

The spot in Mariveles Bay was chosen in the hope that the ship would be protected from air attack by the guns of nearby Corregidor, although there were some misgivings on this score when a bombed and burning merchant ship was observed on The Rock's very doorstep. The CANOPUS moved into a protected cover and, with camouflage netting and green paint, set out to efface herself from prying eyes. Unfortunately, a rock quarry nearby had made a white gash in a cliff which abutted on the shore, and it was impossible to hide the ship completely when viewed from one particular direction. The ship's officers and men were not satisfied with the job, but they had done the best they could.

In this respect they were somewhat like the skipper of a badly damaged cruiser, which was camouflaged with netting, paint and palm fronds in the later Solomons Campaign. When the job was finished the cruiser commander got a naval aviator to take him aloft for a personal inspection of this artistic endeavor. Returning to the airfield, the skipper was bombarded with queries as to how the camouflage job looked from the air. "It looks," said the skipper, "just like a camouflaged cruiser."

To Japan's naval aviators, when they delivered their first major attack on Corregidor on December 29, the CANOPUS must have looked just like a camouflaged submarine tender. The Old Lady's men peered from beneath their ship's disguise as those enemy aviators, with complete contempt for the puny range of Corregidor's antiaircraft guns, came over in wave after wave to plaster The Rock from end to end. All but the last wave of enemy bombers, which plastered CANOPUS—plenty.

Heavy bombs exploded all around the ship, tied up and defenseless. By a miracle CANOPUS took only one solid hit, and by another convenient miracle the ship was not blown to atoms as it properly should have been. The one bomb which hit, an armor-piercing type, went through all the ship's decks and exploded on her steel propeller shaft, starting fires and blasting open the magazines in which were stored quantities of explosives and torpedo warheads. Miracle No. 2, however, was the fact that this blast also cut a large number of steam lines, which immediately wet down the powder bags and helped to put out the fires. Just the same, that night the Old Lady had to busy herself with caring for wounded and burying dead.

Three days after this bombing, on the last day of 1941, the last of the submarines were withdrawn from the Philippines, and now there was apparently no reason for CANOPUS to remain. But higher authority decided that the Japanese were by this time in such force to the southward that a vulnerable vessel like CANOPUS would sail forth only to certain suicide. Besides, although nothing specific was in view at the moment, CANOPUS might come in handy at performing odd jobs. The CANOPUS was to stay, but her officers and men carefully husbanded every ounce of her fuel—they much preferred action at sea to their present role as a sitting duck on which Tojo could train his younger aviators. The officers and men of CANOPUS hoped—a hope that stayed alive to the last—that their orders would be changed and they would be allowed to make a dash outward.

This hope was intensified a week later when the Japanese bombers paid another visit. Again only one bomb struck home. This was a high-explosive fragmentation missile which hit the ship's towering smokepipe and literally sprayed her decks with shrapnel from hawsehole to after overhang. The gun crews had ducked behind their shields at the last possible moment. The shields had provided little protection from the overhead blast, and fifteen men picked up by stretcher parties had to be carried to quarters which the ship's men had set up ashore.

The ship's deck, in addition to its gaping hole from the previous bombing, now was punctured like a sieve in countless places. But conditions below-decks were worse. Several near misses had started seams. The ship's side had been pierced in a number of places, mostly above the waterline; but the hull underwater had been dished in forward, and the ship was taking a serious list.

Well, said the officers and men of CANOPUS, after surveying the damage, there was no use pretending any longer that the ship was so well hidden that it wasn't there, particularly since the Japs were showing no inclination to join in the game. Obviously something else had to be done. It was.

"The tough old girl was not ready for her grave yet," said Commander Sackett, "but if she was to continue a career of usefulness it seemed best to make the Japs think that the last salvo of bombs had done the trick."

The ship's welders carefully sealed up every hole in her side, but they were equally careful not to take off the Old Lady's decrepit list—the water in the hold could be pumped out and the ship righted as soon as the order was given to up anchor and get out of there.

"The next morning when 'Photo Joe' in his scouting plane came over," said Commander Sackett, "his pictures showed what looked like an abandoned hulk, listed over on her side, with cargo booms flapping askew, and with large blackened areas around the bomb holes from which wisps of smoke floated up for two or three days. What he did not know was that the smoke came from oily rags in strategically placed smudge pots, and that every night the 'abandoned hulk' hummed with activity, forging new weapons and patching up old weapons for the beleagured forces of Bataan."

Evidently the deception worked, for the Japanese made only one other halfhearted attempt to attack the ship. This attack, made by dive bombers, was beaten off by the Old Lady's antiaircraft guns, which had been removed from the decks, so as not to draw attention to the ship, and set up on the neighboring cliffs.

In more than one way the Japanese attempts to assault the Old Lady served to draw the ship's officers and men closer together. Men who in the past had been troublemakers, said the skipper's report, now performed prodigies of energy. There was no discipline in the usual sense, such as withholding pay or curtailing shore leave: there was no pay and there was no leave, but neither was there any need for discipline. There was also complete absence of another peacetime commodity—red tape.

The first bombing had completely destroyed all the records and accounts of the ship's supply system.

"From that time on," said Commander Sackett, "our supply system was beautifully simple. What we had we could use without the usual red tape, and if something was lacking nothing could be done about it except devise a substitute or do without. There was nothing for the men to spend their money on, so there were no more pay days. Ice cream and canteen supplies were free as long as they lasted. All clothing became community property, to be doled out to whatever unfortunate should appear in the most nearly naked condition. This Utopian state inevitably led to much closer relations among the crew and officers, and welded us all into a great family working and fighting in a common cause and with only one aim—to do our damnedest to lick the Japs."

The fact that the CANOPUS hummed with activity at night was due, at least in part, to the agility of Bataan's news-bearing grapevine system. The word quickly got around that the men in CANOPUS's shops could fix up anything, and that what they couldn't mend they could replace with something just as good, made by hand. An Air Force second lieutenant wanted a new part for his plane? Can do. An Army dentist was looking for somebody who could make a metal filling? One new set of mouth crockery coming up!

Of course, some sort of living quarters ashore were a necessity if the night workers were to get any rest. This problem was partly solved by taking over a large storage tunnel which the Army had dug into the nearby cliff, just before the coming of war, and which had never been used. The Old Lady's skilled artificers moved in and set up housekeeping. They built bunks, office space, hospital accommodations, a radio and telephone communications center, and an underground galley in which the complement's two meals a day were prepared—and all this before the famous Navy Seabees had yet been dreamed up.

Approximately a hundred of the ship's men moved into these quarters, and the only drawback to their tunnel-with-a-seaside-view was the annoying discovery that the tunnel leaked in several places from seepage through fissures in the rock. Well, said the Old Lady's men, war is hell but, war or no war, the Navy likes its comfort. So they carefully trapped each of the leaks, piped them into a central spillway, and turned them into a shower bath.

3

The Old Lady was not stingy with the comforts she was able to devise by her own ingenuity or which she was able to draw from the refrigerated compartments of her spacious hold. Anybody was welcome aboard CANOPUS or her tunnel adjunct.

Upon his return to the United States as one of the last persons to leave Corregidor before its fall, the skipper of the ship prepared a lengthy narrative of the Old Lady's last days in the Philippines, and this narrative was mimeographed and sent to the families of the Old Lady's men, by that time prisoners of Japan.

"Nearly every evening," wrote Commander Sackett, "Army officers and nurses who were able to snatch a few hours from their duties gathered on board the CANOPUS. We had refrigeration, excellent cooking facilities, and decent living quarters. These seemed heaven to them compared to their hardships in the field. To enjoy a real shower, cold drinking water, well-cooked meals served on white linen with civilized tableware, and greatest luxury of all, *real butter,* seemed almost too much for them to believe. When these favored ones returned to their primitive surroundings and described these 'feasts' topped off with ice cream and chocolate sauce, they were often put in the same doghouse with the optimists who claimed to have seen a rescue fleet steaming in.

"Our visitors repaid us in full for any hospitality with tales of their own adventures. Captain Wormuth, the famous 'one-man army,' often regaled us with graphic and even gruesome accounts of his many encounters. General Casey, Major Wade Cochrane, Major Kircher, Major Lauman, and many others kept us in touch with affairs at USAFFE headquarters and the front lines. Occasionally Marine officers from Corregidor would manufacture reasons for visiting Bataan so that they could visit the CANOPUS and refresh their memories of better days. Bulkeley and other torpedo boat officers in particular enjoyed our ice cream desserts. We were only sorry when our supplies began to fail toward the end, and we could no longer maintain quite as good hotel service for our friends."

But aside from the morale value of this "hotel service," and aside from the work in CANOPUS's night-humming shops, the Old Lady's men also engaged in activities with a grimmer side. One group of men stood watch near the anchorage, in a natural bomb shelter at the base of the cliff, ready to dash aboard as a damage-control party in case their beloved ship should again be damaged from the skies. Other groups manned the guns on the hilltops, groups described by Commander Sackett as "sailors with itchy trigger fingers."

"Finally," he reported, "there were the lookouts and signal stations on the hilltops, with telephone wires reaching throughout the whole system, to spot marauding planes while still far away, and warn their shipmates of impending danger. These men, with little protection for themselves, kept their binoculars coolly trained on the bombers, describing the picture to more sheltered friends. Few will ever forget those quiet voices over the earphones: 'They are heading directly for us—their bomb bay doors are open—don't believe they dropped bombs this time—no, here they come—looks as if they will hit beyond us'—(more words drowned out by a shattering roar)—then, 'lousy shooting—missed us by a quarter of a mile—must have their third team in there today.' "

And many of the Old Lady's men shortly were to become assault troops as part of Bataan's Naval Defense Battalion—a complete misnomer because, perhaps through ignorance of correct land-fighting tactics, the newly created foot-sailors operated along the theory of one of the most familiar orders in their naval textbooks: "Attack and destroy."

4

Of all the naval personnel in Asiatic waters, perhaps none enjoyed greater personal popularity than the operations officer of Patwing Ten, Commander Francis J. Bridget, USN, later to be captured by the Japanese. In informal naval parlance, Bridget was described by close friends as "bright-eyed and bushy-tailed"; and in matters relating to his beloved

Patwing Ten or the war against the Japs he was described as "strictly on the ball." [1]

With all of Patwing Ten's planes operating southward, or damaged beyond repair, Bridget found himself without a job but still in command of about 150 of Patwing Ten's enlisted ground personnel, along with a few of its commissioned pilots.

At that time Mariveles Harbor seemed to be well protected by the small naval craft still afloat and by the naval forces clustered around it. The Army had stabilized a front about 20 miles farther north, on the western side of Mariveles Mountain. This left a considerable stretch of thinly defended seacoast between. Most of this coast was very rugged, and backed up by cliffs or dense jungle, but the road that provided the only avenue of communication to the front lines passed quite close to the sea at several points. Commander Bridget began a series of conferences with senior Army and Navy officers concerning this area, and the result was that he was ordered to form a force charged with its defense.

The 150 stranded sailors of Patwing Ten were ready and waiting, but they were not enough. Bridget "borrowed" 130 men from the CANOPUS, and he "collected" about 100 men from the blasted Cavite ammunition dump, along with another 100 Marines of an artillery outfit with no assignment at the moment. Lieutenant Commander "Hap" Goodall, USN, executive officer of the Old Lady, was named second-in-command. Among the other Marine and naval officers were Lieutenant T. K. Bowers, USN, from Cavite, and Lieutenant Harmon Utter, USN, whom we have already met as a pilot of Patwing Ten. In this same category was Lieutenant (jg) Thomas F. Pollock, USN, communications officer of the strange new outfit. Pollock subsequently was to be taken southward by submarine and still later was to make the last flight from Australia to Corregidor before the fall of The Rock. Two Navy PBYs to make this final rescue trip accomplished what was probably the longest flight over enemy-occupied territory in all the early days of the war.

"Equipment was a serious problem," said Commander Sackett in his

[1] When one naval officer and three Marines were among the first to escape from a Japanese prisoner-of-war camp in the Philippines, they noted, upon their return to the United States, that one of the first questions often asked was: "What happened to Frank Bridget?"

narrative. "The Marines were, of course, ready for field duty. But the others were sailors, and the Navy doesn't provide much equipment for land operations at best, to say nothing of the fact that several of these groups had been separated from their normal supplies by unforeseen circumstances. However, rifles and ammunition of some sort were finally begged, borrowed or stolen for most of the men. Their white uniforms were dyed in coffee grounds to what was supposed to be khaki color, but which turned out to be a sickly mustard yellow. Only about one canteen could be found for every three men, but the great American tin can was pressed into service to make up the deficiency. This had the advantage that the contents could be heated over a fire in case of need, provided care was exercised not to melt out the solder."

Training was the next essential, and here the experienced Marines made a great contribution. These men were spread thinly through the naval ranks, with the sailors being constantly admonished to "keep an eye on the gyrenes—do as they do."

One of the extracurricular activities of the Naval Defense Battalion, according to Lieutenant Pollock, was the operation of a jungle press newspaper, "reported, written, rewritten and edited" by Aviation Radio-man 1/c J. M. Rightmyer. "Receivers were mounted in a station wagon and driven to the tops of the hills to get the best reception," said Pollock. "News was copied for 24 hours a day. Two editions were published, morning and afternoon, until the paper shortage forced a reduction to one afternoon edition. News was copied from all countries, decoded and put into abbreviated form to crowd as much as possible on four or five small pages. A mimeograph machine, dug up from somewhere, was our printing press.

"Our requests for copies grew by leaps and bounds. The supply could not possibly be maintained. The most we could afford to make was 200 copies. A dispatch rider was assigned to deliver them to the scattered Army units. The soldiers were so hungry for news that they would send a representative on a ten-mile hike just to wait along the road to pick up a copy. We would give each unit two copies, and the larger head-quarters units three copies. These copies were nearly always worn out before all hands had finished reading them.

"There were times when there were only enough ink or paper or stencils for one more edition. Short notice would appear in the paper, requesting whatever was necessary to continue the publication; and, sure enough, the messenger would arrive that night with the required items so we could go to press."

When not training or otherwise occupied the men of the Naval Defense Battalion spent considerable time in the effort to get a landing strip prepared for the time when—it was hoped by all and believed by few—carrier planes would come winging to the rescue. The Japanese were completely aware of this effort, however, and they dropped bombs with such regularity that the landing strip was never actually finished.

On a day late in January the officers and men set out on what was intended as an extended field hike. This hike was to develop into the Battle of Longoskawan Point. As the men reached the base of Mount Pucot they were met by a file of retreating soldiers who had been forced by invading Japanese from their lookout stations on the mountain. As Commander Bridget had feared, the Japanese had landed in an effort to cut off the front lines.

Here at last was what they had been training for, and the foot-sailors tried to remember what they had been taught from the book about fighting on land. Soon they were engaged with the Japanese, who were firing from in front of them and on all sides of them and occasionally from behind them. They could remember nothing in the book that seemed to explain or solve this situation, so they threw away the book.

"Five days of what was probably the weirdest jungle fighting in the annals of warfare ensued," said Commander Sackett, "with all accepted principles violated, and no holds barred. Adjacent units were unable to maintain contact with each other during the night, so of course the Japs put to advantage their famous infiltration tactics. However, this did not have the expected results; because our boys, not having been indoctrinated in the ancient military principle that it is fatal to be outflanked, simply held their ground and sent back detachments to clear out the annoying intruders behind their lines.

"The Jap landing party was made up of picked men, larger and stronger than the average, and well equipped for jungle fighting. Had they made a determined assault they undoubtedly could have wiped out completely our whole ragged battalion. But they knew the business of war, and they were sure our front lines must be backed up by powerful reserves somewhere. If they could only find out where these reserves were located they would know where best to make their drive. The big push was held up while their scouts frantically searched for the elusive reserve forces. How could they guess that the crazy Americans were so ignorant of the art of war as to blithely ignore the necessity for reserves? Sixty more Marines with trench mortars were brought over from Corregidor to counteract the advantage the Japs had enjoyed with similar weapons, but they were also used in the front lines and could hardly be called reserves."

Aside from a lack of reserves, the Naval Defense Battalion had en- tered the battle with another important omission: they had not thought to set up a service of supply. A runner was sent galloping back to an- chorage where the skipper of the Old Lady and all his men were anxiously waiting for news. Could the Old Lady lend a hand? She could. Then the message from Commander Bridget was simple: "Send plenty of every- thing."

The order, or request, was lacking in details, perhaps, but on the whole comprehensive.

The Old Lady's men somehow managed to stumble onto some trucks —no detailed information is available, owing to loss of records and so on, as to whether these were some vehicles later reported missing by the Army—and the trucks were rushed to the front with food, ammuni- tion and blankets, and with stretchers and medicines for the wounded. For the next five days the Old Lady dropped all her other work while making certain that the beleaguered foot-sailors got everything they needed "and don't ask any questions about where it came from."

The going was tough, but the foot-sailors were doing all right on their own, with the opposing Japs in a state approaching bafflement. Reported Commander Sackett: ". . . A Japanese officer testified to their complete bewilderment, describing the strange conduct of 'the new type of suicide squads, which thrashed about in the jungles wearing bright yellow uniforms and making plenty of noise. Whenever these apparitions reached an open space they would attempt to draw Japanese fire by sitting down, talking loudly and lighting cigarettes.' "

Commander Sackett had more to say: "Bataan may well have been saved from a premature fall by the reckless bravado of these sailors, be- cause if the Japs had succeeded in cutting off supplies to the western Army front, a general retreat from those prepared positions might have been necessary. The lives lost in that timely effort could hardly have been sacrificed in a better cause."

Despite any different estimate that may be made by historians of the future, with more facts and more perspective to work from, that was Commander Sackett's personal opinion. And Commander Sackett was there.

5

On the fifth day the Naval Defense Battalion was relieved by strong units from the 57th Regiment of Filipino Scouts. These troops were given the highest possible praise by all naval personnel who saw them in action, and who lived or won their way to freedom to tell about it. The Scouts had been a part of the Regular Army, under American officers, since America's entry into the Philippines. Their entrance requirements were most rigid, and they were fiercely proud of their outfit. Best of all, the Scouts were masters of jungle tactics—better at this form of warfare, as they shortly proved, than the Japs themselves.

The relieving Filipinos slipped noiselessly up to the American lines. Many of the foot-sailors were not aware of their presence until they felt a hand on their shoulders and heard the quiet password: "Okay, Joe— I'll take over now."

After three days of the Scouts' deadly marksmanship, and with artillery support from the big guns of Corregidor, the battered and disorganized remnants of the powerful Japanese landing force had been pushed over the cliffs that lined the seacoast, leaving hundreds of dead behind.

Some of the Japs who were pushed over the cliffs were not dead, however, and these remnants holed up in the natural caves in the cliffbank. They still had plenty of food and ammunition, and they resisted all efforts by the Filipino Scouts and Army troops to root them out.

Bridget and his foot-sailors had been relieved of land fighting but they had by no means lost interest in the course of events. Now they began to think as sailors again, and from this angle the problem of the holed-up Japs was simple: the Japs should be shot out of their holes from the sea. Bulkeley and his PT boats were extremely busy elsewhere, and no other craft were available. Of course, mused Commander Bridget, there were some 40-foot launches on the CANOPUS, and . . .

The idea caught on like wildfire.

The Old Lady's shops began to hum again, and soon three of the 40-foot motor launches began to take on a strange appearance. Several machine guns and a light field piece were mounted on each of the boats. Then the Old Lady's artificers snipped up heavy boiler plate, hammered it into shape, and built armored shields around the engines and the guns. By that time the three boats were known to one and all as "Uncle Sam's Mickey Mouse Battle Fleet."

No sooner had the first experimental model been finished than Lieutenant Commander Goodall and a volunteer crew were on their way, with the excess of volunteers loudly claiming "seconds" on the next trip . . . provided the boat came back from the first trip.

There was a 7- or 8-mile run to Longoskawan Point from the CANOPUS anchorage, but Goodall and his volunteers made two round trips the first day, blasting scores of Japs from their hiding place. As evidence of success they brought in two prisoners who were alive but dazed, and a "sample" of three Japanese who had joined their ancestors.

Mickey Mouse Battleship No. 2 was ready for action the second day, and the hunt kept up as long as the Japs lasted.

A week later and there was more work for the tiny warcraft. At about the time Longoskawan was cleared, the Japs had made another landing in force on Quinauen Point, several miles farther north, which was the reason Bulkeley and his PTs were unable to take over at Longoskawan. The PTs had fought valiantly to break up the landing attempt, aided with equal valor by the Army's few remaining P-40s, which dropped small bombs and strafed every enemy in sight. Thirteen loaded barges were reported sunk, and a large destroyer was hit by one of Bulkeley's torpedoes—adding new victories to the PT boats' imposing score—but many of the Japanese invaders got through. Again the Filipino Scouts and their Army brothers-in-arms pushed the enemy into the sea, and again the Mickey Mouse battleships were called upon to disinfect the cliffside caves.

Hap Goodall and his Irregulars did another thorough job, but this time the little expedition was not so lucky. Apparently word of this strange new type of warcraft had seeped back to the Japs, and the Japs showed that they took the threat seriously by sending in dive bombers. Four of these aircraft suddenly hurtled out of the sun as the two Mickey Mouse boats were returning from the scene of their latest triumph. Bombs rained all around the leading boat; it had its bottom blown out, but not before one of the attacking planes was shot down. The other planes strafed as they pulled out of their dives. Commander Goodall, although seriously wounded in both feet, and unable to walk, ordered the other boat beached to prevent the unharmed men from being wounded when the planes returned for another run.

The surviving members of the crew improvised a crude stretcher for Goodall and, hacking their way through the jungle, finally reached the road. There they were picked up by an Army truck driver, who gave them a lift back home to the Old Lady.

At about this time, in mid-February, there began to be indications that the Japanese might be planning a landing attempt on Corregidor, whose beaches were long and loosely defended. The Naval Defense Battalion, the Old Lady's 130 men among them, was now incorporated into the Fourth Marines, commanded by Colonel Samuel L. Howard, USMC, and ordered to duty on Corregidor.

This was all right as far as it went, said the Old Lady's departing men—they were glad to help out where they could, and all that sort of thing. But if CANOPUS's orders not to leave were changed, if the Old Lady suddenly got permission to up anchor and get out of there, those aboard the ship had better let those on Corregidor hear about it first off! Just see that they got the word over there on Corregidor, that was all—they would devise their own ways and means of getting back across Mariveles Bay and getting the Old Lady's decks under their feet again. A number of dark threats and dire imprecations were passed in regard to this warning. As the final clincher, the men departing for Corregidor pointed out that, once there, they would be manning big guns. If the Old Lady should try to go off, leaving them behind with a bunch of gyrenes and soldiers, some shooting might be done.

Well, not that, of course, because they were all still shipmates. But just don't let it happen, see?

That was the way it was as the men heading for Corregidor bade the Old Lady a last and silent good-bye—tough talk, gruff words, and rough gestures. But the situation in the Philippines by that time was becoming ominously clear, and nobody was deceiving anybody else. "Of course," said the skipper of the CANOPUS, "they knew that the situation was just about out of the question, and that any man in either group would gladly give up his own place if fate should give his shipmates a chance to make a dash for it."

6

"Early in March," said Commander Sackett's narrative of the Philippines' last days, "Bulkeley's torpedo craft slipped out of the harbor on their famous dash to the southern Philippines,[1] carrying as passengers General MacArthur and Rear Admiral Rockwell, with their staffs. A few days later the Japanese learned of their departure and started a leaflet propaganda campaign among the Filipinos, claiming that our troops had been deserted by their leaders, that further resistance was foolish, and similar arguments. Fortunately, most of the poison had been extracted from their propaganda by the fact that General MacArthur's departure had already been announced to the troops, as well as the reason for it."

But there was no longer any denying that things had to take a quick turn for the better in the Philippines—or the end would not be long in coming. By the last week in March, after a period of comparative lull, the Japs ended all hopes and suspicions that they might attempt to take Bataan and Corregidor by a process of slow starvation. Perhaps the Japanese knew that American submarines had been sneaking in medicines and vitally needed supplies—not enough, to be sure, but enough to help. (These submarines also brought in a much greater prize, stuffing and stowing it into every available nook and cranny: mail from home.) During the last week in March the Japanese stepped up their offensive to its peak; and by April 6 the remaining officers and men on the Old Lady knew the front lines on Bataan were in serious trouble.

"All reserves were drawn in for the supreme effort," reported the skipper of CANOPUS. "Every remaining tank was thrown into the breach. Even the beaches were left unguarded at some points in order to provide all possible reinforcements, but the task proved too great for the weakened troops. On April 8th came the news that Army forces on the eastern flank were retreating toward Mariveles harbor, destroying stores and ammunition dumps in the path of the victorious Japanese.

"All hope of holding Bataan was gone, leaving us with the grim duty of destroying everything that might be of value to the Nipponese. Early in the day the Commandant had told us that no Navy or Army forces

---

[1] An excellent account of this trip southward, as well as other activities of MTB Squadron Three in the Philippines, is contained in *They Were Expendable* by W. L. White, published in 1942 by Harcourt, Brace & Company, New York.

would be evacuated to Corregidor, since that island was already over-crowded. However, at 10:30 that night he telephoned that General Wainwright had decided to accept on the island one Filipino Scout regiment and the naval forces at Mariveles. These favored units were to augment the beach defenses of Corregidor. Unfortunately, it developed that very few of the Scouts were able to reach an embarkation point before the Japs cut them off.

"Evacuation of the Navy forces had to be completed before dawn brought over more swarms of bombers or an advance guard of Jap tanks. Without defenses and shelters, which were being detroyed, the sailors would be helpless. That wild and horrible, yet weirdly beautiful night must be imprinted forever in the memories of all who lived through its spectacular fury. For miles back on the slope of the mountain, burning ammunition dumps lighted the sky with showers of rocket-like streamers, while the ground shook with the heavy detonations of exploding ammunition. A severe earthquake shock felt on Corregidor was not even noticed on Bataan, which was continually vibrating with man-made earthquakes.

"Roads were choked with retreating troops, often stopped for hours waiting for a dangerously near ammunition dump to burn itself out. Around the shores of Mariveles Bay Navy men blew up the famous old Dewey Floating Drydock, which had served the Asiatic Fleet for so many years, and scuttled the ships which had no part to play in defending Corregidor. The CANOPUS seemed reluctant to go, but her crew could still take pride in the fact that the Japs had been unable to knock her out—she was still able to back out under her own power to deep water. There she was laid to her final rest by the hands of the sailors she had served so faithfully.

"Each man was to be limited almost to the clothes on his back while on The Rock, but we took large supplies of equipment which would be useful in defense. Machine guns, rifles, ammunition, food, and fuel were all on the Urgent list. All through the night long lines of men scurried from storage tunnels to the docks, carrying the precious supplies to evacuation boats, heedless of exploding dynamite all around them, and paying no attention to frequent reports that Jap troops were rapidly approaching. There was no way of knowing that these reports were premature, because the burning ammunition dumps gave a fine imitation of heavy firing.

"As soon as the tunnels were cleared of useful supplies, their entrances were blown in by dynamite charges to prevent the Japs from using them or the equipment necessarily left behind. Just before dawn, all boats had finally been loaded, and the little fleet started off for Corregidor.

"The last three boats, loaded with weary CANOPUS men, had just left the dock when the tortured earth struck back at them. The whole hillside seemed to erupt in an orange burst of flame, hurling huge boulders half a mile out into the bay, lashing the calm waters into stormy, frothing waves. Evidently, gasoline drums stored in one of the tunnels had broken open when the entrance was dynamited, and fumes in the corked-up passage had built up a gigantic explosive charge. Our three boats were squarely in the path of that deluge of destruction. Two of them were struck by massive boulders, one of them sinking instantly under an impact which sheared off the whole stern, leaving three occupants in that section struggling in the water. Fortunately they were not hurt, and were soon rescued by shipmates in the undamaged boat. The other damaged boat did not sink, but boulders crashing down through its canopy killed an officer and three men. Nine other men were wounded by the rain of heavy rocks. However, the battered boat was still able to run, so the interrupted voyage to Corregidor was resumed."

On the day after the fall of Bataan, which came on April 9 (the Netherlands East Indies had fallen a month earlier and Corregidor was to last a month longer), the Japanese began determined aerial attacks on all that remained of the Navy's gunboats and minesweepers. The Japanese hoped to prevent these craft from sweeping mine channels leading to Corregidor, and thereby ending the occasional furtive visits of American submarines, The Rock's last link with the outside world. The Japs were successful in knocking out their targets, but not in their ultimate purpose. The reason was that the ghost of Old Lady CANOPUS was very much on the scene in the form of her motor launches.

These small boats were turned over to experienced Mine Force sailors, who used them as miniature minesweepers. For two weeks these crews worked at night, using hooded navigational lights as uncertain guides. Many times mines exploded near the launches, but without causing serious casualties. At the end of two weeks the channel was clear again, and submarines could bring in their vital supplies and take out key personnel. One who went out on the last submarine before

Corregidor's fall was Commander E. L. Sackett, USN, skipper of the Old Lady, a ship that was dead and gone forever.

But was this true—was it true that there would never be another CANOPUS? *Hell, no, it was not true, said the Navy Department, although perhaps not officially in these words. The Old Lady was too good a ship to die. There would be a new* CANOPUS, *bigger, faster, stronger and—the gods of the sea being kind—almost as stouthearted and true as the Old Lady herself.*

Chapter Eighteen

BATAAN had fallen and now the Japanese were not to be denied in their desire to take The Rock, driving the United States from the Philippines "forever," and ushering in (likewise "forever") the Greater New Order in East Asia. The Japanese had the force to accomplish the conquest. The days of fighting with never enough of anything, the days of fighting with bare hands, the days of heartbreak—all these were about to come to an end for American forces in Asiatic waters.

Commander Melvyn H. McCoy, USN, one of those to surrender on Corregidor, later became one of the first ten American military prisoners to escape from a Japanese prisoner-of-war camp in the Philippines, and Commander McCoy has provided an account of Corregidor's last hours.[1]

"Even in the depths of the solid rock tunnels of Corregidor," said Commander McCoy, "we could feel the vibrations of the almost constant Japanese barrage. One night toward the end of April the barrage lifted for a short time. Hundreds of people went out into the open for a breath of air and a smoke. It was pitch dark. The only light came from the few stars, and the occasional faint glow of a carefully shielded cigarette. Suddenly the group of people around the tunnel entrance seemed to be struck by lightning. There was an awful glare and a mighty crash. A salvo of Japanese 240-mm. shells had landed in the midst of the group. Just that one salvo—no more.

"Fortunately it was dark and the survivors did not have to look on the scene around them. But it was hours later before the hospital staff completed their amputations, transfusions, brain operations and other work.

"About midnight that night I went off duty in the radio shack in

[1] In *Ten Escape from Tojo*, by Commander Melvyn H. McCoy, USN, and Lieutenant Colonel S. M. Mellnik, USA, as told to Lieutenant Welbourn Kelley, USNR; published in 1944 by Farrar & Rinehart, New York.

323

the Navy tunnel, and I went out to the tunnel entrance where the tragedy occurred. There I found one of the nurses who had helped the doctors during the evening. She was crying her heart out on a sandbagged machine gun. I did not know whether she had suffered a personal loss, or whether our situation in general had become too much for her. She obviously had come out into the dark to hide her emotions from the wounded, so I tiptoed away and did not disturb her."

That incident occurred on the night of April 6. By the following day the "situation in general" had reached its last desperate unfolding.

"At 11:55 on May 6, 1942," said Commander McCoy, "I wrote out the Navy's last message from The Rock and handed it to a radioman 1/c at the sending apparatus. 'Beam it for Radio Honolulu,' I said. 'Don't bother with code.' Then the message began to go out: 'GOING OFF AIR NOW. GOODBYE AND GOOD LUCK. CALLAHAN AND McCOY.' . . .

"There were approximately a hundred and twenty-five naval officers and men in the Navy Tunnel when the first Japs came in, some three hours after the surrender. The Japs were ready with bayonets and grenades. (They entered the Army Tunnel with tanks and flame-throwers.) When they saw no sign of opposition they lowered their rifles and became almost jovial as they got down to the pleasant business of looting. This practice is officially forbidden, so Japanese officers made a point of not entering the tunnel for almost two hours after the enlisted men first appeared. By that time everything of value had been taken.

"The Japs seemed to prize above all else our wrist watches. I saw one burly Jap marine with watches all the way up to one elbow, halfway up to the other, and with a bayonet aimed at another Jap who was trying to beat him to an additional prize. Besides watches, fountain pens also were highly prized by our captors. There were numerous scuffles between the Japs over possession of these articles.

"Some of the Japs in the Navy Tunnel could speak a little English. They told us they had been used as assault troops at Hong Kong and Singapore. We were only slightly comforted at being told that we had put up the stiffest resistance they had met.

"The first officers to enter the tunnel were non-coms, sergeants. As the first one entered, a Jap soldier was hopefully searching me—everything of value in my possession had long since been taken away from me. The Japanese sergeant slapped and cuffed this soldier brutally, the soldier standing rigidly at attention, and the sergeant blandly ignoring the evidence of previous looting that was in plain view.

"But Japanese battle action did not end with our surrender. On the day after our capitulation, Japanese planes flew at minimum level over The Rock and dropped bombs, first making sure that their own men were out of the way. Casualties on our side were slight, and the Japs evidently were only bolstering a threat made to General Wainwright that, unless all the forces in the Visayan Islands surrendered, all on Corregidor would be massacred.

"And it did not take us long to learn the temper of our captors. A gun crew on nearby Fort Drum, called 'the concrete battleship,' had fired into a Japanese assault party a few days before Corregidor fell. A high-ranking Japanese officer was killed. This officer's brother, on the Jap headquarters staff in Manila, ordered that the men on Drum be given special attention. They were beaten and hazed unmercifully for forty-eight hours. Another incident occurred when a Japanese sentry began to beat an Army enlisted man without provocation—we did not know at that time that such actions were commonplace. The soldier made as if to hit the sentry with his fists. He was shot dead by another sentry before he could complete the motion."

That was the beginning. Months were to pass before Americans were to hear, from those fortunate few who escaped, of the "March of Death" from Bataan to Camp O'Donnell, of the death and disease at Cabanatuan, of the mistreatment and misery of American military prisoners on Mindanao.

2

Even as Corregidor's people were lining up in surrender, a battle of far more significance was being fought to the south and eastward.

Corregidor's capitulation was announced in Communique No. 76, its officially emotionless words nevertheless conveying a world of sadness and despair.

The first sentence of Communique No. 77, issued on the following day—May 7, 1942—took an entirely different tenor. That sentence read:

"Very excellent news has been received."

The communique went on to tell of the losses and damage sustained by the Japanese in the opening of the Battle of the Coral Sea. The first six months of the war—to the day—had closed with victory, a victory then beyond the estimate of anyone, a victory to be overtopped a month later by the Japanese rout at Midway.

What the communique could not tell in so many words was that the Pacific war's months of desperation and defeat had reached an end. And the communique could not tell, either, of the electric word that was passed (over no known method of communication) from ship to ship throughout the entire fleet: a message in nautical parlance that carried its own world of meaning. It was simple and to the point!

"Stand from under, Tojo—we're headed your way."

THE END

KEY TO ABBREVIATIONS
United States Navy (USN)

	CHIEF	FIRST CLASS	SECOND CLASS	THIRD CLASS
Aerographer's Mate	CAerM	AerM1c	AerM2c	AerM3c
Airship Rigger	CAR	AR1c	AR2c	AR3c
Aviation Machinist's Mate.....	ACMM	AMM1c	AMM2c	AMM3c
Aviation Metalsmith	ACM	AM1c	AM2c	AM3c
Aviation Ordnanceman	ACOM	AOM1c	AOM2c	AOM3c
Aviation Pilot	CAP	AP1c	AP2c	
Aviation Radioman	ACRM	ARM1c	ARM2c	ARM3c
Baker		Bkr1c	Bkr2c	Bkr3c
Boatswain's Mate	CBM	BM1c	BM2c	BM3c
Boilermaker	CB	B1c	B2c	B3c
Buglemaster	CBgmstr	Bgmstr1c	Bgmstr2c	Bgmstr3c
Carpenter's Mate	CCM	CM1c	CM2c	CM3c
Chief Commissary Steward....	CCStd			
Electrician's Mate	CEM	EM1c	EM2c	EM3c
Fire Controlman	CFC	FC1c	FC2c	FC3c
Gunner's Mate	CGM	GM1c	GM2c	GM3c
Machinist's Mate	CMM	MM1c	MM2c	MM3c
Metalsmith	CM	M1c	M2c	M3c
Mineman	CMN	MN1c	MN2c	MN3c
Molder	CML	ML1c	ML2c	ML3c
Motor Machinist's Mate.......	CMoMM	MoMM1c	MoMM2c	MoMM3c
Musician	CMus	Mus1c	Mus2c	Mus3c
Officers' Cook	OCC	OC1c	OC2c	OC3c
Officers' Steward	OCS	OS1c	OS2c	OS3c
Painter	CPtr	Ptr1c	Ptr2c	Ptr3c
Parachute Rigger	CPR	PR1c	PR2c	PR3c
Patternmaker	CPM	PM1c	PM2c	PM3c
Pharmacist's Mate	CPhM	PhM1c	PhM2c	PhM3c
Photographer's Mate	CPhoM	PhoM1c	PhoM2c	PhoM3c
Printer	CPrtr	Prtr1c	Prtr2c	Prtr3c
Quartermaster	CQM	QM1c	QM2c	QM3c
Radarman	CRdM	RdM1c	RdM2c	RdM3c
Radioman	CRM	RM1c	RM2c	RM3c
Radio Technician	CRT	RT1c	RT2c	RT3c
Shipfitter	CSF	SF1c	SF2c	SF3c
Ship's Cook		SC1c	SC2c	SC3c
Ship's Service Man	CSSM	SSM1c	SSM2c	SSM3c
Signalman	CSM	SM1c	SM2c	SM3c

(continued on following page)

United States Navy (USN)

	CHIEF	FIRST CLASS	SECOND CLASS	THIRD CLASS
Soundman	CSoM	SoM1c	SoM2c	SoM3c
Special Artificer	CSA	SA1c	SA2c	SA3c
Storekeeper	CSK	SK1c	SK2c	SK3c
Telegrapher	CT	T1c	T2c	T3c
Torpedoman's Mate	CTM	TM1c	TM2c	TM3c
Turret Captain	CTC	TC1c		
Water Tender	CWT	WT1c	WT2c	WT3c
Yeoman	CY	Y1c	Y2c	Y3c
Boatswain	Boat.			
Chief Boatswain	Chief Boat.			
Chief Carpenter	Chief Carp.			
Coxswain	Cox.			
Electrician	Elect.			
Machinist	Mach.			
Naval Air Pilot	NAP			
Torpedoman	Torp.			
Acting Appointment	AA			
Chaplain Corps	Ch C			
Civil Engineer Corps	CEC			
Dental Corps	DC			
Medical Corps	MC			
Nurse Corps	NC			
Supply Corps	SC			

NON-RATED MEN	FIRST CLASS	SECOND CLASS	APPRENTICE
Hospital Apprentice	HA1c	HA2c	
Fireman	F1c	F2c	F3c
Bugler	Bug1c	Bug2c	
Mess Attendant	MA1c	MA2c	MA3c
Seaman	S1c	S2c	AS

United States Marine Corp (USMC)

Staff Sergeant	S/Sgt.
Technical Sergeant	Tech. Sgt.
Sergeant	Sgt.
Private, First Class	PFC
Private	Pvt.

Awards and Citations*

ADMIRAL CHESTER W. NIMITZ, USN
Commander in Chief Pacific Fleet and Pacific Ocean Areas
Born: 2/24/85, Fredericksburg, Texas

Distinguished Service Medal by Navy

For exceptionally meritorious service as Commander in Chief, United States Pacific Fleet. In that position of great responsibility he exercised sound judgment and decision in his employment and disposition of units of the Pacific Fleet during the period immediately following our entry into war with Japan. His conduct of the operations of the Pacific Fleet, resulting in successful actions against the enemy in the Coral Sea, May, 1942, and off Midway Islands, June, 1942, was characterized by unfailing judgment and sound decision, coupled with skill and vigor. His exercise of command on all occasions left nothing to be desired.

Distinguished Service Medal by Congress

For exceptionally meritorious service to the Government of the United States in a duty of great responsibility as Commander in Chief of the Pacific Fleet since December 31, 1941. At the most critical period of the present war in the Pacific, Admiral Nimitz assumed command in that area and despite the losses at Pearl Harbor and tragic shortage of vessels, planes and supplies, organized his forces and carried on defensive warfare which halted the Japanese advance. As rapidly as ships, personnel and material became available, he shifted from defensive to offensive warfare and, by his brilliant leadership and outstanding skill as a strategist, enabled the units under his command to defeat the enemy in the Coral Sea, off Midway, and in the Solomon Islands; and to capture and occupy the Gilbert and Marshall Islands. As a result of his sound judgment and masterful conduct of naval warfare in the Pacific our forces have assumed a position of dominance in this vital area.

REAR ADMIRAL MILO FREDERICK DRAEMEL, USN
Chief of Staff to the Commander in Chief, Pacific Fleet and Pacific Ocean Areas from December 1941 to June 1942.
Born: 5/30/84, Fremont, Nebraska

Distinguished Service Medal

During the early phases of the war, Rear Admiral Draemel aided immeasurably in the promulgation and furtherance of detailed plans for the reorganization of the Fleet to meet the Japanese threat. By his comprehensive knowledge, broad vision and executive ability he was able to render invaluable assistance in preparing the Fleet for effective and sustained action against the enemy. His tireless energy and steadfast devotion to the accomplishment of a vital task were contributing factors in the success of the Fleet at the Battle of Midway.

* This list is complete as of September 28, 1944.

PEARL HARBOR, DECEMBER 7, 1941

Medal of Honor

KIDD, Rear Admiral Isaac C., USN
Born: 2/26/84, Cleveland, Ohio

Immediately went to bridge and as Commander, Battleship Division One, courageously discharged duties as Senior Officer Present until his flagship, USS ARIZONA, blew up and he lost his life.

BENNION, Capt. Mervyn, USN
Born: 5/5/87, Vernon, Utah

Commanding Officer of the USS WEST VIRGINIA. Though mortally wounded, he evidenced concern only in fighting and saving his ship.

FUQUA, Capt. Samuel G., USN
Born: 10/1/99, Laddonia, Mo.

Despite being stunned and knocked down by explosion of large bomb, he, upon regaining consciousness, directed fighting of fire and rescue of wounded, leaving ship with last boat load.

VAN VALKENBURGH, Capt. Franklin, USN
Born: 4/5/88, Minneapolis, Minn.

Gallantly fought his ship, the USS ARIZONA, until she blew up, resulting in the loss of his life.

YOUNG, Capt. Cassin, USN
Born: 3/6/94, Washington, D. C.

In command of USS VESTAL, took personal command of anti-aircraft gun. After being blown overboard, swam back, and moved ship to anchorage distant from USS ARIZONA.

FINN, Lt.(jg) John W., USN
Born: 7/29/26, Los Angeles, Calif.

Manned a machine gun mounted on an instruction stand in a completely exposed section of the parking ramp at Naval Air Station at Kaneohe Bay, Honolulu, T. H., under heavy enemy machine and strafing fire.

FLAHERTY, Ens. Francis Charles, USN
Born: 3/15/19, Charlotte, Mich.

Remained in turret on USS OKLAHOMA, holding flashlight so remainder of turret crew could see to escape when it was seen that ship was going to capsize and order was given to abandon.

HILL, Chief Boat. Edwin J., USN
Born: 10/4/94, Philadelphia, Penn.

During height of strafing and bombing he led his men of the line handling details of a warship to the quays, cast off the lines, and swam to his ship. Later, while on forecastle attempting to let go anchors, he was blown overboard and killed by explosion of several bombs.

JONES, Ens. Herbert C., USNR
Born: 12/1/18, Los Angeles, Calif.

Organized and led a party, which was supplying ammunition to the anti-aircraft battery after the mechanical hoists were put out of action, when he was fatally wounded by a bomb explosion.

REEVES, Thomas J., CRM., USN
Born: 12/9/95, Thomaston, Conn.

After the mechanized ammunition hoists were put out of commission in the USS CALIFORNIA, he, on his own initiative, in a burning passageway, assisted in maintenance of an ammunition supply by hand to the anti-aircraft guns until he was overcome by smoke and fire, which resulted in his death.

ROSS, Lt. Donald K., USN
Born: 12/8/10, Beverly, Kans.

When his station in the forward dynamo room of the USS NEVADA became almost untenable due to smoke, steam, and heat, he forced his men to leave that station and performed all the duties himself until blinded and unconscious.

SCOTT, Robert R., MM1c, USN
Born: 7/31/15, Massillon, Ohio

The compartment in the USS CALIFORNIA, in which the air compressor to which Scott was assigned as his battle station, was flooded as the result of a torpedo hit. The remainder of personnel evacuated compartment but he refused to leave.

TOMICH, Peter, CWT, USN
Born: 6/3/93, Prolog, Austria

Although realizing that the USS UTAH was capsizing, as a result of enemy bombing and torpedoing, he remained at post in engineering plant until he saw that all boilers were secured, and all fireroom personnel had left stations, and by so doing lost his own life.

WARD, James Richard, S1c, USN
Born: 9/10/21, Springfield, Ohio

Remained in turret of USS OKLAHOMA when it was seen that ship was going to capsize, and order given to abandon ship, holding flashlight so that remainder of crew could see to escape.

Navy Cross

BAKER, Lionel H., PhM2c, USN
Born: 10/26/13, Sheguiandah, Ontario, Canada

Wounded himself, he cared for the wounded.

BOLSER, Lt. (jg) Gordon E., USN
Born: 7/21/10, Boston, Mass.

Voluntarily piloted a JRS amphibian plane, equipped only with Springfield rifles, in search for the enemy forces.

BOTHNE, Boat. Adolph M., USN
Born: 4/18/05, Laporte, Minn.

Rescued survivors and assisted in fighting fires.

BURFORD, Lt. Cdr. William P., USN
Born: 2/12/01, Walla Walla, Wash.

Commanding Officer of the USS MONAGHAN. Despite severe enemy bombing and strafing he maneuvered his ship at high speed in the shoal water and at a bend in the channel.

CHRISTOPHER, Ens. Harald J., USNR
Born: 11/6/19, Dwight, Ill.

Assumed duties on the 5″ broadside battery and effectively controlled his part of that battery until killed by a bomb explosion. USS NEVADA.

CURTIS, Ned B., PhM2c, USN
Born: 5/6/20, Michigan

Despite heavy enemy strafing and bombing he climbed the foremast structure and

disregarding orders of wounded officer to go below, he placed him on a stretcher and with assistance of other men lowered him to boat deck as other means of descent were blocked by serious fire.

DALY, Edward Carlyle, Cox., USN
Born: 4/27/14, Pink Hill, N. C.

Lost life in attempt to save wounded shipmate trapped in flaming compartment of ship.

DARLING, Willard D., Corp., USMC
Born: 12/26/18, Wilson, Okla.

Rescued officer while being evacuated from sinking ship.

DAVIS, Ens. Frederick C., USNR
Born: 10/21/15, Rock County, Wisconsin

Killed by bomb explosion while proceeding to foremast structure to take charge of forward anti-aircraft machine gun battery.

DICKINSON, Lt. Clarence E., Jr., USN
Born: 12/1/12, Jacksonville, Georgia

Piloted plane returning from scouting mission during attack on Pearl Harbor. Lost plane, secured another, started on 175 mile search flight.

DOUGLAS, C. E., GunSgt., USMC
Born: 2/5/06, Zillah, Wash.

Ordered to abandon station after bomb hit caused fire, he and his men continued firing guns until end of action.

DRISKELL, J. R., Corp., USMC
Born: 9/22/16, Terre Haute, Ind.

Seriously wounded, he assisted other wounded men and then joined fire-fighting squads.

DUNLAP, Ens. Ernest H., Jr., USN
Born: 5/7/15, Birmingham, Ala.

Seriously wounded, he assisted with wounded until he collapsed.

EDWARDS, Ens. John Perry, USNR
Born: 3/15/13, Eureka, Kans.

Voluntarily piloted a JRS amphibian plane, equipped only with Springfield rifles, in search for and to obtain information of the enemy force.

ETCHELL, George D., CSF, USN
Born: 4/2/98, New York City

Rescued and carried unconscious shipmate to safety.

FENNO, Lt. Frank W., USN
Born: ——

Attacked and sank enemy merchant vessel, also an enemy patrol vessel.

FISLER, Ens. Frank Moore, USNR
Born: 9/4/16, Bladen Co., N. C.

Rescue of men and officer of Army plane forced down at sea.

FLEMING, W. W., BM1c, USN
Born: 3/28/09, Artesia, Miss.

Although injured, directed his gun crew in such movements as to inspire confidence in men about him.

GOMBASY, L. G., S2c, USN
Born: 10/17/19, Detroit, Mich.

Although wounded, continued clearing mooring lines, caring for other wounded, and fighting fires until the end of action.

GRAHAM, Donald A., AMM1c, USN
Born: 6/17/1900, Scranton, Penn.

Although ordered to abandon ship, he released line of USS VESTAL moored alongside.

HAILEY, Thomas E., Sgt., USMC
Born: 11/13/16 ——

Own ship sunk, swam to another, manned anti-aircraft gun. No previous experience. Later, volunteered and went with plane on search mission.

HANSEN, Alfred Lawrence, CMM, USN
Born: 5/21/98, Cruckston, Minn.

Despite injuries continued assisting Fuel Officer of Naval Air Station, Pearl Harbor.

HUTTENBERG, Ens. Allen J., USNR
Born: 7/5/21, Chatsworth, Ill.

Battery officer on 5" anti-aircraft battery of USS NEVADA. Though wounded and handicapped by heavy casualties to personnel of battery, maintained highly effective fire.

ISQUITH, Lt. Cdr. Solomon S., USN
Born: 8/25/96, New York City

Commanding Officer, USS UTAH. Directed abandonment of ship, when it was capsizing rapidly in such an efficient manner that approximately 90 per cent of crew was saved.

JEWELL, Cdr. Jesse D. (MC) USN
Born: 7/24/91, Leon, W. Va.

Medical Officer USS CALIFORNIA. Although burned about face and arms, continued at post and administered effective first aid.

KAUFFMAN, Lt. Draper L., USNR
Born: 8/4/11 ——

Recovered Jap bomb, used for study by Bureau of Ordnance.

LARSON, Ens. Nils R., USN
Born: 12/13/18, Worcester, Mass.

Voluntarily piloted a JRS amphibian plane, equipped only with Springfield rifles, in search for and to obtain information of the enemy forces.

LEY, F. C., Jr., F2c, USNR
Born: 11/16/19, New Haven, Conn.

Saved officer from drowning in water on which there was a great amount of burning oil.

McMURTRY, Paul James, BM1c, USN
Born: 10/24/19, Waco, Tex.

Assisted materially in maintaining continuous and effective fire against enemy by forming relief gun crews to replace casualties on 5" anti-aircraft battery.

MEAD, Harry R., RM2c, USN
Born: 3/29/21, Bucyrus, Ohio

Performed duties in connection with carrying out radio operations during air attack, and later volunteered to go on search mission as radioman.

MILLER, Doris, MA1c, USN (Negro)
Born: 10/12/19 ——

Stood by Captain on bridge of ship during attack, and assisted in moving his captain when the latter was mortally wounded later. Manned and operated machine gun.

MILLER, Lt. (jg) Jim D., USN
Born: 7/2/17, Van Buren, Ark.

Directed fighting of fires, and supervised rescue of wounded and burned, leaving ship in last boatload.

MOORE, Fred Kenneth, S1c, USN
Born: 12/11/21, Campbell, Tex.

Despite orders to take cover, he remained at his station with two members of gun crew and assisted in keeping anti-aircraft gun in operation until he was killed by an explosion.

OUTERBRIDGE, Lt. Cdr. Wm. W., USN
Born: 4/14/06, Victoria, Hong Kong, China

In command of the USS WARD conducted operations which resulted in the destruction of an enemy vessel.

PARKER, Wm. Whiteford, S1c, USN
Born: 11/2/16, Bannethburn, Ga.

Despite orders to take cover, remained at his station on anti-aircraft gun No. 1 with two other members of gun crew until he was blown overboard by explosion.

PETERSON, Robert J., RM2c, USN
Born: 8/12/17 ——

Extinguished serious fire in one plane, thereby saving it from exploding.

PHARRIS, Jackson C., Gunner, USN
Born: 6/26/12, Columbus, Ga.

Maintained ammunition supply to anti-aircraft guns and rescued many men from oil and vapors.

PHILLIPS, Cdr. John S. USN
Born: ——

Without assistance of tugs got his ship immediately under way from her berth upon realization of fire hazard.

RIGGS, Lt. Cdr. Cecil D. (MC), USN
Born: 3/24/06, Santa Rosa, New Mexico

Organized medical facilities available to care for the many wounded men arriving at station from damaged ships.

ROBB, Lt. (jg) James W., Jr., USN
Born: 9/13/12, Staten Island, N. Y.

Voluntarily piloted JRS amphibian plane on search mission.

ROBERTS, William R., R2c, USN
Born: 7/4/20, Chicago, Ill.

Though himself wounded rescued pilot of his plane which had crashed.

RUTH, Ens. Wesley, H., USN
Born: 11/6/13, DeSmet, S. D.

Voluntarily piloted a JRS amphibian plane on search mission.

SINGLETON, Ens. D. Arnold, USNR
Born: 7/6/12, Birmingham, Ala.

Fuel Officer of Naval Air Station, Pearl Harbor. Although under fire from the enemy, supervised opening of sprinkler valves on fuel tanks. Later assisted in caring for wounded.

SMITH, Harold Francis, BM2c, USN
Born: 4/13/17, Youngstown, Ohio

Transported wounded and burned personnel to shore, thereby saving many lives.

SNYDER, J. L., Y1c, USN
Born: 4/29/17, Rose Hill, Kansas

Opened hot ready-box, removing the ammunition.

TAUSSIG, Ens. Joseph K., Jr., USN
Born: 5/28/20, Newport, R. I.

Although seriously wounded continued control of his battery until forcibly removed.

TAYLOR, Ens. Thomas H., USN
Born: 9/30/15, Lima, Ohio

Assumed control of port anti-aircraft battery of USS NEVADA, and continued to direct efficiently that battery although wounded by shell fragments, and deafened due to broken eardrums.

TEAFF, Ens. Perry L., USN
Born: 4/20/16, Weleetka, Okla.

Took off in plane to search for Japanese.

THATCHER, Albert Curtis, AMM2c, USN
Born: 9/26/20, Chama, N. Mex.

Assisted Fuel Officer of Naval Air Station, Pearl Harbor, in uncoupling all hoses and securing fuel lines.

THOMAS, Lt. Cdr. Francis J., USNR
Born: 10/16/04, Buffalo, N. Y.

Assistant First Lieutenant and Assistant Damage Control Officer of USS NEVADA

Taking command as Senior Officer Present, he displayed excellent judgment in promptly moving his ship from proximity of another which was surrounded by burning oil and afire from stem to stern.

THOMAS, Ens. Robert E., Jr., USN
Born: 7/6/19, Springfield, Ill.

Battery officer on 5″ anti-aircraft battery of USS NEVADA. Although seriously wounded, and handicapped by heavy casualties to personnel of battery, maintained highly effective fire.

VAESSEN, John Barth, F2c, USNR
Born: 7/10/16, San Francisco, Calif.

Although ordered to abandon ship because it was rapidly capsizing, he kept lights burning as long as possible and was later rescued through hole cut in bottom of ship.

Silver Star Medal

KIEFER, Lt. (jg) Edwin H., USNR
Born: 12/13/16, Freeport, Ill.

Helped maintain by hand ammunition supply to anti-aircraft guns, until he was overcome by smoke and fire.

MARSHALL, Lt. Theodore W., USNR
Born: 10/26/17, Kansas City, Mo.

Serving with Patrol Squadron 21, during Japanese attack on Pearl Harbor. Commandeered truck and ferried personnel to battle stations. Later pursued in torpedo bomber, attacking enemy craft for 150 miles.

OWEN, Commodore George Thomas, USN
Born: 9/15/95 ——

Acting commanding officer of the USS CURTIS. Organized his command in a spirited, effective defense.

SHAPLEY, Maj. Alan, USMC
Born: 2/9/03, New York City

Navy and Marine Corps Medal

DAY, Francis D., CWT, USN
Born: 7/25/04, Milburn, N. J.

Assisted fifteen of crew to escape through a submerged porthole. Lost own life.

SCHMITT, Lt. (jg) Ch c Aloysius H., USN
Born: 12/4/09, St. Lucas, Iowa

Assisted shipmates to escape through small porthole. Lost own life.

THOMAS, William S., SF1c, USN
Born: 12/7/16, Fort Kent, Me.

Rescue of a Commander, Medical Corps, from the surf.

WRIGHT, Paul R., CWT, USNR
Born: 12/25/99, Meadville, Mo.

During the attack on Pearl Harbor, assisted shipmates to escape through small porthole. Lost own life.

FOLLOWING PEARL HARBOR (SALVAGE)

Legion of Merit

FURLONG, Rear Admiral William Rea, USN
Born: 5/26/81, Allenport, Penn.

Acting Commandant and later as Commandant of the Navy Yard at Pearl Harbor. By his splendid initiative, sound judgment and untiring efforts in directing the difficult salvage activities, he was largely responsible for the successful and expeditious manner in which the vital operations were completed.

Distinguished Service Medal

WALLIN, Capt. Homer N., USN
Born: 12/6/93, Washburn, N. D.

Fleet salvage officer during period following attack on U. S. Pacific Fleet in Pearl Harbor. Through his tireless and energetic devotion to duty, and benefiting by past experience, he accomplished the reclamation of damaged naval units expeditiously and with success beyond expectation.

Legion of Merit

STEELE, Capt. James M., USN
Born: 8/24/94, Denver, Colorado

Salvage Superintendent following Japanese action at Pearl Harbor. He skillfully organized personnel and expedited the procurement of material and equipment necessary to the accomplishment of the important tasks assigned him.

THOMAS, Capt. Robert Ellsworth, CEC, USN
Born: 8/21/91, Rockford, Ill.

The outstanding accomplishments in Naval base construction in the Pacific Area during 1942 were largely due to Captain Thomas's professional ability, keen foresight and perseverance in the face of almost insurmountable difficulties.

WHITAKER, Capt. Francis H., USN
Born: 10/30/98, Tyler, Texas

Member of the Planning Division and later as Hull Superintendent and Salvage Superintendent following raid on Pearl Harbor.

Navy and Marine Corps Medal

BENNETT, Pryor S., CM1c, USN
Born: 5/19/20, Neguanee, Mich.

Diver, salvage of ships immediately following 7 December 1941.

BESTUL, Morris C., CSF, USN
Born: 4/9/09, Heluatia, Wis.

Diver, salvage of ships immediately following 7 December 1941.

BLACKBURN, Earl S., Carp., USN
Born: 4/2/12, Loris, S. C.

Diver, salvage of ships immediately following 7 December 1941.

BUSCH, Frederick David, SF1c, USN
Born: 1/25/17, Portage, Penn.

Diver, salvage of ships immediately following 7 December 1941.

BUSH, Frank Roy, SF2c, USNR
Born: 7/27/11, Vinitia, Oklahoma

Diver, salvage of ships immediately following 7 December 1941.

CARY, Thomas Henry, SF1c, USN
Born: 2/22/21, St. Ignatius, Montana

Diver, salvage of ships immediately following 7 December 1941.

CLARKSON, Lt. James Stroud, USNR
Born: 12/30/06, Clifton, N. J.

Diver, salvage of ships immediately following 7 December 1941.

DANIEL, Alfred Eugene, CGM, USN
Born: 10/28/12, Murphysboro, Ill.

Diver, salvage of ships immediately following 7 December 1941.

DEVRIES, Peter C., CMM, USN
Born: 7/14/95, Lodi, N. J.

Diver, salvage of ships immediately following 7 December 1941.

DOVER, Nelson H., GM1c, USN
Born: —— Paxton, Ill.

Diver, salvage of ships immediately following 7 Dec. 1941.

DU BOIS, Carl W., SF1c, USN
Born: 6/3/18, Middletown, N. Y.

Diver, salvage of ships immediately following 7 Dec. 1941.

FOWLER, Ralph E., Boat., USN
Born: 7/22/15, Turon, Kansas

Diver, salvage of ships immediately following 7 Dec. 1941.

FRAZIER, Glen, CG, USN
Born: 7/8/01, Magnolia, Ark.

Diver, salvage of ships immediately following 7 Dec. 1941.

GREEN, James William, GM2c, USN
Born: 3/20/22, Detroit, Mich.

Diver, salvage of ships immediately following 7 Dec. 1941.

HAYNES, Lt. Cdr. Howard E., USN
(Ret.)
Born: 1/28/09, Cleveland, Ohio

Officer-in-charge diving activities incident to the salvage of ships.

HENDON, Ens. Robert M., USN
Born: 4/25/12, Choctaw County, Miss.

Leading diver and later officer supervisor of divers, salvage operations.

HENDRICKS, Harold F., CSF, USN
Born: 11/1/15, Liberty, S. C.

Diver, salvage of ships immediately following 7 Dec. 1941.

KATZENSTEIN, Alfred J., CEM, USN
Born: 2/1/17, Las Cruces, New Mexico

Diver, salvage of ships immediately following 7 Dec. 1941.

LEWIS, Hugh D., CM1c, USN
Born: 7/12/16, Ochlocnee, Ga.

Diver, salvage of ships immediately following 7 Dec. 1941.

MAHAN, James R., MM1c, USNR
Born: 12/5/16, Summit, N. J.

Diver, salvage of ships immediately following 7 Dec. 1941.

MANTHEI, Lt. (jg) Roman G., USN
Born: 1/12/12, Plymouth, Wis.

Officer in charge of ordnance Salvage Activities.

MARTIN, Jack Floyd, Carp., USNR
Born: 12/9/11, Goodland, Kansas

Diver, salvage of ships immediately following 7 Dec. 1941.

MULLEN, Robert F., CSF, USN
Born: 12/17/18, Boston, Mass.

Diver, salvage of ships immediately following 7 Dec. 1941.

PACITTI, Louis J., GM1c, USN
Born: 1/17/19, Taylor Springs, Ill.

Diver, salvage of ships immediately following 7 Dec. 1941.

PALMQUIST, Glenn L., CM1c, USN
Born: 1/20/17, Harper, Kan.

Diver, salvage of ships immediately following 7 Dec. 1941.

PETERS, Christian R., CM, USNR
Born: 7/14/16, Stanton, Texas

Diver, salvage of ships immediately following 7 Dec. 1941.

ROBERTSON, William Elmer, GM2c, USN
Born: 10/6/20, Pollock, Louisiana

Diver, salvage of ships immediately following 7 Dec. 1941.

ROCHE, John J., Jr., CM1c, USN
Born: 1/17/18, New York City

Diver, salvage of ships immediately following 7 Dec. 1941.

SAYLES, Harry A., SF1c, USN
Born: 10/13/18, Fruita, Colorado

Diver, salvage of ships immediately following 7 Dec. 1941.

THOMAS, William Houston, SF1c, USN
Born: 8/22/21, Paragould, Ark.

Diver, salvage of ships immediately following 7 Dec. 1941.

TINSLEY, Kenneth F., M1c, USNR
Born: 10/30/15, Salem, Ohio

Diver, salvage of ships immediately following 7 Dec. 1941.

VANDAGRIFF, Tony G., SF1c, USN
Born: 8/15/21, Wellington, Texas

Diver, salvage of ships immediately following 7 Dec. 1941.

VAUGHN, Herbert E., Jr., SF1c, USNR
Born: 10/31/19, Port Arthur, Texas

Diver, salvage operations immediately following 7 Dec. 1941.

WEST, Delbert L., BM1c, USN
Born: 1/24/14, Oakdale, Penn.

Diver, salvage operations immediately following 7 Dec. 1941.

ZAKULEC, Walter, SF1c, USN
Born: 5/27/14, Oakdale, Penn.

Diver, salvage of ships immediately following 7 Dec. 1941.

UNIT CITATIONS

The Commander in Chief, United States Pacific Fleet, takes pleasure in commending:

UNITED STATES NAVAL HOSPITAL,
PEARL HARBOR,
TERRITORY OF HAWAII

for service as set forth in the following:
CITATION:

"For meritorious achievement and distinguished service subsequent to the Japanese Air Attack on the United States Pacific Fleet at Pearl Harbor, Territory of Hawaii, on December 7, 1941. At the time of the attack and afterwards, this unit displayed conspicuous devotion in the line of duty. Its ability to cope with this disaster was responsible for the successful care of all casualties and the saving of many lives. The professional skill displayed and distinguished service rendered by this Hospital Unit were in keeping with the highest traditions of the naval service."

/s/ C. W. NIMITZ,
Admiral, USN

Captain Reynolds Hayden, Medical Corps, USN, was in command of the Naval Hospital at Pearl Harbor at the time of the Japanese attack on December 7, 1941.

The Commander in Chief, United States Pacific Fleet, takes pleasure in commending

USS SOLACE

for service as set forth in the following:

CITATION:

"For meritorious achievement and distinguished service during and subsequent to the Japanese air attack on the United States Fleet at Pearl Harbor, Territory of Hawaii, on 7 December, 1941. At the time of the attack and afterwards, this unit displayed conspicuous devotion in the line of duty. Its ability to cope with this disaster was responsible for the successful care of all casualties and the saving of many lives. The professional skill displayed and distinguished service rendered by this hospital ship were in keeping with the highest traditions of the naval service."

/s/ C. W. NIMITZ,
Admiral, USN

JAPANESE ATTACKS ON MIDWAY ISLAND
December 7, 1941–May 7, 1942

Medal of Honor

CANNON, Capt. George H., USMC
Born: 11/5/15, Webster Groves, Mo.

Command of defense of island against Japanese attack December 7, 1941.

Navy Cross

DICKEY, 2nd Lt. Robert L., USMC
Born: 12/12/06, Neville Island, Penn.

EATON, Lt. John M., Jr., USNR
Born: 3/26/18, Boston, Mass.

HAZELWOOD, Harold R., Corp., USMC
Born: 9/13/20, Butterfield, Mo.

McCARTHY, Capt. Francis P., USMC
Born: 10/13/16, Milton, Mass.

PETERS, Dale L., Corp., USMC
Born: 1/8/17, Breckenridge, Mich.

SOMERS, 1st Lt. Charles W., Jr., USMC
Born: 6/11/16, Salisbury, N. C.

JAPANESE ATTACK ON WAKE ISLAND
December 7, 1941

Navy Cross

DEVEREUX, Maj. James P. S., USMC
Born: 2/20/03, Cabana, Cuba

CUNNINGHAM, Cdr. Winfield Scott, USN
Born: 2/16/1900, Rockbridge, Wis.

´UNIT CITATION

Citation by

THE PRESIDENT OF THE
UNITED STATES

of

*The Wake detachment of the 1st Defense
Battalion, U. S. Marine Corps, under
command of Major James P. S. Devereux,
U. S. Marines*

and

Marine Fighting Squadron 211 of Mar-

*ine Aircraft Group 21, under command
of Major Paul A. Putnam, U. S. Marines*

"The courageous conduct of the officers
and men of these units, who defended
Wake Island against an overwhelming
superiority of enemy air, sea, and land
attacks from December 8 to 22, 1941, has
been noted with admiration by their fel-
low countrymen and the civilized world,
and will not be forgotten so long as
gallantry and heroism are respected and
honored. These units are commended for
their devotion to duty and splendid conduct at their battle stations under most
adverse conditions. With limited defensive
means against attacks in great force, they
manned their shore installations and flew
their aircraft so well that five enemy warships were either sunk or severely damaged, many hostile planes shot down, and
an unknown number of land troops destroyed."

MARSHALL AND GILBERT ISLANDS

Distinguished Service Medal

HALSEY, Admiral William F., Jr., USN
Born: 10/30/82, Elizabeth, N. J.

Commander of Marshall Raiding Force,
U.S. Pacific Fleet. Brilliant and audacious
attack against Marshall and Gilbert
Islands, January 31, 1942.

BROWN, Rear Admiral Wilson Jr., USN
Born: 4/27/82, Philadelphia, Penn.

For exceptionally meritorious service to
the Government of the United States in a
duty of great responsibility as a Task
Force Commander of the United States
Pacific Fleet during a period at sea of
approximately eight weeks in February
and March, 1942, when he displayed the
highest qualities of seamanship, leadership, endurance and tenacity while conducting extensive operations against, and
a successful action with, enemy forces.

BROWNING, Capt. Miles Rutherford, USN
Born: 4/10/97, Perth Amboy, N. J.

Chief of Staff to a Task Force Commander. In addition to contributing immeasurably to the success of our attack
on Marshall and Gilbert and raids on
Wake and Marcus Islands. . . .

Legion of Merit

LEWIS, Rear Admiral Spencer S., USN
Born: 1/8/88, Calvert, Texas

Chief of Staff and aide to Task Force
Commander in Pacific Area for first ten
months of war.

Navy Cross

HOLLINGSWORTH, Cdr. William R., USN
Born: 9/6/03, Ft. Meade, Florida

Commanding Officer of Bombing
Squadron, February 1, 1942. Destroyed

four enemy two-engined bombers and three Japanese fighters being serviced on airfield.

MURRAY, Capt. George D., USN
Born: 7/6/89, Boston, Mass.
February 1, 1942. Commanding Officer of USS ENTERPRISE.

Silver Star Medal

BROWNING, Capt. Miles R., USN
Born: 4/10/97, Perth Amboy, N. J.
Chief of Staff to Task Force Commander, December 6, 1941–June 14, 1942.

BURACKER, Capt. William H., USN
Born: 7/20/97, Luray, Va.
Member of staff of Task Force Commander, December 6, 1941–June 14, 1942.

BURROUGHS, Cdr. Sherman E., Jr., USN
Born: 2/22/03, Manchester, N. H.
Member of staff of Task Force Commander, December 6, 1941–June 14, 1942.

Dow, Cdr. Leonard J., USN
Born: 7/26/02, Bowling Green, Ohio
Member of staff of Commander Task Force, December 6, 1941–June 14, 1942.

GRIGGS, Cdr. Gale E., USN
Born: 11/6/04, Lincoln, Neb.
Member of Task Force Commander, December 6, 1941–June 14, 1942.

MOULTON, Lt. Cdr. Horace D., USNR
Born: 9/29/09, Sabetha, Kansas
Member of staff of Task Force Commander, December 6, 1941–June 14, 1942.

NICHOL, Cdr. Bromfield B., USN
Born: 1/18/04, New Orleans, La.
Member of staff of Task Force Commander, December 6, 1941–June 14, 1942.

ASHFORD, Lt. Cdr. William H., USN
Born: 8/1/03, Carson City, Nev.
Member of staff of Task Force Commander, December 6, 1941–June 14, 1942.

BROWN, Lt. Col. Julian P., USMC
Born: 2/1/97, Belmont, Mass.
Member of staff of Task Force Commander, December 7, 1941–June 14, 1942.

Distinguished Flying Cross

ADAMS, Ens. John P., USNR
Born: 2/20/19, Horton, Kans.
January 31, 1942. While piloting fighter plane, assisted in destruction of enemy four engine patrol bomber seaplane.

BLITCH, Lt. John D., USN
Born: 10/14/14, Charleston, S. C.
Division leader of bombing squadron. On February 1, 1942, scored direct hits on cargo vessel, oil storage tank, enemy heavy bombing plane on ground, and silenced an anti-aircraft gun.

BURCH, Lt. Cdr. William O., Jr., USN
Born: 6/27/04, Paducah, Ky.
Commanding Officer of a scouting squadron. January 31, 1942, led squadron in air attack and personally made direct hit on enemy seaplane tender and sank four engine patrol plane.

DOBSON, Ens. Cleo John, USNR
Born: 11/3/18, Frederick, Okla.
Member of scouting squadron February 1, 1942. One fighter damaged in combat, one submarine sunk by direct bomb hit and one auxiliary vessel damaged by a near miss.

GRAY, Lt. James S., Jr., USN
Born: 2/1/14, Milwaukee, Wis.
Led bombing and strafing attack of his group on Island of Maloelap in most efficient manner. Shot down two fighter planes.

KROEGER, Lt. (jg) Edwin J., USNR
Born: 10/29/13, Akron, Ohio
Despite injury, maneuvered his plane so that gunner might shoot down attacking plane.

KLEISS, Lt. Norman, USN
Born: 3/7/16, Coffeyville, Kans.
Member of a scouting squadron. Scored direct hit on a light cruiser.

McCAULEY, Lt. James W., USN
Born: 10/6/12, Fairbanks, Alaska
Led his section of a bombing squadron in attacks which resulted in sinking a

submarine, destroying several seaplanes, a hangar and other buildings, and damaging the flying field.

McCLUSKEY, Lt. Cdr. Clarence W., Jr., USN
Born: 6/1/02, Buffalo, N. Y.

Commander of Fighting Squadron. February 1, 1942, caused considerable damage to enemy by bombing and strafing. Destroyed one twin engined bomber and damaged another.

McCUSKEY, Lt. (jg) Elbert S., USNR
Born: 2/8/15, Little Rock, Ark.

January 31, 1942, assisted in destruction of an enemy four engine patrol bomber seaplane, which was attempting to attack his ship.

RAWIE, Lt. (jg) Wilmer E., USN
Born: 4/3/15, Staunton, Ill.

February 1, 1942, in attack on Island of Maloelap, shot down an enemy fighter plane.

RILEY, Lt. Paul J., USN
Born: 4/12/13, Hot Springs, Ark.

February 1, 1942, developed the attack of section he was leading against an enemy light cruiser in manner which resulted in destruction of that enemy ship.

VAN BUREN, Lt. John J., USN
Born: 7/22/15, Mukwonago, Wis.

During aerial combat operations February 1, 1942, shot down one of attacking planes, and maneuvered plane so that rear seat gunner might shoot down another.

Air Medal

ANDERSON, Lt. (jg) Edward L., USN
Born: 9/22/14, Claremont, Va.

Pilot of air attack group, February 1, 1942. Obtained direct hit on enemy tanker.

CHECK, Lt. (jg) Leonard J., USN
Born: 3/4/11, Berwick, N. Dakota

Section leader of air attack group, February 1, 1942, rendered seaplane ramp useless and destroyed one enemy seaplane.

DEACON, Lt. Edward T., USN
Born: 9/29/14, Bridgeport, Conn.

Participated in aerial attacks resulting in damage to enemy planes, hangars and other ground installations.

DICKINSON, Lt. Clarence E., Jr., USN
Born: 12/1/12, Jacksonville, Florida

As flight officer of a scouting squadron, he commanded . . . attack which resulted in direct hits on ground installations and on a large enemy ship.

DONNELL, Ens. Earl R., USNR
Born: 9/3/19, Temple, Texas

Participated in initial attack on Kwajalein Atoll February 1, 1942, contributing to damage to enemy installations on Roi Island.

FOGG, Lt. (jg) Carleton T., USN
Born: 8/19/17, Lynn, Mass.

Participated in initial attack on Kwajalein Atoll on February 1, 1942, contributing to damage to enemy installations on Roi Island.

HALSEY, Ens. Delbert W., USNR
Born: 12/8/19, Baker, Montana

Pilot of air attack group, February 1, 1942, made direct hit on and demolished large warehouse.

HOLCOMB, Ens. Keith H., USNR
Born: 12/26/13, Huron, S. Dakota

Pilot of air attack group, February 1, 1942, attacked shore installation which resulted in large fire adjacent to enemy airfield.

LANHAM, Lt. Harvey P., USN
Born: 7/17/13, Chicago, Ill.

As pilot of air attack group February 1, 1942, he obtained direct hits on enemy transport and storage buildings. Later, led his section in bombing attack and scored hits on a hangar and a building.

PATRIARCA, Lt. Frank A., USN
Born: 12/3/13, Providence, R. I.

Participated in attacks on Roi Island February 1, 1942, which resulted in damage to enemy planes, hangars, and other ground installations.

PENLAND, Lt. Joe R., USN
Born: 10/21/11, Concord, N. C.

In aerial attack February 1, 1942, he led his section in attacks resulting in damage to large cargo vessel, and destruction of a hangar and damage to runways.

ROBERTS, Lt. Wilbur E., USNR
Born: 4/17/15, Detroit, Mich.

February 1, 1942. Destroyed enemy two-engined bomber on field.

RUTHERFORD, Lt. Reginald, USN
Born: 8/21/13, Washington, D. C.

February 1, 1942. Led his division in dive bombing attack against enemy ships at Wotje Atoll, which resulted in heavy losses to enemy, including direct hits on two large auxiliary vessels.

SCHNEIDER, Ens. Tony F., USNR
Born: 11/11/17, Hillsboro, Mo.

Attacked enemy ships and shore installations in face of heavy anti-aircraft fire destroying large storehouse and damaging two bombers on ground with near misses.

SEID, Ens. Daniel, USNR
Born: 11/29/18, Brooklyn, N. Y.

Participated in attack on Kwajalein Atoll, February 1, 1942, contributing to the damage to enemy installation on Roi Island.

SMITH, Lt. Lloyd A., USN
Born: 5/3/12, Jacksonville, Fla.

Participated in Marshalls attack February 1, 1942. Scored direct hit on large transport, setting it afire. Near misses scored on large oil tanker and a hangar, causing damage to hangar and destruction of three fighter planes on ground.

STONE, Ens. Reid W., USNR
Born: 1/2/18, Aurora, Ill.

Participated in attack February 1, 1942, which resulted in damage to enemy planes and buildings.

TEAFF, Lt. (jg) Perry L., USN
Born: 4/20/16, Weleetka, Okla.

Participated in initial attack on Roi Island, Kwajalein Atoll, and in subsequent

attack on Wotje Harbor, on February 1, 1942.

TROEMEL, Lt. (jg) Benjamin H., USNR
Born: 6/10/15, Brooklyn, N. Y.

Participated in initial attack on Roi Island, Kwajalein Atoll, and in subsequent attack on Wotje Harbor, on February 1, 1942.

VANDIVIER, Lt. (jg) Norman F., USNR
Born: 3/10/16, Edwards, Miss.

Member of a bombing squadron. On February 1, 1942, attacked enemy ships, shore installations, scoring near miss on cargo vessel and direct hit on small barracks.

WALTERS, Ens. Clifford R., USNR
Born: 11/2/14, Streator, Ill.

February 1, 1942. Destroyed large hangar and radio station power house.

WEST, Lt. (jg) John N., USN
Born: 2/14/14, Forest Grove, Oregon

Participated in attack February 1, 1942, on Roi Island, Kwajalein Atoll, and in subsequent attack on Wotje Harbor.

PRESIDENTIAL UNIT CITATION— USS ENTERPRISE

The President of the United States takes pleasure in presenting the PRESIDENTIAL UNIT CITATION to the UNITED STATES SHIP ENTERPRISE for service as set forth in citation:

"For consistently outstanding performance and distinguished achievement during repeated action against enemy Japanese forces in the Pacific war area, December 7, 1941, to November 15, 1942. Participating in nearly every major carrier engagement in the first year of the war, the ENTERPRISE and her Air Group, exclusive of her far-flung destruction of hostile shore installations throughout the battle area, did sink or damage, on her own, a total of 35 Japanese vessels and shoot down a total of 185 Japanese aircraft. Her aggressive spirit and superb combat efficiency are fitting tribute to the officers and men who so gallantly established her as an ahead bulwark in defense of the American Nation."

Gilbert and Marshall Islands Raid—February 1, 1942
Wake Island Raid—February 24, 1942
Marcus Island Raid—March 4, 1942
Battle of Midway—June 4–6, 1942
Occupation of Guadalcanal—August 7–8, 1942

Battle of Stewart Islands—August 24, 1942
Battle of Santa Cruz—October 26, 1942
Battle of Solomon Islands—November 14–15, 1942

For the President
/s/ FRANK KNOX
Secretary of Navy
April 29, 1943.

USS MARBLEHEAD

Navy Cross

ROBINSON, Capt. Arthur G., USN
Born: 5/21/92, Brooklyn, N. Y.

February 4, 1942. Commanding Officer of the USS MARBLEHEAD on February 4, 1942, during an engagement with superior forces. During which his ship suffered severe damage. Engaged attacking force of Japanese bombing planes, destroyed two enemy planes and saved his badly damaged and crippled ship.

ANDERSEN, Ens. Harvey M., USN
Born: 8/5/01, Chicago, Ill.

February 10, 1942. Although wounded, directed fighting of fires, the rescuing of wounded in forward part of ship and maintaining water-tight integrity of ship.

BARRE, Lester J., QM2c, USN
Born: 2/9/14, Orange, Texas

February 10, 1942. Surrounded by electrical fires, worked tirelessly and with unflinching courage to free the jammed rudder and to lock it amidships.

BECKER, Claude, S1c, USN
Born: 1/22/18, Ogden, Utah

February 4, 1942. Assisted in the removal of powder in the wake of the fire in adjacent compartments. Opened a hot and heavy hatch which permitted men to escape from compartments below the fire.

DRURY, Lt. Cdr., Martin J., USN
Born: 11/6/01, Jamestown, R. I.

February 10, 1942. Directing the work of arresting and repairing damage to the vessel, in fighting fires and assisting in rescue of the wounded.

HOCK, Herman E., CBM, USN
Born: 4/27/12, Galveston, Texas

February 10, 1942. Took charge of operations in the upperdecks, working under many varied conditions, facilitated the evacuation of the wounded, the fighting of fires, clearing of debris and wreckage, maintenance of communications.

JOHNSON, Dale L., MM1c, USN
Born: 7/26/16, Thief River Falls, Minn.

February 10, 1942. After assisting in fighting fires, clearing wreckage, rescuing the wounded, he worked tirelessly and unflinchingly freeing the jammed rudder and locking it amidships.

McCULLEY, Hale T., CSF, USN
Born: 9/26/06, Riverview, Neb.

February 10, 1942. Following bomb explosion, led a party throughout the forward section evacuating flooding magazines. He proceeded to sick bay area, where he brought all fires under control.

MORAN, Martin, M1c, USN
Born: 6/30/16, New Rochelle, N. Y.

February 10, 1942. When the steering engine room was wrecked, he, despite being surrounded by electrical fires, worked to free the jammed rudder and to lock it amidships.

RITTER, Frederick H., CEM, USN
Born: 8/20/02, El Paso, Ill.

February 10, 1942. Directing and assisting in the repair and maintenance of temporary lighting, power and communication circuits.

VAN BERGEN, Cdr. Nicholas B., USN
Born: 5/27/1900, San Francisco, Calif.

February 10, 1942. Gunnery Officer in the early part of the action. Later, assumed the duties of Executive Officer, supervising control of damaged areas, assisting in rescue and care of injured and coordinating the work of all departments.

WASSELL, Lt. Cdr., Corydon M., (MC), USNR
Born: 7/4/84, Little Rock, Ark.

March 1, 1942. Disregard of personal safety while caring for and evacuating wounded under his charge in Java, Netherlands East Indies.

Silver Star Medal

ASCHENBRENNER, Clarence John, SF2c, USN
Born: 5/30/18, New Ulm, Minn.

February 10, 1942. Performed tremendous feats of lifting and moving heavy wreckage ceaselessly for forty-eight hours.

PEARCE, Lt. Hepburn A., USN
Born: 1/3/08, Dorchester, Mass.

February 10, 1942. Voluntarily took charge of Forward Repair Party and assisted in bringing fires under control, checking spread of water in ship and in rescue of wounded.

ACTION AT SALAMAUA-LAE, NEW GUINEA

Navy Cross

ARMSTRONG, Cdr. Robert G., USN
Born: 4/21/04, Wakefield, Neb.

Bombing Squadron Commander, March 10, 1942. He and his squadron inflicted severe damage on enemy. Probable destruction of three hostile ships.

BERRY, Lt. David R., USN
Born: 7/13/15, Owensboro, Ky.

Pilot of bombing plane, March 10, 1942. Seriously damaged and probably destroyed hostile vessel.

BIGELOW, Lt. Lavell M., USN
Born: 11/12/17, Provo, Utah

Pilot of bombing plane, March 10, 1942. Seriously damaged and probably destroyed enemy vessel.

BURCH, Cdr. William O., USN
Born: 6/27/04, Paducah, Ky.

Scouting Squadron Commander, March 10, 1942. He and his squadron scored seven direct hits against hostile vessels— one direct hit being made by him personally.

CALDWELL, Lt. Cdr. Turner F., Jr.
Born: 11/17/13, Narbeth, Pa.

Pilot of scout bomber March 10, 1942. Direct hit on one hostile vessel.

CAMPBELL, Ens. Kendall C., USNR
Born: 7/25/17, Garden City, Kansas

Pilot of scout bomber March 10, 1942. Direct hit on one hostile vessel.

NICHOLSON, Lt. Hugh W., USNR
Born: 2/28/12, Campbellsburg, Ind.

Pilot of scout bomber March 10, 1942. Direct hit on one hostile vessel.

SHORT, Lt. Cdr. Wallace C., USN
Born: 3/26/09, Malone, N. Y.

Pilot of scout bomber March 10, 1942. Direct hit on one hostile vessel.

Distinguished Service Medal

TAYLOR, Cdr. Joe, USN
Born: 7/23/06, Westville, Ill.

Torpedo Squadron Commander, March 10, 1942. He and his squadron destroyed aircraft on deck of enemy carrier, and disabled that vessel.

VEJTASA, Lt. Stanley W., USN
Born: 7/27/14, Paris, Mont.

Pilot of scout bomber March 10, 1942. Obtained direct hit on one hostile vessel, and contributed to destruction of three enemy ships.

Silver Star Medal

SCHINDLER, Cdr. Walter G., USN
Born: 12/10/97, New Glarus, Wis.

Gunnery officer, staff of Task Force Commander for first ten months of war.

SUBMARINE ACTION IN THE PACIFIC

Navy Cross

ANDERSON, Lt. Cdr. William L., USN
Born: 4/10/05, Sylvania, Ga.

AYLWARD, Lt. Cdr. Theodore C., USN
Born: 2/14/03, Cincinnati, Ohio

BACON, Cdr. Barton E., USN
Born: 10/18/01, Rockwood, Tenn.

CHAPPELL, Lt. Cdr. Lucius H., USN
Born: 2/20/05, Columbus, Ohio

DEMPSEY, Lt. James C., USN
Born: 8/30/08, Eastport, Maryland

DETAR, Lt. Cdr. John L., USN
Born: 9/21/06, Lincoln, Nebraska

FENNO, Cdr. Frank Wesley, Jr., USN
Born: 9/11/02, Westminster, Mass.

GRENFELL, Lt. Cdr. Elton Watters, USN
Born: 11/6/03, Fall River, Mass.

HURD, Lt. Cdr. Kenneth C., USN
Born: 11/18/02, Metamora, Mich.

HUTCHINSON, Lt. Cdr. Edward S., USN
Born: 2/14/04, Philadelphia, Pa.

KIRKPATRICK, Lt. Cdr. Charles C., USN
Born: 6/20/07, San Angelo, Texas

LENT, Lt. Cdr. Willis A., USN
Born: 1/5/04, Dorchester, Mass.

McGREGOR, Lt. Cdr. Donald, USN
Born: 10/26/03, Wash., D. C.

McKINNEY, Lt. Cdr. Eugene B., USN
Born: 7/31/03, Eugene, Oregon

MOSELEY, Lt. Cdr. Stanley P., USN
Born: 6/28/03, Mexia, Texas

MUMMA, Lt. Cdr. Morton C., Jr., USN
Born: 8/24/04, Manila, P. I.

PARKS, Lt. Cdr. Lewis S., USN
Born: 4/13/02, Bayport, Long Island

RICE, Lt. Cdr. Robert H., USN
Born: 9/17/03, Pittsfield, Mass.

SAUNDERS, Raymond O., CTM, USN
Born: 8/25/16, Allendorph, Iowa

SAUNDERS, Lt. Cdr. Willard A., USN
Born: 10/25/04, Escanaba, Mich.

SMITH, Lt. Cdr. Chester C., USN
Born: 2/16/05, Bisbee, Ariz.

VOGE, Lt. Cdr. Richard George, USN
Born: 5/4/04, Chicago, Ill.

WARDER, Lt. Cdr. Frederick B., USN
Born: 3/19/04, Grafton, West Va.

WHITE, Lt. Cdr. David C., USN
Born: 11/13/03, Detroit, Mich.

WILLINGHAM, Lt. Cdr. Joseph H., USN
Born: 3/20/05, Pell City, Ala.

WILKINS, Lt. Cdr. Charles W., USN
Born: 8/30/02, Thorofare, N. J.

WRIGHT, Lt. Cdr. William L., USN
Born: 7/19/02, Roby, Texas

Silver Star Medal

BARNARD, Lt. James H., USN
Born: 2/21/14, Webster, Monroe County, N. Y.

CAPECE, Edmund C., CEM, USN
Born: 5/2/08, Providence, Rhode Island

CASLER, Lt. (jg) James B., USN
Born: 8/30/10, Fresno, Calif.

DERAGON, Lt. Cdr. William N., USN
Born: 3/28/11, Albany, New York

HOLDEN, Lt. Cdr. Richard, USN
Born: 12/21/15, Rutland, Vermont

NIMITZ, Lt. Chester W., Jr., USN
Born: 2/17/15, Brooklyn, N. Y.

Navy and Marine Corps Medal

CAIRNS, William R., CTM, USN
Born: 12/10/07, Peekville, Penn.

MEDLEY, Frank H., TM1c, USN
Born: 10/14/18, Middleport, Ohio

PRESIDENTIAL UNIT CITATION— USS GUDGEON

The President of the United States takes pleasure in presenting the PRESIDEN-

TIAL UNIT CITATION to the UNITED STATES SHIP GUDGEON for service as set forth in citation:

"For outstanding performance in combat during eight aggressive and brilliantly executed war patrols in enemy-controlled waters since December 7, 1941. Fighting with remarkable prowess and daring, she achieved an illustrious combat record in the sinking of 19 Japanese ships, including one submarine, which totalled 133,957 tons, and in damaging three more ships totalling 13,944 tons. The superb efficiency and readiness for battle which enabled the GUDGEON to fulfill these vital missions reflects great credit upon her gallant officers and men of the United States Naval Service."

DESTROYER ACTION IN FAR EAST AND PACIFIC

Navy Cross

BERMINGHAM, Lt. Cdr. John M., USN
Born: 7/6/05, New York City

Commanding Officer USS PEARY, in enemy waters, December 10, 1941–February 19, 1942, fought valiantly against enemy.

ABERCROMBIE, Cdr. Laurence A., USN
Born: 10/11/97, Lawrence, Mass.

Commanding Officer USS DRAYTON. Destruction of an enemy vessel December 24, 1941.

Silver Star Medal

FRYMAN, Glenn A., MM2c, USN
Born: 1/15/22, Brooksville, Ohio

USS PEARY, December 28, 1941. When fragment of bomb miss penetrated a 4-inch powder cartridge and set it afire, he unstrapped cartridge from its stowage and threw it overboard.

BATTLE OF MACASSAR STRAIT

January 23–24, 1942

Navy Cross

TALBOT, Cdr. Paul H., USN
Born: 4/3/97, Willoughby, Ohio
Commander of Destroyer Division.

COOPER, Lt. Cdr. Jacob E., USN
Born: 3/20/02, Bristol, Fla.
Commanding USS JOHN D. FORD.

HOURIHAN, Lt. Cdr. John J., USN
Born: 11/3/02, Miami, Fla.
Commanding USS PAUL JONES.

PARKER, Lt. Cdr. Edward N., USN
Born: 7/7/04, Avalon, Pa.
Commanding USS PARROTT.

BLINN, Cdr. Welford C., USN
Born: 10/12/02, Sparta, Ohio
Commanding USS POPE.

COMMANDING OFFICERS OF OTHER DESTROYERS WHICH SANK SUBMARINES

January 28, 1942

Navy Cross

VEEDER, Lt. Cdr. William S., USN
Born: 1/19/03, Washington, D. C.
Commanding Officer USS LONG.

THAYER, Cdr. William K., USN
Born: 5/28/1900, Colorado Springs, Colo.
Commanding Officer USS JARVIS.

BATTLE OF BADOENG STRAIT

February 19–20, 1942

Navy Cross

BINFORD, Cdr. Thomas H., USN
Born: 8/25/96, Durant, Miss.
Commander Destroyer Division.

PARKER, Lt. Cdr. Edward N., USN
Born: 7/7/04, Avalon, Pa.
Commander Destroyer Division.

COOPER, Lt. Cdr. Jacob E., USN
Born: 3/20/02, Bristol, Fla.
Commanding USS JOHN D. FORD.

ECCLES, Cdr. Henry E., USN
Born: 12/31/98, Bayside, N. Y.
Commanding USS JOHN D. EDWARDS.

HUGHES, Lt. John N., USN
Born: 11/28/09, Columbia, Mo.
Commanding USS PARROTT.

SMITH, Lt. Cdr. Harold P., USN
Born: 2/17/04, Grand Bay, Ala.
Commanding USS STEWART.

Gold Star in Lieu of Second Navy Cross

BLINN, Cdr. Welford C., USN
Born: 10/12/02, Sparta, Ohio
Commanding USS POPE.

Silver Star Medal

SEIFERT, Paul R., Mach., USN
Born: 9/26/02 ————.
USS STEWART. Skillful handling of pumping enabled ship to keep station as flagship during enemy action.

SMILEY, Lt. Cdr. Clare B., USN
Born: 1/30/12, Birmingham, Ala.
Executive Officer of USS STEWART. Though wounded persisted in carrying on.

WILSON, Lt. John V., USN
Born: 3/2/18, Sumter, S. C.
Gunnery Officer USS PARROTT. Though wounded, remained at battle station.

NAVAL ENGAGEMENT IN STRAIT OF LOMBOK, N.E.I.

February 19–20, 1942

Navy Cross

POUND, Lt. Cdr. Harold C., USN
Born: 12/20/03, Hutchinson, Kan.
Commanding USS PILLSBURY.
* For additional citations, see page 488.

JAVA SEA*

February 27, 1942

Navy Cross

COLEY, Lt. Cdr. Lewis E., USN
Born: 10/2/99, Alexander City, Ala.
Commanding USS ALDEN in torpedo attack against superior enemy Japanese forces in Java Sea.

DARWIN, AUSTRALIA

February 19, 1942

Silver Star Medal

WILSON, LeRay, MSmTH2c, USN
Born: 2/4/20, Cove, Ore.
USS WILLIAM B. PRESTON. Despite rapidity with which attack developed, and danger of being trapped by explosion, he, in company with a shipmate, went below decks and had just completed closing all doors and hatches when a bomb caused his death.

UNIT CITATION

The President of the United States takes pleasure in presenting the PRESIDENTIAL UNIT CITATION to the UNITED STATES SHIP MAURY for service as set forth in the following CITATION:

"For outstanding performance in combat against enemy Japanese forces ashore and afloat in the Pacific War Area from February 1, 1942, to August 6, 1943. Unique in the comprehensiveness of her service since the commencement of hostilities, the USS MAURY has operated continuously in the most advanced areas, penetrating deep into submarine-infested waters to seek her targets and destroy hostile warships, shore batteries and aircraft with her deadly torpedoes and gunfire. She has furnished powerful fire support for our landing operations and has covered our ships during retirement; she has provided sturdy escort of troops and supplies to our land forces and has frustrated the enemy's attempts to reinforce his own garrisons. Attacking boldly by day and dangerously by night, the MAURY has gallantly fulfilled her missions despite fierce Japanese resistance and by her readiness for combat, has implemented the skill and fighting spirit of her officers and men throughout a crucial period."

For the President,
/s/ JAMES FORRESTAL
Secretary of the Navy

AIR ACTION, PACIFIC AND FAR EAST
December 7, 1941–May 7, 1942

Navy Cross

SHERMAN, Capt. Frederick Carl, USN
Born: 5/27/88, Port Huron, Mich.

Commanding Officer, USS LEXINGTON, on February 20, 1942, when that ship was attacked by eighteen Japanese bombers. As a result of the brilliant performance of the fighting squadrons under his command, eighteen enemy bombers were destroyed, without damage to the USS LEXINGTON.

ALLEN, Lt. Edward H., USN
Born: 3/2/08, Pekin, N. D.

GAYLER, Lt. Noel A. N., USN
Born: 12/25/13, Birmingham, Ala.

Medal of Honor

O'HARE, Lt. Edward H., USN
Born: 3/13/14, St. Louis, Mo.

AIR ACTION
February 4, 1942

Air Medal

HENDRICKS, Lt. (jg) Carl B., USNR
Born: 12/28/12, Thatcher, Arizona

AIR ACTION
February 19, 1942

Silver Star Medal

MOSLEY, Ens. Walter H., USNR
Born: 1/17/16, Waco, Texas

AIR ACTION
February 20, 1942

Navy Cross

HENRY, Lt. Walter Franklin, USN
Born: 11/11/11, Butler, Mo.

LEMMON, Lt. (jg) Rolla Stuart, USN
Born: 11/20/15, Peru, Kansas

PETERSON, Ens. Dale W., USNR
Born: 11/18/19, St. Joseph, Mo.

SELLSTROM, Ens. Edward R., Jr., USNR
Born: 7/19/16, Dayton, Iowa

THACH, Lt. Cdr. John S., USN
Born: 4/19/05, Fordyce, Ark.

Distinguished Flying Cross

CLARK, Lt. (jg) Howard F., USN
Born: 9/15/14, Wilmington, Delaware

EDER, Ens. Willard Ernest, Jr., USNR
Born: 9/27/16, Buffalo, Wyoming

FORWARD, Lt. (jg) Richard Blair, USNR
Born: 10/23/16, Santa Barbara, Calif.

GEORGIUS, Melvin H., ACOM, NAP, USN
Born: 7/21/17, Westside City, Iowa

HAMILTON, Ens. Curtis, USN
Born: 5/3/10, Monroe, Georgia

HURST, Lt. Edwin William, USN
Born: 10/16/10, Falls City, Neb.

LACKEY, Ens. John H., USN
Born: 9/24/13, Cleveland, Ohio

LOVELACE, Lt. Cdr. Donald Alexander, USN
Born: 6/20/06, Scottsburg, Va.

MORGAN, Lt. Robert James, USN
Born: 6/27/13, San Francisco, Calif.

ROWELL, Ens. Richard Merrill, USNR
Born: 8/6/16, Sonoma, Calif.

STANLEY, Lt. (jg) Onia B., USNR
Born: 10/4/14, Clarendon, Texas

STEFFENHAGEN, Ens. Lawrence F., USNR
Born: 10/16/12, Frontenac, Minn.

TALKINGTON, Harley E., Gunner, USN
Born: 8/16/19, Whitehall, Ill.

VORSE, Lt. Albert O., Jr., USN
Born: 8/9/14, Philadelphia, Pa.

WAMPLER, Lt. French, Jr., USN
Born: 9/17/13, Fountain City, Tenn.

AIR ACTION
March 10, 1942

Navy Cross

AURAND, Lt. Evan P., USN
Born: 6/10/17, New York, N. Y.

BASS, Lt. Harry Brinkley, USN
Born: 7/4/16, Chicago, Ill.

BRETT, Lt. Cdr. James Henry, Jr., USN
Born 10/1/05, Cedartown, Georgia

BUCHAN, Lt. (jg) Robert B., USNR
Born: 1/3/16, Portland, Oregon

DIXON, Lt. Cdr. Robert E., USN
Born: 4/22/06, Richland, Georgia

FARRINGTON, Lt. Robert F., USN
Born: 7/12/14, Yonkers, N. Y.

HAMILTON, Lt. Cdr. Weldon L., USN
Born: 12/9/06, Darlington, S. C.

HASCHKE, Ens. Marvin M., USNR
Born: 12/5/16, Austin, Texas

HAYNES, Ens. Leon Wilden, USNR
Born: 2/25/14, Billings, Mont.

LEPPLA, Ens. John Arthur, USNR
Born: 5/7/16, Lima, Ohio

MAZZA, Ens. Harold R., USNR
Born: 11/15/12, Pepaluma, Calif.

NEELY, Ens. Richard F., USNR
Born: 9/17/15, Greensboro, Ala.

QUIGLEY, Ens. Anthony J., USNR
Born: 3/29/15, San Francisco, Calif.

STERRIE, Ens. Norman Anderson, USNR
Born: 11/14/17, St. James, Minn.

WHITTIER, Lt. Mark T., USNR
Born: 2/16/13, Rice Lake, Wis.

GAYLER, Lt. Noel A. M., USN
Born: 12/25/13, Birmingham, Ala.

OTHER ACTION

Navy Cross

CASSEDY, Lt. Hiram, USN
Born: 7/4/08, Brookhaven, Miss.

COOK, Ens. George Carlton, USNR
Born: 2/21/18, Milton, Mass.

DIXON, Harold F., ACMM, USN
Born: 1/10/01, Muskogee, Okla.

EKAR, Ens. Joseph Anton, USNR
Born: 3/17/13, Chisholm, Minn.

MARQUIS, Joseph Thomas, ACMM, USN
Born: 8/17/01, Whitfield, N. H.

WAGONER, Leonard H., AMMIc, USN
Born: 12/6/09, Bakersville, N. C.

Silver Cross

HARGRAVE, Lt. William W., USNR
Born: 11/23/15, Newburgh, Indiana

MOORER, Lt. Cdr. Thomas H., USN
Born: 2/9/12, Mt. Willing, Ala.

Navy and Marine Corps Medal

PECK, John A., Pho2c, USN
Born: 11/6/20, Ft. Worth, Texas

SCHNITZER, Charles E., ACMM, USN
Born: 5/15/01, St. Louis, Mo.

THE PHILIPPINE ISLANDS
December 7, 1941–May 6, 1942

Distinguished Flying Cross

BROWN, Lt. (jg) Ira W., Jr., USNR
Born: 9/6/16, Topeka, Kan.

BULL, Lt. (jg) Richard, USNR
Born: 7/14/14, New York, N. Y.

CAMPBELL, Lt. Duncan Angus, USN
Born: 3/5/14, Grand Rapids, Minn.

DAVIS, Ens. John F., USNR
Born: 9/4/14, Evansville, Ind.

DEEDE, Lt. (jg) LeRoy C., USNR
Born: 2/5/16, Woodworth, N. D.

HOFFMAN, Lt. (jg) Charles C., USN
Born: 10/5/13, Claremore, Okla.

HYLAND, Lt. John Joseph, USN
Born: 9/1/12, Philadelphia, Pa.

KELLER, Lt. Clarence Armstrong, Jr.,
USN
Born: 6/24/10, Wichita, Kan.

PETERSON, Cdr. John Valdemar, USN
Born: 12/22/99, Harlan, Ia.

ROBERTSON, Lt. (jg) John Mott, USNR
Born: 8/13/13, Los Angeles, Calif.

ROBINSON, Lt. (jg) William Sauer, USN
Born: 4/22/14, Zamboanga, P. I.

UTTER, Lt. Harmon T., USN
Born: 8/25/09, Neville, Ohio

Air Medal

BANNOWSKY, Lt. (jg) Clarence J., Jr.,
USNR
Born: 9/14/15, Ballinger, Texas

CHAMBERS, Ens. Russell F., USNR
Born: 6/10/14, Lattabra, Calif.

DOCKERY, Olan L., ARM 1c, USN
Born: 8/13/19, El Centro, Calif.

HALL, Earle B., AMM 2c, USN
Born: 12/25/19, Dawson Springs, Ky.

HILTON, Lt. (jg) Hart D., USN
Born: 5/24/13, Los Angeles, Calif.

MILLER, Lt. (jg) Marsh W., USNR
Born: 9/26/13, Pittsburgh, Pa.

SCRIBNER, James M., RM3c, USN
Born: 6/25/20, Stevens Point, Wis.

Navy and Marine Corps Medal

FRASIER, Clarence A., CPhM, USNR
Born: 3/7/1900, Lebanon Junction, Ky.

GOUGH, Lt. William V., Jr., USNR
Born: 9/13/17, Baltimore, Md.

LOCKLEAR, Thomas E., PhM3c, USN
Born: 1/1/17, Punta Gorda, Fla.

LUTHER, John H., PhM2c, USN
Born: 10/14/15, Orleans, Neb.

STEWART, Russell C., PhM3c, USN
Born: 9/13/19, Astoria, Oregon

U. S. MARINE CORPS
Dec. 8, 1941 to May 6, 1942

Navy Cross

CLARK, Major Max, USMC
Born: 7/9/97, New Britain, Conn.

CLEMENT, Col. William T., USMC
Born: 9/27/94, Lynchburg, Va.

HOGABOOM, 1st Lt. William F., USMC
Born: 9/8/15, Warren Miss.

HOLDREDGE, 1st Lt. Willard B., USMC
Born: 1/7/17, Syracuse, N. Y.

HOWARD, Col. Samuel L., USMC
Born: 3/8/91, Washington, D. C.

SIMPSON, 1st Lt. Carter B., USMC
Born: 11/3/15, Glenn Springs, S. C.

Distinguished Service Cross

BROWN, Robert J., PFC, USMC
Born: 1/26/21, Havana, Ill.

Silver Star Medal (Army)

BAILEY, Melvin D., Corp., USMC
Born: 7/4/18, Rhonesboro, Texas

BAUM, Benjamin G., Corp., USMC
Born: 4/29/19, Grasonville, Md.

BREEZE, John R., Sgt., USMC
Born: 6/9/14, Pocatello, Ida.

BROWN, Capt. Paul A., USMC
Born: 6/7/07, Silsbee, Texas

BUETHE, George M., Corp., USMC
Born: 6/9/17, St. Paul, Minn.

BUNN, Evan F., PFC, USMC
Born: 11/18/18, South Bend, Ind.

CHABOT, 1st Lt. Leon E., USMC
Born: 3/11/17, Gardner, Mass.

CHASTAIN, Joe B., Sgt., USMC
Born: 1/25/20, Irdell, Texas

CLARK, Capt. Golland L., Jr., USMC
Born: 12/2/12, Los Angeles, Calif.

COLLINS, Raymond H., Corp., USMC
Born: 6/27/20, Chicago, Ill.

COOLEY, Richard, Sup. Sgt., USMC
Born: 11/2/01, Columbia, Ky.

CORLEY, John K., FM, USMC
Born: 3/21/21, Junior, W. Va.

DAVIS, Houston L., PlSgt., USMC
Born: 6/29/07, Whitesboro, Texas

DOWNING, Carl E., Sgt., USMC
Born: 10/17/21, San Angelo, Texas

DURBIN, Lloyd T., PFC, USMC
Born: 11/8/18, Kilbourne, La.

FANTONE, 1st Lt. John S., USMC
Born: 11/6/16, Norfolk, Va.

FARNER, Robert P., PFC, USMC
Born: 3/17/21, Hastings, Neb.

FREE, Edward G., PFC, USMC
Born: 4/12/15, Philadelphia, Pa.

GARRETT, Donald J., PFC, USMC
Born: 5/3/20, Mosca, Colo.

GREER, Charles R., PFC, USMC
Born: 7/10/20, Turtle Creek, Pa.

HAYNES, Eugene O., Corp., USMC (with Oak Leaf Cluster)
Born: 10/13/20, St. Joseph, Mo.

HOOPS, James L., PFC, USMC
Born: 3/27/22, St. Louis, Mo.

HUCKABAY, Uri L., Sgt., USMC
Born: 9/1/18, Santo, Texas

JENKINS, J. T., Sgt., USMC
Born: 6/13/1900, Monticello, Ark.

JORDAN, Julian, Sgt., USMC
Born: 11/16/16, Indian Orchard, Mass.

KATCHUCK, Alexander, Pvt., USMC
Born: 2/14/17, New York City

KENNY, Richard D., Sgt., USMC
Born: 6/10/20, Chicago, Ill.

KERNS, James H., Sgt., USMC
Born: 6/14/14, St. Ignatius, Mont.

KLINGBEIL, Herbert G., Pvt., USMC
Born: 3/24/19, Hastings, Minn.

KOENIG, Fred E., Jr., PFC, USMC
Born: 12/16/19, Milwaukee, Wis.

LAKE, Donald E., PFC, USMC
Born: 7/9/19, Taft, Ind.

LANCASTER, Marion B., PFC, USMC
Born: 6/11/21, Greenville, Miss.

LINVILLE, Bert S., PlSgt., USMC
Born: 1/18/08, Mooresville, Ind.

McCLUE, Barney D., Corp., USMC
Born: 12/12/21, Ryder, N. D.

McCORMACK, William N., Corp., USMC
Born: 12/9/15, Mackdou, Texas

MADDEN, Elwood K., Corp., USMC
Born: 3/16/06, Los Angeles, Calif.

MANNING, 1st Lt. Alan S., USMC
Born: 2/7/17, Fall River, Mass.

MILEY, Clifton S., PFC, USMC
Born: 2/5/17, Philadelphia, Miss.

MOORE, Capt. Robert B., USMC
Born: 5/18/14, Cedar Rapids, Iowa

NELSON, George B., PFC, USMC
Born: 11/28/20, Sweden

O'BRIEN, John P., Jr., PlSgt., USMC
Born: 2/18/10, Hattiesburg, Miss.

PARKER, Seymour F., Sgt., USMC
Born: 7/13/20, Deer Lodge, Mont.

PAVLAKOS, James G., Corp., USMC
Born: 7/18/17, Chicago, Ill.

PENICK, 1st Lt. Ralph R., USMC
Born: 8/19/17, Hebron, Ohio

PERRI, Albert, Sgt., USMC
Born: 10/24/16, DuBois, Pa.

PETERSEN, Melvin W., Corp., USMC
Born: 2/21/20, Manitowoc, Wis.

PINTO, Harry W., Sgt., USMC
Born: 4/30/15, San Francisco, Calif.

PROMNITZ, Oliver F., PFC, USMC
Born: 6/10/21, St. Louis, Mo.

RAY, John F., Field Clk., USMC
Born: 2/1/93, Somerville, Mass.

RICE, Kenneth V., PFC, USMC
Born: 2/15/20, Elizabeth, N. J.

ROSSELL, Frank G., Jr., PlSgt., USMC
Born: 12/17/13, St. Louis, Mo.

ROTTER, Edwin J., Field Clk., USMC
Born: 9/7/17, Chicago, Ill.

SHELTON, Herbert R., PFC, USMC
Born: 3/10/22, Macedonia, Iowa

SHOFNER, Capt. Austin C., USMC
Born: 3/3/16, Tyner, Tenn.

SMITH, William A., Sgt., USMC
Born: 1/11/18, San Francisco, Calif.

STEWART, Thomas L., PFC, USMC
Born: 2/12/20, Long Beach, Calif.

SWAHN, Berkley R., PFC, USMC
Born: 8/25/21, Isante, Minn.

TAYLOR, Fred M., Corp., USMC
Born: 12/21/13, Atlanta, Ga.

VAN RAY, 1st Lt. Clarence E., USMC
Born: 9/10/16, Jamestown, N. D.

VINTON, Fred S., PFC, USMC
Born: 8/24/16, Jackson, Mich.

WILLIAMS, Everett S., Corp., USMC
Born: 11/3/16, Plainwell, Mich.

WINTERMAN, Mike, Sgt., USMC
Born: 8/14/14, Boston, Mass.

WITTKE, Donald E., Corp., USMC
Born: 6/12/21, Gunnison, Utah

UNIT CITATIONS

General Orders   WAR DEPARTMENT,
No. 22

Washington 25, D. C., 30 April 1942.
CITATION OF UNITS OF BOTH MILITARY
AND NAVAL FORCES OF THE UNITED
STATES AND PHILIPPINE GOVERNMENTS.
As authorized by Executive Order 9075
(sec. II, Bull. 11, W. D., 1942), a cita-
tion in the name of the President of the
United States, as public evidence of de-
served honor and distinction, is awarded
to all units of both military and naval
forces of the United States and Philippine
Governments engaged in the defense of
the Philippines since December 7, 1941.
By order of the Secretary of War:
G. C. MARSHALL,
Chief of Staff.

General Orders   WAR DEPARTMENT
No. 21

Washington 25, D. C., 30 April 1942.
CITATION OF UNITS IN THE UNITED
STATES FORCES IN THE PHILIPPINES. As
authorized by Executive Order 9075 (sec.
II, Bull. 11, W. D., 1942), a citation in
the name of the President of the United
States, as public evidence of deserved
honor and distinction, is awarded to the
following-named units. The citation reads
as follows:

The HARBOR DEFENSES OF MANILA
AND SUBIC BAYS AND NAVAL AND MARINE
CORPS UNITS SERVING THEREIN, UNITED
STATES FORCES IN THE PHILIPPINES, are
cited for outstanding performance of duty
in action, during the period from March
14 to April 9, 1942, inclusive.
Although subjected repeatedly to intense and prolonged artillery bombardment by concealed hostile batteries in
Cavite Province and to heavy enemy
aerial attacks, during the period above-
mentioned, and despite numerous casual-

ties and extensive damage inflicted on defensive installations and utilities, the morale, ingenuity, and combat efficiency of the entire command have remained at the high standard which has impressed fighting men the world over.

On March 15, approximately 1,000 240-mm projectiles were fired at Forts Frank and Drum, and large numbers of lesser - caliber projectiles struck Fort Hughes and Mills. Again on March 20, over 400 240-mm shells were fired at Fort Frank and a lesser number at Fort Drum, while enemy air echelons made a total of 50 attacks on Fort Mills with heavy aerial bombs.

During the entire period all units maintained their armament at a high degree of efficiency, while seaward defense elements executed effective counter battery action. Antiaircraft batteries firing at extreme ranges exacted a heavy toll of hostile attacking planes, and Naval and Marine units from exposed stations assured the defense of the beaches and approaches to the fortified islands. By unceasing labor and regardless of enemy activity, essential utilities were restored and the striking power of the command maintained unimpaired.

As a result of their splendid combined efforts, ruggedness, and devotion to duty the various units and services comprising the Harbor Defenses of Manila and Subic Bays frustrated a major hostile attempt to reduce the efficiency of the fortified islands.

Units included in above citation:
59th Coast Artillery
60th Coast Artillery (AA)
91st Coast Artillery (PS)
92d Coast Artillery (PS)
Headquarters and Headquarters Battery
Harbor Defenses of Manila and Subic Bays
Medical Detachment
Ordnance Detachment
Quartermaster Detachments (American and Philippine Scouts)
Finance Detachment
1st Coast Artillery (PA) (less 2d Battalion)
Company A
803d Engineer Battalion (Aviation) (Separate)
Detachments DS Army Mine Planter Harrison (American and Philippine Scouts)
4th U. S. Marines
U. S. Navy Inshore Patrol
Manila Bay Area
Naval Force District Headquarters Fort Mills
Naval Forces Mariveles Area Philippine Islands
Battery D, 2d Coast Artillery (PA)
1st Platoon, Battery F, 2d Coast Artillery (AA), (PA)
2d Platoon Battery F, 2d Coast Artillery (AA), (PA)

By order of the Secretary of War:
G. C. MARSHALL,
Chief of Staff.

THE PHILIPPINE ISLANDS, AND FAR EAST
December 7, 1941 to May 6, 1942

Distinguished Service Medal

HART, Admiral Thomas C., USN
Born: 6/12/77, Genesee County, Mich.

As Commander in Chief, United States Asiatic Fleet, for his conduct of the operations of the Allied Naval Forces in the Southwest Pacific Area during January and February, 1942.

Legion of Merit

LEARY, Vice Admiral Herbert F., USN
Born: 5/31/85, Washington, D. C.

Commander, United States Naval Forces, Southwest Pacific, and later as Commander Battleships, Pacific Fleet, from the outbreak of the current war until April 22, 1943.

Distinguished Service Medal

ROCKWELL, Rear Admiral Francis W., USN
Born: 7/28/86, South Woodstock, Conn.

As Commandant of the Sixteenth Naval District, displayed efficiency, leadership, and judgment under difficult, arduous and hazardous circumstances during the Japanese assaults on Cavite, Philippine Islands, in December, 1941, and the subsequent defense of the Bataan Peninsula and the fortified island at the entrance to Manila Bay both by United States Military and Naval Forces.

PURNELL, Rear Adm. William Reynolds, USN
Born: 9/6/86, Bowling Green, Mo.

Chief of Staff to Commander in Chief, Asiatic Fleet, and Commander, U.S. Forces, Southwest Pacific, with duties involving great responsibility connected with formulation plans, counselling their application and aid in directing execution, especially of offensive missions of forces of this command which have resulted in substantial damage to the enemy together with skill and tact displayed in negotiating, conferring and dealing with Commanders of the Allied Forces.

Medal of Honor

BULKELEY, Lt. John D., USN
Born: 8/19/11, New York, N. Y.

Commander of Motor Torpedo Boat Squadron Three, in Philippine waters during the period December 7, 1941 to April 10, 1942.

Distinguished Service Medal

BRYANT, Capt. Eliot H., USN
Born: 8/21/96, Rushville, Ind.

FIFE, Capt. James, Jr., USN
Born: 1/22/97, Reno, Nev.

ROBINSON, Lt. Cdr. James M., USN
Born: 1/19/04, Washington, D. C.

WAGNER, Capt. Frank Dechant, USN
Born: 8/22/93, Pottstown, Pa.

WILKES, Capt. John, USN
Born: 5/26/95, Charlotte, N. C.

WILSON, Cdr. James Dudley, CEC, USN
Born: 10/29/97, Jackson, Tenn.

LINAWEAVER, Cdr. Walter Ellsworth, USN
Born: 1/27/04, Great Cacapon, W. Va.

Navy Cross

BANGUST, Joseph, AMM2c, USN
Born: 5/30/15, Niles, Ohio

BARON, Lt. Cdr. Richard S., USN
Born: 1/22/01, Lowell, Mass.

BOWERS, Lt. Cdr. Thomas K., USN
Born: 2/1/11, Portsmouth, Va.

BOYD, Ens. Eugene Lorell, USN
Born: 2/15/04, Brookhaven, Mass.

BRIDGET, Cdr. Francis J., USN
Born: 8/2/97, Washington, D. C.

BROOKE, Cdr. George Magruder, USN
Born: 3/15/98, Spokane, Wash.

BRUUN, Chief Pay Clerk Othello C., USN
Born: 7/4/03, Van Buren, Arkansas

BULKELEY, Lt. John D., USN
Born: 8/19/11, New York, N. Y.

CHAMPLIN, Lt. (jg) Malcolm, USN
Born: 4/13/11, San Francisco, Calif.

CHAPPLE, Cdr. Wreford G., USN
Born: 2/19/08, Billings, Mont.

CHEEK, Lt. Cdr. Marion C., USN
Born: 10/18/88, Ripley, Tenn.

CHRISTMAN, Lt. (jg) E. L., USNR
Born: 7/14/15, Monitor, Oregon

COX, Ens. George E., USNR
Born: 10/16/14, Niagara Falls, N. Y.

DAVIS, Lt. Cdr. Frank A., USNR
Born: 5/10/96, Boston, Mass.

DAVISON, Lt. Cdr. Thurlow Weed
Born: 1/4/06, Newborn, Pa.

DAWLEY, Lt. Jack Baldwin, USN
Born: 11/3/13, Seattle, Wash.

DEEWALL, Cdr. Raymond Gregory, USN
Born: 9/15/92, Argonio, Kan.

DE LONG, Lt. Edward Grover, USN
Born: 8/20/15, Springfield, S. D.

DIAL, Lt. Cdr. Nathaniel Minter, USN
Born: 3/21/11, Laurens, S. C.

DONALDSON, Lt. (jg) Trose E., USNR
Born: 6/19/14, Tacoma, Wash.

DOWNEY, Ernest Willard, Boat., USN
Born: 11/3/08, Lagootee, Ind.

ENGESET, Lt. Knut, USNR
Born: 4/25/92, Fredrikstad, Norway

FAIRES, Cdr. Carl F., Jr., SC, USN
Born: 1/12/10, Atlanta, Ga.

FERGUSON, Ens. Earl W., USNR
Born: 8/16/13, Houston, Texas

FERRITER, Lt. Cdr. Charles A., USN
Born: 3/14/01, Trenton, Mo.

GRANSTON, Lt. (jg) Robert W., SC, USN
Born: 12/28/16, Seattle, Wash.

GRIFFIN, Lt. Cdr. Edward Raymond
Joseph, USN
Born: 1/19/97, Clinton, Mass.

HANSON, Clifford A., Pay Clerk, USN
Born: 3/4/08, Alexandria, Minn.

HASTINGS, Lt. Burden Robert, USN
Born: 8/1/10, Washington, D. C.

HASTINGS, Cdr. William W., USN
Born 2/18/89, Geneva, Neb.

HAWES, Lt. Cdr. Richard E., USN
Born: 2/21/94, Thomson, Ga.

KELLY, Lt. Robert B., USN
Born: 6/9/13, New York, N. Y.

LURVEY, Don D., ACMM, USN
Born: 7/13/08, Dracut Center, Mass.

MC CRACKEN, Cdr. Alan Reed, USN
Born: 7/14/98, Paxton, Ill.

MC LAWHORN, Evren C., AMMIC, USN
Born: 4/10/21, Lenoir County, N. C.

MITCHELL, Ens. George R., USNR
Born: 8/23/15, Booneville, Miss.

MORRILL, Lt. Cdr. John H., USN
Born: 1/7/03, Miller, S. D.

NASH, Lt. David, USN
Born: 10/12/14, Haddon Heights, N. J.

NEWELL, Lt. (jg) Fred R., Jr., USNR
Born: 3/28/15, Brattleboro, Vermont

OSTER, James C., CBM, USN
Born: 3/26/07, Utica, N. Y.

PETRITZ, Ens. George K., USNR
Born: 8/20/17, Rockford, Ill.

PETTIT, Robert Lee, RMIC, USN
Born: 11/17/06, Clare, Mich.

RAYMOND, Lt. Fred L., USNR
Born: 7/27/99, Worcester, Mass.

ROTH, Lt. Cdr. Egbert Adolph, USN
Born: 12/10/05, Hebron, N. D.

SACKETT, Cdr. Earl L., USN
Born: 3/29/98, Bancroft, Nebraska

SMITH, Lt. Douglas Elwin, USN
Born: 6/12/03, Port Chester, N. Y.

STEWARD, Lt. Cdr. Jerry Alexander, CEC,
USN
Born: 1/27/95, Kirven, Texas

STRAND, Ens. Lowell H., USNR
Born: 11/3/18, Virginia, Minn.

TAYLOR, Gunner Donald C., USN
Born: 6/16/14, Ryegate, Mont.

WALKER, John H., Pay Clerk, SC, USN
Born: 2/3/11, Kaylor, Pa.

WATERMAN, Andrew K., AMMIC, USN
Born: 11/21/13, Lewis County, Ky.

WHITNEY, Lt. Cdr. Rintoul T., USN
Born: 7/11/89, Escanaba, Mich.

WILLIS, Lt. (jg) Meade H., Jr., USNR
Born: 12/13/09, Winston-Salem, N. C.

WINGO, Ens. Peroneau B., USNR
Born: 7/17/18, Richmond, Va.

Army Distinguished Service Cross

BULKELEY, Lt. John D., USN
Born: 8/19/11, New York, N. Y.

COX, Ens. George E., USNR
Born: 10/16/14, Niagara Falls, N. Y.

DONALDSON, Lt. (jg) Trose Emmett, USNR
Born: 6/19/14, Tacoma, Wash.

FULLER, Bert Carl, CRM, USN
Born: 10/3/04, Bennett, Mo.

GOODALL, Lt. Cdr. Henry William, USN
Born: 9/2/1900, Salina, Kan.

KELLY, Lt. Cdr. Robert B., USN
Born: 6/9/13, New York, N. Y.

KRAMB, Charles Herman, Jr., GM3c, USNR
Born: 2/11/19, Edmond, Okla.

SMITH, Charles Edward, CEM, USN
Born: 7/11/04, Cedar Rapids, Ia.

Legion of Merit

BERNATITUS, Lt. (jg) Ann A., NC, USN
Born: 1/21/12, Exeter, Pa.

GILBERT, Lt. Roy D., CEC, USNR
Born: 2/28/01, Albuquerque, N. M.

KNOLL, Lt. Cdr. Denys W., USN
Born: 3/7/07, Erie, Pa.

MORSELL, Capt. Everett G., USN
Born: 7/6/84, Washington, D. C.

USS HERON

Navy Cross

KABLER, Lt. William Leverette, USN
Born: 9/24/08, Roanoke, Va.
Commanding USS HERON.

BROCK, Robert C., MM2c, USN
Born: 12/23/17, DuQuoin, Ill.

JOHNSON, William Harold, Boat., USN
Born: 3/7/09, Ceredo, W. Va.

USS PECOS

Navy Cross

ABERNETHY, Cdr. Elmer P., USN
Born: 6/14/99, Oklahoma City, Okla.
Commanding USS PECOS.

Silver Star Medal

MARCHAND, Roy J., F1c, USN
Born: 9/17/20, Crandall, Miss.

MILLS, Reginald, GM3c, USN
Born: 2/23/20, Franklin County, Orient, Ill.

SAXTON, Luther B., CSK, USN
Born: 7/4/13, Laurel, Miss.

SCHULER, Ralph E., F1c, USN
Born: 3/18/20, St. Louis, Mo.

Silver Star Medal (Navy)

AKERS, Ens. Anthony Bruce, USNR
Born: 10/19/14, Charlotte, Texas

BARNES, William S., AMM2c, USN
Born: 5/29/19, Los Angeles, Calif.

BOSTON, William C., TM1c, USN
Born: 12/21/1900, Elizabeth, Colorado

CHEEK, John M., CTM, USN
Born: 6/25/10, Durham, N. C.

COOK, Ralph W., Gunner, USN
Born: 11/4/11, Block, Tenn.

CUCINELLO, Nicholas G., Machinist, USN
Born: 2/1/11, Bloomfield, N. J.

DAVIS, Harvey O., CTM, USN
Born: 7/25/05, Halls, Tenn.

GAULT, Harry D., Jr., TM1c, USN
Born: 2/8/18, Detroit, Michigan

GUYNUP, Chester A., CY, USN
Born: 9/22/07, Burlington, Vermont

HEAD, George William, Pharm., USN
Born: 12/13/99, La Grange, Kentucky

HERRMANN, Thomas W., CTM, USN
Born: 1/13/03, Winslow, Alabama

HOEFFEL, Capt. Kenneth M., USN
Born: 3/28/94, Oconto, Wis.

MACGOWAN, Lt. Hubert, USNR
Born: 4/1/99, Montreal, Canada

MEEKER, Jack F., Jr., WT1c, USN
Born: 5/10/17, Miami, Fla.

McINTIRE, Raymond K., CTM, USN
Born: 1/20/03, Boston, Mass.

MILLER, Andrew J., Jr., AMM3c, USN
Born: 10/24/13, Greensburg, Mo.

MORALES, Gonzalo, CTM, USN
Born: 12/10/97, Ceiba, Puerto Rico

MULLINS, Ens. Jimmy, USNR
Born: 10/13/15, Jacksonville, Fla.

NASH, Jack K., CTM, USN
Born: 9/2/09, Livingstone, Montana

NELSON, Ens. Ivan G., USN
Born: 4/28/13, Ontario, Ore.

NORTH, Sylvester F., TM1c, USN
Born: 12/30/17, Junction City, Kan.

OLIVER, McKinley, CTM, USN
Born: 9/19/02, Sarcoxie, Mo.

OWENS, Samuel R., TM2c, USN
Born: 4/10/18, Glenville, N. C.

PARO, Cdr. Eugene E., USN
Born: 2/22/04, St. Charles, Mo.

PERRY, Joseph, Jr., TM1c, USN
Born: 10/8/07, Lowell, Mass.

POGREBA, Paul R., BM1c, USN
Born: 1/3/15, Three Forks, Montana

PRELIP, Donald M., CTM, USN
Born: 9/26/08, Kanawha, Iowa

REED, Rollin M., Mach., USN
Born: 2/12/08, ————

SLIPSAGER, Glen F., Phm1c, USN
Born: 1/23/11, Clyde, Kans.

STEELE, James H., CMM, USN
Born: 5/21/11, Philomath, Ore.

TAYLOR, Wayne E., WT2c, USN
Born: 5/7/17, Hundred, W. Va.

THORPE, Ens. Thaddeus, USN
Born: 10/7/06, Lafayette, Ind.

TRUDELL, Lt. (jg) George T., USNR
Born: 3/2/15, Milford, Mass.

VOLL, George W., TM1c, USN
Born: 12/4/11, Springfield, Mo.

WEINMANN, Charles E., CMM, USN
Born: 4/15/09, Atchison, Kan.

WOOD, Samuel, H., CSF, USN
Born: 9/5/11, Philadelphia, Mo.

WORCESTER, Lt. Cdr. Frederick L., USNR
Born: 5/19/98, Ann Arbor, Mich.

Silver Star Medal (Army)

ROCKWELL, Rear Admiral Francis Warren, USN, Commandant, Sixteenth Naval District
Born: 7/28/86, South Woodstock, Conn.
For gallantry in action in the Philippines on March 11, 12 and 13, 1942.

AKERS, Ens. Anthony Bruce, USNR
Born: 10/19/14, Charlotte, Texas

ANDERSON, Lt. Col. Herman R., USMC
Born: 1/15/92, Watson, Mass.

BALOG, John, CPhM, USN
Born: 2/5/14, Stamford, Conn.
Also Oak Leaf Cluster in lieu of second Silver Star Medal (Army).

BANSLEY, Donald E., PhM2c, USN
Born: 4/7/44, Haverhill, Mass.

BARR, Charles James, MM1c, USN
Born: 6/10/13, Magee, Miss.

BARTLETT, George F., F1c, USN
Born: 8/3/13, Montpelier, Idaho

BECKNER, L., PhM3c, USN
Born: 12/13/20, Princeton, Ind.

BENCH, Willie Guy, EM, USN
Born: 5/3/08, Faris, Ark.

BORAGO, Frank Colon, S2c, USN
Born: 12/2/13, Hoehne, Colo.

BOUDOLF, Joseph L., CM1c, USN
Born: 9/2/15, Charleston, S. C.

BOUNDS, Dave W., CAP, USN
Born: 7/2/08, Bluff Dale, Texas

BRANTINGHAM, Lt. (jg) Henry Joseph, USN
Born: 10/29/16, Junction City, Kansas

BROCKMAN, Robert John, TM2c, USN
Born: 11/25/19, Leigh, Nebraska

BULKELEY, Lt. John D., USN
Born: 8/19/11, New York, N. Y.

BURNETT, Robert B., TM2c, USN
Born: 10/27/19, Neponset, Ill.

CASTENGERA, William Joseph, TM2c, USN
Born: 6/27/13, Summitt Hill, Pa.

CHALKER, Joseph C., MM2c, USN
Born: 12/21/16, Redwater, Texas

CLARK, Lt. Albert Hobbs, USN
Born: 12/28/10, Norway, Maine

CLARK, Jesse N., BM1c, USN
Born: 4/10/17, Mountain View, Wyo.

CLIFT, John W., Cox., USN
Born: 1/18/14, Madison, Md.

COBB, Ned M., S1c, USN
Born: 3/19/19, Gonzalez, Texas

CONN, LeRoy G., MM2c, USN
Born: 6/5/18, Marlborough, N. Y.

CORBISIERE, Dominick, SC2c, USN
Born: 6/18/16, New Haven, Conn.

COTE, Raymond Conrad Joseph, FC1c, USN
Born: 9/20/15, Roxbury, Mass.

Cox, Lt. (jg) George E., USNR
Born: 10/16/14, Niagara Falls, N. Y.

CRAIG, Jack Cecil, TM1c, USN
Born: 1/21/14, Sioux City, Iowa

DECKER, Francis Joseph, MM2c, USN
Born: 7/25/15, Cincinnati, Ohio

DEEDE, Lt. (jg) Le Roy C., USNR
Born: 2/5/16, Woodworth, N. D.

DE HOSNERY, Stewart Alexander, MA1c, USN
Born: 3/12/21, San Diego, Calif.

DEVITT, John Albert, CEM, USN
Born: 2/16/14, Buffalo, N. Y.

DE VRIES, Marvin H., TM1c, USN
Born: 12/14/15, Passaic, N. J.

DOWNS, James Thomas, MM1c, USN
Born: 9/11/16, Beltrami County, Minn.

EICHELBERGER, Paul E., MM1c, USN
Born: 2/17/08, Newburg, Pa.

FESTIN, Stanley, S2c, USN
Born: 7/21/21, Salt Lake City, Utah

FISK, Harold Roy, S2c, USN
Born: 10/13/13, Wolsey, S. D.

FRAZER, Jennings Bryan, CMM, USN
Born: 5/2/1900, Colfax, Wash.

FRITSCH, William Harold, EM2c, USN
Born: 7/22/12, Indianola, Neb.

FROGNER, Gordon Ingvald, AS, USNR
Born: 4/27/19, Bellingham, Wash.

GARRETT, Donald J., PFC, USMC
Born: 5/3/20, Mosca, Colorado

GIACCANI, Floyd R., Jr., Bkr., USN
Born: 5/10/16, Lake Village, Ark.
  Oak Leaf Cluster, Second Silver Star
Medal—Army.

GLOVER, DeWitt L., CQM, USN
Born: 3/15/20, Stockton, Calif.
  Oak Leaf Cluster, Second Silver Star
Medal—Army.

GONYER, Alvin Leroy, SM3c, USN
Born: 11/3/19, Howland, Maine

GOODHUE, Theodore Lester, TM2c, USN
Born: 9/22/18, Chicopee, Mass.

GOODMAN, David, RM2c, USN
Born: 5/27/20, Brooklyn, N. Y.
  Oak Leaf Cluster, Second Silver Star
Medal—Army.

GRIZZARD, Herbert W., MM2c, USN
Born: 3/1/17, Nashville, Tenn.

GUNN, Lt. Frederick Arthur, USN
Born: 10/13/11, Enid, Okla.

GUTTERMUTH, John George, F3c, USN
Born: 4/15/23, Akron, Ohio

GUYOT, D., CMM, USN
Born: 12/31/05, Geff, Ill.

HAGOPAN, Jacob, MM1c, USN
Born: 10/5/13, Springfield, Mass.

HANCOCK, Morris W., CMM, USN
Born: 8/7/09, Southport, Ind.
  Oak Leaf Cluster, Second Silver Star
Medal—Army.

HARLFINGER, Lt. Frederick Joseph, II, USN
Born: 9/14/13, Albany, N. Y.

HARRIS, David W., TM2c, USN
Born: 10/10/17, Richmond, Va.

Oak Leaf Cluster, Second Silver Star Medal—Army.

HARRISON, Donald William, EM2c, USN
Born: 4/15/19, Tacoma, Wash.

HAWN, Richard Gatling, MM2c, USN
Born: 12/7/19, New York, N. Y.

HOULEHON, John L., TM1c, USN
Born: 1/18/18, Holyoke, Mass.

HOY, James Elton, F2c, USN
Born: 11/30/18, Happner, Oregon

HUGHES, Robert Luther, EM2c, USN
Born: 6/18/15, Winchester, Tenn.

HUGHES, Walter Robert, Jr., AS, USNR
Born: 9/14/16, Afton, Okla.

HUNTER, Velt F., CMM, USN
Born: 8/22/07, Sivells Bend, Texas

Oak Leaf Cluster, Second Silver Star Medal—Army.

HYATT, Lawson, Jr., S2c, USN
Born: 11/2/22, Lubbock, Texas

IRVIN, Ernest J., PhM2c, USN
Born: 11/30/20, Ged, La.

JACKSON, Billie B., AMM1c, USN
Born: 12/10/16, Portland, Oregon

JACKSON, Lonnie David, MA1c, USN
Born: 4/1/18, Banks County, Ga.

JACKSON, Robert Franklin, F3c, USN
Born: 6/19/21, San Francisco, Calif.

JOHNSON, Ens. C. H., USNR
Born: 7/7/19, St. Joseph, Mo.

JOHNSON, William Harry, S1c, USN
Born: 7/22/20, Amsterdam, N. Y.

JOINER, Thurman Louis, TM1c, USN
Born: 7/28/08, Tennille, Ga.

KAIL, Kenneth Karlyle, S1c, USN
Born: 8/11/20, Stratford, Iowa

KEATH, Harry G., SC2c, USN
Born: 2/24/17, Lancaster, Pa.

KELLY, Lt. Cdr. Robert B., USN
Born: 6/9/13, New York City

KEISELBACH, Arthur Edwin, RM2c, USN
Born: 6/15/18, Jersey City, N. J.

KELTNER, Morris Henry, QM1c, USN
Born: 7/17/14, Hoisington, Kan.

KIEFER, Edwin Arnold, AS, USN
Born: 12/30/21, Akron, Ohio

KING, Homer Lymon, TM2c, USN
Born: 11/18/19, Carlsbad, N. M.

KONKO, William F., RM3c, USN
Born: 7/30/21, Cleveland, Ohio

KUMP, Glen Diever, S2c, USN
Born: 5/11/20, Shelley, Idaho

LANGSTON, Clem L., Cox., USN
Born: 8/7/20, Calhoun, Ga.

LAWLESS, John, MM1c, USN
Born: 10/19/17, Aydlett, N. C.

Oak Leaf Cluster, Second Silver Star Medal—Army.

LEIGHTLEY, Albert Lewis, SM1c, USN
Born: 6/18/12, Boalsburg, Pa.

LEON, Anthony, F1c, USN
Born: 4/9/17, Monroeville, N. J.

LEWIS, John H., MM1c, USN
Born: 9/17/18, Mount Holly, Ark.

LICODO, Benjamin, OS3c, USN
Born: 11/10/09, Rosales, Pengasinan, P.I.

Oak Leaf Cluster, Second Silver Star Medal—Army.

LIGGETT, Clabe, Jr., MM2c, USN
Born: 8/5/20, Lewisburg, Tenn.

LIGHT, James D., CTM (AA), USN
Born: 2/9/20, St. Pauls Valley, Okla.

McCAIN, Lindell H., RM3c, USN
Born: 6/25/18, Murfreesboro, Ark.

McCONNELL, Maurice Leonard, PhM1c, USN
Born: 7/5/11, Peoria, Ill.

McCOY, Charles H., AS, USN
Born: 10/12/24, San Angelo, Texas

McEVOY, James A., Jr., MM2c, USN
Born: 9/10/19, Methuen, Mass.

MARSTERS, John William, CMM, USN
Born: 7/10/10, Everett, Mass.

MARTINEZ, Seraphine Rochel, MM2c, USN
Born: 6/1/09, Manila, P. I.

MARTINO, John, CTM, USN
Born: 11/8/13, Waterbury, Conn.
Oak Leaf Cluster, Second Silver Star Medal—Army.

MILLER, Robert Carl, S2c, USN
Born: 2/10/22, Marinette, Wis.

MOORE, Capt. Robert B., USMC
Born: 5/18/14, Cedar Rapids, Iowa

MORRILL, Lt. Cdr. John H., USN
Born: 1/7/03, Miller, S. D.

MURRAY, Ens. Bond, USNR
Born: 11/6/18, Danielsville, Ga.

NAPOLILLO, Francis J., Jr., SC1c, USN
Born: 4/15/17, Baltimore, Md.

NARDINI, Lt. John E. (MC), USN
Born: 5/4/12, Philadelphia, Pa.

NEARMAN, Kenneth Eugene, S1c, USN
Born: 10/7/20, Missoula, Mont.

NEY, Ralph S., PhM2c, USN
Born: 9/26/18, Minneapolis, Minn.
Oak Leaf Cluster, Second Silver Star Medal—Army.

NOEL, Otis F., QM1c, USN
Born: 8/13/16, Horton, Kansas

OFFRET, Elwood H., CMM, USN
Born: 8/17/11, Park City, Utah

OWEN, Paul A., CMM, USN
Born: 12/6/09, Dora, Ala.

PERKOWSKI, Felix, CTM, USN
Born: 8/17/06, Fitchville, Conn.

PERRY, Ralph Raymond, MM1c, USN
Born: 10/22/09, Rosalia, Wash.

PIERSON, Ernest E., BM2c, USN
Born: 6/14/18, Battle Creek, Mich.

PING, Fred Eugene, S2c, USN
Born: 8/17/23, St. Joseph, Mo.

PITTS, Ens. Raymond Leslie, USNR
Born: 9/2/18, Oxnard, Calif.

POLLOCK, Lt. (jg) Thomas F., USN
Born: 8/8/11, Saticoy, Calif.

POSEY, William H., SC1c, USN
Born: 11/3/18, Cortez, Fla.

RAY, Capt. Herbert J., USN
Born: 2/1/93, Milwaukee, Wis.

REECE, John Daniel, EM1c, USN
Born: 6/4/05, Bridgeton, N. J.

REGAN, Richard A., CMM, USN
Born: 3/6/05, Melvin, Mich.

REYNOLDS, Willard J., CCStd, USN
Born: 12/6/08, Toledo, Ohio
Oak Leaf Cluster, Second Silver Star Medal—Army.

RICHARDSON, Carl C., CMM, USN
Born: 11/2/11, Elbert, Texas
Oak Leaf Cluster, Second Silver Star Medal—Army.

RICHARDSON, Ens. Illiff D., USNR
Born: 4/9/18, Denver, Colo.
Oak Leaf Cluster, Second Silver Star Medal—Army.

RICHARDSON, William Henry, RM1c, USN
Born: 3/18/02, Carthage, N. Y.

ROBERTS, Henry Lee, SC1c, USN
Born: 8/8/10, Savannah, Ga.

ROBINSON, Forest Gordon, CEM, USN
Born: 3/5/04, Temple, Texas

ROOKE, Henry C., SC2c, USN
Born: 12/3/16, Louisville, Ky.

ROSEN, Jacob, Y1c, USN
Born: 5/5/16, Detroit, Mich.

ROSS, Albert P., QM1c, USN
Born: 11/5/19, Bangor, Maine
Oak Leaf Cluster, Second Silver Star Medal—Army.

SAUNDERS, Clifford Harrison, Jr., TM1c, USN
Born: 12/24/08, E. Norwalk, Conn.

SAVOIE, V. A., S1c, USN
Born: ——

SCHOTTLER, Ens. George Henry, USNR
Born: 2/24/20, Baltimore, Md.

SCHUMACHER, Lt. (jg) Vincent E., USN
Born: 7/11/15, Illinois

Scott, Kenneth Irwin, S2c, USN
Born: 10/23/22, Great Falls, Mont.

Scott, Roy Jim, Jr., S2c, USNR
Born: 5/1/20, Waveland, Ark.

Shambora, John, BM1c, USN
Born: 3/28/08, Honeybrook, Pa.

Shepard, George W., Jr., MM1c, USN
Born: 1/15/20, St. Louis, Mo.
   Oak Leaf Cluster, Second Silver Star
Medal—Army.

Shields, John Francis, GM1c, USFNR
Born: 6/5/01, Everett, Mass.

Sims, Watson S., RM3c, USN
Born: 7/9/21, Clyde, Ga.

Southern, Jesse Phillip, CSM, USN
Born: 6/6/04, Forsythe Co., N. C.

Stanford, William Wilson, MM1c, USN
Born: 11/5/10, Gays, Ill.

Strangman, Lt. William L. (DC), USN
Born: 5/28/16, Santa Monica, Calif.

Stroud, Dencil C., CCStd, USN
Born: 7/26/08, Marengo, Ind.

Taylor, Victor LaRue, RM3c, USN
Born: 6/5/12, Van Wert Co., Ohio

Thompson, Robert Moody, AS, USNR
Born: 7/8/20, Wayne, Okla.

Tripp, Harry P., RM3c, USN
Born: 9/7/17, New Bedford, Mass.

Tuggle, John L., MM1c, USN
Born: 3/3/16, Matoaca, Va.
   Oak Leaf Cluster, Second Silver Star
Medal—Army.

Wade, Lt. Cdr. Ernest M. (MC) USN
Born: 10/19/08, Fort Sumner, N. M.

Waworzonek, Louis J., PhM1c, USN
Born: 8/8/18, Poughkeepsie, N. Y.

Willever, Stewart, RM2c, USN
Born: 12/18/20, Easton, Pa.

Willis, Everett Bryant, S2c, USN
Born: 2/12/17, Philadelphia, Miss.

Winget, George W., MM2c, USN
Born: 4/7/14, Hoboken, N. J.

Woodworth, Lt. (jg) Harry Eades, USN
Born: 11/19/15, Spokane, Wash.

Zarzecki, Henry Joseph, F1c, USN
Born: 8/17/22, Milwaukee, Wis.

Zeeman, Chester Bernard, MM2c, USN
Born: 10/1/18, Boston, Mass.

Zubik, Albert, S2c, USN
Born: 5/21/19, Caldwall, Texas

Casualties

MEMORANDUM

September 25, 1944

From: Robert R. Templeton, Head of Casualties Division, OOR-2

To: Commander Walter Karig, USNR
          Lieutenant Welbourn Kelley, USNR

Subject: Action Casualties, first six months of the War.

1. Attached herewith is compilation of war casualties in the Naval services (Navy, Marine Corps, and Coast Guard) released by the Navy Department during the first six months following the attack on Pearl Harbor. They are predominantly casualties in the Pacific area.

2. This list includes only casualties caused directly by enemy action or by operational activities in war zones. Continental deaths or other casualty classifications are not included. Neither are deaths due to disease or ordinary accidents regardless of where they occur.

3. Names are listed alphabetically by States in the respective categories of Dead, Wounded, Missing, and Prisoners of War. The State grouping is on the basis of the residence of Next of Kin when notified and does not necessarily represent the home State, legal residence, or the present address of the family concerned.

4. Rank and ratings of Casualties named are those held at the time of notification.

5. The casualty status in each case is from the current record. Those listed as Missing during this period are still subject to change. Some may be Prisoners of War, or may have been repatriated, some may be otherwise Safe, and others will be officially declared Dead after extensive investigation and under Public Law No. 490.

6. The compilation is summarized in the following figures:

DEAD	4,934
WOUNDED	827
MISSING	2,243
PRISONERS OF WAR	4,109
TOTAL	12,113

ALABAMA

Dead

ABRAMS, Chester Lee, SF3c, USN
ADAMS, Robert Franklin, S1c, USN
BATTLES, Ralph Curtis, F2c, USN
BAUER, Clinton Adam, MM1c, USN
BEANE, Hewlett Warren, ACMM, USN
BELCHER, Kermit Rastus, BM1c, USN
BENSON, James Thomas, S1c, USN
BIBB, Ross Eugene, Jr., ARM3c, USNR
BIBBY, Charles Henry, F2c, USN
BISHOP, Millard Charles, F3c, USN
BLANKENSHIP, Theron Andrew, S1c, USN
BOYD, Charles Andrew, CM2c, USN
BRANNON, Ens. Charles Edward, USNR
BRASHER, Howard Jonnie, SM3c, USN
BROADHEAD, Johnnie Cecil, F2c, USN
BROCK, Ens. John Wiley, USN
BROWN, Eddie Louis, Jr., SC3c, USN
CARPENTER, James Linard, F1c, USN
CATO, Leo Franklin, F3c, USN
COLVIN, Edby M., PFC, USMC
CROOM, James Leo, F2c, USN
COOPER, Claud Cornelius, GM3c, USN
DENMARK, Willie Ray, CM2c, USN
DIXON, Clem Tarrant, OS2c, USN
DUNCAN, Johnny Martin, S2c, USN
ELISBERRY, Julius, MA1c, USN
FERGUSON, Marvin Lee, Jr., AS, USN
FULTON, Robert Wilson, AM1c, USN
FURR, Tedd McKinley, CCM, USN
GARREN, J. B., F1c, USN
GAUTNEY, Willie Burl, S2c, USN
GILBERT, Tom, S1c, USN
GILES, O. H., Jr., AS, USNR
GROSS, Edgar David, WT2c, USNR
HALL, Vaness Frederick, Elect., USN
HALL, William Franklin, Jr., S2c, USN
HARRIS, William Ottis, GM2c, USN
HAWKINS, Anthony, Jr., MA2c, USN
HENDERSON, George Warren, AS, USNR
HENDERSON, Willie Lawrence, MA1c, USN
HINDMAN, Frank Weaver, S2c, USN
HOLLAND, Claude Herbert, Jr., S2c, USN
HOLLIS, Ofris Oliver, S2c, USN
HOLMES, Charles McDonald, S2c, USNR
HOLMES, Lowell D., F3c, USN
HUGHES, Lewis, Burton, Jr. S1c., USN
INGRAM, George Washington, S2c, USN
ISBELL, Robert Lefette, AS, USNR

ISOM, Luther James, S1c, USN
JEMISON, Eugene, MA2c, USN
JOHNSON, Ralph Ezz, SC3c, USN
JOHNSON, Cdr. Samuel Earle, (MC), USN
JOHNSTON, James Edward, F2c, USN
JONES, Daniel Pugh, S2c, USN
JONES, Woodrow Wilson, S2c, USN
KASSEBAUM, Harry John, MM1c, USN
LAURIE, Johnnie Cornelius, MA1c, USN
LINDSAY, James Mitchell, SF2c, USN
LISENBY, Daniel Edward, S1c, USN
MAHAN, John James, S1c, USN
MAYFIELD, Leonard E., Pvt., USMCR
McCARY, William Moore, Mus2c, USN
McCULLUM, Teddy Carl, S2c, USN
McGRADY, Samme Willie, MA1c, USN
McKEE, Quentin Guy, S2c, USN
McKINNEY, Edward Eugene, S2c, USN
MEYER, Virgil Dean, AS, USN
MORRIS, Owen Newton, S1c, USN
MUNTEAN, Samuel Andrew, RM3c, USNR
MURDOCK, Charles Luther, WT1c, USN
MURDOCK, Melvin Elijah, WT2c, USN
NABORS, Paul, S1c, USN
NICHOLS, Alfred Rose, S1c, USN
NICHOLS, Louis Duffie, S2c, USN
PADGETT, Rudder Bernard, S1c, USN
PAIR, George Thomas, S1c, USN
PATTERSON, Elmer Marvin, OC2c, USN
PENNINGTON, Ens. Strudwick Tutwiler, USN
PENTON, Howard Lee, S1c, USN
PHILABERT, Ens. Frank Florestine, USNR
PICKERN, Edgar Verl, AS, USNR
PIKE, James Donald, S1c, USN
PITMAN, Ens. Norman Duplessis, Jr., USNR
PLEMONS, William Thomas, MM2c, USN
PRUETT, George Floyd, S1c, USN
PUTNAM, Avis Boyd, SC3c, USN
PUTNAM, Vernon E., Corp., USMC
REDDOCK, Eldred Eugene, GM1c, USN
ROBERTS, Ens. John Quincy, USNR
ROBERTS, William Francis, S2c, USN
ROBERTSON, David, MA3c, USN
ROGERS, Thomas Spurgeon, CWT, USN
SANFORD, George Edward, MA2c, USN
SHORES, Irland, Jr., S1c, USN
SHOTTS, S. B., S2c, USN
SMITH, Lloyd George, S2c, USN

SMITH, Orlando Randolph, ACOM, USN
SOLLIE, Walter Henry, WT1c, USN
SOUTH, Charles Braxter, S1c, USN
STILLWELL, William Bernard, SF3c, USN
STUBBINS, Ens. Joseph Briggs, USNR
SWEENEY, Paul Robert, Jr., EM3c, USN
TAYLOR, James Carlton, GM3c, USN
TEAL, Johnnie W., Corp., USMC
THORNHILL, Lt. (jg) Leonard Wilson, USN
THORNTON, Cecil Howard, S2c, USN
TRAVIS, Alton John, AMM1c, USN
TRIPLETT, Homer D. C., PFC, USMC
TUCKER, Henry Warren, PhM3c, USNR
TUNNER, Thomas Lanson, S2c, USN
VINSON, Bobby Ford, S2c, USN
VINSON, Carl Nelson, S/Sgt., USMC
WEISS, James Thomas, EM1c, USN
WESTBROOK, James Ross, S1c, USN
WILEY, William Douglas, S1c, USN
WILSON, Comer A., CBM, USN
WINDHAM, Harold Gordon, F2c, USN
WOOLF, Norman Bragg, CWT, USN

Wounded

ADAMS, Napoleon Owens, MA3c, USN
BALTUSNIK, John, CRM, USN
BROWN, James L., Pvt., USMC
CLARK, John William, AMM1c, USN
DEAN, A. C., S1c, USN
DUNLAP, Ens. Ernest Huston, Jr., USN
HARRELSON, Isaac William, Y3c, USN
HARVEY, Charles William, F1c, USN
HARWELL, William Thomas, S2c, USN
HITCHCOX, Onnie, S1c, USN
LAMBERTH, Grady Joe, GM2c, USN
McCURDY, William Aurnee, S2c, USN
MOORE, Theodore Edward, MA3c, USN
PHELPS, Ramon Eugene, S2c, USN
VICE, Ralph M., Corp., USMC

Missing

ARNETTE, Elbert Hugh, F1c, USN
ATKEISON, Warren Ingram, Torp3c, USN
BLACK, James T., Pvt., USMC
BONDS, Woodrow Marshall, S1c, USN
BRASFIELD, William L., Pvt., USMC
CHANDLER, Donald Ross, Pvt., USMC
CREED, Joe, EM2c, USN
DAVIS, Harvey Reid, SM3c, USN
DEMARAIS, Russell Wilfred, CCM, USN
FINCHER, James Gordon, S1c, USN
FLOYD, Joseph Pettus, SF1c, USN
FULTON, Charles Ellis, Jr., F2c, USN
FURR, George Washington, Torp3c, USN

GAINES, Richard Curling, S1c, USN
HALEY, Joe Walker, S2c, USN
HALL, William Franklin, Jr., S2c, USN
HAMBY, Marvin Haynes, S2c, USNR
KNOWLES, Walter Daniel, F1c, USN
LANKFORD, Thomas Woodard, S1c, USN
LEIGBER, Carl Lewis, S1c, USN
LOWERY, Joel William, Jr., CMM, USN
NAISH, Wilbur Lee, S1c, USN
OWEN, Paul Alexandrew, CMM, USN
SESSIONS, Johnnie Clyde, Ptr2c, USN
SHIELDS, Taylor Jones, Jr., RM2c, USN
SMITH, Marcus Malone, S1c, USN
TAYLOR, Glenn Elmo, Torp1c, USN
TERRY, Earlie Freeman, S1c, USN
WEAVER, Ben Earl, GM1c, USN
WEATHERS, John C., Sgt.Maj., USMC

Prisoners of War

BAILEY, Vincent Leonard, SK1c, USN
BOWEN, Emmit Paul, MA1c, USN
CARNLEY, William Douglas, PFC, USMC
CLEERE, Neal C., Corp., USMC
CLEMENTS, Joe Howard, AOM2c, USN
EMBREY, Billy Montgomery, SM2c, USN
GARTMAN, Curtis Sylvester, AMM3c, USNR
GILBERT, Richard Calvin, Pvt., USMC
GODBOLD, Capt. Bryghte David, USMC
GREENE, Lt. George William, USNR
HARRELL, John Allison, Y3c, USNR
HAYNES, James Robert, Pvt., USMC
HEATON, Jesse Clyde, Sgt., USMC
HOGAN, Emmett O'Neal, Pharm, USN
HOWERTON, George Rice, Jr., S2c, USN
JONES, Jack Jessie, Mach., USN
KING, Burton Vernon, S2c, USN
LANGSTON, Clem Lee, Cox., USN
LOCKLEAR, Thomas Eulee, PhM3c, USN
LUCKY, Loyd Vernon, F2c, USN
LYONS, Lt. Cdr. Leonard LeBaron, Jr., USNR
MAXWELL, Frank Lellwyn, PhM1c, USN
ORR, Luther David, Jr., Pvt., USMC
PENOLA, James Leonard, CWT, USN
PITTMAN, William Willoughby, PFC, USMC
REDMOND, Joe G., PFC, USMC
RILEY, William Eston, PhM1c, USN
SMITH, Dempsey, Pvt., USMC
SMITH, Elwood, Pvt., USMC
SMITHEY, Talmadge A., Carp., USN
STEWART, Jimmie Lyn, PFC, USMC
STOWERS, Henry Benjamin, Supply Sgt., USMC

TANNER, James H., PFC, USMC
TURK, William Herbert, PFC, USMC
WHITE, Harold Buford, EM3c, USN

WHITE, Tommie J., PFC, USMC
WILSON, Rex Elwood, EM3c, USN

ARIZONA

Dead

BELL, Robert Edwin, S2c, USN
BERTIE, George Allan, Jr., S2c, USN
COOK, Archie Kennedy, FC3c, USN
CREMEENS, Louis Edward, S1c, USN
CUMMINS, Harold Vernon, S1c, USNR
GILBERT, Ens. George Hellworth, USNR
HOLLOWELL, George Sanford, Cox., USN
HORROCKS, James William, CGM, USN
HUNT, Quince A., Sgt., USMC
JOHNSON, Carl Spencer, S1c, USN
KEITH, George Richard, RM3c, USN
MAST, Albert Charles, AMM2c, USN
McEUEN, Sam L., Corp., USMC
MILLER, Thomas Rudolph, S2c, USN
MONTGOMERY, Warren Anderson, PFC, USMC
MURPHY, James Joseph, S1c, USN
PUGH, John, Jr., SF3c, USN
PYEATT, Merl Andrew, AMM3c, USN
SAFFELL, Morris Franklin, F1c, USN
SEIDEL, Alfred Glenn, EM2c, USN
SKEEN, Harvey Leroy, S2c, USN
VAN HORN, James Randolf, AS, USN
WEBB, William Henry, GM3c, USN
WILSFORD, Clyde Douglas, Sgt., USMC
WRIGHT, Paul Raymond, CWT, USNR

Wounded

GREER, Frederic L., Sgt., USMC
HALL, Lloyd D., PFC, USMC
KREMER, Donald William, S2c, USN
OLDFATHER, William G., PFC, USMC

Missing

ASKEW, Earl Miles Robertson, CQM, USN
BAKER, Lester Leroy, Torp.1c, USN
CLAYTON, James W., F1c, USN
DARTER, Ens. James Roderick, USN
EUSTACE, Milton Jack, MM2c, USN
GAY, Louis H., PFC, USMC

Prisoners of War

ADAMS, Leon C., PFC, USMC
ADAMS, William Lawton, PFC, USMC
AMOS, Robert Aslen, Corp., USMC
ANDREWS, Thomas Jefferson, Jr., Corp., USMC
BARGER, Herman Boris, BM2c, USN
BILLINGSLEY, Jack Morice, PFC, USMC
CLARK, Russell D., RM2c, USN
EDWARDS, Joseph Marvin, PFC, USMC
FOWLER, Harry Park, Corp., USMC
GRANT, Ginner, PFC, USMC
GRUBB, Glenn Elmer, PFC, USMC
HARRIS, James Harvey, Corp., USMC
NOLTING, Harry, Corp., USMC
PARKS, Laurence A., PFC, USMC
SHILL, Wright Painter, Jr., AMM3c, USN
SHORT, Ernest Eugene, S/Sgt., USMC
SPELIMAN, Edward James, Jr., Pvt., USMC
TRUELOVE, William Athol, SM1c, USN

ARKANSAS

Dead

AARON, Hubert, F2c, USN
ALEXANDER, Elvis Author, S2c, USN
ALLEN, C. J., Cox., USN
ANDREWS, Verden G., PFC, USMC
ARNOLD, Thell, SC1c, USN
AUSTIN, Fred Andrew, AMM2c, USN
AUTRY, Eligah T., Jr., Cox., USN
BARNETT, William Thermon, S2c, USN
BOLLING, Gerald Revese, S1c, USN
BOYCE, Milton Lafeyette, F1c, USN

BRIDGES, Paul Hyatt, S1c, USN
CAMM, William Fielden, Y2c, USN
CASH, Lester Monroe, SF1c, USN
CLARKSTON, Leonard O'Neal, S1c, USN
COTHREN, Marshal Foch, F3c, USN
COX, Loyd Franklin, S2c, USN
CRAIG, John William, SK1c, USN
EGBERT, Leon, MA2c, USN
ELDER, Roy Thomas, MM2c, USN
ELLIS, Earl Maurice, RM3c, USN
ERSKINE, Robert C., PFC, USMC
FRANK, LeRoy George, S1c, USN

FREUND, James Thomas, S1c, USN
GATES, Amon Wesley, RM1c, USN
HALL, Elby Loyd, MM2c, USN
HALL, John Rudolph, CBM, USN
HARWELL, Hoyette Irl, CMM, USNR
HINES, Arvel Clay, S2c, USN
HOWARD, James Euell, SK3c, USN
HURST, Marchell Ray, MM1c, USN
JANISE, Vernon Lee, SC3c, USN
JOHNSON, Nathaniel Noble, MA1c, USN
JOHNSON, Thomas Erwin, Jr., GM1c, USN
KENNEDY, Benjamin Franklin, M1c, USN
KENT, Texas Thomas, Jr., S2c, USN
LOCKWOOD, Clarence Marion, WT2c, USN
LUKER, Royle Bradford, F3c, USN
MABRY, Thomas Edward, AMM2c, USN
MANN, 1st Lt. Ralph C., Jr., USMC
MARTIN, Luster Lee, F3c, USN
McGHEE, Lester Fred, S1c, USN
McKAY, Louis Franklin, AS, USN
McKINNIE, Russell, MA2c, USN
MILES, Oscar Wright, S1c, USN
MILLER, Doyle Allen, Cox., USN
MILNER, James William, F1c, USN
NATIONS, Morris E., Corp., USMC
NELSON, Harl Coplin, S1c, USN
O'NEAL, Willie, MA1c, USN
PACE, Millard Clarence, F1c, USN
PARKER, Isaac, MA3c, USN
PETTIT, Robert Lee, CMM, USN
PREWITT, Brady Oliver, S2c, USN
PURKEYPILE, Floyd Richard, S2c, USNR
RAINBOLT, John Thomas, F1c, USN
RAINWATER, Osborn Kieth, F1c, USN
RAMSEY, Maunsel Edward, MM1c, USN
REAGAN, Dan Edward, F1c, USN
REAVES, Casbie, S1c, USN
RELERFORD, Nathaniel Lee, MA1c, USN
RILEY, Lt. Paul James, USN
ROBERTSON, Joseph Morris, S2c, USN
SCARBOROUGH, Frank Allen, Jr., S2c, USN
SCHULTZ, Hobert Farrell, SK3c, USN
SCREETON, James Clark, RM3c, USN
SNOW, William Lansing, BM2c, USN
STEINER, Samuel Cyrus, F1c, USN
STEWART, Thomas Lester, SC3c, USN
TERRELL, John Raymond, F2c, USN
TIPTON, Henry Glenn, S1c, USN
TUCKER, William Marion, Corp., USMC
TUNNELL, Thadeus Oceola, Jr., S2c, USN
TURNER, Billie Gene, MA2c, USN
TURNIPSEED, John Morgan, F3c, USN

WALLACE, Houston Oliver, WT1c, USN
WATTS, Sherman, Maurice, HA1c, USN
WEST, Webster Paul, S1c, USN
WHEELER, John Dennis, F2c, USN
WILLIAMS, Clyde, S1c, USN
YOUNG, Oscar, F2c, USN

Wounded

BARKLEY, Oris Dale, RM3c, USN
BEARD, Bill Joe, S2c, USN
BIDWELL, Frank Shelby, S1c, USN
BOZEMAN, Troy Eugene, GM3c, USN
BUCHANAN, Eris Earnest, F1c, USN
BUTLER, Z. L., Cox., USN
CLEMENT, Robert A., Sgt., USMC
CRAIGG, Thomas A., Jr., PFC, USMC
DAVISON, Ens. Henry Donals, USN
JONES, Ervin B., Pvt., USMC
RAMER, Stephen Howard, GM2c, USN
RICHARDS, Bige, S2c, USN
ROACHELL, James Madison, CWT, USNR
TURNER, Austin P., S2c, USN
WATKINS, Charles Henry, MM2c, USN

Missing

ATTERBERRY, Charles Theodore, S2c, USN
BATTLES, Lawrence F., PFC, USMC
BENNETT, Nyal H., Corp., USMC
BEVEL, Virgil Bill, Jr., Cox., USN
BUICE, William Arthur, F1c, USN
CALAWAY, Rhyman, S1c, USN
CARLON, Walter Raymon, SM2c, USN
CASSADY, Sam Gilbert, RM3c, USN
COOPER, George Ray, SC1c, USN.
COPLIN, Carl Emil, HA1c, USN
DAVIS, Alton Joseph, MM2c, USN
DEHART, Lawrence Raymond, SF2c, USN
GRAVES, Fred Ray, S1c, USN
HARPER, James Obed, GM1c, USN
HOLLAND, Raymond Hamby, F1c, USN
JENKINS, J. T., Sgt., USMC
JONES, Nuel Armstrong, S2c, USN
KENNEY, James, BM2c, USN
LEWIS, John Henry, MM1c, USN
LINDLEY, Aubrey Louis, EM2c, USN
LOFLAND, John Alex, S2c, USN
LYNCH, Charles Leslie, GM2c, USN
McCULLOUGH, Marvin Lee, F2c, USN
McDUFFIE, Lonnie Truman, F1c, USN
NELON, George, Kirkwood, EM3c, USN
PENNINGTON, John Paul, EM1c, USN
ROGERS, Henry Clay, F2c, USN
ROWE, C. L., S1c, USN

Rowe, Sidney Lee, S2c, USN
Saunders, Robert Earl, GM3c, USN
Shook, Shelby C., Pvt., USMC
Sims, Harry L., Pvt., USMC
Tate, Charles Roy, S1c, USN
Tinkle, John Wilson, Y3c, USN
Vance, Charles Wilber, S1c, USN
Watkins, Charles Henry, MM2c, USN
Welch, Delbert Robert, S2c, USN
Williams, John Wilson, CM3c, USN
Wilson, Wayne Scott, AOM2c, USN
Wright, Raymon, Corp., USMC

Prisoners of War

Adams, Charles Speed, RM1c, USN
Bajorek, Aloysius Stanley, F1c, USN
Bearden, Ivan Chester, PFC, USMC
Bennett, James O., Sgt., USMC
Booker, Henry H., PFC, USMC
Bostian, Lester Aran, S1c, USN
Brewer, Artis Travis, PhM2c, USN
Brian, Fowler Morgan, Boat., USN
Brownell, Theodore Richard, CY, USN
Burroughs, Lt. Clement Doss, (MC), USN
Carter, Arthur Floyd, Pvt., USMC
Carter, Harold Bell, SM3c, USN
Chastain, Eldon Tobias, Pvt., USMC
Clement, Robert A., Platoon Sgt., USMC
Collins, Thomas Edward, Corp., USMC
Collins, Wilson Lynn, Boat., USN
Craigg, Thomas Arthur, Jr., PFC, USMC
Crass, Arthur, J., PFC, USMC
Darneal, Dillard Daniel, MM1c, USN
Dodd, Doyle Harding, PFC, USMC
Dollar, John Fulton, S1c, USN
Edwards, Joe F., Tech. Sgt., USMC
Ellis, Leon Malady, Tech. Sgt., USMC
Erwin, Hoyle Medford, Pvt., USMC
Ferriss, James Furr, PFC, USMC
Fields, Marshall Edward, PFC, USMC
Fox, George, Jr., PFC, USMC
Gentry, Mark Nathaniel, PFC, USMC
George, Lt. Cdr. Jack Ruel, (MC), USN
Glover, Ross Madison, S1c, USN

Griffith, Roy Jefferson, CCStd, USNR
Guynn, Marion, PFC, USMC
Hammock, William Lester, Jr., Corp., USMC
Hamrick, John Forrest, Sgt., USMC
Harris, Ens. Robert Bonnell, USN
Harvey, Virgil Carter, CCStd, USN
Holt, James Christopher, Jr., Y2c, USN
Hughes, A. R., Jr., Mess Sgt., USMC
Humphrey, Jack, F2c, USN
Jeanes, Howard, F2c, USN
King, Frank, Cox., USN
Knod, Guy Ellis, SF2c, USN
Levy, Ens. Benjamin Henry, Jr., USNR
Mabry, Jacob Pickett, MM2c, USN
Mathis, Charles Lee, PFC, USMC
May, Earl Vincent, Mach., USN
McCain, Lindell Hosea, RM2c, USN
McKinney, Floyd M., PFC, USMC
McNeil, Alvin Lloyd, S1c, USN
Middleton, William Jeff, S1c, USN
Minton, Olen Cecil, S1c, USN
Moore, Charles Allen, MM2c, USN
Musick, Arthur Benton, F2c, USN
Penter, Loren Boyd, S1c, USN
Price, Dillard, PFC, USMC
Raines, Kirby Newton, SC1c, USN
Rainwater, Dennis Dalton, Jr., PFC, USMC
Ray, Sanford Kelly, Pvt., USMC
Reynolds, James Edward, S1c, USN
Reynolds, Weldon Farrist, GM3c, USN
Rogers, John L., Corp., USMC
St. John, Walter, PFC, USMC
Simpson, Jesse H., PFC, USMC
Stanley, Abram Francis, Jr., PFC, USMC
Storey, James Wilson, PhM1c, USN
Tallant, William Talbert, PFC, USMC
Waisath, Earl Edward, F2c, USN
Webster, Guy Pearson, PFC, USMC
Weems, Charles Monroe, PFC, USMC
Wheat, Patrick Henry, III, F3c, USN
Williams, Henry, Jr., Pvt., USMC
Yeargin, Marion Richard, Torp.2c, USN
Zimmerman, Paul, GM2c, USN

CALIFORNIA

Dead

Abasta, Frank Patrick, AS, USN
Adams, James Wilbur, ACRM, USN
Adamson, Alfred, CFC, USN
Aguirre, Reyner Aceves, S2c, USN
Ahern, Richard James, F1c, USN

Ablerovsky, Francis Severin, B1c, USN
Alderman, Harmon Prive, CRM, USN
Alexander, Lt. Cdr. Hugh Rossman, Dental Corps, USN
Allan, William Frederick, S1c, USN
Allen, William Clayborn, EM1c, USN
Alten, Ernest Mathew, S2c, USN

ALTMAN, Peter William, AMM2c, USN
ANDERSON, Charles Titus, CM2c, USN
ANDERSON, Harry, S1c, USN
ANDERSON, Ens. Leonard S., USNR
ANDERSON, RobertiEmmett, AS, USN.
ANNIS, Beverly, S2c, USN
ANNIS, Bruce, S2c, USN
ANTHONY, Glenn Samuel, S1c, USN
APGAR, Robert Thorne, Y2c, USN
APLIN, James Raymond, CWT, USN
ARMSTRONG, Kenneth Berton, ML1c, USN
ARNEBERG, Harold Raymond, F3c, USN
AUSTIN, James Hiram, F1c, USN
AUSTIN, John A., Chief Carp., USN.
BADILLA, Manuel Donomic, F1c, USN
BAGGARLY, Benjamin Franklin, CCM, USN
BAILEY, Gerald John, S1c, USN
BAILEY, George R., PFC, USMC
BAKER, Henry Ernest, Jr., Cox., USN
BAKER, Lt. (jg) Paul Gerald, USN
BAKER, Robert Dewey, CMM, USN
BANGUST, Joseph, AMM2c, USN
BANKS, Layton Thomas, Cox., USN
BARBEE, Murren Arrel, CMM, USN
BARKER, Charles Sherman, S1c, USN
BARNES, Lt. (jg) Delmar Hayes, USN
BARNES, Herbert McClellan, BM2c, USN
BARR, Joseph Alonza, Jr., RM1c, USN
BARRETT, Raymond L., Corp., USMC
BARTA, Joseph, F3c, USN
BEAL, Albert Quentin, RM2c, USN
BEANE, Hewlett Warren, ACMM, USN
BEASLEY, Douglas Lee, RM3c, USN
BECK, George Richard, S1c, USN
BEDWELL, William T., Gunnery Sgt., USMC
BEECH, Ernest, Jr., S2c, USN
BEGGS, Edward Latchford, CWT, USN
BELCHER, Algie, AMM1c, USN
BELL, Richard LeRoy, S2c, USN
BELLAMY, James Curtis, OS3c, USN
BENFORD, Sam Austin, Bkr2c, USN
BERTIE, George Allan, Jr., S2c, USN
BIENERT, Joseph Benedict, Boat., USN
BIRD, John Arthur, S1c, USN
BLANKENSHIP, Henry Wilbur, PhM1c, USN
BLINCOE, Michael Voltie, S2c, USN
BLOOD, Richard Malcolm, Y3c, USN
BLUE, Edward Charles, F3c, USN
BODECKER, Regis James, Y1c, USN
BOGGESS, Roy Eugene, SF2c, USN
BOHNER, Theodore Roosevelt, S2c, USN
BOLTON, Jack Brixey, F2c, USN

BOMAR, William W., Jr., PFC, USMC
BONNER, Don Cecil, AMM3c, USN
BOOE, James Brazier, Bandmaster, USN
BORGER, Richard, CMM, USN
BOROVICH, Joseph John, S1c, USN
BOUCK, Warren Charles, MM1c, USN
BOURKE, Robert E., PFC, USMC
BRAMSTEDT, Henry John, S1c, USN
BREWER, Robert LeRoy, S1c, USN
BRIER, Claire Raymond, MM2c, USN
BRIGNOLE, Erminio Joseph, S2c, USN
BRITTAN, Charles Edward, S2c, USN
BROADHEAD, Arthur James, AMM1c, USN
BROOKS, Daryl Edward, F2c, USN
BROWN, Charles Martin, S2c, USN
BROWN, Richard Corbett, S1c, USN
BROWNE, Harry Lamont, CMM, USN
BRYANT, Floyd Eugene, Cox., USN
BRYANT, Lloyd Glenn, BM2c, USN
BRYANT, Robert Houghston, AM1c, USN
BUCHANAN, James Rufus, MM2c, USNR
BUCKENDORF, George Washington, CWT, USN
BUCKLEY, Claude Lionel, M1c, USN
BUEHLER, Otto Frederick, RM3c, USN
BULL, Lt. Richard Salisbury, Jr., USN
BULT, Thomas Kyle, QM2c, USN
BURGER, Oliver Kenneth, WT1c, USN
BURNS, William Richard, Y1c, USN
BUSH, James Frederick, MM1c, USN
BUTTS, Rodger Cornelius, SC1c, USN
CAMBRON, John Nelson, CSF, USN
CAMERY, Raymond Ralph, F1c, USN
CAMPA, Ralph, S1c, USN
CAMPBELL, Burdette Charles, S1c, USN
CAMPBELL, Lt. (jg) George Marvin, USN
CAMPION, 2nd Lt. Kenneth O., USMCR
CARLSON, Earl O., 1st Sgt., USMC
CARLSON, Roy Gunnar, Cox., USN
CARPENTER, Elmer Lemuel, BM1c, USN
CARTER, Burton Lowell, S2c, USN
CARTER, Herman Eldrege, MM2c, USN
CARTER, Howard Frederick, Cox., USN
CARTER, Paxton Turner, Acting Pay Clerk, USN
CASIANO, Florencio, OC2c, USN
CASOLA, Riacio, S1c, USN
CASSIDY, Lt. Earl William, USN
CATSOS, George, F1c, USN
CHACE, Raymond Vincent, CSK, USN
CHADWICK, Harold, MA1c, USN
CHAMBERS, Ens. Russell Franklyn, USNR
CHARLTON, Charles Nicholas, WT1c, USN
CHEEVER, Cdr. Sumner Charles, USN
CHESHIRE, James Thomas, CPhM, USN

CHRISTIAN, William Garnett, Bkr2c, USN
CLARK, Alien, CY, USN
CLARK, John Crawford Todd, F3c, USN
CLAYTON, Robert Roland, Cox., USN
COFFIN, Clinton B., PFC, USMC
COLE, Ens. David L., USNR
COLE, Johnnie Ralph, ARM1c, USN
COLLINS, Billy Murl, S1c, USN
CONLEY, Ens. Harry Francis, USNR
CONNELLY, Richard Earl, CQM, USN
CONNOLLY, John Gaynor, Chief Pay Clerk, USN
CONNER, Joseph Ugline, F1c, USN
CONRAD, Robert Frank, BM2c, USN
CONRAD, Robert Frank, S2c, USN
CONRAD, Walter Ralph, QM2c, USN
COOK, Hal, Jr., Corp., USMC
COOPER, Clarence Eugene, F2c, USN
COOPER, Kenneth Erven, F2c, USN
CORBIN, Leon John, GM1c, USN
CORNWELL, Irving Griswald, EM1c, USN
COSTIGAN, James Edward, WT1c, USCG
COTTEN, Clarence John, F1c, USN
COUSE, Earl Irven, SK3c, USN
COVINA, Ross Clifford, S2c, USN
CRAIG, David Bruce, RM3c, USNR
CRANE, Leonard, SK2c, USN
CREAMER, Ens. William W., USNR
CRIDDLE, Leland Richard, GM2c, USN
CRISCUOLO, Michael, Y2c, USN
CRISWELL, Ens. David Wellington, USNR
CROFT, Albert Edward, EM2c, USN
CROFT, Theodore Wheeler, AOM1c, USN
CROWLEY, Lt. Cdr. Thomas Ewing, Dental Corps, USN
CRUM, Lt. (jg) Irvin Stanley, USNR
CRUMBLEY, Byron, CEM, USN
CURRY, William McKnight, EM1c, USN
CYBULSKI, Harold Bernard, S1c, USN
DACUS, Marvin Alvin, WT1c, USN
DALY, Edward Carlyle, Cox., USN
DARRAH, Henry Clay, QM3c, USN
DAUGA, John, WT1c, USN
DAVILLA, Manuel Silva, S1c, USN
DAVIS, Arthur William, S1c, USN
DAVIS, Bruce E., MM1c, USCG
DAVIS, Lt. George Elliott, Jr., USN
DAVIS, Jess Orvel, MM1c, USN
DAVIS, Thomas Ray, SF1c, USN
DAWSON, Merlyn Belmonte, AP1c, USN
DAYO, Tomas, OC1c, USN
DEAL, Delbert Floyd, AOM1c, USN
DE ARMOUN, Donald Edwin, GM3c, USN
DEEDE, Lt. (jg) Leroy Clifford, USNR
DE FUENTES, Stanley Joseph, MM1c, USN

DERE, Philip Avery, SC3c, USNR
DERRINGTON, Ralph Alva, CMM, USN
DE SPARR, Marshall Eugene, Corp., USMC
DIAS, Peter, CBM, USNR
DICK, Ralph R., GM1c, USN
DICKENS, Ernest Boggio, F2c, USN
DINE, John George, F2c, USN
DOBBS, Horace Franklin, CRM, USN
DOHERTY, George Walter, S2c, USN
DORITY, John Monroe, S2c, USN
DOUGHERTY, Robert Edward, PFC, USMC
DOWDY, Kenneth Lloyd, S2c, USN
DOWNEY, John William, RM3c, USN
DRISCOLL, Kevin Emmett, AS, USNR
DUANE, William, CBM, USN
DUCOLON, Fred John, Cox., USN
DUKE, Robert Edward, CCStd, USN
DUNHAM, Elmer Marvin, S1c, USN
DUNHAM, Roland Sumner, S2c, USN
DUNN, Audress Casey, F2c, USN
DUNN, George Sylvester, Jr., S2c, USN
DURKEE, Edward Norman, CMM, USN
DURNING, Thomas Roy, Jr., S2c, USN
DUVEENE, John, 1st Sgt., USMC
EBEL, Walter Charles, CTC, USN
EDLING, Robert Norris, RM3c, USNR
EDWARDS, Harry, CCStd, USN
EDWARDS, Winson Aloysius, EM2c, USN.
EERNISSE, William Frederik, Ptr1c, USN
EFISHOFF, James K., PFC, USMC
ELLIS, Wilbur Danner, RM2c, USN
ELROD, Maj. Henry T., USMC
ELY, Lt. Arthur Vincent, USN
EMBREY, Bill Eugene, F3c, USN
EMBROGNO, Joseph, BM2c, USN
EMERY, Ens. Jack M., USNR
ENGLAND, Ens. John Charles, USNR
ESTES, Forrest Jesse, F1c, USN
EVANS, Clyde Harold, AMM1c, USN
EVANS, Ens. Evan F., USNR
EWELL, Alfred Adam, WT1c, USN
FALLIS, Alvin E., PhM2c, USN
FELOSOFO, Fermin, OC3c, USN
FELSHEIM, Marcus George, PFC, USMC
FERRARI, Attilio John, S2c, USNR
FESS, John Junior, F1c, USN
FIEBERLING, Lt. Langdon Kellogg, USN
FIFE, Ralph Elmer, S1c, USN
FIRTH, Henry Amis, F3c, USN
FIRTH, Howard, MM1c, USN
FISHER, Paul William, PFC, USMC
FISHER, Robert Ray, S2c, USN
FISK, Charles Porter, III, Y1c, USN
FLOYD, Charles Eliott, CBM, USN

FORD, Jack C., S1c, USN
FORD, Raymond D., Pvt., USMC
FOTH, Jack, EM1c, USN
FOX, Lt. Col. Daniel R., USMC
FRANCHERE, Evariste Gabriel, S1c, USNR
FREEMAN, Ray Amos, MM2c, USNR
FRENCH, Lt. Cdr. John Edmund, USN
FRIZZELL, Robert Niven, S2c, USN
FRUIT, Albert David, MM1c, USN
FUGATE, Fred, CCStd, USN
GALL, Thomas Leroy, RM3c, USN
GANAS, Nickolas Steve, S2c, USN
GANDRE, Melvyn Amour, QM1c, USN
GANTNER, Samuel Merritt, BM2c, USN
GARCIA, Claude Ralph, SF2c, USN
GARLINGTON, Raymond Wesley, S1c, USN
GARTIN, Gerald Ernest, S1c, USN
GAVER, 2nd Lt. Harry Hamilton, Jr., USMC
GEBSER, Paul Heino, MM1c, USNR
GEER, Kenneth Floyd, S2c, USN
GEORGE, Paul Fredrick, F2c, USN
GIFT, Kenneth Mace, BM2c, USN
GILBERT, George, FC2c, USN
GILBERT, Lt. Roy Del, CEC, USNR
GILMORE, Cdr. Walter William, Supply Corps, USN
GLOVER, William John, ARM2c, USN
GOBBIN, Angelo, SC1c, USN
GOFF, George Wesley, F3c, USN
GOGGIN, Daryl Henry, Mach., USN
GOLDEN, Glen Tiery, S2c, USN
GOLDWATER, Jack Reginald, RM3c, USNR
GONZALEZ, Ens. Manuel, USNR
GORDON, Duff, CM, USNR
GORDON, William, Sgt., USMC
GOULD, Howard Stanton, SK3c, USNR
GOVE, Rupert Clair, S1c, USN
GOWDEY, William James, CM1c, USN
GRAVES, Jack H., PFC, USMC
GRAY, William James, Jr., S1c, USN
GREENWOOD, Lt. George Hamilton, CEC, USNR
GREER, Charles R., PFC, USMC
GREGORY, Robert Francis, SM3c, USN
GRIFFITHS, Robert Alfred, EM3c, USN
GRISHAM, Kenneth Floyd, Y3c, USN
GROGG, David Franklin, AMM3c, USN
GROSS, Milton Henry, CSK, USN
GROW, Vernon Neslie, S2c, USNR
GRUNDSTROM, Richard Gunnar, S2c, USN
GUNN, Ralph Eugene, M1c, USN
GURGANUS, William Ike, CEM, USN
GUSTI, Robert Lee, MM2c, USN

GURIERREZ, Luis, S2c, USN
GUY, George Hormer, S2c, USN
HAAS, John William, CMM, USN
HAGEDORN, 2nd Lt. Bruno P., USMCR
HAINES, Robert Wesley, S2c, USN
HALEY, Gifford L., S/Sgt., USMC
HANSON, Charles, MoMM2c, USNR
HARRIS, Daniel Fletcher, CFC, USN
HARRIS, Ens. Willard E., USN
HART, Lt. Patrick Henry, USN
HASTINGS, Lt. Burden R., USN
HAUGEN, Albin Marvin, MM1c, USN
HAVINS, Harvey Linfille, S1c, USN
HAWKINS, Sidney Percy, F2c, USN
HAYES, John Doran, BM1c, USN
HAYES, Kenneth Merle, F1c, USN
HAZDOVAC, Jack Claudius, S1c, USN
HEAD, Frank Bernard, CY, USN
HEALY, Lt. Cdr. Howard Raymond, USN
HEATH, Fred Theo., S2c, USN
HEBEL, Lt. (jg) Francis Frederick, USN
HEDGER, Jess Laxton, S1c, USN
HEDRICK, Charles Edgar, RM2c, USN
HEDRICK, Paul Henry, BM1c, USN
HEIDT, Edward Joseph, F1c, USN
HEIDT, Wesley John, F1c, USN
HELDOORN, Johannas Cornileus, AMM1c, USNR
HENDERSON, Maj. Lofton R., USMC
HENNESSY, Capt. Daniel J., USMC
HERBERT, George, GM1c, USN
HERMANN, Lt. (jg) Gayle Louis, USN
HERZOG, Robert A., Corp., USMC
HIGHTOWER, Willis Herbert, AS, USNR
HILBERT, Ernest Lenard, AOM3c, USN
HILL, Bartley Talor, AOM3c, USN
HILL, Edwin Joseph, Chief Boat., USN
HILL, Everett Clyde, RM2c, USN
HODGES, David William, SK2c, USN
HOFFMAN, Donald K., PFC, USMC
HOFSTRA, George Jesse, S2c, USN
HOLLIS, Lt. (jg) Ralph, USNR
HOLMES, Irving E., PFC, USMC
HOLMES, John Martin, CMM, USNR
HOMER, Samuel Byers, CMM, USNR
HOOD, Lt. Clark Alexander, Jr., USN
HOPPER, Ens. George Aurand, Jr., USNR
HOUDE, Emery Lyle, Bkr2c, USN
HOUSE, Clem Raymond, CWT, USN
HOWARD, Harry M., Corp., USMC
HUDGELL, Alfred William, BM1c, USN
HUDSON, Charles Eugene, WT1c, USN
HUDSON, John Cecil, F3c, USN
HUGHES, Lt. (jg) Richard Beverly, USN
HUNT, William Evan, AOM3c, USN
HUNTER, Ens. Robert M., USNR

HUNTINGTON, Henry Louis, S2c, USN
HUNTINGTON, Robert Kingsbury, ARM3c, USN
HURST, Lt. Edwin William, USN
HYMAN, Lt. Cdr. Willford Milton, USN
IAK, Joseph Claude, Y3c, USN
IBBOTSON, Howard Burt, F1c, USN
IFFLAND, Charles William, FC2c, USN
IRVIN, Stuart, F1c, USN
IVERSEN, Earl Henry, S2c, USN
IVERSEN, Norman Kenneth, S2c, USN
IVEY, Charles Andrew, Jr., S2c, USN
JACKSON, Billie Burke, AMM1c, USN
JACKSON, Willie, OC1c, USN
JACOBS, Alfred Deitrick, AS, USNR
JAMES, Ens. Will Roy, Jr., USN
JANZ, Lt. Clifford Thurston, USN
JARVIS, William Hector, SF1c, USN
JEFFERY, Edward Julian, QM1c, USN
JEFFREYS, Romie Lloyd, CMM, USN
JENSON, Jesse Bennett, GM3c, USN
JOHNSON, Arthur, Bkr3c, USN
JOHNSON, Edmund Russell, MM1c, USN
JOHNSON, Elbert McKinley, CSF, USNR
JOHNSON, Ernest Ralph, WT1c, USN
JOHNSON, Gordon Kenneth, SC1c, USN
JOHNSON, Melvin Walfred, RM2c, USNR
JOHNSON, Parham Screeton, ARM2c, USN
JOHNSON, Ray Berhard, F3c, USNR
JOHNSTON, Lt. Cdr. Philip Devereux, USNR
JONES, Fred "M", MM1c, USN
JONES, Harry Edward, Jr., Pvt, USMC
JONES, Henry, Jr., MA1c, USN
JONES, Ens. Herbert C., USNR
JONES, Homer Loyd, S1c, USN
JONES, Hugh, Junior, S2c, USN
JONES, Leroy Henry, S1c, USN
JORDAN, Lt. Julian Bethune, USN
JORDAN, Wesley Vernie, S1c, USN
JOSEN, William Adler, AMM1c, USN
JUEDES, William Arthur, SC2c, USN
KAELIN, John Louis, Y3c, USNR
KAGARICE, Harold Lee, CSK, USN
KANE, William John, SK3c, USN
KARLI, John Albert, S1c, USN
KATT, Eugene Louis, S2c, USN
KAUFMAN, Harry, BM1c, USN
KEFFER, Howard Verne, RM3c, USNR
KELLER, Kenneth Merton, RM1c, USN
KELLEY, Harold Gene, S2c, USN
KELLEY, Joe Marion, S2c, USN
KELLY, Robert Lee, CEM, USN
KENT, William Harrison, S1c, USN

KENYON, Ens. Henry Russell, Jr., USNR
KERESTES, Elmer Tom, F1c, USN
KESLER, David Leland, Bkr2c, USN
KIEHN, Ronald William, MM2c, USN
KIESELBACH, Charles Ermin, CM1c, USN
KILCOYNE, Thomas Philip, EM3c, USNR
KING, Edward Windsor, Chief Torp., USN
KINNEY, Gilbert Livingston, QM2c, USN
KLEINSMITH, Charles, WT1c, USN
KOENIG, Kenneth Oliver, MM1c, USN
KOSEC, John Anthony, BM2c, USN
KOSMIDER, Daniel, CY, USN
KRIENER, Bob Bernard, SK3c, USN
KRISSMAN, Mac Sam, S2c, USN
KRUGER, Richard Warren, QM2c, USN
KRUPLACK, Joseph Francis, AMM1c, USN
KUEHNLE, Ens. Lowell Franklin, USNR
LAKE, John Ervin, Jr., Acting Pay Clerk, USN
LAKIN, Donald Lapier, S1c, USN
LAKIN, Joseph Jordan, S1c, USN
LA MAR, Ralph B., FC3c, USN
LAMB, George Samuel, CSF, USN
LAMONS, Kenneth Taft, BM2c, USN
LANE, Lewis Lee, F2c, USN
LANE, Lyman Lyle, PFC, USMC
LANGE, Richard Charles, S1c, USN
LANSING, William Henry, AMM1c, USN
LARIOS, Milton T., Mess Sgt., USMC
LATIMER, Philip Elisha, SM2c, USNR
LAWE, William Clare, AM3c, USN
LAWHON, George Frank, ACMM, USN
LEIGHT, James Webster, S2c, USN
LEROY, John Smith, Jr., Radio elect., USN
LE VAN, Francis Burns, MM1c, USN
LEVAR, Frank, CWT, USNR
LEVY, Harold Walter, S2c, USN
LEWIS, John Earl, SK1c, USN
L'HEUREUZ, Edwin Eugene, MM1c, USN
LINDSAY, James E., PFC, USMC
LINDSEY, Lt. Cdr. Eugene Elbert, USN
LINDSEY, Harold William, S2c, USN
LITTLE, Lt. (jg) John Grubbs, III, USN
LITTLEFIELD, Lauren Evan, AMM2c, USN
LOCKLIN, Eugene Debb, Tech. Sgt., USMC
LOEHNBERG, Louis Melvin, WT1c, USN
LONG, Benjamin Franklin, CY, USN
LONG, Guy Edward, S2c, USN
LORENZ, Allen John, MM1c, USN
LOVE, Carl Robert, S2c, USN

LOVELACE, Lt. Cdr. Donald Alexander, USN
Low, Donald Banks, F1c, USN
LUCAS, 2nd Lt. John D., USMCR
LUKE, Vernon Thomas, MM1c, USNR
LUNDY, Harold Cheuvront, Jr., ARM1c, USN
LURVEY, Merle F., Platoon Sgt., USMC
LUTSCHAN, William Edward, Jr., Sgt., USMCR
LUZIER, Ernest Burton, MM2c, USN
LYNCH, Donald William, F1c, USN
LYON, Benjamin Malcolm, Jr., RM1c, USN
MacDONALD, Frederick Windthrope, SF3c, USN
MacDONALD, Sherman Price, 1st Sgt., USMC
MacLACHLAN, Robt. Wallace, RM1c, USN
MADDEN, Elwood K., Corp., USMC
MADDEN, Herbert Cecil, AS, USNR
MADDOX, Raymond Dudley, CEM, USN
MADOLE, 2nd Lt. Eugene P., USMCR
MADRID, Arthur John, S2c, USN
MADSEN, Paul, AMM1c, USN
MAFFEI, Amelio, ARM2c, USNR
MAHONEY, Joseph Francis, Platoon Sgt., USMC
MALECKI, Frank Edward, CY, USN
MALFANTE, Algeo Victor, SF2c, USN
MANLOVE, Arthur Cleon, Elect., USN.
MAPLE, Chester Ansel, SK2c, USN
MARABLE, Malroy Culpepper, WT2c, USN
MARCOTTE, Thomas Norman, CEM, USN
MARSH, Walter L., Jr., Pvt., USMCR
MARSHALL, Thomas Donald, S2c, USN
MARTIN, Dale Lewis, SC1c, USN
MARTIN, Frank Anthony, BM1c, USNR
MARTIN, James Orrwell, S2c, USN
MARTIN, Seeley Douglas, S2c, USN
MARTINEZ, Rudolph Machado, EM3c, USN
MASSEY, Lt. Cdr. Lance Edward, USN
MASTEL, Clyde Harold, S2c, USN
MASTERSON, Cleburne Earl Carl, PhM1c, USN
MAURER, Ens. William Edward, USNR
MAXWELL, Clyde, SF1c, USN
MAYBEE, George Frederick, RM2c, USNR
MAYER, Charles, CRM, USN
McALLEN, John Scott, S2c, USN
McCALL, Herbert Harper, CM, USN
McCOLLOM, Lawrence Jennings, MM2c, USN

McCONCHIE, James Carson, CCStd, USN
McCUTCHEON, Warren Harrell, S2c, USN
McFADDIN, Lawrence James, Jr., Y2c, USN
McFARLAND, William, QM3c, USN
McINTOSH, Harry George, S1c, USN
McKINNEY, Richard E., Platoon Sgt., USMC
MEDOW, Ray Eugene, S2c, USN
MELTON, Herbert Franklin, BM2c, USN
MERRELL, Lawrence Wesley, PFC, USMC
MEYER, Walter W., Corp., USMC
MICHAEL, Lt. Cdr. Charles O., USNR
MICHELSWIRTH, Anthony George, CEM, USN
MILBOURNE, Jesse Keith, AS, USN
MILLER, Forrest Newton, CEM, USN
MILLER, J. B. Delane, Cox., USN
MILLIMAN, Ens. Richard Diver, USNR
MILLS, Emery Oren, WT1c, USN
MITCHELL, Wallace Gregory, S1c, USN
MITWALSKY, Robert William, Sgt., USMC
MOLPUS, Richard Preston, CM, USN
MONTGOMERY, Robert Eugene, S2c, USN
MONTGOMERY, William Andrew, GM3c, USN
MOORE, Elijah Winston, MM1c, USN
MOORE, Harold Martin, F2c, USN
MOORE, Lt. Raymond Austin, USN
MOORMAN, Lee Russell, S2c, USN
MORAN, Arthur Patrick, CMM, USN
MORGAN, Henry Morris, S2c, USN
MORGAN, Wayne, S1c, USN
MORRIS, William Francis, F1c, USN
MORSE, Francis Jerome, BM1c, USN
MORTON, Seldon Edward, S2c, USN
MOULTON, Gordon Eddy, F1c, USN
MOULTON, J. Earl, TM1c, USN
MUGGY, Denzel Eddy, CCStd, USN
MUNCY, Claude, MM2c, USN
MURRAY, John Edward, BM1c, USNR
NATION, Israel Luther, ACMM, USN
NAUGLE, John Wesley, CRM, USN
NEIPP, Paul, S2c, USN
NELSON, Lawrence Adolphus, CTC, USN
NEVILLE, John Joseph, BM1c, USN
NICHOLS, Clifford LeRoy, TC1c, USN
NIDES, Thomas James, EM1c, USN
NIELSEN, Arnold Madsen, BM1c, USN
NIELSON, Hal Arnold, S2c, USN
NIGHTINGALE, Joe Raymond, S1c, USN
NOFTSGER, Ernest Howard, GM2c, USN
NORMAN, John Willis, QM3c, USN
NORRIS, Maj. Benjamin W., USMC
NORVELLE, Alwyn Berry, CSK, USN

Nunes, William Warren, S2c, USNR
Nye, Frank Erskine, S1c, USN
O'Connell, Melvin Donald, CEM, USN
Ogilvie, Ernest Ephrom, MM1c, USN
O'Gwin, Cecil Neil, AMM1c, USN
Oliver, Raymond Brown, S1c, USN
Orcutt, Robert Yale, BM2c, USN
Orr, Dwight Jerome, S1c, USN
Otterstetter, Carl William, S2c, USN
Overley, Lawrence Jack, FC2c, USN
Owen, John Edward, EM1c, USN
Owens, Arley Royce, GM3c, USN
Owens, Lt. James Charles, Jr., USN
Owsley, Warren Vanus, Pvt., USMC
Pace, Amos Paul, BM1c, USN
Paciga, Walter Joseph, S2c, USN
Paguirisgan, Sinforoso, OS2c, USN
Palmer, Calvin Harry, S2c, USN
Palmer, Joseph Ronald, SF3c, USN
Palmer, Wilfred Dewey, S2c, USN
Parker, Elmer Anthony, CSK, USN
Parkes, Harry Edward, BM1c, USN
Parks, Chester Lloyd, S1c, USN
Parmenter, Melvin Wayne, F2c, USN
Paroli, Peter John, Bkr3c, USN
Pavini, Bruno, S1c, USN
Pearson, Norman Cecil, S2c, USN
Peck, Eugene Edward, S2c, USN
Peery, Max Valdyne, S2c, USN
Pennington, Raymond, Pvt., USMC
Pepe, Stephen, WT1c, USN
Perdue, Charles Fred, SF1c, USN
Perry, Leo Edward, ACRM, USN
Peterson, Elroy Vernon, FC2c, USN
Peterson, Francis, GM2c, USN
Peterson, Oscar Verner, CWT, USN
Peterson, Roscoe Earl, S2c, USN
Pettit, Charles Ross, CRM, USN
Petway, Wiley James, B2c, USN
Phillips, John Wesson, CBM, USN
Pinkham, Arthur William, S1c, USN
Pitcher, Walter Giles, GM1c, USN
Platts, Frank Leroy, AS, USN
Poirier, Roger Phillippe, TC1c, USN
Polidori, Bennie John, EM1c, USN
Ponce, Julian, F3c, USN
Poole, Harry Ellington, SC1c, USN
Portillo, Damian Maraya, SC1c, USNR
Posey, Thomas Charles, MA3c, USNR
Post, Darrell Albert, CMM, USN
Powers, Roy Wallace, SF2c, USN
Quatrara, Anthony Dominic, B1c, USN
Raby, Edward Wesley, MA1c, USN
Radzinski, George Smith, MM2c, USN
Radzinski, Victor Frederick, MM2c, USN

Ramsey, Carl Raymond, GM2c, USN
Ramsey, Capt. Frederic H., USMC
Ramsey, Garry Wayne, AMM3c, USN
Rasmussen, Arthur Severin, CM1c, USN
Ratkovich, William, WT1c, USN
Ray, Don Edison, GM3c, USN
Ray, Harry Joseph, BM2c, USN
Raymond, Elza L., Sgt., USMC
Re, Frank Anthony, F2c, USN
Reed, James Buchanan, Jr., SK1c, USN
Reese, Alexander, WT2c, USN
Regan, Leo Basil, WT2c, USN
Register, Lt. Cdr. Paul James, USN
Rentz, Cdr. George Snavely, USN
Reynolds, William Leroy, CWT, USN
Rich, Benjamin Butler, F3c, USN
Richison, Fred Louis, GM3c, USN
Rickel, James Wilson, Jr., EM3c, USN
Rico, Guadalupe Augustine, S1c, USN
Riganti, Fred, SF3c, USN
Riggins, Gerald Herald, S1c, USN
Rinehart, Lt. (jg) Clark Franklin, USN
Roberts, McClellan Taylor, CPhM, USN
Roberts, Orren Augustus, AMM1c, USN
Robinson, Frederick Webb, CWT, USN
Robinson, Harold Thomas, S2c, USN
Robinson, James William, S2c, USN
Rogers, Cecil Otis, MM1c, USN
Romero, Newman, MM2c, USNR
Rose, Ernest Claude, SC1c, USN
Rose, Joseph Edmons, GM3c, USN
Routledge, Gerald William, S2c, USN
Rowell, Ens. Richard Merrill, USNR
Roy, Alfred, Pvt., USMC
Rozar, John Frank, WT2c, USN
Runckel, Robert Gleason, Bug1c, USN
Runyan, Garvyn Delno, CCStd, USN
Ruse, Charles Lee, Mus2c, USN
Russell, Robert, 1st Sgt., USMC
Sanderson, James Harvey, Mus2c, USN
Sandoval, 2nd Lt. William B., USMCR
Santos, Filomeno, OC2c, USN
Saravolatz, Joseph Milan, MM2c, USN
Sather, William Ford, PM1c, USN
Scheib, Robert R., Corp., USMCR
Schmitt, Henry Louis, MM2c, USN
Schneider, Robert Clark, Torp. 2c, USN
Schoonover, John Harry, PhM1c, USN
Schulze, Francis Benjamin, SF1c, USN
Schumacher, Stanley Joseph, CBM, USN
Schuman, Herman Lincoln, SK1c, USN
Schwarting, Herbert Charles, S1c, USN
Scott, Donald F., PFC, USMC

SCRUGGS, Jack Leo, Mus2c, USN
SEARS, Horance Thomas, CEM, USNR
SEDGWICK, John Szewczyk, EM1c, USN
SEID, Ens. Daniel, USNR
SESSIONS, Herman Maxwell, MM1c, USN
SEVIER, Charles Clifton, S1c, USN
SHAFER, William Kenneth, F2c, USN
SHARON, Lewis Purdie, F1c, USN
SHARP, Elmer, M1c, USN
SHELTON, Donald Leroy, F2c, USN
SHIVE, Gordon E., PFC, USMC
SHIVE, Malcolm Holman, RM3c, USNR
SHOOK, Willis Charlie, MM1c, USN
SHRIDER, Lt. (jg) Harold Demar, USN
SHROPSHIRE, Ens. William Bryan, Jr., USNR
SHULER, Joseph Clifton, AM2c, USN
SILVA, William Garfield, GM1c, USN
SILVA, William Howard, S2c, USN
SILVEIRA, Joaquin Vierra, Mach., USNR
SIMPSON, Frederick Jefferson, AMM1c, USN
SINDEL, Ens. Edwin Coleman, Jr., USNR
SKAGGS, Eugene Mitchell, SM1c, USN
SKIDMORE, Lt. (jg) Chester Hugh, II, USN
SLIFER, Martin Reuben, GM1c, USN
SMITH, Lt. (jg) Albert Joseph, USN
SMITH, Ens. Gerald Seckner, USNR
SMITH, Gordon Ellsworth, SK2c, USN
SMITH, Harry, S2c, USNR
SMITH, John Edward, S1c, USN
SMITH, John Howell, CEM, USN
SMITH, Leonard Ferdnay, M1c, USN
SMITH, Ens. Leonard Leroy, USNR
SMITH, Richard Charles, F1c, USN
SMITH, Robert Lavelle, BM2c, USN
SMITH, Rowland Hampton, Music, USN
SMITH, Walter Raymond, Jr., S2c, USN
SNELLINGS, Herman Lee, QM Clerk, USMC
SNYDER, William A., PFC, USMC
SOARES, Henry George, BM2c, USNR
SOENS, Harold Mathias, SC1c, USN
SPEICHER, Ernest Edward, Jr., EM2c, USN
SPOONER, Terry Heath, S2c, USN
SPRINGER, Charles Harold, S2c, USN
STAFFORD, Gordon William, S2c, USN
STAGG, Roy Joseph, SC3c, USN
STAMBAUGH, William Henry, ARM1c, USN
STANLEY, Colen Merkerson, MM1c, USN
STAUDT, Alfred Parker, F3c, USN

STEINHOFF, Lloyd Delroy, S1c, USN
STENMAN, LaVerne Pendrel, AS, USN
STEPHENS, Benjamin Robert, WT1c, USN
STEPHENS, Eugene Winston, CRM, USN
STEVENS, Theodore R., AMM2c, USN
STEVENSON, Ens. Burt Manning, Jr., USNR
STEWART, Donald Archie, S2c, USN
STEWART, Raymond, MM2c, USN
STEWART, Ralph William, Jr., PhM2c, USNR
STEWART, Thomas Ayers, SK3c, USN
STEWART, Thomas Lincoln, PFC, USMC
STOCKDALE, Ens. Lewis Stephens, USNR
STOCKSTILL, Lt. (jg) Eugene William, USN
STOCKTON, Louis Alton, S2c, USN
STOCKTON, Maurice E., Sgt., USMC
STORM, John Victor, S2c, USN
STORM, Laun Lee, Y1c, USN
STORER, Max Clifford, CRM, USN
STRINZ, Gerald Victor, F3c, USN
STUMPF, Bernard William, F1c, USN
SUMMERLIN, Bennie Richard, AM1c, USN
SUTTON, Clyde Westly, CCStd, USN
SWANSBERGER, 2nd Lt. Walter W., USMCR
SWANSON, Charles Harold, MM1c, USN
SWEENEY, Thomas F., Sgt. Maj., USMC
SWISHER, Charles Elijah, S1c, USN
SWORTFIGUER, Arthur Frank, S2c, USN
SYMONETTE, Henry, OC1c, USN
TAPIE, Edward Casamiro, MM2c, USN
TARG, John, CWT, USNR
TAYLOR, Aaron Gust, MA1c, USN
TAYLOR, Palmer Lee, MA1c, USN
TEELING, Charles Madison, CPrtr, USNR
TEER, Allen Ray, EM1c, USN
TEMTE, Robert, CSM, USNR
TEW, Douglas Holcomb, MM2c, USN
THAU, Willard Albert, MM1c, USN
THEILLER, Rudolph, S1c, USN
THEISE, Walter John, Field Cook, USMC
THEW, Richard Ridley, FC1c, USN
THOMAS, Vincent Duron, Cox., USN.
THOMPSON, Charles William, F1c, USN
THOMPSON, Leland Earl, S2c, USN
THOMPSON, Ralph William, F3c, USN
THOMPSON, Robert Gary, SC1c, USN
THOMPSON, Thurman, WT1c, USN
TIBBS, Ernie Ewart, CMM, USN
TIMEUS, Gerald, S2c, USNR
TINDALL, Lewis Frank, F1c, USNR
TISDALE, William Esley, CWT, USN
TOKRYMAN, Paul, Corp., USMC

Tomich, Peter, CWT, USN
Treanor, Frank Parnell, RM3c, USN
Trovato, Tom, S1c, USN
Turner, Walter Joseph, QM2c, USN
Valente, Richard Dominic, GM3c, USN
Van Atta, Garland Wade, MM1c, USN
Vanderkamp, Burton Louis, RM3c, USNR
Van Valkenburgh, Capt. Franklin, USN
Vass, Frank Imery, Jr., S2c, USN
Vaughan, William Frank, PhM2c, USN
Vernon, Walter, GM1c, USN
Vest, Jack Robert, S2c, USN
Vogt, Ens. John Henry Leon, Jr., USN
Vosti, Anthony August, GM3c, USN
Wagner, Mearl James, SC2c, USN
Waite, Everett Fred, MM2c, USN
Walker, Harry Earnest, SK1c, USN
Walpole, Eugene Anderson, S2c, USN
Walters, Clarence Arthur, S2c, USN
Walters, Ens. Clifford Raymond, USNR
Walton, Ivan Irwin, Cox., USN
Ward, Oliver, CMM, USN
Waterman, Andrew Kenneth, AMM1c, USN
Watson, Ens. John C., Jr., USNR
Watson, Miad Irving, S2c, USN
Weaver, Luther Dayton, S1c, USN
Weber, John Aloysius William, MM2c, USN
Weeden, Ens. Carl Alfred, USN
Weller, Ludwig Fredrick, CSK, USN
Wells, Harvey Anthony, SF2c, USN
Westerfield, Ivan Ayers, S1c, USN
Westlund, Fred Edwin, BM2c, USN
Wetherington, Thomas L., PFC, USMC
White, Lester John, GM2c, USN
Whitman, Lt. (jg) Robert Scott, Jr., USN
Whittington, Arthur B., PFC, USMC
Wiegand, Lloyd Paul, Mus2c, USN
Wilke, Ens. Jack Winton, USNR
Williams, Joseph Anthony, CBM, USN
Williamson, William Dean, RM2c, USN
Wilson, John James, S1c, USN
Wilson, Ens. John Woodrow, USNR
Wilson, Nelson Maynard, SC1c, USN
Winfield, Starring Brooks, RM3c, USNR
Winn, Easton Carl, MM1c, USN
Winters, Lt. Cdr. Robert Chalmers, USN
Wise, Joseph Hill, SM1c, USN
Witter, William Leonard, CPrtr, USN
Wojtkiewicz, Frank Peter, CMM, USN

Woodruff, David E., Corp., USMC
Woodside, Joe Lamont, SC1c, USN
Woodson, Lt. (jg) Jeff Davis, USN
Woodward, Ardenne Allen, MM2c, USN
Woody, Harlan Fred, S2c, USN
Wortham, John Layman, GM2c, USN
Wright, Johnalson E., Platoon Sgt., USMC
Wright, Malcolm Carlisle, CMM, USN
Young, Vivan Louis, WT1c, USNR
Yurko, Joseph John, WT1c, USN
Yzelman, Charles Ray, S1c, USN
Zampatti, Roger William, S1c, USNR
Zech, Daniel Myron, AMM3c, USN
Zuckerman, Abraham, PFC, USMC
Zvansky, Thomas, CSM, USNR

Wounded

Aldridge, Fred Aquilla, EM1c, USN
Allred, Donnell William, S2c, USN
Ambrosini, Leo Alfonso, MM2c, USN
Anderson, Oliver Fred, S2c, USN
Arthur, Robert O., S/Sgt., USMC
Ball, James Ray, SC3c, USN
Ballauf, Charles, ACMM, USN
Beckner, Raymond Isaac, CFC, USN
Boek, Archie Adolph, AMM3c, USN
Borghetti, Thomas, Jr., FC1c, USN
Brandt, David Samuel, S1c, USN
Brindell, Charles T., Gunner, USN.
Brown, Frank Addison, CWT, USN
Bubb, Maurice Rodger, S1c, USN
Burge, Earl Stewart, MM1c, USN
Burkett, Horace Springer, CEM, USN
Burnett, Joe Burney, Cox., USN
Card, Eugene T., Corp., USMCR
Carlin, Thomas Gerald, 1st Mus., USN
Carroll, Michael, WT1c, USN
Christy, Francis Venert, ACMM, USN
Ciepiewicz, John Charles, CGM, USN
Clark, Robert Harris, F1c, USN
Coffman, Harry Joseph, SC1c, USN
Collie, Winfrey, Jr., Acting Pay Clerk USN
Cossitt, Douglas Marvin, RM3c, USNR
Covert, Billy C., Pvt., USMC
Cranston, Edward Robert, Cox., USNR
Crawford, Claude C., Jr., Corp., USMC
Curtis, Ned Bigelow, PhM1c, USN
Dawson, George Dake, ACM, USN
Dick, Gene Roundy, HA1c, USN
Dietz, Harry Walter, CPhM, USN
Donahue, Richard Andrew, AS, USN
Dunn, James Edward, MM1c, USN
Fill, John, SC1c, USN
Fishell, Harvey Clyde, S2c, USN

FOSTER, James Park, Jr., S1c, USN
Fox, Henry Wesley, S1c, USN
FUCHS, William Robert, CBM, USN
FURTADO, Robert Louis, S2c, USN
GAINES, Robert Yantis, EM1c, USN
GAUNTT, Fred Forrest, Bkr2c, USN
GIDEON, John Edward, S2c, USN
GILLEN, Ens. Earle Clinton, USNR
GLADDEN, Chester Leroy, AS, USNR
GOGGINS, Cdr. William Bernard, USN
GRAHAM, James Robert, Jr., S2c, USN
GRANNELL, James Brown, Sgt., USMC
GRAY, Theodore Boyd, BM2c, USN
HALE, Willard, GM3c, USN
HAMM, Willie Irvin, Cox., USN
HARPER, Donald Egbert, S2c, USN
HARRISON, Glendon Cecil, AMM3c, USN
HAUK, George Lincoln, RM3c, USNR
HEICK, Albert James, F3c, USN
HEIN, Ens. Douglas, USN
HERMAN, Hugh Patrick, Jr., S1c, USN
HOHENSTEIN, Lt. (jg) Raymond Charles, USN
HOLDREN, Ellis Leo, S1c, USN
HUBBARD, Arthur George, RM1c, USN
HUNT, James E., Gunner, USMCR
HUNTER, Harold Leroy, MM2c, USN
HURRLE, Gwen Edison, AMM3c, USN
HUTTENBERG, Ens. Allen John, USNR
IRWIN, Oscar Ray, RM3c, USN
JOHNSON, Charles Alfred, SF2c, USN
JONES, Hubert Hayes, CWT, USN
JORDAN, Fred William, AS, USN
JUDY, Forrest Jack, S2c, USN
KAISER, Chester Roland, RM3c, USNR
KEMP, Ralph Lloyd, MM2c, USN
KENT, Howard Kankins, S2c, USN
KENWORTHY, Lyle Franklin, PhM1c, USN
KERSHNER, Ens. Arthur William, USN
KUHLOW, Frank Carl, BM1c, USN
LAMB, Edmund Wier, SC1c, USNR
LA VACK, Lloyd Frederic, MM1c, USN
LINNARTZ, Peter Paul John, CGM, USN
LINNARTZ, Robert Edward, GM3c, USN
LOONEY, Clyde Vergil, Cox., USN
MAHONEY, Timothy, Jr., MM2c, USN
MALRIN, Cecil Smedsvig, AMM2c, USN
MALTBY, LeRoy George, S1c, USN
MANNWEILER, Leslie Carl, FC2c, USN
MARDUENO, Robert Clements, S2c, USN
MARKS, Jack William, HA1c, USNR
MARSH, LaMoine Francis, S1c, USN
MAUDLIN, Gilbert Leroy, RM1c, USN
McBRIDE, James Frederick, SF1c, USN
McCORMICK, Raymond Edgar, F1c, USN

McDONALD, James Roderick, S2c, USN
McFEELY, Gordon R., PFC, USMCR
McNUTT, Benjamin Harrison, S1c, USN
MEADOWS, Lee Herbert, Jr., AS, USN
MILLER, Voyle, F2c, USN
MITCHELL, Ralph, Jr., RM3c, USN
MITSKY, Vincent Walter, S2c, USN
MOE, Norvil, Pvt., USMC
MOHLE, Ens. Robert Lieurance, USNR
MOORE, William Foster, Jr., F3c, USN
MOUTRAY, James Theodore, MM1c, USN
MYERS, James Loral, F1c, USN
NASH, James Joseph, ACMM, USN
NEWBERG, Walter George, AS, USN
NEWMAN, Jacob Lafayette, CTC, USN
NOCITA, Emilio Ralph, S1c, USN
NORTON, Ens. Robert S., Jr., USNR
OLEJARCZYK, Anthony Joseph, BM2c, USN
ORLET, David Jaffray, AS, USN
PADEN, John Aldred, MM2c, USN
PEDERSEN, Francis Neilsen, F3c, USN
POLK, Woodrow A., Sgt., USMC
PULLIAN, Lester Everette, BM2c, USN
RAIDY, James Martin, CEM, USN
RASCHBACHER, Ens. John L., USNR
REDDICK, Alfred Leroy, S2c, USN
RENKEN, Elmer, GM2c, USN
ROBBINS, Tommie Roland, S1c, USN
ROBINSON, Charlie Edward, BM2c, USN
ROHOW, Cdr. Fred Merten, (MC), USN
RUDIE, Oscar Magnus, MM2c, USN
SANDERS, William, AMM3c, USN
SCHLENDERING, 2nd Lt. Harold G., USMCR
SEAVER, Lt. (jg) Joseph H., USNR
SIERAD, Gustav, S1c, USNR
SIGMAN, James Michael, S2c, USN
SLATTENGREN, Carl Albert, F2c, USN
SMITH, DeWitt V., PFC, USMC
SMITH, Jay, Chief Boat., USN
SMITH, Richard Robert, AS, USN
STANEK, Douglas Arthur, S2c, USN
STAPH, William L., Marine Gunner, USMC
STOCKER, Robert Francis, F1c, USN
STRATTON, Stanley Cramer, HA2c, USN
SWIFT, Gilbert Robertson, RM3c, USNR
THOMPSON, Ens. Paul Vance, USN
TILLMAN, Rogers Lee, EM2c, USN
VAN KEUREN, Melvin Warren, S1c, USN
WALKER, William Edward, CMM, USNR
WATSON, Robert Nethery, S2c, USN
WAUGH, Robert W., Platoon Sgt., USMCR
WEEKS, John Cleland, AMM2c, USN

WELLS, Russell Glenn, SF2c, USN
WHALEY, Robert Elroy, EM2c, USN
WIEBE, Ernest, Jr., S2c, USN
YATES, Cecil Marshall, BM1c, USN
YOUNGBLOOD, Henry Roy, CM, USN
ZUEHLKE, Arthur Robert, WT1c, USN

Missing

ADAMS, Charles B., Pvt., USMCR
ADRIAENSEN, Joseph A., 1st Sgt., USMC
ALLEN, Henry Andrew, Jr., S2c, USN
ANDERSON, Herbert Edgar, Jr., Gunner, USN
ANTHONY, Arthur Lee, S1c, USN
ASDELL, Ens. John R., USNR
BAILEY, Lester William, S2c, USN
BARR, George Melvin, GM1c, USN
BARTLETT, David W., Corp., USMC
BARTLETT, George Francis, F1c, USN
BAUMKER, Robert Joseph, Boat., USN
BELLIS, Lewis John, AMM2c, USN
BENTLEY, Bryant Edwin, CSK, USN
BERGER, Leslie Leo, WT2c, USN
BERREY, Wright Jenning, Jr., F1c, USN
BIGGS, Clyde Hillis, Y1c, USN
BOEGER, Maurice August, WT2c, USN
BOOTH, Charles Williard, S1c, USN
BORIS, Alphonse, MM1c, USN
BOROWICZ, John Joseph, CEM, USN
BORREGO, Peter, WT1c, USN
BOSLEY, Kenneth Pershing, F2c, USN
BOWMAN, Byrl Gay, S2c, USN
BOYNTON, Dwight Eugene, S2c, USN
BRAINARD, John T., Marine Gunner, USMC
BRANUM, George Milton, MM1c, USN
BRAY, Lloyd Allen, SF1c, USN
BRAZZI, Gaston Silverio, MM2c, USN
BREITBACH, Anton George, SC1c, USN
BRIDGES, Carl Cecil, Jr., EM1c, USN
BRINKHURST, Clyde, Prtr3c, USN
BRISLIN, Charles Michael, Jr., RM1c, USN
BROILES, Benjamin Ralph, F2c, USN
BROOKS, Harold Russell, S2c, USN
BROWN, Ellis Richard, Torp.2c, USN
BROWN, Harold Francis, BM1c, USN
BURCHETT, Howard Hadley, Boat., USN
BURGE, Jack, S1c, USN
BURNETT, Sidney Addison, CRM, USN
BURRELL, Delbert Franklin, S2c, USN
BURRELL, Roy Bouton, Jr., S1c, USN
BUSHNELL, Edgar Wayne, CSK, USN
BUTLER, Lt. (jg) Charles Gleason, (MC), USN
BUTTS, Floyd Edwin, Mach., USN

BYRNE, Dan Joseph, WT1c, USN
CALVERT, Arthur Madison, S2c, USN
CARLSON, Clarence Edward, F1c, USN
CARNEY, George Roland, Cox., USN
CARTER, Fredrick Lester, Jr., QM3c, USN
CARTER, Gilbert Grant, S1c, USN
CASEY, Leonard Francis, MM2c, USN
CATON, Laverne Francis, SK3c, USN
CHITWOOD, Joe Capers, AMM1c, USN
COGGINS, Loyd Raymond, CPhM, USN
COLLIER, Walter Leon, PFC, USMC
COLLINS, Robert Emmet, S1c, USN
CONKLING, Ens. Robert Charles, USNR
CONRAD, William Henry, Cox., USN
COOLEY, Willie Spence, CGM, USN
COOPER, Harmon, CBM, USN
COPELAND, George Paul, RM1c, USN
CULLEY, Robert Ramsey, CEM, USN
CURTIS, Col. Donald, USMC
CZADO, Louis Joseph, Mach., USN
DAVIS, Stephen Clair, S1c, USN
DELONG, Lt. Edward Grover, USN
DEMOEN, Achiel Rene, CEM, USN
DE SHIELDS, William Martin, QM1c, USN
DEUSCHLE, Rudolph Harold, ACMM, USN
DEWALD, William Charles, AMM2c, USN
DEWES, Philip James, CPhM, USN
DEXTER, Robert Edwin, S1c, USN
DISNEY, Alfred Clyde, S1c, USN
DOBLER, Robert Joseph, QM1c, USN
DORRELL, Tony Rusher, MM1c, USN
DUNN, Wallace Peter, F1c, USN
DUPLER, Harley H., 1st Sgt., USMC
DURLER, Ogden John, CMM, USN
DUTTON, Archibald John, CBM, USN
DUVAL, Ivan Wheeler, F2c, USN
DYE, Ens. Harvey S., Jr., USNR
ELLIOTT, Alton Edward, CCStd, USN
ELLIOTT, Clarence Ferrit, CFC, USN
ELLIOTT, Floyd Francis, CWT, USN
ELLIS, William, MM1c, USN
EMLAW, James Edwin, B1c, USN
FAGUNDES, Harry F., PFC, USMC
FAIRCHILD, Clarence DeVere, Jr., MM1c, USN
FARNSWORTH, Thomas Wilkinson, S1c, USN
FERRARI, Arthur Philip, F1c, USN
FINNEY, Don Merle, Torp.1c, USN
FISHER, Lt. (jg) Allen Jack, Supply Corps, USN
FISHER, George Lewis, F1c, USN
FLEURY, Elmer George, F1c, USN

FLOWERS, Homer Lloyd, WT1c, USN
FREY, Lt. Nat Brownfield, USN
FULLER, Orlan Elwin, SM2c, USN
GEIKEN, Albert Henry, CRM, USN
GIAMBRUNO, Philip, SC2c, USN
GIESE, Arthur John, CY, USN
GILBERT, Robert James, TM3c, USN
GILHART, Bernard Anthony, F2c, USN
GILLET, Frank Aloysius, Radio elect., USN
GOFF, Ens. Douglas Lawrence, USNR
GOUSSE, Albert, S2c, USN
GOVERNALE, Anthony Lonnie, M1c, USN
GRANGER, Charles Howard, F1c, USN
HAIGH, Alvin Floyd, S1c, USN
HALLIDAY, Fred Earl, Jr., RM2c, USN
HANSON, Clarence J., PFC, USMC
HANSON, Hohlaus Hirtzel, RM3c, USN
HARMON, William D., PFC, USMC
HARNDEN, Robert Delno, Jr., EM1c, USN
HARRUFF, Arthur Edwin Albert, WT1c, USN
HART, William Lynn, WT2c, USN
HASSELBRINK, Harold Chris, EM1c, USN
HATFIELD, Clark Charles, S1c, USN
HAYES, Carl H., SM3c, USN
HAYES, Obie Dee, Jr., F3c, USN
HAYS, Lt. (jg) John Wythe, USN
HEINTZ, Jack, F1c, USN
HIGHFALL, Denzil Delaine, Cox., USN
HOAGLAND, James Murray, WT2c, USN
HODGE, Lt. Ernest Debbes, USN
HOEKSTRA, Edwin Wallace, HA1c, USN
HOLDER, Alden James, AMM1c, USN
HOUSTON, Dwight Aird, GM2c, USN
HOWARD, Jay M., Platoon Sgt., USMC
HOWARD, Col. Samuel L., USMC
HOWARD, Wilson, RM2c, USN
HUBBARD, William Beardon, S1c, USN
HULT, Sydney Eugene, S1c, USN
IMLAY, James Fred, S1c, USN
INGERSON, Clarence John, Gunner, USN
INGRAM, Ernest Dale, QM2c, USN
JACKSON, Charles R., Sgt. Maj., USMC
JEROME, Samuel Raymond, Torp. 2c, USN
JOHNSON, Douglas Roger, S2c, USN
JOHNSON, Simon Ray, S1c, USN
JONON, Claude William, Jr., AMM1c, USN
JONTZ, Jay Burdeen, Music, USN
KAMLER, Thomas James, S1c, USN
KEARNEY, Walter Robert, S2c, USN
KEELER, Floyd Chester, CEM, USN
KEENEY, Leon Don, MM2c, USN
KEERAN, Richard King, PhM1c, USN
KEIFER, Karl C., Pvt., USMCR
KELLEY, Floyd Thomas, PhM3c, USN

KERFOOT, Gerald Richard, EM2c, USN
KERICH, Thomas Leslie, F3c, USN
KERN, William Ernest, WT2c, USN
KIELTY, Martin Thomas, SC1c, USN
KING, David Lester, RM1c, USN
KING, John William, CMM, USN
KIRK, Robert Alexander, CMM, USN
KLEIN, Ralph Grant, Y3c, USN
KOEHLER, Leslie Warren, Torp.3c, USN
KOEPKEY, Fred Emanule, MM2c, USN
KOLLER, John Rudolph, Music, USN
KUNOLD, Richard Louis, CEM, USN
KVACH, Clarence Duane, RM3c, USN
LACOMBE, Lt. Joseph Leer, USN
LAMBERT, Homer, OC2c, USN
LANG, Richard Nicholas, CMM, USN
LANGDON, Van Victor, CSF, USN
LANN, Carl Jefferson, CBM, USN
LANTRIP, Lelon Howard, S1c, USN
LATTIN, Claude William, RM2c, USN
LAURIDSEN, Wilbur Christian, RM3c, USNR
LAWRENCE, James, MM2c, USN
LAYA, Jose, OS3c, USNR
LEDGERWOOD, Walter Raymond, MM2c, USN
LEE, Roy, S1c, USN
LEONARD, Leland Edward, CRM, USN
LEWIS, Joseph Leonard, CM3c, USN
LITTLEFIELD, Albert Dale, BM1c, USN
LOE, Orville Leonard, CEM, USN
LOGAN, Carl E., PFC, USMC
LOOMER, Ens. Vernon Frederick, USNR
LOVE, Edward L., Corp., USMC
LOWMAN, Capt. Kenneth Earle, (MC) USN
MACUMBER, Frank Leslie, CY, USN
MAHER, Lt. Francis Xavier, Jr., USN
MARTIN, Andrew Martin, SK3c, USN
MARTIN, John Theron, Y3c, USN
MARTINEZ, Alfred, S1c, USN
MARTINEZ, Evans Vernon, F1c, USN
MATZ, Harold T., PFC USMC
MAYNARD, James Louis, MM1c, USN
McCOOL, Felix J., Sgt., USMC
McCUTCHEON, Russell Deen, CMM, USN
McGEE, James Earl, QM2c, USN
McKINDSEY, Kenneth Blain, F3c, USN
McKINSTRY, John Hunt, S1c, USN
McMULLEN, Sidney A., Corp., USMC
McNEALY, Jack Gerald, MM1c, USN
MEKKELSON, Carol Oswald, CMM, USN
MEREDITH, Earl Jefferson, Asst. cook, USMC
MEYERS, Delmer V., Field music, USMC

MEYERS, Lt. Richard William, USN
MILLER, Edward Byron, F3c, USN
MILLER, James V., PFC, USMC
MILLETT, Weaver James, SM2c, USN
MINEAR, Richard J., Jr., PFC, USMC
MONROE, Elmo Paul, EM2c, USN
MORELAND, Ted, RM1c, USN
MORTON, Robert George, S2c, USN
MOUNT, Cecil Vernon, WT2c, USN
MOXHAM, Raymond F., PFC, USN
NETTER, Harold Nickolis, Chief torp., USN
NIX, Lt. Joshua James, USN
NOEL, Otis Frank, QM1c, USN
NOLATUBBY, Henry E., PFC, USMC
NOVAK, Antone, CRM, USN
NUNNELLEY, Robert Buddy, MM1c, USN
OED, John Joseph, MM2c, USN
OLSON, Oscar Albert, B1c, USN
O'NEAL, Joe Sonnier, CSF, USN
ORDUNG, Wyott Thomas, CQM, USN
OSBORNE, Robert Lannom, QM2c, USN
OVERCASH, Jack Blaine, S2c, USN
PARKER, Clyde Norman, BM2c, USN
PARKS, Harold George, CMM, USN
PARKS, James Delos, MM2c, USN
PATAYE, John Edward, S2c, USN
PATTON, Farrel Leon, CY, USN
PATTY, Lt. John Cockrell, Jr., USN
PECK, James Harvey, QM1c, USN
PECK, William George, MM1c, USN
PEDERSEN, Victor Sigward, EM1c, USN
PETERS, Charles Albion, FC1c, USN
PETERSON, Raymond Eugene, SK3c, USN
PETROFF, John, Jr., CBM, USN
PIERCE, Arthur Donald, MM1c, USN
PIGGOTT, Harold H., Corp., USMCR
PINKERMAN, William Edwin, CWT, USN
PLUMB, Ens. Ralph Peter, USNR
POLK, Farest Gerald, WT1c, USN
POULSEN, Hans Hansen, AMM2c, USN
POUND, Lt. Cdr. Harold Clay, USN
POWELL, Jack S., PFC, USMC
POZANAC, Charles John, RM1c, USN
PRENTICE, Jack Howard, Cox., USN
PROUTY, Walter Raymond, Chief torp., USN
PROUTY, William Dewey, S2c, USN
PROWS, James Walter, S1c, USN
RARDIN, Irvin Stanley, PFC, USMC
REBURN, Paul Alexander, EM2c, USN
REEVES, Arthur Joseph, S1c, USN
REH, Theodore John, RM1c, USN
REHNER, Robert Joseph, BM2c, USN
REICHERT, Theodore John, MM2c, USN
REISINGER, Robert Richard, S1c, USN

RICHARDSON, Ens. Illiff David, USNR
RIDDLE, Merrill B., PFC, USMC
ROACH, Harold Doyt, BM2c, USN
ROBE, Walter, WT1c, USN
ROBERTS, Cdr. David Wells, USN
ROBERTSON, Lt. (jg) John Mott, USNR
ROLF, Albert, SF3c, USN
ROOT, Lee Franklin, FC1c, USN
ROSS, Lt. Russell Roosevelt, USN
ROSSI, Daniel Armand, F2c, USN
ROUSH, Cleo Leroy, Y3c, USN
RYAN, David William, Chief Torp., USN
SANDERSON, George Henry, CQM, USN
SAUTER, Joseph Gregory, RM2c, USN
SAWYER, Archie Carroll, CMM, USN
SAWYER, Richard Calvin, S1c, USN
SCHMITT, Erwin Edward, CPhM, USN
SCHONBORG, Harold Carl, RM3c, USN
SCHRODER, John Henry, Jr., MM1c, USN
SCOTT, Bill, RM2c, USN
SEGO, Donald Wagner, MM1c, USN
SHARP, Cliff Alton, AMM3c, USN
SHAW, Herbert Dennis, CM1c, USN
SHEARER, Lloyd Oswald, CWT, USN
SHEEDY, Ralph Marcus, WT1c, USN
SHEEHAN, Robert John, S2c, USN
SHEFFIELD, Leroy Arthur, MM2c, USN
SHELTON, Van Lewis, AMM, USN
SHOUSE, Claude F., Pvt., USMC
SILER, Burdetter Basil, AMM2c, USN
SIMMONS, Tyrus Raymond, MM1c USN
SIMPSON, Clifford Emmett, QM3c, USN
SIVESIN, Arthur William, CMM, USN
SMART, Harry James, F1c, USN
SMITH, Chester Ballentyne, F1c, USN
SMITH, Chester Millard, SC1c, USN
SMITH, Edwin Jack, S2c USNR
SMITH, Elton Buck, CWT, USN
SMITH, Jack Leroy, WT2c, USN
SMITH, Lloyd Leslie, EM2c, USN
SMITH, Walton Quinby, MM2c, USN
SMITH, Warren H., PFC, USMC
SOLOMON, Bertram, S1c, USN
SOLOMON, L. W., SF3c, USN
SONIGA, Ambrocio, OC3c, USN
SORENSEN, Edwin Richard, EM2c, USN
SOULE, Lt. Cdr. Arthur W., USNR
SPOO, Henry Herbert, CWT, USN
STANDISH, Walter, Gunnery Sgt., USMC
STANTON, Joseph Oscar, GM3c, USN
STARR, Melvin Cecil, S1c, USN
STEEN, Ellwood Howard, CMM, USN
STEINMAN, William Burr, AMM1c, USN
STERLING, Cleo Clifford, MM2c, USN
STEWARD, Ens. Glen Spencer, USNR
STONER, Lowell Ross, SM1c, USN

STUMPFF, Darrold William, GM2c, USN
SULLIVAN, Thomas Joseph, SM1c, USN
SWEET, Harry George, RM1c, USN
TADLOCK, Malcolm Grayham, Jr., Prtr1c, USN
TAGLIERE, Lewis, S1c, USN
TALBOT, Charles James, S1c, USN
THAW, Henry Franklin, EM1c, USN
THOMAS, Harold R., RM1c, USN
THOMPSON, Robert Beyrl, Acting Pay Clerk, USN
TIMMONS, Orlando Emery, F1c, USN
TODD, Grover Earl, MM2c, USN
TOOHIG, Thomas D., Jr., Corp., USMC
TRAMMELL, James Borman, Cox., USN
TRAVER, Robert Nelson, Jr., S1c, USN
TRESKON, Stephen J., PFC, USMC
TUCKER, Robert Edward, MM2c, USN
UKENA, Jewell, Junior, S2c, USN
VAN SLYKE, Richard Merrill, F1c, USN
VISHNESKY, Edward John, Mach., USN
VITALE, Peter Joseph, S2c, USN
WADLEY, Chris Hoover, CCStd, USN
WALKER, Perry Appling, CRM, USN
WARREN, Irel James, S1c, USN
WEBBER, Harry W., Jr., PFC, USMC
WEGER, Stanley A., Pvt., USMC
WESTERFIELD, Donovan Harris, EM1c, USN
WEYL, Joe Warren, S2c, USN
WHEELER, Larkin Haywood, S2c, USN
WHIPPLE, Walter Fred, S2c, USN
WHITE, Leo, PFC, USMC
WHITE, Warren Clifton, MM2c, USN
WHITEFORD, Jack Edward, SM3c, USN
WICKHAM, Arthur Keith, CBM, USN
WILD, Lt. Phillip Grant, Jr., USN
WILKINSON, Henry E., PFC, USMC
WILLIAMS, Fred Clinton, MM2c, USN
WILLIAMS, Orville Burton, B1c, USN
WILLIAMS, Ted R., Corp., USMC
WILSON, Charles F., PFC, USMC
WILSON, Robert Frederick, S2c, USN
WINCHESTER, John Edwin, AMM2c, USN
WISE, Ray Haynon, Jr., S2c, USN
WOOD, Harry Joseph, MM1c, USN
WOOD, William Edwin, CM1c, USN
YATES, Henry Strickland, CMM, USN
ZELLER, William Lewis, Cox., USN
ZULL, Irwin L., Sgt., USMC

Prisoners of War

ACKLEY, Edwin M., Sgt., USMC
ADAMS, Jewett F., S/Sgt., USMC
ADAMS, Joseph John, BM2c, USN
ADAMS, William H., Field music, USMC

ALBERTAZZI, Dorman Vernon, PhM1c, USN
ALBRITTON, Amos Hermon, CWT, USN
ALLEN, Sherman L., PFC, USMC
ALLEN, Stanley G., PFC, USMC
ALVARADO, Baldwin C., Jr., Pvt., USMCR
AMES, Jack C., Pvt., USMC
AMIRANT, Raymond J., PFC, USMC
ANDERSEN, Holger Hans, CM1c, USN
ANDERSON, Albert A., PFC, USMC
ANDERSON, Lt. Col. Herman R., USMC
ANDERSON, John Brown Leslie, RM3c, USN
ANDERSON, Lt. Richard Kerfoot, USN
ANDERSSEN, Arnold, Corp., USMC
ARMSTRONG, Robert Lewis, Corp., USMC
ARNAUD, John Bertram, BM2c, USN
ARNOLD, Joseph Stephen, PhM1c, USN
ATWOOD, Laurence Maybank, PhM2c, USN
AUGUSTUS, Ralph Lloyd, EM1c, USN
AUTREY, Benjamin Franklin, Chief torp., USN
AVERILL, Bernard June, WT1c, USN
AVERY, Roy Elvin, HA1c, USN
BALEN, Louis, S1c, USN
BALLINGER, Richard Willis, PFC, USMC
BALTZLY, Lt. Cdr. Frederick, USN (Ret.)
BANGERT, Ronald Frederick, MM1c, USN
BARFIELD, Burke Hugh, CCStd, USN
BARNES, Carl Ellis, WT2c, USN
BARNES, Earl Harry, Corp., USMC
BARNES, James Edward, BM1c, USN
BARNES, William Sewell, AMM2c, USN
BARRICKLO, Lyle Bud, Bkr1c, USN
BEAUREGARD, Linwood L., PFC, USMC
BEECHER, Lt. Col. Curtis T., USMC
BENDER, George Frederick, S2c, USN
BENDER, Jack Eugene, MM1c, USN
BENNETT, Arthur King, PFC, USMC
BENSON, Arthur Wise, Bkr2c, USN
BERRY, Edward L., Corp., USMC
BERTELS, Alton Jewel, Sgt., USMC
BERTZ, Louis Stetson, PFC, USMC
BEVEL, Virgil Bill, Jr., Cox., USN
BICKNELL, Cdr. Walter Herbert, Supply Corps, USN
BIECHLIN, Louis Emil, Carp., USN
BIGELOW, Elwin Earl, Corp., USMC
BINGHAM, Cordell, B2c, USN
BIRD, Edwin Alvin, RM3c, USN
BIRD, James, SC3c, USN
BIRD, Leo Clarence, F1c, USN
BISHOP, Raymond Eugene, MM2c, USN
BJORK, Clarence L., Mstr. Tech. Sgt., USMC

BLANKENHORN, Harry Yeager, CSM, USN

BOGUE, Douglas W., Sgt., USMC

BOONE, Lt. Cdr. James Daniel, (MC), USN

BOOTS, Morris A., Pvt., USMC

BORTH, Harold Clarence, Marine Gunner, USMC

BOSCARINO, James Frank, Platoon Sgt., USMC

BOSCH, Ralph, SC1c, USN

BOWERS, Kenhard, QM2c, USNR

BOWERSOX, James Donald, BM1c, USN

BOWNE, Frank G., Corp., USMC

BOYD, Eugene Lorell, Chief Boat., USN

BRADSHAW, A. Z., Corp., USMC

BRAIN, Donald Carl, S2c, USN

BREWER, Ens. Norman Arthur, USNR

BREWSTER, Lt. (jg) Earl Ray, USNR

BRODERICK, Albert R., Sgt., USMC

BROOKE, Cdr. George Magruder, USN

BROUSSARD, Henry Maxie, CMM, USN

BROWN, Charles Milton, RM1c, USN

BROWN, James F., Pvt., USMC

BROWN, James Richard, Corp., USMC

BROWN, Roy Eugene, CRM, USN

BROWNE, Edward R., 1st Sgt., USMC

BRUUN, Othello Christian, Chief Pay Clerk, USN

BRYAN, Alton B., GM3c, USN

BUCHANAN, Gerald Earnest, PFC, USMC

BUELL, Earl Edward, WT2c, USN

BUNDY, John A., PFC, USMC

BURKE, John Joseph, F2c, USN

BURLAGE, George E., PFC, USMC

BURNS, 1st Lt., John A., USMC

BUSSELL, Norman E., Asst. cook, USMC

BYERS, Elmer Guy, Jr., Gunner, USN

CALANCHINI, Arthur James, PFC, USMC

CALDWELL, Richard Rossiter, PFC, USMC

CALDWELL, Robert Edward, S2c, USN

CALLAHAN, Lt. Cdr. Fort Hammond, USN

CAMPBELL, Fred Levi, Pay Clerk, USN

CARR, Gerald John, Mess Sgt., USMC

CARRILLO, Andrew James, Jr., QM1c, USN

CARSON, George R., Jr., PFC, USMC

CARY, Ralph James Y1c, USN

CASSELL, Robert Pershing, Torp.2c, USN

CASTRO, Manuel, S1c, USN

CATHER, Frederick Kirby, Jr., S1c, USN

CAVALLERO, Raymond Peter, EM3c, USN

CESSNA, Harry Junior, PFC, USMC

CHAMBERLAIN, Russell Delos, PhM3c, USN

CHAMBLISS, Jesse Royce, PhM3c, USN

CHAPMAN, Henry Herbert Walter, PFC, USMC

CHASE, Chester Oliver, EM1c, USN

CHAVES, Ernest Thomas, AMM1c, USN

CHERRY, Ralph W., Platoon Sgt., USMC

CHRISTIE, Martin S., Corp., USMC

CILULLA, Michael Angelo, SC3c, USN

CLACK, Roy Lee, EM3c, USN

CLARK, Edgar Rohr, Prtr2c, USN

CLARK, Ernest Emil, CRM, USNR

CLARK, 1st Lt. Golland L., Jr., USMC

CLARK, Russell Paxton, Sgt., USMC

CLOUGH, Harold Elmer Guy, CRM, USN

COBB, George Edgar, SC1c, USN

COHEN, Ray E., Corp., USMC

COLBY, Harold Gould, Pvt., USMC

COLE, James Hector, PFC, USMC

COLLMAN, James Walton, MM2c, USN

COMBS, Claude Dewitt, CBM, USN

COMMANDER, Eugene C., Mstr. Tech. Sgt., USMC

CONDON, Clifford Kain, Pharm., USN

CONNELL, Lt. Cdr. James Aloysius, Dental Corps, USN

COOK, Collins White, PhM3c, USN

COOPER, Clarence Gilbert, Jr., Corp., USMC

COOPER, Robert Earl, PFC, USMC

CORBIN, Leonard Roy, Corp., USMC

COSTA, Anthony, PFC, USMC

COTTON, Ens. Percy MacDonald, USNR

COVERT, Phillip Gilbert, Pvt., USMC

CRAFTS, Glen Francis, Corp., USMC

CRAWFORD, Robert Clark, PhM3c, USN

CREWS, Jeremiah Valentine, Pharm., USN

CRISPI, Eugene Carl, Y3c, USN

CRONIN, Thomas James, PFC, USMC

CROWDER, Harvey Burnham, RM2c, USN

CUNNINGHAM, Cdr. Winfield Scott, USN

CURTIS, Louis N., Pvt., USMC

CYR, Clifford Charles, Torp. 1c, USN

DAHLGREN, Jack Adolf, CRM, USN

DALE, Dewey Nelson, PFC, USMC

DAMON, Walter Leroy, Mess Sgt., USMC

DANIEL, Horace Holden, CY, USN

DANIELS, Reginald Ernest, SK1c, USN

DANIELS, Robert Emmet, S1c, USN

DAVIDSON, Arthur C., Corp., USMC

DAVIS, Lt. Cdr. Frank Alfred, USNR

DAVIS, Lt. (jg) James Edward, Chaplain Corps, USN

DAVIS, Lt. James Robert, CEC, USN

Davis, John Earl, Chief torp., USN
Davis, Robert Josephus, ACMM, USN
Day, Robert, F1c, USN
Decker, James Ralph, CPhM, USN
Dehaan, Harmen, Tech. Sgt., USMC
De La Hunt, Remes E., Gunnery Sgt., USMC
Demanio, Joseph Jack, RM3c, USN
Dennis, Francis Henry, Torp. 2c, USN
Desaulniers, Armand Claude, PFC, USMC
Dial, Lt. Nathaniel Minter, USN
Dieball, Charlie W., PFC, USMC
Dietrich, Clyde Chalmer, CEM, USN
Dietz, Herman Godfrey, Jr., F1c, USN
Dillard, Everett Robert Love, Chief torp., USNR
Dilley, Frank David, CRM, USNR
Dimond, Clark Whiting, Jr., QM1c, USN
Dixon, John F., Sgt., USMC
Dobler, Herbert Eugene, Mach., USN
Dobson, Roy Alvin, Sgt., USMC
Dodge, Bernard Angelo, PFC, USMC
Dodson, Earl Caleb, Field cook, USMC
Doherty, John Albert, MM2c, USN
Doke, Cecil Emmett, AS, USN
Dreasher, Charles Earl, Corp., USMC
Drown, Jearuld Jeston, MM1c, USN
Dubois, William L., Pay Clerk, USMC
Duggan, Edward J., PFC, USMC
Dunlap, Wilson Willard, HA1c, USN
Dunlavy, Harry Craft, Field music, USMC
Dunn, Garth Grafton, Jr., PFC, USMC
Dutro, Harold William, F2c, USN
Easton, Chester J., Pvt., USMC
Eby, Richard L., PFC, USMC
Eeccles, Raymond Erhard Wilson, Sgt., USMC
Eckstein, Charles Lloyd, Sgt., USMC
Edwards, Willie, PFC, USMC
Egelston, Douglas Wayne, EM2c, USN
Eggers, Robert, Junior, Pvt., USMC
Ehrhart, Robert William, Pvt., USMCR
Elliott, Bruce Gordon, S1c, USN
Ellis, Frank Dopson, CWT, USN
Elvestad, Henry Alfred, S/Sgt., USMC
Engeset, Lt. Knut, USN
English, Irvin Frank, Gunner, USN
English, Merle Lee, MM2c, USN
Eppley, Lt. (jg) James Edward, (MC), USN
Erdman, Joseph James, RM1c, USN
Espy, Lt. (jg) Cecil Jefferson, Jr., CEC, USN

Erickson, Lt. Cdr. Hjalmar August, USNR
Evans, Everett Ludington, CRM, USN
Evans, Glenn G., PFC, USMC
Fansher, James Reginald, EM1c, USN
Fariss, Luther Albert, CY, USN
Farkas, Milton, SK2c, USN
Faulkner, Stuart Thomas, RM2c, USN
Feilzer, Frederick William, WT1c, USN
Feliz, Jack Martin, MM1c, USN
Fellom, James B., PFC, USMC
Finken, William Herman, PFC, USMC
Finley, Lloyd Benjamin, PFC, USMC
Finn, Lt. (jg) Charles Reuben, USNR
Fish, Jack Erwin, PFC, USMC
Fisher, Lt. Douglas Robin, USNR
Flagg, Morris Alton, QM2c, USN
Foley, Joseph Albert, MM1c, USN
Foss, Clarence Stewart, F3c, USN
Fowler, Charles Peter, Jr., F2c, USN
Fox, Norman Lee, RM1c, USN
France, Kenneth Carl, MM2c, USN
Francis, George, Corp., USMC
Franzen, Roy Oscar, S1c, USN
French, Ens. Paul Wadhams, USNR
Freuler, Capt. Herbert Caspar, USMC
Frontis, Irving, CPhM, USN
Fuerst, Morris Vernon, Sgt., USMC
Fuller, Bert Carl, CRM, USN
Fulton, James Wesley, S/Sgt., USMC
Fulton, Judson Paul, PhM3c, USN
Gabler, Albert, Jr., PFC, USMC
Gagnon, Augustin Raoul, MM1c, USN
Gahan, Sidney Vernon, Prtr2c, USN
Gaines, Lt. Cdr. Oliver Wallace, USN
Galbavy, Theodore John, CM2c, USN
Garwick, Lt. Warren Arthur, USNR
Gayler, Robert William, Pvt., USMC
Geisman, Capt. Willis Taubert, USMCR
Ghuzman, Louis, PFC, USMC
Giaccani, Floyd Rego, Bkr2c, USN
Gibson, Wallace Elvie, RM2c, USN
Gibson, William Johnithan, MM2c, USN
Giffin, Levis Edgar, Mstr. Tech. Sgt., USMC
Giglio, Charles Salvatore, CM3c, USN
Gilbert, Richard Henry, PFC, USMC
Gilmore, Orville Earl, PFC, USMC
Glass, William Henry, Mach., USN
Goldstein, Harry, PFC, USMC
Golich, George C., PFC, USMC
Gomez, Frank, Cox., USN
Gooding, George Brewer, Mach., USN
Gordon, Carl Burke, PhM2c, USN
Gorski, Ens. Alexander Alfred, USNR
Graf, Lt. Cdr. Paul Mason, USN

GRANT, Willard Virgil, Chief Torp., USNR
GREY, James Edward, Pay Clerk, USN
GRIFFIN, Earl Dennis, Jr., PFC, USMC
GROOM, Percy Wilmet, Jr., MM1c, USN
GUERRA, Domingo, WT1c, USNR
GUIRAUD, Jean Auguste, PFC, USMC
GUIREY, Ernest Lincoln, SF1c, USN
GULLICKSON, Oscar Theodore, CEM, USN
GUTIEREZ, Anthony Aralio, EM1c, USN
HALLMAN, Leonard E., RM1c, USN
HALLMARK, Kenneth Lee, PFC, USMC
HAMAS, John, Marine Gunner, USMC
HAMILTON, Claude Amos, S1c, USN
HAMILTON, Lt. Col. George D., USMC
HAMILTON, William John, Tech. Sgt., USMC
HAMMETT, Orion Alexander, Boat., USN
HANSEN, Kenneth Russell, PFC, USMC
HANSEN, Richard Cleveland, SF3c, USN
HANSON, Clifford Austin, Pay Clerk, USN
HAPPY, Walter Evans, Jr., F2c, USN
HARMAN, Leroy, Tech. Sgt., USMC
HARRALSON, Richard Aynard, RM1c, USN
HARRINGTON, Mary Rose, NC, USN
HARRIS, Adrian Forrest, Corp., USMC
HARRIS, Lanson Harold, AMM1c, USN
HARRISON, Lt. Cdr. George Gustave, USNR
HARTSELL, Earl Tasker, CEM, USN
HARVESTON, 'J. Harold, Ptr2c, USN
HARVEY, Luis Worden, CEM, USN
HASLETT, John Charles, Pvt., USMC
HASSLER, Earl Augustus, Corp., USMC
HASTINGS, Edward Warren, CPhM, USN
HEATLEY, Charles D., Jr., Pvt., USMC
HEDE, Lt. Cdr. Adolph, USN
HEDMARK, Earl Orlo, Corp., USMC
HEIN, Ens. Herbert Ross, Jr., USNR
HENDRICKS, Edward Charles, CRM, USN
HENDERSON, Ralph L., Jr., PFC, USMC
HENKE, William Leonard, S1c, USN
HENSLEY, Howard Grant, PFC, USMC
HERNANDEZ, Pedro Rodriguez, Pvt., USMC
HERNDON, Donald Whitehead, MM1c, USN
HESSON, James Frank, AMM1c, USN
HESTER, Capt. James Raymond, USMC
HIGLEY, George Roswell, S2c, USN
HINKLE, Robert Moore, Pvt., USMC
HILDRETH, Lester James, Jr., S2c, USN
HILTON, Lt. (jg) Hart Dale, USN
HIPPLER, Ross Eldon, PM2c, USN

HITTLE, Robert Glen, SK3c, USN
HOGG, Forrest Glenn, RM1c, USN
HOGUE, Dallas Eliga, MM1c, USN
HOLMES, Jesse Godfrey, CMM, USN
HOLTMAN, Louis Forrest, Sgt., USMC
HOOKUM, Francis Robert, CY, USN
HOOPER, Harold Everett, RM1c, USN
HORN, William Ellery, PFC, USMC
HORNING, Ferdinand Warner, QM2c, USN
HOUSCHILDT, Frank Henry, PFC, USMC
HOUSE, William Charles, Aer1c, USN
HOWE, Edward H., Pvt., USMC
HOYT, Leroy Leander, Gunner, USN
HUBLEY, George Gaston, PFC, USMC
HUFFMAN, James Walter, Cox., USN
HUGHES, Albert Neal, Torp. 1c, USN
HUGHES, Lawrence Thomas, MM2c, USN
HUNT, Ens. Wylie Mallory, USNR
HUNTER, William Albert, Y1c, USN
HUTCHISON, William Adolphus, Mach., USN
JACKSON, Frederick L., PFC, USMC
JACKSON, Harry William, CRM, USN
JACKSON, Wilbur Joseph, CEM, USN
JANES, Howard A., Y1c, USN
JELINSKI, Alfred Valentine, CMM, USN
JENKINS, Alvin, Radio Elect., USN
JENKINS, 1st Lt. Sidney Ford, USMC
JENSEN, Maj. Owen Ernest, USMCR
JESSE, John Henry, PFC, USMC
JESSUP, John Joseph, PFC, USMC
JOHNSON, Edward Eugene, S2c, USN
JOHNSON, Edwin Leroy, MM1c, USN
JOHNSON, Ellis J., Tech. Sgt., USMC
JOHNSON, Elmer R., PFC, USMC
JOHNSON, Lt. Harlan Thode, USN
JOHNSON, Irving Erick, MM2c, USN
JONES, Alex N., Chief cook, USMC
JONES, Leon Gilbert, Sgt., USMC
JONES, Roy Dillard, PhM1c, USN
JONES, William Beecher, S2c, USN
JUDY, Mark Chesley, Mach., USN
KAIL, Maj. Charles William, USMC
KANAE, John Edward, S1c, USN
KANIG, John F., Corp., USMC
KASH, Edward, Corp., USMC
KEECH, Richard Eugene, PFC, USMC
KEENE, Cdr. Campbell, USN
KELLY, John B., 1st Sgt., USMC
KENNARD, Richard Frank, MM2c, USN
KENNEDY, Walter T., S/Sgt., USMC
KERBOW, Harry Jack, CPhM, USN
KERR, William A., Corp., USMC
KIDDER, Francis Richard, M1c, USN
KIRKLAND, Jack R., PFC, USMC

KIRKPATRICK, Bill Howard, RM3c, USN
KLINE, Lt. Cdr. Edward Franklin, (MC), USN
KLEPONIS, Vincent, QM, Sgt., USMC
KOVIAK, Howard William, CMM, USN
KUBETH, Joseph, Pvt., USMC
KUCHTA, Joseph George, SM1c, USN
KUHLMAN, Edward William, PFC, USMC
KUNDERT, Emanuel, AM1c, USN
LA CHAPPA, John Emilio, PFC, USMC
LADE, Lt. Cdr. Charles Grant, USNR
LAFFERTY, John Weldon, MM2c, USN
LA FLEUR, George Noel, PFC, USMC
LA FRANCE, Earl Albert, F3c, USN
LA HEIST, Vernon Gordon, MM1c, USN
LANE, Arthur Verlie, Ptr1c, USNR
LANE, Lloyd George, PFC, USMC
LANE, Robert Bruce, CBM, USN
LANNING, John Riley, PhM1c, USN
LATHAM, John Pershing, Pvt., USMC
LAZCANO, Arthur William, SK1c, USN
LEBER, Hal Taylor, PFC, USMC
LECOMTE, Lt. Charles Frederick, (MC), USN
LEE, Allen William, MM1c, USN
LEE, Charles Raymond, PFC, USMC
LEE, Jesse Earl, Boat., USN
LEHMAN, Paul Clifford, Y2c, USN
LEININGER, Jack, WT1c, USN
LEON, Antonio, Chief cook, USMC
LEWIS, Claude Raymond, PFC, USMC
LIGHT, James Dawson, Chief torp., USN
LINDSEY, George Giles, Corp., USMC
LINN, Frank King, Bandmaster, USN
LIPPINCOTT, Lt. Joseph Reading, USNR
LITTIG, Lt. John Cassell, USNR
LOCARNINI, Peter Renaldo, S1c, USN
LOCHBIHLER, Edward, ACCM, USN
LOFTIN, Clarence Albert, Pvt., USMC
LOVE, Wilbur Everett, SC2c, USN
LOWE, Lt. Mason Richard, USNR
LUDLOW, Charles Crittenden, PFC, USMC
LUFKIN, Sewell Robert, Corp., USMC
LUNDBERT, Harold Tenney, WT2c, USN
LUTZ, Frederick C., Pvt., USMC
LYLE, Wanger Dewitt, AMM1c, USN
LYON, Otto James, S1c, USN
MACK, Alvin Jay, PFC, USMC
MACNULTY, Lt. Col. William Kirk, USMC
MAGEE, Lt. (jg) Thomas 3rd, USNR
MALICK, Sam Rashid, Jr., RM3c, USN
MALONE, Clifford Bernard, PhM3c, USN
MANISTA, Anton, CGM, USN
MARECHAL, Robert BM1c, USN

MARSHALL, William Elmer, Gunnery Sgt., USMC
MARTYN, Donald Joseph, Pvt., USMC
MASELLI, Leo J., PFC, USMC
MASELSKIS, Frank William, Corp., USMC
MASSINGILL, Harvey Lee, CQM, USN
MATHIESEN, Maj. Andrew J., USMC
MATTHEWS, Raymond Leon, PFC, USMC
MAY, Earl Vincent, Mach., USN
MAYBERRY, Richard Henry, PhM2c, USN
MAYHEW, Richard Coe, Y3c, USN
MAYNARD, Sherman Daniel, Corp., USMC
MCCALL, James Franklin, F1c, USN
MCCLARY, Carl Rollo, PFC, USMC
MCCOLLUM, Thomas Donahue, Pvt., USMC
MCCORD, George W., PFC, USMC
MCCOY, Mas M., CY, USN
MCCOY, Lt. Cdr. Melvyn Harvey, USN
MCCOY, William Hardy, S2c, USN
MCCUNE, Don Lee, RM2c, USN
MCCUSKER, Chester F., PFC, USMC
MCDOUGALL, Donald Bruce, SC1c, USN
MCGRATH, Ens. James Merrill, USNR
MCMAKIN, Capt. Benjamin Lee, USMC
MCMILLIN, Capt. George Johnson, USN
MCMURRY, Cloyd Carter, Sgt., USMC
MCQUILLING, Robert Edgar, Corp., USMC
MCREYNOLDS, Wendell Walter, SK2c, USN
MEEK, Sidney Warren, AMM3c, USN
MEIGS, Maj. Carl Warren, USMC
MELETIS, Paul John, PFC, USMC
MELLOW, Ens. Hugh Robert, USNR
MELOTT, Edward Lewis, EM2c, USN
MERCURIO, John, Gunnery Sgt., USMC
METCALF, Ens. John Coughlin, USNR
MEYERS, Adolph Wessel, CPhM, USN
MIDDLETON, Edward Henry, Sgt., USMC
MILET, John Donald, Corp., USMC
MILLER, Donald Wayne, CM, USN
MILLER, Ens. George Henry, USNR
MILLER, Jack Z., PFC, USMC
MILLER, Robert Carl, RM1c, USN
MILLER, Wayne Kenneth, 1st Sgt., USMC
MOFFETT, Kenneth Preston, PhM2c, USN
MOMBERG, Arnold William, CY, USN
MONNIE, Joseph Fred, F2c, USN
MONOOGAN, Weston H., PFC, USMC
MONROE, Robert Hayes, CMM, USN
MONTGOMERY, Leland Holzhauer, PFC, USMC
MOORE, Carl, Jr., AS, USN
MOOTE, Lt. Leslie Elmer, USNR

MORAN, James Patrick, PFC, USMC
MORENO, Alfonso Joseph, Field Mus. 1c, USMC
MORGAN, Capt. Glenn Dean, USMC
MOSS, Wynn Thomas, Jr., Pvt. USMC
MOSTOWSKI, Paul Arthur, CY, USN
MOURAL, James, Jr., AS, USN
MULLIS, Fred William, SM1c, USN
MURDOCK, Austin Matthew, WT1c, USN
MURPHY, William, SM1c, USNR
MUSSELWHITE, Otis Warren, RM1c, USN
MYERS, Hugh Hadley, CRM, USN
MYERS, Malvern R., PFC, USMC
NAHAS, Richard, PFC, USMC
NATIONS, Johnie Washington, CGM, USN
NELSON, George B., PFC, USMC
NESTLE, Lt. (jg) Leahmon Beecher, USNR
NEWSOM, Robert S., PFC, USMC
NEWTON, Robert Alysious, Corp., USMC
NICHOLS, Glenn Edward, Corp., USMC
NICHOLSON, Bruce, PhM, USN
NICKEL, Henry, BM1c, USN
NOLAN, Emmett F., Mess Sgt., USMC
NORDELL, Robert Lorenzo, QM3c, USN
NORDYKE, Curtis Alvin, RM3c, USN
NORRIS, Charles Douglas, PFC, USMC
NOYES, Glen Vernon, PFC, USMC
NUTTER, Capt. Hugh R., USMC
OLEN, Leo James, RM1c, USN
OLIVER, Melville Louis, MM2c, USN
OLIVER, William Melburn, Jr., S1c, USN
OSBORNE, Howard Robinson, Sgt., USMC
O'TOOLE, Edward Morris, PFC, USMC
OTTEN, Kenneth Herman, CQM, USN
OTTO, Leon John, Gunner, USN
OVERLEY, Clyde Hayes, PhM2c, USN
PACE, Harvey Lecota, Jr., AMM3c, USN
PAGET, Richard Edward, S1c, USN
PAIGE, Eldene E., NC, USN
PAREDES, Rudolph Alvin, AOM2c, USN
PARKS, Edgar G., PFC, USMC
PARKS, Frank James, Pvt., USMC
PARKS, Harold Pontius, Boat., USN
PARRISH, Albert Henry, BM1c, USN
PARRISH, Francis Marion, BM2c, USN
PASINI, John Dymond, GM1c, USN
PATTERSON, Billy Leroy, Sgt., USMC
PATTERSON, Rae, CWT, USN
PAUL, Archie T., PFC, USMC
PAULSEN, Frederick G., Corp., USMC
PEART, Cecil Jesse, PhM2c, USN
PEDIGO, Jess Leroy, PFC, USMC
PERMENTER, Donald Oscar, PhM3c, USN
PERRY, William Bridgeman, Y1c, USN

PETERSON, Harold Albert, Pvt., USMCR
PHILLIPS, Edward Walter, MM1c, USN
PICKERRELL, Paul Vernon, S1c, USN
PIERCE, Carlton Earl, ACMM, USN
PIKE, Donovan S., PFC, USMC
PINKHAM, Lucius Shepherd, MM1c, USN
PINTO, Harry William, Platoon Sgt., USMC
PIPPI, Louis, PFC, USMC
PITCHFORD, Robert William, CMM, USNR
PITZEL, Daniel John, Sgt., USMCR
PLANT, Ens. William Hendry, USNR
PODRIES, Anthony Joseph, MM1c, USN
POHLMAN, Lt. (jg) Max Edward, USNR
POLITO, Leon Anthony, Pvt., USMC
POLLARD, Lt. Eric George Frederick, Dental Corps, USN
POTTER, Frank Jay, EM2c, USN
POWERS, Theodore Howard, F2c, USN
PRATT, Robert Merritt, PFC, USMC
PRATTE, Ralph, PFC, USMC
PRICE, Theodore J., Jr., PFC, USMC
PUTNAM, Maj. Paul Albert, USMC
RAFALOVICH, Daniel Spiro, S1c, USN
RAMSEY, Marvin Clyde, PFC, USMC
RAUHOF, Jackson Price, Drum Maj., USMC
RAY, John Patrick, WT1c, USN
REARDON, Joseph J., QM Clerk, USMC
REIFSCHNEIDER, Wilmer James, Corp., USMC
REITER, William Lloyd, F2c, USN
REMME, Orville Dean, S1c, USN
REYES, Donald B., PFC, USMC
RICE, John Hill, Pay Clerk, USMC
RICE, William Thomas, Chief torp., USN
RICHARDS, David G., PFC, USMC
RICHARDS, Hugh Nelson, PFC, USMC
RITTER, Jack L., Corp., USMC
RIVERA, Anthony S., PFC, USMC
ROACH, Homer Eugene, Cox., USN
ROBERTS, Capt. Lyle Jay, (MC), USN
ROBERTS, Morton Edmun, CQM, USN
ROEPKE, Fred Conrad, CPhM, USN
ROGERS, Lt. (jg) Leon William, USN
ROMAN, Oldrich Bohumil, PFC, USMC
ROSE, Charles Ancill, CSM, USN
ROSS, Howard Defracca, PFC, USMC
ROSS, Robert Arnold, Corp., USMC
ROUTT, Melvin Leland, F2c, USN
RUEL, Henri, MM2c, USN
RUNCK, John Frederick, Sgt., USMC
RYAN, Robert F., S/Sgt., USMC
SAALFIELD, Herbert Albert, Jr., S2c, USN
SADO, John Eugene, Corp., USMC

SAGER, William Henry, Aer1c, USN

SALM, Alma Ernest, Chief Pay Clerk, USN

SANDERS, Clifton Cleo, PFC, USMC

SANDERS, Philip Earl, CBM, USN

SAVAGE, William Otto, SC1c, USN

SAWYER, Leslie Duane, Sgt., USMC

SCHNABEL, Charles William, CPhM, USN

SCHRADER, Arthur Henry, PhM3c, USN

SCHWARTZ, Lt. (jg) Jack William, USNR

SCHWEIZER, Earl Godfrey, Radio elect., USN

SEEGER, Harold Aloysius, PFC, USMC

SEVERTSON, Luther Donald, MM2c, USN

SHANE, George Joseph, Sgt. USMC

SHAUL, Emmitt Wane, Corp., USMC

SHIMMEL, Eugene R., Sgt. USMC

SHIRE, Norman Oliver, Pvt., USMC

SHOOK, James Henry, Jr., WT2c, USN

SHUGART, Eugene Weslie, Platoon Sgt., USMC

SIEGEL, Charles, 1st Sgt., USMC

SIGMAN, Carter Enloe, CCStd, USN

SILLIPHANT, Lt. Cdr. William Merrill, (MC), USN

SIMMERS, James Thomas, PFC, USMC

SIMO, Marino Joseph, PFC, USMC

SKAGGS, Owen N., Pvt., USMC

SKIVER, Russell Elwood, CM1c, USN

SKWIRALSKI, Frank, 1st Sgt., USMC

SLANE, Lt. (jg) Charles Littleton, USNR

SMALL, Vernon McCoy, CMM, USN

SMALLING, Hollis, PFC, USMC

SMALLWOOD, Thomas Edward, SK2c, USN

SMITH, Lt. Cdr. Carey Miller, (MC), USN

SMITH, Sassius Edward, AS, USN

SMITH, Frank Eugene, SC3c, USN

SMITH, Frederic Ferguson, RM1c, USN

SMITH, George, Platoon Sgt., USMC

SMITH, Mack, PFC, USMC

SMITH, Newell Whitney, Jr., RM1c, USN

SMITH, Raymond Eldon, S/Sgt., USMC

SMITH, Walter Clifford, Mach., USN

SMITH, William A., Sgt., USMC

SMITH, William Porter, QM, Sgt., USMC

SOUZA, Lawrence McNear, Pvt., USMC

SPARKS, Wainard Hoover, SK1c, USN

SPECHT, Eugene Leonard, PFC, USMC

SPICER, Lt. Col. Donald, USMC

SPRIGGS, Lt. Cdr. Morris Homer, USN (Ret)

STALCUP, Lewis Joseph, QM2c, USN

STALKER, Leo Hazelton, Jr., Pvt., USMC

STANBAUGH, William Allen, CY, USN

STAMP, Loren Elmer, PhM2c, USN

STANDLEA, William Dale, Pvt., USMC

STARR, Capt. Marvin Tipton, USMC

STEMMER, Frank Herman, CMM, USN

STEVENSON, Sperry, MM2c, USN

STILL, Dorothy, NC, USN

STOCKS, William Samuel, WT1c, USN

STOCKTON, Frank Denton, PFC, USMC

STOCKTON, Lewis Irvin, SC3c, USN

STOKES, John Blanchard, PFC, USMC

STONE, George Burwell, Jr., Corp., USMC

STOWE, Joe Morris, Platoon Sgt., USMC

STRANGMAN, Lt. William Leigh, Dental Corps, USN

STRAUCH, Henry Ernest, CMM, USN

STREETER, Ernest Orville, GM2c, USN

STROMSTAD, Erick, Sgt., USMC

STROSCHEIN, Vernon Kenneth, SC2c, USN

STUBO, Lt. Cdr. Knuty Christianson, USNR

SUMMERS, George Robert, Jr., PFC, USMC

SWEET, Clifford Eugene, Gunner, USN

SWIFT, William D., Corp., USMC

SWITZER, Raymond Clelan, PFC, USMC

TATE, James Pope, RM1c, USN

TAYLOR, Fred Martin, Corp., USMC

TAYLOR, Harry Orlo, EM1c, USN

TAYLOR, Lt. Cdr. Herbert Harold, USN

TAYLOR, Jacob Eugene, CSK, USN

TEMPLEMAN, Edward John, S1c, USN

TENNANT, Walter Ray, CWT, USN

TERRY, Arthur Franklin, Corp., USMC

TERRY, James Hurtial, Mach., USN

THEW, Henry Prior, FC1c, USN

THOMAS, Edward William, PFC, USMC

THOMAS, Stilvel Emory, SC1c, USN

THOMPSON, Arthur Robert, SC1c, USN

THOMPSON, Charles Russell, S1c, USN

THOMPSON, Jack Dempsey, PFC, USMC

THORSEN, John Thomas, S2c, USN

TICKSMAN, Paul Frederick, PFC, USMC

TIPTON, Wiley Edward, Sgt., USMC

TOBIAS, James Edward, CRM, USN

TODD, C. Edwina, NC, USN

TOLOSKO, Raymond Henry, B2c, USN

TOWSEND, Homer Lamar, CBM, USN

TREGO, Carroll Elwood, Corp., USMC

TRIBUKAIT, George Bertram, EM1c, USN

TRIM, Donald Paul, Cox., USN

TROTH, Leslie Raymond, PFC, USMC

TROWBRIDGE, Harry Anthony, Jr., F1c, USN

TUCK, Erville Raymond, Pvt., USMC

TUCKER, William Edward, Mus2c, USN
TULLOCH, Paul Sanford, WT2c, USN
TURNER, Joseph Lyle, SM2c, USN
TURNIPSEED, Jess, Pharm., USN
TUSA, Joe Nashen, PFC, USMC
TYSINGER, Raymond Luther, AMM1c, USN
ULMER, John Cassady, PhM1c, USN
UNGER, John Ignacious, PhM3c, USN
VALOIS, Robert Leslie, PhM2c, USN
VAN BUSKIRK, Wilburn V., Corp., USMC
VAN NESTE, Omer Leon Gaston, CWT, USN
VAN PEENAN, Lt. Cdr. Hubert John, (MC), USN
VERGA, Vincent Henry, PFC, USMC
VICENTINI, Tullio Vincent, Corp., USMC
WADE, Lt. Cdr. Ernest Marion, (MC), USN
WAGNER, Capt. Lloyd Ernest, USMCR
WALKER, Joseph L., Jr., Pvt., USMC
WARD, Robert Eugene, CM2c, USN
WASH, Jack Lawrence, S1c, USN
WASHBURN, Roy McDonald, WT2c, USN
WATERS, Arthur Dale, MM2c, USN
WATSON, Max Howard, SC1c, USN
WEBBER, Lawrence Edward, Corp., USMC
WEEKS, Maj. George Roland, USMC
WEEKS, Roy Santos, MM2c, USN
WEIDEL, Leonard August, CCStd, USN
WELCH, Lt. John Lytle, USN
WELKER, Charles Joseph Garfield, S1c, USN
WELLS, Frederick Porter, Y3c, USN
WELLS, Paul J., Tech. Sgt., USMC
WELSH, Thomas Patsy, PFC, USMC
WEMMER, Virgil Charles, EM2c, USN

WEST, Lawrence Elmer, RM3c, USN
WHARTON, Herbert R., PFC, USMC
WHEELER, Lt. (jg) Kenneth Ray, Supply Corps, USN
WHIPPLE, John Worthington, PFC, USMC
WHITMIRE, Leland Perry, ACMM, USN
WHITNEY, Leonard Vincent, Bkr1c, USN
WILLIAMS, Donald, S1c, USN
WILLIAMS, Edwin Derby, CY, USN
WILLIAMS, George Ernest, CEM, USNR
WILLIAMS, George Rudd, CQM, USN
WILLIAMS, James Morgan, RM2c, USN
WILSON, Carl Malone, MM1c, USN
WILSON, Cecil Earl, Elect., USN
WILSON, Elmer Wallace, PhM3c, USN
WILSON, Franklin Marquette, S2c, USN
WINKLER, James William, MM1c, USN
WINSOR, Willard Ira, CY, USN
WINTERS, Jack, Pvt., USMC
WISE, James Oran, S1c, USN
WISNIEWSKI, Valentine Stanislaus, RM2c, USN
WOLF, Joseph William, S2c, USN
WOLFE, Clarence Eugene, S1c, USN
WOOD, Jack Walter, Corp., USMC
WOOD, Jimmie, S1c, USN
WOOD, Kenneth Charles, F1c, USN
WOODSIDE, Ens. John Stewart, USNR
WOODWARD, Theodore Herman, PFC, USMC
WRATHALL, John Courtney, Corp., USMC
WYNNE, Marion Lee, PFC, USMC
YORK, Lewis Marvin, PFC, USMC
YOUNG, Edmund Clarence, RM1c, USN
YOUNG, Jack Robert, PhM3c, USN
YOUNG, James Clifton, CPhM, USN
ZYCH, Felix Stanley, CSK, USN

COLORADO

Dead

ALBERTS, Charles F., PFC, USMC
ALLEN, George Russell, PhM3c, USN
AMBROSE, Edward Frank, AMM3c, USN
AMICK, Leroy Arthur, S2c, USN
ANDERSON, Glen Willard, EM2c, USN
BERRY, Gordon Eugene, F2c, USN
BEUCHAT, Eugene Philip, PFC, USMC
BOHLENDER, Sam, GM3c, USN
BRUNNER, William Frank, F3c, USN
BUCHER, Carroll Wilson, Field Mus. Corp., USMC
BUTLER, 2nd Lt. John M., USMC
CALLAGHAN, James Thomas, BM2c, USN

CAMPBELL, Ens. Kendall Carl, USNR
CARMACK, Harold Milton, F2c, USN
CLARK, Vernon Floyd, SK1c, USN
COMIN, Howard D., Sgt., USMC
CONWAY, Edward LeRoy, EM1c, USN
CORNING, Russell Dale, RM3c, USNR
CROXEN, Russell Leroy, S2c, USN
CUNNINGAM, Harold Day, AMM2c, USN
DAVAULT, James Beal, S1c, USN
DAVIS, Allen Arthur, F3c, USN
DENNIS, Otis Lee, RM3c, USN
DURANT, Howard Elza, Jr., S2c, USNR
EAKES, Wallace Eldrid, SK3c, USN
ELLIS, Louis Claud, S1c, USN
ERRECA, Louie Rupert, ACMM, USN

FISHER, Ronald Joseph, ARM2c, USN
FRENCH, Joy Carol, S2c, USN
GOMEZ, Edward, Jr., S1c, USN
GONZALES, Bibian Bernard, S1c, USN
GOODWIN, William Arthur, S2c, USN
GORDON, Peter Charles, Jr., F2c, USN
GUSSENHOVEN, Raymond Allen, Sgt.,
   USMC
HAMILTON, Edwin Carrell, S2c, USN
HANIS, George Leroy, S1c, USN
HARMON, Raymond Donald, Corp.,
   USMC
HEELY, Leo Shinn, S2c, USN
HORTON, Edward Francis, S/Sgt., USMC
HULSE, Ellis M., Pvt., USMC
JENKINS, Jay William, RM3c, USN
JENKINS, Myron Lewis, Mach., USN
JOHNSON, Donald Walter, S2c, USN
JOHNSON, Ens. Joseph Philip, USNR
JONES, Edmon Ethmer, S1c, USN
KNIPP, Verne Francis, Cox., USN
LANDWEHR, Mathew L., Pvt., USMC
LEWIS, Guy William, SK3c, USN
LINDSAY, James Mitchell, SF2c, USN
LYON, Arnold Eugene, GM3c, USN
MASSEY, James Edward, AS, USN
MAYFIELD, Lester Ellsworth, F1c, USN
McCLELLAND, Ens. Thomas A., USNR
McMANUS, Ens. James Edward, USN
MORRISSEY, Edward F., PFC, USMC
NICHOLSON, Hancel Grant, S1c, USN
NORBY, Clarence Johanas, Jr., AMM3c,
   USN
OFF, Virgil Simon, S1c, USN
O'MALIA, Edward Robert, F1c, USN
O'NEALL, Rex Eugene, S1c, USN
OWENS, Richard Allen, SK2c, USN
PHILBIN, James Richard, S1c, USN
PHILLIPS, Milo Elah, WT1c, USN
PRENTICE, Richard Merlin, F1c, USN
REECE, John Jeffris, S2c, USN
REININGER, Lee W., Corp., USMC
RESLEY, Floyd Theadore, F3c, USNR
REYNOLDS, Earl Arthur, S2c, USN
ROBINSON, James Henry, S2c, USN
SAYLES, Orville Crawford, MM2c, USN
SCHLECT, Benjamin, RM2c, USN
SHIDLER, Arthur Seth, EM1c, USN
SHROYER, Robert Walter, S2c, USN
SHUGART, Marvin John, S1c, USN
SMITH, George Hoyle, BM2c, USN
SMITH, Ronald Bell, Corp., USMC
THOMAS, Howard Griffith, BM2c, USN
THOMAS, William Dwayne, SK3c, USN
WEBSTER, Harold Dwayne, S2c, USN
WHITELEY, Robert Leland, Bkr3c, USN

WILL, Joseph William, S2c, USN
WISE, Glen Edgar, FC3c, USN
WOOD, Harold Baker, Cox., USN
YANKS, Charles Robert, SM2c, USN
YERIAN, Kenneth Eugene, FC1c, USN
ZEILER, John Virgel, S1c, USN

Wounded

ANDREW, Marion Edgar, F2c, USN
BIELSER, Robert William, S2c, USN
CADY, Ome Edward, S2c, USN
GOODWIN, Charles Ralph, S2c, USN
MARTINEZ, Joseph Alfonso, AS, USN
MUSSELMAN, 2nd Lt. John C., Jr.,
   USMCR
SEXTON, William Stewart, S2c, USN
SIMMONS, Claude William, Jr., S1c, USN
VEZINA, Samuel Alexander, S2c, USN

Missing

BIGGERSTAFF, Hugh Vernon, S1c, USN
BRUST, James Lloyd, Cox., USN
BRYANT, Clyde Ora, MM1c, USN
BUENO, Narciso Benito, S2c, USN
CANTRIL, Thomas Stephen, F1c, USN
CONOVER, Leland, F2c, USN
EPSTEIN, Cdr. William Abraham, (MC),
   USN
FETTERHOFF, Charles Kirtlie, CY, USN
GENNER, Wilford Jacob, BM2c, USN
HIRSCH, Adolph Alexander, WT1c, USN
HIRSCH, Harry, F1c, USN
HODGE, Robert R., PFC, USMC
HUBERT, Earl Guy, MM1c, USN
HUNTER, Lowell Clinton, CPhM, USN
JAMES, Howard E., PFC, USMC
LAMMON, Francis A., PFC, USMC
LARSON, Coleman Leroy, GM1c, USN
LEE, Walter Glenn, Aer1c, USN
LOONEY, Douglas R., Pvt., USMC
MORRISON, Clark William, AP1c, USN
NISWONGER, Duel L., PFC, USMC
O'HAYRE, Eddie Paul, RM3c, USN
PAPISH, Paul Ernest, SK3c, USN
PHILLIPS, Stanley, Junior, S1c, USN
POUND, Lt. Kenneth Edward, USN
RICHIE, Elmer Thomas, Jr., EM3c, USN
ROWAN, Raymond Hobson, Jr., F1c, USN
SANDERCOOK, Theodore, BM1c, USN
SANGER, Harold Henry, SC1c, USN
SHIPPY, Clair Howard, S1c, USN
SIBERT, Lawrence James, RM2c, USN
VAN HORN, Edward, EM1c, USN
WARD, Frank Calvin, EM3c, USN
WILKERSON, Clyde Leonard, S1c, USN

WILLIAMS, Bazel Ozell, SK2c, USN
WOLF, Frank Henry, GM2c, USN
WYMAN, Duncan Arthur, Jr., Cox., USN
YOUNG, Troy Findland, F1c, USN
ZEILER, Jerry Hollice, Jr., Torp. 2c, USN

Prisoners of War

AMES, Bayard Powers, EM3c, USN
AMIDEI, Levio, Bkr3c, USN
ARNOLD, Floyd Virgil, S2c, USN
BALDWIN, George William, PFC, USMC
BARTLETT, Jess A., Corp., USMC
BRUCE, George Douglas, PFC, USMC
BURCH, Webster Eugene, PFC, USMC
CALVIN, Andrew Reese, PFC, USMC
CASTOR, Melvin Hershman, PFC, USMC
CHARLESWORTH, Gilbert, Jr., Cox., USN
COOK, Alonzo Edgar, Jr., BM1c, USN
COPELAND, Frank Emory, Corp., USMC
CULP, James Daniel, Gunner, USN
CUTTER, Verle D., PFC, USMC
DAVIES, James Edward, PFC, USMC
DE LANEY, William Burnerd, Corp., USMC
DILLON, J. D., Corp., USMC
ERWIN, Victor Charles, CM1c, USN
FARNER, Robert P., PFC, USMC
FITZGERALD, Bernard Joseph, PFC, USMC
FORREST, Dale E., PFC, USMC
Fox, Edwin Spencer, PhM1c, USN
GAMMON, Eugene Arthur, Boat., USN
GARRETT, Donald J., PFC, USMC
GOLIGHTLY, Robert Lee, F3c, USN
GOODIER, Lt. Benjamin Doolittle, CEC, USNR
GRAY, Robert Leo John, PFC, USMC
GRUENBERG, Arthur Howard, PFC, USMC
HERRON, Carl Roy, Corp., USMC
HERRON, Wendell M., PFC, USMC
HIXSON, Arthur Louis, PFC, USMC
HOBBY, Jackson Scott, Pvt., USMC
HOOVER, Harold Henry, Pvt., USMC
HOTCHKISS, Richard Lewis, S2c, USN

HUEBLER, Eugene Alfred, Jr., Bug1c, USN
HUMMELL, William Allen, SF1c, USN
HUNT, Ens. Wylie Mallory, USNR
JENSEN, Francis Erland, PFC, USMC
JENKINS, Gilbert Daniel, Jr., F2c, USN
JONES, Robert William, Aer2c, USN
LAFFOON, Arthur Lee, PFC, USMC
LEASE, Raymond Elmo, PFC, USMC
LEAVERTON, John Milton, AMM2c, USN
MALLORY, Robert Victor, Torp. 2c, USN
MANION, Tommy, Jr., S1c, USN
McANNALLY, Winford Jennings, Corp., USMC
McDOWELL, Jack W., Sgt., USMC
McELHINNEY, Jack Raymond, PFC, USMC
McGEE, James Robert, PFC, USMC
MELLIES, Warren Harding, Corp., USMC
MIDDLETON, Elmer Arthur, PFC, USMC
MORROW, Clifford Virgle, Pvt., USMC
MURPHY, Frank, Jr., Corp., USMC
NEUMANN, Herbert Carl, MM1c, USN
NEVILL, Willard Wiley, S2c, USN
NOLLETTE, David Daniel, GM2c, USN
PINSON, Barton Franklin, Aer3c, USN
RILEY, John Hamilton, SM1c, USN
RUSSELL, William G., Corp., USMC
SCHROEIER, Richard Ruper, PFC, USMC
SCOTT, Donald Jackson, Corp., USMC
SHEARER, Clarence, Pharm., USN
SHIVELY, David Thomas, Pvt., USMC
SHUSTER, John F., PFC, USMC
SKAGGS, Viktor Vincent, SC2c, USN
SMITH, Ralph Lowell, MM2c, USN
SMITH, Salem Irvin, Corp., USMC
STEARMER, Ivan Max, M2c, USN
STEINBRECHER, William Frederick, Jr., PFC, USMC
STIVERS, Ens. John Bell, USNR
TOWNSDIN, J. Roy, PFC, USMC
WHELAN, Charles P., Corp., USMC
WILKINSON, Eugene Thomas, S2c, USN
WOODWARD, Floyd Stanley, S1c, USN
YAKOVICH, Anthony, PFC, USMC

CONNECTICUT

Dead

ALSOP, Leo James, Cox., USN
BAILEY, Lt. Walter Clyde, USN
BRANDENBERGER, James Herbert, S1c, USNR
BROWN, Lon Alexander, Jr., RM1c, USN
BUSKY, Albert John, GM3c, USN

CARLSON, Harry Ludwig, SK3c, USN
CARVER, Warren J., PFC, USMC
CZINKY, William Joseph, MM2c, USN
DENTE, Gerald James, BM2c, USN
EVANS, David Birch, CMM, USNR
FETKO, Joseph, S2c, USN
GILL, Joseph Mathew, Chief Torp., USN
GILLIE, Lt. (jg) James Ross, USNR

GRAHAM, Ens. Robert Parmelee, USNR
HEALEY, Lawrence Vincent, BN2c, USN
HOLLADAY, John Anthony, S2c, USN
HOLT, Robert Earl, QM2c, USN
HOWARD, George Fielding, F1c, USN
JONES, Richard Harrison, S2c, USNR
KANE, Frederick William, CBM, USN
KELLY, Lester, MM1c, USN
LANOUETTE, Henry John, Cox., USN
LOUGHLIN, Thomas Philip, Torp. 2c, USN
LUNTTA, John Kallervo, S1c, USN
MALINOWSKY, Alexander Frank, F1c, USN
MARCINAK, Stanley James, S2c, USNR
McKEE, Albert, CMM, USNR
MONTANARI, Eugene James, S1c, USN
NOBLE, Wilson Porter, SM3c, USN
O'NEILL, Ens. William T., USNR
ORZECH, Stanislaus Joseph, S2c, USN
PATTERSON, Richard, Jr., SF3c, USN
PEARSON, Raymond Bertis, F1c, USN
PINKERTON, 2nd Lt. David W., Jr., USMC
POVESKO, George, S1c, USN
POWELL, Reese, F1c, USN
QUARTO, Mike Joseph, S1c, USN
QUEY, Mario, Gunner, USN
RATTI, Raphael Joseph, F1c, USN
REBUZZINI, John Claudio, WT1c, USN
REEVES, Thomas James, CRM, USN
ROBERTS, Sidney Ewing, Jr., MM2c, USN
ROWLEY, Richard Harvey, MM1c, USN
RUSSELL, George Gilbert, EM2c, USNR
SEELEY, William Eugene, S1c, USN
SCHMUT, John Michael, CRM, USN
TAYLOR, Ens. Harry Landau, USNR
TRAPP, Ens. Wilson Beaumont, USNR
VALENTE, Kenneth Franklin, S1c, USN
WHITEHEAD, Ens. Ulmont Irving, Jr., USN
WHITHAM, John Edwin, Gunner, USN
WOLGER, Lewis Harvey, SC3c, USN
ZILINEK, Victor Joseph, GM3c, USN
ZOSS, Otto Julius, WT2c, USN

Wounded

HYLAND, Everett Joseph, S2c, USN
ISYK, Henry Peter, AMM3c, USN

Missing

ABATE, Leo Carmelo, S1c, USN
AQUINO, Anthony Frank, CY, USN
BOUCHER, Arsen Louis, MM2c, USN
CARRARA, Malcolm Anthony, SC1c, USN

CASE, George B., Mstr. Gunnery Sgt., USMC
DAVIS, Lt. (jg) Lewis Olcott, Supply Corps, USN
DOMBROWSKI, Edwin Stanley, S1c, USN
DRABB, Andrew Joseph, CCStd, USN
GIRET, Andrew Joseph, FC1c, USN
HIRSCHBERG, Louis, FC2c, USN
LATAUSKAS, Edward John, PhM2c, USN
MARETTE, Earnest Hanson, SM2c, USN
MOORE, Thomas, S1c, USN
MUIR, Linwood Robert, QM1c, USN
PICKHARDT, Thomas Vincent, GM3c, USN
SZALKEVICZ, Felix, Gunnery Sgt, USMC
SZYMASZEK, Edward Joseph, CWT, USN
VITELLI, Louis, SF3c, USN
WILSON, Oscar Waldimar, CRM, USN

Prisoners of War

ANDREWS, Joseph, S/Sgt, USMC
ASHTON, Henry Jay, BM2c, USN
BAIREY, Verne Nicholas, MM1c, USN
BARNES, Stanley Davenport, S1c, USN
BEALE, Ens. Arthur George, USNR
BERIO, Alfred Edward, Chief Torp., USN
BOTHAM, Willard Robert, S1c, USN
BOWEN, Charles Augustus, PhM1c, USN
BURT, Robert Arthur, Jr., RM2c, USN
CARPENTER, Thomas Royal, Platoon Sgt., USMC
CHAISON, Marshall Frederick, RM2c, USN
CHAMBERS, Capt. Robert Jr., USMC
CHOPCHIK, George John, BM1c, USN
CONOVER, William Lawrence, CEM, USN
DERUSSO, John August, MM2c, USN
DIMAIO, Charles, Torp.1c, USN
DUNN, Lt. (jg) John Edward, USN
FRASER, Harry Stuart, S2c, USN
GORDON, Harvey, PhM2c, USN
HOEFFER, Frank Hart, Jr., SC2c, USN
HOLLIS, Frank Peter, EM1c, USN
JAKUBIELSKI, Raymond Joseph, BM1c, USN
KARKUT, Walter John, WT1c, USN
KOBLISH, Joseph Francis, WT2c, USN
KOSSYTA, Frank Joseph, Sgt., USMC
LANGDON, Lt. (jg) Benjamin Bruce, (MC) USN
LASER, Henry Frederick, Supply Sgt., USMC
NIKKONEN, Rudolph, Gunner, USN
PAWLOWSKI, Louis Stanley, S1c, USN
PEARCE, Herbert Neal, Corp., USMC
PELTIER, William Nelson, Jr., F3c, USN

PERNAL, Edward Anthony, CWT, USN
REARDON, Thomas Joseph, S1c, USN
RISTAU, Herbert Paul, ACOM, USN
RYE, Jens Olaf, PhM1c, USN
SMITH, Lt. Cdr. Douglas Elwin, USN

THOMAS, Earl A., Corp., USMCR
VAITKUS, Benedict Anthony, CM2c, USN
WAYNE, Phillip, AMM3c, USN
WINSLOW, Lt. (jg) Walter Gillespie, USNR

DELAWARE

Dead

GOSNELL, Paul Gustavus, GM1c, USN
HOLZMUELLER, Charles Donnan, Jr., S1c, USNR
PENUEL, George Ames, Jr., BM2c, USN
SHELDON, Eli Erb, MM2c, USNR

Wounded

(None)

Missing

MARVEL, Thomas Henry, CMM, USN

Prisoners of War

CONAWAY, Woodrow Wilson, S2c, USN
HAGERTY, Oliver Parker, Jr., Sgt., USMC
KANE, John Woodward, S1c, USN
LONG, Walton F., F1c, USN
WILLIAMS, Maj. Francis H., USMC
WILSON, Wesley Wood, SM1c, USN

FLORIDA

Dead

ALMOND, Jule Patterson, F3c, USN
ARMSTRONG, Tramble O., PFC, USMC
ARRANT, John Anderson, MM1c, USN
ATCHISON, Willis Dudley, AMM1c, USN
ATKINSON, John Lawrence, CEM, USN
BARNETT, Edwin Ryland, CWT, USN
BELLAMY, Woodrow, MA1c, USNR
BLANTON, Atticus Lee, SF3c, USN
BOLTON, John Alden, RM1c, USN
BOYKIN, David Samuel, S2c, USN
BREWER, John Tol, S1c, USN
BROOKS, Oscar Russell, Jr., AS, USN
BROWN, Thomas Hayward, AS, USN
BULL, Ens. Richard, USNR
BURDICK, Allen Frost, S2c, USN
CAMPBELL, James Matthews, S2c, USNR
CATO, James Henry, AS, USN
CHEYNE-STOUT, Ronald, Jr., AS, USN
CLOSE, Thomas Sheldon, AOM2c, USN
COOK, William Ernest, MM1c, USN
COWART, Melvin Wright, SM3c, USN
CRAIG, Lt. Cdr. James Edwin, USN
CREACH, Edsel David, SC3c, USN
CROFT, Franklin Harwell, S2c, USN
CULPAN, Raymond, Bkr1c, USN
DAILEY, Jim, OC1c, USN
DANA, Edwin Legrand, Y1c, USN
DAVIS, Chester Arthur, OC2c, USN
DOSICK, Stanley Daniel, S1c, USN
FIELDS, Retiford, MA2c, USN
FLANAGAN, James Monroe, S2c, USN

GARCIA, Manuel, Jr., S2c, USN
GEIGER, Frank Drake, Jr., AP1c, USN
GOFF, William Lorenzo, S1c, USN
GRIFFIN, Robert Edward, AS, USNR
HARRIS, Lt. Cdr. Andrew Earl, USN
HOLL, Donald Dean, S2c, USN
HOLTON, Ens. Ralph Lee, USN
JONES, Quincy E., PFC, USMC
KRAKER, Ens. Donald J., USNR
LANE, William Gerald, F2c, USN
LEE, Donald Ernest, RM2c, USN
LISH, Eugene Victor, Mus3c, USN
LLOYD, Ens. William Rees, USNR
MAEGER, Sherrill Galt, RM3c, USN
MATTHEWS, John Raymond, SC3c, USN
MATTOX, James Durrant, AM3c, USN
MAYO, Milburn William, S2c, USN
MAYO, Rex Haywood, EM2c, USN
McKAY, Chester Rufus, BM2c, USN
McMILLAN, Thomas Edward, S2c, USN
MEARES, Cuthbert Wayne, F1c, USN
MERANDA, Thomas Robert, S2c, USN
MILLIMAN, Ens. Richard Diver, USNR
MIXON, John Marion, S2c, USN
MIXON, Thomas Clay, S2c, USN
MORGAN, Charles Arnold, RM3c, USNR
MORRIS, Ronald Bernard, Cox., USN
MUSHINSKI, Edwin John, ARM2c, USN
NEWTON, Orville Yuths, S1c, USN
NICHELSON, Oliver D., Corp., USMC
NOBBS, Harrison Schilling, ACRM, USN
O'NEIL, Stephen Michael, S2c, USN
PENTON, Fred Wilkerson, RM3c, USN

PLANT, Burel Lemar, F3c, USN
POINDEXTER, Herbert Joseph, Jr., S1c, USN
PREVATT, Barden Willis, S2c, USN
PRINCE, Pearl Greison, S2c, USN
PRYOR, A. D., AS, USN
PUTNAL, Clabe Winston, F3c, USN
RICH, Claude Edward, S1c, USN
RIPPEY, Lt. (jg) Wilson Bloom, USNR
ROSS, Harold Eugene, F3c, USN
RUTTAN, Dale Andrew, EM3c, USN
SINGLETARY, Grady R. M., S2c, USN
SKALING, Howard Douglas, GM3c, USNR
SMITH, Earl Walter, FC3c, USN
SMITH, Ens. Frederick Andrew, USNR
SOOTER, Lt. (jg) Cecil Dean, USN
SUGGS, William Alfred, S1c, USN
THOMAS, Horace B., PFC, USMC
TOWNSEND, Curtis, S2c, USNR
VARNUM, John Wesley, SC3c, USN
WATSON, Claude Bridger, Jr., S1c, USN
WATSON, William Lafayette, F3c, USN
WERT, Charles Reo, S1c, USNR
WHITE, Woodrow Wilson, WT2c, USN
WING, Arthur Ray, SK2c, USN
WOLFF, Henry Edward, AMM2c, USN

DURRANCE, Donald Carlos, RM2c, USN
FRINK, Ens. Marvin Polk, USNR
FUSSELL, Donald Eldridge, MM2c, USN
FUSSELL, Jack Hale, F2c, USN
GONZAGA, Ramon, CMM, USNR
HAMLIN, Lt. (jg) Harold Sherwin, Jr., USN
HARRIS, Raymond John, S2c, USN
HEDRICK, George Randolph, Jr., QM2c, USN
KEENE, 1st Lt. James William, USMC
MACKEY, Donald Dale, EM1c, USN
MAINEY, Ens. Lawrence Hugh, Jr., USNR
MALLIAS, Santiago, MA1c, USNR
MENTEN, Charles Edward, MM1c, USN
MORRIS, James Clifford, AMM3c, USN
OLIVER, Herbert Leo, ACMM, USN
PAUTSCH, Philip Walter, WT2c, USN
PIERSON, Ernest Earl, Cox., USN
POSEY, William Henry, SC1c, USN
POSTON, John Turner, CGM, USN
WALSER, James Odes, S1c, USN
WARNES, Paul Dale, AM2c, USN
WATKINS, Charles Oscar, S1c, USN
WATKINS, Dodd Wayne, AMM3c, USN
WINBURN, Paul Andrew, S1c, USN

Wounded

BLAIN, Capt. Richard L., USMCR
BLENMAN, Lt. Charles, Jr., USN
CROWNOVER, Joseph Talley, RM1c, USN
FERGUSON, Dwight Lindsay, PhM1c, USN
HENDERSON, William Riley, Bkr3c, USN
HOYLE, William Sherlock, AM3c, USN
IVERSON, 1st Lt. Daniel, Jr., USMC
KINLAW, Emmett Gregory, CB, USN
POSTLETHWAITE, Paul Orrin, S2c, USN
RAINES, James Guy, RM2c, USN
SMATHERS, Hilliard Claud, ACMM, USN
TOWNSEND, Alvis Rennel, RM1c, USN
WILSEY, Murray E., Jr., PFC, USMC

Missing

ADKINSON, David Lang, S2c, USN
ARGO, Charlie Duke, Jr., S2c, USN
BETHEA, William, S2c, USN
BLINN, Lt. Cdr. Welford Charles, USN
BRYAN, Lamar A., Platoon Sgt., USMC
CALPO, Feliciano, CBM, USN
COOK, William Earl, CMM, USN
CULPEPPER, John Eutus, QM1c, USN
CUMMING, George Hosmer, Jr., ACMM, USN
DOMINGUES, Joe M., PFC, USMC
DUNN, James Archie, Jr., S1c, USN

Prisoners of War

ADDISON, Hugh, F2c, USN
ATKINS, Ralph Perry, F2c, USN
BOSWELL, John Ray, Corp., USMC
BRANHAM, Lawrence Randolph, S2c, USN
BROWN, Lt. Hugh, USNR
CARDEN, Tom Hayes, ACMM, USN
CARLSON, August W., QM Clerk, USMC
FORD, Cecil Cassells, S/Sgt., USMC
FORSYTH, Frank Ray, Corp., USMC
FOSHA, Charles Edward, ACMM, USN
GAINEY, Gilbert, PFC, USMC
GODWIN, William Flavious, Platoon Sgt., USMC
HALL, Clarence George, GM1c, USN
HAMMON, Charlie, CBM, USN
HARRELL, Roland Eugene, CEM, USN
HAUN, Robert Clinton, Pay Clerk, USN
HICKS, Thomas R., Sgt., USMC
HILL, Charles Callis, PFC, USMC
HILL, Robert Austin, RM1c, USN
HUTCHISON, Dick, PFC, USMC
JARRELL, Lee Farris, Carp., USN
JOHNSON, Leon Curtis, CMM, USN
JOYCE, John William, Torp. 1c, USN
JUNE, Randolph Marlin, Tech. Sgt., USMC
LOCKE, Henry Clay, PFC, USMC
MASSEY, Cecil Frederick, BM1c, USN

McHugh, Frederick George, PFC, USMC
McKnight, Charles Jackson, Y3c, USN
Merritt, Lonnie Cleophas, CPhM, USN
Morgan, Lt. (jg) Wade Hampton, Jr.,
  Dental Corps, USN
Morrison, George Alton, CRM, USN
Mott, Charles Thomas, PFC, USMC
Mott, John J., Corp., USMC
Moye, Holland O., Asst. Cook, USMC
Mullins, Ens. Jimmy, USNR
Parker, John Jackson, CBM, USN
Pierce, Charles Daniel, Jr., Tech. Sgt.,
  USMC
Pierce, Laurence Richard, RM1c, USN
Pringle, Joseph Alton, CPho, USN

Ragan, Rudolph Clyatt, S1c, USN
Rowe, Abner Peter, Jr., PhM1c, USN
Sealey, Armon James, Gunnery Sgt.,
  USMC
Serra, Miguel, Corp., USMC
Skipper, Sterling Preston, SC1c, USN
Smith, Donald Lonnie, MM1c, USN
Stalls, Henry Mansfield, SK1c, USN
Stewart, Al Raymond, AMM3c, USN
Strickland, H. S., F1c, USN
Teem, Linzia Coy, Chief Torp., USN
Thompson, Robert Edward, S2c, USN
Wells, George Bernard, Boat., USN
Whitaker, Kenneth Francis, CWT, USN
Winburn, Paul Andrew, S1c, USN

GEORGIA

Dead

Allmond, Dennis, CQM, USN
Anderson, Lt. (jg) Charles Edison, USN
Bagley, Hollis Fred, WT2c, USN
Blaylock, Fred Powell, F1c, USN
Booze, Asbury Legare, BM1c, USN
Bragg, Lenton, AS, USNR
Butler, David Eugene, AS, USNR
Chapman, Robert Fred, GM3c, USN
Coates, Willie, MA2c, USN
Croft, Theodore Wheeler, AOM1c, USN
Crowe, Lemuel Zebulon, Jr., F2c, USN
Curry, Pinkney Leroy, Jr., S2c, USN
Dixon, Ens. Sherman Frederick, USNR
Donald, John Malcolm, SF3c, USN
Dozier, Paul Pittman, Jr., S2c, USN
Echols, Edward Wesley, Cox., USN
Ellington, Stanford Edison, S2c, USN
Fair, James Hammond, MM1c, USN
Fleming, Hosea McCall, S2c, USNR
Foskey, Thurman Clarence, S2c, USN
Freeman, Lewis Edward, Jr., S2c, USN
Grantham, Hugh Milton, ARM3c,
  USNR
Hadden, Hoyt Harry, GM3c, USN
Harris, Hiram Dennis, S1c, USN
Harrison, Woodrow Wilson, S2c, USN
Hart, Thomas Harold, S2c, USN
Henderson, William Glenn, AS, USNR
Hill, Clarence Edwin, S2c, USN
Hodges, Ens. Flourenoy Glen, USNR
Jordan, James Cleon, ARM3c, USN
Kelley, Sanford V., Jr., GM3c, USN
Kimberly, Frank David, WT2c, USN
Knight, Milton Jewel, Jr., F1c, USN
Koontz, Benjamin D., Corp., USMC
Lasseter, Fain McCord, AS, USNR
Lester, Jesse Augustus, PhM2c, USN

Maddox, Thomas Emmett, F1c, USN
Manning, Walter Benjamin, EM1c, USN
Mathews, Charles Calvin, Jr., Torp.2c,
  USN
Mathis, Jacob, S1c, USN
Matthews, Hoyt Garward, Torp.3c,
  USN
Mims, Robert Lang, S1c, USN
Minton, Maurice Windell, S2c, USN
Montgomery, James Nelson, AS, USNR
Moore, Tommy Howell, S2c, USN
O'Donnell, Jack Thomas, FC1c, USN
Parkerson, Clifford Harrison, SM3c,
  USN
Parramore, Robert Travis, F3c, USN
Peacock, Harold Clayton, S2c, USN
Pike, Harvey Lee, EM3c, USN
Pike, Lewis Jackson, S1c, USN
Pittman, Allen Coleman, F2c, USN
Reddick, Troy Johnson, AMM3c, USN
Reich, Ens. William Owens, Jr., USNR
Roberts, Ennis Lee, MM2c, USCG
Rodgers, Curtis, S1c, USN
Scarborough, Hiram Alton, S2c, USNR
Scott, James Robert, AS, USN
Scott, Thomas B., Jr., Pvt., USMC
Shirley, Anthony Bradford, Jr., S1c,
  USN
Snow, Jep, CMM, USN
Speer, John Ralph, AS, USNR
Stewart, William Purnell, S2c, USNR
Sutton, Theodore Roosevelt, M2c, USN
Vining, George Eugene, MA2c, USN
Wall, Ralph John, S2c, USN
White, Jack Bufford, AS, USNR
Wilcox, Rear Adm. John Walter, USN
Worsham, John Murry, Torp.3c, USN
Wright, Robert Allen, Torp.1c, USNR

Wounded

CASTLEBERRY, Lewis Odum, S1c, USN
HALL, Ens. Benjamin C., USN
JAMES, Archie Ray, S2c, USNR
KNIGHT, Eugene Haywood, Jr., GM3c, USN
RHODEN, Earl Milton, S2c, USN

Missing

BALDWIN, Ens. Justin Ousley, Jr., USNR
BAXTER, Rufus James, SC2c, USN
BONNELL, James Everett, MM1c, USN
BOONE, Evans LeRoy, S2c, USN
BURNETTE, Grady Harold, SM3c, USN
CLARK, William Thomas, F1c, USN
EDWARDS, Ausburn Revis, SC1c, USN
FLEEMAN, James D., 1st Sgt., USMC
GINGRAS, Lt. Cdr. Richard Hermus, USN
GINWRIGHT, Lee Edward, EM1c, USN
GRIGGS, Howard Lee, Jr., SC2c, USN
GRINSTEAD, Ray Monroe, F2c, USN
HARRIS, Ens. William Henry, USNR
HERREN, William Fiedler, AMM1c, USN
KOLB, Lt. Otto Ferdinand, Jr., USN
LATHAM, Raymond Alpheus, GM2c, USN
MALLORY, Ens. Fred Ferguson, USN
McGIBONY, Ens. William Noel, Supply Corps, USN
MURRAY, Ens. Bond, USNR
NEW, Kinsley Roscoe, F3c, USN
NISEWONGER, Fred Edward, MM2c, USN
O'NEAL, James Percy, GM3c, USN
PITTMAN, John William, RM1c, USN
PURCELL, Mack Clinton, M1c, USN
ROGERS, Floyd, SK1c, USN
ROOKE, Henry Casher, SC2c, USN
SMITH, Duane Lonnie, QM3c, USN
TAYLOR, John Henry, WT1c, USN
TERRY, Huse Bogus, MM2c, USN
TOOTLE, James Auburn, Sgt., USMC
TURNER, Marion McDaniel, EM2c, USN
WEED, Arthur Goodwin, MM2c, USN
WHITE, Robert Doyle, MM2c, USN
WORLEY, Randolph Emerson, Torp.3c, USN

Prisoners of War

ANDREWS, Austin Lamar, SK3c, USN
BIGGERS, Huey A., PFC, USMC

CARMICHAEL, Otis Andrew, Pay Clerk, USN
CASH, Holland, Platoon Sgt., USMC
CLEMENT, Cecil Albert, CY, USNR
COUCH, Asmon Jordan, AMM1c, USN
COX, William A., Pvt., USMC
DALZELL, James Walter, RM1c, USN
DAVIS, Lt. (jg) James Joseph, Jr., Supply Corps, USN
DE LOACH, Emett Dan, Pvt., USMC
DIXON, Vernon Grady, Asst. Cook, USMC
FEDER, Lt. (jg) John George, (MC), USN
FOREHAND, James Morgan, WT1c, USN
FOUCHE, Chandler Edwin, Corp., USMC
GILLELAND, Jesse Paul, WT2c, USN
GLENN, John Lewis, Y1c, USN
GORDON, Ens. Jack Benjamin, Jr., USNR
GORDY, Tom Watson, RM1c, USN
GRAY, Harry Thomas, RM3c, USN
GRAYSON, Elton, Mach., USN
HARRIS, John Soloman, Torp.2c, USN
HAWKINS, Defoix Wilson, S1c, USN
HERREN, Albert Felix, Jr., AMM1c, USN
JONES, Osborne Joseph, CSM, USN
KIMBELL, James Marvin, MM2c, USN
KING, Nathan Hughes, RM1c, USN
LEWIS, Robert S., S1c, USN
MANRY, Duke Richmond, CSK, USN
McCRANIE, William Thomas, S1c, USN
McMULLEN, Doster Lee, Y1c, USN
MEGGINS, Harry Othnal, BM2c, USN
MORGAN, Theodore Lawton, MM1c, USN
MURCHISON, Lt. (jg) William Jervis, USNR
O'NEAL, Elza Cohen, PFC, USMC
ORR, James Irwin, CMM, USN
PATE, Ralph Edward, AMM3c, USN
POWELL, Felix Doyal, F1c, USN
RAWLINS, Russell Nathaniel, AMM3c, USN
SCOTT, James Colquitt, F3c, USN
SHAW, Kenneth L., Pay Clerk, USMC
SMITH, Alvin Gracy, CGM, USNR
SMITH, Lt. Cdr. Columbus Darwin, USNR
SMITH, James Madison, Jr., F2c, USN
WALL, Thomas Edwin, S1c, USN
WEBB, Wallace Cornelius, RM1c, USN

IDAHO

Dead

BRADLEY, Carl Merrill, F2c, USN
BRIGGS, Lyle Lee, EM3c, USN
CHARLTON, Davis Milton, S2c, USN

CREECH, Lynn Joseph, F3c, USNR
CROWLEY, Rex Blaine, RM3c, USN
EDMISTON, John Wallace, CSF, USN
EVANS, William Orville, S2c, USN

EVERSOLE, Lt. (jg) John Thomas, USN
FRIESEN, Kenneth Cornwall, AOM3c, USN
HALSEY, Ens. Delbert Wayne, USNR
HANSEN, Louis Dale, RM2c, USN
HAYNES, Curtis James, QM2c, USN
HOLCOMB, Byron Eugene, SK3c, USN
HUNTSMAN, David Gratten, S2c, USN
JACOBS, Richard William, S2c, USN
JOLLEY, Berry Stanley, S2c, USNR
KENNARD, Kenneth Frank, GM3c, USN
LINDSAY, 2nd Lt. Elwood Q., USMC
LIPE, Wilbur Thomas, S2c, USN
LONG, Ens. Robert Gene, USNR
LOVELAND, Frank Crook, S2c, USN
MARSH, William Arthur, S1c, USN
MASON, Byron Dalley, S2c, USN
OWSLEY, Thomas Lee, SC2c, USN
PETERSON, Ens. Oscar Joel, USNR
PHELPS, Herbert La Verne, F3c, USN
ROSENAU, Howard Arthur, S2c, USN
ROWELL, Marshall Leland, S2c, USN
RUPERT, Dale Elton, SF3c, USN
RUSCOE, Jackson, GM1c, USN
SHIAVE, John D., Pvt., USMC
STOCKMAN, Harold William, FC3c, USN
THROCKMORTON, Lester Lee, SC3c, USN
VARIAN, Ens. Bertram Stetson, Jr., USNR
VEEDER, Gordon Elliott, S2c, USN
ZACEK, Laddie John, S1c, USN

Wounded

BALLOU, Robert Warren, S2c, USN
GREER, Stanley D., Sgt., USMC
KEIPER, Fred Albert, S2c, USN
MABEY, Kember Dee, Pvt., USMCR
MATTOX, Milo, S2c, USN
TANNLUND, Ronald Edgar, S2c, USN

Missing

DRAKE, Charles Virgil, S2c, USN
HARMANING, Harry Ervin, S2c, USN
LANDON, Kenneth Leon, F1c, USN
MOSTEK, Francis C., PFC, USMC
OWENS, William Lawrence, SM2c, USN

SNAPP, Edward Nolan, BM1c, USN
TAGGART, Ross Arthur, EM1c, USN
WAITE, Walter Warren, Elect., USN
WARNER, John Chester, Music, USN
WILLIAMS, Earnest Dale, S2c, USN

Prisoners of War

ADAMS, Raymond Charles, PFC, USMC
BALLEW, James Letcher, S2c, USN
BOWLER, Samuel Gaston, ACMM, USN
BREEZE, John Robert, Sgt., USMC
BROWN, Gene Edward, Corp., USMC
CHANDLER, Melvin Wesley, SK1c, USN
CHRISTENSEN, Sidney Myron, PFC, USMC
CLARK, Henry R., GM1c, USN
COLLINS, Earl Robert, RM1c, USN
CREAMER, Carl Edward, AOM3c, USN
DE MOUTH, Lester Jacob, PFC, USMC
DOWNEY, Ernest Willard, Boat., USN
ENGBLOM, Edward Howard, F1c, USN
FAWCETT, Albert W., PFC, USMC
FELTON, Melvin Everett, S2c, USN
GIRARD, Maurice P., Corp., USMC
HENRY, Andrew Allen, QM3c, USN
JONES, John S., PFC, USMC
KIBBLE, Dare Keane, F2c, USN
LORING, Lance Edward, S1c, USN
McCANDLESS, George Clyde, SF3c, USN
McKASSON, Glenn William, PFC, USMC
McKENNA, Chester R., PFC, USMC
MERCER, Kenneth Oliver, Tech. Sgt., USMC
MILLER, Thomas Orlan, S1c, USN
MORRIS, Orland Otis, PFC, USMC
NASLUND, Charles Edward, PFC, USMC
OSTERMILLER, Leo Glenn, PFC, USMC
RATHBUN, Lorenzo Everett, RM2c, USN
SCOTT, Charles Francis, PFC, USMC
SENFTEN, Daniel David, S1c, USN
SMITH, John W., PFC, USMC
STEPHENS, Lawrence Byron, CCStd, USN
WILKER, Max Wallentine, S1c, USN
WRIGHT, Edgar Baird, PhM2c, USN

ILLINOIS

Dead

ADAMS, Leonard William, MM1c, USN
ALBEROVSKY, Francis Severin, B1c, USN
ANDERSON, Harry Edward, Corp., USMC
ANTMAN, Irving, PFC, USMC
APPLE, Robert William, F1c, USN

ARBUCKLE, William Dellano, S2c, USNR
AVES, Willard Charles, F1c, USN
BACKMAN, Walter Howard, RM2c, USN
BAILEY, Floyd Dean, S2c, USNR
BAILEY, Forrest Augustus, PhM1c, USN
BAJORIMS, Joseph, S1c, USN
BALAKAS, Victor B., PFC, USMC

BARNARD, Robert Douglas, S2c, USN
BAUER, Lee Anthony, F1c, USN
BAUM, Earl Paul, S1c, USN
BELL, Hershel Homer, FC2c, USN
BENNETT, William Edmond, Jr., Y3c, USN
BERTRAM, William P., PFC, USMC
BOLEN, Albert James, F1c, USN
BRADLEY, Bruce Dean, S2c, USN
BRODIE, Walter, F2c, USN
BROWN, Charles Darling, EM3c, USN
BROWN, Robert J., PFC, USMC
BULL, Lt. (jg) Richard, USNR
BUCK, Joseph Almerian, Jr., S1c, USN
BURROUGHS, George Owen, F2c, USN
BYRD, Virgil, CQM, USN
CABAY, Louis Clarence, S1c, USN
CAPPORELLI, John, S1c, USCG
CASE, Lt. (jg) Frank David, Jr., USN
CAUDLE, Donald, S1c, USN
CHRISTOPHER, Ens. Harald Jensen, USNR
CLARK, George Francis, GM3c, USN
CLARKE, Ens. Francis Xavier, USNR
CLAYTON, Joseph Dwight, S2c, USN
CONLEY, Harold Francis, Jr., SK3c, USNR
CONLIN, Bernard Eugene, S2c, USN
CONLIN, James Leo, F2c, USN
COOK, Carl Wayne, S2c, USNR
COTNER, Leo Paul, S2c, USN
COTTIER, Charles Edwin, F1c, USN
COX, Gerald Clinton, Mus2c, USN
CREPS, Lawrence Raymond, AS, USN
CROSS, Clark Butler, WT1c, USN
DANFORTH, Lt. (jg) James Walker, USNR
DELLES, Leslie Phillip, EM3c, USN
DITT, Robert A., Corp., USMC
DOLATA, Casimir Simon, RM3c, USN
DONAHUE, John Gerald, MM1c, USN
DOUBLE, John Fention, Corp., USMC
DUFFY, Lt. Leonard Vincent, USN
DUKES, Lonnie William, S1c, USN
DUNCAN, Robert Thomas, RM2c, USNR
EDWARDS, Floyd Lee, S1c, USN
EDWARDS, Kenneth Orville, SF3c, USN
EGNEW, Robert Ross, S1c, USN
ELDEN, Lt. Ralph Waldo, USN
ETCHASON, Leslie Edgar, S1c, USN
EVANS, Paul Anthony, S1c, USN
EVANS, Raymond Glenn, AM3c, USN
FARRELL, Fred Howell, Torp.1c, USN
FISCHER, William H., Sgt., USMC
FITZSIMMONS, Eugene James, F3c, USN
FLACK, James Wilfred, Jr., SM2c, USNR
FLEEK, Donald James, F3c, USN
FLOEGE, Frank Norman, S2c, USN

FREELAND, Owen William, SF1c, USN
FRYDLE, Daniel J., Pvt., USMC
FUNK, Lawrence Henry, S1c, USN
GALAJDIK, Michael, F1c, USN
GAULTNEY, Ralph Martin, GM3c, USN
GAUS, Harold Lawrence, Y2c, USN
GEORGE, Kelton B., Corp., USMC
GIOVENAZZO, Michael James, WT2c, USN
GLUBA, Evan Frederick, AOM2c, USN
GOOD, Leland, S1c, USN
GOSSELIN, Ens. Edward W., USNR
GOULD, Harry Lee, S1c, USN
GRISSINGER, Robert Beryle, S2c, USN
GROSS, Roy Arthur, F1c, USN
GULLACHSON, Arthur Kenneth, S2c, USN
GURLEY, Jesse Herbert, SK3c, USN
GUSIE, William Fred, FC3c, USN
HAFFNER, Floyd Bates, F1c, USN
HALTERMAN, Robert Emile, S1c, USN
HANUS, George, AS, USNR
HARR, Robert Joseph, F1c, USN
HARRIS, George Ellsworth, MM1c, USN
HARSHBARGER, John R., Corp., USMC
HAWKINS, Russell Dean, SM3c, USN
HEBEL, Robert Lee, SM3c, USNR
HELLSTERN, William Francis, GN2c, USN
HILL, Donald W., Pvt., USMC
HISSEM, Ens. Joseph Metcalf, USNR
HOLL, George J., Jr., SM3c, USCG
HOMER, Henry Vernon, S1c, USN
HOOVER, James Howard, F3c, USN
HUBNER, Edgar Eugene, S1c, USN
HUFFINE, Howard E., PFC, USMC
IVANTIC, Joe John, RM3c, USN
IVANTIC, Paul Valentine, RM3c, USNR
JACOBS, Richard Frederick, SF3c, USN
JACOBSON, Herbert Barney, F3c, USN
JANSEN, Robert O., Pvt., USMC
JURASHEN, Thomas Valentine, S2c, USN
KALEMBA, Frank Michael, F2c, USN
KALISZ, Edwin Jacob, QM3c, USN
KAMPER, Roger Walter, AMM2c, USN
KELLER, Robert J., PFC, USMC
KENNEY, Richard D., Corp., USMC
KLASING, William August, EM3c, USN
KNUTH, Donald, S2c USN
KOCH, Curtis Herman, S2c, USNR
KOEPPE, Herman Oliver, SC3c, USN
KONESKY, Leon, Tech. Sgt., USMC
KOVAR, Robert, S1c, USN
LANE, John Udell, RM2c, USN
LAWRENCE, Edward Stephen, PFC, USMC
LEARNER, Robert B., S2c, USCG
LINDBERG, Henry Norman, S1c, USN
LINDSLEY, John Herbert, F3c, USN
LIPOVSKY, Lawrence P., PFC, USMC

LITTLE, Clarence J., F1c, USCG
LOCKARD, Joseph Robert, S2c, USN
LOEBACH, Adolph John, FC3c, USN
LOUGH, Ens. John Cady, USNR
LOUNSBURY, Thomas William, S2c, USN
LOVE, Henry Stewart, Jr., S2c, USN
LUND, Archie Marvin, AS, USNR
LYNCH, Clyde Bertis, WT1c, USN
MacDOUGALL, Eugene Rodger, Y2c, USN
MADAY, Anthony J., Pvt., USMC
MAHONEY, Francis P., PFC, USMC
MALEK, Michael, S2c, USN
MANCL, Frank J., PFC, USMC
MANION, Edward Paul, S2c, USN
MARTENAS, Bruce Alfred, MM2c, USN
MARTIN, Earl Wolfner, SK3c, USN
MATHEIN, Harold Richard, B2c, USN
MATHIEU, James Michael, S1c, USN
MATTESON, James E., PFC, USMC
McCLAIN, Charles W., PFC, USMC
McCARTHY, Thomas Joseph, AS, USNR
McDANIEL, James Benjamin, Torp.1c, USN
McGLASSON, Joe Otis, GM3c, USN
McGRANE, James Bernard, WT2c, USCG
McINTOSH, Dencil Jeoffrey, S2c, USN
McLAIN, Clayton O'Dell, SC2c, USNR
McQUADY, Kieth Lloyd, S2c, USN
McQUILKIN, Gerald F., PFC, USMC
MESSICK, Harvey, Corp., USMC
MEYERS, Joseph, S2c, USN
MILLER, Marvin Eugene, S2c, USN
MILLER, William Oscar, SM3c, USN
MOODY, Leonard, Jr., S1c, USN
MORLEY, Eugene Elvie, F2c, USN
MUSSON, James Harrington, Jr., QM3c, USNR
MYRICK, Wyvon L., Sgt., USMC
NANNINGA, Henry D., Sgt., USMC
NATZKE, Leonard Frank, S2c, USN
NINNESS, Paul Giltner, F1c, USN
NIX, Charles Edward, SM3c, USN
NORRIS, Peter S., PFC, USMC
OEHLER, Victor William, S2c, USNR
O'FARRELL, William Hubert, RM3c, USN
OSMUS, Ens. Wesley Frank, USNR
PARKER, June Winton, QM3c, USN
PENROSE, Marsdon O'Dell, S1c, USN
PETERSON, Robert Lee, S2c, USNR
PHELPS, Bernard Phillip, ARM2c, USN
PIERCY, Ralph Delbert, MM2c, USN
PITT, Howard William, Jr., S1c, USN
POLAK, Henry Joseph, F3c, USN
POWELL, Thomas George, S1c, USN
PRICE, George Franklin, F1c, USN
PROTZ, Christian Fred, Jr., F2c, USN

PRYMULA, Aloysius Walter, S2c, USN
PULLEN, Roy Alfred, S2c, USN
RALL, Lt. (jg) Richard Redner, (MC), USN
RANDALL, Lt. (jg) Gardner Durfee, USNR
REED, George E., PFC, USMC
ROSENBERY, Orval Albert, SF2c, USN
RUARK, John Wesley, Corp., USMC
RYCKEGHEM, Maurice Julius, GM1c, USN
SANDALL, Merrill Keith, SF3c, USN
SCHOENWOLF, Lt. Fred Lewis, USNR
SHAULL, Donald M., Sgt., USMC
SHELTON, Russell Lee, S1c, USN
SIDELL, John Henry, GM3c, USN
SIENICKI, Valentine Bill, S2c, USNR
SILVERSTEIN, Lt. Max, USN
SIMCOX, John David, S1c, USN
SKOKOWSKI, Joseph Florian, Prtr3c, USN
SMITH, Edward, GM3c, USN
SMUKSTA, John William, S2c, USNR
SNYDER, Robert C., PFC, USMC
SOLIDAY, Sam Henry, S2c, USN
SOLLIS, Milton Bernell Frank, S2c, USN
SPENCER, Melvin Everett, CMM, USN
SPOTZ, Maurice Edwin, F1c, USN
STARKS, Henry I., Pvt., USMC
STEELE, John M., PFC, USMC
STEELE, Mack Eugene, Bkr3c, USN
STEFFAN, Joseph Philip, BM2c, USN
STREET, Charles Raborn, F1c, USN
SUTHERLAND, Robert David, S1c, USN
SWAN, George Washington, F3c, USNR
SWEANY, Charles Edward, EM1c, USN
TAYLOR, Charles Benton, EM3c, USN
THOMPSON, Charles Leroy, S1c, USN
THOMPSON, Thomas Calvin, SC2c, USN
THUNHORST, Lee Vernon, S2c, USN
TIPSWORD, Keith Warren, MM1c, USN
TOBIN, Patrick P., PFC, USMC
TOW, Paul Herbert, Torp.3c, USN
TRIBBLE, Davis, Jr., AS, USNR
TYLOCH, Stanley Joseph, FC3c, USNR
VINCENT, Jesse C., Jr., Corp., USMC
VOZAK, Leo Carl, RM3c, USNR
WALTERS, Ens. Clifford Raymond, USNR
WALTS, Howard Lester, S1c, USN
WARD, William E., Cox., USN
WEBER, Ens. Frederick T., USNR
WEIER, Bernard A., Pvt., USMC
WELLS, Alfred Floyd, MM1c, USN
WENE, Ens. Carl Leon, USNR
WILLIAMS, Albert Luther, Mus2c, USN
WILLIAMSON, Mansfield Curtis, MA3c, USN
WODARSKI, Steven Joseph, S1c, USN

WRIGHT, Edward Henry, S2c, USN
YATES, James Allen, EM1c, USN
YATES, Orin Arthur, EM2c, USN
YEATS, Charles, Jr., Cox., USN
YOMINE, Frank Peter, F2c, USN
YOUNG, Robert Verdun, S1c, USN
ZAJAC, Theodore R., Pvt., USMC
ZEBROWSKI, Edward Francis, AS, USNR
ZEDDIES, Vernon Adrien, S2c, USNR
ZEMOLA, Henry, PFC, USMC
ZURCHAUER, Robert, Jr., Sgt., USMC

Wounded

ALLRED, Edwin F., PFC, USMCR
BARKER, James Bernard, S1c, USN
BAXTER, Gerald Francis, S2c, USN
BICE, Robert Krieg, S1c, USN
BLAKE, Billie Eugene, S1c, USN
BOZEK, Walter John, Pvt., USMCR
BROWN, Harry Verde, MM2c, USN
BUSH, Harry Paul, Bkr3c, USN
CARTER, Hillis D., Pvt., USMCR
CLINARD, Richard, S2c, USN
COTNER, Francis Eugene, S2c, USN
CRAYNE, Charles Richard, S1c, USN
CUMMINGS, 2nd Lt. Daniel L., USMC
CUNNINGHAM, Allen Eugene, AMM2c, USN
CURRY, Albert Earl, S1c, USN
DIENES, Walter Lawrence, SM3c, USNR
DIETZ, Edward Joseph, S1c, USN
DRABEN, Warren C., Pvt., USNCR
ELLIOTT, Nelson Warner, S2c, USN
FECHT, James Henry, S1c, USN
FRIZZELL, John William, GM3c, USN
GAULDEN, Paul Edward, F2c, USN
HUBER, Charles W., Pvt., USMC
KEENAN, Charles E., Pvt., USMC
KERR, Hugh Oliver, AMM3c, USN
KIEFER, Ens. Edwin Herman, USNR
LANE, Thomas Spencer, Jr., AM2c, USN
LANSING, Alfred M., S1c, USCG
LINDSAY, Thomas Derstine, S2c, USN
LOOMIS, Merrett Frances, S2c, USN
LORING, Alvin Leroy, S2c, USN
LOUCK, Marion Allen, S2c, USN
McFALL, Ens. John T., USNR
McKENZIE, Earl Eugene, S1c, USN
MENN, Robert Oliver, SF2c, USN
MERTZ, Robert Frederick, SF2c, USN
MITCHELL, Eldon Roscoe, S2c, USN
NICHOLS, Roy A., PFC, USMCR
PATTERSON, Cleone B., PFC, USMC
PERTLE, Walter H., S1c, USCG
POPP, Louis, S2c, USN

POZDRO, Ignatius, CBM, USNR
READY, Floyd Eugene, S2c, USN
SHELBY, Carl Edward, S2c, USN
STONE, Frank Herman Magnus, S1c, USN
SWEET, Granville George, Corp., USMC
THOMAS, Ens. Robert Ellsworth, Jr., USN
WILHITE, Teman, Pvt., USMC
WILK, Carl Joseph, S1c, USN
WILSON, Arlie Valley, S1c, USN
WILSON, Charles Leo, S1c, USN
YOUMANS, Clifford Reeves, AMM3c, USN

Missing

ABRAHAMSON, Chester Elmer, BM1c, USN
ADAMS, Richard Lee, S2c, USN
ALDERMAN, Chester C., Corp., USMC
ALLABAUGH, Everett Weldon, S2c, USN
ASHTON, James Clifford, F2c, USN
BAILEY, James Harold, RM3c, USN
BARTOSZEWICZ, Richard George, S1c, USN
BENJAMIN, Leslie Russell, S1c, USN
BLOCH, Francis William, Jr., S1c, USN
BOERSMA, Sidney Henry, QM1c, USNR
BRANDT, Lester F., PFC, USMC
BRANDT, Theodore, Jr., Cox., USN
BROWN, Allie Overton, F2c, USN
BRUCHERT, Layton Earl, SF3c, USN
BUBINS, Joseph Anton, S1c, USN
BYRAM, William Howard, RM2c, USN
CANTRALL, Guy Nard, CMM, USN
CARRADION, Albert Joseph, Cox., USN
COLBERT, Urban Harrison, Cox., USN
COOPER, Lloyd Franklin, S2c, USN
CORNISH, Robert Joseph, S1c, USN
CRAWFORD, Lawrence Orville, Y2c, USN
DALEY, Robert Martin, GM3c, USN
DAVIS, Capt. Robert G., (MC), USN
DAVIS, Virgil D., Pvt., USMC
DE FRATES, Emmanuel Edward, S2c, USN
DEKREON, Joseph Martin, S2c, USN
DELAY, Archie Junior, F3c, USN
DELL, Lt. (jg) Russell Clark, USN
DOTY, Carl, WT1c, USN
DREESBACH, Herbert A., PFC, USMC
DURFEE, Edgar Clark, F2c, USN
EARLYWINE, Virgil Elmo, GM1c, USN
ENGELLAND, Peter, MM1c, USN
FALLUCCA, Joseph, S2c, USN
FENCHEL, Gerald Erwin, S1c, USN
GILLINS, Robert Eugene, S2c, USN
GOODBERLET, William F., Pvt., USMCR

GRAHAM, Joe Butler, F2c, USN
GRASS, Earl Fabian, Cox., USN
GRAY, Marion Kenneth, S1c, USN
GREEN, Albert L., Jr., Sgt., USMC
GRUSH, Fred Joseph, Jr., S2c, USN
HAMEL, Don E., Field Mus., USMC
HARPER, George Plitt, Chief Torp., USNR
HARPER, Earl Rector, S1c, USN
HARRIS, Douglas Fairbanks, S2c, USN
HASKELL, William Dale, SC3c, USN
HAYS, Roy E., PFC, USMC
HEEREN, George March, QM1c, USN
IMBUSH, Leo Rufus, Y1c, USN
INGRAM, William, Jr., S2c, USN
IWANICKI, John Joseph, S2c, USN
IWANICKI, Stanley Joseph, S2c, USN
JIMERSON, Floyd B., Corp., USMC
JOHNSON, Elmer Elisworth, S1c, USN
JONES, Frank Joseph, CRM, USNR
KEEN, Owen J., Jr., F2c, USN
KELLER, William Robert, Bkr3c, USN
KIRINCICH, Joseph Nicholas, F3c, USN
KOZIOL, Paul W., Corp., USMC
KRAMER, Michailis, F1c, USN
KUPCZAK, Frank, Cox., USN
LAFFERTY, John Andrew, Pay Clerk, USN
LANDERS, Paul Herbert, RM3c, USN
LEDBETTER, Arthur V., PFC, USMC
LESZCZYNSKI, Anthony, Jr., S1c, USN
MAHER, Cdr. Arthur Laurence, USN
MARTIN, James Eugene, Cox., USN
MASSIONGALE, Frank Myers, SC1c, USN
McCARRENS, James F., Corp., USMC
McCOY, Harley Allen, F2c, USN
MENSCHING, Wilfred H., PFC, USMC
MESNER, Lawrence Richard, S1c, USN
MIDDLESWART, John Franklin, PFC, USMC
MILLER, William David, S2c, USN
MIRRE, Herman Adolph, F1c, USN
MOGA, Rome Joseph, S2c, USN
MORRIS, James Isaac, S1c, USN
MORRIS, Ralph Edgar, Mus2c, USN
MOSELEY, Lt. George Harley, (MC), USN
MULLINS, William Donald, S1c, USN
MYERS, Loren Stanford, S2c, USN
NORTHCUTT, James Albert, S1c, USN
NORVELLIS, Albert Frank, S1c, USN
NOVICKI, Stanley Edward, MM1c, USN
O'BRIEN, Joseph Bernard, PFC, USMC
PENNESSY, Thomas Patrick, AS, USNR
PETERSON, Lennart Oley, GM2c, USN
PRINCE, Arthur Martin, S1c, USN
RANGER, John William, AMM2c, USN
RATAJIK, Richard Paul, Y3c, USNR

REHFELD, Lester William, S1c, USN
ROARKE, Francis Joseph, F1c, USN
ROLAND, Junior Wayne, S2c, USN
RUZICKA, Albert, PFC, USMC
SADOWSKI, Henry John, EM2c, USN
SANDERS, Carl Murry, RM2c, USN
SCHNEIDER, William J., Pvt., USMC
SCHNITZIUS, Woodrow Bud, S2c, USN
SCOTT, Charles Duane, S2c, USN
SEIBERT, Jesse P., PFC, USMC
SHUBERT, Raymond Houston, S2c, USN
SHUMAKER, Clarence William, S2c, USN
SIKKEMA, Richard Duane, SM2c, USN
SMALL, George James, S2c, USN
SMITH, Hobert Lee, Jr., Field Music, USMC
SMITH, Raymond Jennings, MM2c, USN
SNIFF, Jack B., Field Mus. Corp., USMC
SPARKS, Paul William, S1c, USN
STECKENRIDER, Arnold Ray, CM1c, USN
STROUP, Paul Edwin, GM2c, USN
SWANSON, Edwin C., Corp., USMC
SWIONTEK, Stanley S., Field Cook, USMC
TARASZKIEWICZ, Stanley, F2c, USN
TERRY, Claude Harry, GM1c, USN
THOMAS, Frederick, PFC, USMC
THOMPSON, Lyle Wilson, S2c, USN
TIERNEY, Walter Richard, S1c, USNR
TOFT, Arthur Clarence, S2c, USN
UNTERKIRCHER, George Leroy, S2c, USN
VACCA, Babe Joe, AS, USNR
VALLIS, George, F1c, USN
VAUGHAN, Joseph H., Pvt., USMC
VLAHON, Samuel, Pvt., USMC
WALDRON, Richard Martin, Jr., S1c, USNR
WALLEN, Richard T., Pvt., USMCR
WALLS, Otto Ray, S2c, USN
WEIS, Leonard Michael, RM3c, USN
WILES, Robert Austin, F1c, USN
WINDLE, Robert England, Pvt, USMC
WOLLACK, Raymond J., PFC, USMC
WOOD, John Foster, CMM, USN
WRIGHT, Forrest E., PFC, USMC
WUERST, Edwin A., PFC, USMC
YAKOWCHYK, William, PFC, USMC
ZAJAC, Joseph F., Corp., USMCR
ZUROWSKI, John J., PFC, USMC

Prisoners of War

ADAMS, John C., PFC, USMC
ALBERT, Philip, PFC, USMC
ANDERSON, Robert L., PFC, USMC
ANDREWS, Arthur Dale, PFC, USMC
AUGUST, Alfred G., Pvt., USMC

AUTON, Lowell Everett, Y2c, USN
BAGGETT, Raymond, PFC, USMC
BARBATTI, Henry Thomas, S1c, USN
BARNES, Roy F., Jr., PFC, USMC
BATCHELDER, Walter Dale, Corp., USMC
BAZEWICK, Casey T., Corp., USMC
BEECHER, Lt. Col. Curtis T., USMC
BENDENSKI, Joseph Bond, PFC, USMC
BENNETT, Donald R., Platoon Sgt., USMC
BENNISON, Elroy Lawrence, PFC, USMC
BERLEY, Lt. Ferdinand Victor, (MC), USN
BIALEK, Leon G., Pvt., USMC
BIELA, Ralph E., PFC, USMC
BLACK, Robert S., Pvt., USMC
BLOSSER, Kenneth, Pvt., USMC
BOEHME, Arthur Alexander, GM2c, USN
BORCHERS, Orville Noy, PFC, USMC
BOWEN, James William, RM1c, USN
BOYD, Eugene Lorell, Chief Boat., USN
BOYDEN, William Henry, Jr., PFC, USMC
BRECKENFELD, Herbert George, F2c, USN
BREESE, Paul R., PFC, USMC
BRUNNER, Harold D., Pvt., USMC
BUCKLE, William Bernard, Jr., Pvt., USMC
BUDZYNSKI, John Joseph, PFC, USMC
BUEHLER, William Finkbiner, PFC, USMC
BUHLMAN, Clarence Nelson, S2c, USN
BURKEY, Hilary Francis, Pvt., USMC
BYRUM, Harry Edward, Jr., PFC, USMC
CALKINS, Joseph Valton, S1c, USN
CEMERIS, John, Gunnery Sgt., USMC
CHANDLER, Arthur William, S1c, USN
CHAPMAN, George Thompson, GM3c, USN
CHAPMAN, Mary F., NC, USN
CHARLESTON, Clarence G., PFC, USMC
CHITTENDEN, William Howard, Corp., USMC
CHUCK, Harris, PFC, USMC
CHUDZIK, Joseph Thomas, Pvt., USMC
CIARRACHI, Victor Frank, Sgt., USMC
COLLINS, Raymond H., PFC, USMC
COLLINS, William Marion, F3c, USN
COX, Joseph Theodore, S1c, USN
DEEDE, Truman J., Field Music, USMC
DE GROAT, Dudleigh Eugene, PhM3c, USN
DEPORE, Anthony, Pvt., USMC
DIECKOW, Clyde H., Pvt., USMC
DIEDERICH, Aloysius Michael, PhM2c, USN
DI MEO, Carmen M., PFC, USMC
DITEWIG, Wilbur Edward, PFC, USMC

DONOHUE, John Thomas, F1c, USN
DUDLEY, William A., Gunnery Sgt., USMC
DUNHAM, Estille Fay, PFC, USMC
EICHMAN, Martin David, Field Music, USMC
ELLISTON, John C., PFC, USMC
FELDMANN, Harry O., Pvt., USMC
FELDT, Everett Roy, EM1c, USNR
FERGUSON, Lt. George Theodore, (MC), USN
FICK, Joseph James, PFC, USMC
FINCH, Le Roy A., Corp., USMC
FISHER, George N., Jr., PFC, USMC
FORD, James D., Jr., PFC, USMC
FORD, James P., Pvt., USMC
FRAZIER, John H., PFC, USMC
FREHR, Joseph John, PFC, USMC
GERHARD, Ens. Edward Ashley, Jr., USNR
GIBBS, Wayne, SC2c, USN
GILBERT, Ross Henry, F1c, USN
GIRTMAN, Lawrence Herbert, Jr., S1c, USN
GLENNON, David, F1c, USN
GORDON, George William, CM3c, USN
GORDON, John P., PFC, USMC
GOUDY, Ralph Harris, PFC, USMC
GREENMAN, George E., PFC, USMC
GREENMAN, Lt. Robert Brownell, (MC), USN
GRUNWALD, Darwin D., PFC, USMC
GUSSAROFF, Jacob M., Sgt., USMCR
GUSTAFSON, Clarence P., Pvt., USMC
GUYOT, Dale, CMM, USN
HAIDINGER, Robert Fernand, Corp., USMC
HALE, Ralph H., Corp., USMC
HALE, Waldo Stedem, S1c, USN
HALL, Erwin LeRoy, S1c, USN
HALL, Richard Thomas, PFC, USMC
HARMON, Robert W., Pvt., USMC
HARRIS, Walter Lloyd, S1c, USN
HARRISON, Vernon Frank, Y2c, USN
HASKELL, Jenness Pearly, MM1c, USN
HATLEN, Edwin Arthur, S1c, USN
HAYDEN, Otis C., Field Music, USMC
HENRY, John Owen, CRM, USN
HETTGAR, Earl W., Corp., USMC
HICKS, William D., PFC, USMC
HIRSCHKAMP, George, PFC, USMC
HULL, Ralph L., PFC, USMC
INGRAM, Robert Francis, SM3c, USN
IOVINO, Neil P., Corp., USMC
JACOBS, Abe, Jr., S1c, USN
JANECEK, John C., PFC, USMC
JASPITS, John, Corp., USMC

JENKINS, Jack Wilbur, PhM2c, USN
JOHANNSEN, Fred, PFC, USMC
JOHNSON, Walter C., Sgt., USMC
JOHNSON, Wayne, S2c, USN
JOHNSON, Willis A., Corp., USMC
JOHNSTON, Herbert A., Corp., USMC
JONAITIS, Charles F., PFC, USMC
JONES, Harold Eugene, Y3c, USN
JURKOVIC, Paul, PFC, USMC
KATAUSKAS, Frank J., PFC, USMC
KAZ, Norman Nathan, PFC, USMC
KEITH, Robert Vincent, Corp., USMC
KERSKE, Arno F., CBM, USNR
KEY, Paul E., Pvt., USMC
KILLEBREW, William Edgar, Jr., Corp., USMC
KIRBY, Jack Pershing, QM3c, USN
KIRK, Terence Sumner, Corp., USMC
KLISS, John Stanley, Jr., PFC, USMC
KNIPPENBERG, Theodore Roy, Torp.1c, USNR
KOON, John Leland, F1c, USN
KOOPER, Leonard William, S1c, USN
KOPACZ, Joseph J., PFC, USMC
KOVALCIK, John P., PFC, USMC
KOZLOWSKI, Leonard Stanely, PFC, USMC
KOZUCH, Stephen T., Pvt., USMC
KRASS, Raymond George, B2c, USN
KREKAN, Albert, F1c, USN
KRIGAS, George M., S/Sgt., USMC
LANG, William J., PFC, USMC
LANGER, Robert Irving, RM3c, USN
LASCH, Lewis E., Asst. Cook, USMC
LAW, Phinas Allen, Asst. Cook, USMC
LEE, Robert Earl, Corp., USMC
LEHNER, James J., PFC, USMC
LEWIS, Charles Joseph, F1c, USN
LITTLE, Lt. Edward Neal, USN
LOEWE, Emmerson G., PFC, USMC
LOGAN, Wilfred Edward, S1c, USN
LORENZ, Henry Donald, PFC, USMC
LOWMAN, Ralph Seaton, SC3c, USN
LUTHER, William G., PFC, USMC
LUTZ, Eugene Joseph, PFC, USMC
MAASS, Edward, PFC, USMC
MAHLANDT, Melvin Henry, FC2c, USN
MALONE, James H., Asst. Cook, USMC
MARKWELL, Norman Ray, CBM, USN
MARRS, Wilbur Mason, PFC, USMC
MASA, Rudolph Emil, Boat., USN
MATES, Arthur Franklin, PFC, USMC
McAFOOS, Charles Basil, SM2c, USN
McCALLA, Marvin Paul, PFC, USMC
McGHEE, Darrell Eugene, S1c, USN
McMAHON, Ronald Oliver, PFC, USMC

McNEECE, Lee Anderson, SF3c, USN
MIKUCKI, Walter F., PFC, USMC
MOE, Lt. Cdr. Tilden Iver, (MC), USN
MOORE, Howard Carson, Corp., USMC
MORTVEDT, Carl, PFC, USMC
NASH, Louis, SF2c, USN
NEEDHAM, Ens. John Collier, USNR
NEGRO, John, Jr., PFC, USMC
NICHOLS, Frank, Jr., Pvt., USMC
O'CONNELL, John Joseph, Pvt., USMC
O'CONNOR, James Aloysius, WT1c, USN
OELBERG, Christian, Jr., Corp., USMC
OGNIBENE, Samuel S., PFC, USMC
OLDS, Marion B., Chief Nurse, USN
OLECHNO, Ray Albert, MM2c, USN
OLSON, Richard H., PFC, USMC
O'SHEA, John Joseph, Platoon Sgt., USMC
OVINGTON, Matthew, GM2c, USN
OWEN, Lester Charles, PFC, USMC
PADBURY, Edward A., Corp., USMC
PAINTER, John Scott, Corp., USMC
PAVLAKOS, James G., PFC, USMC
PEARCE, Lt. (jg) William Mansfield, USNR
PELLEGRINI, Alfred Frank, PFC, USMC
PETERS, James Orval, S2c, USN
PETRITZ, Ens. George Karl, USNR
PHILLIPS, Glen Neal, Pvt., USMC
PISTOLE, Frank Lyle Harold, S1c, USN
PRICKETT, Capt. William F., USMC
PRINCE, Frank W., Jr., PFC, USMC
PROCHASKA, Albert Joseph, PFC, USMC
PROTZ, Albert L., Mess Sgt., USMC
PULLEN, Robert Harold, S1c, USN
QUINN, Fenton R., PFC, USMC
RASCHICK, Ens. Richard Emil, USNR
RAYMOND, Samuel William, Corp., USMC
REBUFFATTI, Louis Domnick, SC1c, USN
REYNOLDS, Burrel James, S2c, USN
REYNOLDS, Victor Corey, Jr., S1c, USN
RICHARDSON, James M., PFC, USMC
RIGAS, Peter T., PFC, USMC
RITTER, Lt. Edward Francis, Jr., (MC), USN
ROBERTS, Albert William, F1c, USN
ROBERTSON, Virgil, Pvt., USMCR
ROBINSON, James William, Jr., S2c, USN
ROBINSON, John Walter, Jr., F2c, USN
RODENBURG, Harry, PFC, USMC
ROSS, William, Jr., F3c, USN
ROTTER, Edwin J., Field Cook, USMC
ROZYCKI, Stanley Joseph, PFC, USMC
RUCKER, John Dooley, PFC, USMC
RUNDLE, Clayton T., PFC, USMC

SAWYER, Alvin Ernest, Corp., USMC
SCHERTZ, Joseph William, Jr., S1c, USNR
SCHNEIDER, Leroy Nicholas, PFC, USMC
SCHROEDER, Robert Arnold, PFC, USMC
SCHULZE, Chal H., Sgt., USMC
SEDENBERG, Leslie, PFC, USMC
SETTLES, Edward Wayne, S1c, USN
SHEALY, Paul Louis, S1c, USN
SHOAFF, Forrest Kenneth, CBM, USN
SHORT, William Lawrence, CGM, USNR
SIMON, Adolph, PFC, USMC
SINKS, Arlie Theron, CMM, USN
SKWAREK, Stanley A., PFC, USMC
SLEZAK, Rudolph Mathew, Pvt., USMC
SLOWIAK, Walter Lawrence, Corp., USMC
SMITH, Lt. Cdr. Carey Miller, (MC), USN
SMITH, Noble Frank, Corp., USMC
SMITH, Lt. Stanley W., Dental Corps, USN
SONTAG, Louis E., PFC, USMC
SPARKMAN, Eldon Ellis, PhM1c, USN
SPRINKLE, Kenneth, S2c, USN
STARR, Larry Gordon, PFC, USMC

STOLLEY, Frederick Theodore, Corp., USMC
STONE, Frank Marion, Platoon Sgt., USMC
STONE, Harry H., SC2c, USN
STORY, Jerold Beers, Corp., USMC
STRAMA, Matthew Bruno, PFC, USMC
STUDNICKI, Edward Joseph, PFC, USMC
STURGEON, Edward Vinson, Pvt., USMC
TATTRIE, Norman Sidney, MM1c, USN
TAYLOR, James Leon, S1c, USN
TERFANSKY, Joseph Edward, PFC, USMC
THOMPSON, Francis Earl, Sgt., USMC
THOMSON, Peter, Pvt., USMC
TIRITILLI, Rosindo Albert, PFC, USMC
WARSHAFSKY, Jack, Corp., USMC
WHITE, Wilbur W., PFC, USMC
WILLIAMS, Carl H., Pvt., USMCR
WILSON, Lt. William Ritchie, Jr., USN
WIRTZ, Carl, PFC, USMC
WOLOS, Alex James, S2c, USN
WOOD, Ens. Edwin Allen, USNR
WROBLE, Fred, MM1c, USN
ZARENGA, Joseph Dominic, PFC, USMC

INDIANA

Dead

ADKINS, Bruce, S2c, USN
ALBRIGHT, Galen Winston, S1c, USN
ALLEN, Harold Raymond, S2c, USN
BAIRD, Billy Byron, S1c, USN
BAKER, Richard Harold, S1c, USN
BARGERHUFF, Benjamin Ernest, Jr., SF3c, USN
BATES, John Hail, RM3c, USN
BLACKBURN, Louis Raymond, S1c, USN
BLUM, Carl Homer, MM1c, USN
BLUNDELL, John Melville, ARM3c, USN
BOYER, Fred Hunter, F1c, USN
BRANDT, Oris Vernelle, S1c, USN
BROONER, Allen Ottis, S1c, USN
COCKRUM, Kenneth Earl, MM1c, USN
COFFMAN, Marshall Herman, GM3c, USN
COSTIN, Louis Albert, F1c, USN
CRAWLEY, Wallace, Dewight, Cox., USN
CRIPE, Donald John, CRM, USN
CRISWELL, Wilfred John, S1c, USN
CROMWELL, Howard Don, CM2c, USN
DAVIS, Loren P., PFC, USMC
DEETZ, John Wesley, GM3c, USN
DE REAMER, Ens. Robert W., USNR
DIERKING, Raymond Anthony, CEM, USN

DOBBINS, Albert James, S1c, USN
DRAKE, Virgil Stewart, MM2c, USN
DUNWAY, Marvin Boone, S1c, USN
EHRMANTRAUT, Frank, Jr., S1c, USN
EMERY, Wesley Vernon, SK2c, USN
EVANS, Ens. William Robinsen, Jr., USNR
EYED, George, SK3c, USN
FLORY, Dale Frederick, WT2c, USN
FLORY, Max Edward, S2c, USN
FOREMAN, Elmer Lee, F2c, USN
GARR, Robert Francis, Jr., Sgt., USMC
GIPSON, Ferrell Myron, BM2c, USN
GLENN, Arthur, MM1c, USN
HANNON, Francis Leon, SF3c, USN
HARKER, Charles Ward, FC3c, USN
HATHAWAY, John Harvey, AMM1c, USN
HUNTER, Robert Thomas, MM2c, USN
HURLEY, Wendell Ray, Mus2c, USN
JACKSON, Lester Dale, S1c, USN
KIDD, James William, SC3c, USN
KRAMER, Robert Rudolph, GM2c, USN
LEMOND, Edward Aden, F1c, USN
LIVINGSTON, Alfred Eugene, F3c, USN
McINTYRE, Warren W., PFC, USMC
MILLER, Robert Francis, F2c, USN
MINIX, Orville Ray, S1c, USN
NASH, Paul Andrews, FC1c, USN

NEWTON, Wayne Edward, S1c, USN
OWENS, Glenn Franklin, S2c, USNR
PALMER, Gilbert E., S2c, USN
PIERCE, Clifford Ben, S2c, USN
POLLITT, James Durham, S2c, USN
POOL, Elmer Leo, S1c, USN
PROFFITT, Charles McKindred, CGM, USN
ROYSE, Frank Willard, RM3c, USN
SHAIM, Donald Robert, S1c, USN
SHEFFER, George Robert, S1c, USN
SHERON, Arthur Lee, S1c, USN
SMITH, Gerald Owen, SK1c, USN
SMITH, Glenn Wesley, S2c, USN
SPENCER, Delbert James, S1c, USN
STEWART, Orval Lee, EM3c, USN
STRANGE, Charles Orval, F2c, USN
STRATTON, John Raymond, S1c, USN
TAYLOR, Harry Theadore, GM2c, USN
THOMPSON, Wilbur Thomas, AMM2c, USN
THURSBY, Wallace Edmund, S2c, USN
TODD, Dana P., Pvt., USMC
TRAPP, Harold Frank, FC2c, USN
TRAPP, William Herman, EM3c, USN
TUCKER, Raymond Edward, Cox., USN
VANDIVIER, Ens. Norman F., USNR
WESTCOTT, William Percy, Jr., S1c, USN
WILCOX, George James, Jr., S2c, USN
WILTROUT, Glen Erwin, BM2c, USN

Wounded

ARY, DeForest, EM3c, USN
CLEPHANE, Harry Clifford, S2c, USN
DAVIS, Earl Emery, SK3c, USN
DRISKELL, Joe Richard, Corp., USMC
DUFFIN, Woodrow Wilson, S1c, USN
FRANKLIN, Jesse Eugene, MM2c, USN
GOUGH, Harold Joseph, Cox., USN
HALEY, Robert Bruce, EM1c, USN
HAWKINS, Alan Chester, Torp.1c, USN
JOHNSON, Frank Vincent, S2c, USN
KING, Gifford Allen, S2c, USN
LYNCH, Robert O'Keefe, EM3c, USN
MARTIN, Donald Eugene, SF2c, USN
MEWES, Joseph Albert, MM2c, USN
MURCH, Douglas "A", SM1c, USN
QUINN, John Patrick, S1c, USN
SMITH, James Shirley, MM1c, USN
WIGGAM, Richard Edwin, SK3c, USN

Missing

ANSPAUGH, George Bell, S2c, USN
ARTHURHOLTZ, Harley R., PFC, USMC
BAKER, George Dewey, S2c, USN

BLALOCK, Cecil Glenn, SC2c, USN
BRAY, James Francis, Jr., PhM3c, USN
BROWN, Fred Louis, F3c, USN
CASSADAY, William H., Pvt., USMCR
CRAVENS, John Francis, Chief Mach., USN
CLINE, Gilbert Charles, Y3c, USN
CRABILL, Larry Andrew, B1c, USN
CRAIG, Nelson Leroy, MM2c, USN
CRAIG, Russell Harris, F2c, USN
CROXTON, Wilfred George, F1c, USN
DAGGETT, Harley William, FC3c, USN
DARLING, William Earl, S1c, USN
DOBKINS, Mack, MM2c, USN
DRAGO, Donald Thomas, S1c, USN
DYE, DeForest, SK3c, USN
DYMANOWSKI, Severyn Frank, Mus1c, USN
HACKER, Calvin, Jr., S2c, USN
HANNAH, Russell Carl, AOM1c, USN
HIATT, William Lincoln, S1c, USN
HOLLINGSWORTH, John William, F2c, USN
HOWELL, Leroy, Cox., USN
HUNTLEY, William Walter, S2c, USN
HUYS, Arthur Albert, S1c, USN
JORDAN, Howard A., Corp., USMC
LINVILLE, Bert S., Platoon Sgt., USMC
LUTES, Eugene Thomas, S1c, USN
MALSON, Harry Lynn, SK3c, USN
MASON, Evert Lee, F1c, USN
McCOY, Ralph Eugene, GM2c, USN
McFEE, Eugene Ambrose, F1c, USN
McKEE, Harold Rex, F1c, USN
McKENZIE, Norman Lawrence, S2c, USN
MERKEL, Alvin J., PFC, USMC
MEYERS, Lt. Richard William, USN
MIETH, William Clemens, F1c, USN
MILLER, Leslie Omer, M2c, USN
MILLS, Carl, F2c, USN
NEWTON, Paul Eugene, S1c, USN
NICKELSON, Raymond, MM2c, USN
OMO, Harold Frank, AOM1c, USN
PATTERSON, Ray Winfred, Corp., USMC
PURL, Andrew Archibald, CBM, USN
RAYMANN, James Eugene, F1c, USN
REED, Clarence Oscar, RM2c, USN
SANDERS, Roy, CMM, USN
SHELTON, Raymond Emette, EM3c, USN
SHIREMAN, Raymond Leon, MM1c, USN
SHORT, Chester Alonzo, WT2c, USN
SINGLETON, Arthur Edward, S2c, USN
SOFRANOFF, Mike, PFC, USMC
STOLLER, James William, Y3c, USNR
TUCKER, Clarence Solomon, CM3c, USN
WARINNER, John Warren, AS, USN

WEBBER, Arthur, S2c, USN
WEIBEL, Albert R., QM Sgt., USMC
WHITE, Walter Leland, MM2c, USN
WOLFE, Glendon Ray, S2c, USN

Prisoners of War

ALLEN, David Garland, GM2c, USN
ANTRIM, Lt. Richard Nott, USN
ARNETT, Lowren Augustus, S1c, USN
BAILEY, Jack F., Corp., USMC
BEAM, Richard Allen, S1c, USN
BEARDSLEY, Marvin Monroe, S2c, USN
BENNETT, John William, Gunner, USN
BINGHAM, Joseph Lee, S1c, USN
BLACK, Arthur Robert, S2c, USN
BOBOR, Andrew, Jr., MM2c, USN
BOOTHROYD, Owen, Jr., M2c, USN
BOWSHER, Walter Allen, Jr., Sgt., USMC
BROUSE, Wayne W., PFC, USMC
BROWN, Robert Lawrence, Corp., USMC
BROWN, Wilbur D., PFC, USMC
BYERLY, Eldon Lee, SK3c, USN
CASEY, John Franklin, MM1c, USN
CHERRY, Thomas Dwight, Y1c, USN
CIBOCH, George B., PFC, USMC
CLUBINE, Robert M., PFC, USMC
COCHRAN, Mortland, CMM, USN
COMINUS, Gus Jim, PFC, USMC
COOPER, Dale Rogers, Pho3c, USN
CORDELL, Doyle Dewitt, Y3c, USN
CRAGO, Donald M., PFC, USMC
CRAIG, Charles Frank, Cox., USN
CRAMER, Clinton Jerald, RM1c, USN
CUFFLE, Kermit S., PFC, USMC
DARLING, James Hollie, PhM2c, USN
DAVIS, Floyd Henry, Corp., USMC
DAVIS, Jack Edward, PFC, USMC
DAY, Clarence Nixon, S1c, USN
DEMMON, Bernard C., PFC, USMC
DE ROLF, Dell R., PFC, USMC
DEUITCH, Richard Henry, Bkr3c, USN
DE VOSS, Wilson Herbert, S2c, USN
DINAPAS, Joseph P., Asst. Cook, USMC
ELLIOTT, Jesse E., Jr., S1c, USN
GAFF, Max S., Corp., USMC
GRAHAM, Richard Gresham, Y3c, USN
GWINNUP, Ralph Henry, EM1c, USN
HARRINGTON, John LeRoy, RM3c, USN
HICKS, Albert, Jr., PFC, USMC
HOWARD, Edward Neal, WT2c, USN

IREY, James Earl, Prtr1c, USN
JONES, Leslie, CBM, USN
KIMBLEY, Rodney Miller, RM1c, USN
KLUEMPER, Edwin Herman, RM3c, USN
KRASMIZEH, Tony, F1c, USN
KRUCZEK, Walter John, Corp., USMC
LACH, Joseph Frank, F3c, USN
LANNARELLI, Anthony Nicholas, PhM2c, USN
LEONHARDT, Corwin Dean, GM3c, USN
McCOY, Lt. Cdr. Melvyn Harvey, USN
McDOWELL, Basil, MM2c, USN
McINTOSH, Edward Archie, S1c, USN
MEFFORD, Claude A., PFC, USMC
METZCAR, Emerson George, Y3c, USN
MILLER, Charles Ervin, S1c, USN
MROZ, Stanley, Torp.2c, USN
MUNIZ, Angel, Jr., Corp., USMC
MURPHY, Joseph Cornelius, PFC, USMC
MURPHY, William C., PFC, USMC
NASH, Lt. David, USN
NULL, Harley Theodore, EM1c, USN
O'MALLEY, James Marcellus, CM2c, USN
PERRY, Marion Leon, S1c, USN
PETTY, Warren Gamaliel, S1c, USN
RAUCH, Benjamin Nathan, Jr., S2c, USN
RAYMER, Francis Marion, Cox., USN
REED, Dick Leon, PFC, USMC
REGG, Norman Maxwell, PFC, USMC
RICHWALSKI, Edward Melcher, PFC, USMC
RIDER, Neil Orlando, PFC, USMC
RUGE, Capt. Robert F., USMC
SHEARER, James Monroe, S1c, USN
SMITH, Howard Bruce, CFC, USN
SMITH, Julio Forest, MM2c, USN
SMITH, Markle Tobia, RM1c, USN
SNYDER, Arthur Owen, S2c, USN
SOICE, Rae H., Corp., USMC
SPICER, Walter T., Corp., USMC
STANCZAK, John, MM2c, USN
STURGEON, Richard Donaldson, GM2c, USN
THACKERY, Elza Russell, CQM, USN
TURNER, Gerald A., Sgt., USMC
WAMPLER, Carl Amos, F1c, USN
WILLIAMS, David Marvin, S1c, USN
WILLIS, Donnis Wayne, S1c, USN
WILSON, Earl Vance, MM1c, USN
WINGER, Ira Robert, Cox., USN

IOWA

Dead

ALLARD, William Fabian, S1c, USN
ANDERSON, Lt. Elmer Dean, USN

ANDERSON, Ens. Lawrence D., USNR
ARICKX, Leon, S1c, USN
BAKER, Delmar Eugene, F1c, USN

BALDRIDGE, Norman Dean, S1c, USN
BALL, William V., S1c, USN
BARKER, Loren Joe, Cox., USN
BAUMBACK, Alvin Charles, F3c, USN
BEITZ, Carl Owen, S2c, USN
BELLOWS, Glenn Cedric, PFC, USMC
BELTHIUS, Lafern Winston, F2c, USN
BENNETT, Robert James, F3c, USN
BENSON, 2nd Lt. Thomas W., USMCR
BERSCH, Arthur Anthony, S1c, USN
BOOTON, Charlie Vinton, S1c, USN
BOSLEY, Kenneth LeRoy, EM3c, USN
BOWMAN, Howard Alton, S2c, USN
BRADSHAW, Harry Frederick, S1c, USN
BRANHAM, George O'Hara, ML1c, USN
BRAUN, Harold Ervin, F1c, USN
BREEDLOVE, Jack Asbury, FC3c, USN
BRIDIE, Robert Maurice, F1c, USN
BROWN, Wesley James, F1c, USN
BURCH, Earl George, Bkr3c, USN
BURGER, Dennis Daniel, CM3c, USN
BURKE, James Francis, QM, USN
BURKE, William A., Pvt., USMCR
BUTLER, James Warren, F2c, USN
CALLAHAN, James Albert, S1c, USN
CARNEY, Harold Francis, MM1c, USN
CARROLL, Guy Wayne, QM2c, USN
CHRISTENSEN, John Kenneth, S2c, USN
CLARK, Darwin Lawrence, ARM2c, USN
COLLINS, James Perry, M2c, USNR
CRABTREE, Joseph James, AS, USN
DAVIS, Myrle Clarence, F3c, USN
DE VORE, George Robert, S2c, USN
DRURY, Morris Frank, AS, USCG
EULBERG, Richard Henry, FC2c, USN
FERRIS, Donald Vance, S2c, USN
FIELD, John Henry, S1c, USN
FOOTE, George Perry, SK3c, USN
FORD, George Calvin, F2c, USN
FOX, Gilbert Roy, F1c, USN
FRICKE, Morris Edward, AMM3c, USN
FRISBIE, Harold Arthur, FC3c, USN
GARDNER, Ralph, S2c, USN
GEUDER, Roland Ernest, RM1c, USN
GESELL, Walter Alfred, S1c, USN
GIESEN, Karl Anthony, Y2c, USN
GOODWIN, Robert, SC3c, USN
GRANGER, Raymond Edward, F3c, USN
GRISWOLD, Ens. Don T., Jr., USNR
GROMAU, Harold George, SF3c, USN
GROSNICKLE, Warren Wilbert, EM2c, USN
GRUNDER, John Dale, AS, USN
HAAG, Donald Edwin, MM2c, USN
HEBEL, Bernard Ferdand, F2c, USN
HEIM, Gerald Leroy, S2c, USN

HENDERSON, William Walter, S2c, USN
HERRING, James, Junior, S3c, USN
IRISH, Robert Clemet, S2c, USN
JACKSON, Robert Woods, Y3c, USN
JANTE, Edwin Earl, Y3c, USN
JAVONOVICH, Anthony, Mach., USN
JERRISON, Donald D., Corp., USMC
JOHANN, Paul Frederick, GM3c, USN
JOHNSON, Arthur Weller, WT2c, USN
KEAT, Harry Martin, GM2c, USN
KELLOGG, Wilbur Leroy, F1c, USN
KENINGER, Leo Thomas, F1c, USN
KENNEDY, William Henry, F1c, USN
KERNDT, Ens. Gustave Frederick, USNR
KINNEY, Kenneth Harold, RM3c, USN
KJOLHEDE, Gerhardt Marvin, B1c, USN
KLEIST, Norman Arthur, F2c, USN
KUKLENTZ, Carl John, GM2c, USN
KVIDERA, William Lester, CM3c, USN
LANGENWALTER, Orville John, SK2c, USN
LEEDY, David Alonzo, FC2c, USN
LETTOW, Charles Austin, Cox., USN
LINCOLN, John William, F1c, USN
LIVESAY, Earnest Sherman, S2c, USNR
LOUSTANAU, Charles Bernard, S1c, USN
LUKOWICZ, Casimir John, M2c, USN
MANSKE, Robert Francis, Y2c, USN
McCARTY, Wallace E., PFC, USMC
McCORD, Willis Edward, S1c, USN
McKEEMAN, Bert Eugene, F1c, USN
MOORE, Robert James, F2c, USN
MOWREY, Robert E., PFC, USMC
MULICK, John Mark, HA1c, USN
MURPHY, Verle W., Corp., USMC
MYERS, Ray Harrison, S2c, USN
NICHOLS, Harry Ernest, SK3c, USN
NIEMOTH, Donald W. M., PFC, USMC
O'DELL, Charles Henry, S2c, USN
ODGAARD, Edwin Nelson, EM2c, USN
ODLE, Charles Thomas, S1c, USN
OLSEN, Eli, SK3c, USN
PALIDES, James, Junior, Mus2c, USN
PATTERSON, Lt. (jg) Donald Delos, USN
PEAVEY, William Howard, QM2c, USN
PENCE, John Wallace, R3c, USN
PENNOCK, Ralph Ira, GM3c, USN
PERRY, Forrest Hurbert, SC3c, USN
PETERS, Max Vestal, AOM2c, USN
PIERCE, Ens. Walter Edward, USNR
PLOFF, John Frederick, S1c, USN
REIMER, John William, Jr., ACM, USN
RICHARDSON, Robert Curtis, S2c, USN
RICHARDSON, Warren Jay, S2c, USN
ROBINSON, Clifton LeRoy, SK2c, USN
SAXTON, Glen Dwayno, BM1c, USN
SCHMIDT, Adam Joseph, F1c, USN

SCHMITT, Lt. (jg) Aloysius Herman, USN
SCHOLL, Raymond Earl, AM1c, USN
SCHRADER, Herbert A., Pvt., USMC
SCHULTZ, Leo Franklin, SF3c, USNR
SCOTT, Ralph Edward, S1c, USN
SEAMAN, Russell Otto, F1c, USN
SEARLE, Erwin LeRoy, GM3c, USN
SELLSTROM, Ens. Edward Robert, USNR
SHANAHAN, William James, Jr., SM3c, USNR
SHELDEN, Edward Judson, FC1c, USN
SPILMAN, Thomas Ponchard, RM3c, USN
STANLEY, Eugene Robert, S2c, USN
STOTT, Donald Alfred, S1c, USN
STRANATHAN, Dale Chester, CMM, USN
STROZDAS, Craig Leo, S2c, USN
STUBBE, Harris Blake, F1c, USN
SUESENS, Lt. (jg) Richard Wayne, USN
SWARTZ, Donald Miles, AS, USN
SZABO, Theodore S., Pvt., USMCR
TAYLOR, Robert Denzil, Cox., USN
TEMPLE, Monroe, S1c, USN
THORMAN, John Christopher, EM2c, USN
THUMAN, John Henry, PhM3c, USN
TIDBALL, David Franklin, S1c, USN
TITTERINGTON, Everett Cecil, F1c, USN
TUCKER, William David, F1c, USN
TURNER, William G., Pvt., USMC
ULRICH, George Vernon, F1c, USN
WAGNER, Thomas George, S1c, USN
WATT, James Ervin, F3c, USN
WEST, Ernest Ray, F1c, USN
WETRICH, Vernard Oren, FC1c, USN
WHISLER, Gilbert H., PFC, USMC
WILCOX, Arnold Alfred, QM2c, USN
WILLIAMS, Lester Lee, MM2c, USN
WILSON, Ray Milo, RM3c, USNR
WOODSIDE, Darrel D., AMM1c, USN
WORKMAN, Creighton Hale, F1c, USN
ZEIGER, Joseph M., BM2c, USN
ZOBECK, Lester Frank, S1c, USN

Wounded

ADKINS, John Robert, S1c, USN
ANDREWS, John Edward, RM2c, USN
BAUGOUS, Richard Carroll, EM2c, USN
CARROLL, Richard Charles, Y3c, USN
CARTWRIGHT, Julius Maxwell, F2c, USN
CHRISTENSEN, Henry Dewaine, CMM, USN
CLINGENPEEL, Donald Oscar, S1c, USN
DOWNING, Jack Merrill, Bkr2c, USN
FRANCIS, Hollis B., PFC, USMC
GOLDSBERRY, William Joseph, S1c, USN

GORDON, Roger A., Pvt., USMC
HUEY, Dennis Leroy, RM2c, USN
MANNING, Harry Keith, S2c, USN
PIERCE, Tedy Thomas, S1c, USN
POTTS, Garfield Collier, S2c, USN
PRICE, Leonard Anson, S1c, USN
ROSE, Lloyd M., Field Music, USMC
SAYRE, Bernard Joseph, SF2c, USN
STITES, Irvin Stanley, AMM3c, USN
VANCE, James Milton, S1c, USN
WADE, Harold Eugene, S2c, USNR
WARNER, Frederick Charles, S1c, USN
WATERS, Gerdon Marlowe, S1c, USN

Missing

ALLEN, Glen Lewis, S2c, USN
ARMSTRONG, Donald B., PFC, USMC
ASHMEAD, Morris Leland, S1c, USN
BARRETT, Branson Warren, S1c, USN
BERRY, Harley Leo, QM1c, USN
BLACK, Isaac Albert, S1c, USN
BLACKSMITH, Robert Lee, S1c, USN
BOEDING, Louis H., PFC, USMC
BRAATHEN, John William, S2c, USN
BROWN, Edgar Mark, MM2c, USN
BUNS, Arnold Herman, S1c, USN
BYRNE, Harold Leo, SC3c, USN
CARNES, Gordon Oliver, RM1c, USN
CHRISTENSEN, Lester Angus, S2c, USN
COON, Joseph Harry, S2c, USN
COYNE, Joseph Michael, F1c, USN
CRIPPEN, Marshall Ernest, Cox., USN
DAVIS, Joseph Simpson, S1c, USN
DEBORD, Mark Andrew, Music, USN
DILLON, Joseph Errol, S1c, USN
DONALDSON, Donald Gustav, F1c, USN
ENDORF, Conrad Nelson, F2c, USN
FAULKNER, Willard Serge, Y3c, USN
FAUST, Ervin Claire, S1c, USN
FLEETWOOD, Donald E., PFC, USMC
FRAME, Paul, S2c, USN
GERDES, Hans Heinrich, S1c, USN
GILBRECH, Earl Wilber, EM3c, USN
GORDFISH, Peter W., Jr., MM2c, USN
GRAPER, Edgar Allen, S1c, USN
GUERNSEY, Charles Edwin, S1c, USN
GUYER, Floyd Galon, S1c, USN
HALL, Joseph Murry, S2c, USN
HARTJE, Lamar Hugo, M1c, USN
HEY, Raydeen, B1c, USN
HINMAN, Earl Edward, Cox., USN
HOBBS, Merle Halver, S2c, USN
HORTON, Otto Farrell, S1c, USN
JENN, Henry, Platoon Sgt., USMC
JOHNSON, Burlen Gaylord, GM2c, USN
JOHNSON, Harold Arnold, Y2c, USN

KADLEC, Joseph, Pvt., USMCR
KAISER, Bernard Richard, Y2c, USNR
KETMAN, Robert Earl, Jr., S1c, USN
KNOWLTON, James Thomas, GM3c, USN
KOELLING, Vernon Louis, Mus2c, USN
KOLLMYER, Lt. (jg) Kenneth Leon, USN
LAIRD, Jay R., SC3c, USN
LAMPE, Theodore William, Cox., USN
LANGFITT, Perry E., S2c, USN
LEE, Harley Mowery, GM2c, USN
LENTS, Robert Wayne, Torp.3c, USN
LINDSTROM, Jonas Andrew, S1c, USN
LOCHNER, Francis John, GM3c, USN
LUNDGREN, Victor C., Jr., PFC, USMC
MANN, Harry Raymond, Torp.1c, USN
McFADDEN, Elmer Lewis, GM2c, USN
MIHALOVICH, John, MM2c, USN
MONTGOMERY, Recil L., PFC, USMC
MORROW, Sam Clement, SK2c, USN
MOYLE, Alfred Charles, PhM1c, USN
MUSSER, John Dolson, Jr., MM2c, USN
NEWTON, William Dow, S1c, USN
PATTERSON, Lewis Irl, CM1c, USN
QUIGLEY, Raymond Aloysius, F1c, USN
RAINS, Joseph Earl, S2c, USN
RHOADES, Robert Jack, S1c, USN
ROBERTS, Howard Grover, F1c, USN
ROMEO, Edward Vincent, CMM, USN
ROSZELL, Lyle Thomas, S2c, USN
ROTH, John Thomas, MM2c, USN
SCHNECK, Walter Karlton, Mus2c, USN
SCHRAM, Theodore, Bkr2c, USN
SCHWERS, Julius Francis, S1c, USN
SCOTT, James Chester, S1c, USN
SEATON, Leslie Frederick, S1c, USN
SMITH, Robert Louis, S1c, USN
SPRAGLE, Glenn Wesley, GM3c, USN
TUBBS, Robert Lee, RM2c, USN
VAUGHN, Leonard Leslie, F1c, USN
VOLZ, Vernon J., Pvt., USMC
WEATHERMAN, Dean, EM2c, USN
WEAVER, David Oscar, CMM, USN
WEISS, Virgil Charles, S1c, USN
WICKHAM, Clifford C., Pvt., USMC
WIDKIE, Gerald Wayne, S2c, USN
WILSON, James E., PFC, USMC
WILSON, Stuart Stanley, HA1c, USN
WINGER, Ancil Wayne, EM3c, USN

Prisoners of War

ANDERSEN, Lloyd G., Field Cook, USMC
APPENZELLIER, Marshall J., PFC, USMC
ATHEY, John Francis, Pay Clerk, USN
ATTEY, James J., Jr., Corp., USMC
BARBER, Leroy Frederick, GM3c, USN
BARNETT, Carroll Dale, PFC, USMC

BEESE, Fred Allen, PFC, USMC
BLACKFORD, Sidney Earl, S2c, USN
BLAYDES, Wilbur Kassel, Jr., PhM3c, USN
BOECK, Harvey H., PFC, USMC
BRIDGES, John Douglas, AMM3c, USN
BROWN, Kenneth LeRoy, PFC, USMC
BUCHENAU, LaVerne Andrew, S1c, USN
CAIN, Orville James, Sgt., USMC
CANNELLA, John D., PFC, USMC
CARDAMON, Frank, PFC, USMC
CARR, Edward W., Pvt., USMC
CARY, Oran Francis, RM1c, USN
CLAPSADDLE, Harold Kilburn, GM1c, USN
CONN, Floyd Ottis, Cox., USN
COOLEY, Delmar Earl, PFC, USMC
COON, Benjamin Franklin, CM3c, USN
DAGUE, Lawrence William, MM2c, USN
DAMERVILLE, Floyd, BM2c, USN
DAVIDSON, Gordon William, WT2c, USN
DITCH, William Irving, HA1c, USN
DITTO, Walter A., Pvt., USMC
DRENNEN, Homer K., Field Cook, USMC
DULLARD, Edward James, RM2c, USN
EADS, Lyle Willis, Y1c, USN
EMERICK, Billie Edward, PFC, USMC
EPPING, Kenneth Joseph, S1c, USN
EXLINE, Frank Victory, S1c, USN
FLEENER, Gene Allen, PFC, USMC
FORSMAN, Melfred LaVerne, S1c, USN
FREIBERGER, Walter Edward, PFC, USMC
GEORGE, Joseph Emanuel, Jr., Corp., USMC
GODFREY, Donald Francis, S1c, USN
GRANT, Larry Sherman, Cox., USN
HAMBLEY, Louis Clark, SM1c, USN
HANSEN, Ralph Robert, S1c, USN
HERRON, Joseph Edward, BM2c, USN
HERRON, Merle Lee, Pvt., USMC
HOOD, John Edward, S1c, USN
HOOVER, John Horsford, PhM2c, USN
HOUGH, Hubert Dwight, Y2c, USN
HUMPHREY, Earl Chapman, S1c, USN
HUMPHREY, Herbert Joseph, PFC, USMC
JAHN, Edwin Henry, S2c, USN
JOHNSON, Harold Martin, S1c, USN
JOHNSON, Harland Rayford, PFC, USMC
JOHNSON, Thomas Wesley, Corp., USMC
JORGENSON, Warren G., PFC, USMC
KERNES, Wilfred, PFC, USMC
KIJAK, Henry, Supply Sgt., USMC
KING, Orville William, PhM3c, USN
KLISE, James Glenn, AOM2c, USN
KRUPP, Russell J., Pvt., USMC
LAVIA, Emilio Anthony, QM1c, USN

LEWIS, Henry George, S2c, USN
LOWE, Lt. Mason Richard, USNR
MASON, George Frank, S1c, USN
McCUEN, Walter Rea, MM2c, USN
McDOLE, Glenn W., PFC, USMC
McFALL, William Edward, PFC, USMC
McGOWAN, James William, Prtr2c, USN
McMANUS, Harold Edward, S1c, USN
McMANUS, O. C., Ptr2c, USN
McQUEEN, Russell Orvill, RM2c, USN
McSHANE, George LeRoy, PFC, USMC
MICHELS, Glen Eugene, S1c, USN
MILES, William Ridgeway, S1c, USN
MOLLOY, George Donald, Sgt., USMC
MOORE, Capt. Robert B., USMC
MORLEY, Hubert Raymond, S1c, USN
MORRIS, John L., Corp., USMC
MURPHY, Leroy Vernon, PFC, USMC
NAESE, Durwald Alfred, S1c, USN
NIELSEN, Clare W., PFC, USMC
NIELSEN, Milford, Y3c, USN
O'CONNOR, James T., PFC, USMC
ORCUTT, Lyle Forrest, CMM, USN
PETERSON, James Lyle, Y2c, USN
PITCHER, Susie J., NC, USN
REDENBAUGH, Carl Eugene, PFC, USMC
REED, Robert P., PFC, USMC
RICHARDSON, Harold LaVerne, F1c, USN
RITTER, William Lee, BM2c, USN
ROBINSON, William Fredrick, CMM, USN
ROBINSON, Milo W., PFC, USMC
ROMANELLI, Joseph Michael, Sgt., USMC
ROUSH, Howard, Jr., S1c, USN

RUSSELL, Conrad G., PFC, USMC
SCHNEIDER, Loren Oscar, S/Sgt., USMC
SHOVE, Robert Glenn, F2c, USN
SMITH, George H., Jr., PFC, USMC
SORENSEN, Steve Michael, CBM, USN
SPENCER, George Raymond, MM1c, USN
STEARNS, Willard R., Corp., USMC
STECK, Rudolph Paul, CCStd., USN
SYDOW, Alan A'Dale, Sgt., USMC
TAYLOR, Robert E., PFC, USMC
THOMAS, Donald H., Pvt., USMC
THOREN, Oscar, Corp., USMC
TIEFEL, Dale Joseph, S1c, USN
TOMLINSON, Darrell E., PFC, USMC
TOMPKINS, Raymond Maurice, PFC, USMC
TRIMBLE, Linville Clyde, S1c, USN
TURNER, Keith Charles, MM2c, USN
VAALE, Ernest Christian, PhM3c, USN
WALKER, Paul Mohon, Y2c, USN
WALSH, Vance W., PFC, USMC
WATSON, Bruce Ezra, S1c, USN
WESTCOTT, Paul Leverne, Cox., USN
WESTBERG, William Bastian, BM2c, USN
WILLARD, Louis Arthur, F1c, USN
WILLERTON, Robert Paul, Y2c, USN
WILLIAMS, Harold Raymond, MM2c, USN
WRIGHT, William Jesse, BM2c, USN
WYATT, Dudley Duane, S1c, USN
WYMORE, Willis Dale, RM1c, USN
YODER, John Edward, S1c, USN
ZAGAR, Rudolph E., PFC, USMC

KANSAS

Dead

ABERCROMBIE, Ens. William Warner, USNR
ALDRIDGE, Willard Henry, S1c, USN
ARMSTRONG, Robert Benton, B2c, USN
BARNCORD, Cecil Everett, EM3c, USN
BARNETT, William Leroy, F3c, USN
BARRETT, Wilbur Clayton, S2c, USN
BARTHEL, Paul Richard, AS, USNR
BATES, Harold Eugene, F1c, USN
BAUER, Harold Walter, RM3c, USNR
BECKER, Marvin Otto, GM3c, USN
BECKER, Wesley Paulson, S1c, USN
BELT, Walter Sidney, Jr., F1c, USN
BIDDLE, John Cunningham Brakey, S1c, USN
BIERI, Harry Vernon, CFC, USN
BONEBRAKE, Buford Earl, F2c, USN

BRIGHT, Kenneth Ray, S2c, USN
BRONSTON, Jason S., Sgt., USMC
BROWN, Elwyn LeRoy, EM3c, USN
BROWN, Walter Scott, AMM2c, USN
BROWNE, Frederick Arthur, GM3c, USN
BURCHART, Edwin Bruno, MM1c, USN
CHESTER, Chris, Sgt., USMC
CHESTER, Edward, S1c, USNR
CHRISTIANSEN, Edward Lee, Bkr3c, USN
CLARKE, Robert Eugene, S1c, USN
CLIFFORD, Floyd Francis, S2c, USN
CORN, Robert Livingston, FC1c, USN
CONWAY, Ens. Paul Robert, USNR
CROMWELL, Anderson Burton, CMM, USN
CULBREATH, Andrew LeRoy, MM2c, USN
DANIELS, Theodore Duane, S1c, USN
DAVIS, Milton Henry, S1c, USN

DAY, Shirley Otis, WT2c, USN
DEAN, Lyle Bernard, Cox., USN
DOWNING, Eugene Victor, S2c, USN
DOYLE, Bernard Vincent, S2c, USN
DUVALL, Lawrence Dea, S2c, USN
EAKES, Wallace Eldred, SK3c, USN
EATON, Louis Merl, PFC, USMC
FANGHOR, Gene, GM3c, USN
FARR, Earl Benton, AOM2c, USN
GAGER, Roy Arthur, S2c, USN
GIBSON, Billy Edwin, S1c, USN
GIBSON, George Harvey, EM3c, USN
GILES, Doyle B., PFC, USMC
HADEN, Samuel William, Cox., USN
HAMPTON, J. D., F1c, USN
HARDESTY, Blaine Elijah, S2c, USN
HAYS, Victor Otis, S2c, USN
HAYS, William Henry, SK3c, USN
HEAVIN, Hadley Irvin, F1c, USN ·
HEINZMAN, Ens. Thomas McFarland,
  USNR
HESLER, Austin Henry, SM3c, USN
HOPE, Willard Herman, Y2c, USN
HOWELL, Frederick Christopher, S2c,
  USN
HUNSINGER, Wilbur Clare, RM3c, USN
INGRAHAM, David Archie, FC3c, USN
JONES, Edgar Richard, AMM3c, USN
JONES, Harry Cecil, GM3c, USN
KELLER, Ens. Robert Franklin, USNR
LINKE, Harold F., PFC, USMC
MAHANNAH, 2nd Lt. Martin E., USMCR
MAY, Louis Eugene, SC2c, USN
MIDDLETON, Edward Eugene, PFC,
  USMC
MOORHOUSE, William Starks, Mus2c,
  USN
MORRELL, Keith Noel, SK3c, USN
MYERS, Clair Clifton, S1c, USN
NAASZ, Erwin H., SF2c, USN
NAIL, Elmer Denton, F1c, USN
NEHER, Don Ocle, EM3c, USN
NIES, Dick Kinzer, S1c, USN
NUNN, Bertram Lavant, Bkr2c, USN
O'GRADY, Camillus Michel, S1c, USN
OLSEN, Ens. Edward E. K., USNR
PEARCE, Dale Ferrell, S2c, USN
PEARCE, LeRoy Deely, F3c, USN
PETERS, Lt. Thomas Videtto, USN
PERRY, Paul Edward, S1c, USN
PIRTLE, Gerald Homer, F1c, USN
PURINTON, Howard William, S1c, USN
PURVIS, John Fletcher, S1c, USN
REID, Earl Hilton, Jr., Sgt., USMC
RENNER, Francis J., Sgt., USMC
ROBERTS, Dwight Fisk, F1c, USN

SALTZGAVER, Robert LeRoy, Pho3c, USN
SAWYER, Cecil D., S2c, USN
SCHENCK, Eugene, EM2c, USN
SCHURR, John, EM2c, USN
SMITH, Elwin E., Field Music Corp.,
  USMC
STEVENSON, Frank J., PFC, USMC
STRICKLAND, Charles Emerson, S1c, USN
STUKEY, Bertie McClellan, S2c, USN
SWEENEY, Willis Harold, S2c, USN
TANNER, Ranger Faber, Jr., S2c, USN
TAYLOR, Thomas Russell, WT1c, USN
TINGLE, Ray Delbert, S2c, USNR
TRIPLETT, Thomas Edgar, S1c, USN
TURK, Pete, S2c, USN
VELIA, Galen Steve, SM3c, USN
VOGAN, Jack C., MM2c, USN
WAGONER, Lewis Lowell, S2c, USN
WEGENER, Ens. Leonard George, USNR
WHITE, Charles William, F3c, USN
WILBUR, Harold, CM3c, USN
WINDLE, Everett Gordon, S2c, USN
WISE, Rex Elwood, F1c, USN
ZANE, Squire Boone, WT1c, USN

Wounded

BERNDSEN, Simon B., F3c, USN
CARSON, Carl Melvin, S1c, USN
CHILES, Edward "C", CM3c, USN
CHRISTIANSEN, Harlan Carl, AS, USN
CONNERS, Elden Fay, S2c, USN
DOBSON, Clarence, Jr., GM3c, USN
GREER, Jefferson Gideon, S1c, USN
KEENAN, Harold Patrick, GM3c, USN
KRAPES, Glenn Huber, AS, USNR
LONG, Donald Ernest, S1c, USN
McGEE, Glenn LeRoy, S2c, USN
SCHUBERT, Lt. Cdr. Anthony Robert,
  USN
SHULTS, Ray Oscar, S2c, USN
SNYDER, Max Eldon, RM2c, USN
SOLTIS, Frank Anthy, SF1c, USN
STEMAS, William Leo, S1c, USN
WISEMAN, Harold Allen, GM1c, USN
WYRICK, Clifton Walter, Mus2c, USN

Missing

ALBERS, Harold Sidwell, AMM1c, USN
ALFORD, Charles Wilbur, Bug1c, USN
ANDERSON, Roy A., Field Cook, USMC
BELCHER, Jessie Glen, S1c, USN
BIRD, Oscar Huron, S2c, USN
BOONE, William Albert, SC2c, USN
BRUCE, Herbert Lyle, S1c, USN
CAMPBELL, James Enos, S1c, USN

DRAKE, Maryle LeRoy, RM2c, USN
EARHART, Marion Thomas, SM2c, USN
ESBAUGH, Elmer Marcena, SM2c, USN
FAIRBANKS, Carl Douglas, F2c, USN
FAST, John Arthur, PhM3c, USN
FEESE, Harold Chester, CEM, USN
FERREIRA, Lee Francis, S2c, USN
FOSTER, Clarence Clifton, MM2c, USN
FRAME, Charlie Morgan, RM1c, USN
FRANTZ, Harlan Milton, SK3c, USN
GIESELMAN, Gerald Victor, EM3c, USN
GILMORE, Morris B., PFC, USMC
GOODALL, Lt. Cdr. Henry William, USN
HARTENBERGER, Ramon Charles, BM2c, USN
HOOFER, Edwin Fay, S1c, USN
HOOPER, Lloyd Raymond, AMM2c, USN
HOWREY, George Alva, Jr., EM2c, USN
KING, Donald Paul, M1c, USN
KLYMASZEWSKI, Raymond Lee Roy, SC2c, USN
KOVARNIK, William Jacob, CMM, USN
LOCKHART, Ray Herman, S1c, USN
McCLASKEY, James Elroy, S2c, USN
MONK, Herbert Walter, F2c, USN
PRICE, William G., Corp., USMC
REVES, Elbert Leister, RM3c, USN
ROBBINS, Dale E., Sgt., USMC
SALYER, Harry Woodrow, S1c, USN
SHARP, Purdy Adolf, PhM2c, USN
SHETTER, Warren G., SK3c, USN
SMITH, Carl Francis, S1c, USN
SMITH, Loren Robert, F2c, USN
STEELE, Raymond C., Tech. Sgt., USMC
TAYLOR, Lee Ervin, SK3c, USN
THOMPSON, Eldro Walter, S2c, USN
TUNIS, Glenn Edward, GM3c, USN
VAUGHN, Noah David, MM1c, USN
WARD, Robert Elwood, GM2c, USN
WEISS, Lawrence Gray, SF1c, USN
WESTWOOD, Dale Edwin, RM2c, USN
WHAN, Howard Omar, Torp. 3c, USN
WHITFORD, William Franklin, S2c, USN
WILLIAMS, John G., PFC, USMC
WOOD, Sam Wesley, CWT, USN
WOODS, Harold Melvin, S1c, USN

Prisoners of War

ABRAHAMS, Franklin Edward, Field Music 1c, USMC
ADAMS, Edwin Birdene, PFC, USMC
ALBERS, Aaron Milo, SK2c, USN
ANDREWS, Alvin Anthony, F1c, USN
ARNOLDY, Arthur A., PFC, USMC
BARRETT, Lt. Arthur Miller, (MC), USN
BELL, Elmer Marsden, MM2c, USN

BENNETT, Lester C., PFC, USMC
BINNS, Donald Adair, Cox., USN
BISHOP, Charles Acle, SC3c, USN
BLACKBURN, Wilbur Burdett, Torp. 2c, USN
BLUMA, Lawrence, BM2c, USN
BRAWDY, Ira Melvin, Field Music 1c, USMC
BUCHANAN, Vernon Edward, F1c, USN
BURNETT, Von Pershing, EM3c, USN
CAPELL, Henry August, Jr., SK2c, USN
CHARLES, Howard R., PFC, USMC
COBB, Laura M., NC, USN
COULSON, Dale D., PFC, USMC
DANIELSON, Dewey Curtis, Field Music 1c, USMC
DEEDS, Buferd Alvin, PFC, USMC
DE MOSS, Donald Dean, S2c, USN
DENNING, James Thomas, PFC, USMC
DOBBS, Francis Eugene, AMM2c, USN
EATON, Edward Franklin, PFC, USMC
EBAUGH, Forest Vergil, S2c, USN
ECKLES, Le Thayer Edwin, GM3c, USN
FAGER, Burl Dwain, SM3c, USN
FRANKLIN, Edwin Eugene Kreimer, Corp., USMC
GARDNER, Glen G., Sgt., USMC
GIBSON, Donald C., Platoon Sgt., USMC
GOSLIN, Edgar Henry, F2c, USN
GUTHRIE, Frank A., Corp., USMC
HALE, Robert Lee, PFC, USMC
HART, Lewis William, MM2c, USN
HARTER, Harlan D., PFC, USMC
HECKEL, John Edward, PFC, USMC
HERNDON, Joseph Guy, MM1c, USNR
HOLL, Bernard Thomas, PFC, USMC
HOLLENBECK, William John, S1c, USN
HOUSE, LeRoy Christian, Jr., F1c, USN
JARRET, Elmer Pery, S/Sgt., USMC
JOHNSON, Nelson Laverne, FC1c, USN
KEAST, William Sheldon, S1c, USN
KELLER, Joseph J., Jr., Pvt., USMC
KELLEY, Harry Theron, S2c, USN
KING, James Orlo, PFC, USMC
LOHMAN, Benny Lee, PFC, USMC
LOUIS, Laurence Gilbert, GM3c, USN
MARTIN, Virgil Edward, PFC, USMC
McAMIS, Terrence Theo, Corp., USMC
McQUILLIAM, Raymond Cornelius, PFC, USMC
METTSCHER, Leonard Glenn, PFC, USMC
MILLER, Hayward Kenneth, MM2c, USN
MILLER, Robert Louis, B1c, USN
MIZE, Kenneth W., Sgt., USMC
NEVANS, Wesley B., PFC, USMC

NORTH, Sylvester Farrington, TM1c, USN
ODNEAL, Harley Miles, PhM2c, USN
ORTH, Harold Peter, Bkr2c, USN
OXENDINE, William Thomas, S1c, USN
PARKER, Claude Eugene, S1c, USN
PARSONS, Franklin R., PFC, USMC
PETERS, Donald Archie, PFC, USMC
POUNTAIN, James E., Pvt., USMC
PRICE, Fred Dalton, S1c, USN
PURLING, Donald Theodore, Y3c, USN
QUICK, Fred B., Jr., Pvt., USMC
REBENSCHIED, William E., PFC, USMC
RECTOR, Earl Woolsey, B2c, USN
REECE, Ernest Ivan, BM1c, USNR
REED, William James, F2c, USN
RHODES, Frank, WT2c, USN
RIEDEL, Frank F., PFC, USMC
ROBINSON, George Leroy, PFC, USMC
ROE, James Howard, S2c, USN
RYAN, Eugene Roy, PFC, USMC
SCHNEICKERT, George Arthur, MM2c, USN

SKRIPSY, Gerald L. J., Corp., USMC
SPENCER, Charles T., PFC, USN
SPROWLS, J. A., Corp., USMC
STAFFORD, Virgil Duane, PFC, USMC
STEARMAN, Guy, Jr., RM3c, USN
STEGMAIER, Carl Edward, Jr., PFC, USMC
STERLING, William Thomas, Pharm., USN
STEWART, William John, S1c, USN
STILL, John Howard, RM2c, USN
STONE, Wendell William, S1c, USN
THAIRE, Grover Ernest, PFC, USMC
THOMPSON, Harold Ray, CEM, USN
THOMPSON, Wendell Dwyer, Torp. 1c, USN
WARREN, Howard Edgar, Platoon Sgt., USMC
WASHBURN, Harold Estes, RM2c, USN
WEBER, Leo Henry, F3c, USN
WEIMER, Jacob George, PFC, USMC
WILSON, LeRoy Aaron, F1c, USN
WRIGHT, Robert S., PFC, USMC

KENTUCKY

Dead

ALLISON, Hal Jake, F2c, USN
ASHBY, Welborn Lee, F3c, USN
BARLOW, Woods Richardson, S2c, USN
BARNES, Frank, S2c, USNR
BARNETT, George Edward, F1c, USN
BECKMAN, William Joseph, SC3c, USN
BEDFORD, Purdy Renaker, F1c, USN
BINGHAM, Ernest Roy, GM1c, USN
BLACKBURN, Harding Coolidge, Y3c, USN
BOLLING, Walter Karr, F3c, USN
BOYD, Charles Seldon, MM2c, USN
BROCK, Hobert, MM1c, USN
BROCK, Walter Pershing, S1c, USN
BROWN, Pallas Franklin, S2c, USNR
BUCKLEY, Jack C., FC3c, USN
BURK, Millard, Jr., S1c, USN
BURNS, John C. Feltner, Cox., USN
CHANEY, George Reece, F3c, USN
COLLINS, Austin, SF3c, USN
COLLINS, James Earl, S1c, USN
COLLINS, Thomas Wickliffe, F3c, USN
CONLEY, Galen William, SK2c, USN
COUCH, Winslow, Tech. Sgt., USMC
COX, William Milford, S1c, USN
CROSBY, Louis Bertrand, SM2C, USN
CROWDER, Samuel Warwick, F1c, USN
CROWE, Cecil Thomas, GM2c, USN

DAWSON, James B., Pvt., USMC
DOYLE, Wand B., Cox., USN
EDWARDS, Harry Lee, S1c, USN
FARMER, Luther James, MM1c, USN
FERGUSON, Russell Alexander, MM2c, USN
FIELDS, Ira Pod, GM3c, USN
FORD, William Walker, EM3c, USN
FRASURE, Hershell Douglas, S2c, USN
HALCOMB, Roy Boneparte, RM3c, USN
HALL, Earle Boitnott, AMM2c, USN
HALL, Hubert Preston, S2c, USN
HARRIS, Lt. Cdr. Andrew Earl, USN
HELTON, Floyd Dee, S2c, USN
HIBBARD, Robert Arnold, Bkr2c, USN
HINTON, Carson Kinks, Cox., USN
HOWARD, Elmo, S1c, USN
HUMFLEET, Lowell E., Pvt., USMCR
JEWELL, James Buford, RM3c, USN
JOHNSON, Flavous B. Martin, GM3c, USN
JOHNSON, Henry Cecil, Jr., BM2c, USN
KUZEE, Ernest George, S1c, USN
LACY, Elbert Finley, SM1c, USN
LAING, William Bernard, AP1c, USN
LAMBERT, Willard H., F2c, USN
LAWRENCE, Elmer Patterson, S1c, USN
LAWSON, Willard Irvin, F3c, USN
LEOPOLD, Ens. Robert L., USNR
LILE, Roy Thompson, CSK, USN

LYNCH, Emmett Isaac, Mus2c, USN
MAGERS, Howard Scott, S2c, USN
MANNING, Leroy, S2c, USN
MATTHEWS, Clifton Edward, RM2c, USN
MATTINGLY, Philip, S2c, USN
MEADOWS, Elvin Lee, F1c, USN
MENGES, Ens. Herbert Hugo, USNR
MOORE, Robert Lee, CY, USN
MOSS, Tommy Lee, MA2c, USN
NELSON, Charles W., PFC, USMC
OAKLEY, Arthur Elwood, S2c, USNR
O'BRYAN, George David, FC3c, USN
O'BRYAN, Joseph Benjamin, FC3c, USN
OSBORNE, Mervin Eugene, F1c, USN
OTTER, Lt. (jg) Bethel Veech, USNR
OWSLEY, Alphard Stanley, EM3c, USN
PAYTON, Walter Collis, S1c, USN
PHILLIPS, James William, S1c, USN
PRIDE, Ens. Lewis Bailey, Jr., USN
PUCKETT, Edwin Lester, SK3c, USN
RECCIUS, Kenneth Melton, S2c, USNR
RECTOR, Clay Cooper, SK3c, USN
REDFERN, Doyle Glover, RM2c, USN
REEVES, Oscar, MA1c, USN
RICE, William Hurst, GM3c, USN
RICHARDSON, Warren John, Cox., USN
RICKARD, Len Crundy, F1c, USN
RITCHIE, Julius, S2c, USN
ROSE, Chester Clay, BM1c, USN
SCOTT, George William, SK2c, USN
SNYDER, Ens. Russell, USNR
STEELY, Ulis Claud, MM1c, USN
SUTTON, George Woodrow, SK1c, USN
TAPP, Lambert Ray, GM3c, USN
TARRENCE, Earl Leonard, S2c, USN
TEMPLETON, Chester Hendon, S2c, USN
THOMPSON, John, MM2c, USN
TREADWAY, Shelby, GM3c, USN
WALTHER, Edward Alfred, FC3c, USN
WATKINS, Lenvil Leo, F3c, USN
WHITAKER, Manuel Owen, AMM3c, USN
WHITE, Ens. Robert G., USN
WHITMER, Moses Jimmie, S2c, USN
WHITT, William Byron, GM3c, USN
WILLIAMS, Alter Lee, MA1c, USN
YOUNG, Martin Raymond, F2c, USN

Wounded

BERRYMAN, Charles Allen, S2c, USN
BRANT, Felix, S1c, USN
BROOKS, Earnest Raymond, S2c, USNR
EVANS, Henry Herbert, Jr., S1c, USN
GOSHEN, William Eugene, S1c, USN
HARPER, Eugene Everett, Cox., USN
HARRELL, Rupert Egbert, GM3c, USN

JOHNSON, Henry Engelbert, MM2c, USN
JOHNSON, William Lawrence, S2c, USN
KROULIK, Frank William, S2c, USN
LACEY, Herbert Paul, SF3c, USN
LOGSDON, Raymond Louis, HA1c, USN
LUKE, George Robson, S2c, USN
MULLINS, Edward, S2c, USN
NICHOLS, James Renfro, S1c, USN
PFEIFFER, Louis Edward, S1c, USN
REAGAN, Eddie, M1c, USN
WILEY, Norman Eugene, S1c, USN

Missing

ABRAMS, Russell Eugene, Y3c, USN
ALBIN, Blumer Thomas, F3c, USN
ALEXANDER, Clyde Marshall, CM2c, USN
ANGLIN, Roy Wilford, SM2c, USN
ANGLIN, Rudell Houston, S1c, USN
BAIZE, Talbert Wade, S1c, USN
BELK, Raymond Hays, F1c, USN
BELK, William Bailey, WT1c, USN
BRAUNER, Arthur Frederick, F1c, USN
CAMERON, J. R., MM2c, USN
CAMPBELL, Robert Earl, F3c, USN
CARR, John Richard, SM3c, USN
CHANDLER, Richard Carlysle, S2c, USN
CHANDLER, Thomas Kaiper, F1c, USN
CLEVINGER, Gordon Bennett, S1c, USN
CRIDER, Forrest Wayne, Cox., USN
DICK, Herbert Ethard, Cox., USN
DODDS, Lewis Chester, S1c, USN
DOWELL, Thomas Albert, Cox., USN
EIDEN, Herman George, F1c, USN
EWING, Charles Earl, WT1c, USN
FREEBURGER, Charles William, EM2c, USN
GILLIAM, Jesse James, SK3c, USN
GRASHAM, Stanley Jason, S2c, USN
HAWKINS, John Burks, S2c, USN
HERMAN, Richard James, S1c, USN
HOFFMAN, Chris Porkins, AMM3c, USN
HORNBECK, Louis Edward, S1c, USN
ISAACS, Edwin Charles, S1c, USN
JOHNSON, Robert Rance, S2c, USN
LAWSON, Eugene, S1c, USN
LOYD, Denver Wright, WT2c, USN
MARTIN, Pete, WT2c, USN
McCARTY, Orville Thomas, CWT, USN
McCLAIN, Robert Bruce, S2c, USN
McNABB, James Wilbur, S1c, USN
MOBERLY, James Grubbs, WT2c, USN
MOORE, Lt. Jack Cobb, USN
MOORE, Henry Elton, S2c, USN
NORRIS, Jack, F1c, USN

PERKINS, Jesse, BM3c, USN
POWERS, Fred Edward, Y3c, USN
REED, Norman, F1c, USN
RIFFLE, James William, SM3c, USN
ROBISON, Jessie Holland, EM2c, USN
SANDERS, William Howard, Bkr2c, USN
SCHMIDT, Albert George, Jr., S2c, USN
SHUBERT, Kyle Charles, S2c, USN
SMILEY, William Woodrow, F2c, USN
SMITH, George Walter, Jr., S2c, USN
STURGILL, Ollie James, S1c, USN
TACKETT, James A., PFC, USMC
VAUGHN, Charles William, MM2c, USN
WHISMAN, Herman Leo, SK3c, USN
WHITE, Glen Dail, S2c, USN
WILSON, James Marvin, PhM1c, USN

Prisoners of War

ANDERSON, Gerald Lee, S1c, USN
ANDERSON, Lt. Richard Kerfoot, USN
BEISLER, Joseph John, CMM, USN
BEURIS, George Washington, Jr., GM3c, USN
BISHOP, Jack Lupton, Y3, USN
BOAZ, Fern Gray, CMM, USN
BOLT, Clarence Leonard, S2c, USN
CALDWELL, Daniel Alfred, BM1c, USN
CALLIS, James Allen, Supply Sgt., USMC
CARNES, John Edward, SC1c, USN
CHRISTIAN, John Robert, Torp. 3c, USN
COOLEY, Richard, Supply Sgt., USMC
COX, James Leslie, RM2c, USN
FORRESTER, John Edgar, S1c, USN,
FROST, Clair Benton, SF2c, USN
FROST, Lawrence Karl, SF3c, USN
GAYHART, Clarence Irvin, EM1c, USN
GIRARD, William, F3c, USN
GOODMAN, Lt. Shields, USN
HEITMEYER, Charles Frederick, S1c, USN
HIRST, Allen Albert, EM3c, USN

HOLBROOKS, Benjamin, MM1c, USN
HOWARD, Reese, S1c, USN
HUGHES, Jess Willard, MM3c, USN
JUSTICE, Harold Morrice, S1c, USN
KNIGHT, Chester Brown, S1c, USN
KNIGHTEN, Jesse Willard, Supply Sgt., USMC
KRATZMEIER, August Frank, S1c, USN
MARKS, Capt. Mortimer A., USMC
MARSHALL, John Homer, SK3c, USN
MITCHELL, Walter Herschel, CBM, USN
MOFFETT, 1st Lt. Albert W., USMC
PARKER, Gerald C., PFC, USMC
PEAK, Martin Henry, PFC, USMC
PENCE, Earl W., Corp., USMC
POWELL, Odeen Delano, PhM3c, USN
POWERS, Marcellus Vinson, AM2c, USN
PRIMM, Charles Hubert, S1c, USN
PROFFIT, Leonard Melvin, PhM3c, USN
RAY, James Edward, F1c, USN
RICKERT, Albert Powhattan, Corp., USMC
RIGGS, Selby Bert, QM3c, USN
RIGHTMYER, Jackson Madison, RM1c, USN
ROBERTSON, James L., PFC, USMC
ROBINSON, James E., PFC, USMC
SATTERFIELD, Frank Allen, CCStd, USN
SHROUT, Sanford, WT2c, USN
SIMS, Hugh Ranceford, S1c, USN
STEVENS, Loranzo Dow, F2c, USN
SULT, Alfred Paul, Jr., S1c, USN
TAYLOR, Lt. Marion Woodrow, USNR
VANCE, Evans, SM3c, USN
VANCE, Shelby Nolan, CRM, USNR
WALTERS, Wyman, SM1c, USN
WHALEY, Joseph Hoyt, S1c, USN
WILLIS, Harry Paul, CGM, USN
WILSON, Lee Erick, S1c, USN
YANKEY, Ens. William Ross, USNR

LOUISIANA

Dead

ALFORD, Elwin, S2c, USN
ALFORD, Oscar Jep, RM3c, USN
ANDING, William Thomas, QM1c, USN
ARNAUD, Achilles, F3c, USN
ARNAUNE, Ens. Wilson Preston, USNR
ARNOLD, Claude Duran, Jr., F3c, USN
ASHMORE, Wilburn James, S2c, USN
AYDELL, Miller Xavier, WT2c, USN
BEATTY, James Alfred, S1c, USN
BELLARD, Theodore Allen, MM1c, USN
BLOUNT, Andrew, Jr., PFC, USMC

BOUDREAUX, Charles Camille, MM2c, USN
BOUDREAUX, Ralph McHenry, MA1c, USN
BOWEN, LeRoy Melvin, S1c, USN
BRISTER, Ens. Robert Earl, USNR
BROWN, Clarence Elmon, S2c, USN
CLARK, Malcolm, Bkr3c, USN
CONNER, Joseph Ucline, F1c, USN
CUTRER, Lloyd Henry, S2c, USN
DARCE, Raymond Joseph, ARM3c, USNR
DAVIS, John Quitman, S1c, USN
DILLON, George J., Jr., PFC, USMC

Dugre, Bernard Herman, MA3c, USN
Dugrest, Louis Felix, S1c, USN
Dusset, Cyril Isaac, MA1c, USN
Farley, Alfred Jack, S2c, USN
Fontenot, Elmo, Torp. 3c, USN
Fontenot, Woodrow Andrew, RM3c, USN
Foss, Ens. Rodney S., USNR
Frederick, Charles Donald, EM2c, USN
Gandy, Charley Woodrow, S1c, USN
Glover, Frank Adrion, S2c, USN
Glover, William Lucian, Jr., S2c, USN
Gomez, Charles Clay, Jr., S2c, USN
Gomez, Perique, Jr., AS, USNR
Graves, Dewitt Osborn, GM3c, USN
Hale, Lt. (jg) Roy Orestus, Jr., USN
Hardy, Arthur Hornsbur, AS, USNR
Harris, Charles Houston, EM3c, USN
Harveson, Lt. (jg) Harold Aloysius, USN
Holland, Thomas Jefferson, S1c, USN
Holmes, Charles, MA1c, USN
Howard, William A., PFC, USMC
Huval, Ivan Joseph, S1c, USN
Jones, Floyd Baxter, MA2c, USN
Jones, Ens. Thomas R., USNR
Kynerd, Marvin Earl, S2c, USN
Landry, Andre Joseph, AS, USNR
Landry, Kenneth Urban, S2c, USN
Legros, Joseph McNeil, S1c, USN
LeRouge, Merlin Fred, MM1c, USN
Lindup, Joseph John, AS, USNR
Marchand, Roy Joseph, F1c, USN
Marmande, 2nd Lt. James H., USMCR
Mayo, Marvin William FC2c, USN
McNeely, Herman Macune, S2c, USN
Michel, Victor Samuel, Jr., RM1c, USN
Miller, Ray Aubry, AS, USNR
Murphy, Jessie Huell, S1c, USN
Naylor, "J" "D," SM2c, USN
Perkins, Avery Evander, S1c, USN
Piacun, Nicholas Frank, F1c, USN
Picou, Ashwell Lovelace, S2c, USNR
Poole, Gradie C., PFC, USMC
Pribble, Robert Lams, FC3c, USN
Pritchett, Robert Leo, Jr., S1c, USN
Rasberry, Mahlon Eldridge, S2c, USN
Rice, Lenard B., PFC, USMC
Roane, Don S., PFC, USMC
Roberts, Nathan Anthony, F1c, USN
Roberts, Wilburn Carle, Bkr3c, USN
Savage, Ens. Walter S., Jr., USNR
Schanzbach, Donald J., PFC, USMC
Smith, Henry Clay, F2c, USN
Stoddard, William Edison, S1c, USN
Temples, Houston, S1c, USN

Thompson, Clarence, SC1c, USN
Tubre, Henry Oran, S1c, USN
Tyson, Robert, FC3c, USN
Waldman, Aaron J., Pvt., USMC
Walker, Prosper Edward, Jr., MA3c, USNR
Watson, Richard Leon, S1c, USN
Webre, Clarence Joseph, S2c, USNR
Wheaten, Joseph, Jr., MA2c, USN
Whitaker, John William, Jr., S1c, USN
Williams, Adrian Delton, S1c, USN
Willis, Robert Kenneth, Jr., S1c, USN
Woods, Vernon Wesley, S1c, USN
Zeringue, Philip John, MM1c, USN

Wounded

Bankston, William Homer, S1c, USN
Charlton, Hubert Huddlen, S1c, USN
Davis, Harold Richard, SK1c, USN
Doherty, John Andrew, CGM, USN
Faciane, Russell Bernard, S2c, USN
Lewis, Ermon Trellis, PFC, USMC
Simmons, Otto Leo, RM1c, USN
Williams, Louis Mitchener, PhM3c, USN

Missing

Andrews, David Zack, Jr., S2c, USN
Bachert, John Wilson, SK3c, USN
Barron, Floyd W., Pvt., USMC
Brown, Allen Ramsey, Jr., Y3c, USN
Cherry, Travis Joshua, GM1c, USN
Conner, William Andrew, F1c, USN
Cook, Howard James, S1c, USN
Durio, Russel J., Pvt., USMC
Evans, David D., PFC, USMC
Fontenot, Walter Joseph, F2c, USN
Funck, Louis John, Cox., USN
George, Marion E., PFC, USMC
Germany, Lt. Robert William, Jr., USN
Griffin, Lawrence J., PFC, USMC
Harder, Jack Henry, WT1c, USN
Hargrave, Dunice, PFC, USMC
Harrington, Preston, QM3c, USN
Hart, Charles Arthur, Jr., CBM, USN
Hebert, Melvin Ray, S1c, USN
Hinkson, Elmer Joe, F3c, USN
Hogan, James Elmore, Gunner, USN
Hux, Leslie C., PFC, USMC
Kraemer, Clyde Albert, Cox., USN
Lacombe, Lt. Joseph Leer, USN
La Fauci, Rosario Anthony, MM2c, USN
Maher, Ens. Albert Clinton, USNR
Murphy, Cdr. Joseph Augustine, USN (Ret.)
Nagele, Philip Raymond, F3c, USN

NETHKEN, Ens. Alva Freeman, USN
NIGHTLINGER, Ivan Clifford, F3c, USN
PENTON, Gibb G., Pvt., USMC
ROACH, George Louis, S2c, USN
SENTELL, John Mercer, III, S1c, USN
STARK, John Henry, RM2c, USN
STRICKLAND, Henry Wiley, Jr., S2c, USN
THAXTON, William LeRoy, F2c, USN
VERZWYVELT, James Joseph, S1c, USN
WELLS, Verdie O., Jr., PFC, USMC
WERNER, Joseph F., Pvt., USMC
WISECUP, John H., Pvt., USMC

Prisoners of War

ALFANO, Frank P., PFC, USMC
ANDERSON, Allison Leonard, PFC, USMC
BALLARD, Louis R., Corp., USMC
BERTHEAUD, Lionel Aloysius, Pvt., USMCR
BISHOP, Paul, PFC, USMC
BORNE, Joseph Edwin, PFC, USMC
BRENT, Claude L., Sgt., USMC
BROUSSARD, Lee Euel, RM2c, USN
BROWN, Fred Howard, PFC, USMC
BUGBEE, Karl A., PFC, USMC
BYALL, San J., Pvt., USMC
CARRIER, Wilton M., Pvt., USMC
CARRINGTON, James W., PFC, USMC
CARTER, Charles E., PFC, USMC
CHANDLER, Adrian P., Pvt., USMC
COHEN, Sam Lears, Jr., PFC, USMC
COLLINS, John Porter, CMM, USN
COLLINS, Nathan Mayo, MM1c, USN
COLVIN, Charles A., Jr., PFC, USMC
CONSTANTINEAU, Frank W., Corp., USMC
COOK, Henry H., Pvt., USMC
COURVILLE, Willard J., Pvt., USMC
DAVIS, H. D., Pvt., USMC
DEES, William J., PFC, USMC
DOMINGUE, Alton Joseph, Corp., USMC
DORAND, Henry Edward Francis, MM2c, USN
DUPONT, Joseph E., Jr., PFC, USMC
DUPUIS, Edward Charles, Field Music., USMC
DURBIN, Lloyd T., Pvt., USMC
FISCHER, Culver L., Pvt., USMC
FRALEIGH, Lt. Claud Mahlon, Dental Corps, USN
FROST, Jack, PFC, USMC
GAYNOR, James T., Corp., USMC
GILBERT, Oliver C., PFC, USMC
GOULD, Earl Vester, Pvt., USMC
GRAY, John Douglas, MM1c, USN

GREGOUIRE, Sylvester, PFC, USMC
GRICE, Walter L., PFC, USMC
GRIFFIN, Freddie J., Pvt., USMC
GUILBEAUX, Stanley Paul, PFC, USMC
HALEY, Philip R., PFC, USMC
HART, Bernice Clifford, Boat., USN
HATHORNE, Walter W., PFC, USMC
HEARD, James M., PFC, USMC
HEBERT, Philton J., PFC, USMC
HELLMERS, John Anthony, CCStd, USN
HERBERT, Thomas, PFC, USMC
HUTCHINSON, Hardy J., Pvt., USMC
IRVIN, Ernest Joseph, PhM3c, USN
JOHNSON, Aubrey P., PFC, USMC
JOHNSON, Wilmer, S2c, USN
KIDD, Walter, PFC, USMC
KING, Kirby Kermit, Corp., USMC
LEMOINE, Ernest Murrell, S2c, USN
LYLES, John Henry, Sgt., USMC
MADERE, Joseph Anthony, Pvt., USMC
MANCEAUX, Sylvestre P., PFC, USMC
MARTIN, Paul Joseph, Corp., USMC
MASON, Ralph T., Field Cook, USMC
MATHENY, Wilfred R., Pvt., USMC
MAY, Robert C., Pvt., USMC
McWIGGINS, James Collins, Corp., USMC
MELTON, Oliver Stephen, Corp., USMC
MILLER, Cody Aloysius, PFC, USMC
MORGAN, Clyde V., PFC, USMC
MOUTON, Grover E., Jr., Pvt., USMC
NIXON, James D., PFC, USMC
ORDOYNE, Eulice Joseph, Pvt., USMC
ORGERON, Edwin J., PFC, USMC
ORGERON, Lyonal Joseph, AOM3c, USN
OUBRE, Tony Theodule, PFC, USMC
PINGNO, Luke Marino, S1c, USN
PITTMAN, Cooper, MM1c, USN
PORCHE, William R., PFC, USMC
PRESLAR, Lyndal B., PFC, USMC
PROCELL, Clifton, S1c, USN
REBOWE, Joseph J., PFC, USMC
REDMOND, Russell J., PFC, USMC
REEMES, Willie, PFC, USMC
RYAN, Matthew J., Jr., Pvt., USMC
SARTIN, Cdr. Lea Bennett, (MC), USN
SILK, Allen L., Sgt., USMC
SINGLETARY, James Emerson, Torp.3c, USN
SMITH, Dick Richard, PFC, USMC
SMITH, Jack W., PFC, USMC
SMITH, James Albert, S2c, USN
STAHL, Rudolph William, Jr., PFC, USMC
STEADMAN, Edwin S., PFC, USMC
STODDARD, Harry Gordon, RM2c, USN
TATE, Willis, PFC, USMC

TERRY, Mabry Armster, Sgt., USMC
TOUCHET, Wilson, PFC, USMC
TRASCHER, Floyd Lance, PFC, USMC
TREUIL, Edward John, Corp., USMC
VICE, Bernard Lloyd, SK1c, USN

WAGGONER, Doyle Winslow, AOM1c, USN
WILKS, Zack Ezell, SF3c, USN
WILLIAMS, Luther, PFC, USMC
WILSON, James R., Pvt., USMC

MAINE

Dead

ALLEN, Ens. Stanley W., USNR
BELANGER, Maurice A., PFC, USMC
CUMMINGS, Fred W., Jr., PFC, USMC
DOBBINS, Richard Henry, EM1c, USN
FOGG, Lt. (jg) Carlton Thayer, USN
GENTHNER, George William, CSK, USN
GROVES, Ens. Stephen William, USNR
HARTFORD, Leon Winslow, Y3c, USN
JEWETT, Euan Lochel, S2c, USNR
MALEAR, Serbert Price, CSM, USN
McINTIRE, Raymond Kermit, Chief Torp., USN
MURRAY, John Francis, Cox., USNR
RANKIN, Galen Belmont, S2c, USN
SHANE, Lt. Cdr. Louis, Jr., USN
WALKER, Harold Rutledge, Cox., USNR
WELCH, Bradford Dearbon, SM2c, USN

Wounded

(None)

Missing

DUNPHEY, Claire Frederic, EM1c, USN
LANIGAN, Arthur Webster, S1c, USN
LAROCK, Sherwood H., Corp., USMC
RANDALL, Andrew James, Pay Clerk, USN

Prisoners of War

DEARBORN, Harvey Willis, CMM, USN
MERGENTHALER, John Joseph, PFC, USMC
OSTER, James Charles, CB, USN
STEVENS, James Jackson, PhM1c, USN

MARYLAND

Dead

ADAMS, Lt. Samuel, USN
ARNOTT, Robert Everett, PhM2c, USN
BELL, Sylvester Carroll, Jr., RM3c, USN
BROWN, Ens. Frank Snowden Ridgely, USNR
BROWN, Harry Allen, Y1c, USN
BURTH, Frank Anthony, PhM1c, USN
CHRONISTER, 2nd Lt. Mason F., USMC
CLARK, Lt. (jg) Howard Franklin, USN
CRUMPTON, James Theodore, AOM1c, USN
DOBBINS, Lawrence Spencer, MM1c, USN
ESTES, Roland Ashby, EM1c, USN
GAMBRILL, Raymond Alfred, S2c, USN
GATES, Lt. Albert Eugene, Jr., USN
GUSTAFSON, Lt. Arthur Leonard, USN
HARDIN, Minor Newton, Jr., AS, USNR
HARRINGTON, Lt. Thomas J., USNR
HAYDEN, Albert Eugene, CEM, USN
HEATLEY, Joseph Burke, S2c, USN
HILL, Roger Marvin, MM2c, USN
KELLY, Ens. Charles Markland, Jr., USNR
KELBAUGH, Mahlon John, S2c, USN

KIDD, Rear Adm. Isaac Campbell, USN
KING, Curtis Perryman, Mstr. Tech. Sgt., USMC
KOWALEWSKI, Charles Stanley, MM2c, USN
LANHAM, Roy Willis, S2c, USNR
LAWNICKI, Walter Sebastion, AMM3c, USN
MATEO, Macario, OS2c, USN
McKINNEY, John Edward, F3c, USCG
MILLER, Richard Carroll, Y3c, USNR
PHINNEY, Nelson, AMM1c, USN
RAWSON, Clyde Jackson, BM1c, USN
RESTIVO, Jack Martin, Y2c, USN
RICHARDS, James A., PFC, USMC
ROOP, Gordon Leroy, Mus1c, USN
SCHULER, Max Newton, F2c, USN
STEFANSKI, Albert Clemments, Torp.2c, USN
TAMBOLLEO, Victor Charles, SF3c, USN
TISDALE, Cdr. Ryland Dillard, USN (Ret.)
VAN ORMAN, Dennis Ray, WT2c, USN
WEIDNER, Louis Herman, SM3c, USN
WILCOX, Rear Adm. John Walter, USN
WORTHINGTON, Lt. Edward Hicks, USN

Wounded

BALODIS, Felix Vladimir, S1c, USN
DOMBROWSKI, Robert Edward, SF3c, USN
HOFFMAN, Joseph Daniel, CRM, USN
JOYNER, Walter George, F2c, USN
MORRIS, Thomas Redmond, GM3c, USN
NICHOLS, William David, CPhM, USN
WILLIS, Ens. Charles Fountain, Jr., USNR

Missing

BAUM, Benjamin George, PFC, USMC
BLINN, Lt. Cdr. Welford Charles, USN
BRITT, Lt. Cdr. Jacob William, USN
BURTON, Filmore Ernest, F1c, USN
FORTNER, James, MM1c, USN
GILMORE, Lt. (jg) Morris Davies, Jr., USN
GULLIVER, Lt. Louis Joseph, Jr., USN
HOLMS, William Edward, Jr., S1c, USN
HURT, Lt. Cdr. David Albert, USN
JOHNSON, Warren Larry, MM1c, USN
LAIRD, Charles Wesley, Jr., CMM, USN
LONG, Elmer E., Jr., PFC, USMC
MARSHALL, Robert Henry, Torp.3c, USN
NAPOLILLO, Francis Joseph, Jr., SC1c, USN
PHILLIPS, Paul Eugene, SK1c, USN
PRICE, Lee Costin, Jr., F1c, USN
SERAFINO, Saturnino, SC1c, USNR
SIGELKO, Robert Charles, S2c, USN
STEWART, Lt. Andrew Patrick, USN

STORM, Donald Edward, Cox., USN
UCZYNSKI, Alfred Adam, Torp.1c, USN
WETHERELL, Thomas Addison, CPhM, USN
ZUKOWSKI, Chester Joseph, PhM2c, USN

Prisoners of War

BOWMAN, George Raymond, AMM3c, USN
BROOK, Lt. Charles Bates, USN
COCHRANE, Donald Fraser, SK1c, USN
COLLINGS, Charles Mitchell, SF2c, USN
DALTON, Lt. Joseph Francis, USN
DABROWSKI, Bernard Alfred, F1c, USN
DUNCAN, Louis E., Sgt., USMC
EDWARDS, George Verl, SK3c, USN
FREENY, Lt. Col. Samuel W., USMC
GILES, Cdr. Donald Theodore, USN
HANDY, Harry Gray, SK1c, USN
HESS, Robert William, BM2c, USN
KAIN, Walter Louis, CBM, USNR
LANG, Earl Walter, ML2c, USN
MADSEN, Lt. Elwood Christian, USN
MERTEN, Frederick Rudolf, CCStd, USNR
PEARMAN, Charles George, GM1c, USN
QUINN, Lt. David Long, Chaplain Corps, USN
ROBINSON, Lt. James Burnham, USNR
TYREE, Lawrence Franklin, PhM2c, USN
VERBRIC, Anthony Henry, Cox., USN
WATTS, Edwin Allan, QM1c, USN
WILLIAMS, Lt. (jg) Richard Bland, Jr., (MC), USN

MASSACHUSETTS

Dead

ADAMS, Lt. Samuel, USN
ALVORD, Capt. John R., USMC
BALLOUGH, Rudolph, MM1c, USN
BANCROFT, Harold Wendell, S1c, USN
BARON, Lt. Cdr. Richard Swan, USN
BEAN, Howard Warren, RM3c, USN
BISHOP, John James, S1c, USN
BLACK, Lt. Cdr. Hugh David, USN
BORUS, Felix Edward, CMM, USN
BRAGA, Charles, Jr., Y2c, USN
BRANNAN, Thomas Leo, S1c, USN
BRENNAN, Ralph John, S1c, USN
BUNKER, Marshall Alton, WT1c, USN
BUTTERWORTH, William Edmund, RM2c, USN
CABANA, Napoleon Joseph, Mach., USN
CAMPBELL, Albert Ferguson, CQM, USNR

CASELLA, Mark Anthony Cornelius, QM2c, USN
CHAMBERLAIN, Russell Delano, Y2c, USN
CHAPMAN, Ens. Charles Edmund, USNR
CLEMENS, Finch Woodrow, MM1c, USN
COADY, Wilfred Albert, F1c, USCG
COGAN, Joseph Harold, PFC, USMC
COYNE, Walter, WT2c, USN
CRUZA, Joseph, Jr., MM2c, USNR
DARCH, Phillip Zane, S1c, USN
DAVIS, Ens. Alton Wood, USNR
DEFRANCE, John, MM1c, USN
DI CASSIO, Daniel John, Pvt., USMC
DOHERTY, Ens. John J., USNR
DORROUGH, Charlie Lee, CEM, USN
DOUCETTE, Joseph Francis, Jr., EM3c, USN
DOUGHERTY, Ralph McClearn, BM1c, USN

DUMOULIN, Dorant Henry, SK1c, USN
DUNN, Edmund Louis, Jr., RM3c, USNR
EDMONDS, Clifton Earle, S1c, USN
EMANUELLI, Joseph Angelo, AS, USCG
FISHER, Henry Joseph, Jr., SM3c, USNR
FORSYTH, William James, CMM, USNR
FRENCH, Harold Eaton, Jr., S1c, USNR
FRENCH, Ens. Joseph Luther, USNR
GALUSHA, Lawrence Albert, SK1c, USN
GAUDRAULT, Joseph Lucien Bernard, S1c, USN
GELINAS, Joseph Alphonse Raymond, WT1c, USN
GENETTI, Frederick Alfred, S2c, USN
GIONCARDI, Ralph Joseph, SC3c, USN
GOSSELIN, Joseph Adjutor Alfred, RM1c, USN
GREENWOOD, Arnold, FC3c, USN
GREGOIRE, Charles Normand, S2c, USN
GRINDLE, Ens. Arthur McIntyre, USNR
GUYNUP, Chester Arthur, CY, USN
HAGAN, 1st Lt. Frederic N., Jr., USMC
HALL, Norman Francis, F2c, USN
HAVEN, Edward Stanley, Jr., S1c, USN
HEALY, Lt. Cdr. Howard Raymond, USN
HEBERT, Edward Omer Patrick, EM1c, USN
HILLMAN, Merle Chester Joseph, PhM2c, USN
HRYNIEWICZ, Frank Alphonse, S1c, USN
IVERSON, James Andrew, F1c, USN
JOHNSON, John Russell, S1c, USN
JOHNSON, Robert Edwin, FC3c, USN
JONES, Clifford Earl, Torp.1c, USN
KANGAS, Eino William, S2c, USNR
KEOUGH, Harry, CWT, USN
KERICHENKO, John, Jr., S2c, USNR
LANDRY, James Joseph, Jr., Bkr2c, USN
LATTIN, Bleecker, RM3c, USN
LEARY, Thomas Francis, F1c, USN
LEBLANC, Edward Stephen, F1c, USN
LEE, Richard Joseph, EM2c, USN
LEMIRE, Joseph Sam Leonide, S1c, USN
LESCAULT, Lionel Wilfred, Bugmstr2c, USN
LEWIS, Ens. Victor Alan, USNR
LISI, Charles, Torp.3c, USN
LONDERGAN, Joseph Edwin, Jr., WT1c, USN
LORENTE, Walter Garcia, EM1c, USN
LUKE, Walter, RM1c, USN
MALYSICWSKI, Joseph, RM3c, USN
MASTROTOTARO, Maurice, S1c, USN
McCARTHY, Capt. Francis P., USMCR
McGRANN, Robert Phillip, EM2c, USN
McLEAN, Cornelius Francis, S2c, USNR

McMILLEN, Charles Wendell, CBM, USN
MOREAU, Raymond George, MM1c, USN
MORRILL, William E., Corp., USMC
MULKERRIN, Michael Joseph, S1c, USNR
NELSON, Robert Edward, AS, USN
O'BRIEN, Cdr. Thomas Francis, USN
O'CONNELL, William David, Jr., CSK, USN
OUELLETTE, Armand Raymond, CM2c, USN
PACE, Joseph Wilson, RM3c, USNR
PARKER, Reed Barnard, Y2c, USN
PARKER, Roy Abbott, S1c, USN
PATCH, Clifton Francis, CMM, USN
PEASE, Harry Norman, AS, USNR
PELLETIER, Paul Romeo, S2c, USN
PHARMER, Paul Daniel, WT2c, USN
PICHETTE, Norman Mitchell, S2c, USNR
PIDINKOWSKI, Anthony Frank, S1c, USN
POIRIER, Roger Phillippe, TC1c, USN
POPP, Walter Eugene, MM2c, USNR
RATHSACK, Walter Carl, CRM, USN
RAY, Howard, Torp.1c, USN
RAY, Lt. Martin Hasset, Jr., USN
REYNOLDS, Willard Jay, SC1c, USN
ROBERTS, Raymond Jack, GM1c, USN
ROCK, Robert Frederick, MM1c, USN
SADLOWSKI, Roman Walter, EM3c, USN
ST. MARTIN, Chester Albert, AS, USNR
SANTON, Howard Marshall, S1c, USN
SOLOMON, Robert Wesley, AS, USNR
SPEAR, Herman Alder, S1c, USN
STOPYRA, Julian John, RM3c, USN
TABAROWSKI, Joseph John, AS, USNR
TARSA, Peter Walter, AS, USN
TAYLOR, Donald Coates, AS, USNP
THOMAS, Stanley Horace, F3c, USN
TROXIL, Joseph George, MM2c, USN
TWEEDY, 2nd Lt. Albert W., Jr., USMCR
VEATOR, Manuel Cardoz, MM2c, USNR
VEZINA, Roderique Dolar, F2c, USN
VIBERT, Ovila Napoleon, S1c, USN
WHITE, Robert Leon, SC2c, USN
WICKETT, Ray Franklin, Jr., MM2c, USN
WORSTER, Richard Nealon, S2c, USN
YATES, James Allen, EM1c, USN
ZERVAS, Charles George, RM3c, USNR

Wounded

BARTLETT, Edwin Carl, MM2c, USN
BROWN, John Stephen, SK3c, USN
COOPER, Lt. Cdr. George Randolph, USN
DAUPLAISE, Arthur Joseph, S2c, USN
DONAHUE, John Joseph, S1c, USN
FERRIER, Harry Hackett, RM3c, USN
HAMILTON, Julian, RM3c, USNR

HARING, Ens. Philip S., USNR
HARRINGTON, John Dennis, SK3c, USN
JEZIORSKI, Stephen Peter, F1c, USN
LOWE, John Livingston, AMM3c, USN
MANOOGIAN, Mesag, S1c, USN
McCARRON, John Harry, GM2c, USN
MURCH, Robert Lyman, S2c, USN
NOBLE, Charles Wesley, Jr., F2c, USN
O'CONNELL, William Francis, GM1c, USN
RAGUSZ, Ernest John, S2c, USN
RILEY, John Bernard, CBM, USN
ROUISSE, Raymond Victor, SK3c, USN
ROUSSELL, Woodrow Albert, WT2c, USN
SARFDE, Edward, S1c, USN
SHEBAK, Joseph, S1c, USN
SPRAGUE, Paul Alexander, AM2c, USN
TRZCINKA, Raymond Joseph, F2c, USN
VALERA, John Anthony, SK3c, USN
WALKER, Horace Allen, RM1c, USN
WILSON, Robert, F1c, USN

Missing

BALASKI, Walter Joseph, Bkr2c, USN
BARGIEL, Stanley, SK1c, USN
BLAIR, Kenneth Sutherland, CSM, USN
BROWN, Charles Newton, MM2c, USN
BURNS, Charles Joseph, SF3c, USN
CARRIER, Raymond, Y1c, USN
CIPOLLA, Eugenio, MM2c, USN
CLAUDE, Henry L., Sgt., USMC
CODERRE, Ernest Joseph, WT1c, USN
COLLINS, John Floyd, RM3c, USNR
CROSS, Charles Leonard, Jr., Torp.1c, USN
CUMMINGS, Thomas William, S1c, USN
CZYZEWSKI, Charles, Ptr1c, USN
DALTON, Charles Edward, S1c, USN
DAY, Raymond, PhM2c, USN
DI GIULIO, Gori, CMM, USN
EARLYWINE, Roland Ilo, Y2c, USN
EKBERG, Oscar Donald, MM1c, USN
FELICE, Olindo, WT1c, USN
FISCHER, Ernest Otto Conrad, CBM, USN
GLASSETT, Francis Joseph, Jr., S1c, USN
GUGLIETTI, Albert David, GM2c, USN
IRVING, Arthur Richard, RM1c, USNR
JACKSON, Charles Henry, Jr., CRM, USNR
KERR, William James, EM3c, USN
KIERTIANIS, Stephen, MM1c, USN
KRAUS, John Ernest, CMM, USN
LITCHFIELD, Arthur Joseph, GM2c, USN
LONG, Joseph Freeman, AOM1c, USN

LYNCH, William J., Sgt., USMC
LYONS, Alfred Gregory, GM3c, USN
MacDONALD, Robert Joseph, Jr., S1c, USN
MacKILLOP, Donald, RM1c, USN
MATTILA, Martti Olavi, CSK, USN
McPEAKE, Lt. Cdr. Lawrence John, USN
MOFFETT, Joseph, PhM2c, USN
NORMAND, Joseph Raymond, RM2c, USN
PATINGRE, Joseph Edward, WT2c, USN
RUSEK, Leonard, Aer1c, USN
SARACINA, Joseph John, B2c, USN
SCOTT, David Edward, GM2c, USN
SULKIS, Ens. Leonard Stephen, USNR
TOBIA, Solvino Paul, AMM2c, USN
TSENDEAS, Elias, F3c, USN
TUSCHER, Joseph W., Pvt., USMC
USTASZEWSKI, Sigmund Henry, PhM2c, USN
WHITNEY, Gaylord Hill, CM2c, USN
WOJAS, Julian J., PFC, USMC
WOLKOWICZ, Joseph, S1c, USN
WOODRUFF, Lt. (jg) John Ford, USN
WYNNE, Edmund Griffith, F2c, USN

Prisoners of War

ALLAIN, Joseph Alban, MM1c, USN
ANDERSON, Earl Gustav, F1c, USN
ASHURST, Col. William W., USMC
BASTIEN, James Sanquinet, Pvt., USMC
BRODSKY, Charles, CBM, USN
BURRIDGE, George Thayer, RM1c, USN
CALLAHAN, Leo Augustus, S2c, USN
CARON, Henry Lawrence, PFC, USMC
CASEY, Leo Francis, F1c, USN
CHABOT, 1st Lt. Leon Edmond, USMC
CHARLES, Myron Winston, SK2c, USN
CLARK, Ens. Preston Richter, Supply Corps, USN
COHEN, Mitchell, Corp., USMC
COOK, Lt. (jg) Whitney Mowvry, USNR
CUSTER, Edwin Morton, CPhM, USN
DALESANDRO, Nicholas, F2c, USN
DEC, Mieczyslaw, MM2c, USN
EARLY, James Duignen, WT1c, USN
EWELL, Parker Thomas, RM2c, USN
FARWELL, Edward Pierce, GM2c, USN
FENN, Frank Lewie, Jr., PhM1c, USN
FITZGERALD, John Patrick, Sgt., USMC
FOSTER, Abner Ellsworth, Mstr. Gunnery Sgt., USMC
FREEMAN, Lawrence Irving, MM2c, USN
GABOURY, George Napoleon, CM1c, USN
GIBBONS, Robert Emmet, S2c, USN
GORHAM, Martin Joseph, CM1c, USN
GRAVES, Leon Adelbert, Corp., USMC

GREELEY, 2nd Lt. Robert Willis, USMC
GRESKA, Martin Andrew, Corp., USMC
GRIBBONS, George Thomas, CCM, USN
GRIFFIN, Lt. Cdr. Edward Raymond Joseph, USN
HADLEY, Samuel William, AMM3c, USN
HANNA, 2nd Lt. Robert Melton, USMC
HERBERT, Alfred Joseph V., BM1c, USNR
HOOKER, Francis Charles, Corp., USMC
IANUZZO, George Robert, PFC, USMC
JOHNSON, Earl Russell, HA1c, USN
JORDAN, Julian, Sgt., USMC
KENNEY, John, Torp.2c, USN
KESSLER, 1st Lt. Woodrow Milton, USMC
KNEELAND, Harold William, SM3c, USN
KOWALL, William Joseph, Jr., Sgt., USMC
KREBS, Phillip Charles, Torp.3c, USN
LA FLEUR, Albert Henry, RM3c, USN
LAFORET, Marshall John, EM3c, USN
LA MOUNTAIN, Arthur Lawrence, S1c, USN
LAREAU, Robert Armond, Corp., USMC
LILLEY, John, CBM, USN
MALOOF, George Meetry, BM1c, USN
MANNING, 1st Lt. Alan Shearer, USMC
MANNING, William Henry, Jr., S1c, USN
MARGIOTTO, Frank Joseph, Y2c, USN
MAXWELL, William Daniel, MM2c, USN
McANAUGH, John William, WT2c, USN
McCARTHY, James Henry, F2c, USN
McEVOY, James Arthur, Jr., MM2c, USN
McKINISTRY, Clarence Brown, Marine Gunner, USMC
MELANSON, Clarence Francis, AM2c, USN
MOORE, John Paul, PFC, USMC

MOREY, Edward Raymond, SK1c, USN
MORIN, Joseph Ernest Arthur, SC1c, USN
NIKKONEN, Rudolph, Gunner, USN
NORCROSS, Roger Merrill, Corp., USMC
PAIVA, Gabriel Dias, Jr., Torp.1c, USN
PARMENTER, Alan Weldon, RM1c, USN
PAYNE, Lt. Thomas Benjamin, USN
PERRY (PEREIRA), Joseph, Jr., Torp.1c, USN
PICKERING, George Fiander, SK3c, USN
PINKHAM, Paul Webster, F2c, USN
PORTER, Chester Avard, Corp., USMC
PROVENCHER, Raymond Joseph, Corp., USMC
RAY, John Francis, Asst. Cook, USMC
RAYMOND, Lt. Fred Luman, USNR
SANGIORGIO, Emil, QM3c, USN
SAWYER, Lt. Joseph Harlan, USNR
SELIGA, Martin Edward, CQM, USNR
SILVERMAN, Carl, AMM1c, USN
SOSVIELIE, Clarence Henry, CQM, USN
STANKATIS, Anthony, Corp., USMC
STEVE, John, CBM, USN
STRONG, Lt. Cdr. Robert Cowan, Jr., USN
TAYLOR, Lt. Cdr. Herbert Harold, USN
TRIPP, Harry Preston, RM3c, USN
TRUDELL, Ens. George Thomas, USNR
WALASZEK, Edward Thadeus, S1c, USN
WELCH, Martin F., Corp., USMC
WELLS, William, CGM, USN
WHITE, Lt. Alfred Fitzgerald, Dental Corps, USN
WROBLOWSKI, Thaddeus, WT2c, USN
YAMOLOVICH, Albert John, Corp., USMC
ZORZANELLO, Baselio Gesippe, EM1c, USN

MICHIGAN

Dead

ADAMS, Otto Frank, F1c, USN
AMON, Frederick Purdy, S1c, USN
AULD, John Cuthbert, S2c, USN
BALLANCE, Wilbur Frank, S1c, USN
BATTENFIELD, Stuart Clair, F3c, USN
BENSON, Walter Amburn, S1c, USN
BIEBUYCK, William Paul, S1c, USN
BITSON, Robert Lewis, S2c, USN
BOLAN, Fred Christian, F3c, USN
BONEBRIGHT, Jerold Ed, Cox., USN
BOSOM, Clarence John, AS, USN
BOYNTON, Raymond Devere, S2c, USN
BRANDEL, Ens. Bernard E., USNR
BUCK, Kenneth Mortimer, RM2c, USNR

BUDD, Robert Emile, F2c, USN
BUGMRA, Albert Lewis, S2c, USN
CANNON, 1st Lt. George H., USMC
CARLSON, Albert Earl, CM3c, USN
CARR, Nelson Leo, AM3c, USN
CLASH, Donald, F2c, USN
COLE, Wilson Burnett, F3c, USNR
COOPER, Kenneth James, FC3c, USN
COPELAND, Rex Edmund, GM3c, USN
CORBETT, Charles Corneilus, F2c, USNR
CRINELLA, Albert Bertin, F1c, USN
CRONCE, Paul R., MM2c, USCG
CROUSORE, Verlin Dorré, GM3c, USN
CYCHOSZ, Francis Anton, S1c, USN
CZARNECKI, Stanley, F1c, USN

Czekajski, Theopil, SM3c, USNR
Deguehery, Hans Werner A., SK3c, USN
Denby, Lt. Edwin, Jr., USN
Despres, Virgil Joseph, SM3c, USN
Diamos, Thomas Nick, F2c, USNR
Doll, Ens. George Lakemond, USNR
Eastman, Carl Edwin, S2c, USN
Egan, Phillip O., PFC, USMC
Ellis, Gerald James, GM3c, USN
Faddis, George Leon, GM3c, USN
Figurski, Theodore Joseph, S1c, USN
Finnegan, Ens. William Michael, USN
Flaherty, Ens. Francis C., USNR
Fox, Elmer Clarence, S1c, USN
Frazier, John William, Cox., USN
Fuzi, Eugene Dash, FC3c, USN
Gaylord, Delvan Clair, EM2c, USN
Gaynier, Ens. Oswald Joseph, USNR
Giles, Thomas Robert, EM3c, USN
Gisner, Robert James, Torp.3c, USN
Glass, Lawrence Carlton, S1c, USN
Goddard, John Dougall, F2c, USN
Graham, Wesley Ernest, S1c, USN
Gregg, Russell Emmett, F1c, USN
Griffin, Ralph, S2c, USN
Hallmark, Johnie Winfield, S1c, USN
Harris, James Edward, S1c, USN
Harris, Louis Edward, Jr., Mus2c, USN
Haverstick, George Francis, F2c, USN
Headington, Robert Wayne, S1c, USN
Hendriksen, Frank, F2c, USN
Henry, Otis W., Pvt., USMCR
Hickok, Warren Paul, S2c, USN
Holden, Charles Merle, S2c, USN
Holton, Ens. Ralph Lee, USN
Hopkins, Homer David, S1c, USN
Howard, Alvin Virgil, S2c, USN
Janke, John Charles, S2c, USN
Jastrzemski, Edwin Charles, S1c, USN
Jones, George Edwin, RM3c, USNR
Judd, Albert John, Cox., USN
Jugle, Lawrence William, WT2c, USNR
Juszkowski, Edward, PFC, USMC
Keeler, Louis Raymond, EM2c, USN
Keller, Paul Daniel, ML2c, USN
Kern, Reinhardt William, S2c, USN
Kinchsular, James Joseph, Jr., RM3c, USN
Kirt, Glenn Bork, AMM3c, USN
Klann, Edward, SC1c, USN
Klett, Lloyd Elmer, Jr., MM2c, USN
Koivisto, Lt. Martin Mathew, USN
Kovar, Robert, S1c, USN
Kowal, Chester Joseph, F1c, USN
Kowalski, Leonard Thomas, S2c, USN

La France, William Richard, S1c, USN
Lalonde, Eldo Frank, S1c, USN
Landman, Henry, AMM2c, USN
Landry, Gail, SF2c, USN
Latimer, Homer Price, Jr., Cox., USN
Lehman, Gerald George, F3c, USN
Lipke, Clarence William, F2c, USN
Lohman, Earl Wynne, S1c, USN
Lowe, Chauncey C., PFC, USMC
Lucas, Allen R., Pvt., USMC
Maillette, Paul Vincent, AS, USNR
Marsh, Ens. Benjamin R., Jr., USNR
Mason, John B. A., Pvt., USMC
Mattice, Roy Gordon, AS, USNR
McGuire, Francis Raymond, SK2c, USN
McNeil, Robert Travis, S1c, USN
Miller, Chester John, F2c, USN
Morse, Edward Charles, S2c, USN
Myers, Orval James, S1c, USN
Noah, Howard Joshua, S2c, USNR
Noonan, Robert Harold, S1c, USN
Olesnevich, George John, S2c, USN
O'Neel, James LeRoy, BM2c, USN
Ostrowski, Joseph, AS, USNR
Owen, Ens. William Lea, USNR
Paul, Vallentyne Lester, EM3c, USN
Petz, Robert Albert, S1c, USN
Pitcher, Jack Arthur, S1c, USN
Platschorre, Daniel Paul, S2c, USN
Powers, Joe Oneil, SK3c, USN
Powers, Ens. Oswald Aaron, USNR
Pursley, Robert Henry, S2c, USN
Raimer, Stanley Earl, SC3c, USN
Rice, Irvin Franklin, RM3c, USN
Riddell, Eugene Edward, S1c, USN
Ripley, Edwin Herbert, S2c, USN
Ross, Norman Carl, F3c, USN
Secord, David Duane, S1c, USNR
Shiffman, Harold Ely, RM3c, USNR
Shipp, Delbert Ray, S2c, USNR
Shively, Benjamin Franklin, F1c, USN
Simbulan, Quirino Cruz, Jr., AS, USN
Simmons, Tceollyar, S2c, USN
Sims, Laurence, ARM2c, USN
Smith, Lawrence, AS, USNR
Preeman, Robert Lawrence, GM3c, USN
Stebbins, Carl Cadmus, S1c, USN
Stegenga, George, AS, USN
Stephenson, Lionel, S2c, USN
Stinchombe, Guy, Jr., S2c, USN
Stretch, Robert Eugene, F1c, USN
Symons, Richard L., PFC, USMC
Turner, William James, F1c, USN
Uhlmann, Ens. Robert W., USNR
Ulrich, Elmer Herbert, F3c, USN

VALLEY, Lowell Earl, F2c, USN
VANDER GOORE, Albert Peter, F1c, USN
VAN SICKLER, William Glenn, F3c, USN
VERGNOCKE, Albert Rene, AS, USNR
WAGDA, Teddy, S1c, USCG
WASIELEWSKI, Edward, S1c, USN
WEATHERFORD, Charlie Fred, AS, USNR
WEEMAN, Lynn Clayton, Mach., USN
WESOLEK, Joseph Paul, F2c, USN
WETZEL, Orien R., F1c, USN
WHITCOMB, Cecil Eugene, EM3c, USN
WILLETTE, Laddie James, S2c, USN
WOLCHOK, William Frank, GM3c, USNR
WOOD, George Alan, S1c, USN
YUGOVICH, Michael Charles, EM2c, USN
ZIEHR, Ens. Carl Halley, USN
ZUK, Raymond John, S2c, USN

Wounded

AUGUSTINE, Merle Lloyd, AS, USN
COLE, John Claude, FC3c, USN
CONKLIN, Leo Ethan, Jr., S1c, USN
DE FIELDS, John B., Y3c, USN
EGGEMAN, Henry Bernhardt, M2c, USN
FAYTEK, James Michael, S2c, USN
FISHER, Wilson, S2c, USNR
FLETCHER, Ernest Phoenix, Jr., S1c, USN
GOMBASY, Louis George, S2c, USN
GOODHUE, Lt. Arthur Archibald, USN
GROOMER, Ray Manlius, Jr., RM3c, USN
HUBBARD, Thomas Henry, Jr., PM1c, USN
LECLAIR, Richard Joseph, S2c, USN
LUKASAVITZ, Steven Jerome, S1c, USN
McCLELLAND, Charles William, S2c, USN
McCLELLAND, James Allison, FC3c, USN
McCURDY, Russell J., Pvt., USMCR
McKENZIE, Colin, S2c, USN
PALMER, Robert Allen, S2c, USN
REED, Daniel Leon, S2c, USN
SMITH, Hilton Lewis, S2c, USNR
VANCE, Edward, S1c, USN
WOODS, Raymond James, S2c, USN

Missing

ALBRECHT, Edward A., PFC, USMC
BACHER, Albert Jacob, S2c, USN
BARAGA, Joseph, Sgt., USMC
BARNEY, Dwight M., Sgt., USMC
BOURGEOIS, Ens. Frederick Joseph, USNR
BREEN, Robert Phillip, F3c, USN
BROWN, Robert Clayton, F1c, USN
BUCKNER, Leroy Alvin, SC3c, USN
BUNKER, Wallace Harry, F3c, USN
CEBELAK, Sylvester Joseph, S1c, USN

CHORMANN, Chester Lewis, S1c, USNR
CLEMENS, Lyman Edward, S2c, USN
DEWEY, Henry Wissel, F3c, USN
DUNCAN, Richard, 1st Sgt., USMC
EGRI, George John, SC2c, USN
EUGATES, John Michael, S1c, USN
FARQUHAR, Warren G., S1c, USN
FREEMAN, Robert James, S1c, USN
GAGNON, Gilbert, Jr., S2c, USN
GILL, Benjamin Swartz, F3c, USN
HANDY, David Dix, S1c, USN
HARPER, David J. S., Pvt., USMCR
HAZEN, Glenn, E., Pvt., USMCR
HERGERT, Norman Clyde, MM1c, USN
HILLIARD, Robert Curtis, SM2c, USN
HOGUE, John Joseph, WT2c, USN
HORTON, Leonard A., PFC, USMC
HUSEK, George Earnest, M2c, USN
HUTZEL, Cecil Clarence, S1c, USN
KANE, Charles Joseph, CSK, USN
KULIKOWSKI, Leopold A., Corp., USMC
LEWALL, Zygmunt Stanley, AMM1c, USN
LEWIS, Robert S., Corp., USMC
LOVERIX, Campbell, Corp., USMC
MARSH, LeRoy Wilbur, BM2c, USN
MATHEWS, Donald Howard, MM2c, USN
McARDLE, Robert F., Corp., USMC
McDIARMID, Vincent C., Pvt., USMC
McFARLANE, Thomas James, PhM2c, USN
NELSON, Floyd Kenneth, S1c, USN
NELSON, James David, F3c, USN
OLSON, Avon Carl, S2c, USN
OSTROWSKI, George Peter, F2c, USN
PARKS, Theodore Junior, S2c, USN
PLUDE, Leo Edmond, S2c, USN
PONNIETZKY, John E., PFC, USMC
RACINE, John "J", GM2c, USN
REXIN, Frank Leo, S2c, USN
ROE, John Elmer, S2c, USN
RUTLEDGE, Eugene Leon, S1c, USN
SASS, Chester August, FC3c, USN
SEALE, Don Edward, AM3c, USN
SEIFERT, Paul Richard, CMM, USN
SELLERS, Lewis Earl, S2c, USN
SEWARD, William Rigby, EM3c, USN
SIMONSON, Randall Douglas, SK2c, USN
SKIDMORE, Lt. Bruce Delbert, USN
SLEGT, William, Jr., MM2c, USN
SMITH, Russell Van, S2c, USN
SMITH, Willard Andrew, PhM3c, USN
STONE, Merle Roy, S1c, USN
TREAT, Dayton William, AMM1c, USN
TUTTLE, Raymond Morris, BM1c, USN

VALLO, Robert Ralph, AMM3c, USN
VANDER MOLEN, Robert, Jr., F2c, USN
WATERS, Eugene Clayton, SK3c, USN
WELCH, Roscoe Wilber, S2c, USN
WESTON, Charles Henry, Cox., USN
WILEMON, Roy Haskell, S2c, USN
WISE, Howard Robert, F2c, USN
WOOTEN, Melvin Eugene, S1c, USN

Prisoners of War

ADAMS, Richard Paul, Pvt., USMC
ANDREWS, Leland M., Platoon Sgt., USMC
BARNES, Robert Allen, CM3c, USN
BELL, Ferris D., PFC, USMC
BENNIE, Woodrow W., Corp., USMC
BISHOP, Jack Roland, Platoon Sgt., USMC
BLACK, Joseph W., Corp., USMC
BLISS, Richard Wentworth, Y3c, USN
BUDZAJ, Zygmond, CGM, USN
BURNETT, Robert Benjamin, Torp.2c, USN
BURTON, Donald LeRoy, S1c, USN
BUSCH, Nelson A., PFC, USMC
BYER, Lawrence Marion, PFC, USMC
BYRNE, Herbert Richard, PFC, USMC
CARPENTER, James Edward, S2c, USN
CASSADY, Frank Leslie, HA1c, USN
CHROUCH, L. B., S1c, USN
CLARK, Duane J., PFC, USN
COOK, Harry, Aer1c, USN
CORNETT, John, Pvt., USMC
COX, James Henry, F1c, USN
CUNNINGHAM, Ray, GM3c, USN
DENSON, James Edward, Prtr3c, USN
DOLSEN, John C., PFC, USMC
DONOHUE, Joseph F., Sgt., USMC
DOYASH, Harold W., PFC, USMC
DUQUETTE, William George, S1c, USN
FELDSCHER, Johann Philipp, GM1c, USN
FERGUSON, Robert Allen, PFC, USMC
GAMBILL, William C., Chief Cook, USMC
GOODSON, Ray, S1c, USN
GRANT, Marion DeWitt, CBM, USN
GUITH, Frederick Gorman, Prtr1c, USN
HAHN, Dale Francis, S1c, USN
HANEY, Robert E., Corp., USMC
HARPER, Raymond J., Y1c, USN
HARVEY, Thomas E., PFC, USMC
HASKINS, Thomas Theron, S2c, USN
HENDRICKS, Robert Harry, S1c, USN
HENDRICKSON, Sulo Raymond, EM1c, USN
HERSHEY, William Louis, S2c, USN

HOLEWINSKI, Ralph Joseph, Corp., USMC
HUIZENGA, 2nd Lt. Richard Marvin, USMC
HUTCHINSON, Bill Martin, S2c, USN
JOHNSON, Earl Clarence, RM1c, USN
KAPPLINGER, Jarvis M., Corp., USMC
KEISER, Dean E., Corp., USMC
KINNEY, Harold E., PFC, USMC
KRUPA, Bennie, EM2c, USN
KRUTSCH, Arthur Franklin, S2c, USN
KUTCHEY, Edward Ferdinand, CMM, USN
LAUFF, Ens. Bernard J., USNR
LAVICTOIRE, Lt. Isaac Newton, USNR
LEE, Robert H., PFC, USMC
LUDWICK, Kirby, Jr., BM2c, USN
LUKINS, Richard Nesbitt, S2c, USN
MAJEWSKI, Joseph, Jr., F2c, USN
MARSH, Philip C., Jr., Corp., USMC
McCUTCHEON, Donald Nesbit, MM1c, USN
McDOWELL, William Stewart, Chief Torp., USN
McDUFFIE, William Gordon, CM3c, USN
McGARVEY, Albert Emery, FC2c, USN
McINTOSH, Edward Archie, AMM3c, USN
McLEOD, Wilifred Norman, Corp., USMC
MILLIKEN, Emerson John, Torp.1c, USN
MOLENDA, Steve A., PFC, USMC
NEVENZEL, Jay, Corp., USMC
OLMSTED, James N., Mstr. Gunnery Sgt., USMC
OSS, Michael Anthony, Platoon Sgt., USMC
PARRISH, Lloyd G., PFC, USMC
PATRICK, Edward Newell, Corp., USMC
PEPLINSKI, Matthews V., Pvt., USMC
POULIN, Lawrence Everett, F2c, USN
RICE, Kenneth V., PFC, USMC
RIDER, Russell Dale, CY, USN
RIETZLER, Hugo, Jr., Pvt., USMC
RODY, Leo, S1c, USN
SALYER, Joseph L., PFC, USMC
SCHULTZ, Glenn Robert, Chief Cook, USMC
SCHUMACHER, William Thomas, PFC, USMC
SPENCER, Mason Dale, S2c, USN
SPOONER, David R., PFC, USMC
STOCKWELL, Byron D., Jr., Pvt., USMC
SUOMI, Sulo Walter, S1c, USN
TARDIF, Paul Bernard, S1c, USN
TEBO, Floyd L., Sgt., USMC
TERVOLIS, Donald S., PFC, USMC

TIEFENBACH, Roger Evart, MM1c, USN
TOBIN, John D., SK1c, USNR
TRUPIANO, Michael A., PFC, USMC
TRUPIANO, Peter J., Corp., USMC
VIEAU, Euclid A., Asst. Cook, USMC

VINTON, Fred S., PFC, USMC
VONTOM, Sherwood Richard, Sgt., USMC
WHITMAN, Ens. Harry Gill, Jr., USNR
WOOD, Ludlow George, CSM, USNR
YOUNG, Kenneth Asa, S1c, USN

MINNESOTA

Dead

ALTO, Eino John, EM1c, USN
ANDERSON, Delbert Jake, BM2c, USN
ASCHENBRENNER, Clarence John, SF2c, USN
BLANCHARD, Albert Richard, Cox., USN
BRAIOVICH, John Dyshon, RM2c, USN
BRANCHAUD, Fred Ervin, MM1c, USN
BREKKEN, Evan Benhart, S1c, USN
BRICK, Frederick Raymond, MM2c, USN
BUKOVICH, Anthony, Y3c, USN
BYKLOM, Bennie, S1c, USN
CARROL, Ens. John Bennet, USNR
CHRISTIANSON, Harris Curtis, SK3c, USNR
CIHLAR, Lawrence John, PhM3c, USN
CLAFFY, Charles Porter, F3c, USN
CLAPP, Marvin John, SC3c, USN
CYRLACK, Glenn Gerald, SK2c, USN
DAHLHEIMER, Richard Norbert, S1c, USN
DREWETT, Robert Edward, Y3c, USN
DUOOS, Lester Wendell, F3c, USN
DVORAK, Alvin Albert, BM2c, USN
EBERHART, Vincent Henry, Cox., USN
ENGER, Stanley Gordon, GM3c, USN
ERBES, Leland Earl, F2c, USN
ERICKSON, Scott Walter, F2c, USN
FALZONE, Anthony John, S2c, USN
FILKINS, George Arthur, Cox., USN
FLEMING, Capt. Richard E., USMC
FUGATE, Kay Ivan, S1c, USN
GIFFORD, Quentin John, RM2c, USN
GRATZEK, 2nd Lt. Thomas J., USMCR
GREATHOUSE, Lt. (jg) John D., Jr., USNR
HALLQUIST, William Lowell, S1c, USN
HAM, Harold William, MM2c, USN
HAMPTON, Walter Lewis, BM2c, USN
HANSEN, Richard Mathew, ARM3c, USNR
HANSON, Carl Henry, S1c, USN
HANZEL, Edward Joseph, WT1c, USN
HELM, Merritt Cameron, S1c, USN
HOLM, Kenneth Laurence, F3c, USN
HOWARD, Rolan George, GM3c, USN

IVERSON, Glaydon Ignatius Clement, F3c, USN
JARRETT, Kenneth R., Pvt., USMC
JEFFERY, Ens. Ira Weil, USNR
JOHNSON, Aaron Luverne, SF3c, USN
JOHNSON, Lt. (jg) Earl Vincent, USN
JOHNSON, George E., PFC, USMC
JOHNSON, Joseph Morris, S1c, USN
KOCH, Walter Ernest, S1c, USN
KOEP, Mark John, S2c, USN
KRAUSE, Fred Joseph, S1c, USN
KVALNES, Hans Christian, S2c, USN
LABEEUW, Edward J., Pvt., USMC
LARSEN, Donald Clifford Vincent, RM3c, USN
LEIGH, Robert Blair, S1c, USNR
LEWANDOWSKI, Arthur Anthony, ML2c, USN
LIDGERDING, William Charles, RM2c, USN
LIEN, Kenneth Frank, S2c, USN
MACKNICKI, Stanley Walter, F2c, USN
McINNIS, John Adam, S1c, USNR
McQUADE, Robert Cameron, S1c, USN
MEUERS, Arnold Theodore, Prtr2c, USN
MIX, Raymond Frederick, AMM2c, USN
MRACE, Albin John, WT2c, USN
NELSON, Henry Clarence, BM1c, USN
NICHOLS, Robert Donald, S2c, USN
NIGG, Laverne Alious, S2c, USN
NORMAN, Orris Nate, F2c, USN
OSTRANDER, Leland Grimstead, PhM3c, USN
PARSONS, Thomas R., PFC, USMC
PETERSON, Lester Norman, GM2c, USN
PIELES, Edward Mitchell, S2c, USN
PREINER, Gerald P., PFC, USMC
QUESENBERRY, Willis Edward, AS, USN
RASMUSSON, George Vernon, F3c, USN
RICH, Ens. Ralph McMaster, USNR
ROBERTSON, Douglas Stuart, PFC, USMC
ROCHE, Ens. David John, USNR
ROGALLA, Emil Joseph, GM1c, USN
ROUSER, Charles Wayne, Jr., ARM2c, USN
RUNKEL, Carl Wayne, F1c, USN
SAL PETER, Harding Irving, AS, USNR
SAMPSON, Sherley Rolland, RM3c, USNR

SCHADL, Frank George, AMM3c, USN
SCHMIDT, Vernon Joseph, S1c, USN
SCHWARTZ, Richard Gerry, Pvt., USMC
SEYMOUR, John Gilbert, Mus1c, USN
SLETTO, Earl Clifton, MM1c, USN
SMALLEN, Robert LeRoy, S1c, USN
SMESTAD, Hagle Hojem, RM2c, USN
SOMMERS, John Joseph, PFC, USMC
STAHL, John A., Supply Sgt., USMC
STANLEY, Dayton Orlando, SC3c, USN
STORKSON, Julian Almer, AMM1c, USN
STROM, Burton James, ARM3c, USN
SULIER, Durwood Rupert, Sgt., USMC
THOLEN, Edward Henry, S1c, USNR
TIMM, Lloyd Rudolph, S2c, USN
TINI, Dante Sylvester, RM3c, USN
TODD, Neal Kenneth, F1c, USN
VOJTA, Walter Arnold, S1c, USN
VOLLUM, Ole Christopher, CBM, USN
WEIDELL, William Peter, S2c, USN
WEST, Ens. William Price, USNR
WICKLUND, John Joseph, S1c, USN
WIGEN, Henry Benjamin, Paymstr. Sgt., USMC
WILKENS, Paul John, S1c, USN
WILLIS, Ens. Walter Michael, USNR
WINTER, Ens. Edwin Ray, USNR
WITTENBERG, Russell D., Pvt., USMC

Wounded

ANDERSON, Wallace Dale, S1c, USN
CAMPBELL, Robert Francis, S1c, USN
CAREY, Capt. John F., USMC
COVER, Woodland Henry, SC3c, USN
DESSO, Ralph R., Pvt., USMCR
EUE, Gordon A., PFC, USMC
FLANAGAN, Ens. Guy S., Jr., USNR
GUTTERMANN, John Robert, SF3c, USN
HENDRICKSON, William Harlan, S1c, USN
JANIKOWSKI, Edward Joseph, Cox., USN
KUEHL, Russell K., Pvt., USMCR
LANE, Glenn Harvey, RM3c, USN
LANG, Donald Francis, SK2c, USN
LONG, Donald Berton, S2c, USN
McCARTHY, Ens. John R., USNR
McFALL, John H., Pvt., USMCR
MONROE, William, Pvt., USMC
MORRELL, Robert William, MM2c, USN
PETERSON, Kenneth Wayne, PFC, USMC
PROFT, Paul Donald, S1c, USN
REMPEL, Henry M., PFC, USMC
RODLAND, Bert W., Pvt., USMCR
SNOWBECK, Llewellyn Francis, S2c, USN
STEWART, John Baker, F2c, USN
ST. MARIE, Phillip Joseph, S2c, USN

TROWBRIDGE, Lyle D., Pvt., USMC
VOLK, Harvey Cecil, F2c, USN

Missing

BARRETT, Norval Sell, SF3c, USN
BELKNAP, Gordon Bernard, WT2c, USN
BETTINGER, Phillip James, QM2c, USN
BOOKOUT, Lt. (jg) Alton Coleman, (MC), USN
BOUCHER, Donald Lester, RM3c, USN
BOWLER, Morris Richard, WT1c, USN
BRICKLEY, Roy Lusch, F1c, USN
BUJAK, Stanley Frank, S1c, USN
BUNNELL, Victor Lionel, TC1c, USN
CLYMER, Shelton Henry, BM1c, USN
CREPPS, Harry Ernest, Jr., S1c, USN
EICHERS, Armund Joseph, S1c, USN
FRASER, Richard Louis, S2c, USN
GELINEAU, John Henry, CRM, USN
GOLYER, Paul Eugene, S1c, USN
HAGEN, Victor Palmer, S2c, USN
HANSEN, Arvid George, CQM, USN
HARVEL, Joseph, PFC, USMC
HENRIKSEN, Max "T", MM1c, USN
HOUT, Melville August, F1c, USN
HULTMAN, Donald S., PFC, USMC
JACOBS, Paul Joseph, Jr., MM1c, USN
KJORNESS, Charles Morris, S1c, USN
LAMM, Frederick William, EM2c, USN
LEE, Earl Henry, S1c, USN
LEITNER, Otto J., Jr., PFC, USMC
LHEUREUX, Henry James, SC3c, USN
LOVSHIN, William J., PFC, USMC
MAMER, George Ferdinand, S1c, USN
MILLER, Homer E., PFC, USMC
MOHN, Ralph Clifford, S2c, USN
MORISETTE, William Henry, Jr., F3c, USN
NELSON, Kenneth Lyle, S1c, USN
NICOLAO, Anthony, S1c, USN
O'NEIL, James Leroy, MM1c, USN
PERSONIUS, Glen C., Mstr. Tech. Sgt., USMCR
POFFENBERGER, John Charles, F2c, USN
PRESCHER, Harold Harry, EM1c, USN
RAINEY, Vernon Durant, S1c, USN
RASSATT, Urban Phillip, S2c, USN
ROBINSON, Harry Franklin, CY, USN
SAVOIE, Victorian Albert, SM2c, USN
SKRAMSTAD, Alvin Grover, Jr., S2c, USN
SMITH, Neil Leroy, S1c, USN
SOLLBERGER, Roland Anton Richard, GM1c, USN
SWANSON, Howard S., PFC, USMC
SZARKE, Andrew Steve, S1c, USN

THORPE, Carlton Wayne, GM3c, USN
THORSON, Harold Oscar, MM1c, USN
TREANOR, Halloran James, WT1c, USN
VAN DEN BERG, Suverns Ernest, GM3c, USN
WALCHUK, John, GM3c, USN
WATTERS, Donald Franklin, F2c, USN
WENHOLZ, Roy Arthur, MM2c, USN

Prisoners of War

AGIN, Gerald Leon, S2c, USN
ANDERSON, Ralph W., PFC, USMC
ANDERSON, Victor S., Corp., USMC
BACKHAUS, Fred Herman, SC3c, USN
BARTZ, John Edward, S1c, USN
BECKER, Robert Clifford, PFC, USMC
BENSON, John Nichols, S1c, USN
BIGGER, Delwone Buret, S2c, USN
BUETHE, George Merton, Corp., USMC
CARSON, Morris Anthony, PFC, USMC
CHRISTLE, Merrit Mashvils, Asst. Cook, USMC
CROTEAU, Edgar Arthur, PFC, USMC
DAVIS, Homer Eugene, GM2c, USN
DENNIG, Richard Alphonse, SK2c, USN
DIXON, Elmer, Sgt., USMC
DOBERVICH, 1st Lt. Michel, USMC
DORAN, William Daniel, PFC, USMC
FEELY, James John, S2c, USN
FINSETH, Halvor Edward, PFC, USMC
FISH, Cyrus Douglas, Corp., USMC
FLATHERS, Thomas A., PFC, USMC
FLYNN, David Charles, RM2c, USN
GALBRAITH, LeRoy, EM3c, USN
GALLATI, Boyd Edward, PFC, USMC
GARROW, Everett Charles, Field Cook, USMC
GILBERTSON, Homer Alva, PFC, USMC
GLISCHINSKI, Frank Arthur, PFC, USMC
GRUBER, Walter John, Corp., USMC
HAGEMO, Olaf William, Sgt., USMC
HANLEY, Robert Leon, S2c, USN
HANSON, Knute Clarence, PFC, USMC
HAUGEN, Henry, Sgt., USMC
HAUGO, Morris Sherman, Sgt., USMC
HENDRICKSON, Russell Warren, PFC, USMC
HITCHCOCK, Wallace Patrick, Corp., USMC
HOSLER, James Chauncey, PFC, USMC
HOYNY, Walter George, Cox., USN
JOHNSON, George Leroy, PFC, USMC
KALLGREN, Harry Marshall, Pvt., USMC
KARPEN, Edward Thomas Aquinis, Corp., USMC

KLINGBELL, Arthur Earl, PFC, USMCR
KLINGBELL, Herbert George, Pvt., USMCR
KLUSENDORF, William Alvin, Field Cook, USMC
KRUEGER, Marius Cartier, RM2c, USN
KUMM, Emmett Elmer, Pvt., USMC
LA CROIX, Orin A., Pvt., USMC
LARSON, Leonard E., Sgt., USMC
LARSON, Robert Vernon, S2c, USN
LATVALA, Einer Alvin, PFC, USMC
LAUER, Willard Lessle, RM1c, USN
LEE, Robert James, Corp., USMC
LEMBECK, Urban William, F1c, USN
LEWIS, Norman Lee, Jr., M1c, USN
MACKIE, Robert Jave, AS, USN
MACKNICKI, Stanley Walter, F2c, USN
MANN, Philip LeLand, BM2c, USN
MANSON, Lt. Emmet Loring, USNR
METCALF, Ens. John Coughlin, USNR
NORDINE, Karl Lawrence, Pvt., USMC
ODDEN, William M., PFC, USMC
O'HAVER, Goldia A., NC, USN
ORSMETH, Russell Bernard, PFC, USMC
PEARSALL, John Edward, PFC, USMC
PERRY, Ralph John, Corp., USMC
PETERSEN, Shannon Lester, EM2c, USN
PLATE, William Orville, F1c, USN
PRYATEL, Charles Joseph, F2c, USN
PYZICK, Maj. Frank Peter, USMC
READER, William Dwayne, PFC, USMC
ROSLANSKY, Marvin Arthur, Pvt., USMC
SCHILLING, Floyde Oscar, Platoon Sgt., USMC
SCHLEGEL, Alfred Arlington, PFC, USMC
SELVIG, Donald Allen, RM2c, USN
SILVERLIEB, Irving Bernard, PFC, USMC
SMITH, Bert Loraine, F2c, USN
SNATER, Bernard Jake, Mach., USN
SNYDER, Charles Francis, PFC, USMC
STIMAC, Joe Edward, Pvt., USMC
STRAND, Ens. Lowell Hall, USNR
SWAHN, Berkley Rodger, PFC, USMC
SWANSON, Dorsey Guy, S1c, USN
TAYLOR, Claude Harold, PFC, USMC
TAYLOR, Leonard Andrew, CGM, USNR
TUOMALA, Reino William, PFC, USMC
VAN BLAIR, Bernard Charles, Corp., USMC
VIDAL, Donald C., Pvt., USMC
WILSON, Willie Lee, S1c, USN
WITTKOP, Lawrence Henry, F1c, USN
WOOD, Cecil L., Marine Gunner, USMC
WORKING, Nelson A., PFC, USMC
ZECH, Peter Frank, CMM, USNR

MISSISSIPPI

Dead

BARKLEY, Troy C., ARM3c, USN
BOND, Burnis L., Corp., USMC
BRAMLETT, Adrian, GM3c, USN
BRATU, Cecil Victor, RM3c, USCG
CAMPBELL, Warren Edmond, S1c, USN
CHADWICK, Charles Bruce, MM2c, USN
CLARK, Cullen Benjamin, F1c, USN
CLEMENTS, Henry B., PFC, USMC
COOLEY, John Paul, MM2c, USN
COVINGTON, Cecil Lavelle, Y3c, USCG
CURTIS, Herbert Smith, Jr., S2c, USN
DAVENPORT, James Watson, Jr., F1c, USN
DAVIS, Donald Avil, Torp.2c, USN
DAVIS, Leland Lafroy, Mach., USN
DIAL, John Buchanan, S1c, USN
DISMUKE, Wilfred Julius, S2c, USN
DUCKWORTH, Thomas, S2c, USNR
FERGUSON, Charlton Hanna, Mus2c,
    USN
FORTENBERRY, Alvie Charles, Cox., USN
GILMORE, Purvis Wayne, S2c, USN
GONIA, Hugh Tracy, S1c, USN
GRAY, Robert Henry, Jr., CGM, USN
GREEN, Glen Hubert, S1c, USN
HENDERSON, James Webster, S2c, USN
HOLDER, Ens. Randolph Mitchell, USNR
HOWELL, Reubin Hollis, F1c, USN
JOHNSTON, George Sebron, B1c, USN
JOHNSTON, Jim Hal, F1c, USN
JONES, Jerry, MA3c, USN
KNOX, Jefferson Elmer, AS, USNR
LETORT, Francis Vernon, S1c, USNR
LOTT, Garland, S2c, USNR
MELTON, John Russell, S1c, USN
MENEFEE, James Austin, S1c, USN
MISTER, Joe Eddie, MA1c, USN
MOODY, Robert Edward, S1c, USN
NESBITT, Judge R., PFC, USMC
NORWOOD, Gus Hayward, Cox., USN
OGLESBY, Lonnie Harris, S2c, USN
ROBERTSON, John Allen, S2c, USN
ROLAND, Earnest Frank, F3c, USN
RUDDOCK, Cecil Roy, S1c, USN
SMITH, Gordon Cleveland, FC1c, USN
SMITH, Ens. Richard Mark, USNR
SMITH, Walter Tharnel, MA1c, USN
STEPHENS, Robert Houston, S1c, USN
SYKES, William David, MM1c, USN
THORNTON, George Hayward, GM3c,
    USN
TONEY, Victor Nally, S1c, USN

WADE, Durell, AMM2c, USN
WHAYNE, Thomas Samuel, RM2c, USN
WHITE, Volmer Dowin, S1c, USN

Wounded

BRATTON, Rufus Port, WT2c, USN
BROPHY, Ens. James M., Jr., USNR
CROSBY, Mulford Cullon, S1c, USN
DALTON, Nathan Coats, F3c, USN
FIELD, Ens. Jennings Pemble, Jr., USNR
FORTINBERRY, Adrian Woodrow, FC3c,
    USN
KINCAID, William Owen, PhM3c, USN
McKNIGHT, Philip Felix, S2c, USN
NUNNALLY, Bruce W., Pvt., USMC
PARKS, Ames, MA2c, USN
RATCLIFF, Lolies, MA3c, USN

Missing

BEALL, Benton Wilson, MM1c, USN
BECK, Oree Charles, Asst. Cook, USMC
BECKETT, Robert A., PFC, USMC
BEESON, Walter LeRoy, S1c, USN
BURT, Larkin J., Corp., USMC
COLLINS, Vernon C., EM3c, USN
COSTELLO, Leonard Wilfred, RM2c, USN
DETHLOFF, Frank Albert, WT2c, USN
GARY, James Crisler, Jr., CFC, USN
GASKIN, Earl H., PFC, USMC
HAYES, Charles Sidney, SK2c, USN
HEGWOOD, Cecil C., Corp., USMC
HOWELL, Ernest P., PFC, USMC
JOHNSON, David L., PFC, USMC
LANCASTER, Marion Barnett, Pvt., USMC
LANDRUM, James O., Corp., USMC
LASETER, Marion K., Corp., USMC
LOCKLEY, Rufus W., PFC, USMC
McMAHEN, William Cooper, EM3c, USN
MURFF, Andrew Rogers, WT2c, USN
PARISH, Bartow Harrison, AMM2c, USN
PATTY, Lt. John Cockrell, Jr., USN
RIGNEY, Elbert L., PFC, USMC
SELLERS, Allen J., F2c, USN
WHITE, James Henry, SF1c, USN
WHITE, John T., Platoon Sgt., USMC
ZEIGLER, William L., Pvt., USMC

Prisoners of War

ALLEN, Carl Lee, MM2c, USN
AUSTIN, Rufus Baker, Pvt., USMC
BAGGETT, Ralph Newell, PFC, USMC

BOYD, Berdyne, PFC, USMC
BROWN, Joseph C., PFC, USMC
BURKETT, Claude L., Platoon Sgt., USMC
BYNUM, Cecil W., PFC, USMC
BYRD, Frank M., PFC, USMC
BYRD, Jack Rudolph, PhM1c, USN
BYRD, Malcolm L., Pvt., USMC
CARPENTER, Herman Oliver, Corp., USMC
CARRAWAY, Charles Berton, S2c, USN
CAVIN, James T., PFC, USMC
CHAMBLIS, Julius Cecil, MM2c, USN
COMFORT, Floyd Herman, PFC, USMC
CONERLY, Albert M., PFC, USMC
COPELAND, Clifton E., Corp., USMC
CORNETT, Ruble H., Pvt., USMC
CURET, Fred, Jr., Corp., USMC
DETHLOFF, Robert Lee, F2c, USN
FOWLER, Miles Bailey, S1c, USN
GLAZE, James Edwin, PFC, USMC
GOFF, Harold E., Pvt., USMC
GORDON, Edward S., Pvt., USMC
GRANT, Everand Meade, PFC, USMC
GREEN, Cecil, Pvt., USMC
GRIFFING, Deever Hooker, CEM, USN
GULLEDGE, Inman, PFC, USMC
HAGGARD, Fred Daniel, PFC, USMC
HALFORD, William T., PFC, USMC
HARPER, Joel Eligh, Pvt., USMC
HARRINGTON, Lt. William Birt, USNR
HARTZOG, Shelton, PFC, USMC
HINTON, Cecil Edmond, CM1c, USN
HODGE, Roy Ray, Pvt., USMC
HOGABOOM, 1st Lt. William F., USMC
HOLLAND, Thomas G., PFC, USMC
HOLLOWAY, Carl Milner, Corp., USMC
HUBBARD, A. G., PFC, USMC
INGRAM, Osburn Furr, S2c, USN
JOHNSON, William Rhett, Sgt., USMC
JONES, Artis Willis, PFC, USMC
JONES, Douglas Charlie, Pvt., USMC
JONES, Joel, Corp., USMC
JONES, Otis Terrell, PFC, USMC
JOYNER, Earl E., PFC, USMC
KEYES, Johnny P., Pvt., USMC
KIDD, John H., Jr., Corp., USMC
LEE, George Waldon, S1c, USN
LEGGETT, Marion K., Asst. Cook, USMC
LEWIS, Clifton Henry, PFC, USMC

MADDOX, Morrison B., PFC, USMC
MALONE, Thomas Jefferson, Jr., PFC, USMC
McALISTER, 2nd Lt. John Alexander, USMC
MILEY, Clifton S., Pvt., USMC
MILLER, William D., PFC, USMC
MITCHELL, Ens. George Robert, USNR
MITCHELL, James Paul, Pvt., USMC
MOORE, J. W., PFC, USMC
MORGAN, R. C., PFC, USMC
MOSLEY, Harvey Lee, PFC, USMC
MURRAY, Grady, PFC, USMC
NETTLES, Howard, Pvt., USMC
O'BRIEN, John P., Jr., Platoon Sgt., USMC
PICKETT, Wilbert, PFC, USMC
POWERS, Claude D., PFC, USMC
PRICE, William M., PFC, USMC
RATLIFF, Owen R., PFC, USMC
RAWLS, James C., PFC, USMC
RIDGWAY, William Harold, Torp.1c, USN
SCARBOROUGH, Carlton E., Corp., USMC
SEAL, William Riley, SK3c, USN
SEYMOUR, Charles Ray, PFC, USMC
SHEDD, Homer L., PFC, USMC
SMITH, Herman E., Corp., USMC
SMITH, John Marvin, Pvt., USMC
SMITH, Gordon Lester, Pvt., USMC
SMITH, Wilbur Kellie, Torp.1c, USN
STEPHENSON, David M., Field Mus.1c, USMC
STEWART, Glenn E., Pvt., USMC
SWAIN, Dixon H., PFC, USMC
TAYLOR, James E., Sgt., USMC
TAYLOR, Marion Alexander, PFC, USMC
THOMPSON, Thomas R., PFC, USMC
THORNTON, George B., PFC, USMC
TRONEY, Norris Henry, S1c, USN
TURNIPSEED, Truman Elliott, Radio Elect., USN
VANCE, Guy, F2c, USN
VAUGHN, James, PFC, USMC
VAWTER, Olice J., Sgt., USMC
WALTON, Felix Burrell, MM2c, USN
WARD, James Sample, Corp., USMC
WARREN, John O., PFC, USMC
WILLIAMS, Clyde Perry, Y3c, USN
WILLOUGHBY, Lloyd C., PFC, USMC

MISSOURI

Dead

AGOLA, Mathew Joe, S2c, USNR
ALLISON, J. T., F1c, USN

AMMONS, Cecil Eugene, AS, USN
ANDERSON, Richard T., PFC, USMC
ANDERSON, Robert Adair, GM3c, USN
ANDREWS, Mitchell Edwin, S1c, USN

Bagby, Walter Franklin, SF3c, USN
Bailey, Ira Wendell, Cox., USN
Ball, James William, F2c, USN
Balzer, Frank, S2c, USN
Bandy, Wayne Lynn, Mus2c, USN
Barnes, Charles Edward, Y3c, USN
Barnes, Herbert McClellan, BM2c, USN
Bazetti, Michael Louis, S1c, USN
Beggs, Harold Eugene, F1c, USN
Belter, Warren H., PFC, USMC
Best, Roy Sidney, S/Sgt., USMC
Bingham, James Robert, S2c, USN
Birdsell, Rayon Delois, F2c, USN
Blake, James Monroe, F1c, USN
Boemer, Paul Louis, Cox., USN
Brendlinger, Ralph Emery, MM1c, USN
Bristow, Don Baily, S1c, USN
Brown, Raymond R., PFC, USMC
Brown, Robert Van Buren, SK3c, USN
Brownfield, Voris Vane, S1c, USN
Brune, James William, RM3c, USNR
Bunch, Arthur Jr., S2c, USN
Burnam, Denver W., Pvt., USMC
Caldwell, Charles Jr., S2c, USN
Cantrell, Fred D., Corp., USMC
Casinger, Edward Eugene, F2c, USN
Christian, David Albert, F3c, USNR
Clift, Ray Emerson, Cox., USN
Clippard, Lloyd Dale, S2c, USN
Coleman, Donald Earl, S2c, USN
Coose, John, S1c, USN
Cowan, William, Cox., USN
Craven, Noel Elwood, S2c, USN
Curlin, Robert Buriel, EM3c, USNR
Curtis, Lloyd "B", S1c, USN
Davis, Walter Mindred, F2c, USN
Diamond, Theodore Lee, S2c, USN
Duffy, James Richard, F1c, USNR
Dupree, Arthur Joseph, F2c, USN
Duren, Frank Edward, AOM3c, USN
Durham, John W., Jr., Pvt., USMC
Dye, Tommy, F1c, USN
Evans, Ferdinand Alois, MM2c, USN
Evans, Mickey Edward, S1c, USN
Fain, Truman J., PFC, USMC
Farrell, Robert I., PFC, USMC
Funk, Frank Francis, BM2c, USN
Gardner, Cecil Eldon, F2c, USN
Garrett, Orville Wilmer, SF2c, USN
George, George Themistocles, S2c, USNR
George, Roy Patrick, S1c, USN
Gibbs, Lawrence Junior, EM3c, USN
Givens, Harold Reuben, Y3c, USN
Gooch, George Merton, EM3c, USN
Goodwin, Clifford George, S1c, USN
Gowen, John Leonard, AS, USN

Grant, Lawrence Everett, Y3c, USN
Graves, 1st Lt. George A., USMC
Gray, Ens. John P., USNR
Gray, Lawrence Moore, F1c, USN
Haas, Curtis Junior, Mus2c, USN
Halpin, Joseph Ambrose, CM1c, USN
Hames, William, S1c, USN
Hardin, Charles Eugene, S1c, USN
Harrington, Keith Homer, S1c, USN
Harris, James William, F1c, USN
Harris, Noble Burnice, Cox., USN
Hartman, Otis Henry, F1c, USN
Hartsoe, Max June, GM3c, USN
Head, Harold Lloyd, S2c, USN
Heckendorn, George Richard, F1c, USN
Hensley, Charley Francis, S2c, USNR
Hicks, Ralph Ducard, Ptr2c, USN
Hirzy, Joseph Frank, F3c, USN
Hoard, Herbert John, CSK, USN
Hon, William Jerry, S1c, USNR
Hord, Chester George, SK3c, USN
Hough, Grover Herbert, S2c, USN
Housel, John James, SK1c, USN
Huie, Doyne Conley, HA1c, USN
Humbargar, Richard T., Asst. Cook, USMC
Hunstein, Carl John, F1c, USN
Hyde, William Hughes, Cox., USN
Jaques, Ray Leon, Y3c, USN
Johnson, Billy James, F1c, USN
Johnson, Roger Adran, M1c, USN
Jones, Marshall William, B2c, USN
Jordan, Joseph Franklin, MM2c, USN
Joyce, Ens. Philip Michael, USNR
Kaiser, Robert Oscar, F1c, USN
Keener, Arlie Glen, SK3c, USN
Kempf, Warren Joseph, RM3c, USN
King, Horace Edward, F1c, USN
King, Orveil Vaniel, Jr., PFC, USMC
Kirby, James David, AOM2c, USN
Kirchhoff, Wilbur Albert, S1c, USN
Kirkpatrick, Capt. Thomas LeRoy, (Chaplain Corps), USN
Knubel, William, Jr., S1c, USN
Kuchemeister, Edward William, BM2c, USN
Kutz, William Irwin, SF3c, USN
Lee, Melvin E., Pvt., USMC
Livingston, Samuel David, F2c, USN
Lormis, Robert Lee, S2c, USN
Manges, Howard Ellis, FC3c, USN
Manning, Milburn Alexander, AMM3c, USN
Marlow, Urban Herschel, Cox., USN
Marshall, John Andrew, WT2c, USN
Mathis, Jewell Asa, F1c, USN

MAXSON, Richard B., PFC, USMC
McCOLLUM, Alfred Edward, F1c, USN
McCREARY, Frank Elmer, MM1c, USN
MEYER, Theodore Henry, SK2c, USNR
MILLER, Earl Jesse, F3c, USNR
MONROE, Donald, MA2c, USN
MONTGOMERY, Wallace Alford, MM2c, USN
MORGAN, Harold Lavern, GM2c, USN
MYERS, James Gernie, SK1c, USN
MYERS, Martin B., Corp., USMC
NECESSARY, Charles Raymond, S1c, USN
NEWTON, Wilbur Francis, S1c, USN
OGLE, Charles Ralph, F1c, USN
O'NEAL, Morris Allen, S1c, USN
PARKER, Richard Edward, MA2c, USNR
PAYNE, Kenneth Morris, S1c, USN
PECKHAM, Howard William, F3c, USN
PETERSON, Ens. Dale William, USNR
PETERSON, Herbert Richard, SM2c, USNR
POLSTON, Francis Samuel, S1c, USN
PUMMILL, Nolan Eugene, MM2c, USN
RADFORD, Harry M., PFC, USMC
RANDOL, Mack Warren, S1c, USN
RANDOLPH, Robert Lee, S1c, USN
RECKE, Charles W., Sgt., USMC
RICHESIN, Franklin Delano, RM3c, USN
RICHEY, Ens. Joseph Lee, USNR
RIGGS, Lt. Cdr. J. Clark, USN
RINEHART, Lt. (jg) Clark Franklin, USN
ROBERTS, Walter Scott, Jr., RM1c, USN
ROEHM, Harry Turner, MM2c, USN
RUSHER, Orville Lester, MM1c, USN
RUSSLER, Clifford Edward, SM1c, USN
SAMPSON, Kenneth Harlan, S1c, USN
SANFORD, Thomas Steger, F3c, USN
SCHMIDT, Vernon John, RM3c, USN
SCHMITT, Jerome U., Pvt., USMC
SCHULTZ, Ray, GM3c, USN
SCREETON, James Clark, RM3c, USN
SHERWOOD, Gail L., Pvt., USMC
SKILES, Charley Jackson, Jr., S2c, USN
SKILES, Eugene, S2c, USN
SKILES, Gerald LeRoy, S2c, USN
SMITH, Clarence Edward, CM1c, USN
SMITH, Earl, Jr., S1c, USN
SMITH, Edward O., PFC, USMC
SNYDER, Glenn Latrell, S1c, USN
SOOTER, Lt. (jg) Cecil Dean, USNR
STAPLETON, Kirby Roy, S1c, USN
STAUSEBACH, Clarence Albert, Jr., AMM3c, USN
STOUT, Robert Thomas, FC3c, USN
TABER, George Edward, MM2c, USN
TARTWATER, Vincent Francis, S2c, USN

TERHUNE, Benjamin C., F2c, USN
THOMPSON, Robert Earl, PhM1c, USN
THOMURE, Harold Cyril, PFC, USMC
THORPE, Leonard Arnold, F3c, USNR
TORTI, Natale Ignatius, S1c, USN
TRANBARGER, Orval Austin, S1c, USN
TRAXLER, Harold William, AS, USN
TUCKER, Joseph Mark, Jr., AS, USN
TUTTLE, Ens. Joseph Morton, USNR
UFFORD, Russell Orville, S2c, USN
VANDERPOOL, Payton L., Jr., F2c, USN
WARD, 2nd Lt. Maurice A., USMCR
WEBB, James Cecil, F1c, USN
WEBB, Rupert Cleo, SK3c, USNR
WELLS, Raymond Virgil, Jr., S1c, USN
WELLS, William Bennett, S1c, USN
WHITE, Jack Dewey, S1c, USN
WISE, Clarence Alvin, F3c, USNR
WORTHINGTON, Ens. Robert Stearns, USNR
YATES, Herbert Wilson, MM2c, USN
ZEORLIN, Harold, Torp.2c, USN
ZIMMERMAN, Loyd McDonald, S2c, USN

Wounded

ANDERSON, Walter D., Corp., USMCR
ARNOLD, Charles Garrett, S2c, USN
ARNOLD, Warren Woodrow, SK3c, USN
AUXIER, Gerald Thomas, F1c, USN
BEAMAN, Delbert William, S1c, USN
BESS, Donald Niclos, S2c, USN
COSLETT, Audrey Gerald, RM3c, USN
CROWDER, Burl Franklin, F1c, USN
CUNNINGHAM, Chester Earl, PhM2c, USN
DAFFRON, Daniel Bennett, Cox., USN
GARRETT, William Robert, S2c, USN
GRAY, William Wilbur Burl, SM2c, USN
GREGG, Ens. Max Eugene, USNR
HAZELWOOD, Harold R., Corp., USMC
HILL, William Riley, Pvt., USMC
HOLMAN, Nelson R., Pvt., USMC
HUEBNER, Paul F., Jr., PFC, USMC
HUX, Travis Dale, PhM2c, USN
KABLE, Ens. Donald Mark, USN
KUNZ, 2nd Lt. Charles M., USMCR
LOVE, Joseph E., Pvt., USMC
MARTIN, William Newton, S2c, USN
MILLER, Posey, GM3c, USN
MYERS, James Leonard, AS, USN
NOEL, Clyde Clinton, WT1c, USN
PENNELL, Lowell, GM3c, USN
PITTMAN, Delbert Leroy, S2c, USN
RAY, Buel, RM3c, USN
READER, Earl Thomas, Cox., USN
REID, Wallace J., PFC, USMC

Schiller, Walter Alex, S1c, USN
Smith, Francis Lafayette, GM2c, USN
Smith, Leonard Dale, S2c, USN
Teaff, Lt. (jg) Perry Lee, USN
Warren, Clifton Lee, SK3c, USN
Wells, Arthur W., PFC, USMC

Missing

Aders, Frederick Charles, SC3c, USN
Atchison, John C., Pvt., USMC
Atkinson, Carl Douglas, S1c, USN
Baker, Wayne Stratton, S2c, USN
Baughn, Norvel Wilbert, EM2c, USN
Beattie, William Dildine, F2c, USN
Belt, Everett R., Jr., PFC, USMC
Bernasek, Albert C., Jr., Pvt., USMC
Boswell, Robert B., GM2c, USN
Bristow, Charles Winfred, RM2c, USN
Brockman, Clarence Allen, F2c, USN
Button, Charles James, S2c, USN
Campbell, Joel Evans, CM2c, USN
Clifton, John Bradford, Jr., S2c, USN
Coble, Joseph Robert, S1c, USN
Connell, James Harold, F2c, USN
Cook, Joseph Fletcher, F3c, USN
Copeland, James Love, S1c, USN
Dale, Loren Eugene, F2c, USN
Darling, Lloyd Lee, MM1c, USN
Dietrich, Normand William, MM2c, USN
Dinan, Charles Patrick, F2c, USN
Donahue, Everett Kae, MM1c, USN
Dowell, Harry, BM2c, USN
Fisher, Howard Rex, S1c, USN
Fornkahl, Raymond Wallace, S2c, USN
Gann, Howard L., PFC, USMC
Garrett, Jordan Joseph, S1c, USN
Gilmore, Charles Eugene, S2c, USN
Hale, Robert, F3c, USN
Hall, Billy Hugh, F3c, USN
Hall, Ted, Pvt., USMCR
Handley, Lt. James Franklin, Jr., (MC), USN
Hayes, Charles Sidney, SK2c, USN
Helms, Eugene Edward, S1c, USN
Himmelmann, Leroy Rudolph, Torp. 2c, USN
Himmelmann, Otto Kenneth, S2c, USN
Holsinger, Frank O., Corp., USMC
Howard, Raymond R., PFC, USMC
Hunter, Lowell R., Sgt., USMC
Hyser, Wayne Henry, S1c, USN
Ivey, Jack, S2c, USN
Jackson, Edward, B1c, USN
Jones, Harry Bross, AMM3c, USN
King, Paul Grant, GM3c, USN

Klefisch, Frederick Francis, S1c, USN
Klick, Kenneth A., PFC, USMC
Knowles, Wesley Smith, RM1c, USN
Kocsis, Frank, GM3c, USN
Kraisser, Michael Jerome, FC3c, USN
Kurz, Nicholas Murray, S1c, USN
Laster, Eddie Lee, S1c, USN
Lenz, Paul Dunbar, MM1c, USN
Llewellyn, Robert Thomas, F1c, USN
Martin, Virgle, MM2c, USN
Miles, Rodney Winfred, Torp. 3c, USN
Mitchell, Earl Archer, MM2c, USN
Montgomery, Edward Joseph, S1c, USN
Newton, Willard Alvin, S1c, USN
Overturf, James Glen, EM1c, USN
Parsons, Charles Earl, S2c, USN
Parsons, Loys Aloysius, S2c, USN
Paul, Robert Ross, S1c, USN
Pedrotti, Francis J., Pvt., USMC
Pool, Virgil William, F1c, USN
Potter, William L., Sgt., USMC
Reynolds, James Arthur, MM2c, USN
Riddlesperger, Ralph, S2c, USN
Riley, Ens. John James, USNR
Schmitt, Milton W., Pvt., USMC
Schuler, Ralph Edward, F1c, USN
Schwamle, Theodore, SM2c, USN
Scott, Crawford E., PFC, USMC
Shettlesworth, Clinton Anderson, BM2c, USN
Singleton, Thornton Elborn, S2c, USN
Smith, George, Jr., AMM2c, USN
Smith, Robert William, RM3c, USN
Spotts, Harold G., Corp., USMC
Stratton, Joseph Richard, S2c, USN
Swearingen, Lonnie Dowl, S2c, USN
Talley, Henry Olin, S2c, USN
Terry, Archie Harrison, CWT, USN
Thomas, Jack Tindall, S1c, USN
Thurman, Ens. James, USNR
Turman, Russell Clay, Y3c, USN
Vancil, Kenneth Alvie, S2c, USN
Van Voorhis, Merrel Ellis, F3c, USN
Waddell, George McClelland, PFC, USMC
Waltrip, Dennis Shaw, F3c, USN
Werner, Paul William, Jr., S1c, USN
Wild, Lt. Phillip Grant, Jr., USN
Williams, Harold, MM2c, USN
Williams, Robert Eugene, S2c, USN
Windish, Robert J., Pvt., USMC

Prisoners of War

Armour, Floyd, S1c, USN
Arnold, Harry, Gunnery Sgt., USMC
Baker, Francis Earl, PhM1c, USN

BALES, Ernest J., PFC, USMC
BARKLEY, James Allen, M1c, USN
BARNES, Silas K., PFC, USMC
BARTHEL, James P., PFC, USMC
BATTLES, Connie Gene, PFC, USMC
BEAL, John Leonard, F1c, USN
BEATTY, Paul Erskin, S2c, USN
BEAVER, Harold K., Corp., USMC
BEESON, Darrell Milton, PFC, USMC
BELL, Richard Eugene, Cox., USN
BINKO, Stanley, PFC, USMC
BOGLER, Leo J., Corp., USMC
BOLLIN, George W., Jr., Y2c, USN
BOOTH, Donald F., Pvt., USMC
BOYLE, Martin, Corp., USMC
Box, Robert Smith, Jr., Sgt., USMC
BRANNAN, John W., PFC, USMC
BRETHOLD, Calvin Edward, S1c, USN
BRIGHAM, William Joseph, PFC, USMC
BROWN, Buell Stanley, PFC, USMC
BROWN, Joseph Rust, S2c, USN
BUERGER, Burdell Oscar, PFC, USMC
BUNYARD, Basil Corbin, EM1c, USN
BURNS, William, CBM, USN
BUSSE, Wilbur John, PFC, USMC
CAUDELL, Robert Norman, RM2c, USN
CAWTHON, Hugh Dane, RM2c, USN
CLAYPOOL, Edward B., PFC, USMC
COMBS, Jay B., Mess Sgt., USMC
CONNER, Warren David, PFC, USMC
CONNOR, Dennis Clifford, PFC, USMC
COOPER, James Noel, RM3c, USN
COSTELLO, Robert M., PFC, USMC
Cox, Roy Thomas, PFC, USMC
CRAIG, Jennings B., PFC, USMC
CUMMONS, Clarence A., Pvt., USMC
CURRY, Robert Eaves, PFC, USMC
DAPRON, George Ivan, S1c, USN
DARR, Charles Henry, Chief Cook, USMC
DARTER, Harold Leslie, Pvt., USMC
DAVIS, Charles Brown, MM1c, USN
DAVIS, Elmer Loyd, RM1c, USN
DAVIS, Eschol Eugene, Corp., USMC
DAVIS, Harvey Oliver, Chief Torp., USN
DAWSON, Harvey Louis, PFC, USMC
DEADRICK, James E., Pvt., USMC
DENNIS, Edward D., Sgt., USMC
DURRWACHTER, Henry Louis, Jr., Corp., USMC
ECKEL, Harold Eugene, RM2c, USN
EHRHARDT, Melvin Edward, EM3c, USN
ELLIS, Robert Reid, RM1c, USN
ESTES, James Henry, Y2c, USN
EVANS, Charles E., Corp., USMC
EWING, James Chatham, S2c, USN
FANNON, Buel Ragan, SM3c, USN

FARGIE, Oscar S., PFC, USMC
FICHTENMAYER, Fred George, CCM, USN
FITCH, Elvin T., PFC, USMC
FITZPATRICK, James Alburn, PFC, USMC
FREY, Robert LeRoy, PFC, USMC
GARDNER, Douglas Dean, PFC, USMC
GLACKEN, Joseph C., Jr., Pvt., USMC
GOLDEN, Marion Eugene, S2c, USN
GRIFFIN, James Sullivan, RM3c, USN
GROSS, Franklin David, Corp., USMC
HALL, LaFayette E., PFC, USMC
HAM, Ralph Erman, CRM, USNR
HANSON, Charles W., PFC, USMC
HAWKINS, Hal W., PFC, USMC
HAYNES, Eugene O., PFC, USMC
HERD, Leo, Asst. Cook, USMC
HIBBS, Richard G., Pvt., USMC
HINKLE, Walter M., PFC, USMC
HOBBS, Earl R., Sgt., USMC
HOOD, Virgil B., Jr., Corp., USMC
HOOPS, James L., PFC, USMC
HOOVER, Frank W., PFC, USMC
HULL, Richard Henry, MM1c, USN
HUNT, Arthur L., PFC, USMC
HYDER, Luther E., S/Sgt., USMC
ISENHOWER, Harold William, RM3c, USN
JENKINS, Frederick Charles, S2c, USN
JOHNSON, John Stewart, Jr., Corp., USMC
JOHNSON, Morris H., Pvt., USMC
JONES, John Henry, PFC, USMC
JONES, Raphael Odon, AOM2c, USN
JONES, Vincent Young, Y2c, USN
JORDAN, Howard C., Platoon Sgt., USMC
JORDAN, Raymond George, FC1c, USN
KEITZER, Harold A., Corp., USMC
KELLEY, Albert Manuel, Mus1c, USN
KELLOGG, Harvey Guy, RM1c, USN
KILMER, Emmett Lee, EM3c, USN
KING, Lloyd Sterling, PFC, USMC
KIRK, John Travis, PFC, USMC
KIRK, William Albert, WT2c, USN
KNIGHT, Aubrey Arthur, CEM, USN
LAPORTE, Ewing Emile, Pvt., USMC
LARSON, William Carl, PFC, USMC
LEBOVITZ, Harry Benjamin, PhM1c, USN
LEHNHOFF, Eugene Elmer, S1c, USN
LEPPERT, Roy Williams, PFC, USMC
LINHARDT, LeRoy M., PFC, USMC
LONG, Ens. Andrew Willison, Jr., USNR
MADISON, Jack Julian, F2c, USN
MANNING, Bernard H., Sgt., USMC
MARSHALL, Peter B., Jr., PhM3c, USN
MARTINEAU, Robert J., PFC, USMC
McCARTHY, Roy Bernard, PFC, USMC

McCullough, George Wesley, GM2c, USN
McDaniel, Alvie, Field Cook, USMC
McGee, Thomas Lowell, PFC, USMC
McKenzie, James J., PFC, USMC
McKinley, William J., Corp., USMC
McMillian, John Russell, Corp., USMC
Meier, Gilbert C. M., Pvt., USMC
Milbourn, Ival Dale, Asst. Cook, USMC
Miller, Andrew Jackson, Jr., AMM3c, USN
Moeder, Dale E., PFC, USMC
Mount, Alfred W., PFC, USMC
Murphy, Jimmie R., PFC, USMC
Oliver, McKinley, Chief Torp., USN
Osborn, Max Bernard, Pvt., USMC
Page, Robert Edward Lee, Corp., USMC
Parker, Ted, Jr., S1c, USN
Peukert, Herman W., Pvt., USMC
Ploke, John Francis, PhM1c, USN
Prange, Edward Herman, PhM3c, USN
Promnitz, Oliver F., PFC, USMC
Puckett, Albert E., PFC, USMC
Ragan, Robert G., Corp., USMC
Rieken, Vernon E., PFC, USMC
Rogatch, John F., PFC, USMC
Rogers, Leo L., Corp, USMC
Rose, Earl Brigham, S2c, USN
Rosenthal, Lt. Herbert Jerome, USNR
Rossell, Frank G., Jr., Platoon Sgt., USMC
Roster, John F., PFC, USMC
Sanders, Richard L., Pvt., USMC
Schlegel, Stanley R., Corp., USMC
Schneider, William Theodore, Cox., USN
Schubert, Arthur George, PFC, USN

Shaw, Virgil, S2c, USN
Shepard, George Walter, Jr., MM1c, USN
Shumard, Gene David, PFC, USMC
Sickels, Percy Henry, PFC, USMC
Silar, Joseph David, PFC, USMC
Sirota, John F., PFC, USMC
Slipsager, Glen Frederick, PhM1c, USN
Smart, Doyle James, QM2c, USN
Smith, Lee Thomas, Pvt., USMC
Smith, Norval Giles, SM1c, USNR
Stephenson, Joseph Earl, Boat., USN
Stewart, Charles Albert, Jr., PFC, USMC
Strickland, Eldon K., PFC, USMC
Tabor, Buford E., PFC, USMC
Taylor, James C., PFC, USMC
Thomas, James Alexander, PFC, USMC
Thomas, William Harold, PFC, USMC
Thurmon, Buford E., PFC, USMC
Tihen, Herman Joseph, EM1c, USN
Tistadt, 1st Lt. Hugh A., Jr., USMC
Tripp, Glenn Eugene, Y3c, USN
Tucker, Richard, S2c, USN
Van Horn, Ray Earl, PFC, USMC
Vaughan, Churchill Edison, SK1c, USN
Vincent, Oland Melvin, PhM2c, USN
Vining, Virgil Vernon, GM1c, USN
Walker, Dorsey Robert, EM1c, USN
Warsing, John Wesley, Jr., Sgt., USMC
Watts, Willard William, PFC, USMC
West, Wallace Raymond, Pvt., USMC
Wheatly, Rankin Wallier, Cox., USN
Wilder, Robert Lee, S1c, USN
Williams, Maurice S., Jr., Sgt., USMC
Zollinger, Harold W., Corp., USMC

MONTANA

Dead

Andrews, John Blake, F1c, USN
Barrows, Robert Leon, S1c, USN
Daniel, Lloyd Maxton, Y1c, USN
D'Hondt, August Maurice, S1c, USN
Doherty, George Walter, S2c, USN
Doherty, John Albert, MM2c, USN
Dullum, Jerald Fraser, EM3c, USN
Dunn, James Earl, BM1c, USN
Fehr, Raymond Emanuel, AMM3c, USN
Hundley, Frank, Corp., USMC
Jackson, Lowell Bruce, S2c, USN
Johnson, Ernest Claude, S2c, USNR
Marling, Joseph Henry, S2c, USN
Matzdorf, Darrel Francis, F3c, USNR

McCreedy, Orin Clell, F1c, USN
Meyers, Joseph, S2c, USN
Micheletto, Carlo Anthony, Sgt., USMC
Morrison, Earl LeRoy, S1c, USN
Morse, George Robert, S2c, USN
Parks, Donald Edward, SM3c, USN
Pearson, Robert Stanley, F2c, USN
Ronning, Emil Oliver, Cox., USN
Scilley, Harold Hugh, SF2c, USN
Sellong, William Lawrence, S2c, USN
Shelton, Ens. James A., USNR
Sloan, John C., Platoon Sgt., USMC
Smart, George David, Cox., USN
Smith, Robert Arthur, ARM3c, USNR

TRUJILLO, Richard Ignacio, PFC, USMC
VAN BRAMER, Ens. Glenn Rudolph, USNR

Wounded

CHOSE, William Burt, S2c, USN
FOX, J. L., S2c, USN
OUELLETTE, Clarence Matt, S2c, USN
VODEN, Gerre Stewart, RM3c, USNR

Missing

AIRHART, Albert Edward, S2c, USN
FORMAN, Ens. Percy Wendell, USNR
GILLEN, John Arthur, CGM, USN
JEFRIES, George T., Asst. Cook, USMC
JENSEN, Robert James, SM1c, USN
KINNEY, Lawrence Calvin, F1c, USN
LACHMAN, Joseph Frederick, S2c, USN
NELSON, John William, RM2c, USN
SCHENK, Richard John, S1c, USN
SEVERIN, James Allen, SC2c, USN
SHELTON, Girard David, CGM, USN
VANCE, Lyle L., Pvt., USMC

Prisoners of War

ARENTZEN, Charles, AM2c, USN
BARTON, Wallace Arthur, BM2c, USN
BEAN, Russell Chase, CRM, USN
BISHOP, John Joseph, PFC, USMC

BUTLER, George Dwight, SF3c, USN
COVEY, Donald L., PFC, USMC
DAVIDSON, Harry Willard, WT2c, USN
DAVIS, Richard J., Sgt., USMC
DAWSON, Jasper Frank, PFC, USMC
DICKOVER, Floyd A., Sgt., USMC
EGAN, Willmont Edward, SC1c, USN
HINRICHSEN, Merlin Freeland, S2c, USN
HUTCHISON, William Adolphus, Mach., USN
KENNEY, Don W., Mess Sgt., USMC
KEOUGH, Stanley J., PFC, USMC
LARSEN, William Keith, Pvt., USMC
LEGATO, Albert, Sgt., USMC
MARSHALL, Donald Roupert, Corp., USMC
McCLUE, Barney D., Corp., USMC
McCONE, James, PFC, USMC
MIKKELSON, Melvin W., Field Music, USMC
MOCABEE, Cecil J., CBM, USN
MORRILL, George J., PFC, USMC
NASH, Jack Kenneth, Chief Torp., USN
NELSON, Stevephen, Pvt., USMC
OWENS, Floyd I., PFC, USMC
PACKER, Richard S., PFC, USMC
ROGERS, Charles Gertus, PFC, USMC
RUSSELL, Ens. Robert Enson, USNR
WARD, Jack Charles, S1c, USN
WILLEY, Lloyd V., Pvt., USMCR

NEBRASKA

Dead

ATKINS, Gerald Arthur, HA1c, USN
BAIRD, Carl Frantz, S1c, USN
BARTEK, Frank Joseph, Jr., F1c, USN
BICKEL, Kenneth Robert, F1c, USN
BLITZ, Leo, MM2c, USN
BLITZ, Rudolph, F1c, USN
BOCK, John George, Jr., S2c, USN
BOND, Dwaine Gale, ML1c, USN
CALKINS, Max Arthur, ARM3c, USN
CARLSON, John Benjamin, SK2c, USN
CHAPMAN, Naaman N., S1c, USN
CHRISTENSEN, Lloyd Raymond, F1c, USN
CLAYTON, Gerald Lee, SK2c, USN
CLOUGH, Edward Jay, GM1c, USN
COOK, Grant Clark, Jr., F1c, USN
COX, Kenneth L., Pvt., USMC
CURTIS, Robert Alvin, Carp., USN
DICKEY, Shirley Ray, F1c, USN
DURR, Clement Edward, S1c, USN
EBERHARDT, Fred Lorrence, F1c, USN

ELLIS, Richard Everrett, S2c, USN
EPPERSON, Ben Price, PFC, USMC
EVANS, Truman Floyd, Torp.1c, USN
FRY, Irvin Francis, S1c, USN
GAISER, William Frederick, Sgt., USMC
GIBSON, Clayton Leon, S2c, USN
GOODWIN, Myron Eugene, S2c, USN
GROUND, Orla Lester, F3c, USN
HAASE, Clarence Frederick, S1c, USN
HANSEN, Martin Lavern, S1c, USN
HARRIS, Peter John, Cox., USN
HART, Ens. John Paul, USNR
HASL, James Thomas, F1c, USN
HISKETT, Denis Hubert, F1c, USN
HOELSCHER, Lester John, HA1c, USN
HOLLEY, Paul Elston, S1c, USN
HOLMAN, Veryl Raymond, AMM3c, USN
JACOBSEN, Donald Roy, S2c, USN
JONES, Charles Alan, S2c, USN
JONES, Warren Allen, Y3c, USN
KMENT, Joseph Frank, F3c, USN
KULA, Stanley, SC3c, USN

KUNTZ, John Henry, F2c, USN
LACKEY, John Delmar, ARM3c, USN
LA RUE, George Willard, GM3c, USN
LOMAX, Ens. Frank Stuart, USN
LUNSFORD, Jack L., Pvt., USMC
MARINO, Joseph James, F2c, USN
MARVIN, Neil Eugene, RM1c, USN
MAULE, Joseph Keith, S1c, USN
McLAUGHLIN, Lloyd Elden, S2c, USN
McMAHON, Kenneth Eugene, S2c, USNR
MORRELL, Elmer R., PFC, USMC
MUDGE, Arthur George, RM1c, USN
PATTERSON, Truman, CQM, USN
PENTICO, Walter Ray, S2c, USN
PURVIS, Gordon W., Sgt., USMC
RADFORD, Neal Jason, Mus2c, USN
RICHTER, Walter Max John, RM3c, USN
SANKO, Francis Phillip, S1c, USN
SAVIN, Tom, RM2c, USN
SCHLUND, Elmer Pershing, MM1c, USN
SHANNON, William Alfred, S1c, USN
SHERIDAN, Emmett Martin, Corp., USMC
SHUNK, Donald Frederick, S2c, USNR
SIDLO, Vencil Frank, S1c, USN
STONE, Donald E., PFC, USMC
TATGE, Clifford Christopher, S2c, USN
TESAR, Henry, CM3c, USN
THOMPSON, George Allen, S2c, USN
TRAMPE, Ervin Erick, RM3c, USNR
TUSHLA, Louis James, F1c, USN
WHIPPLE, Eugene Edwin, S2c, USN
ZIMBA, Louis John, GM3c, USN
ZONIK, John Dan, S2c, USNR

Wounded

ANSTINE, Keith Clark, F2c, USN
BADER, Wilmer L., Corp., USMC
BROOKS, 2nd Lt. William V., USMCR
DICKAU, Glenn Arthur, PhM3c, USN
DUNCAN, Eugene Rager, Cox., USN
JACKSON, Ronald Warren, AMM2c, USN
KAPPELMAN, George E., PFC, USMC
LARSON, Raymond Decius, WT1c, USN
PRIEST, Eugene Oneal, Y3c, USN
SMITH, John Bennet, GM2c, USN
STRATTON, Donald Gay, S2c, USN
WILLIAMS, Charles Raymond, MM2c, USN

Missing

ARNOLD, Mac William, S2c, USN
BEAN, Lloyd Charles, AMM2c, USN
BENNER, Calvin William, EM3c, USN
BOOTHE, Merton Alva, MM2c, USN

BRILL, Richard Jack, GM3c, USN
CHRISTIE, Burnard Sinclair, SM1c, USN
CLINGINGSMITH, Dale, S1c, USN
FISHER, George R., Cox., USN
GALUSHA, Eugene Rex, HA1c, USN
GLEESON, Milton Francis, AMM3c, USN
GREEN, Billy Eugene, S1c, USN
HOSTICK, Ellis Burton, GM3c, USN
JEROME, Charles Clare, Cox., USN
KOENIG, Vincent Gerhart, SK2c, USN
MARSH, Samuel Joseph, S2c, USN
MAYFIELD, Harry Leroy, CM3c, USN
MEAD, Chester Victor, AMM2c, USN
MENICHETTI, August, RM2c, USN
MILLS, Keith Leroy, SC3c, USN
NITZ, William Glen, SK3c, USN
RICHTER, Herman Anton, CM3c, USN
ROCHFORD, Eugene D., Corp., USMC
ROHRBAUGH, Mansfield Joseph, S1c, USN
SCHROER, Kenneth Edward, S2c, USN
SHAFFER, Herbert Keith, BM2c, USN
SKUDLAS, John Joe, S1c, USN
SMERSH, Randolph Dale, F1c, USN
URBAUER, Merton G., PFC, USMC
VAN HOENACKER, Jerome A., PFC, USMC
VERLEY, Ralph Austin, EM3c, USN
VERSAW, Donald L., PFC, USMCR
WHEELER, Glenn A., 1st Sgt., USMCR
WHITE, Charles Edwin, S2c, USN
YOUNG, Ralph William, F1c, USN

Prisoners of War

ASCHENBRENNER, Reinholdt, PFC, USMC
BALLARD, William Lynn, WT1c, USN
BAMFORD, Roger Dick, Pvt., USMC
BAYER, Lt. (jg) Edward W., USNR
BEAVERS, Dean Leo, Torp.3c, USN
BLAHA, Joseph Henry, CY, USN
BROWN, Lyle J., PFC, USMC
CALLAHAN, Myron James, S2c, USN
CECHA, Cdr. Albin H., USN
COMBS, Charlie Allen, Jr., PFC, USMC
DANEHEY, Donald E., PFC, USMC
DAVIS, Kenneth William, PFC, USMC
EDWARDS, Ranall Stokes, RM1c, USN
FARR, Morris Cecil, PhM2c, USN
FUGATE, Robert Tebo, PFC, USMC
GARDEN, Wendell N., PFC, USMC
GASPER, Tony, Corp., USMC
GEARHART, Harold Gerald, S1c, USN
GORZELANSKI, Helen C., NC, USN
HENRY, Pemberton Dee, SK2c, USN
HUSTON, James Leon, PFC, USMC

JENSEN, Harold Chris, S1c, USN
JOHNSON, Phillip Wesley, PFC, USMC
JOHNSON, Ralph Edward, S/Sgt., USMC
LAURSEN, Norman James, Corp., USMC
LINDSAY, Wilford John, PFC, USMC
LOWREY, John Jackson, S2c, USN
MALLECK, Donald Reed, Sgt., USMC
McCAULLEY, Wade B., Pvt., USMC
MINNICK, Ray J., PFC, USMC
NIEDERHAUS, George, S1c, USN
NYE, Marvin Donald, PFC, USMC
PHILSON, Clark Allen, HA1c, USN
PICK, Frank Edward, Sgt., USMC
PLUGGE, Lowell Jonathan, Y3c, USN
PULOS, 1st Lt. Ted E., USMC
RHINE, Lloyd Raymond, S2c, USN
RICE, John W., Jr., PFC, USMC
RIDER, Richard, PFC, USMC
SCHIFFBAUER, Robert Arnold, SK1c, USN
SCHULZ, Richard Paul, SM3c, USN
SHAW, Gilbert James, PhM1c, USN

SHELLHORN, Melvin Winford, Sgt., USMC
SHELTON, Herbert Raymond, Pvt., USMC
SHIPP, John Stanley, PhM2c, USN
SIEGEL, Benjamin Ford, Y1c, USN
SILLMAN, Otto A., PFC, USMC
SMITH, Lyle Edwards, Torp.2c, USN
STAHLECKER, Harold Rienhart, Corp., USMC
STANSBERY, Clifford Devine, S1c, USN
STOHLMAN, Mathew Herman, PFC USMC
SUMMERS, Verble LeRoy, Torp.2c, USN
TAYLOR, Ralph Albert, PFC, USMC
TAYLOR, Ray Fred, PFC, USMC
TRAMPOSH, Charles Edward, PFC, USMC
WHITE, James Francis, RM1c, USN
WILLIAMS, Everett Smith, Corp., USMC
WILLIAMS, Roy Oscar, GM1c, USN
WOODS, Chester John, Corp., USMC
YATES, Donald Ralph, F2c, USN

NEVADA

Dead

GILL, Richard Eugene, S1c, USN
O'FLAHERTY, Ens. Frank W., USNR
RADCLIFFE, Lt. Melvin Ernest, USN
ROSE, John Joseph, Jr., S1c, USN
WEAVER, Richard Walter, S1c, USN
YATES, Elmer Elias, SC3c, USN
YOUNG, Ens. Eric Reed, USN

Wounded

THOMAS, Weisner F., Gunnery Sgt., USMC

Missing

BARKER, James LeRoy, S1c, USN
HUSTON, James T., Jr., PFC, USMC

Prisoners of War

DILLON, Charles W., PFC, USMC
GARRISON, Alfie T., PFC, USMC
GEORGE, Perlie Monroe, S2c, USN
GIRARDOT, Carl F., Jr., Field Music, USMC
KIMBALL, Murry Bryan, MM1c, USN
LEAHIGH, Lt. Stanley Adelbert, USNR

NEW HAMPSHIRE

Dead

BRONSTEIN, Lt. (jg) Ben Richard, USNR
CLOUSE, Ens. Edward Blanchard, USN
CROSSETT, David Lloyd, S1c, USN
EDMUNDS, Bruce Roosevelt, Y2c, USN
GADBOIS, Oscar, CMM, USN
HOPKINS, Edwin Chester, F3c, USN
MANDEVILLE, Joseph Emile, S2c, USN
OSBERG, Ens. Carl August, USNR
ROGERS, Ens. Robert F., USNR
ROZMUS, Joseph Stanley, S1c, USN

UNDERWOOD, Chester Dexter, MM2c, USN
VARJABEDIAN, Benjamin, EM2c, USN
WILLSON, Charles Edward, SC3c, USN

Wounded

JODOIN, Robert Joseph, F3c, USN
MERRILL, Capt. Herbert T., USMC

Missing

GREBENSTEIN, William Arthur, MM1c, USN

Prisoners of War

BELIVEAU, Clayton Norman, QM2c, USN
BRABEC, Joseph John, Jr., F1c, USN
BRADLEY, Maj. James V., Jr., USMC
BROKENSHIRE, Lt. Cdr. Herbert Cecil, USNR

DOUGLASS, Lt. Francis Malcolm, USN
HODKINS, Ray King, Jr., S2c, USN
KECK, Truman Wilber, PhM1c, USN
MORRISSETTE, Roy Leon, CQM, USN
NELSON, Harold Roy, PhM3c, USN
PLANTE, John Joseph, S1c, USN

NEW JERSEY

Dead

ALLSOPP, Lt. (jg) Robert Thomas, USN
APGAR, John Parker, S2c, USNR
ARNESEN, Robert Arne, F1c, USNR
BAKER, Ens. John Drayton, USNR
BARRY, Michael Francis, Elect., USN
BINDER, William Eugene, Jr., S2c, USN
BISHOP, Wesley Horner, Jr., RM3c, USNR
BROWN, Ens. Richard Earl, USNR
BUNDY, George, GM2c, USN
BURDETTE, Ralph Warren, Mus2c, USN
CALLAHAN, Archie, Jr., MA2c, USN
CAMERON, Thomas Henry, GM3c, USN
CAMPBELL, John Judson, CEM, USN
CANNON, Clyde Cecil, S2c, USN
CARLISLE, Thomas Kelsey, S2c, USNR
CARO, Joseph, F2c, USN
CLARK, Edwin Post, CBM, USN
CLARK, Harold, SM2c, USN
COOK, Franklin Michael, MM2c, USN
CORDES, Raymond Frederick, RM3c, USN
COSTILL, Harold Kendall, F3c, USN
CURTIN, Capt. Robert E., USMC
DAY, Francis Daniel, CWT, USN
DEVRIES, Peter Cornelius, CMM, USN
DUSAK, Andrew Michael, Cox., USN
EBERHARDT, Eugene Keller, MM1c, USN
EISENMAN, Irving, S2c, USNR
FREDERICKS, Harry Carl, Jr., Cox., USN
GABRIELE, Angelo Michael, F1c, USN
GLOVER, Charles Francis, M1c, USN
GRAICHEN, Edmund, CMM, USNR
HILL, Edwin Joseph, Chief Boat., USN
HITTORFF, Ens. Joseph Parker, Jr., USN
HOLDEN, 2nd Lt. Frank J., USMC
HOLZWORTH, Walter, Mstr. Gunnery Sgt., USMC
HYNES, William Patrick, F1c, USN
IDAROLA, Charles Angelo, F1c, USN
JABLONSKI, Alfred John, S1c, USN
JECK, Frederick Charles, RM3c, USN
JEWETT, Phillip Loren, M2c, USN
KAHN, Harold Barton, MM2c, USN

KAPPES, Joseph Michael, MM1c, USN
KAUPP, William Frederick, Torp2c, USN
KELLY, Charles Raymond, BM2c, USN
KERRIGAN, Raymond Joseph, MM2c, USN
KLENK, Edwin John, S2c, USNR
KNOX, Ens. Leslie Lockhart Bruce, USNR
LA BRIE, William Charles, WT2c, USN
LANE, John Joseph, QM3c, USNR
LEIGRAF, Theodore Joseph, CMM, USN
LINDGREN, Arthur Richard, RM2c, USN
LLOYD, Edward James, SM2c, USN
LUCEY, Neil Jermiah, S1c, USN
MAXWELL, Ens. Herbert William, USNR
McDONALD, Thomas William, GM2c, USN
McGEEHAN, John Henry, Jr., S2c, USN
MEGLIS, John Anthony, F1c, USN
MELTON, Earl Rudolph, MM1c, USN
MICHALOWSKY, Henry, S1c, USN
NUTT, Harold Lester, S2c, USN
OJSERKIS, Charles, S2c, USNR
OPDENCAMP, William, FC2c, USN
OSTERMIER, Robert David, AMM1c, USN
OVERHOLT, Walter, Torp.3c, USN
PARKS, Floyd David, F1c, USN
PHIFER, George Hendrick, EM2c, USN
PICCOLO, Charles Louis, S2c, USN
PIRANEO, Joseph T., PFC, USMC
ROBERTS, John Joseph, SC2c, USN
ROWE, Eugene Joseph, S1c, USN
RUNIAK, Nicholas, S1c, USN
RYAN, Edmund Thomas, Y3c, USN
SANDMAN, Karl Lother, Y2c, USN
SANZARI, Alfred Angelo, F3c, USN
SAVIDGE, John Edwin, S1c, USN
SCHOLTEN, Lyle Joseph, ACOM, USN
SCHROEDER, Henry, BM1c, USN
SHATTUCK, Herbert Fred, Chief Torp., USNR
SIMON, Walter Hamilton, S1c, USN
SOKOLSKY, Myron, Cox., USNR
SPERLING, Joseph, SF1c, USN
STROUSE, Ernest, WT2c, USN

TACEY, George Edmonds, F2c, USN
THOMPSON, Ens. William M., USNR
THROMBLEY, Robert Leroy, S2c, USN
VAN ANTWERP, Daniel Kelley, F1c, USN
VANNATTA, Thomas O., Corp., USMC
WILLETT, Edward George, GM2c, USN
WOLF, Edward Norman, F3c, USNR
WOLFE, Maurice Arthur, Jr., S2c, USN
WOOL, Meyer Theodore, AS, USN
WYCKOFF, Robert LeRoy, F1c, USN
ZWARUN, Michael, Jr., S1c, USN

Wounded

ABATE, Vincent, Jr., ARM3c, USN
COBURN, Ens. Charles Hamond, Jr., USNR
DANIELS, Earl Charles, S1c, USN
FERRAIOLO, John Sam, F1c, USN
GAYNOR, William E., Jr., Pvt., USMC
JONES, Earl Leslie, S2c, USN
MINKWITZ, Vernon Cecil, S2c, USN
PURVIS, William Robinson, F3c, USN
STILLWELL, James Francis, BM2c, USN
WILKINSON, Howard Lyman, SK1c, USN

Missing

ALLEN, Harper Basil, S1c, USN
ANDERSON, Clarence Bernhardt, SM3c, USN
BORKOWSKI, Edward Joseph, RM3c, USN
BROWN, Douglas Raymond, RM3c, USN
CHISHOLM, Lt. Cdr. John Kielkopf, Supply Corps, USN
CROTTY, Ens. William Blackwood Joseph, USNR
DALE, Peter John, RM1c, USN
DELPRETE, Louis Andrew, S1c, USN
DE VRIES, Marvin Henry, Torp.1c, USN
DI GIACOMO, Dominick John, F1c, USN
FEUCHACK, Stephen, MM1c, USN
GLASSBERG, Seymour Bernard, S1c, USN
GRODZKI, Henry Stanley, S1c, USN
HARTPENCE, Earl Nixon, S2c, USN
HICKMAN, Frank Robert, Jr., S1c, USN
HOLTZMAN, Harry, Prtr1c, USN
KULESH, Michael, S1c, USN
LEAMING, Jack, PhM2c, USN
LEWIS, William Edward, Jr., F2c, USN
MARTON, Bela, BM2c, USN
MILLS, Fredrick Joseph, S2c, USN
MONNETT, John, F3c, USN
MOORER, Harry Joseph, F2c, USN
PARKIN, Edward Joseph, S1c, USN
PEDEN, Joseph, Jr., S1c, USN
PIENCIAK, John Peter, F1c, USN

REILLY, John David., SM3c, USN
ROBERTS, Cdr. David Wells, USN
SCHLOSSER, Charles Martin, S1c, USN
STEWART, Albert Conrad, S1c, USN
STIRES, George Edward, F2c, USN
UR, Dazider E., Corp., USMCR
WALLING, Nelson Chester, F1c, USN
WILSON, Robert Archibald, FC1c, USN
WILSON, Lt. Samuel Joseph, USNR
ZULLO, Nicholas Joseph, S1c, USN

Prisoners of War

ACKERMAN, James, Bkr1c, USN
AXELSON, Walter Chris, S2c, USN
BACSIK, Stephen Charles, BM2c, USN
BALCER, Julian Henry, Corp., USMC
BARNES, Darrell LeRoy, F2c, USN
BLUEMKE, George Louis, Sgt., USMC
BRIDGET, Cdr. Francis Joseph, USN
BRONSON, Clarence Edmund, MM2c, USN
BROWN, James Monroe, III, S2c, USN
BROWN, Robert McCulloch, Corp., USMC
CASE, Alexander, GM3c, USN
CERRUTI, Julius Elmer, CPho, USN
CHAMBERS, Philip Speck, PFC, USMC
CHRISTENSEN, Arthur, ML1c, USN
CRAFT, George A., Corp., USMC
DAVIS, Herman, PhM3c, USN
DAVIS, Jack, 1st Sgt., USMC
DONOVAN, John Francis, S1c, USN
DU HAIME, Arthur Raymond, S1c, USN
EPPERSON, Bobbie, RM2c, USN
EVENSEN, Merle James, MM2c, USN
FABIAN, Henry, Jr., MM2c, USN
FINE, Reuben, CSM, USNR
GLATT, Ens. Robert Louis, USNR
GREERY, Lt. Cdr. Elmer Blomfield, USNR
GRONECK, George Martin, MM2c, USN
IRVIN, William Tallman, CMM, USNR
JOHNSON, Lt. Robert Henry Glass, USN
KELSEY, Paul Van, F1c, USN
KLINE, Lt. Cdr. Edward Franklin (MC), USN
LEE, John Wilson, S1c, USN
LOWNDES, Lt. William Rawlins, USN
McCAMBRIDGE, John, S1c, USN
MITRO, Albert Fred, SK3c, USN
NASH, Lt. David, USN
NELSON, Clarence Hampton, Jr., S1c, USN
NEWHOUSE, Gerald Arthur, 1st Sgt., USMC
O'GRADY, Joseph Patrick, SF1c, USN

PEARCE, Lt. (jg) William Mansfield, USNR
PEPPITONE, Vito, PFC, USMC
POLIDORO, Vincent Florentino, S2c, USN
RAWLINGS, William, CBM, USN
ROGALSKI, Joseph F., Corp., USMC
RUSSELL, Otha Knight, Gunner, USN
SCHUSTER, Adolph, CMM, USNR
SCHWARZ, Otto Carl, S2c, USN
SKIDMORE, William B., PFC, USMC
SMITH, Edward D., Sgt., USMC

SMITH, Robert Alexander, Sgt., USMC
SMOLEN, George, S2c, USN
SNOW, Ens. Russel Wakefield, Jr., USNR
STAFF, Jack Wadsworth, S1c, USN
STEINGART, Meyer Martin, CSF, USN
VANDERGRIFT, Lt. (jg) Jacob Jay, Jr., USN
WALKER, Robert R., PFC, USMC
WILLEVER, Stewart, Jr., RM2c, USN
WINFREY, Walter Monroe, Aer2c, USN

NEW MEXICO

Dead

BLOCK, Ivan Lee, PhM2c, USN
BUHR, Clarence Edward, S1c, USN
GARA, Martin Anthony, F2c, USN
GILBERT, Lt. Roy Del, USNR
GILMAN, Earl Wilton, RM2c, USN
JONES, Ens. Robert D., Jr., USNR
LIVERS, Raymond Edward, S1c, USN
LIVERS, Wayne Nicholas, F1c, USN
RAMOS, James Flores, S2c, USNR
SCOTT, C. W., Jr., CM2c, USN
SORENSEN, Holger Earl, S1c, USN
SUMNER, Oren, S2c, USN
VALENCIA, Juan, S1c, USN
WALTERS, William Spurgeon, Jr., FC3c, USN

Wounded

GARCIA, Willie, AS, USN
HENSLEY, Ovid Alvy, AS, USNR
KLINE, Elmer LeRoy, Jr., AMM3c, USN
MILLS, Leon Eugene, S2c, USN

Missing

EATON, Andrew Deloss, Torp.2c, USN
ELMS, Leo Gore, RM3c, USN

ESTES, Victor William, S2c, USN
WALKER, Uzelle D., S/Sgt., USMC
WETSEL, William Douglas, S1c, USN

Prisoners of War

BRANNIN, Tom Adams, PFC, USMC
BUSTAMENTE, Lawrence Robert, PFC, USMC
CHRISTIAN, Jesse Earl, PFC, USMC
CLAYBOURN, Charles Vance, S2c, USN
DOW, Benjamin James, MM2c, USN
GONZALES, Joseph Vincent, Corp., USMC
GREGORY, Robert Amis, RM3c, USN
KINISTER, Bert Franklin, GM3c, USN
LAKE, Donald E., PFC, USMC
LEES, Paul C., PFC, USMC
LILLARD, George Edward, Pvt., USMC
LINDERFELT, William Robert, Corp., USMC
MARQUEZ, Trancito Garcia, PFC, USMC
PRICKETT, Hiram Jefferson, QM1c, USN
PRINGLE, William John, AMM3c, USN
SANFORD, Egbert Everett, PFC, USMC
TODD, Herman Albert, PFC, USMC

NEW YORK

Dead

ALBANESE, Salvatore Joseph, F2c, USN
ALTIERI, John Joseph, Jr., ARM3c, USN
ANDREN, Robert Francis, F1c, USN
ANNUZIATO, Frank John, S1c, USN
APREA, Frank Anthony, Cox., USN
AUSTIN, Laverne Alfred, S1c, USN
BARANICK, George, F2c, USN
BARBIERI, Stephen, S1c, USNR
BARON, William Kraft, S1c, USNR

BASSETT, Ens. Edgar Reese, USNR
BATES, Ens. Edward M., Jr., USNR
BATOR, Edward, F1c, USN
BECKETT, Lt. Harold James, USNR
BECKWITH, Thomas Stewart, SF2c, USN
BERMINGHAM, Lt. Cdr. John Michael, USN
BIRGE, George Albert, S1c, USN
BLACK, Thomas Francis, S1c, USN
BLAIS, Albert Edward, RM3c, USNR
BONFIGLIO, William John, EM1c, USN

BORODENKO, Michael, Cox., USN
BRABBZSON, Oran Merrill, Mus2c, USN
BRANCHEN, William, Jr., CGM, USN
BROM, Walter William, SM1c, USN
BUDKA, William, WT2c, USNR
BUNKER, Ens. William Logan, Jr., USNR
BUONASSISI, Michael, Torp.2c, USN
BUSSO, Frank, WT2c, USN
BUTLER, William Thomas, ARM1c, USN
CAREY, Francis Lloyd, SK3c, USN
CARLSON, Daniel William, CMM, USN
CASILAN, Epifanio Miranda, OS3c, USN
CHAJHOWSKI, Anthony John, WT1c, USN
CHEENEY, Bartholomew Ambrose, RM1c, USN
CHERNUCHA, Harry Gregory, Mus.2c, USN
CHRYSANTHEM, George, S1c, USNR
CLARK, Ens. Louis Crawford, USN
CLAFLIN, Carl Rex, F2c, USN
COHN, Mitchell, RM3c, USNR
COLLIER, Leland Ross, EM3c, USN
CORBIN, James J., Jr., Pvt., USMC
CORCORAN, Gerald John, S1c, USN
COUGHLIN, Leo Fred, B2c, USN
COVATI, Joseph Frederick, Cox., USN
CRISAFULLI, Charles Carman, GM2c, USNR
D'ANGELO, John, S1c, USN
DENNEY, Lt. Edward Francis, USN
DE ROSA, William Anthony, Bkr3c, USNR
DE SEVE, Joseph, GM2c, USN
DE TORO, Nicholas Joseph, S1c, USN
DIECKMANN, Albert Wilbur, Cox., USN
EDWARDS, James, Jr., Torp.3c, USN
EHRLE, Elwood, GM3c, USN
ELLISON, Ens. Harold John, USNR
ENGLISH, Leonard Post, Cox., USN
ESTABROOKS, Louis Ervin, QM3c, USN
EVERETT, Hilton Hardin, F1c, USN
FENTON, Willard Chapman, Torp.3c, USN
FERRACANE, Anthony William, Y2c, USN
FIELD, George Arthur, ARM3c, USN
FIELDS, Bernard, RM3c, USNR
FIELDS, Ira Ped, GM3c, USN
FISCHER, Lt. (jg) Carl Otto, USNR
FISCHER, William Frederick, Jr., S1c, USN
FLANNERY, Robert Joseph, FC3c, USN
FLECHSENHAAR, Howard, SK3c, USNR
FOLEY, Walter Charles, S1c, USN
FOSTER, Sterling Cecil, CEM, USN
FURMAN, Burton J., SK3c, USNR
GATES, Nelson Edward, SK3c, USNR

GENTILE, Lawrence V., Pvt., USMCR
GHILONI, John Primo, CM1c, USN
GIESA, George Edward, F2c, USN
GOEBEL, Henry James, CBM, USN
GOLDYCH, John, Torp.2c, USN
GORNEY, Roman Theodore, S1c, USN
GOULD, Arthur, RM3c, USNR
GRACEY, Robert Kennedy, F1c, USN
GRANES, Joseph Anthony, CGM, USN
GRAY, Augustus Henderson, Torp.1c, USN
GREENE, Ens. Eugene Allen, USNR
HALVORSEN, Harry John, F1c, USN
HAMMER, Edward Earl, AMM3c, USN
HARTLEY, Kenneth Jay, F1c, USN
HAYMAN, Harvey Joseph, AMM3c, USN
HERTHNECK, Lt. (jg) Robert George, Dental Corps, USN
HIA, Magnus, S1c, USNR
HILL, James Thomas, S1c, USN
HOLLENBACH, Paul Zepp, S1c, USN
HOLMES, Harry Randolph, F3c, USN
HOMIC, Bennie Stephen, MM1c, USNR
HOPPING, Lt. Cdr. Hallsted Lubeck, USN
HORVATH, Edward Joseph, S1c, USN
HOUSTON, Earl Frederick, MA2c, USN
HOYT, Edward, RM3c, USN
HUBAL, Ernest John, S2c, USN
HUDSON, Ira Duane, F3c, USN
HUNT, Robert Elwyn, F2c, USN
HUNTLEY, John Foster, Jr., S2c, USNR
HUOT, Robert Joseph, Aer3c, USN
HYMAN, Lt. Cdr. Willford Milton, USN
IESSI, Frank Patsy, RM3c, USN
INGALLS, Richard Fitch, SC3c, USN
INGALLS, Theodore A., SC3c, USN
IZZO, Mario Fred, F1c, USNR
JAMES, Harvey Weldon, Jr., S1c, USN
JAYNE, Kenneth Lyle, F3c, USN
JAYSON, David, RM2c, USNR
JENISON, Eugene Richard, AS, USNR
JOHANNES, Charles John, CM3c, USN
JORDAN, Ens. John Anthony, USN
JOYCE, Lt. (jg) Edgar Thomas, USNR
KAISER, Harry Franklin, F2c, USNR
KAST, Warren Harding, SK3c, USN
KAVANAUGH, Lawrence William, MM2c, USN
KEILSON, Herbert, Sgt., USMC
KENNEDY, George Francis, SM3c, USN
KENNEY, David Owen, F1c, USN
KENYON, Ens. Henry Russell, Jr., USNR
KIEB, Ens. Norman H., Jr., USNR
KILLELEA, Charles Francis, S1c, USNR
KING, Ens. Robert N., Jr., USNR
KLINE, Robert Edwin, GM2c, USN
KOSBOB, James Clark, S2c, USN

KRAM, Leonard, AS, USN
KRAMB, Charles Herman, Jr., GM3c, USN
KRAMB, James Henry, S1c, USN
KRAMB, John David, M1c, USN
KUGEL, Eugene, Jr., CQM, USNR
KWIATKOSKI, Franklin Stanley, S2c, USN
LAZAREK, George, PFC, USMC
LEE, Ens. Kenneth Gordon, USNR
LIBBY, Robert Leroy, SF3c, USN
LOCK, Douglas A., S1c, USN
LOVERING, Ens. William Bacon, USNR
LUND, Paul Odell, Torp.1c, USN
LYNCH, Francis Frederick, Torp.3c, USN
LYNCH, Hubert Joseph, AS, USN
MacNAUGHTON, Donald Martin, CY, USN
MAGEE, Gerald James, SK3c, USN
MANGER, Peter, S1c, USNR
MARANO, Joseph Charles, AS, USN
MARTINO, Pasquale Joseph, AS, USN
MASON, Ens. Newton Henry, USNR
MASSEY, Lt. Cdr. Lance Edward, USN
MAURICE, Walter Homer, GM3c, USN
McCORMACK, Nicholas Joseph, S1c, USN
McGOWAN, Stephen Joseph, Jr., S1c, USNR
MENZENSKI, Stanley Paul, Cox., USN
MERINGOLO, Ferdinand Frank, S1c, USN
MERKL, John William, Jr., SK3c, USN
MILLER, John Joseph, Jr., EM3c, USN
MILLER, Ens. Marsh Weston, Jr., USNR
MILLIMAN, Ens. Richard Diver, USNR
MINNECI, Charles, F1c, USN
MONDI, Anthony Mike, F2c, USN
MONTANO, Christopher Frank, Ptr3c, USN
MORINCELLI, Edo, MM2c, USN
MULLER, Robert Elmo, AMM2c, USN
NADEL, Alexander Joseph, Mus2c, USN
NAMMINGA, Henry Vanderwood, Cox., USNR
NANCK, Edward, F2c, USNR
NEE, Edwin Thomas, Chief Torp., USN
NEWMAN, Lt. Arthur Lester, USN
NOCE, Emile Salvatore, EM2c, USN
NOWOSACKI, Ens. Theodore L., USNR
O'BRIEN, John Patrick, SM3c, USN
O'BRIEN, Thomas Francis, FC2c, USN
O'CONNOR, Maurice Michael, MM1c, USN
O'GORMAN, Charles Patrick, F1c, USN
O'KEEFE, Eugene Francis, F3c, USNR
ORZECHOWSKI, Leo, GM1c, USN
PALERMO, James William, F2c, USN
PARKINSON, Stanley George, BM1c, USN

PAWLOWSKI, Raymond Paul, S1c, USN
PELESCHAK, Michael, S1c, USN
PETERSON, Albert Hendrix, Jr., FC3c, USN
PETERSON, Arthur Burnett, F1c, USN
PHELPS, George Edward, S1c, USN
PHILLIPS, John Joseph, WT1c, USNR
PODRES, Ladislaus, WT2c, USN
POLHEMUS, Willis, F3c, USN
POLOMARES, Manuel Francis, AS, USNR
POTTER, Ens. Charles Kirby, USNR
POWERS, Lt. John James, USN
PRICHARD, Charles Lloyd, Jr., CM3c, USNR
QUIRK, Edward Joseph, F1c, USN
RAPOZA, Leonard, AS, USNR
RAY, James Thomas, SC1c, USN
RAY, Lt. Martin Hasset, Jr., USN
REED, Capt. Willard, Jr., USMC
REILLY, Robert Emmet, Bkr3c, USN
REISTETTER, John Steven, CGM, USN
REITER, Lt. (jg) Charles, USNR
RENGER, Lawrence Harold, FC3c, USN
REYBOLD, Lt. Cdr. John K., USN
REYNOLDS, Jack Franklyn, S1c, USN
RICHTERS, Joseph William, F2c, USN
RIFKIN, Steven Samuel, F1c, USN
RIORDAN, James Joseph, Jr., Y2c, USNR
ROBUSTO, Louis Joseph, S1c, USN
ROMERO, Vladimir Mendoza, S1c, USN
ROSENBLATT, Murray, S1c, USNR
ROSENTHAL, Alfred Aaron, RM3c, USNR
ROSS, Deane Lundy, S2c, USN
ROSS, Robert Alexander, SM3c, USN
ROSS, William Frazer, GM3c, USN
RUEHL, Virgil L., PFC, USMC
RUGGERIO, William, FC3c, USN
RYAN, George Patrick, FC2c, USN
RYCHLEWSKI, Walter Leo, F2c, USN
SANDERS, Ens. Eugene Thomas, USN
SAVAGE, Lyal Jackson, S1c, USN
SCHANTZ, Lloyd Houghton, MM2c, USN
SCHUERHOFF, Ens. Elmer C., USNR
SCHUSTER, John Charles, Jr., GM3c, USN
SHARP, Wade Elmer, EM3c, USN
SHADINGER, Lt. (jg) Gail Jenner, USNR
SHEELEY, Arnold Glenford, GM3c, USN
SIBLER, Donald J., PFC, USMC
SIBLEY, Delmar Dale, S1c, USN
SIMPSON, Albert Eugene, S1c, USN
SMITH, Allen Frederick, AS, USN
SMITH, Carlyle George, Ptr3c, USN
SMITH, Robert Daniel, S2c, USN
SMITH, William Everett, SM1c, USN
SMITHIES, Donald Abram, SK3c, USN

SPATA, John Justin, S2c, USN
STANKEWICZ, Frank, WT2c, USN
STAPLETON, John Charles, F1c, USN
STASKO, John, Jr., SF3c, USN
STEINIGER, Charles Edward, F2c, USN
STEPHENSON, Hugh Donald, S1c, USN
STERN, Ens. Charles M., Jr., USNR
STRIEGLER, Herman Frederick, EM1c, USN
SWEENEY, Francis John, F1c, USN
TACHNA, Ens. Lionel Judah, USNR
TANCREDI, Michael Anthony, S1c, USNR
TAYLOR, Lynn Anson, F3c, USN
TERP, Perry Jens, F2c, USN
THOMAN, Ferdinand Lewis, S2c, USN
TORTORICI, Acursio, S1c, USNR
TROTTER, Neal Junior, WT2c, USN
UMPLEBY, Eugene Edgar, WT1c, USN
URBAN, John Joseph, MM2c, USN
UNDERHILL, Ens. Samuel Jackson, USNR
VAN BUREN, Lt. (jg) John James, USN
VANUCCI, Eugene John, F2c, USN
VILLA, Michael William, F3c, USN
WAINWRIGHT, Silas Alonzo, PhM1c, USN
WANDLER, Lawrence H., PFC, USMC
WARBURTON, William Henry, Jr., RM2c, USN
WARD, William John, Y2c, USNR
WARDZINSKI, Bernard Joseph, CM3c, USN
WARE, Lt. Charles Rollins, USN
WATERS, Ens. Robert John, USNR
WERNER, Edward Theodore, AMM2c, USCG
WHITE, Ernest, S2c, USN
WHITE, William Alloyous, WT2c, USNR
WHITMAN, Lt. (jg) Robert Scott, Jr., USN
WILLIAMS, Earl John, S1c, USN
WILLIAMS, Richard Samuel, S1c, USN
WILSON, Bernard Martin, RM3c, USNR
WOLL, Louis Joseph, SC3c, USN
WOODS, William Anthony, S2c, USN
YANNY, William Joseph, WT1c, USN
ZACHARIAS, Lt. Casper, USNR
ZAJKOWSKY, Benjamin, F1c, USN
ZIEMBICKI, Steve Anthony, S1c, USN
ZON, Edward Valentine, S2c, USN

Wounded

AMBROGIO, Joseph John, AMM3c, USN
BAUMEISTER, William Nicolas, ACMM, USN
BELL, Joseph William Howard, F1c, USN
BELLINGER, Lloyd, Aer3c, USN

BERGNES, Paul Alvin, Cox., USN
BUREK, Walter George, F2c, USN
CIACCIA, Patsy, S2c, USN
CIOFFI, Charles, S1c, USN
CITO, Alfred Frederick, S2c, USNR
CLARKE, George William, S1c, USN
CUMMINGS, John Joseph, Jr., F2c, USN
CYMERMAN, Raymond Alfred, S2c, USN
DE LALIO, Capt. Armond H., USMCR
DE NEEF, James Peter, S1c, USN
DORFELD, Walter Ernest, SM2c, USN
DWYER, John Francis, ARM3c, USN
GOOD, Robert, Jr., F1c, USN
GRISHAM, Lester Alvin, ACOM, USN
GUINESS, Christian, AMM3c, USN
HENNESSEY, William Francis, F2c, USN
ISCHIA, Herbert "N," F1c, USN
LAMBERT, Richard Carl, Jr., EM1c, USN
LEHR, Willard Albert, S1c, USN
McDADE, Joseph Michael, AMM3c, USN
McGREGOR, Allister Matthew, S1c, USNR
MESISCA, Fred Carmine Joseph, HA1c, USN
MOORE, 2nd Lt. Thomas F., Jr., USMCR
O'GRADY, John Lawrence, S2c, USN
PASK, William Frederick, F1c, USN
PERKINS, Ellsworth Clark, F1c, USN
ROBINSON, Lawrence David, SC2c, USN
ROCKWELL, Cdr. Joseph Perkins, USN
TRONOLONE, Ens. John J., USNR
WEISSMAN, Daniel, S1c, USN
WELLS, Duncan, AOM1c, USN
WILSON, George Emiel, S1c, USNR
YURKUS, Walter Casper, EM2c, USN

Missing

ABRAMS, Bernard, RM1c, USN
ADOLFI, Jack Joseph, SC3c, USN
ASHTON, Charles Edward, MM1c, USN
BAKER, George Wilson, WT1c, USN
BALCEREK, Casimer Alfred, Jr., Cox., USN
BELLINGER, Lt. George Lieinberger, USN
BURGOYNE, John Leo, Cox., USN
BYERS, Walter Kohler, Jr., S1c, USN
CAPLICKI, Joseph, F1c, USN
CARLIN, William Francis, CEM, USN
CARLYLE, Edward Thomas, S1c, USN
CARSON, Ens. John Douglas, Supply Corps, USN
COLLITON, Luke Dunbar, MM1c, USN
CONN, LeRoy Ghear, MM2c, USN
CONWAY, Raymond Leonard, F3c, USN
COSEY, Victor Joseph, RM3c, USN

CRUM, Walter Gerard, S1c, USN
DWYER, William Joseph, WT2c, USN
EDMONDS, Phillip Riley, S2c, USN
EMMERTH, William Herbert, Cox., USN
EVANS, Roger Milton, S1c, USN
FERRERO, John, S2c, USN
FISCHER, Lt. (jg) Howard Philip, USN
GALLAGHER, 2nd Lt. Frank E., Jr., USMC
GARDINER, George Earnest, RM1c, USN
GILMAN, Wallace Bertram, RM2c, USN
GRECO, John, Torp2c, USN
GROSSE, George, MM1c, USN
GUARINO, Alfred Kenneth, RM3c, USNR
HAAS, Albert Chester, S2c, USN
HEAVEY, Thomas Vincent, Cox., USN
HICKS, Lt. Cdr. Harry Lynwood, USN
INGERSON, Clarence John, Gunner, USN
KATCHUCK, Alexander, Pvt., USMC
KAUTTER, Charles Anthony, EM2c, USN
KORSAK, William Paul, S1c, USN
KURTZ, Albert Joseph, S2c, USN
LIEBLA, Sylvan Sprague, EM1c, USN
LONGO, Joseph Leo, S1c, USN
MAYO, Ens. Caswell Armstrong, III, USNR
McCORMACK, Lt. John Joseph, Jr., USN
McLAUGHLIN, Robert Paul, F3c, USN
MENCHUK, Ens. Walter Michael, USNR
MORRA, Mario Anthony, F3c, USN
MULDOWNEY, Frank Alexander, Jr., QM2c, USN
O'NEIL, Bernard Joseph, S1c, USN
ORLYK, Stephen Michel, MM1c, USN
PAPA, Anello Dominick, F2c, USN
POLLAK, Ens. Edward George, USNR
POSTMAN, Hyman, AMM2c, USN
PUSKAS, James, S1c, USN
RIGGIO, Filippo, SM1c, USN
RISI, Bernard, AS, USNR
SCHAFFER, Eugene John, F1c, USN
SHEA, Richard John, EM3c, USN
SKINNER, Alfred Jerome, BM3c, USN
SMOLINSKY, Rudolph Raphael, F2c, USN
SNODGRASS, Lt. (jg) Ray Arvel, USN
STETTLER, Robert Frederick, S2c, USN
STONE, Lt. Archibald, Jr., USN
SWINEGAR, John Paul, S2c, USN
TAFURO, Frank Thomas, MM2c, USN
THURSTON, Robert Allen, S2c, USN
TOWNLEY, Walter Harris, Jr., SK3c, USN
VALEK, Antone George, Jr., AMM1c, USN

VILLARI, Andrew Joseph, S1c, USN
WELKER, John Stewart, SK2c, USN
WELLBOURN, Arthur Frederick, BM1c, USN
WELLER, Maurice Elgin, CCM, USN
WEYGANT, Robert, S1c, USN
WHALEN, Aloysius F., PFC, USMC
WOLVEN, Francis John, S1c, USN
ZAZZARA, James Joseph, SK3c, USN
ZEALE, Edward Paul, EM3c, USN
ZINK, Lt. (jg) Oswald Arthur, USN

Prisoners of War

ALLEVA, Joseph George, S1c, USN
AUSTIN, Ens. Donald E., USNR
BANSLEY, Donald Edmond, PhM2c, USN
BASSETT, Lt. Robert Vanrensselaer, Jr., USN
BAUMGARDNER, Lt. Earl Gearhart, USNR
BENEDETTO, Michael Angelo, Pvt., USMC
BENEDICT, Donald Andrew, PhM3c, USN
BERGEN, James Timothy, S2c, USN
BERKERY, James Michael, Jr., PFC, USMC
BLAIR, Rollie Heym, CM3c, USN
BONDAR, Harry, WT2c, USN
BOOKMAN, Lt. (jg) John Jacob, USNR
BORNT, Harold Merritt, AMM3c, USN
BOUCK, Ralph Richtmyer, Cox., USN
BRETTMAN, John William, Corp., USMC
BROHMAN, Henry George, PhM1c, USN
BUTTERFIELD, George Bronson, MM1c, USN
CAHOON, Weldon Charles, CEM, USN
CARPENTER, William Theodore, BM, USN
CARSCALLEN, Edwin William, PhM2c, USN
CASIMIRI, Nunzio Nichols, S1c, USN
COURTENAY, Madison Leroy, Jr., RM3c, USNR
COVERT, Lawrence William, RM1c, USN
COX, Wilbur Gorden, Jr., MM2c, USN
CROVAT, Lt. Philip Stuart, USNR
CURRY, Edwin Doyle, Sgt. Maj., USMC
DAUGHERTY, Elwood Alonzo, Cox., USN
DAVIS, Lt. James Robert, CEC, USN
DAWSON, Harold Rosmond, CBM, USN
DeBLASIO, John J., PFC, USMC
DEISINGER, George Michael, S1c, USN
DEVEREUX, Maj. James Patrick Sinnot, USMC
DIETZ, Cecil Morton, Sgt. Maj., USMC
DIMENTO, Frank, Pvt., USMC
DOUGHERTY, John Ready, M1c, USN

ERIKSSON, Roger Vilhelm, MM2c, USN
FERGUSON, Ens. Earl Walton, USNR
FERGUSON, John Andrew, F2c, USN
FOLEY, Warren John, S1c, USN
FOLEY, Lt. (jg) William Thomas, USN
FOY, James Walter, CRM, USN
FRISING, William Albert, Pvt., USMC
GALOWSKI, Leon Herbert, F2c, USN
GANS, Philip Thomas, MM1c, USN
GLUSMAN, Lt. (jg) Murray, USNR
GOODMAN, David, RM1c, USN
GRIFFITHS, William E., Sgt., USMC
GROSSE, William Frederick, CMM, USNR
GUSTAFSON, Wilbert Theodore, Ptr1c, USN
GUYON, Charles Ambrose, SF1c, USN
HABERMAN, Robert Ray, PFC, USMC
HARRINGTON, Cdr. Wilson Hempfield, USNR
HAUSMAN, Edwin John, BM1c, USNR
HEDE, Lt. Cdr. Adolph, USN
HENRY, John Owen, CRM, USN
HILLMAN, Robert Stephen, F1c, USN
HIRSHBERG, Harold Edward, SM1c, USN
HOLDREDGE, 1st Lt. Willard B., USMC
JANSON, Lt. (jg) John Ragnar, USNR
JAQUIN, Howard Frank, MM2c, USN
JORDAN, James Joseph, Sgt., USMC
KELLY, Joseph Allen, PFC, USMC
KING, Irven Ray, PFC, USMC
KIRKPATRICK, Lt. Harlan Good, USN
KUCHARSKI, Leo Frank, BM1c, USN
KUCK, Edward Nolan, EM3c, USN
LADY, Dennie Guy, Corp., USMC
LAMBERT, Lt. Gordon Kenneth (MC), USN
LAPOINTE, Henry D., Pvt., USMC
LEVITT, Ens. Herbert Alfred, USNR
MACDOUGALL, Daniel, CPhM, USN
MADSON, Quentin Christian, Cox., USN
MARCLEY, James Irving, GM1c, USN
MARINOS, Matthew Michael, S1c, USN
MARTIN, Ens. Joseph, Jr., USNR
McCARTHY, James Benjamin, CY, USN
McCAVANAGH, Patrick John, CWT, USN
MICELI, Joseph, PFC, USMC
MICHEL, Lt. (jg) John Joseph Aloysius, USN
MOHR, Frederick Balthasar, Sgt., USMC
MORVAN, Laurence E., PFC, USMC

MUNSON, Gerald Vincent, S2c, USN
MUSTO, James William, S2c, USN
NEWELL, Alfred Harry, Torp3c, USN
NICHOLSON, John Thomas, RM1c, USN
O'BRIAN, Ens. William Joseph, Jr., USNR
O'BRIEN, John Francis, Chief Carp., USN
O'BRIEN, Robert Louis, CGM, USN
O'CONNOR, Thomas John, S2c, USN
PARKS, William Alexander, S1c, USN
PASSARETTI, Thomas Anthony, Y3c, USN
PEKARICH, Joseph Stevens, Platoon Sgt., USMC
PERRY, Elbert James, Mach., USN
PHILLIPS, Frank Patrick, PFC, USN
PICKUP, Capt. Lewis Herman, USMC
PITCHON, Salvatore, S1c, USN
PONESS, Ralph Carlo, SK2c, USN
POWELL, John Michael, BM1c, USN
RAPP, Ray Emmett, PFC, USMC
RIND, Alfred T., Jr., S/Sgt., USMC
ROSENTHAL, Lt. Herbert Jerome, USNR
RYAN, John Francis, PhM3c, USN
RYAN, John Patrick, SF2c, USN
SOLOMON, Morris, BM1c, USN
SOROCCO, John, CSM, USN
SWARTZ, Lowell Wendell, PhM2c, USN
TIGHE, James Gustavus, Jr., Sgt., USMC
TIRK, Ens. Richard Enoch, USNR
TYBUR, Albert John, PhM1c, USN
ULRICH, George, CWT, USNR
VAN BUSKIRK, Lt. Beverly Robinson, USN
VISSARIS, Christopher, Pvt., USMC
WALTER, Henry M., Jr., Sgt., USMC
WALTZ, John, CBM, USN
WARD, John Carlton, MM1c, USN
WAWRZONEK, Louis Joseph, PhM2c, USN
WEBB, 2nd Lt. Henry Gorham, USMC
WHITE, Edward W., Tech. Sgt., USMC
WILLIAMS, Ens. Belmont Murray, CEC, USNR
WILSON, Alfred James, Cox., USN
WINTERMAN, Mike, Sgt., USMCR
WOLF, Herman, Sgt., USMC
WRESINSKI, Thaddeus, PM1c, USN
ZELAZNY, Leo Frank, S2c, USN
ZIMBA, John Patrick, Corp., USMC
ZUNDELL, Lt. Cdr. Joseph La Monte, (MC), USN

NORTH CAROLINA

Dead

ALDRIDGE, Thomas Elwood, S2c, USN
ALLEN, Joseph Bright, AS, USNR
ALLEN, Moses Anderson, MA1c, USN
ALLEY, Jay Edgar, GM1c, USN
AYCOCK, William Henry, F1c, USN
BALLEW, Charles William, F2c, USN
BALLEW, James Robert, F1c, USN
BAME, Thomas Wiley, AMM3c, USN
BATSON, Charles Horace, AS, USNR
BEAN, Leslie Elmer, AS, USNR
BOWDEN, Edward Daniel, F1c, USN
BRASWELL, Shelton Parker, S1c, USN
BRITT, Prentiss Gaston, F1c, USN
BROOKS, Leon Murl, CM2c, USN
BROOKS, Livingston Ward, WT2c, USCG
BROTHERS, Walter Eugene, Jr., RM3c, USN
BUCKWELL, Crowell Harding, AS, USNR
CAMPBELL, James Matthews, S2c, USNR
CARGILE, Murry Randolph, S1c, USN
CARROLL, Robert Lewis, S1c, USN
CLAWSON, George Rome, Jr., F2c, USN
COLLIER, Samuel Mims, Jr., MM2c, USNR
COMPTON, Lewis de Liessiline, QM1c, USN
CONDERMAN, 2nd Lt. Robert J., USMC
DEWEESE, Richard Charles, S2c, USNR
DOBBINS, Lawrence Spencer, MM1c, USN
DODSON, Benjamin Ross, Jr., ARM3c, USN
DRUM, Donald Landford, F2c, USN
DURHAM, William Teasdale, S1c, USN
EDWARDS, Dupree Lee, F3c, USN
EDWARDS, Roland Wayne, F2c, USN
EFFIRD, Edward Lee, S2c, USNR
EVANS, Milton P., Corp., USMC
FIELDS, Robert Auswell, EM3c, USN
FISHER, Ernest Clifton, Y2c, USN
FRYE, Neil Daniel, MA3c, USN
GARRIS, Eugene, MA2c, USN
GARRISON, James Alexander, PhM1c, USN
GASHAW, James K., S1c, USN
GLOVER, Wilmer Thomas, AOM3c, USN
GREENE, Edgar James, S1c, USN
GRIFFITH, Carrol Alexander, S2c, USNR
HALL, Raymond Allgood, MM1c, USN
HAYNES, John Dennis, GM3c, USN
HERRING, Henry Edward, F1c, USN
HILTON, Wilson Woodrow, GM1c, USN

HODGES, Howard David, F1c, USN
HOLLIDAY, Louis Thomas, MM1c, USN
HOOD, Joseph Earnest, F1c, USN
HORRELL, Harvey Howard, SM1c, USN
HOYLE, Carl Edward, AS, USN
JACKSON, Austin Randolph, S1c, USN
JACKSON, Claudius Solomon, S2c, USN
JACKSON, William Clarence, EM3c, USN
JAMES, Edward Foster, S1c, USN
JONES, Clifton Cleo, S2c, USN
JONES, James Linwood, AS, USNR
JONES, Willie Everett, S2c, USN
KING, Lewis Meyer, F1c, USN
LEIGH, Malcolm Hedrick, GM3c, USN
LOVEGROVE, Edwin Calvin, S2c, USN
LOVELACE, Lt. Cdr. Donald Alexander, USN
MANN, Charles Willis, S1c, USN
MARSHALL, Ens. Hunter, III, USNR
MAY, Robert Elias, Cox., USN
McARTHER, Ernest Kestler, Jr., S1c, USN
McCABE, Edwin Bonner, WT1c, USN
McGINNIS, Bill Mark, AS, USNR
McGINNIS, Jackson Delaney, SC3c, USN
McLEOD, William Desmond, S2c, USN
McNEIL, Jesse Elwyn, MA1c, USN
MEADOWS, Percy, S2c, USN
MIDGETT, Darius Thomas, F2c, USN
MILLER, William Cicero, RM1c, USN
MITCHELL, Vimmy McKlies, MA2c, USN
MOORE, Clyde Carson, RM2c, USN
MOOSE, Samuel E., Tech. Sgt., USMC
NELON, David Edward, EM3c, USN
NICHOLS, Burton Keeth, S2c, USN
OUTLAND, Jarvis Godwin, F1c, USN
OWNBEY, Ernest Josiah, Jr., F3c, USN
PARIS, Edward Dill, AMM2c, USN
PARKER, Arthur Reuben, CPhM, USN
PEIFFER, Ens. Carl David, USNR
PIERCE, Carl Willard, AMM2c, USN
PIKE, Charlie Boyd, Jr., F3c, USN
PINKHAM, Albert Wesley, S2c, USN
POWELL, William Jeremiah, MA2c, USN
RAWLS, Wheeler Holden, AMM2c, USN
RAY, Patrick Henry, S2c, USN
RHODES, Mark Alexander, S1c, USN
ROBERSON, John Baxter, MA2c, USN
ROBERTS, Earl Reed, S1c, USN
ROEBUCK, George Benjamin, S1c, USN
ROUSE, Joseph Carel, S1c, USN
SHEEP, Harry Hinton, RM3c, USN
SMITH, Clen Newton, S2c, USN

SMITH, George Hoyle, BM2c, USN
SMITH, George Randolph, MA1c, USN
STALLINGS, Kermit Braxton, F1c, USN
STEVENSON, David Rex, S2c, USNR
SURRATT, Milton Reece, S1c, USN
SWINDELL, Thurman Randolph, AOM1c, USN
TALBERT, Carl Leonard, F1c, USN
TAYLOR, James Robert, S2c, USN
THOMPSON, Jessie Daniels, SC3c, USN
TILGHMAN, Henry Edward, F1c, USN
TUSSEY, Lloyd Harold, EM3c, USN
WARREN, Bryan Little, S1c, USN
WELCH, Robert Hiram, AMM, USN
WILKINS, Kenneth Paul, F1c, USN
WILLIAMSON, Randolph, Jr., MA1c, USN
WORLEY, Pink, S2c, USN

Wounded

COPELAND, Thomas Bailey, MA1c, USN
CRUMPLER, Charles Leroy, Jr., S1c, USN
GREENE, William Henry, MA2c, USN
JACOBS, James Hursley, S1c, USN
JOYNER, Cicero Elzin, S2c, USNR
LEWIS, Robert Howard, AS, USNR
MORRIS, Comelis, F1c, USN
MORRIS, Vernon, S1c, USN
O'NEAL, Dallas E., F1c, USCG
PARKER, Linwood Perry, GM3c, USN
PORTER, Ernest Clifton, Jr., EM2c, USN
SHAW, James Odell, GM3c, USN
SPAINHOUR, Thamer Elmo, S1c, USN
TALBERT, Carl Leonard, F1c, USN
TARLTON, Dennis Clarence, SC3c, USN
TEAGUE, Robert W., Platoon Sgt., USMC
TEMPLE, Charlie Wilson, F1c, USN

Missing

BARNHILL, Elmon, S1c, USN
BLACK, Joseph Grady, Jr., S1c, USN
BOLTON, Wilbur, Jr., F1c, USN
BUCHANAN, Henry Thomas, S1c, USN
CHERRY, Claude Marvin, Jr., FC3c, USN
DUNN, Clarence Preston, S2c, USN
FRASER, Meldean, F2c, USN
GIBSON, Lewis, S2c, USN
GRAHAM, Joyner Page, BM2c, USN
GRAY, Herbert, AS, USNR
HARPER, James R., PFC, USMC
HELSABECK, Robert Filmore, Jr., S2c, USN
HILL, Clyde Garfield, MM2c, USN
LANCASTER, Henry Franklin, S1c, USN
MILLER, William Curtis, S1c, USN

OZMENT, Andrew Franklin, CGM, USN
PARKER, William Wendell, S1c, USN
PRINCE, Charles William, S1c, USN
RHODES, William Anderson, TC1c, USN
RICHARDSON, Joseph Randolph, S1c, USN
SMITH, Charlie Culberth, CCStd., USN
SMITH, Stacey Hugh, S2c, USN
SMITH, Timothy Boswell, S2c, USN
STEINBECK, Edwin Dickson, SM1c, USN
STORIE, Luther Thomas, CMM, USN
SULLIVAN, Charles William, SC3c, USN
SWINK, Clifton Allen, SC2c, USN
TETTERTON, William Ellodious, F2c, USN
WOLEVER, Benjamin Harrison, Chief Pay Clerk, USMC

Prisoners of War

BARBOUR, Stewart Gordon, RM2c, USN
BERRY, Bryan Webster, PhM3c, USN
BOWMAN, LeRoy Wilson, PhM3c, USN
BRIMMER, Charles Walton, Corp., USMC
BRUTON, Harold Glenn, MM1c, USN
BUNCH, Jerry Judson, RM1c, USN
CAHOON, Celon L., PFC, USMC
CARAWAN, Benaga Greene, PhM3c, USN
CAUSEY, Fred Odell, GM1c, USNR
CHEEK, John Marvin, Chief Torp., USN
CLARK, Dallas Rhea, MM1c, USN
CLIFT, John White, Jr., CY, USN
COX, Emmette Grover, SC1c, USN
DARDEN, James Bizzell, S1c, USN
EUDY, Ernest Franklin, WT1c, USN
FARMER, Randolph Perry, Sgt., USMC
FENNELL, John Miller, F1c, USN
FLOURNOY, Capt. Walter Nevins, USMC
GARRIS, Eugene Alfonza, Pvt., USMC
HARVELL, Edward Lassiter, SM3c, USN
HOGGARD, Grady Lee, WT1c, USN
HOGGARD, Pritchard Rudolph, Cox., USN
HONEYCUTT, James Willard, S1c, USN
HOWERTON, Vance Bryan, SF2c, USN
HUNTLEY, Ted Douglas, AOM2c, USN
HYDE, Claywell Thomas, PhM2c, USN
JOHNSON, John David, BM2c, USN
JORDAN, Lt. Cdr. Francis Dixon, USN
KING, Clifton Earle, SC2c, USN
LANGDON, Lt. (jg) Benjamin Bruce (MC), USN
LINEBERRY, Capt. William Taylor (MC), USN
LYON, 1st Lt. Julian Venson, USMC
MUNN, Anderson Mitchell, EM3c, USN
NORKET, Jay Wiley, GM3c, USN
OWENS, Samuel Robert, Torp2c, USN

PICKETT, Leonard Virgil, CRM, USN
PORTIS, Walter Edward, BM2c, USN
REAVES, John Robert, CSK, USNR
ROBINSON, Bobby Gerrel, MM2c, USN
ROBINSON, David Mason, Jr., Torp2c, USN
ROTH, Lt. Cdr. Egbert Adolph, USN
SCATTERGOOD, Roderick Davidson, RM2c, USN
SEARCY, Ralph Norfleet, Torp1c, USN
SIMMONS, Robert Dorus, F1c, USN
SIMPSON, Greeley Lee, CBM, USN

STALKER, Bennie Lindon, CMM, USNR
STAPP, Kenneth W., Pvt., USMCR
STEVENS, Curtis Richard, Jr., SC3c, USN
UNDERWOOD, John Bunard, Jr., Torp1c, USN
WEBB, Royce Talmadge, MM2c, USN
WILKES, Robert Archie, CM3c, USN
WILLIS, Lt. (jg) Meade Homer, Jr., USNR
YOUNG, Thomas Wesley, AM2c, USN

NORTH DAKOTA

Dead

ALLEN, Lt. Edward Henry, USN
ANDERSON, Howard Taisey, F2c, USN
BENDER, Melvin Eugene, PFC, USMC
BERNARD, Frank Peter, SF2c, USN
CONLON, David William, PFC, USMC
COOL, Orlan Robert, S1c, USN
DEEDE, Lt. (jg) Leroy Clifford, USNR
EIDSVIG, Vernon Jerome, S1c, USN
EMERY, John Marvin, GM3c, USN
FECHO, Lawrence Herman, F1c, USN
FISCHER, Nicholas, MM2c, USN
GEBHARDT, Kenneth Edward, S1c, USN
GLEASON, Charles William, S1c, USN
HAMMERUD, George Winston, S1c, USN
HANSON, Rodger Jonas, S1c, USN
HUBER, Lowell Henry, MM2c, USN
JOHANNES, Charles Homer, S2c, USN
JOHNSON, Edward Dale, F1c, USN
KLEIST, Chester Fredrick, Cox., USN
KUKUK, Howard Helgi, S1c, USN
KUSIE, Donald Joseph, RM3c, USN
LANGELIERS, Terrance Henry, Cox., USN
LESMEISTER, Steve Louis, F3c, USN
LONDON, James Edward, SK1c, USN
LUND, Arnold Raymond, MM1c, USN
MATTERN, John A., Pvt., USMC
NELSON, Richard Eugene, F3c, USN
NERMOE, Earl Tilman, S1c, USN
NEUENSCHWANDER, Arthur Clarence, GM1c, USN
NICHOLSON, Glen Eldon, EM1c, USN
O'DONNELL, Ignatius Peter, F2c, USN
O'DONNELL, John Patrick, F1c, USN
OLDS, Clifford Nathan, F1c, USN
OLSON, Kermonth Norris, PhM3c, USN
PFAFFENGUT, Harold, F1c, USN
REGISTER, Lt. Cdr. Paul James, USN
RENNER, Albert, F2c, USN
ROSE, Paul Raymond, MM1c, USN

SCHDOWSKI, Joseph, S1c, USN
SEVERINSON, Everett Iven, SF1c, USN
SHERVEN, Richard Stanton, EM3c, USN
SHOCKMAN, James P., PFC, USMC
SIMENSEN, 2nd Lt. Carleton E., USMC
SUMMER, Verlin Bernard, S2c, USN
TUNTLAND, Earl Eugene, S1c, USN
WELLS, Floyd Arthur, RM2c, USN
WOHL, Oswald Carl, S2c, USN
ZIMMERMAN, Fred, Cox., USN

Wounded

BLEILE, Peter Ralph, S2c, USN
CHECK, Lt. (jg) Leonard J., USN
ENGEN, John Klaboe, Music, USN
GERSZEWSKI, Sebastian Leo, S1c, USN
KIHL, Tracy Gerald, SK3c, USN
KNUDSON, Reo Irvin, S1c, USN
KOHL, William Peter, GM3c, USN
PALMER, Roy Andrew, S2c, USN
ZETTEL, Alvin Francis, ARM3c, USN

Missing

BERGLY, Kenneth Bernhard, AM3c, USN
BORUSKY, Edwin C., Corp., USMC
CHARBONEAU, Paul Orland, S2c, USN
COLBERT, Patrick Leo, MM2c, USN
FEIGLE, Lawrence James, S1c, USN
GIBBON, Leland Arthur, S1c, USN
GOLDMANN, Paul Jacob, SF2c, USN
JONES, William Sylvester, FC2c, USN
KOPP, Alois, PhM2c, USN
KRAHN, James A., PFC, USMC
KRENZEL, Maxmilian, S1c, USN
LEIGH, Junior Howard, PhM2c, USN
PORTER, John Robert, Y3c, USN
RICHTER, Adolph, PFC, USMC
RUDDY, James Roy, F1c, USN
SALMELA, James Leroy, S2c, USN

SHEMANSKI, Sylvester Walter, S1c, USN
SWEHLA, Donald Miles, S1c, USN
TYLER, Floyd E., 1st Sgt., USMC
WHITE, Robert Frank, SK3c, USN

Prisoners of War

BIGELOW, Frank Herndon, S2c, USN
CICHA, John Rudolph, S1c, USN
DANIELS, Warren Wesley, Bkr3c, USN
ENGLER, Irvin Jacob, Corp., USMC
FAY, Henry Lewis, S2c, USN
FOSTER, Roland Daniel, AMM2c, USN
GESSNER, Maurice Ernst, PFC, USMC
GUY, James Andrew, S2c, USN
HAASE, Howard Lester, PFC, USMC
HASSIG, Edwin Ferdinand, Tech. Sgt., USMC
HOLCOMB, Max E., Corp., USMC
HURD, Maurice Charles, RM3c, USN
KELNER, John R., PFC, USMC

KLUPP, Adam Jack, EM2c, USN
KRINGLER, Orvin Gerald, WT2c, USN
LAPLANTE, William Arsene, S1c, USN
MAILLOUX, Donald Victor, F1c, USN
McCONN, Donald Woodrow, Aer2c, USN
MYERS, Harold Burkett, Jr., PFC, USMC
MYERS, Keith T., PFC, USMC
NIEFELDT, Jack Earnest, MM2c, USN
ROTH, Lt. Cdr. Egbert Adolph, USN
SAEFKE, Frederick Edward, Jr., PFC, USMC
SCHULTZ, Donald Leroy, SF3c, USN
SHAFFER, Woodrow Trygve, S1c, USN
SWARTZ, Merle Edward, PFC, USMC
VAN ALST, Willard F., PFC, USMC
VAN RAY, 1st Lt. Clarence Edward, USMC
VINJE, Harold Morris, S1c, USN
WARCKEN, August Nichols, S2c, USN
WILSON, Robert Woodrow, CSK, USN

OHIO

Dead

ANDREWS, Charles LeRoy, RM3c, USN
BAILEY, Robert Edward, SF3c, USN
BAKER, Glen, S2c, USN
BANCROFT, William Emerson, F1c, USN
BARRETT, Donald Patrick, S1c, USN
BERRY, James Winford, F2c, USN
BLACK, Lt. (jg) John Edward, USN
BLACKBURN, John Thomas, F2c, USN
BLAINE, Robert Earl, S2c, USNR
BONNESS, Charles Joseph, S2c, USN
BORING, James Bryce, F2c, USN
BROWN, Bernard Oscar, F1c, USN
BRUNSON, Theodore Raymond, AS, USNR
BULLOCK, Lt. James Earl, Supply Corps, USN
BUNN, Virgil S., PFC, USMC
BURDEN, Ralph Leon, RM3c, USN
BUSICK, Dewey Oleny, F3c, USN
CAMPBELL, William Clarence, Cox., USN
CAPLINGER, Donald William, SC3c, USN
CASSIDY, Lt. Earl William, USN
CASTO, Charles Ray, F1c, USN
CASTO, Richard Eugene, F2c, USN
CHAFFEE, Ens. Davis Elliott, USNR
CHAMBERS, Edward A., Pvt., USMC
CHAPMAN, John Foster, Jr., Torp3c, USN
CHAPMAN, Thomas A., Sgt., USMC
CHERNEK, John, RM3c, USNR
CHESTNUTT, George, Jr., S2c, USN

CLARK, Carl Cecil, MM2c, USN
CLEMENS, Finch Woodrow, MM1c, USN
COCHRAN, Donald Ivan, SK3c, USNR
COLE, Francis Eugene, M2c, USN
COLSON, Virgil Willis, S2c, USN
CONRAD, Homer Milton, Jr., S1c, USN
COOK, Joseph William, GM3c, USNR
COON, Ernest Lyle, QM3c, USN
CORZATT, Beoin Hume, F1c, USN
DANIK, Andrew Joseph, S2c, USN
DAUGHERTY, Paul Eugene, EM3c, USN
DAVIS, Murle Melvin, RM2c, USN
DECKELMAN, Lt. Daniel Bernard, USN
DEVON, Robert Henry, RM3c, USN
DUTTON, William Francis, Cox., USNR
DYER, Buford Harvey, S1c, USN
EDWARDS, James David, SK3c, USNR
EMBREUS, George Robert, SK2c, USN
ERWIN, William Stokes, F1c, USN
FARBER, Richard Paul, S2c, USN
FIELDS, Bernard, RM3c, USNR
FLANNERY, James Lowell, SK3c, USN
FREY, Edward, Jr., F3c, USN
GALASZEWSKI, Stanley Casmier, S2c, USN
GALLAGHER, Thomas Alvin, ARM2c, USN
GAVIN, Thomas Vincent, Jr., AS, USNR
GEMIENHARDT, Samuel Henry, Jr., MM2c, USN
GRIFFITH, Thomas Edward, RM3c, USN
HAAS, Robert Arthur, AS, USN

HALLORAN, Ens. William I., USNR
HANN, Eugene Paul, GM3c, USN
HAVERFIELD, Ens. James W., USNR
HEEG, George Bernard, Jr., QM2c, USN
HEFFELBOWER, Charles Robert, S1c, USN
HERMANN, Lt. (jg) Gayle Louis, USN
HITRIK, Albert Joseph, F2c, USN
HIXSON, James Henry, AS, USNR
HOFFMAN, Joseph Warren, Mus1c, USN
HORN, Melvin Freeland, F3c, USN
HOSLER, John Emmet, S1c, USN
HOUSEHOLDER, Dallas Eugene, RM1c, USN
HUDSON, Norman, Jr., OC3c, USN
HUFFMAN, Clyde Franklin, F1c, USN
HUNTER, Robert Frederick, S1c, USN
JACKSON, Ens. David W., USNR
JAMES, Challis Rudolph, S2c, USN
JOHNSON, Lemuel, S1c, USN
JOYCE, Calvin Wilbur, F2c, USN
KAISER, George James, GM2c, USN
KASSELMAN, John Anthony, S1c, USN
KEANEY, Lee Edward John, S1c, USN
KELLER, Donald Garrett, S1c, USN
KENISTON, Donald Lee, S2c, USN
KENISTON, Kenneth Howard, F3c, USN
KENNEY, Bernard John, RM1c, USN
KIRKHAM, Fred, EM1c, USN
KLOPP, Francis Lawrence, GM3c, USN
KLUEH, Jerome Jacob, WT2c, USN
KNIGHT, Robert Wagner, EM3c, USN
KOLLAR, Elmer Mike, S2c, USN
KOZELEK, Leonard Joseph, RM3c, USN
KUBINEC, William Paul, F2c, USN
KUHLMANN, Walter Louis, Jr., AMM3c, USN
LAMB, James Earl, S1c, USN
LANEY, Durward Allan, PhM2c, USN
LOVE, Lloyd Milford, Cox., USN
LYONS, Harold Vivian, EM1c, USN
MAILER, William Granville, S1c, USN
MARKIN, Loran Robert, F2c, USN
MARRIOTT, Herbert Lloyd, AS, USN
MATTES, Raymond Charles, Torp3c, USN
McCLAFFERTY, John Charles, BM2c, USN
McGUCKIN, Edward Lawrence, S1c, USN
MELE, Albert Gene, S1c, USN
MEYER, Elmer Arthur, S2c, USN
MEYERS, Paul Cutler, AOM3c, USN
MILLER, George Stanley, S1c, USN
MILLER, Jessie Zimmer, S1c, USN
MOLLOY, John E., Pvt., USMC
MURPHY, James Palmer, F3c, USN
MYER, Warren Hasting, MM2c, USN

NEU, Russell Eugene, MM2c, USN
NEUENDORF, William Frederick, Jr., S1c, USN
ORWICK, Dean Baker, RM2c, USN
OSWALD, Harvey Emerson, MM2c, USN
OTT, Peter Dean, S1c, USN
OVERBERG, John Albert, ARM2c, USN
OWSLEY, Arnold Jacob, S1c, USN
PANCAKE, Toney Chilton, F1c, USN
PAULIN, Kenneth R., PFC, USMC
PELTIER, John Arthur, EM3c, USN
PISKURAN, Rudolph Victor, S2c, USN
POLAND, Eugene Richard, S2c, USN
POOLE, Ralph Ernest, S1c, USN
PORTERFIELD, Robert Kirk, AMM3c, USN
PRESSON, Wayne Harold, S1c, USN
PURVIS, Ens. Roy Wallingford, USNR
QUIGGEN, Jack, MM2c, USN
REID, George Beard, SF1c, USN
RIDENOUR, Clyde, Jr., RM3c, USN
ROACH, Russell Clyde, S1c, USN
ROBISON, Mark Clifton, MA1c, USN
ROE, Eugene Oscar, S1c, USN
ROMBACH, Ens. Severin Louis, USNR
ROOT, Melvin Leonard, S1c, USN
ROTH, Louis, S1c, USN
ROYER, Howard Dale, GM3c, USN
RUNYAN, Joseph Bashford, SK3c, USNR
RUPERT, William Frederick, Jr., S2c, USN
SABELLI, Nick, MM1c, USN
SANDER, Rudolph Andres, Pvt., USMC
SAWHILL, William Franklin, ARM3c, USN
SCHLEITER, Walter Ray, F1c, USN
SCOTT, Robert Raymond, MM1c, USN
SELLET, George Rudolph, F3c, USN
SETTLEMIRE, Alonzo Russell, WT2c, USN
SHAW, Clyde Donald, S1c, USN
SHAW, Wendell Arnold, Cox., USN
SIDDERS, Russel Lewis, S1c, USN
SIMMONS, Frank Leroy, MA2c, USN
SMALLEY, Jack "G," S1c, USN
SMISEK, Lada, CMM, USNR
SMITH, Jack, F3c, USN
SMITH, John "A," SF3c, USN
SMITH, Keith V., Pvt., USMCR
STAPLER, Leo, MA1c, USN
STEIGLEDER, Lester Leroy, Cox., USN
STIEF, Frank William, Jr., SC2c, USN
SULSER, Frederick Franklin, GM3c, USN
SUMMERS, Harold Edgar, SM2c, USN
SUTTON, George Cornelius, S1c, USN
SYPECK, Simon Joseph, MM1c, USN
THOMAS, Lt. (jg) Lloyd, USN

THOMPSON, Irven Edgar, S1c, USN
TRICHLER, George Phillip, F1c, USN
TUROCZY, John Alfred, SC1c, USN
VARGA, Arnold, F1c, USN
VOGELGESANG, Joseph Junior, F2c, USN
VRABEL, Joseph, CGM, USN
WALTERS, Charles Edward, S2c, USN
WARD, James Richard, S1c, USN
WEIANT, Ens. Carl Andrew, Jr., USNR
WELCH, William Edward, S1c, USN
WHITSON, Ernest Hubert, Jr., Mus2c, USN
WILLIAMS, Henry Irvin, F2c, USN
WILLIAMS, Ens. Lawrence A., USNR
WILSON, John Louis, MM2c, USN
WOLFE, Herbert William, SM1c, USN
WOOD, Frank, S2c, USN
WORRICK, George J., Jr., Corp., USMC
YOUNG, Julius Raymond, S1c, USN
ZOLLER, Russell Alvin, Y3c, USNR
ZWIR, Michael Simon, SC3c, USN

Wounded

ANDERSON, William, SM2c, USN
ANKROM, Roy Maxwell, S2c, USN
BODISH, Francis Alexander, S1c, USN
BOWEN, Samuel Franklin, S1c, USN
BUCHANS, Ens. John Anthony, Jr., USNR
CRAWFORD, Lawrence Edward, F3c, USN
CURTISS, William Frank, S2c, USNR
DIMMIT, Calvin, S2c, USN
FADICK, Carl E., PFC, USMC
FEEMAN, Charles Clark, S2c, USN
GASCOIGNE, Richard Frank, SK1c, USN
GOODWIN, Robert James, S2c, USN
HENERY, John Joseph, F2c, USN
HOFF, Howard Lawrence, WT2c, USN
KELLEY, Ralph Sterling, S1c, USN
KISKER, Kenneth Kermeth, S1c, USN
LLEWELLYN, Fred Morgan, RM2c, USN
MARIN, Fredrick Harris, S1c, USN
McVEY, David Glenn, S1c, USN
MILLER, Merle Leroy, F2c, USN
MILSOP, George Robert, PFC, USMC
PESCHEL, Robert Frank, S1c, USN
PRUNNER, George Philemon, S1c, USN
SCHERER, Carl Edward, F2c, USN
SEEDLOCK, Ens. Walter Francis, USN
SMITH, Joseph Lawrence, CEM, USN
TAYLOR, Ens. Thomas Hart, USN
WALLACE, Ens. Maurice R., USNR
WARDLE, William James, S2c, USN
WELLS, Donald Lewis, S2c, USN
WHITCHER, Henry Edward, S1c, USN

WHITCOMB, William J., Pvt., USMC
WILLIAMS, Frederic George, AMM3c, USN
WILT, Clyde Kenneth, S1c, USN
WISE, James Louis, S1c, USN

Missing

ALEX, Andrew, S1c, USN
ALLEN, Roy Richard, S2c, USN
ARAND, Leroy Edward, MM2c, USN
ARTZ, John William, SC3c, USN
BARNA, James G., PFC, USMC
BARROWS, Paul Albert, WT2c, USN
BENNETT, Walter Lee, Y2c, USN
BIECHLIN, Louis Emil, Carp., USN
BIECHLIN, Neal Conrad, Y2c, USN
BINGLEY, Harold LeRoy, S1c, USN
BOOROM, Richard William, S1c, USN
BROWN, Howard Edwin, EM2c, USN
BRUBAKER, Joseph Henry, Y2c, USN
BURCHER, William Garfield, EM2c, USN
CALLAND, John R., PFC, USMC
CHAY, William, S1c, USN
CONNOR, Robert M., Corp., USMC
COX, George Bowen, SC3c, USN
CURRAN, Thomas William, Jr., AM2c, USN
DE LONG, Frederick E., Corp., USMC
DETZEL, Elmer John, MM1c, USN
FAHNESTOCK, Merrill Harry, B1c, USN
FRONKIEUGYZ, Walter John, S1c, USN
FROST, Robert Lee, Jr., PhM3c, USN
FURNARI, Biacio Horlando, SM1c, USN
GOOD, Edward David, S2c, USN
GORE, James Patrick, F1c, USN
GRAY, Charles Leroy, F3c, USN
GROTE, Harry Frank, Jr., MM1c, USN
HAMMOND, William Browning, S2c, USN
HANSEN, Guredon Junior, S2c, USN
JOHNSON, Clarence Earnest, B2c, USN
JOHNSON, James Clifford, F2c, USN
KALINOWSKI, Henry, Pvt., USMC
KENNEDY, Bernard Hayes, F2c, USN
KONKO, William Francis, RM3c, USN
KORMOS, John, F3c, USN
KUNKE, Czeslaus John, GM2c, USN
LEGGETT, Woodford Ross, S1c, USN
LEININGER, Paul W., Platoon Sgt., USMC
LEMON, Albert S., QM Sgt., USMC
LEWDANSKI, Joseph, WT2c, USN
LEWIS, Vernon Bradley, F1c, USN
LINDSLEY, Albert John, S1c, USN
MARKELL, Ralph Allen, SC2c, USN
MARTIN, Jack Eugene, S1c, USN
MATHIAS, David Ellis, PhM3c, USN

METZGER, Alvin Willis, MM2c, USN
MITTENHOLZER, William, Y2c, USN
NOE, Jack Grant, F2c, USN
NOWAK, Edward Bernard, Mus1c, USN
O'NEAL, Robert Shilling, S1c, USN
PALMER, James Edwin, EM3c, USN
PAYNE, Thomas Emerson, Cox., USN
PHELPS, Raymond Allan, BM2c, USN
POOL, Wilbur Edward, CMM, USN
PORTER, John Joseph, Mus1c, USN
RAGAN, Donald Robert, Torp2c, USN
RAWERS, Paul, F2c, USN
REAS, John Clifford, Y2c, USN
ROBINSON, John, S1c, USN
ROSELLE, Richard J., Pvt., USMC
ROSS, Mark Elliot, MM2c, USN
SATTERFIELD, Richard Lewis, F3c, USN
SCHAEFER, Gilbert Eugene, S1c, USN
SCHANTZ, Dale Edward, RM3c, USN
SEASHOLS, Bob Stuart, SC2c, USN
SHEETS, Alfred Edwin, S2c, USN
SOKE, Charles Daniel, AMM3c, USN
STAFFORD, Frankland Fish, Jr., SM3c, USN
STAHL, James Cox, EM2c, USN
STANSBURY, Walter Allan, S2c, USN
STATEN, Thomas Franklin, F3c, USN
STEVENS, Roscoe Clayton, CCM, USN
STEVENSON, Harold Victor, S1c, USN
STOVER, Charles William, RM3c, USN
STOWER, Donald Godfred, S2c, USN
TERRY, Kenneth Gordon, Jr., SC3c, USN
TOWNSEND, Lawrence William, SF1c, USN
TRUMMER, Harold, Sgt., USMC
VANDIVER, Larry, F2c, USN
VAN TILBURG, Frank Ernest, S1c, USN
VILLERS, Donald D., Mus2c, USN
WALLACE, John Gardner, Jr., Cox., USN
WALLACE, Robert Ray, S2c, USN
WOLF, Adrian William, F2c, USN
WREN, Howard Richard, F1c, USN
YANNUCCI, Chester, Mus1c, USN
YUREK, Louis Eugene, ARM2c, USN

Prisoners of War

ADAMS, Harry Edward, S1c, USN
ANDERSON, Willis Willard, Corp., USMC
BARRETT, Russell Edward, PFC, USMC
BAY, William Russell, PFC, USMC
BEAN, Glen Taylor, F2c, USN
BEEMAN, Gerald Leroy, Corp., USMC
BENTZ, Roy Howard, MM2c, USN
BIGLEY, Joseph Regis, F1c, USN
BLISS, Tasker Homer, Field Mus. Sgt., USMC

BOZ, Wallace Stephen, S2c, USN
BROYLES, Earl Morris, Pvt., USMC
BRYK, Chester John, Pvt., USMC
BURFORD, Philip Leo, PFC, USMC
BUSHILLA, Frank Francis, EM3c, USN
BUTLER, Ray Smith, CEM, USN
CALHOUN, Waid Bert, S1c, USN
CARLSON, Carl Anian, Jr., Gunner, USN
CHANDLER, Paul Guy, QM Clerk, USMC
CLAFLIN, Francis Marion, Cox., USN
COLEDANCHISE, Mercurio, PFC, USMC
COOKE, Lawrence, EM2c, USN
DAVENPORT, Jesse M., PFC, USMC
DAVIDSON, Adrian Clyde, Corp., USMC
DAVIES, Robert Thomas, Jr., Corp., USMC
DAVIS, David, S2c, USN
DAVIS, Capt. Howard L., USMC
DE TALLENTIRE, Gibson Alexander, Sgt., USMC
DETRE, George Elen, F1c, USN
DORAN, Peter Robert, Jr., F2c, USN
DUDLEY, Noble Clementyne, MM2c, USN
ELLIOTT, Ens. John William, USNR
ELLIS, Clifford Lee, Gunnery Sgt., USMC
ERDMAN, Edwin, MM2c, USN
ESTEP, Norman Ray, PFC, USMC
FEHER, Arthur Joseph, MM2c, USN
FINK, Nelson Harold, Prtr3c, USN
FLANIGAN, George Portman, SK2c, USN
FLOOD, Donald Russell, PhM2c, USN
FOGARTY, Virginia J., NC, USN
FOUST, Carl W., Pvt., USMC
GRANT, Walter LeRoy, F2c, USN
HARDWAY, James Edward, Corp., USMC
HOFFMAN, John Mathew, Chief Torp., USNR
HOFFMAN, Raymond Frederick, RM3c, USN
HOWERTON, George Rice, Jr., S2c, USN
JACKSON, Cloyd Walter, S1c, USN
JACKSON, Leona, NC, USN
JACKSON, Paul, Pay Clerk, USN
JEFFRIES, William Floyd, SK2c, USN
KAZMIERCZAK, Chester, MM2c, USN
KIRHGESNER, Peter Joseph, F2c, USN
KOCHER, Bernard Fred, S2c, USN
KRUSZYNA, Anthony, SC1c, USN
LALLY, Lt. (jg) Robert William, USNR
LARSON, Theodore William, Pvt., USMC
LINN, Wilbur Bush, S1c, USN
LUCAS, Dwight Richard, Chief Torp., USN

MARKOWITZ, Lt. (jg) Herbert Abraham (MC), USN
MARSHALL, William Lloyd, PhM3c, USN
MARTIN, Charles Thomas, Sgt., USMC
MARTIN, Clarence Roderick, RM1c, USN
McDONOUGH, Raymond Peter, S1c, USN
McGEE, Robert Harold, PFC, USMC
McGINNIS, Albert Hazard, S1c, USN
McKINNON, Richard Lewis, HA1c, USN
McMANUS, Lt. Francis Joseph, Chaplain Corps, USN
MOREY, Corwin Raymond, Pvt., USMC
MUENICH, Gustav Joseph, RM1c, USN
O'DONNELL, John J., Jr., Pvt., USMC
OLEKSA, John, Jr., SC3c, USN
OLSON, Gordon Erland, PhM2c, USN
OLSON, John Carney, Marine Gunner, USMC
PAQUIN, James Oscar, S2c, USN
PARR, Charles William, Corp., USMC
PECHACEK, Thomas Joseph, Corp., USMC
PENICK, 1st Lt. Ralph Roger, USMC
PEPPERS, Frederick Earl, QM2c, USN
PETERS, Irving Eugene, F2c, USN
PIPER, Robert W., PFC, USMC
PLECKER, McPherson, F2c, USN
POINDEXTER, 2nd Lt. Arthur Andrews, USMC
PROVOST, Theodore Foch, MM2c, USN
REEVES, Solomon, CWT, USN
ROGERS, Clinton William, RM1c, USN

ROSE, Guy Michell, MM2c, USN
RUPNIK, Eugene Frank, F2c, USN
SALAY, Steve Alex, PFC, USMC
SAWYER, John Wilbur, S1c, USN
SCHICK, Michael Jacob, S/Sgt., USMC
SCHMITZER, Frank William, PFC, USMC
SELBY, William Arthur, EM2c, USN
SHIELDS, Harold Eugene, RM1c, USN
SKIVER, Russell Elwood, EM1c, USN
SMITH, Robert Nunley, PFC, USMC
SNYDER, Earl Joe, S1c, USN
SPILAK, Alexander John, BM2c, USN
STEFANEK, John Bartholemew, Cox., USN
STEMEN, John Isaac, S2c, USN
STURGELL, Stephen Ray, Elect., USN
TANBERG, Albert Neal, Bkr3c, USN
TARKANISH, George, S1c, USN
TARNOWSKI, Zeno Chester, Aer1c, USN
TAYLOR, Forest Lee, PhM3c, USN
THOMAS, Harold Eugene, S1c, USN
TODD, 1st Lt. Charles Solen, USMC
TRUMP, Lt. Cdr. Herbert Ray, Chaplain Corps, USN
TURVEY, Thomas, S2c, USN
VAUGHAN, Richard, S2c, USN
WEBER, John Joseph, S1c, USN
WELLS, Noble W., 1st Sgt., USMC
WEST, Max Lancaster, S1c, USN
WHITE, Capt. John A., USMC
WIDMEYER, Harry Clark, S1c, USN
WRIGHT, Robert Sanford, S2c, USN
ZIMMER, Robert William, F2c, USN

OKLAHOMA

Dead

ADAMS, Jesse Leroy, S1c, USN
ALLEN, Jack V., Tech. Sgt., USMC
ANGLE, Clifford Jackson, S2c, USN
ATCHISON, Ernest D., PFC, USMC
BAIRD, Earl Thomas, S1c, USN
BAKER, J. W., Torp3c, USN
BARDON, Charles Thomas, S2c, USN
BARR, Jack Farrill, S2c, USN
BLEDSOE, Herman, MA2c, USN
BOHLANDER, Frank Woodworth, Jr., S2c, USN
BRITTON, Thomas A., Corp., USMC
BROOME, Loy Raymond, SM3c, USN
BUCKLEY, Willis Oregon, S/Sgt., USMC
CAMDEN, Raymond Edward, S2c, USN
CAMPBELL, Ovid W., Corp., USMC
CHAPIN, Ora Eugene, PFC, USMC

CHRISMAN, Ollie O., PFC, USMC
CLEMMENS, Claude Albert, S1c, USN
COBURN, Walter Overton, S1c, USN
COLLETTE, Allie, S2c, USN
COULTER, Arthur Lee, S1c, USN
CRUMP, Marvin Earl, AMM3c, USN
DANGERFIELD, John Merril, PFC, USMC
DAVIS, Billy Rex, F2c, USN
DRIVER, Bill Lester, RM3c, USN
DUNAWAY, Kenneth Leroy, EM3c, USN
EATON, Emory Lowell, F3c, USN
EDWARDS, Robert P., Sgt., USMC
EWELL, Paul Phillip, Jr., RM2c, USN
FANSLER, Edgar Arthur, S1c, USN
FLORENCE, Robert Clay, S1c, USN
FORBES, William Kenneth, RM3c, USNR
GELLER, Leonard Richard, F1c, USN
GOFF, Wiley Coy, S2c, USN
GRAHAM, William Jacob, Jr., S1c, USN

GREER, Alwyn L., PFC, USMC
HALL, Leon, RM2c, USN
HAMILTON, William Holman, GM3c, USN
HAMPTON, Ted "W," Jr., S1c, USN
HARBIN, Mike, Torp3c, USN
HARTLEY, Alvin, GM3c, USN
HENDRICKS, Jesse I., S2c, USN
HILL, Clifford Dale, S2c, USN
HOWARD, David Carroll, Cox., USN
JAMES, Ens. Will Roy, Jr., USNR
JOHNSTON, Warren Goulden, RM2c, USN
KELLEY, James Dennis, SF3c, USN
KIMBREL, Berlyn Marconi, Torp1c, USN
KYSER, D. T., S2c, USN
LANE, Mancel Curtis, S1c, USN
LEE, Roy E., Jr., Pvt., USMC
LOCKE, Chester Hayes, AMM1c, USN
LUCY, Herbert Roddy, WT1c, USN
LUNA, James Edward, S2c, USN
LYON, Thomas Frank, F3c, USNR
MATHEWS, Forest Cortlan, WT1c, USN
McKOSKY, Michael Martin, S1c, USN
McMURTREY, Aaron Lloyd, S1c, USN
MILLER, Carl Julius, PFC, USMC
MINOR, Alvia Lee, S2c, USNR
MONTGOMERY, William Hueston, WT2c, USN
MOORE, George S., Jr., Pvt., USMC
NEVILL, Sam Douglas, Y3c, USN
OGLE, Victor Willard, S2c, USN
PICKLE, Sterling Dunn, PFC, USMC
PITTS, Cecil Charles, AS, USN
PITTS, Lewis William, Jr., S2c, USN
REED, Ray Ellison, S2c, USN
ROGERS, John Richard, CM2c, USNR
ROLLINS, Edward Earl, F2c, USN
ROOKER, Stanley Irvin, F3c, USN
SCHINDLER, Richard Calvin, AS, USN
SCROGGINS, Ted Harry, RM2c, USN
SELBY, Nyal M., PFC, USMC
SHIPMAN, Ferlin Fonzo, S1c, USN
SHOFFSTALL, Webster R., PFC, USMC
SHOUSE, Henson Taylor, F1c, USN
SMITH, Mack Lawerence, S1c, USN
SMITH, Ens. Orville Stanley, USN
SMITH, Richard Charles, F1c, USN
TODD, Cecil Leon, SC3c, USN
TRUAX, Albert Danvers, Torp1c, USN
TURNER, Billy, S1c, USN
VASSAR, Benjamin Frank, S2c, USN
VIRGIN, Stanley Polhill, CEM, USNR
WARD, Albert Lewis, S1c, USN
WARREN, Roland Henry, MM2c, USN
WEBB, James Cecil, F1c, USN

WICKER, Eugene Woodrow, S1c, USN
WIGHT, Capt. Cecil W., USMC
WINSLOW, James Herbert, RM3c, USN
WOOD, Roy Eugene, F1c, USN
YOUNG, Charles Robert, ARM3c, USN

Wounded

ARMSTRONG, George Arthur, S1c, USN
BINGHAM, Albert Warren, S1c, USN
DUNCAN, Sherman Lee, AMM3c, USN
ESLICK, Garlen William, S2c, USN
EYMAN, Lawrence Oliver, S1c, USN
FOGELSTROM, Wayne Alexander, S2c, USN
FRY, Thomas Charles, S2c, USN
GARDNER, Woodrow Wilson, S2c, USN
GERMANY, Thurman D., PFC, USMC
HARDY, Charles L., Pvt., USMC
HARGER, Harvey Allen, S1c, USN
HARRELL, Allen Boyd, S1c, USN
HUMES, Warren George, S1c, USN
JONES, Arthur W., PFC, USMC
KNUCKLES, Claude Franklin, S1c, USN
LAUGHLIN, Raymond "J," PFC, USMC
McALLISTER, Ernest Edward, S2c, USN
MORRIS, Lester A., Pvt., USMC
PEMBERTON, Marvin Hansford, S2c, USN
POE, John Dewitt, Jr., SK1c, USN
RINER, Earl William, GM3c, USN
RISNER, Grady William, GM3c, USN
SLATON, Everett Joe, RM3c, USN
TRAMMELL, J. R., S1c, USN
TROUT, Coleman Marcelle, S2c, USN
WALTERS, James Elwyn, AOM3c, USN
WILDEY, Robert Freman, S2c, USN

Missing

BARNETT, Roger Irvin, F1c, USN
BEATON, Freddie, Pvt., USMC
BERRIDGE, Robert Channing, RM3c, USN
BETTINGER, David Albert, S1c, USN
BLAKE, Paul Revere, GM3c, USN
BOCK, Dudley Charles, PhM3c, USN
CHILDERS, James Henry, S1c, USN
CLARKE, Harry Clinton, EM1c, USN
CRAIN, Kenneth E., Pvt., USMC
DAVIDSON, Thomas Alvin, S1c, USN
DAVIS, James Bradford, Jr., RM2c, USN
DONAHOU, George Washington, Bkr1c, USN
DOWLING, William Lester, S1c, USN
ELLIOTT, Leslie Lee, Cox., USN
FAULK, Joseph H., Corp., USMC
FETERLY, Allen Miles, S2c, USN
FRAZIER, Warren Vernon, F3c, USN

Gray, James D., Pvt., USMC
Hamby, Thaddies LaVerne, Bug1c, USN
Harold, William Russell, S1c, USN
Hazen, William Earnest, S1c, USN
Holly, Lt. Charles William, Jr., Dental Corps, USN
Kendrick, Arlando W., PFC, USMC
Killgore, Raleigh Wayne, Torp. 2c, USN
Kyle, Grady Henry, MM1c, USN
Lantz, William Collins, S1c, USN
Lynch, Randle Ray, F3c, USN
Malone, Aubrey K., PFC, USMC
McDonald, Paul Morris, S1c, USN
McGehee, Lesley Vernon, EM3c, USN
Mills, Sylvester, S1c, USN
Moon, Carl Irvin, S2c, USN
Neal, Osman Wofford, MM1c, USN
Oxford, Ernest Preston, WT2c, USN
Peak, Robert H., Pvt., USMC
Peppers, Cheston Gibson, SC3c, USN
Power, Abner F., Pvt., USMC
Reed, Reuben W., Sgt., USMC
Roberson, Norman Lee, S2c, USN
Rowland, Ralph Turner, S1c, USN
Sanderson, Con Albert, Jr., GM2c, USN
Scott, Earnest, F2c, USN
Shillings, George Allen, S1c, USN
Slocum, Jim E., PFC, USMC
Smalley, Harold Bigheart, S1c, USN
Smith, Harold Peck, EM1c, USN
Smith, William Amos, S2c, USN
Sowder, Jack Dunham, S1c, USN
Taylor, Charles R., PFC, USMC
Williams, Paris Dola, S1c, USN
Wilson, Wayne Leonard, RM1c, USN
Yancy, Everett Preston, F3c, USN
York, Clyde Ladelle, Torp. 3c, USN

Prisoners of War

Baker, Elvie Eugene, Corp., USMC
Beaurman, William, Jr., F1c, USN
Beavers, John, PFC, USMC
Bell, Paul Albert, SM3c, USN
Bennett, Pat Foster, Pvt., USMC
Benson, Benjamin Robert, Field Cook, USMC
Bentley, Joseph Miller, PFC, USMC
Berry, Ens. William Aylor, USNR
Bible, James Edward, Field Cook, USMC
Biggs, Chester Maxwell, Jr., PFC, USMC
Black, Loy Joseph, PhM1c, USMC
Brewington, William Iven, MM1c, USN
Brittingham, Richard Cloyd, CY, USN
Bryan, Pershing B., Asst. Cook, USMC

Bumgarner, Alvin Aaron, Platoon Sgt., USMC
Burden, Joe D., PFC, USMC
Bush, Elmo Arnton, AOM3c, USN
Byard, Lester Carl, PFC, USMC
Camp, Charles Hayward, Corp., USMC
Campbell, Rollin Lee, S2c, USN
Carl, Jeff Charles, GM3c, USN
Carter, Walter Wade, SM3c, USN
Case, Alvin Lynn, Sgt., USMC
Childers, Mitchell Keen, S2c, USN
Clark, Owen C., PFC, USMC
Clemons, Aaron Lee, PFC, USMC
Coffelt, Clarence E., PFC, USMC
Cook, Jack Beasom, Sgt., USMC
Cook, Thomas Jefferson, Jr., GM3c, USN
Cooper, Paul Carlton, PFC, USMC
Couch, Claude Chester, PFC, USMC
Couch, Elbert Theodore, PFC, USMC
Crouch, James Aron, Pvt., USMC
Cutler, Jack Marvin, Pvt., USMC
Dale, John Raymond, Corp., USMC
Daniels, Alfred Lee, HA1c, USN
De Munbrun, Elmo Gordon, Pvt., USMC
Douglas, Griff Lazell, HA1c, USN
Douglass, Lt. Francis Malcolm, USN
Dye, Clyde Wilbur, PFC, USMC
Enyart, Clinton Hudson, Pvt., USMC
Etter, Frank Gabriel, PFC, USMC
Faulkner, James O., PFC, USMC
Fleming, Manton Leon, Pvt., USMC
Franklin, Lewis, PFC, USMC
Frazee, Russell Edward, S1c, USN
French, Edward William, PFC, USMC
Garrison, Everett, PFC, USMC
Giddens, George Githon, Pvt., USMC
Gilliam, Preston Solan, PFC, USMC
Gillihan, Rex Ross, S1c, USN
Gilmore, Orville Earl, PFC, USMC
Gordon, Byron Carl, PFC, USMC
Gray, James Fredrick, RM2c, USN
Gwartney, James Cornelious, PFC, USMC
Hainline, John William, F1c, USN
Harris, William Newton, PFC, USMC
Harrison, Charles Lee, PFC, USMC
Hartung, Arvel Nelson, PFC, USMC
Haynes, William, Platoon Sgt., USMC
Hill, Ollie H., Corp., USMCR
Hobbs, Richard A., Pvt., USMC
Hodgens, Floyd Willie, PFC, USMC
Hoskinson, Larence Odell, PFC, USMC
Howard, John Robert, PhM1c, USN
Humphreys, Howard Winston, PFC, USMC

JARRETT, Jess Thomas, CM, USN
JENKINS, Louis, PFC, USMC
JENNINGS, Hugh Dale, PFC, USMC
JOHNSON, Dick Maple, Corp., USMC
JOHNSON, Orville Arthur, SK1c, USN
JONES, Bobby Spears, Field music, USMC
JONES, Howard Mitchell, PhM1c, USN
KING, Charles Fain, PFC, USMC
KOHLMAN, Eugene Marvin, Corp., USMC
LEE, Jack Boggan, SC3c, USN
LEE, Jesse Earl, Boat., USN
LEHMAN, Clarence Albert, F2c, USN
MARTIN, Max Holland, Pvt., USMC
MAZE, Elvin Lawrence, S2c, USN
McDANIEL, George Washington, PFC, USMC
McFARLAND, George Woodrow, Corp., USMC
McINNIS, Lt. (jg) Harry Burford, USN
McLEOD, Marvin Donald, HA1c, USN
MORLAN, Jack D., PFC, USMC
MULLEN, James Monroe, Jr., S2c, USN
NORMAN, Robert B., PFC, USMC
NOWLIN, James Alex, PFC, USMC
ODOM, Wilson Willard, AS, USN
PARR, Rexford Gerald, RM2c, USN
PERCY, R. C., PFC, USMC
PERRYMAN, Floyd Loree, Pvt., USMC
PESHEK, 1st Lt. Michael Emil, USMC
PORTER, Louis H., PFC, USMC
PRATER, Frank Paskal, PFC, USMC
PRYOR, Ray Sherman, MM1c, USN
RASOR, Herman Lee, PFC, USMC
REEVES, Joe Morris, Pvt., USMC
ROARK, Clyde Edward, Corp., USMC

RUSHER, Arthur, Jr., PFC, USMC
SCOGGIN, Leslie Raymond, PFC, USMC
SCOTT, Burton Elmer, SF3c, USN
SELBY, Harold Vernon, PFC, USMC
SHELTON, Clifford Eldon, PFC, USMC
SHORES, Robert, PFC, USMC
SIMPSON, Claud Ernest, Corp., USMC
SKAGGS, Jack Robert, PFC, USMC
SMITH, John Clarence, Pvt., USMC
SNOW, Arthur Otto, S1c, USN
SPARKS, Raymond LeRoy, S1c, USN
SPRAGUE, J. Wilson, PhM2c, USN
STANDIFER, Ole Owen, Field Cook, USMC
STEPHENS, Shedric William, Jr., PFC, USMC
STEVENS, Norman Eugene, FC3c, USN
STRINGFIELD, George William, PFC, USMC
SWISHER, Morris Denver, F1c, USN
THOMAS, Charles P., PFC, USMC
TOWRY, J. B., Pvt., USMC
VARDELL, Virgil Pierce, Asst. Cook, USMC
WALDREP, John David, Y3c, USN
WALLER, Clyde Roy, Corp., USMC
WARDLOW, Pierce Lillard, PFC, USMC
WARNER, Jack Doyle, PFC, USMC
WESTMORELAND, Jack L., Chief Cook, USMC
WHEELER, Mackie Lee, PFC, USMC
WHITE, Seldon T., PFC, USMC
WILEY, Andrew Newell, AMM2c, USN
WILLIAMS, Clyde Richard, Mus2c, USN
WILLIAMSON, Jack Russell, PFC, USMC
WRIGHT, Elmer Ray, QM Sgt., USMC

OREGON

Dead

ADKINS, Marvin Birch, GM3c, USN
ALLEN, Robert Lee, SF3c, USN
ALMASIE, John Homer, S2c, USN
ANDERBERG, William Robert, F2c, USN
ANDERSEN, Walter Pat, PFC, USMC
ANDERSON, Ens. Alfred William, USNR
ANDERSON, Donald William, SM3c, USN
ANDERSON, James Pickens, Jr., S1c, USN
APPLEGATE, Gilbert Betts, S1c, USN
AULT, Cdr. William Bowen, USN
BAHR, Harold Valentine, S2c, USN
BARNES, Lt. (jg) Delmar Hayes, USN
BATES, Ens. James Parker, Jr., USNR
BENNETT, Orville Don, S1c, USN

BROWN, Frank George, QM3c, USN
BROWN, Herman Franklin, CBM, USN
BROWN, William Howard, S2c, USNR
BURGESS, John Edwin, Jr., S2c, USN
BUTZ, Joe Oliver, PFC, USMC
CAMPBELL, Lt. (jg) George Marvin, USN
CAMPBELL, Raymond Stewart, RM3c, USN
CLINKINBEARD, Willis, GM3c, USN
COLLIER, John, F2c, USN
COTTON, Harry Franklin, Jr., CSM, USN
COWDEN, Joel Beman, S2c, USN
CRAFT, Harley Wade, CM3c, USN
CURRY, William Joseph, WT2c, USN
DEWITT, Charles Franklin, GM3c, USN
DODD, William Donald, CM1c, USN

DYKEMAN, Harold Everett, F2c, USN
EDMONSTON, David Bell, S2c, USN
ELDEN, Lt. Ralph Waldo, USN
EVANS, Woodrow Wilson, GM3c, USN
FELIX, Irving Arthur, Y1c, USN
FREDERICKSON, Robert Lee, S1c, USN
FRY, Irvin Francis, S1c, USN
GAMBLE, Robert Francis, MM2c, USN
GILMAN, Merrill Ray, CMM, USN
GILLETTE, Warren Clayton, S1c, USN
GOWEY, Claude Olliver, F1c, USN
GREENFIELD, Carroll Gale, S1c, USN
GROVER, William Dell, S2c, USN
GUTHRIE, Dale Winston, F3c, USNR
HEATER, Verrel Roy, S1c, USN
HOLVERSTOTT, Charles Clynard, SM2c, USN
HOWE, Darrell Robert, S2c, USN
JEANS, Victor Lawrence, WT2c, USN
JOHNSON, Adolph Herman, RM1c, USN
JONES, Rodney Wallace, S2c, USN
JONES, Ens. William S., USNR
KING, Virgil Newton, S2c, USN
KURTZ, Stanley Robert, S2c, USN
LAWRENCE, Charles, AMM2c, USN
McKINNEY, Kenneth Ernest, EM2c, USN
MILES, Archie Theodore, MM2c, USN
MILLER, Charles Alva, RM3c, USN
MILLER, John Henry, SC2c, USN
MILLER, Raymond, Pvt., USMC
MILLER, Robert Emmett, RM1c, USN
MYERS, Alfred Francis, RM2c, USN
PAGE, Warren William, S1c, USN
PARKS, Clyde Gerald, CRM, USN
PFEIFER, Robert William, PFC, USMC
PREWITT, Lt. Vance Carlyle, USNR
PRICE, Arland Earl, RM2c, USN
QUESSETH, Alfred Oliver, CMM, USN
RICH, Porter Leigh, WT2c, USN
RICHTER, Leonard Claiver, MM1c, USN
ROBINSON, John James, EM1c, USN
ROSSITER, Paul James, S1c, USN
RUSHFORD, Harvey George, S2c, USN
SACHTER, Jake, ARM1c, USN
SANDERS, Ens. Eugene Thomas, USN
SAWTELL, Kenneth James, S2c, USNR
SEDERSTROM, Ens. Verdi D., USNR
STUBBLEFIELD, Donald Ferris, S1c, USN
TEATS, Ens. Grant Wayne, USNR
WALLACE, Ralph LeRoy, F3c, USN
WALLAN, Arthur Junior, AS, USNR
WESTIN, Donald Vern, F3c, USN
WHITE, Glen Albert, F1c, USN
WICK, Everett Morris, FC2c, USN
WIENERT, Ralph Marvin, CEM, USN
WILLIAMS, James Clifford, S1c, USNR

WILSON, LeRay, M2c, USN
WYMAN, Ens. Eldon Paul, USNR
YOUNG, Glendale Rex, S1c, USN

Wounded

CARVER, Robert Allan, Jr., F1c, USN
DEPEE, Freddie Emerald, S2c, USN
FOOS, Walter Edward, S2c, USNR
FRANCIS, Melvin Russell, S2c, USN
FULGHUM, Philip LeRoy, AOM2c, USN
HENSON, Willard Edgar, S1c, USN
IVERSON, David Wright, SM3c, USN
JEWELL, Cdr. Jesse D., (MC), USN
LUCAS, George Marvin, Jr., Y3c, USN
McKINNEY, Delbert Edward, S1c, USN
MISHLER, Willis Hawley, S2c, USN
ROBERTS, Lt. (jg) Howard Gordon, USNR
ROGERS, George Hiram, MM1c, USN
ROWLAND, William Eugene, AOM2c, USN
WARDEN, Edgar Frank, S1c, USN

Missing

BEST, George Harold, Cox., USN
BREON, Floyd Lloyd, Cox., USN
COLVIN, Cecil Garland, Y1c, USN
COOPER, Lyle Dee, F1c, USN
CRAWFORD, Reynold Clyde, F1c, USN
DAVIDSON, Vernon William, F2c, USN
DAVIS, Clayton Theodore, F1c, USN
DECAMP, Laco Edwin, S2c, USN
DOIG, William MacPherson, S1c, USN
DRAPER, Jack Dyke, S1c, USN
FINCHER, Dexter W., Sgt., USMC
HARDY, Beverly E., PFC, USMCR
HODGE, Lt. Ernest Debbes, USN
HOOPER, Harry Hershell, S2c, USN
HUMBLE, Ray K., PFC, USMC
JOHNSON, Totsie Jesse, EM3c, USN
LEADERS, John G., PFC, USMC
LEWIS, Donald Max, S2c, USN
LEWIS, Jesse Adelbert, Y2c, USN
McCLUNE, Donald Keith, CPhM, USN
McCONNELL, Joseph Liggett, CRM, USN
MORIARTY, Thomas Howard, S1c, USN
NORVEL, Richard, S2c, USN
READ, Herman Richard, S1c, USN
RIGGS, Merle Arthur, S1c, USN
SMITH, Joseph Festine, PhM2c, USN
VALLIERE, Harry Fred, SM3c, USN
VANDER AUWERA, Robert Joseph, FC3c, USN
VAUGHAN, Houston A., Field Music Sgt., USMC

WAGONER, Leo Albert, S1c, USN
WEST, Steve Charles, Torp.2c, USN
WILSON, Phillip Earl, S2c, USN
WOLFE, John Bertrand, WT1c, USN
ZAHLER, Melvin John, Field Music, USMC

Prisoners of War

ABBEY, Edgar Chester, S2c, USN
ADAMS, E. O. Stephen, Pvt., USMC
ADKINS, Robert A., Corp., USMC
ALLEN, Frank Rilea, PFC, USMC
ANKROM, Merlin Winfield, PFC, USMC
AUST, Richard, Jr., Pvt., USMC
BAKER, Roger D., Field Music, USMC
BARNUM, Donald Warren, CRM, USN
BASS, George Lornce, PFC, USMC
BEERS, Thomas Delbert, CY, USN
BELLSTROM, Leonard Olof, MM2c, USN
BENGE, Clyde Addison, Corp., USMC
BENNETT, Keith Leighton, Pvt., USMC
BLACK, Jack, F1c, USN
BOLEY, Kenneth Conrad, PFC, USMC
BORDWELL, James Douglas, SK1c, USN
BOSTICK, William Frank, PFC, USMC
BUNN, Douglas A., PFC, USMC
BURGARD, Carl Norton, S2c, USN
BUSCH, Richard Charles, S1c, USN
BUSEIMEIER, Rudolph Matthew, RM1c, USN
BUSTER, Ivan L., Mstr. Tech. Sgt., USMC
BYRD, Hershel Wayne, HA1c, USN
CAMPBELL, Andy Nyal, Corp., USMC
CAMPBELL, Vern Delowis, TM2c, USN
CARSON, Erbert Earl, S1c, USN
CHENOWETH, Joseph Gordon, TM2c, USN
CLOUSE, John Jacob, PFC, USMC
CONSER, Herbert Raymond, F3c, USN
CROWE, Veral Harris, S/Sgt., USMC
CRUMPACKER, Lloyd E., Pvt., USMC
CUNNINGHAM, Kenneth Eugene, Pvt., USMC
DAINS, Albert Jacob, PFC, USMC
DAVIS, Paul E., Field Music Sgt., USMC
DODSON, John D., PFC, USMC
DOUTHIT, Harry Fitzgerald, PFC, USMC
DRAKE, Elmer Sidney, Jr., Corp., USMC
DRIVER, Francis Marion, F1c, USN
DROLETTE, James Alexander, Pvt., USMC
EDDY, Merritt Volney, CM2c, USN
ENGEBRETSEN, Wilbert Ferdinand, CM1c, USN

ESHLEMAN, Donald Berton, Corp., USMC
ESPY, Lt. (jg) Cecil Jefferson, Jr., CEC, USN
EVANS, Bertha R., NC, USN
FUNK, Sidney Earnest, Corp., USMC
GAFFEY, Wilford Ivan, S2c, USN
GARLICK, Elmer Hugh, PFC, USMC
GRENZ, Jesse E., Pvt., USMC
GREWE, Carl Otto, GM1c, USN
GRIGSBY, George Edward, PFC, USMC
HARRIS, Kenneth Louis, RM1c, USN
HEINZ, Fred, SF3c, USN
HOBLITT, Fredrick M., Corp., USMC
HOFF, Ruben S., Field Music Corp., USMC
HOGSHIRE, Lt. Cdr. George Riley, Jr., (MC), USN
HOGUE, William Austin, EM2c, USN
HORSTMAN, Herbert Jack, S2c, USN
HUNDLEY, Robert Gordon, PFC, USMC
HYZER, Morris Forgery, PFC, USMC
JOHANSEN, Carl Oscar, Corp., USMC
KINDEL, Julius H., PFC, USMC
KLIEWER, 2nd Lt. David Donald, USMC
KNIGHT, Lt. Henry Carlisle, Dental Corps, USN
KNIGHT, Oscar Osborne, F1c, USN
LAMB, Robert Verne, S1c, USN
LARSON, Ernest Theodore, Jr., Field Music, USMC
LEAHIGH, Lt. Stanley Adelbert, USNR
LITTLE, Wesley C., Corp., USMC
LOVERING, Lauren Lionel, CEM, USN
LUSK, Thomas Vernon, PFC, USMC
MacBAIN, Arthur Glenn, PhM1c, USN
MARTIN, Marion K., Supply Sgt., USMC
McFARLANE, Jack D., PFC, USMC
McMURPHY, Frank Buerk, RM2c, USN
McVITTIE, Ernest Chester, Platoon Sgt., USMC
MILLER, Robert L., Corp., USMC
MITCHELL, Robert Russell, PFC, USMC
NIXON, Harbart C., PFC, USMC
OLCOTT, Ens. Chester W., USNR
OSBORNE, Raymond Daniel Alfred, RM2c, USN
PALMER, Milo Gardner, S2c, USNR
PLUMMER, Nathan Smith, PFC, USMC
RAVIN, Frederick Scott, TM2c, USN
RAYMOND, Robert Lawrence, PFC, USMC
RICE, Granville J., Corp., USMC
RICHTER, Eugene Vearl, PFC, USMC
RUTH, Philip Nicholas, TM1c, USN
RYDER, Lt. John French, USN
SANDERS, Fred Richard, PhM2c, USN

SATTERFIELD, Lonnie Morse, F1c, USN
SCHLATTER, Wilfred Adee, Corp., USMC
SCHNEIDER, Jacob Victor, Corp., USMC
SHUMWAY, Kenneth Woodrow, PhM2c, USN
SMITH, Cassius Edward, AS, USN
SMITH, David Walter, RM1c, USN
SYLVESTER, Valleon, CQM, USN

TRUELOVE, David Marshall, F1c, USN
VINSON, Benjamin H., Jr., PFC, USMC
WALLACE, Ray Walker, PFC, USMC
WILLIS, Harry Kirtley, CGM, USN
WINSLOW, Robert Erwin, Pvt., USMC
WOLF, Edward Gustave, Pvt., USMC
WOODIN, Lt. (jg) Charles Wesley, USNR
YOUNG, Joe Robert, CRM, USN

PENNSYLVANIA

Dead

ASHENFELDER, Harold Henry, S2c, USNR
BANGERT, John Henry, FC1c, USN
BARBA, Tony, Jr., SC1c, USN
BEARDSLEY, Loren Leigh, EM3c, USN
BENDER, Joseph Stephen, GM3c, USN
BERKANSKI, Albert Charles, Cox., USN
BEVIS, Carl Douglas, Jr., S1c, USNR
BILYI, Anthony, SC3c, USN
BIRCHER, Frederick Robert, RM3c, USNR
BODKIN, Robert Eugene, S2c, USNR
BONSALL, John Joseph, CM3c, USNR
BRAUN, Charles Richard, F1c, USN
BRENNAN, Ens. John Joseph, USNR
BRIGHT, Lt. Graham Paul, Supply Corps, USN
BROCKWAY, Marvin Spencer, WT2c, USNR
BULL, Lt. Richard Salisbury, Jr., USN
BURNS, John Edward, F1c, USN
CAMPBELL, Robert Claude, S2c, USN
CARPENTER, Robert Nelson, MA1c, USN
CARSON, Arthur W., Pvt., USMC
CINOWALT, William Joseph, WT2c, USN
CLARK, Robert William, Jr., FC3c, USN
COURIS, Thomas Phillip, EM2c, USNR
CRESSON, Caleb, VI, S2c, USN
DEATRICH, Ray Luther, CCStd, USN
DEATRICK, Ralph Morgan, F2c, USN
DIETRICH, Lester William, AMM1c, USN
DECK, Leonard Joseph, SC2c, USN
DINEEN, Robert Joseph, S1c, USN
DI BACCO, Vincent Joseph, S2c, USN
DOYLE, Charles Francis, F1c, USN
DURIK, Joseph Edward, AS, USN
ELMES, Ens. Clyde Collamore, Jr., USN
ELY, Lt. Arthur Vincent, USN
ENRIGHT, Ens. Robert Paul Francis, USNR
ERNEST, Robert William, S2c, USN
FIELDS, Evan Lee, HA1c, USN
FOX, Ens. Lee, Jr., USNR

FOX, Maurice Donald, MM2c, USN
GARDNER, Arthur Joseph, WT2c, USN
GILMORE, Cdr. Walter William, Supply Corps, USN
GLAZE, Levi, MA3c, USNR
GORMAN, William Francis, MM1c, USN
GRAHAM, Harry Carl, S2c, USN
GREENWALD, Robert Donald, S1c, USN
GREWCOX, Charles Elbert, F1c, USN
HAAS, Walter Joseph, Cox., USN
HAK, Frank Joseph, SK3c, USNR
HAMPTON, Walter Lewis, BM2c, USN
HAPPEL, Frederick Jacob, Jr., F1c, USN
HASKIN, John E., Supply Sgt., USMC
HAYES, James Patrick, S2c, USCG
HEIDEN, Richard Oscar, F1c, USN
HENDRICKSON, William E., PFC, USMC
HENRY, Joseph Lewis, Jr., S1c, USNR
HOLUBEC, Nicholas T., AS, USCG
HOLLAND, Francis Crowley, S2c, USN
HOOK, William Cahill, Jr., S2c, USNR
HOWARD, Ens. John Martin, USNR
HUDSINUS, Charles, MM2c, USN
HUFF, John Roland, S2c, USNR
HUGHES, Bernard Thomas, Mus2c, USN
HUNTER, Lt. (jg) John Charles, USN
HUNTER, Lt. (jg) Samuel Howard, USN
JABKOWSKY, Edward Vincent, CBM, USN
JARDEL, Thomas Edward, F1c, USN
JASON, Albert Stanley, BM2c, USN
JEFFRIES, Keith, Cox., USN
KAMMERER, Lt. (jg) Christian Albert, USNR
KAPP, George Wilson, Jr., Cox., USN
KATCHAK, John, Corp., USMCR
KEMP, William Bedell, M1c, USN
KENDIG, John Richard, MM1c, USN
KENNEDY, Howard Matthew, MM2c, USN
KLONIN, Hoarce, S2c, USN
KONNICK, Albert Joseph, CM2c, USN
KRAUSE, John Horace, MM2c, USN
KRUPINSKI, Walter Francis, S2c, USN

LEIDY, Edward William, EM2c, USN
LIPPLE, John Anthony, SF1c, USN
MAGAN, Jack Francis, GM3c, USN
MANNING, David Charles, S2c, USN
MARSHALL, William Faudie, AMM3c, USN
McCARTHY, Joseph Benedict, Y2c, USNR
McCLUNG, Ens. Harvey M., USNR
McCOMB, Fred, GM2c, USN
McPEEK, Norman John, F1c, USN
MESTICHELLI, Philip Joseph, S1c, USN
MILLER, Sylvester Vernon, WT1c, USNR
MIRELLO, Bernard Joseph, S1c, USN
MLINAR, Joseph, Cox., USN
MONTGOMERY, Charles Andrew RM3c, USNR
NANNOS, Ens. George, USNR
NEWBERRY, John Alfred, EM2c, USN
NEWMAN, Charles Paul, ML2c, USNR
OSBORN, Robert, ACOM, USN
OWENS, James Patrick, RM3c, USNR
PARRISH, Irvin Emerson, S2c, USNR
PEARCE, Stanley Barker, S2c, USN
PENSYL, John Campbell, GM2c, USN
PERRY, Leroy Ellsworth, BM1c, USNR
PERRYMAN, Paul, GM2c, USN
PETYAK, John Joseph, S1c, USN
PIERCE, Aloysius Joseph, CSM, USN
PINKO, Andrew Anthony, EM3c, USN
PLETO, Tony Roger, ARM3c, USN
POLLOCK, Charles Kimball, S2c, USNR
POTTS, Howard Green, S2c, USNR
POTTS, John Pershing, S2c, USN
PUZIO, Edward, S1c, USN
QUINAUX, Kenneth Eugene, S1c, USN
RABYK, Andrew, GM2c, USNR
RACISZ, Edward Stanley, S1c, USN
REAM, Roland Emery, GM2c, USNR
RECKHOUSE, William Henry, S2c, USN
REX, William Henry, F1c, USN
RHODES, Wilburn Everett, Jr., SF3c, USN
RICE, John, Jr., CM3c, USNR
RICHAR, Raymond Lyle, S1c, USN
ROBY, Raymond Arthur, S1c, USN
RODGERS, John Dayton, S1c, USN
ROGERS, Warren Livingston, Jr., S1c, USN
ROTH, Richard, CPhM, USN
ROWE, Kenneth George, S1c, USN
RUCHINSKY, Stephen, PhM1c, USN
RUDDEROW, Lt. Cdr. Thomas Wright, USNR
RUTKOWSKI, John Peter, S1c, USN
SAMBOREK, Edward Joseph, S2c, USN
SANDERS, Dean Stanley, CMM, USN
SAUL, James Edward, Cox., USN

SAVINSKI, Michael, S1c, USN
SCANLON, Francis, S2c, USNR
SCHEUERLEIN, George Albert, GM3c, USN
SCHLICITING, George Rothenhause, EM2c, USNR
SCHRENK, Lt. (jg) Edward Lawrence, USNR
SEIBERT, William Chester, TM2c, USN
SESTACK, Albert Joseph, S1c, USN
SHARBAUGH, Harry Robert, GM3c, USN
SHEDLOCK, Victor Frank, WT1c, USN
SHELLY, Russell Kenneth, Jr., Mus2c, USN
SHILEY, Paul Eugene, S1c, USN
SHIMER, Melvin Irvin, S1c, USN
SLAPIKAS, Edward Frank, S1c, USN
SMETANA, Pete, BM2c, USN
SNYDER, John J., Corp., USMCR
SOMMERVILLE, Guy Wilbur, AS, USNR
STEMBROSKY, George Joseph, S2c, USN
SUGARS, Mickee, Platoon Sgt., USMC
THOMAS, William John, F2c, USNR
TOMS, George A., PFC, USMC
TROUTNER, Milburn Emmerson, MM2c, USNR
TURNER, Daniel M., Jr., S1c, USCG
TYRPAK, Elias, GM1c, USN
VARCHOL, Brinley, GM2c, USN
VAS, Michael T., MM2c, USCG
VDOVIN, John, S1c, USN
WEIDLICH, Paul Clement, S1c, USN
WEST, Harold Richard, S1c, USN
WILSON, James, S1c, USN
WOLF, Ens. George A., Jr., USNR
WOOD, James Alan, S1c, USN
WYDILA, John Charles, SF3c, USN
WYLIE, Howard Eugene, AS, USNR
YANEK, John Joseph, Jr., GM3c, USN
YANOV, Michael, GM3c, USN
YOUNG, Robert William, F1c, USN
YUKAS, Steve John, S2c, USN
ZAJAC, Walter Paul, MM2c, USCG
ZEIGLER, Harry Daniel, Y3c, USN
ZIZAK, Frank Edward, MM2c, USN

Wounded

BRENDLE, Louis Joseph, FC2c, USN
CASSERLY, Clyde Milton, S1c, USN
GILBERT, Charles Clifford, S1c, USN
GIRARD, Allen Joseph, S2c, USN
GROSS, William Edward, F2c, USN
HENDERSON, Russell, AMM3c, USN
JOLLY, Ranall H., Corp., USMC
LEINWEBER, Joseph Rudolph, S2c, USN
LOWEY, Michael Eugene, GM3c, USN

MANCUSO, Joseph, S1c, USN
McDONALD, Eugene Francis, S1c, USN
MILLER, William Edward, SK3c, USN
MONZO, Angelo Anthony, FC3c, USN
MOORE, John H., Corp., USMC
NELSON, John Joseph, MM1c, USN
NUNEMACHER, Robert Lewis, S2c, USN
SAUERWINE, Richard Walter, S2c, USN
SOFIA, Lawrence Anthony, Cox., USN
WATERS, Robert Bolden, S2c, USN

Missing

ADAMS, Lt. Col. John P., USMC
BEREZNY, George, MM2c, USN
BOLDEN, Sidney, SC3c, USN
BONKOSKI, John Anthony, GM1c, USN
BYRNES, Thomas Francis, Jr., MM1c, USN
CARSILLO, Romeo Leone, S1c, USN
CHISHOLM, Lt. Cdr. John Kielkopf, Supply Corps, USN
EKMAN, Frank Hubert, S1c, USN
FEDICO, Paul, S2c, USN
GARWOOD, Edward Dering, RM2c, USN
GINGRAS, Lt. Cdr. Richard Hermus, USN
GLIPTIS, John Mark, F2c, USN
GRAHAM, George, Cox., USN
GYUGO, Paul, Jr., WT2c, USN
HARRON, Lamar Folk, S1c, USN
HAUSMAN, Quinton Edwin, TM3c, USN
HOWELL, Rupert Ellsworth, F1c, USN
JANTZ, Carl J., Corp., USMC
KEPHART, John Edgard, Jr., Y1c, USNR
KUBILUS, Raymond, Chief Cook, USMCR
LEARISH, Jesse William, CSF, USN
LEINTHALL, Daniel Franklin, F2c, USN
LILLEY, Paul Reed, MM1c, USN
LYDIC, Wilson, PFC, USMC
MADDEN, Ens. John Aloysius, Jr., USNR
MARTIN, Paul Bernard, F2c, USN
McCASLIN, Truman Everett, BM1c, USN
McGARRITY, Lt. (jg) John Joseph, USNR
McMILLAN, William L., PFC, USMC
MERKEL, George Calvin, CY, USN
MORASKI, Alexander Joseph, BM1c, USN
MUMMEY, Charles Isaac, CMM, USN
PHILLIPS, David Scott, S2c, USN
PRICE, Joseph Warner, S1c, USN
ROBINSON, Lt. (jg) William Saner, USN
ROMAN, Walter Anton, GM3c, USN
RYDER, Grafton Green, MM3c, USN
SELLERS, Ens. Coleman, IV, USN
SMITH, Andrew Joseph, MM1c, USN
SNYDER, Earl Robert, S2c, USN
SOLAR, Adolfo, BM1c, USN

SOWERS, Paul Albert, S2c, USN
STOUTEN, James, CBM, USN
SURA, Michael, QM3c, USN
SZYMALA, Victor John, MM2c, USN
UDITSKY, Samuel Lable, WT1c, USN
VANO, George Joseph, CCStd, USN
WEILER, Lt. (jg) Francis Brooks, USN
WEIMER, Albert Gohn, SK2c, USN
WILLIAMS, Robert Arthur, QM3c, USN
ZBURA, Michael, S1c, USN
ZINK, Joseph J., Platoon Sgt., USMC

Prisoners of War

ALDEN, John, Pay Clerk, USN
AMBRO, Eugene Allen, PhM2c, USN
ARCURI, Louis, RM2c, USN
AUGUSTYN, Anthony A., PFC, USN
BALABAS, John Edward, GM1c, USN
BARNUM, Thomas Elmer, F1c, USN
BASSETT, Lt. Robert Van Rensselaer, Jr., USN
BENNETT, 1st Lt. Charles H., USMC
BERGAM, Samuel Joseph, CWT, USN
BINDER, Martin, Boat., USN
BLANDY, John Frederick, S/Sgt., USMC
BOBROWNICKI, Walter Joseph, S1c, USN
BOYER, Franklin, Corp., USMC
BRADLEY, Joseph John, PhM3c, USNR
BRYAN, Lt. Cdr. Arthur Melven, Supply Corps, USN
BURTZ, John, SK1c, USN
BUTLER, Francis Edward, CMM, USN
BUTTERBAUGH, Robert Earl, AMM1c, USN
CHARLTON, Monford P., PFC, USMC
CLIMIE, Capt. James F., USMC
CONNELL, Lt. Cdr. James Aloysius, Dental Corps, USN
CONNER, Marion Ellis, AMM2c, USN
CONNOR, James Harry, CQM, USNR
DEAN, John Robert, SC3c, USN
DEAN, Oscar C., S/Sgt., USMC
DELEMAN, Bernard, MM2c, USN
DI SERIO, John D., PFC, USMC
EICHELBERGER, Paul Earl, MM1c, USN
FEINBERT, Morton, PFC, USMC
FRY, Robert Gregory, Torp.3c, USN
FRYAR, William F., PFC, USMC
FULLER, Andrew Augustine, S2c, USN
GALLAGHER, Lt. Robert Anthony, USN
GERBERDING, Oliver Laird, Jr., RM3c, USN
GOTHIE, Lt. Daniel Shinton, USN
GOTTLIEB, Lt. Mack Leonard, (MC), USNR
GUARIN, Joseph, Jr., PFC, USMC

HAGSTROM, Alfred Staples, PhM2c, USN
HANZSEK, Joseph, MM1c, USN
HEIN, Christian William, MM1c, USNR
HORVATH, Charles S., PFC, USMC
HULINA, Milton F., Corp., USMC
HUMPHREY, Thomas Sylvester, PFC, USMC
JAMES, Walter J., Jr., PFC, USMC
JENKINS, 1st Lt. Robert F., Jr., USMC
KALYNYCH, Nicholas Richard, MM1c, USN
KEATH, Harry Grant, SC2c, USN
KIRKPATRICK, Lt. Harlan Good, USN
KLECKY, Rudolph, MM2c, USN
KLEPEK, Joseph Edward, S1c, USN
KRAWIE, John Walter, Mstr. Gunnery Sgt., USMC
KRENITSKI, William, PFC, USMC
KROPTAVICH, James Simon, PFC, USMC
LECHLER, William Richard, S1c, USN
LINTON, Herbert Milton, F3c, USN
LITZ, Eugene Harold, PFC, USMC
LOHRIG, Charles Woodrow Wilson, F2c, USN
MACDONALD, Edward L., Sgt., USMC
MARKAROVICH, John, Corp., USMC
MANCUSO, Ernest Joseph, PFC, USMC
MASCAVAGE, Anthony Alfred, EM2c, USN
McCANDLESS, John Cameron, SC2c, USN
McCLUNG, William John, III, Sgt., USMC
McCLURE, Ens. John Francis, USNR
McCORMICK, Edward Merle, Sgt., USMC
McELHENNY, Joseph, Y1c, USN
McMASTER, Samuel Thomas, BM1c, USN
MIKULA, Joseph Edward, Corp., USMC
MILLER, Howard DeWald, Aer3c, USN
MILLER, Roy, Boat., USN
MORGAN, Jack Payne, PhM1c, USN
MURCHISON, Lt. (jg) William Jervis, USNR
NARDINI, Lt. John Edward, (MC), USN
NASH, Margaret A., NC, USN

NOVAK, Louis, Jr., PhM2c, USN
NULL, Robert Nelson, S/Sgt., USMC
OLENOWSKI, Michael, PFC, USMC
PANTALONE, Guiseppe, SC1c, USNR
PEARLSTEIN, Joseph, 1st Sgt., USMC
PEDA, Charles John, SC1c, USN
PERRI, Albert, Corp., USMC
PFEIFFER, James Augustin, Pharm., USN
PRICE, William Joseph, S1c, USN
REED, Rollin Maurice, Mach., USN
REGAN, Richard Arthur, CMM, USN
REHM, Orville Everett, QM Sgt., USMC
RINKER, Lynn Koch, Torp.1c, USNR
RUSH, William Evans, RM1c, USN
SCOTT, Lt. Warwick Potter, USNR
SEIFERT, Clifford Wilson, MM1c, USN
SENCHUK, Ens. Walter, USNR
SHAMBORA, John, BM1c, USN
SHAPUTNIC, Walter Adam, Carp., USN
SHEARER, Clarence, Pharm., USN
SHIMEL, James B., QM Clerk, USMC
SLATER, Thomas Arthur, GM1c, USN
SMITH, Elwood Marks, S/Sgt., USMC
STROUSE, Milton Harold, SF3c, USN
TAYLOR, Rudolph Joseph, PFC, USMC
TAZZANI, John, Jr., S1c, USN
THOMAS, Wesley Ernest, CSM, USN
VACCHIANO, Lewis John, MM1c, USN
WAGHER, Frank C., Jr., PFC, USMC
WALKER, John Henry, Pay Clerk, USN
WALL, Raymond Edward, SK2c, USN
WALLACE, Verne Lorton, PFC, USMC
WANGER, Lt. James Linford, Dental Corps, USN
WARONKER, Alvin Jacob, Field Music, USMC
WATERLOO, Francis Charles, RM3c, USN
WEBER, Capt. Richard D., USMC
WESCHLER, Lt. Charles John, USN
WILLIAMS, Robert Lee, S1c, USN
WILMER, James H., Corp., USMC
WOJTKIELEWICZ, William, S1c, USN
WUEST, Lt. (jg) Robert Richard, USNR
YETTER, Doris M., NC, USN
YURCHAK, Stephan, SK1c, USN

RHODE ISLAND

Dead

BLAIR, Eugene, CMM, USN
BRENNER, Wayne Earl, AMM1c, USN
BUCKLEY, John Daniel, AOM3c, USN
CUTNER, Alec, CWT, USN
DALTON, John Francis, CQM, USN

FAY, Charles Joseph, Chief Torp., USNR
FAZZI, Victor Armiss, F2c, USNR
GAYDE, Peter Albert, CSK, USN
GOODYEAR, Ens. Bradley, Jr., USNR
GREENWOOD, James, BM1c, USN
LA CROSSE, Henry Eugene, Jr., SK2c, USN

LUNDGREN, Oscar Albert, CGM, USN
LYONS, Edward Francis, PhM2c, USN
MARTIN, Michael Francis, CWT, USNR
McGOVERN, John Michael, AMM2c, USN
MORSE, Edward Clarence, CMM, USN
MURPHY, Thomas Joseph, Jr., SK1c, USN
NEVILLE, Joseph Patrick, WT1c, USNR
PALIOTTI, Victor, Corp., USMC
PAOLUCCI, James Alfred, S2c, USN
PERKINS, George Ernest, F1c, USN
RICE, Wilson Albert, S1c, USN
RUSSO, Albert, S1c, USN
VIEIRA, Alvaro Everett, S2c, USN
WOODRUFF, Ens. James Gordon, USNR

Wounded

BARAN, Sylvester Frank, CM1c, USN
DENNETT, John Simeon, Jr., F1c, USN
DODGE, Harold Robertson, CPrtr, USN
ROLLINS, Howard Taft, ACRM, USN

Missing

ALBEE, Clyde William, Jr., SM1c, USN
BENTON, Theron Taft, CBM, USN

GENTRY, Samuel Allison, WT1c, USN
GRIFFIN, Earl Bradford, EM1c, USN
HURLOCKER, Eddie Monrow, CM1c, USN
JOHNSON, Warren Edwin, F2c, USN
MOREY, Ernest Allen, BM2c, USN
SULLIVAN, George Byron, S2c, USN
URBANO, Camilo, OS3c, USNR

Prisoners of War

BENJAMIN, Armand Emile, PFC, USMC
CARNEY, Ens. Francis Joseph, USNR
COLAVECCHIO, Felix Anthony, BM1c, USN
COWAN, Alva Roberts, CPhM, USN
DUNSMOOR, Earl Worcester, Pay Clerk, USMC
GORSKI, Ens. Alexander Alfred, USNR
GROVE, Lt. Cdr. Alfred Edgar, USN
KENYON, Hugh Andrew, AMM3c, USNR
LUSIGNAN, Charles, BM1c, USN
McRAE, George, PFC, USMC
MENNA, William Albert, S1c, USN
SANBORN, Ens. Philip H., USNR

SOUTH CAROLINA

Dead

ARLEDGE, Kenneth Ulver, CBM, USN
BARNARD, William G., Sgt., USMC
BIELKA, Lt. Cdr. Rudolph Paul, USN
BROOKS, Robert William, F2c, USNR
BUSH, Samuel Jackson, MA1c, USN
CHRISTENSEN, Ens. Stratton, USNR
CLEMENT, Hubert Paul, FC1c, USN
COONER, Ens. Bunyan Randolph, USNR
COOPER, Furman Cleveland, S2c, USN
DORR, Carl David, F2c, USN
DYER, William Harold, RM3c, USN
EDWARDS, Thomas David, GM3c, USN
EVANS, Alfred, MA3c, USN
GIBBS, Nathaniel, MA3c, USN
GILLIARD, Benjamin Edward, MA1c, USN
GINSBERG, Robert, Chief Torp., USNR
GODDARD, James Warren, III, SF3c, USN
HALL, John Victor, S2c, USN
HARKINS, James Waymon, AS, USNR
KAMPMEYER, Eric Theodore, GM3c, USN
LEE, Henry Lloyd, S1c, USN
LEONARD, Ens. Edwin Madison, USNR
LEWIS, Wayne Alman, CM, USN
MATTHEWS, Lewis Raymond, MM1c, USN

MAYFIELD, Frazier, MA1c, USN
McBEE, Luther Kirk, S1c, USN
McCLARY, John Marion, S1c, USN
McMURRY, William, AS, USNR
MEARES, John Morgan, S2c, USN
MOORE, Douglas Carlton, S1c, USN
MOORE, James Carlton, SF3c, USN
NATIONS, James Garland, FC2c, USN
ORR, Manley Stribling, EM2c, USN
PICKENS, Cecil J., Sgt., USMC
PLYLER, Hazel "B", MM2c, USN
POWERS, Davis Morrell, F1c, USN
PRIVETT, Johnnie Lee, S2c, USNR
RHODES, William Glenn, AS, USNR
SENN, Harold Anderson, AS, USNR
SIMPSON, Ansel King, PhM1c, USN
WEBB, Durward, CY, USN
WEST, Broadus Franklin, S1c, USN
WHEELER, James B., S2c, USNR
WHITE, Vernon Russell, S1c, USN
WILLIAMS, Jack Herman, RM3c, USNR

Wounded

HUBER, Lawrence John, Cox., USN
SANDERS, Fred Jack, BM2c, USN
SMITH, Robert Lewis, AMM3c, USN

Missing

ANDERSON, John Wilson, Jr., S2c, USN
ANDERSON, Wayne Ellie, Torp.1c, USN
BRANDT, Rudolph Otto, Cox., USN
CLIPPARD, Maxie, EM2c, USN
Fox, Julian Edward, S1c, USN
HARRIS, Lester Cleveland, Jr., S1c, USN
PATTERSON, William Jackson, F1c, USN
POSTIGLION, Angelo, MM2c, USN
TOWILL, Ens. Richard Judson, USNR
USSERY, Frank, Platoon Sgt., USMC
WEEKS, George Thomas, Jr., S1c, USN

Prisoners of War

BOUDOLF, Joseph Louis, CM1c, USN
BUCKLER, Demaree, CBM, USN
BURNETT, Wilburn, CMM, USN

COOPER, Claude Bernard, Y1c, USN
CROCKER, Ralph James, Cox., USN
ELLISON, John Henry, Corp., USMC
FULTON, Lt. Robert Burwell, II, USN
HARRIS, Otto Bennefield, S2c, USN
HUFFMAN, Forest, Platoon Sgt., USMC
JOHNSON, Edward Irvin, SK3c, USN
NEELY, Robert Odell, BM2c, USNR
OLASKY, Charles, CY, USN
PETERS, Raymond Charles, CWT, USN
PHILLIPS, William Joseph, SC1c, USN
PLATT, Capt. Wesley McCoy, USMC
PURSLEY, Lester Frank, Chief Torp., USN
ROBERTS, Austin J. V., 1st Sgt., USMCR
SALLEY, Ansel Arthur, PhM1c, USN
WALKER, George M., PFC, USMC
WOOD, Jeff Calvin, Pvt., USMC

SOUTH DAKOTA

Dead

ANDERSON, Arnold Leo, S1c, USN
DAVIDSON, 2nd Lt. Carl R., USMC
DILL, Leaman Robert, EM2c, USN
EKBERG, Ens. Alvin Lendall, USNR
FULTON, Jess E., Gunnery Sgt., USMCR
GOETSCH, Herman August, S1c, USN
GRANDPRE, Arthur Matthew, F2c, USN
GUSTAFSON, Lt. Arthur Leonard, USN
HANSON, Wendell Herbert, SM2c, USN
HENRICHSEN, Jimmie Lee, S2c, USN
JARDING, George William, F3c, USN
LEHMAN, Myron Kenneth, S2c, USN
LEWIS, Lloyd Warren, Y2c, USN
McPHERSON, Stuart Richard, F3c, USN
MULHAIR, James Joseph, F3c, USN
O'LEARY, Edward Lewis, S1c, USN
QUANDE, Kenneth Melvin, S1c, USN
RIVERS, Alvin J., PFC, USMC
ROESCH, Harold William, S1c, USN
ROGERS, Walter Boone, F1c, USN
SELLE, Harry Gamaliel Morland, S2c, USN
SMITH, Leonard Quintion, Bkr3c, USN
SMITH, Thayne Charles, Torp2c, USN
SUTTON, Wayne George, S2c, USNR
WALDRON, Lt. Cdr. John Charles, USN

Wounded

BOHR, LeRoy Francis, EM2c, USN
GOEDEN, Leonard F., Pvt., USMCR
LOVELACE, Clair Beveridge, HA1c, USN

MARESH, Frederick Raymond, S2c, USN
SCHLEVE, Clifford Edward, S2c, USN
VALDER, Lester Alvin, S1c, USN

Missing

BARRINGER, Elra Franklin, FC2c, USN
BELL, John Roger, WT2c, USN
DELONG, Lt. Edward Grover, USN
GIESEN, Frank Joseph, Chief Torp., USN
HALL, Meredith Carrol, S1c, USN
HALVERSON, Elmer Charles, S1c, USN
HEADLY, Lawrence, MM1c, USN
HEHN, Clifford Emil, S1c, USN
WINCE, Dwyce Donald, MM2c, USN

Prisoners of War

BAHR, Edwin Henry, CM1c, USN
BINGHAM, John Coleman, Jr., Sgt., USMC
BROWN, Morris Carl, PFC, USMC
BROWN, Robert MacLean, SK3c, USN
GLODERY, Alvin Gilbert, Pvt., USMC
HAGEMO, Olaf William, Corp., USMC
HAIR, Steven Yellow, Pvt., USMC
JAEGER, Cletus Wilfred, RM3c, USN
JAEGER, John Edward, Jr., MM2c, USN
MATHIAS, Robert A., PFC, USMC
SILK, Herman J., PFC, USMC
STOBER, Mell J., PFC, USMC
WELCH, Lt. Cdr. Cecil Charles, (MC), USN
WHITBY, Ellwood Pierce, PFC, USMC
WILLIAMS, Lt. Richard Beebe, USN

TENNESSEE

Dead

ALLEN, Thomas Benton, GM2c, USN
ALLISON, Andrew K., F1c, USN
ARMSTRONG, Paul E., Corp., USMC
ATKINSON, Edgar Blannam, QM2c, USN
BOLEN, Henry Howard, GM3c, USN
BRIDGES, James Leon, S1c, USN
BROOKS, William, S1c, USN
BROWN, Lon Alexander, Jr., RM1c, USN
BRUNET, Frank, Cox., USN
BURNETT, Charlie Leroy, S2c, USN
BYRD, Charles Dewitt, S1c, USN
CAMPBELL, William Vane, S2c, USN
CHAPMAN, Henry Thomas, F1c, USN
CISCO, Luther Elver, S2c, USN
CRIM, Warren Harding, F3c, USN
DAWN, Grant Ulysses, RM3c, USN
DERRINGTON, John Porter, WT2c, USN
ECHOLS, Charles Louis, Jr., EM3c, USN
FARMER, John Wilson, Cox., USN
FORTNER, Roscoe Leland, SK3c, USN
FOSTER, James Henderson, MA3c, USN
GREEN, Cecil Johnson, S1c, USN
GREER, James Oscar, AS, USNR
HAYNES, Elliott David, GM2c, USN
HENRY, Joel Quinn, S2c, USN
HODGES, Kermit Ward, M1c, USN
HORNSBY, Marshall Thomas, WT2c, USN
HOWE, Ens. William Henry, USNR
HUGHEY, James Clynton, S1c, USN
HURD, Willard Hardy, MA2c, USN
IVEY, Everett Leon, F1c, USN
JACKSON, Ens. Marion Francis, Jr., USNR
JAMISON, William George, MM2c, USN
JOHNSON, Lee Edward, GM1c, USN
JOHNSON, Gordon Molone, F2c, USN
JONES, Ernest, MA3c, USN
JONES, Leland, S1c USN
JONES, Willard Worth, S1c, USN
KENNINGTON, Charles Cecil, S1c, USN
KING, Gordon Blane, S1c, USN
KWAPINSKI, Stanley Edwin, Jr., PhM3c, USN
LANG, Maj. Harry C., USMC
LITTLE, James Lloyd, SF2c, USN
LOVELL, George Robert, S2c, USN
LUNN, David Martin, Cox., USN
MANSFIELD, George Henry, RM1c, USN
MARTIN, John Winter, F3c, USN
McMILLAN, Harrison Edwin, S1c, USN
McPHERSON, John Blair, S1c, USN

MEDLEY, James Edward, AS, USN
MILAM, L. B., S1c, USN
MILLER, Whitman Senter, GM1c, USN
PARRISH, Jack, ARM2c, USN
PATTERSON, Charles Henry, RM3c, USN
PENNYBACKER, Frank Harwood, SF3c, USN
PERRY, Earl, S2c, USN
RAY, Eldon Casper, SK3c, USN
RAY, Sanford Farris, CM3c, USN
RHODES, Birb Richard, F2c, USN
ROBERTSON, James Milton, MM1c, USN
ROSE, Harold Lloyd, AS, USNR
RUFFNER, Harold Gilbert, FM2c, USN
RUSHING, Harold Anderson, M2c, USN
SAULSBURY, Theodore Hilliard, OC2c, USN
SAYLOR, Paul Edd, F1c, USN
SCHUON, Richard Martin, Jr., S1c, USN
SMITH, Clarence Eugene, S2c, USN
SMITH, Frank William, S1c, USN
SMITH, Luther Kent, S1c, USN
SMITHSON, Charles Estyl, F3c, USNR
SNEED, William Marion, S2c, USN
SPENCE, Merle Joe, S1c, USN
STERLING, Otis Delaney, MA1c, USN
STEUART, George Alexander, S2c, USNR
TACKET, Walker, S2c, USNR
WALLACE, Stuart Henry, S2c, USN
WARE, Lt. Charles Rollins, USN
WHITE, Claude, CWT, USN
WHITTEMORE, Andrew Tiny, MA2c, USN
WILLIAMS, Paul, S2c, USN
WIMBERLEY, Paul Edwin, GM3c, USN
WINNETT, Selmer Ray, F3c, USN
YOUNG, Carl Curtis, S1c, USN
ZIMMERLE, Edward William, GM3c, USN

Wounded

HARRIS, Henry Sherman, S1c, USN
KIRBY, Roy Hail, Jr., S1c, USN
KNIGHT, William, S1c, USN
RUTH, Ernest Richard, Jr., S1c, USN
STEWART, Ens. Richard Lewis, USN
TURNER, James Wesley, F2c, USN
WEBB, William Carson, S1c, USN

Missing

ADCOCK, Curtis, CSK, USN
ALLEN, Earl Tyson, SK1c, USN
AWTREY, Palmer Sanford, S1c, USN
BAILEY, Fred, WT2c, USN
BARNES, Otis Belton, SK3c, USN

BOARDMAN, Rex Gale, SK2c, USN
CAMPBELL, John Franklin, CM2c, USN
DODD, Ernest Ambrow, S2c, USN ·
ELLZEY, Luther Earl, QM3c, USN
FINLEY, Woodrow W., PFC, USMC
FISHEL, Ens. Myron Philip, USN
FOWLKES, William West, Cox., USN
FRENSLEY, Claude Eugene, CMM, USN
HILL, Jessie James, MM1c, USN
HOLDER, Robert McKinney, S1c, USN
HOLMES, Jason Hunter, Jr., WT2c, USN
HOOD, Charles Harvey, S2c, USN
HUBBARD, Atwood Albert, S1c, USN
KNIGHT, Fred Maxwell, F1c, USN
LAMB, James Shelton, Jr., S2c, USN
LEEDY, William Edward, F1c, USN
MARKS, Mitchell Henry, S1c, USN
McKIBBEN, William Frank, S1c, USN
MILLER, Carl William, CGM, USN
O'BRIEN, Howard, SC2c, USN
RIDGEWAY, William Henry, S1c, USN
SALLIS, James Homer, SM1c, USN
SILER, Joseph Hubert, S1c, USN
STOVER, Lloyd Wayne, EM3c, USN
SWANN, Harry Lee, SK1c, USN
TEMPLE, Murrel Robert, S1c, USN
THORNBURG, Hubert Denzil, F1c, USN
WATKINS, James Howard, S1c, USN

Prisoners of War

BALLINGER, James McClain, S1c, USN
BENNETT, Raymond Osborne, PFC, USMC
BOSTIC, Hobert Edward, F2c, USN
BROOKS, Howard Eugene, EM3c, USN
BURNETTE, Earnest Michael, Jr., S1c, USN
COLLINS, William Irven, Ptr1c, USNR
FERGUSON, Frank William, QM Clerk, USMC
FISHER, Walter Howell, CBM, USN
FOX, William Earl, CWT, USN
FREEMAN, Clarence Anderson, S2c, USN
GALBRAITH, Lt. Cdr. William Jackson, USN

GOODALL, Lt. Cdr. Henry William, USN
GRANT, William, Platoon Sgt., USMC
GRIZZARD, Herbert Wayne, MM2c, USN
HAMMETT, Orion Alexander, Boat., USN
HODGE, Allen Jones, S1c, USN
HOLDEN, Wesley James, S2c, USN
HOWARD, Robert Leroy, RM1c, USN
HURST, Herman D., Ptr2c, USN
JAMERSON, Joseph Paul, Sgt., USMC
JONES, Claude Anderson, AM1c, USN
JONES, David Estle, AMM3c, USN
KING, Otis Hocker, PFC, USMC
LATHAM, David Lexton, S2c, USN
LAWSON, Gains Willard, AMM3c, USN
LYNCH, Roy Elmons, PhM2c, USN
MALONE, Luther Harry, Cox., USN
MARKHAM, Roy Holman, PFC, USMC
McCAGE, Harvey Eugene, PFC, USMC
MILLER, Clifford Lochert, Jr., RM1c, USN
MOUNT, Walter Eugene, AMM3c, USN
NORRIS, Charles Douglas, F1c, USN
PATRICK, William Harrison, BM2c, USN
PAYNE, Harry Lee, HA1c, USN
PEMBERTON, Ralph Cumming, AMM2c, USN
PETWAY, Ens. Edwin Sayle, Jr., USNR
PING, Robert, S1c, USN
PRUITT, Charles Lester, S1c, USN
SHOFNER, Capt. Austin Conner, USMC
SMITH, Charles Carlyle, Jr., SM2c, USN
SMITH, Ens. Charles Donovan, II, USN
SMITH, Nathan Alexander, Corp., USMC
SOMERS, James Mitchell, Corp., USMC
STEARNS, Lt. Benton Hammond, USNR
TAYLOR, Clarence Mariet, Boat., USN
TAYLOR, John F., Corp., USMC
TAYLOR, Ralph, F1c, USN
WALLACE, Albert Victor, F1c, USN
WALSH, Justin C., PFC, USMC
WATSON, D. H., CY, USN
WOFFORD, Ira Luther, S1c, USN
WOODY, Stanley Dorch, S2c, USN
WORD, Roscoe C., Jr., Sgt., USMC

TEXAS

Dead

ABERCROMBIE, Samuel Adolphus, S1c, USN
ADAMS, Jesse Leroy, S1c, USN
ADKINSON, James Dillion, S1c, USN
ALBRECHT, Charlie Martin, MM1c, USN
ALLEN, William Lewis, SK2c, USNR
ANDERSON, Von R., Corp., USMC

ASHING, Carl Blake, FC3c, USN
AUTRY, Eligah T., Jr., Cox., USN
AYERS, Dee Cumpie, S2c, USN
BAGGETT, Paul Reginald, S2c, USN
BAGWELL, Will Clarmond, WT2c, USN
BAILEY, Wilbur Houston, S1c, USN
BAKER, Arthur Chester, F1c, USN
BALLARD, Robert John, S1c, USN

BARNER, Walter Ray, S2c, USN
BARRON, Thomas N., Corp., USMC
BARTLETT, Paul Clement, MM1c, USN
BATES, Robert Alvin, PhM3c, USN
BAUMGARTEN, Thomas Edgar, RM3c, USN
BEAUMONT, James Ammon, S2c, USN
BIGHAM, Virgil Cornelius, S2c, USN
BISHOP, Grover Barron, MM1c, USN
BLAYLOCK, Clarence Arvin, F3c, USN
BLOUNT, Wayman Boney, S1c, USN
BLOXOM, Harvey Lee, Sgt., USMC
BOYDSTUN, Don Jasper, S2c, USN
BOYDSTUN, R. L., S2c, USN
BRISCO, Onie Richard, Pvt., USMCR
BROOKS, Ennis Edgar, F1c, USN
BROWN, Riley Mirville, F1c, USN
BRYAN, Leland Howard, S1c, USN
BURKE, Frank Edmond, Jr., SK2c, USN
BURT, William H., Pvt., USMC
BUTLER, John Dabney, F1c, USN
BYUS, Grady G., Jr., MM1c, USN
CAMP, Ens. Jack Hill, USNR
CAMPBELL, Phillip Mangum, AMM2c, USN
CARLISLE, Robert Wayne, S1c, USN
CARRINGTON, Carl Ulysses, MA2c, USN
CARROLL, Joseph William, F2c, USN
CASTLEBERRY, Claude William, Jr., S1c, USN
CAVENDER, Jack Frank, CEM, USN
CHASTAIN, Joe Bill, Sgt., USMC
CHERRY, Dorsey Elwayne, PhM2c, USN
CLARK, David, Jr., S2c, USN
CLARK, Milton Wayne, AMM2c, USN
CLARK, Richard Clarence, S2c, USNR
CLARY, Alva Leroy, S2c, USN
COBB, Ballard Burgher, S1c, USN
COKE, George Anderson, S1c, USN
COLLIER, Linald Long, Jr., Bkr3c, USN
COMPTON, Thomas Grenville, S2c, USN
CONE, Arthur Benjamin, S1c, USN
CORBIN, Andy, PFC, USMC
CORNELIUS, P. W., S2c, USN
CRABB, Vincent Weathers, Jr., F2c, USNR
CRAIN, John Reeves, F1c, USN
CROUCH, Loren Bailey, SK2c, USNR
CROW, Ens. Howard Daniel, USNR
CURRIE, Osa, Corp., USMC
DAUGHERTY, Vaughn Wood, PFC, USMC
DAVIS, Edward Hope, SK1c, USN
DAVIS, Ens. Frederick C., USNR
DAVIS, Reginald Henry, RM1c, USN
DAVIS, William Priere, S2c, USN
DAWSON, James Douglas, RM3c, USN

DAY, James R., Pvt., USMC
DENNIS, Leroy, S2c, USN
DOBEY, Milton Paul, Jr., S1c, USN
DONNELL, Ens. Earl Roe, Jr., USNR
DOSSER, William Hugh, S2c, USN
DRAUGHON, Alonzo Owen, AS, USNR
DUDLEY, Roland Quinton, Jr., S2c, USN
DUGGER, Guy, F1c, USN
DUKE, Lee Herwin, S2c, USN
DUKES, Billie Joe, S1c, USN
DUPREE, William Joseph, F3c, USN
ELLIS, James Harvy, F3c, USN
ELWELL, Royal, S1c, USN
ENGLAND, Richard Boyd, MM2c, USN
ERWIN, Stanley Joe, MM1c, USN
ERWIN, Walton Aluard, S1c, USN
ESTEP, Carl James, S1c, USN
ESTES, Carl Edwen, S1c, USN
FAIR, Charles Edison, AOM3c, USN
FARRAR, Herbert D., S/Sgt., USMC
FITCH, Simon, MA1c, USN
FOWLER, George Parten, S2c, USN
FRAYER, Chester Henry, MM2c, USN
FRAZIER, George G., PFC, USMC
FREE, Thomas Augusta, MM3c, USN
FREE, William Thomas, S2c, USN
GARCIA, Robert Stillman, SK3c, USN
GARLOFF, James Maurice, MM2c, USN
GARY, Thomas Jones, S2c, USN
GHOLSTON, Roscoe, Y2c, USN
GLENN, Wilburn Forrest, ARM2c, USN
GOLDMAN, Herman Eugene, Y3c, USN
GREEN, Harold Thigpen, F1c, USN
GREGSTON, Brevis Manuel, S1c, USN
GRIFFIN, Reese Olin, S2c, USN
GUEST, Vernon Wayne, EM3c, USN
HACKWORTH, William Conrad, F1c, USN
HALL, Dee, S2c, USN
HAMRICK, Charles Albert, S2c, USN
HANNA, David Darling, EM3c, USN
HARDWICK, James William, S2c, USN
HARRIS, Freddy H., PFC, USMC
HARRIS, John Lawrence, RM3c, USN
HARRIS, Tommie, MA2c, USN
HARRISS, Hugh Braddock, HA1c, USN
HARTSON, Lonnie Moss, SM3c, USNR
HARVEY, Eddie Louis, MA3c, USN
HARVEY, Harold Milburn, S1c, USN
HEATH, Francis C., PFC, USMC
HECKENDORN, Warren Guy, S1c, USN
HENDRIX, Walter Powell, Jr., S2c, USNR
HENSON, William Edward, Jr., S2c, USN
HERRIN, Billy Blythe, AMM2c, USN
HERRIOTT, Robert Asher, Jr., S1c, USN
HILL, Burton Adolphus, PFC, USMC
HILL, Ens. George Russell, Jr., USNR

HILTON, Lynn, AS, USNR
HODGES, Garris Vada, F2c, USN
HODNETT, R. J., S1c, USN
HOFFER, Robert Franklin, CBM, USNR
HOLLAND, Clayton Louis, Jr., PFC, USMC
HOOD, Lt. Clark Alexander, Jr., USN
HOOKS, William Mickins, SK2c, USNR
HORTON, William David, S1c, USN
HOWARD, James Kale, S2c, USNR
HOWARD, John Lynn, Carp., USN
HOWELL, Robert Lee, S1c, USN
HUNTER, Lt. (jg) John Charles, USN
HUVAL, Robert Anthony, Pvt., USMC
JACKSON, David Paul, Jr., S1c, USN
JAMES, John Burditt, S1c, USN
JENKINS, Robert Henry Dawson, S2c, USN
JINKS, Edgar Phelan, RM3c, USN
JOHNSON, Don Lee, PFC, USMC
JOHNSTON, Joe, Jr., Pvt., USMC
JOHNSTON, Valmer Clark, PFC, USMC
JONES, Sloan Joyce, Torp3c, USN
KAATZ, Albert Henry, S2c, USNR
KANE, Albert Utley, F1c, USN
KEITH, Ellis Judson, Jr., S2c, USNR
KELLEY, Ferris Elbern, Jr., RM3c, USN
KILSBY, Thomas Bryant, BM2c, USN
KING, John McElree, EM1c, USN
KING, Leander Cleaveland, S1c, USN
KITE, T. J., Corp., USMC
KOLAJAJCK, Brosig, S1c, USN
KRUPPA, Adolph Louis, S1c, USN
LAND, Harold Clifford, AS, USN
LEE, Carroll Volney, Jr., S1c, USN
LEGRANT, Charles Clinton, AS, USNR
LIGHTFOOT, Worth Ross, GM3c, USN
LINDSEY, Ens. Charles Vinson, USNR
LONG, Jack Bobbie, AMM2c, USN
LOWE, Robert S., S2c, USN
LYNCH, James Robert, GM3c, USN
LYNCH, Kenneth Lee, S2c, USN
LYNCH, William Joseph, Jr., S1c, USN
MANRY, Winston Taylor, S2c, USNR
MANSKER, Charles R., Pvt., USMCR
MARIS, Elwood Henry, S1c, USN
MARSHALL, James Kenneth, AMM1c, USN
MARSHALL, William Earl, Jr., S2c, USN
MARTIN, James Albert, BM1c, USN
MARTIN, John Timothy, Jr., AS, USNR
MASTERS, Dayton Monroe, GM3c, USN
MATNEY, Vernon Merferd, F1c, USN
McALISTER, Glenn Cruse, AS, USNR
McBRIDE, James Earnest, PFC, USMC
McCORMICK, Flake Vernon, AS, USNR

McDONALD, James Oliver, F1c, USN
McELROY, Rex Edgar, EM2c, USN
McKISSACK, Hale, S1c, USNR
McMEANS, Clyde Clifton, S1c, USN
MEANS, Louis, MA1c, USN
MEEKS, Joseph Sherman, AS, USN
MILLER, Franz la Verne, S1c, USN
MILLER, John David, S1c, USN
MILLIGAN, Weldon Harvey, S1c, USN
MINTER, James Dewey, S2c, USN
MONTGOMERY, Nathan, Jr., PFC, USMC
MOORE, Charles Lee, ARM3c, USN
MOORE, Fred Kenneth, S1c, USN
MOSLEY, Ens. Walter Harold, USNR
NEAL, Tom Dick, S1c, USN
OWEN, Fredrick Halden, S2c, USN
PACK, Leslie O., PFC, USMC
PADILLA, Joe, F1c, USCG
PARKER, Charles Darnell, S2c, USN
PATTERSON, Harold Lemuel, S1c, USN
PEARCE, Alonzo, Jr., S1c, USN
PIERCE, Sidney, RM3c, USN
PILGRAM, Walter Edward, CEM, USN
POPEJOY, Sim A., Field Mus.1c, USMC
PORCH, Troy Wayde, RM2c, USN
POWELL, William J., Corp., USMC
PUCKETT, Ray V., S/Sgt., USMC
PUE, Jasper Langley, Jr., F3c, USN
RAIMOND, Paul Smith, S1c, USN
REEVES, James Olen, S2c, USN
RENCH, Bernice Neal, S2c, USN
ROGERS, Joe B., EM2c, USN
ROSS, Joe Boyce, RM2c, USN
ROWELL, Frank Malcom, S2c, USN
RUSH, Richard Perry, S1c, USN
RUSSELL, Benjamin Nelson, AS, USN
SAHL, Glenn Dawain, F3c, USN
SAUNDERS, Charles Louis, S2c, USN
SAUNDERS, Sidney Melvin, AS, USN
SCHILLER, Ernest, AS, USN
SCHNEIDER, Albert Joseph, F1c, USN
SCHRANK, Harold Arthur, Bkr1c, USN
SCOTT, A. J., S2c, USN
SCOTT, Richard Elsworth, S1c, USN
SEELY, William Henry, EM3c, USN
SELF, Eugene Hal, Y3c, USNR
SENTER, Asa Bob, S2c, USN
SHAW, Robert K., Mus2c, USN
SHERRILL, Warren Joseph, Y2c, USN
SIKES, William Lee, Jr., F1c, USN
SILVEY, Jesse, MM2c, USN
SMALLWOOD, James Earl, S2c, USN
SMARTT, Ens. Joseph Gillespie, USNR
SMITH, Marvin Ray, S1c, USN
SMITH, Raymond Curtis, AM3c, USN
SMITH, William Lance, S2c, USN

SOLOMON, James Cleve, S1c, USN
SOOTER, James Frederick, RM3c, USN
SPAETH, Johnnie Herbert, S2c, USN
SPENCER, William Lee, MA1c, USN
SPILLERS, M. L., SC3c, USN
STALLCUP, Ens. Vance William, USNR
STEVENS, Jack Hazelip, S1c, USN
STEWART, Floyd D., PFC, USMC
STONE, David Griffith, ARM2c, USNR
STOVALL, Richard P., PFC, USMC
STRAUS, David H., Jr., SK2c, USNR
STRICKLAND, Perry William, S1c, USN
TENNELL, Raymond Clifford, S1c, USN
THERIAC, John Edward, F3c, USN
THOMAS, Houston O'Neal, Cox., USN
THOMSON, Richard Joseph, S2c, USN
TINER, Robert Reaves, F2c, USN
TULEY, Melvin O., Corp., USMC
TUMLINSON, Victor Pat, FC3c, USN
TYLER, Clarence Fredric, S1c, USN
UHLIG, Edward Bruno, S2c, USNR
VINSON, James, F3c, USN
WADE, George H., Jr., Pvt., USMC
WADLEY, Othello Fred Douglas, MA2c, USN
WALKER, Bill., S1c, USN
WALKER, Noel James, F1c, USN
WALTERS, Bethel Elbert, F1c, USN
WARNER, Joe Harvey, F1c, USN
WATTS, Victor Edward, GM3c, USN
WATKINS, Vernon Castle, SF2c, USN
WEBB, Carl E., PFC, USMC
WEDERBROOK, Roy A., PFC, USMC
WEIDEMEYER, Hal J., S1c, USN
WEST, George Willis, S1c, USN
WHITE, James Clifton, F1c, USN
WHITLOCK, Paul Morgan, S2c, USN
WIGAND, Eldridge, AS, USNR
WILKERSON, Claude Marion, SK3c, USN
WILSON, Milton Sloss, F3c, USN
WISE, Charles Ramsey, S1c, USN
WOOD, Horace Van, S1c, USN
WOOD, Lloyd Haven, B2c, USN
WOODS, Francis M., PFC, USMC
WOODS, Lawrence Eldon, F1c, USN

Wounded

ALDRIDGE, Howard, BM1c, USN
BEALE, Jerome Kearby, S2c, USN
BOARD, Woodrow Wilson, Pvt., USMC
BROWN, Frank Addison, CWT, USN
BRUMLEY, Edwin Jack, Cox., USN
CARPENTER, Herman Lansing, SC3c, USN
CARSON, Louis Edgar, GM3c, USN
CHILDS, Tilden Robert, SF1c, USN

COOK, Willie Edwin, S1c, USN
CURRY, Buford E., PFC, USMC
DALE, Tommie Jackson, PFC, USMC
DE PAUL, Vence, S1c, USN
FAULKNER, Charles Edwin, AS, USN
FINLEY, James Melvin, AS, USNR
FOMBY, Robert Emmett, SF3c, USN
FOWLER, Eugene, MA1c, USN
GOLEMON, Joseph T., PFC, USMC
GOTCHER, Estel Hendrix, F2c, USN
HARRISON, Alva Allen, Jr., S2c, USN
HIX, Ewing William, RM3c, USN
LACKEY, James Thomas, S2c, USNR
LAGESSE, Lewis Emil, S1c, USN
LOWE, John Edward, Jr., SK3c, USNR
LUTZ, Carrol Fredrick, S2c, USN
MAHONE, Maurice Flourney, S2c, USN
MARTIN, Lynn Clovis, S2c, USN
McCOOL, George Odell, S1c, USN
MILES, Wyatt Samuel, Jr., S1c, USN
MUCKLEROY, Robert Leon, S2c, USN
MUSICK, Clay Henry, S1c, USN
NICHOLSON, D. V., F1c, USN
O'SHAY, Donald Edward, WT1c, USN
POLK, William McAdoo, AMM2c, USN
RAMSEY, Charles Patrick, F2c, USN
REGER, James Edward, Jr., S1c, USN
ROBINSON, Jack Welton, FC2c, USN
ROBINSON, Richard Clemence, ARM1c, USN
ROGERS, Robert Edward, S2c, USN
ROMAGOSA, Garland Claude, S1c, USN
ROUNTREE, Joseph Carl, S2c, USN
SELLERS, Leslie Aubrey, SK2c, USN
SHENKIR, William Henry, SC3c, USN
SPRADLING, Douglas Reid, S2c, USN
STEWART, Carl Frank, S2c, USN
STRAIT, Ellis Duncan, S2c, USN
TACKETT, Samuel Freston, S3c, USN
TEER, Artie Loren, S2c, USN
WAINSCOTT, Robert Eugene, S2c, USN
WALTERS, Eugene Lloyd, S2c, USN
WAYLAND, James Weldon, EM1c, USN
WEBSTER, William P., Jr., PFC, USMCR
WHITAKER, Erby Lewis, FC2c, USN
ZOELLER, Frederick Louis, S1c, USN

Missing

ALLEN, Willie Louis, S1c, USN
ANDERSON, Carl Brown, WT2c, USN
ANDRUS, Horace Wilbern, MM1c, USN
AUSTIN, Roy Earl, S2c, USN
AYERS, Roy Lee, RM3c, USN
BAUMGARTEN, Howard Fritz, Torp3c, USN
BELCH, Thomas E., S/Sgt., USMC

BISHOP, Viva A., Corp., USMC
BLACK, Walden, Pvt., USMC
BOLTON, Vernon, SC2c, USN
BRADLEY, Leonard Earl, S2c, USN
BREEDING, David Henry, Jr., SC2c, USN
BRICKLEY, Eugene, Pvt., USMC
BRIDGES, James Roy, MM2, USN
BRYAN, Alexander Washington, S1c, USN
BURNS, James Leroy, MM2c, USN
BYRD, J. R., F1c, USN
CARUTHERS, Charles Hennen, S2c, USN
CASEY, Virgil Edward, F1c, USN
CHALKER, Joseph Charles, MM2c, USN
COMPTON, Hubert Ray, F3c, USN
DAVIS, George D., Pvt., USMC
DEAN, Benjamin J., Jr., PFC, USMC
DEBELL, Asa Wallingford, S2c, USN
DEEB, William, S2c, USN
DIETRICH, Bloomfield August, F2c, USN
DITTOE, Thomas Patrick, S2c, USN
DOTSON, Robert, F1c, USN
DUDLEY, Gary Lamar, Bug1c, USN
DUMAS, Roy Robert, S2c, USN
DUNNAM, Robert W., Pvt., USMCR
DUPLICHAIN, Eldridge Joseph, MM2c, USN
EDGE, John Wesley, F2c, USN
ENGELMAN, Carl William, S1c, USN
ENGLISH, Henry Anon, BM2c, USN
EVANS, Arnold Napoleon, F3c, USN
FIELDS, Earnest Lamoss, Cox., USN
FINCHER, Allen B., Asst. Cook, USMC
FRITZSCHING, Richard L., PFC, USMC
FROELICH, Raymond William, BM2c, USN
GARNER, Clifford Duncan, S1c, USN
GARRETT, William Everett, MM2c, USN
GAYLOR, Welch, Torp3c, USN
GENTRY, Stacy George, Jr., S1c, USN
GILL, George Clarence, SK1c, USN
GREER, Fred Wylie, AMM3c, USN
GRIFFIN, Everette Presley, CPhM, USN
GRIFFITH, Hubert Edwin, WT2c, USN
HALEY, Jack Colman, S2c, USN
HAM, John Harold, AM1c, USN
HARE, Robert John, CSK, USN
HARP, Frank Neal, S2c, USN
HARRELL, Dero H., Jr., PFC, USMC
HENDERSON, Buddy, Pvt., USMC
HENLEY, Doyle Franklin, SF3c, USN
HILGER, Lt. Ted Adair, USN
HOLLINGSWORTH, Leonard Nathaniel, WT3c, USN
HOPE, Harold W., Pvt., USMC
HOWARD, Fred Marshall, S1c, USN
HUDNALL, Robert C., PFC, USMC

HUDSON, William Lee, RM3c, USN
HUFF, Robert G., Pvt., USMC
HUGHES, Marvin A., Pvt., USMC
JARRELL, James Edgar, RM3c, USN
JARVIS, Charles Frank, F1c, USN
JOHNSTON, Lucius F., Jr., PFC, USMC
JOHNSTON, Phillip Raymond, CFC, USN
JONES, Morris Lamar, S1c, USN
JONES, Robert Jackson, S2c, USN
KEATON, Vernon P., Pvt., USMC
KEEN, Billy Mack, Pvt., USMC
KEITH, Lt. Cdr. Farrel Wilber, USNR
KENT, James L., Pvt., USMC
KEYES, Robert Carl, AS, USNR
KING, F. H., Pvt., USMC
KIRKPATRICK, William Adrian, SC3c, USN
LASS, Robert Merriett, S2c, USN
LAYNE, Guthrie Fitzhugh, Jr., S2c, USN
LEE, Jack F., Field Music, USMC
LEE, Presnell, Corp., USMC
LEE, Samuel Mason, Jr., S1c, USN
LEE, Wilson Pershing, MM1c, USN
LINNSTRAEDTER, Ben Zilmon, S1c, USN
LUSK, Joe M. T., Sgt., USMC
MASSENGALE, Ben Dotson, F3c, USN
MASSEY, Allen Otis, Cox., USN
MATHIS, Claud Allan, F2c, USN
MATTSON, Johnnie Ralph, CM2c, USN
MAULDIN, Woodrow Wilson, S1c, USN
MAY, Milton Robert, S1c, USN
McCORMACK, William N., PFC, USMC
McCRARY, Kenneth, AMM3c, USN
McFARLAND, Thomas J., Pvt., USMC
McKENZIE, Cletius Julius, S2c, USN
MOORE, Howard Lewis, MM2c, USN
MORGAN, G. P., F2c, USN
MORRIS, Marvin D., PFC, USMC
OLSEN, James Lee Arthur, F1c, USN
OWEN, Gerald Neal, S2c, USN
PALMER, Robert Lewis, S2c, USN
PARKER, Louis Newman, CBM, USN
PECENA, Thomas Frank, RM3c, USN
PENNINGER, William Robert, S2c, USN
PETTIT, William Robert, PFC, USMC
POOL, Grover W., Pvt., USMC
PRYOR, Charley L., Jr., Sgt., USMC
RADNEY, William Doyle, F2c, USN
RANEY, Doc Bradford, Jr., S1c, USN
REESE, Sheldon Dortez, S1c, USN
RICHTER, Paul Richard, Jr., EM2c, USN
ROBINSON, Louis M., S1c, USN
RODGERS, Louis, S2c, USN
RUSHING, Robert C., S2c, USN
RUSSELL, Milton Bland, S2c, USN

SANDERLIN, Robert Benjamin, RM2c, USN
SAWYER, Charles, S1c, USN
SCOTT, DeWitt Talmadge, Jr., S1c, USN
SISK, Joe Sam, S2c, USN
SITTON, Troy Lee, F2c, USN
SKILLEN, Donald Douglass, S1c, USN
SLONE, Emory Dale, SK2c, USN
SMITH, Horace Porter, Jr., FC3c, USN
SMITH, Sammie David, SK2c, USN
SPRAYBERRY, James Gregory, SC3c, USN
STAFFORD, William Francis, S1c, USN
STEPHENS, George Loudolphus, F3c, USN
STEVENS, Errol Francis, S2c, USN
STEVENS, William Wright, Jr., EM2c, USN
STONECIPHER, Vernon Harold, SK3c, USN
STUBBLEFIELD, Claude, CWT, USN
TAYLOR, Cecil Luther, S1c, USN
TEDFORD, Clois Winford, GM2c, USN
THEDFORD, Edwin Henly, S2c, USN
TIMMONS, Frank Lee, CGM, USN
TOONE, Jack Dale, QM2c, USN
TYRE, Arlie Winston, F2c, USN
VAN DYKES, Birdine, FC3c, USN
VAUGHN, James Harold, Jr., F2c, USN
VORPAHL, Lt. Arthur Henry, USN
WEAVER, Charles Turner, EM2c, USN
WEISSINGER, William J., Jr., S1c, USN
WESTFALL, Billy Louis, S1c, USN
WEYL, Joe Warren, S2c, USN
WHITELEY, John W., PFC, USMC
WILEY, George Marcus, Jr., MM1c, USN
WILLENBERG, Walter Oscar, S1c, USN
WILLIAMS, Alfred Truman, CTC, USN
WILLIAMS, Arlie, S1c, USN
WILLIAMS, Benjamin M., PFC, USMC
WILLIAMS, Isaac Clarence, Jr., Pvt., USMC
WILLIAMS, John Marshall, S2c, USN
WILSON, Noah Jacob Andrew, Jr., S2c, USN
WRIGHT, Sidney T., Pvt., USMC
WYATT, Wilson, SK3c, USN

Prisoners of War

ABBOTT, Samuel Woodrow, SK2c, USN
ADAMS, John Markham, AMM3c, USN
ALLEN, Arthur Larry, Corp., USMC
ALLEN, Billy Wandall, Corp., USMC
ALLEN, David Martin, GM3c, USN
ALLEN, Walter Carlton, PFC, USMC
ALLENDER, Thomas Baldwin, PFC, USMC

ANDERSON, Jimmie B., Asst. Cook, USMC
ARMSTRONG, Wade Hampton, Jr., PFC, USMC
ARNEY, Billy J., Pvt., USMC
ARNEY, Travis Bee, Pvt., USMC
AUTREY, James Gilbert, S2c, USN
AWALT, George Thomas, Jr., PFC, USMC
AWALT, Sidney Owen, BM1c, USN
BABB, James Woodrow, PFC, USMC
BACK, Col Adison, Jr., SF3c, USN
BACON, Bobby T., PFC, USMC
BAGLEY, James Monroe, Pvt., USMC
BAGWELL, Woodrow Lattin, PFC, USMC
BAILEY, Melvin D., PFC, USMC
BAILEY, William W., PFC, USMC
BAKER, S. L., PFC, USMC
BAREFIELD, Samuel Thomas, PFC, USMC
BARKER, Russell Pershing, PFC, USMC
BARNES, Ray Hershel, PFC, USMC
BARNETT, Ira Ray, PFC, USMC
BARRETT, John William, Jr., F1c, USN
BEDFORD, Windell J., S1c, USN
BENTON, Willie Lee, PFC, USMC
BICKLEY, Robert Gray, SC3c, USN
BIDDY, Floyd Acy, PFC, USMC
BILBO, Harry Arnold, WT2c, USN
BLAHUTA, Alvin Henry, Corp., USMC
BLANCETT, Jesse Ralph, PhM3c, USN
BORISKIE, Robert Oliver, Y2c, USN
BOSHER, Raymond Richard, Corp., USMC
BRECKENRIDGE, Albert Harold, PFC, USMC
BRITAIN, Mark Floyd, BM1c, USN
BROWN, Capt. Paul A., USMCR
BROWN, Roy T., PFC, USMC
BROWN, Sharkey, CWT, USN
BRUMLEY, James Richard, Torp2c, USN
BUCHANAN, Knox A., Bkr2c, USN
BUKOWSKY, Emil G., Pvt., USMC
BULLARD, Delmar Albert, S1c, USN
BURGE, Jack Orman, MM2c, USN
BYRD, Harry Joseph, PFC, USMC
CALDWELL, Sammy Lee, Pvt., USMC
CALLAHAN, Melvin Carl, S1c, USN
CALVIN, Taylor Pershing, PFC, USMC
CANTRELL, James Albert, S2c, USN
CARROLL, Charles Edward, S2c, USN
CARUTHERS, Arvon Ewing, GM2c, USN
CASTLETON, John Vallie, PhM1c, USN
CHIPMAN, Marvin Lee, F1c, USN
CLARK, Emery Thomas, Pvt., USMC
CLARK, Maj. Max, USMCR
CLEBASKI, Leon Adam, PFC, USMCR

CLEM, Onnie Ellsworth, Jr., Corp., USMC
COLEY, Robert Lee, S/Sgt., USMC
COLVIN, Joe Leonard, PFC, USMC
CONDER, Archie Wesley, PFC, USMC
CONDRA, Charley Henry, Chief Cook, USMC
CONNELL, Arthur L., S1c, USN
CRAIG, Kermit Elmer, Corp., USMC
CRAWFORD, Boyd William, Pvt., USMC
CRAY, Hampton R., Jr., Pvt., USMCR
CREWS, T. G., Corp., USMC
CROSS, Charles G., PFC, USMC
CULP, Joseph Cicro, PFC, USMC
CURLEE, Albert Coleman, PFC, USMC
DAVIS, Avril James, S1c, USN
DAVIS, Hillman Albert, PFC, USMC
DAVIS, Houston L., Platoon Sgt., USMC
DAVIS, Thomas Allen, PhM1c, USN
DEDMON, Theodore Roosevelt, Corp., USMC
DEEDES, Robert Leon, PFC, USMC
DEFIBAUGH, George Lexington, F3c, USN
DIXON, Floyd Alton, S2c, USN
DORMAN, Roger, Pvt., USMC
DOWNING, Carl E., Corp., USMC
DRURY, John Lanoid, GM1c, USN
DUNN, Aubrey C., Y2c, USN
ELAM, Richard Wade, S2c, USN
ERLER, Otto Charles, Jr., PFC, USMC
FERRELL, Harold Marion, Marine Gunner, USMC
FITZGERALD, James Russell, F2c, USN
FLIPPEN, Melton C., Jr., PFC, USMC
FLYNN, Jack Burton, BM1c, USN
FOURNET, George Joseph, Jr., S2c, USN
FRASIER, James Henry, Jr., Pvt., USMC
FREDERICK, Revice Noble, Field Music, USMC
GANDY, M. Z., Jr., SM1c, USN
GANN, Carl Burke, EM2c, USN
GARRISON, John Brackenridge, PFC, USMC
GARZA, Frederick, S1c, USN
GATEWOOD, Martin Alna, PFC, USMC
GEAR, Joe Bailey, S1c, USN
GEE, James W., PFC, USMC
GEORGE, John F., PFC, USMC
GEORGE, Pete, PFC, USMC
GILLESPIE, Bill Edmond, S2c, USN
GLEESON, Pleas, Pvt., USMC
GLENEWINKEL, Elmer Paul, PFC, USMC
GLOVER, Herbert Preston, PhM3c, USN
GOETZ, Howard Clarence, PhM1c, USN

GOLDMAN, Luther Earl, PFC, USMC
GRAGG, Dellerd Kester, RM3c, USN
GRAVES, Elmo Elsey, Corp., USMC
GRAY, Martin Lewis, Field Mus., Corp., USMC
GRIFFIN, Mark James, Cox., USN
GUESS, Odell Clifford, S1c, USN
HAGOOD, Fletcher Marvin, Corp., USMC
HALBROOK, Alton, PFC, USMC
HALL, Alton Henry, EM2c, USN
HAMBY, Thornton Estill, Pvt., USMC
HAMILTON, Lt. Col. George Durell, USMC
HARBISON, Leonard Sam., PFC, USMC
HARKINS, John Owen, Pvt., USMC
HARRELL, Claude H., Sgt., USMC
HARRINGER, Ewald, Jr., PFC, USMC
HARROD, Reid Donald, PhM1c, USN
HATFIELD, Bazil Muse, Jr., Torp1c, USN
HAWKINS, 1st Lt. Jack, USMC
HAYNES, Stephen Samuel, PFC, USMC
HEARN, Jack Doyle, PFC, USMC
HEIMS, William Arnold, PhM3c, USN
HENDERSON, Henry Clay, CMM, USN
HENDERSON, James Cullens, Corp., USMC
HENDERSON, Roy L., PFC, USMC
HINES, Gerald Woodie, Bug1c, USN
HINKLE, James Edwyn, PFC, USMC
HOFFSETZ, Robert Faye, SK2c, USN
HOLMES, Charles Ardon, S/Sgt., USMC
HOLT, Elmer Clearance, AMM1c, USN
HOLT, Johnson Porter, PFC, USMC
HOOTEN, Aubrey Lee, Corp., USMC
HOOTEN, James Herron, S2c, USN
HOOTEN, William Thomas, III, S1c, USN
HORNSBY, Jack Clay, PFC, USMC
HOUSE, Joy Albert, Cox., USN
HOWTON, John Isaac, Cox., USN
HUCKABAY, Uri L., Jr., Corp., USMC
HUFSTUTLER, Raymond Anderson, Corp., USMC
HURTA, Oscar Milburn, PFC, USMC
IVY, Jon Ted, S1c, USN
JACKSON, Chester S., PFC, USMC
JAY, John Patrick, PhM3c, USN
JENKINS, Haley B., Pvt., USMC
JOHANSON, Willie, PFC, USMC
JOHNSON, Solon Lamar, PFC, USMC
JOHNSTON, Lillard Louis, Jr., Corp., USMC
JOYNER, Alvin Durwood, Corp., USMC
JOYNER, Paul Clifton, PFC, USMC
KAHN, Lt. (jg) Gustav M., USNR
KALINOWSKI, Robert John, F3c, USN
KENNEDY, Albert Elmo, F1c, USN

KENNEY, James, BM2c, USN
KIDD, Darwin Frost, S2c, USN
KILLIAN, Charles Henry, BM2c, USN
KING, Earl, S1c., USN
KIRKLEN, Charles Alton, PFC, USMC
KOEHLER, Linroy, PFC, USMC
KROESEN, Paul Bernard, PFC, USMCR
LA GRONE, Harry John, Pvt., USMC
LANGLEY, Edgar Nelson, PFC, USMC
LATHAM, Joe Teague, PFC, USMC
LEWIS, Cecil Walter, Pvt., USMC
LIGON, Lane Everett, Pvt., USMC
LIPPARD, John Bryan, PFC, USMC
LONG, Joseph Wilson, AOM2c, USN
LOWERY, John Clark, Y2c, USN
MARTIN, Robert Irvin, S1c, USN
MAXWELL, James Perry, Jr., Corp., USMC
McBRAYER, 2nd Lt. James David., Jr., USMC
McCLANAHAN, Wilbur Clyde, PFC, USMC
McCOY, Marvin Marshall, PFC, USMC
McNALLY, Theodore, CMM, USN
McWILLIAMS, Howard Weldon, RM1c, USN
MELTON, Kenneth Linon, PFC, USMC
MILES, Walter J., PFC, USMC
MILLER, Albert Ray, Pvt., USMC
MILLER, Arthur, AM1c, USN
MILLER, Hershal Lopez, Corp., USMC
MILLER, Roy Waltman, PFC, USMC
MILLER, William Floyd, Y3c, USN
MILLIGAN, Howard Lee, PFC, USMC
MITCHUM, Winfred Allan, CY, USN
MONK, Matthew David, PFC, USMC
MOON, Harley Russel, S1c, USN
MOORE, Elvis Richard Lee, Corp., USMC
MORGAN, Jack Barksdale, PFC, USMC
MORRIS, E. C., PFC, USMC
MURPHY, John W., Jr., F1c, USN
MURRAY, Sylvester Elmo, PFC, USMC
MUSICK, Lawson Arnold, PFC, USMC
MYERS, Alfred Franklin, Pvt., USMC
NALLS, Nathan Cass, Jr., PhM1c, USN
NEAL, Gayle, Pvt., USMC
NEITSCH, Alfred Raymond, MM2c, USN
NELSON, Ens. John Blount, USN
NEUSE, Max Henry, PFC, USMC
NEWMAN, Junior Howard, PFC, USMC
NIXON, David, Jr., S2c, USN
NORTHAM, Douglas, S2c, USN
NOWLIN, Jessie Elmer, PFC, USMC
O'BRIEN, Johnny F., Pvt., USMCR
OSBORNE, J. D., SM2c, USN
PAGE, Bert E., Jr., Pvt., USMC

PAINE, Robert, Jr., CGM, USN
PARHAM, Thomas Eugene, S1c, USN
PATTERSON, Charles E., Field Mus., Corp., USMC
PATTERSON, George Scott, S2c, USN
PATTERSON, Woodrow David., EM1c, USN
PERMENTER, Calvin Lafayette, PFC, USMC
PHIPPS, Ralph Edward, PFC, USMC
PISTOLE, Erwin D., PFC, USMC
PITNER, John Dee, Corp., USMC
PITTS, Bernie B., Jr., Field Mus. Corp., USMC
POGUE, Bill Barton, Pvt., USMC
PRUETT, Johnnie Martin, PFC, USMC
PUCKETT, Vernon Fate, CMM, USN
PYE, Guy Edgar, GM3c, USN
RAY, Daniel Woodrow, PFC, USMC
REDDICK, Clifford Arthur, PFC, USMC
REED, Billy Gillette, PFC, USMC
RICHARDSON, J. W., Corp., USMC
ROBERSON, Felix M., Jr., Corp., USMC
ROBERTS, James E., Pvt., USMC
ROBERTS, Valdon Stephen, F2c, USN
ROBERTSON, Ted J. D., Cox., USN
ROBINSON, Albert J., PFC, USMC
ROBINSON, Francis Edward, PFC, USMC
ROBINSON, Marvin E., Pvt., USMCR
RODRIGUEZ, Fernando Cantu, PFC, USMC
ROOK, Edward Baron, Sgt., USMC
ROSE, Lewis Oran, Corp., USMC
ROSIER, Warren W., CEM, USN
SANDERS, Jacob Rex, PFC, USMC
SANDERS, Lawrence Wayne, PFC, USMC
SAPP, Charles Walter, Pvt., USMC
SAUTTER, Albert G., PFC, USMC
SCOTT, Irvin C., Jr., PFC, USMC
SCRUGGS, Lloyd, PFC, USMC
SEAGRAVES, Raymond Lewis, PFC, USMC
SENTER, Claude Davis, S2c, USN
SIEGER, Norman Patrick, Corp., USMC
SIMMONS, Dorris Pickett, CPhM, USN
SINDERS, John Walter, Corp., USMC
SLOMAN, Wiley Winfield, PFC, USMC
SMITH, Jack Dale, S1c, USN
SMITH, Rufus W., PFC, USMC
SOBEY, William Henry, Sgt., USMC
SOCKWELL, Wesley Hammack, F2c, USN
SPARKMAN, Orville Reid, PFC, USMC
SPARKS, Raymond Thomas, Tech. Sgt., USMC
SPURLOCK, Gid Howard, Jr., S1c, USN

STANDEFER, John Young, PhM3c, USN
STEWARD, Lt. Cdr. Jerry Alexander, USNR
STINSON, John Reynolds, F2c, USN
SUBLETT, Henry W., Pvt., USMCR
SWEATMAN, Charlie Calvin, PFC, USMC
SWOR, Sam Roscoe, Corp., USMC
THOMASON, R. B., CPhM, USN
THOMPSON, Clarence A., Corp., USMC
THOMPSON, Jack Edward, PFC, USMC
TRICE, Ernest M., Pvt., USMC
USHER, Rexford Deming, S2c, USN
VARDEMAN, William H., Pvt., USMC
VENABLE, James Cameron, PFC, USMC
WADE, Q. T., Sgt., USMC
WALDRUM, Everett R., PFC, USMC

WASHBURN, Claude William, Jr., S1c, USN
WATSON, Richard J., Pvt., USMC
WEAVER, James Walter, PFC, USMC
WELCH, Robert Harold, Cox., USN
WHITE, Clyde, Jr., AS, USN
WHITWORTH, Laurel Woodrow, SC1c, USN
WICKHAM, John Edwin, PFC, USMC
WILKERSON, Melvin Cecil, S1c, USN
WILLIAMS, Henry Belmont, PhM3c, USN
WILLIAMS, John B., PFC, USMC
WILSON, James Clark, PFC, USMC
WISKOCHIL, Robert Irving, PFC, USMC
WYNN, Marvin Anglous, S1c, USN
YARBRO, Robert Lee, GM1c, USN

UTAH

Dead

ANDERSEN, Randers Hassa, CBM, USN
ANDERSON, Venoy Merrill, AS, USNR
ARCHIBALD, Edmund Wayne, S2c, USN
BENNION, Capt. Mervyn Sharp, USN
BRAZIER, Robert Boyd, ARM2c, USN
CARDY, Louis Ray, S2c, USNR
CRACRAFT, Arthur Levi, FC3c, USN
CRUZAN, James Franklin, Jr., MM2c, USN
DEAN, William Robert, QM3c, USN
DONOHUE, Ned Burton, F1c, USN
GARGARO, Ernest Russell, S2c, USN
HANSEN, Carlyle B., MM2c, USN
HESS, Darrel Miller, FC1c, USN
JENSEN, Keith Marlow, EM3c, USN
JENSEN, Theodore Que, RM3c, USN
LARSEN, Elliott Deen, Mus1c, USN
MARINICH, Steve Matt, Cox., USN
MARTIN, Hugh Lee, Y3c, USN
MERRILL, Ens. Howard Deal, USN
MITCHELL, Harold, F2c, USN
NELSON, Harry William, Jr., ARM1c, USN
NIELSEN, Floyd Theadore, CM3c, USN
PIERCE, Eldon F., Pvt., USMCR
REID, William Henry, F1c, USN
STEELE, Earl William, S2c, USN
SUTTON, Mack P., Corp., USMC
WALTON, Alva Dowding, Y3c, USN
WHITE, Charles William, Mus2c, USN
WILSON, Ens. John Woodrow, USNR
YOUNG, Jay Wesley, S1c, USN

Wounded

GAISFORD, Robert Kenneth, SK3c, USN
HANSEN, Keith, S1c, USN

HOLT, William Clark, Jr., S1c, USNR
PYPER, Joseph D., Jr., PFC, USMC

Missing

ALLRED, Max Joseph, SM2c, USN
CROSLEY, Verlin James, WT2c, USN
DICKINSON, Ordell, S2c, USN
FITZGERALD, Kent B., Pvt., USMC
FROST, Wilson Lester, Cox., USN
GIBSON, James Elwood, S2c, USN
HALL, Raymond Frank, HA2c, USN
HOLMES, Robert K., PFC, USMC
JONES, Ernest Arthur, MM1c, USN
McLEAN, Robert Wallace, Bkr2c, USN
McMULLIN, Mark Douglas, S1c, USN
NICHOLL, Joseph Junior, WT2c, USN
NIELSEN, Lester Russel, MM2c, USN
NORDSTROM, Layne, PFC, USMC
OSBORNE, Robert Willis, S1c, USN
PATTEN, Kenneth Bingham, S1c, USN
REINHOLD, Rudolph H., Pvt., USMC
SNYDER, Samuel Elmer, S1c, USN
SPILLMAN, Andrew John, GM3c, USN
STEWART, William Nielsen, Torp1c, USN
STOKER, Floyd Earl, EM3c, USN
STREET, Raymond Alford, CY, USN
TANNER, Wilford Richards, CWT, USN
VIRCHOW, Harry Huzen, GM3c, USN
WEST, Max Leroy, SC1c, USN
WITTKE, Donald Eldon, PFC, USMC

Prisoners of War

BARGER, Lester LeRoy, PFC, USMC
BARTA, Fern Joseph, RM2c, USN
CHEW, Hoyle E., PFC, USMC

CHRISTIANSEN, Lorraine, NC, USN
CHURCH, Ray Howard, PFC, USMC
CRAVEN, Jerry Albert, RM2c, USN
DANA, Max, Jr., PFC, USMC
DAVIS, Rex V., Field Cook, USMC
DRAPER, John William, PFC, USMC
FRANDSEN, Andrew Jay, PFC, USMC
HALE, Edward Everett, EM2c, USN
HAMEL, Fred Mack, Pvt., USMC
HAWKES, Warren Karl, F2c, USN
HEPWORTH, Joseph Mabey, Y2c, USN
HOCK, Peter Nicholas, RM1c, USN
JONES, Paul Robert, Pvt., USMC

MANNING, Don Knighton, Asst. Cook, USMC
NEWTON, 1st Lt. George R., USMC
PRATT, Alma Glenn, S1c, USN
SEEWER, Glen R., Pvt., USMC
SHEATS, Robert Carlton, Torp1c, USN
SHEYA, Melvin, PEC, USMC
SLATER, Floyd Lester, Cox., USN
SMITH, Jay Durfey, Pvt., USMC
STOCKS, Artie James, PFC, USMC
STODDARD, George DeWitt, S1c, USN
WALLACE, Howard Earl, Corp., USMC
WEBBER, Edward Clarence, CEM, USN

VERMONT

Dead

ALLEN, Lt. (jg) Eric, Jr., USN
ANDREWS, Brainerd Wells, CCM, USN
BEAN, Donald Ralph, F1c, USN
BROPHY, Myron Alonzo, F2c, USN
CAPISTRAND, Kenneth Joseph, Y3c, USN
CONANT, Samuel Kenyon, AMM1c, USN
EDWARDS, John Owen, ARM2c, USN
FOURNIER, Bernard Peter, CRM, USN
PERRIER, Leo Paul, AS, USN
SMITH, Ens. Norman Carl, USN
WISELL, Stanley F., PFC, USMC

Wounded

BESSETTE, Chester Leon, CCstd, USN
CHURCHILL, Winston Maro, S1c, USN

Missing

LAMPHERE, Fayette Anthony, S1c, USN
MANSFIELD, Tracy Henry, S1c, USN
SHARROW, Robert James, S1c, USN
TARQUINIO, Coffredo, SM2c, USN

Prisoners of War

ECONOMOU, Michael Nicholas, Corp., USMC
LIETZ, Theodore Comerford, Y1c, USN
NEWELL, Lt. (jg) Fred Rising, Jr., USN
ORTH, Eugene, PhM2c, USN
REILLY, Walter James, Sgt., USMC
TAYLOR, George Arthur, RM1c, USN
VON DETTE, Robert Francis, S2c, USN

VIRGINIA

Dead

ANDERSON, Irwin Corinthias, MA1c, USN
ANTHONY, Everette Vincent, AS, USNR
BATES, Ens. Clayton Elmer, USNR
BOOTH, Julian Callaway, F3c, USCG
BOSTON, Victor Reid, S2c, USN
BOYD, Sherman Taft, WT1c, USN
BREWER, Randall Walter, MA1c, USN
BRISTOW, Howard Earl, CQM, USN
BROWN, Benjamin Lee, S2c, USN
BROWN, Charles James, AS, USNR
BRYANT, Raymond Willard, S2c, USN
BUNCH, Kenneth Cecil, ARM1c, USN
BURTON, John Garland, S1c, USNR
CAHALAN, Frank Ray, CCStd, USN
CARPENTER, Robert Nelson, MA1c, USN
CASEY, Robert Lee, S2c, USN

CELIS, Lyle Francis, F3c, USN
CLARK, Ens. Louis Crawford, USNR
CLOUGH, Richard Kenneth, MM2c, USN
CREASY, Otway David, Jr., ARM3c, USNR
CUSHMAN, Ens. John Herbert, USNR
DAVIS, Lt. (jg) Joel Archibald, Jr., USN
DAVIS, Marvin Burton, CWT, USN
DAVIS, William Pink, WT2c, USN
DICKERSON, Lacy Lee, Jr., S1c, USN
DRUMMOND, Bowdoin Mears, Cox., USNR
ELLIOTT, Roland Charles, QM3c, USN
ELLISON, Ens. Harold John, USNR
EWING, Alex Alexander, CM, USN
FIDLER, Charles William, CMM, USN
FISHER, James Anderson, MA1c, USN
FLETCHER, Charles Herbert, S1c, USCG

Foresman, Edward V., Sgt., USMC
Freeman, William Raymond, Jr., AS, USNR
French, Harold Dolphin, CQM, USN
Gault, Duke Davis, CMM, USN
Goodwin, Charles Woodrow, AS, USNR
Goolsby, Rawley M., Jr., Pvt., USMC
Hankinson, Delray Miller, CCstd, USN
Harris, Carson Moss, AS, USN
Harris, David Woodson, Torp2c, USN
Harris, Thomas Cecil, Jr., AS, USNR
Henderson, Gilbert Allen, MA2c, USN
Hendricks, James H., S/Sgt., USMC
Herold, Andrew Clyde, Jr., SK2c, USN
Hildebrand, John Arthur, Jr., F1c, USN
Hladilek, Charles Andrew, ARM1c, USN
Holzhauer, James William, S1c, USN
Hubbard, Haywood, Jr., MA2c, USN
Hutchison, Edward Jennings, Jr., S1c, USN
Ingersoll, Lt. Royal Rodney, USN
Jones, Melvin Lafayette, S2c, USN
Johnson, David Andrew, Jr., OC2c, USN
Julian, Herbert, APho1c, USN
Kanach, Charles Edward, CMM, USNR
Kauffman, John W., Jr., PFC, USMC
Knox, Ens. Leslie Lockhart Bruce, USNR
Lane, Elmer Vernon, SC2c, USN
Langston, Henry Garett, OS3c, USN
Lanning, Roland Ross, PhM2c, USN
Lentsch, William Joseph, B2c, USN
Letterman, Charlie Alford, CWT, USN
Liebra, Otto, CMM, USCG
Little, James Norman, Ptr1c, USNR
Littlefield, Harold Francis, ARM2c, USN
Mabine, Octavius, MA1c, USN
Major, Ens. Charles Nance, USNR
Mantel, Julius Arthur, Prtr1c, USN
Marks, George Andrew, BM1c, USN
Martin, James Wilton, AMM2c, USN
McCord, Langford Scott, S1c, USN
Miles, Robert Bruce, AMM1c, USN
Miles, Samuel Willard, F3c, USN
Miller, James Marshall, CWT, USN
Moore, Lt. Raymond Austin, USN
Morgan, Thomas Gale, CWT, USN
Morse, Norman Roi, WT2c, USN
Morton, Lt. (jg) Harry Sankey, USNR
Musselwhite, Edwood F., AS, USCG
Ogden, William Stephen, MM2c, USN
O'Neal, Charles Bertram, CMM, USN
Palumbo, Patrick Nick, S2c, USN
Pamperin, Robert Walter, SF2c, USN

Parks, Maj. Floyd B., USMC
Peterson, Harvey, AMM1c, USN
Pitt, Guyler Storm, SC2c, USN
Pitts, Joseph Lennon, Jr., F1c, USN
Raines, Horace Franklin, SM1c, USNFR
Reynolds, George W., CMM, USCG
Ricketts, Lt. Milton Ernest, USN
Robertson, Edgar, Jr., MA3c, USN
Romano, Simon, OC1c, USN
Royals, William Nicholas, F1c, USN
Scott, Bernard Oliver, MA1c, USN
Self, George Luther, S2c, USNR
Sieck, Lt. (jg) Ludwig V. T., USCG
Skidmore, Lt. (jg) Chester Hugh, II, USN
Sligh, Thomas Edward, S2c, USN
Smith, Donald Blake, RM1c, USN
Smith, George Blane, GM1c, USN
Snow, William Kelly, CWT, USN
Talbott, Alvin Thornton, S2c, USNR
Taylor, Donald Charles, CM1c, USN
Thomas, Charles Robert, OC3c, USN
Thomason, Matthew Louis, GM3c, USN
Thornton, Edward Douglas, MA3c, USNR
Twillie, Clarence Alton, FC3c, USN
Venable, Hoge Cralle, Jr., SK2c, USN
Waldron, Lt. Cdr. John Charles, USN
Walker, David, MA3c, USN
Wells, Cleo, AMM1c, USN
Williams, George Washington, S1c, USN
Williams, Wilbur Slade, OS3c, USN
Wingfield, Ens. John David, USNR
Wyatt, Ens. Clifton Fontaine, Jr., USNR
Yackee, Raymond Francis, CM2c, USN

Wounded

Bowlin, James Franklin, S2c, USN
Bradford, Gordon F., S1c, USCG
Damron, Harry Woodrow, PM1c, USN
Dominici, Lewis Richard, SF3c, USN
Ford, John A., Jr., S1c, USCG
Helm, Thomas William, III, RM1c, USN
Johnson, Leon Earl, F2c, USN
Moore, Grover Cleveland, Jr., S1c, USN
Robinson, Bertram Monroe, AOM2c, USN
Taussig, Ens. Joseph Knefler, Jr., USN
Zahradka, Joseph, Jr., EM3c, USN

Missing

Albertson, Wallace Marshall, EM3c, USN
Amory, Sidney Griffith, F2c, USN
Ayers, Ray Charley, CQM, USN

BARLOW, Joseph Eddie, F2c, USN
BRIZENDINE, David Steve, Cox., USN
CASERIO, Ebo Raymond, CMM, USN
CASH, James Ludwell, S1c, USN
CASON, Ralph Hamon, AOM2c, USN
COMER, Joseph Guy, CEM, USN
GARDNER, Howard Nathaniel, EM1c, USN
GAY, William Burton, MM1c, USN
GILMORE, Charles Campbell, CRM, USNR
HARRIS, 1st Lt. William F., USMC
HASKINS, Cecil William, S2c, USN
HAYES, Cdr. Thomas Hirst, (MC), USN
HOLLOWELL, Cdr. John Ambrose, Jr., USN
HUGHES, John F., Jr., Platoon Sgt., USMC
HURRELL, Leslie Taylor, AM2c, USN
HURT, Lt. Cdr. David Albert, USN
JACKSON, John Clifford, BM2c, USN
LANIER, Julian, MM2c, USN
LINDSAY, Emmitt Warren, S1c, USN
MASSEY, Andrew Jackson, F2c, USN
MILES, Lt. Lion Tyler, USN
MYERS, Sidney Franklin, 1st Mus., USN
NEWSOME, Albert Kenneth, CMM, USN
SHARP, James Henry, S1c, USN
SIMPSON, Samuel Ford, Torp1c, USN
SMITH, William Stanley, S1c, USN
SPRAGUE, Robert Messinger, CMM, USN
TATE, John Abner, Jr., F2c, USN
TAYLOR, James Franklin, AM3c, USN
TAYLOR, James Underhill, Cox., USN
THOMPSON, James Francis, ARM3c, USN
TUGGLE, John Lincoln, MM1c, USN
VOLK, Russel James, FC2c, USN
WIDDIFIELD, James Thomas, F1c, USN
WILMOTH, Johnnie Richard, Jr., FC2c, USN
ZINI, Andrew Linn, CMM, USN

Prisoners of War

AKERS, Irving Nile, PFC, USMC
BAKER, Dousey E., Sgt., USMC
BATCHELOR, William Charles, S1c, USN
BEACH, Joseph Evan, RM2c, USN
BEGALA, June B., Platoon Sgt., USMC
BLEVINS, George Junior, S1c, USN
BRADLEY, Maj. James V., Jr., USMC
BUNCH, Jerry Judson, RM1c, USN
BURKHOLDER, Arthur Watson, Jr., SK2c, USN
CALLAHAN, Samuel Sanders, AMM3c, USN

CASTEEL, Lacy Love, CPhM, USN
COE, John O., 1st Sgt., USMC
DIXON, George Raby, PhM1c, USN
DOWDY, Charlie Windfred, S1c, USN
DUNN, Carl Rhea, MM2c, USN
DUNN, Glenn Gillespie, F1c, USN
EDWARDS, Karl Winfred, CRM, USN
ENOS, Lawrence, CMM, USN
ERCANBEACK, Earl Benson, 1st Sgt., USMC
FANTONE, 1st Lt. John S., USMC
FOWLKES, Hubert Arthur, ACM, USN
GALE, Thomas Oakley, EM3c, USN
GOLDEN, Lt. (jg) Francis Xavier Philip, USNR
GOODWIN, William Rufus, HA1c, USN
HALL, Ens. Stuart Hopkins, USNR
HAMPTON, Rupert Lee, MM2c, USN
HAVILAND, Lt. James William, III, USN
HYLTON, Isaac George, Cox., USN
JACKSON, Frederick Lawrence, Chief Torp, USN
JOHNSON, Robert Edward, CBM, USN
KAHL, William Albert, Sgt., USMC
KEETON, Charles W., Supply Sgt., USMC
KING, Maj. Stuart Waller, USMC
KNIGHT, Lyle Gray, GM2c, USN
LEE, William A., Chief Marine Gunner, USMC
LEWIS, 1st Lt. William Wallis, USMC
MANNEY, William L., PFC, USMC
MERRITT, Henry Hugh, Jr., Torp3c, USN
MILLER, Brooks, Corp., USMC
MONTGOMERY, Talton B., PFC, USMC
NESTOR, Lt. John Louis, USN
ODOM, Harry Edward, RM3c, USN
ODUY, Jessie Lee, S2c, USN
PAYNE, Lt. Thomas Benjamin, USN
RHODES, Herman Edgar, SK1c, USN
RICE, William Edward, PhM1c, USN
RIDGELY, Maj. Reginald H., Jr., USMC
ROCHER, Jack Jerome, F1c, USN
ROGERS, Ernest George, S/Sgt., USMC
SCHAEFFER, Maj. Max William, USMC
SHEPHERD, William Frederick, CSK, USN
SIMPSON, 1st Lt. Carter B., USMC
SMITH, Lt. Alfred Littlefield, (MC), USN
STALEY, Darrell S., 1st Sgt., USMC
TAYLOR, Clarence Mariet, Boat., USN
TOWNSEND, Paul Derrickson, QM3c, USN
TURNER, James LeRoy, Aer2c, USN
VAIDEN, William S., Platoon Sgt., USMC
VEST, Ralph Marvin, BM2c, USN

WALMER, Dan, PhM1c, USN
WANGER, Lt. James Linford, (Dental Corps), USN
WESCHLER, Lt. Charles John, USN
WILKINSON, Alexander Roberts, PhM3c, USN

WILLIAMS, Lt. (jg) Richard Bland, Jr., USN
WILLIAMS, Robert L., Pay Clerk, USMC
WINGO, Ens. Personneau Brown, USNR
WRIGHT, Damon Haley, F1c, USN

WASHINGTON

Dead

AARHAUS, David Louis, SF2c, USN
ALLEN, James Douglas, MM2c, USN
ARTLEY, Daryle Edward, QM2c, USN
ARVIDSON, Carl Harry, CMM, USN
BAILEY, James Edward, RM3c, USNR
BAIR, Frederick Franklin, Jr., HA1c, USN
BAK, Joe, Cox., USN
BAKER, Frank James, S2c, USN
BARRY, Edward Merritt, F3c, USN
BEERMAN, Henry Carl, CM3c, USN
BERCHOT, Delbert Glenn, AM3c, USN
BERG, David Donald, ARM3c, USN
BERRY, Theodore Stanley, CWT, USN
BICKNELL, Dale Dean, S1c, USN
BIRKS, Frank Edward, S1c, USN
BLANCHARD, William Eugene, B1c, USN
BLIEFFERT, Richmond Frederick, S1c, USN
BOWEN, Albert Philip, F1c, USN
BOWERS, Ens. Robert K., USNR
BRAKKE, Kenneth Gay, F3c, USN
BRENDLE, Hayden Fred, MM2c, USN
BROMLEY, George Edward, SM3c, USN
BROMLEY, Jimmie, S1c, USN
BROOKS, Ens. Robert N., USNR
BUTCHER, David Adrian, F2c, USN
CADE, Richard Esh, S2c, USN
CARROLL, Ens. John Bennett, USNR
CARTER, Cyrus David, MM2c, USN
CARTER, William John, S2c, USN
CASEY, James Warren, S1c, USN
CASKEY, Clarence Merton, S1c, USN
CHESS, Patrick Lloyd, SF3c, USN
COFFIN, Robert, SF3c, USN
COLEGROVE, Willett Stillman, Jr., S2c, USN
COMSTOCK, Harold Kenneth, S1c, USN
CONRAD, Lt. (jg) Robert Ive, USNR
CORDOVA, Nicholas Guerra, EM1c, USN
COREY, Ernest Eugene, PhM3c, USN
COX, Pearlin Grant, S2c, USN
CRAWFORD, David Warren, MM1c, USN
CROSS, Lawrence Jackson, CQM, USN
DAY, Cyril Avery, AMM1c, USN
DAY, William John, S2c, USN
DERITIS, Russell Edwin, S1c, USN

DIBBLE, Harold Vernon, F1c, USN
DICK, Francis Edward, Mus2c, USN
DONALDSON, Lt. (jg) Trose Emmett, USNR
DOMPIER, Marshall Leonard, SK2c, USN
DOOLEY, Martin Joseph, Jr., CM2c, USN
DOUGLAS, Norman W., S1c, USN
ECHTERNKAMP, Henry Clarence, S1c, USN
EK, 2nd Lt. Bruce H., USMCR
ELLISON, Bruce Harry, RM3c, USN
ELY, Robert Charles, S1c, USN
ENDICOTT, Ronald Burdette, F3c, USN
ERICKSON, Robert, S2c, USN
FINUCANE, 2nd Lt. Arthur E., USMCR
FORMOE, Clarence Melvin, AMM1c, USNR
FOSTER, Howard James, F2c, USN
FROHNHAFER, Heman Austin, S2c, USN
GADROW, Lt. (jg) Victor Marvin, USN
GAUDETTE, William Frank, S1c, USN
GILLIS, Arthur Thomas, AMM1c, USN
GRAY, Albert James, S1c, USNR
GREEN, Edward Flowers, Cox., USN
GUISINGER, Daniel Luther, Jr., S1c, USN
GYORFI, Albert John, AP3c, USN
HALL, Robert Vernon, S1c, USN
HAMILTON, Clarence James, MM1c, USN
HAMLIN, Dale Reuben, GM3c, USN
HANSEN, Henry G., Jr., PFC, USMC
HARDY, Dewey Lee, B1c, USN
HARGRAVES, Kenneth William, S2c, USN
HARRIS, Franklin Rosecrans, QM1c, USN
HERBER, Harvey Christopher, EM1c, USN
HERRMANN, Clarence Albert, S2c, USN
HESSDORFER, Anthony Joseph, MM2c, USN
HICKMAN, Arthur Lee, SM3c, USN
HICKS, Elmer Orville, GM3c, USN
HOAG, Frank Samuel, Jr., RM3c, USN
HOFLACK, Gabriel Marcelle, AMM3c, USN
HOLCOMB, Allen Dale, S2c, USN
HOLLIDAY, Jasper L., PFC, USMC
HOLSBO, Robert L., PFC, USMC
HOUSTON, Albert Lee, ACMM, USN

HOWARD, Lt. (jg) Curtis William, USN
HOYER, Ens. Glenn Allan, USNR
HULTGREN, Lorentz Emanuel, MM2c, USN
HUTCHINSON, Lt. George Leland, USN
HYDE, Don Ellsworth, S2c, USNR
IRONS, Henry Augustus, F2c, USNR
JAMES, John D., PFC, USMC
JARED, Benjamin Elmer, CM3c, USN
JOHNS, Ens. Paul Howard, USNR
JOHNSON, Melvin Grant, RM3c, USN
JOHNSON, Robert, S2c, USN
JOHNSON, Sterling Conrad, Cox., USN
KEENER, Russell Eldon, CM1c, USN
KEIL, Ralph Henry, S1c, USN
KELLEY, Ronald Lawrence, SK3c, USN
KENNAUGH, Gilbert Thomas, GM1c, USN
KERR, James Howard, QM1c, USN
KING, Andrew, AS, USN
KINNEY, Frederick William, 1st Mus., USN
KNISLEY, Kenneth Melburn, CWT, USN
KOENEKAMP, Clarence Dietrich, F1c, USN
LANCASTER, John Thomas, PhM3c, USNR
LARSON, Leonard Carl, F3c, USN
LARSON, Llewellyn Liene, S1c, USN
LA SALLE, Willard Dale, S1c, USN
LEGGETT, John Goldie, BM2c, USN
LEVAR, Frank, CWT, USNR
LINBO, Gordon Ellsworth, GM1c, USN
LODIK, William, WT1c, USN
LYMAN, Ens. Chauncey, USNR
LYNN, Estus Lee, SF3c, USN
MANN, William Edward, GM3c, USN
MANNING, Jay Darrell, AMM3c, USN
MARTIN, Hollis, ARM3c, USN
MASON, Henri Clay, 1st Mus., USNR
MATHISON, Donald Joseph, FC3c, USN
McHUGHES, John Breckenridge, CWT, USN
McLAIN, Robert Mathew, CEM, USN
MEYERS, Erwin Frederick, MM1c, USN
MILLER, Robert Athelbert, Sgt., USMCR
MITCHELL, Ens. Albert Edward, USNR
MITCHELL, Henry Maclaren, AMM1c, USN
MYERS, James Gernie, SK1c, USN
MYLER, James Melvin, SM1c, USN
NAFF, Hugh Kenneth, S2c, USN
NELSEN, George, SC2c, USN
NELSON, Marlyn Wayne, F2c, USN
NICHOLS, Bethel Allan, S2c, USN
NORMAN, Donald Charles, S2c, USN

OCHOSKI, Henry Francis, QM2c, USN
OHLER, William George, CEM, USN
OLSON, Glen Martin, S2c, USN
O'TYSON, Donald Clayton, F2c, USN
PARADIS, George Lawrence, PhM3c, USN
PATRICK, Hugh Alexander, Corp., USMC
PATTERSON, Harry Joseph, EM2c, USN
PENDARVIS, George Eugene, F3c, USN
PETERSON, Hardy Wilbur, FC3c, USN
PHILLIPS, William Albert, Jr., ARM3c, USNR
PHIPPS, James Norman, S2c, USN
PONDER, Walter Howard, MM1c, USN
PRESTON, Lee Arnold, Sgt., USMC
RAMSDEN, Martin Lee, Cox., USN
RANKERT, George Robert, QM3c, USN
RAY, Glen Edward, RM3c, USN
RICE, William Albert, S2c, USN
RICH, Otto Vernon, PhM1c, USN
RICHTER, Albert Wallace, Cox., USN
ROBERTS, Kenneth Franklin, BM2c, USN
ROMBALSKI, Donald Roger, S2c, USN
ROOKS, Capt. Albert Harold, USN
RUARK, Ervin Ellsworth, AMM1c, USN
RUSKEY, Joseph John, CBM, USN
SCHULER, Norman Frank, MM2c, USN
SEATON, Chester Ernest, F1c, USN
SITTON, Quentin Ray, Pvt., USMC
SMITH, Merle Andrew, EM3c, USN
SOUSLEY, Joseph Byron, S2c, USN
SPARKS, Neal Richard, RM3c, USN
SPARKS, Wendell Clark, ARM3c, USNR
STARKOVICH, Charles, F3c, USN
STARKOVICH, Joseph, Jr., F2c, USN
STEELE, Garvin G., Field Cook, USMC
STEPHENS, Woodrow Wilson, EM1c, USN
STEVENSON, Wilbur William, S1c, USN
STEWART, Orval Lee, EM3c, USN
STILLINGS, Gerald Fay, F2c, USN
STOCKSTILL, Lt. (jg) Eugene William, USN
STRONG, David Edward Roaldo Walter, CM2c, USNR
SUMMERS, Glen Allen, Y1c, USN
SURBER, Merle Duane, AS, USN
TANNER, Russell Allen, GM3c, USN
TAYLOR, Arthur Lionel, BM2c, USN
THUMME, Arthur Joseph, CM2c, USN
TONER, Philip James, S2c, USN
TROWBRIDGE, Robert Edgar, S1c, USN
UMALI, Donato, OS1c, USN
VAIRETTA, Stephen Paul, S1c, USN
VAMMEN, Ens. Clarence Earl, Jr., USNR
VANDERPOOL, Marion Frank, S2c, USN
WAIT, Wayland LeMoyne, S1c, USN

WHITE, James Kenneth, GM1c, USN
WHITSON, Alton Walter, EM3c, USN
WILLIAMSON, Melvin Dale, S1c, USN
WILSON, John Gilbert, SK2c, USN
WINTER, Edward, Mach., USNR
WINTER, Ens. Edwin Ray, USNR
YARROW, Richard Arthur, PFC, USMC
ZELLER, Martin Henry, S2c, USNR

Wounded

ALVESTAD, Roy Lyle, S1c, USN
BATES, Walter Edward, CBM, USN
BRUNER, Lauren Fay, FC3c, USN
CULP, Donald Arthur, S2c, USN
DALY, John J., PFC, USMC
FARQUHAR, Lawrence Albert, FC2c, USN
FLEMING, William Sloan, BM1c, USN
FOLAND, Raymond Glen, GM3c, USN
GRANA, Carmel Albert, MM1c, USN
HOMAN, William Carl, S2c, USN
JACOBS, William Foster, EM3c, USN
JENSEN, James Harold, S2c, USN
LAKE, Harold Jessie, QM1c, USN
LA ROCK, Thomas Perdon, S2c, USN
MARS, William Henry, MM2c, USN
MARSH, Virgil Ruel, AMM1c, USN
MASLOWSKI, Louis, S2c, USN
MERCER, Dean Chabran, S1c, USN
MOSER, Richard Robert John, RM3c, USN
NEAL, Frank Emanuel, GM1c, USN
OTTE, Lyman Gerald, AS, USNR
POLER, Howard Alexander, S1c, USN
REVI, James Earnest, AS, USN
RITCHIE, Eugene Robert, S2c, USN
SANDERS, Elmer Larimore, GM1c, USN
SKINNER, John W., Pvt., USMC
SMITH, Eugene Frank, S1c, USN
VESEY, Vernon Arthur, S1c, USN
WHITE, Ebed Howell, S2c, USN
WHITEMAN, Earl Myron, S2c, USN
WHITNEY, Loren Carlos, S2c, USN
WISNER, Wallace R., Pvt., USMC

Missing

ALBONEY, Francis, Torp3c, USN
AUSTIN, James H., PFC, USMC
AUTIO, Lauren Edward, S2c, USN
BARNHART, Othar Colburn, Cox., USN
BARRETT, 2nd Lt. Edward M., USMC
BARRETT, Raleigh, S2c, USN
BATCHELDOR, William Wallace, F2c, USN
BENNETT, Phillip Lawrence, MM1c, USN
BERG, Alfred Harold, MM2c, USN
BOWLBY, Wilbur Eugene, S1c, USN
BRENNAN, John Clark, MM1c, USN

BROWN, Donald Charles, S2c, USN
BULLA, John, Jr., MM1c, USN
BUSHELL, Alfred, CMM, USN
CALLISON, Charles Thomas, WT2c, USN
CHEADLE, Clarence Richard, S1c, USN
CHRISTOPHER, Robert Lovie, SC1c, USN
CLARK, Capt. John W., Jr., USMC
COFFIELD, Rolland Leroy, PhM1c, USN
COLE, Charles Warren, Pvt., USMC
COMLEY, Sydney Paul, MM2c, USN
CUSICK, Lt. (jg) Jean Clare, USN
DEAN, Maurice Frederick, SC3c, USN
DESART, Boyd I., F2c, USN
DUFF, Elmore Earl, Cox., USN
FAILER, Vernon, RM2c, USN
FARNSWORTH, Franklin Monroe, S1c, USN
GALE, James Marion, AMM3c, USN
GRANSTON, Ens. Robert Wyatt, Supply Corps, USN
GRIFFIN, Everette Presley, CPhM, USN
HAGEL, Alfred LeRoy, CMM, USN
HASHAGEN, Wayne D., PFC, USMC
HERNDON, William Thomas, SC3c, USN
HIGGINS, Louis William, Cox., USN
HOEY, Allen Nelson, S1c, USN
HOLM, Herbert Clayton, F2c, USN
HOWELL, Walter Theodore, QM1c, USN
JACKSON, Robert Allen, F1c, USN
JENNINGS, Lynn Logan, S2c, USN
JOHNK, Merle Warren, AMM3c, USN
JONES, Dwight Winston, GM1c, USN
JONES, Harold Edmund, Bkr3c, USN
JONES, Kenneth Archie, RM2c, USN
KELLAM, Robert William, S1c, USN
LAMBERT, Carl Healy, F1c, USN
LEO, Nicholas, CEM, USN
LITTLE, Jopaul, S1c, USN
LONDO, Joseph Lewis, F3c, USN
LUSSIER, Alfred Joseph, BM1c, USN
MASON, Willard Paul, MM1c, USN
MILLER, Kearney Elbert, SF2c, USN
MILLER, Samuel Donald, BM1c, USN
MILLER, Truman Wilson, RM1c, USN
MOORE, Clayton Lloyd, MM2c, USN
MOORE, Lt. Jack Cobb, USN
PERRY, Willard Orland, AMM3c, USN
PRATICO, Louis, EM3c, USN
RHODES, Lyon Ralph, F1c, USN
RINGS, Lt. (jg) Glen Robert, Supply Corps, USN
ROHLETTER, James Barry, S1c, USN
ROWLEY, James Richard, F1c, USN
SCHACHT, Lt. Kenneth George, USN
SCHMIDTMAN, Robert E., 1st Sgt., USMC
SCHUELKE, John Harry, SC3c, USN

SCHUFFENHAUER, Louis Otto, S1c, USN
SCOTT, George H., Pvt., USMC
SELFRIDGE, Henry Adolph, WT1c, USN
SHARP, John Robert, TM1c, USN
SHEALY, Mendel Worth, EM1c, USN
SIEGEL, John Jacob, Jr., EM2c, USN
SMITH, Wilbur George, S1c, USN
SOULE, Lt. Cdr. Arthur W., USNR
SOULE, Irvin George, GM3c, USN
SPENCER, Charles Le Roy, S1c, USN
STEWART, Glenn Smith, QM1c, USN
STONE, Lt. Archibald, Jr., USN
TANA, Flaviano, OS2c, USN
TISDALE, William Vernon, Bkr1c, USN
TUTTLE, John Sherwood, QM1c, USN
WARREN, James Verlin, S1c, USN
WELFELT, Edward Abraham, MM2c, USN
WHEELER, Robert Lee, QM2c, USN
WILDER, Charlie, PFC, USMC (Ret.)
WILLIAMS, John David, F2c, USN
WOODS, Winfred Oral, MM1c, USN
WYNNE, James Celus, CMM, USN

Prisoners of War

ATHEY, John Francis, Pay Clerk, USN
ATKINS, Leslie M., Jr., PFC, USMC
ATWOOD, Clayton Woodron, PhM2c, USN
BAERMAN, Donald George, S2c, USN
BAILEY, Ivon John, S1c, USN
BALLETTI, Herbert Charles, Sgt., USMCR
BECK, Lewis Graffin, CPhM, USN
BENDER, Edward, PFC, USMC
BENDER, Jack Val, PFC, USMC
BERG, Norman James, Corp., USMC
BLOOMINGDALE, Leslie Frank, HA1c, USN
BOWMAN, Rupert Orrin, PFC, USMC
BRONK, Stanley Edward, 1st Sgt., USMC
BROWN, David Joseph, S1c, USN
BROWN, Harold Phylander, PFC, USMC
BURTON, Robert Vernon, F1c, USN
CARLSON, Lt. Arnold John, USN
CARSON, Frank Lewis, BM1c, USN
CATLOW, Lloyd Andrew, Corp., USMC
CHRISTENSEN, Robert Melvin, RM2c, USNR
CHRISTIAN, Clifford Howard, Cox., USN
CHURCH, Paul Clark, S1c, USN
CLARK, E. Lee Rae, PFC, USMC
CLARK, Kenneth Robinson, PFC, USMC
CLOUGH, James Burton, PhM3c, USN
COGHLAN, William A., PFC, USMC
COLE, Walter Willis, SC2c, USN
COX, Marlin Owen, S1c, USN
CRAIG, Willard Homer, BM2c, USN

CRIMMINS, Clayton Alfred, Pvt., USMC
CROCKER, Harry Delmore, PFC, USMC
DALRYMPLE, Russell Edward, Pvt., USMC
DAUL, Arthur Percival, Pharm., USN
DESCAMPS, Clarence Camille, PFC, USMC
DIAL, William Thomas, S1c, USN
DIEMERT, William Adrian, PFC, USMC
DOCKWEILER, Lt. Cdr. Edward Vincent, USN
DUNNING, Laverne Harley, M1c, USN
EHRHART, William Thomas, MM2c, USN
ELFSTROM, Robert Clarence, EM1c, USN
ELKINS, Jack Orin, PFC, USMC
EMARD, Arthur Delores, MM2c, USN
ENGLIN, Milton A., Sgt., USMC
ERDMAN, James, Pvt., USMC
EVERIST, Joseph L., Tech. Sgt., USMC
FOOTE, Arthur Earnest, MM1c, USN
FRASIER, Clarence Alvin, CPhM, USNR
GALDE, Burton Conrad, S1c, USN
GALYEAN, George Lee, Bandmaster, USN
GRAGG, Raymond, Sgt., USMC
GRAHAM, Paul George, Sgt., USMC
GRAHNERT, James D., PFC, USMC
HADDON, James Richard, CBM, USN
HALL, Claude Beryl, Asst. Cook, USMC
HALL, Elison Kendall, CPhM, USN
HALL, Jack Quenten, Sgt., USMC
HANNAH, Clyde William, Sgt., USMC
HARMON, Jack Buchanan, PFC, USMC
HAUSAM, Alfred William, TM1c, USN
HEFLING, William Wesley, PFC, USMC
HEIM, Joseph George, Jr., CSM, USN
HEMMELGARN, Francis Paul, S/Sgt., USMC
HENDERSON, Robert D., Pvt., USMC
HENRY, Lt. (jg) Floyd Clifford, USNR
HERTHNECK, Lt. (jg) Robert George, Dental Corps, USN
HETZLER, Marvin Leroy, PhM2c, USN
HETZLER, Melvin Ray, PhM1c, USN
HIGGIN, William Dabney, PFC, USMC
HILL, James Russell, Corp., USMC
HIMELRICK, John Robert, PFC, USMC
HONAN, Thomas Raymond, Sgt., USMC
HOWARD, William Hanson, Sgt., USMC
HUGHES, Lyall Arthur, RM1c, USN
HURTT, Thomas Braxton, SM1c, USN
HUTCHINSON, A. C., WT2c, USN
HUTCHISON, William Adolph, Mach., USN
IVARSEN, William C., PFC, USMC
JACKSON, Paul, Pay Clerk, USN
JAMES, Edward Richard, EM2c, USN

Jansen, Shirk George, PFC, USMC
Jensen, Arthur Wallace, CSK, USN
Johnson, Milton Orville, Corp., USMCR
Johnson, Lt. Willard Carroll, Supply Corps, USN
Johnston, Robert Wilfred, S2c, USN
Joslin, Harold Eugene, RM2c, USN
Kaye, Lt. (jg) William Rollo, Supply Corps, USN
Kelly, Bernard Francis, Corp., USMC
Kerns, James H., Sgt., USMCR
Kieffer, Joseph Henry, Sgt., USMC
Kinney, 2nd Lt. John Franklin, USMC
Kuonen, Charlie Robert, PFC, USMC
La Casse, John Joseph, PhM1c, USN
Lange, Carl Leo, Gunnery Sgt., USMC
Letson, Lt. (jg) Charles Francis, USNR
Lightfoot, Lt. (jg) Charles Joseph, Supply Corps, USN
Logan, Emit Francis, PFC, USMC
MacGowan, Lt. Hubert, USNR
Marshall, Kenneth John, PFC, USMC
Martin, Gerald James, PFC, USMC
Marvin, Kenneth Leo, Corp., USMC
Mathews, Edward Harrison, F1c, USN
McCotter, Roy Wommack, RM1c, USN
McCoy, Charles Francis, SK1c, USN
McGuire, Albert C., PFC, USN
McKechnie, Robert Peter, PFC, USMC
McLean, Arnold Edward, PFC, USMC
Mix, William Gerald, Corp., USMCR
Moore, Richard Kenneth, Pvt., USMC
Morgan, Albert James, Sgt., USMC
Moritz, Leroy Glenwood, PFC, USMC
Moritz, Melvin Clyde, F2c, USN
Morrissey, Thomas Leroy, EM2c, USN
Mosher, Alfred Raymond, PhM3c, USN
Mueller, George John, AMM1c, USN
Netter, Jack Gordon, S2c, USN
Ney, Ralph Stephen, PhM3c, USN
Nies, William Wayne, CM1c, USN
Norris, Jack Carl, RM1c, USN

Nye, Burl Lee, MM1c, USN
Omoth, Robert Engman, S1c, USN
Packwood, Walter, Jr., S1c, USN
Page, Harold Lloyd, S1c, USN
Parker, Ray D., PFC, USMC
Parker, Seymour F., Corp., USMC
Parr, George Wilson, Asst. Cook, USMC
Patton, William Anderson, SK2c, USN
Peterson, Lewis Martin, AMM2c, USN
Ramsey, Edgar Allen, Corp., USMC
Rasmussen, Harland Bonnell, WT2c, USN
Ratzman, Earl Martin, S1c, USN
Reed, Reginald Walter, SM1c, USN
Rogers, Leonard Lee, PFC, USMC
Rossetto, Otto, Sgt., USMC
Sandvold, Julian Keith, S2c, USN
Sauers, Virgil Laverne, BM1c, USN
Schilperoort, Clarence Harold, EM2c, USN
Schwab, Albert John, PhM2c, USN
Sharer, David Mitchell, S1c, USN
Shelley, Lawrence Wesley, SM2c, USN
Slagle, Edward E., S/Sgt., USMC
Sparks, George W., PFC, USMC
Stewart, Leon Radimar, Mess Sgt., USMC
Stewart, Russell Clifton, HA1c, USN
Tarter, Ernest Clinton, PFC, USMC
Volgamore, Millard Wenzen, F1c, USN
Waller, Murray Arthur, PFC, USMC
Warren, Roy Levi, S2c, USN
Weaver, Roy Madison, PFC, USMC
Welsh, Lt. Cdr. Clyde Lionel, (MC), USNR
White, Elmer James, SF2c, USN
White, James Frederick, TM2c, USN
Wilkins, Ens. Charles Meredith (Supply Corps), USN
Williams, Leo Harry, F1c, USN
Wilson, John David, Mach., USN
Wood, Ivan Sidney, S1c, USN

WEST VIRGINIA

Dead

Adkins, Golden, AS, USNR
Adkins, Howard Lucas, F1c, USN
Alderman, Raymond Alfred, F3c, USNR
Amburn, Richard Lyle, AMM3c, USN
Angie, Earnest Hersea, F2c, USN
Baldwin, Virgil Kenneth, MM2c, USN
Bennett, Dennis Howard, S2c, USNR
Branson, John Richard, S2c, USN
Browning, Tilman David, S1c, USN

Burkett, Ens. Howard Roy, USNR
Bush, Ray Jr., WT2c, USN
Carroll, Joseph William, F2c, USN
Clark, John Franklin, F1c, USN
Corbitt, George Albert, S1c, USN
Crabtree, Eugene Oscar, S1c, USN
Crawford, Billy Brant, F3c, USN
Dawson, Claude Dailey, F2c, USN
Dawson, William Thomas, EM2c, USN
Dillmore, Wilbur Asbury, Jr., AS, USNR

DRWALL, Stanislaw Frank, PM1c, USN
DUNN, John Joseph, F3c, USN
EDDY, George William, Jr., AMM2c, USN
EMERICK, Floyd Preston, AS, USNR
GARLITZ, George Austin, MM2c, USN
GAY, Samuel Lee, SK2c, USN
GIBSON, Rupert Glennville, S1c, USN
HADDAD, Nathan, Jr., S2c, USNR
HALIER, Thomas Darwin, MM2c, USN
HEDRICK, Charles Marion, S2c, USNR
HUTCHINSON, Robert Lee, S1c, USN
IGNATIOUS, William B., Platoon Sgt., USMC
KENNEDY, Herbert, S2c, USNR
KERNS, Lester Lurensel, AM1c, USN
KINDER, Murhl Franklin, SC3c, USN
KING, Fred Pierce, AOM1c, USN
KINZER, Ens. Edward Blaine, USNR
KNIPP, Stanley Wayne, SC2c, USN
KORMAN, Frank, F3c, USN
LADERACH, Robert Paul, FC2c, USN
McCLOUD, Donald Robert, FC2c, USN
McComAS, Clarence William, S1c, USN
McGRAW, George Vincent, F1c, USN
McKINNEY, Harold Leroy, S2c, USN
McKINNEY, Nathan Lorain, S2c, USN
MOORE, Ens. Ulvert Mathew, USNR
NICHOLS, Carl, S2c, USN
PETTRY, Tom Hartsel, ARM2c, USN
PLYBON, Robert Theodore, BM2c, USN
PLYMALE, Dorsel E., S2c, USN
PRATT, Lyman Milford, F1c, USN
PRICE, Lt. (jg) Edward Max, USN
REED, Frank Edward, SF3c, USN
ROBINSON, Robert Warren, PhM3c, USN
SEIVERTSON, Charles Edward, AS, USNR
SHAFFER, Charles Lenard, AS, USN
SMITH, Carl, WT2c, USN
STELLER, Alfred William, Jr., MM2c, USN
THOMAS, Randall James, S1c, USN
TINNEY, Roland Herald, FC3c, USN
TRENT, Garard Humphrey, F3c, USNR
TYLER, Charles Hylbert, SK3c, USN
WEBB, Joseph Clifford, CMM, USN
WEEKS, Virgil Lewis, PhM2c, USN
WHITE, Rush Truman, SK2c, USNR
WILSON, Clyde Richard, S1c, USN
WIMMER, Bernard Ramon, FC1c, USN
YOUNG, Carroll Fletcher, RM2c, USNR

Wounded

GARRETT, Isaac Lawrence, Jr., S2c, USNR
KING, Wilford McCutcheon, F1c, USN

ROBEY, Earl Albert, F3c, USN
RODGERS, Ens. Robert Reese, USNR
WORKMAN, Carl, GM2c, USN

Missing

BASSETT, Robert Alexander, MM2c, USN
CAMPBELL, Creed Bruce, EM1c, USN
CORNUTTE, Marion Franklin, MM2c, USN
DAVIS, Lawrence Byrd, EM3c, USN
ELKINS, Dorsey Junius, S2c, USN
HARPER, Paul Bernard, F2c, USN
HAYES, Gilbert Wayne, S1c, USN
HENDERSON, Howard Glen, CM2c, USN
LAMBERT, Van Rolo, S1c, USN
LILLY, Willard S., Sgt., USMC
MATHIS, Chester Marion, F2c, USN
MAZE, Ralph F., PFC, USMC
MERCURI, Antonio James, RM3c, USN
MILGEL, John Lewis, S2c, USN
PETERS, Orvel Vincent, F2c, USN
PLANTZ, Ernest Virgil, S1c, USN
ROUWSEY, Lewis Winston, S2c, USN
SNODGRASS, Lt. (jg) Ray Arvel, USN
SPERANDIO, Ricardo James, CBM, USN
SWIGER, Everett Boyd, S2c, USN
WARD, Willard G., SF1c, USN
WILLIAMSON, Waldo Ray, QM3c, USN
WILSON, Allen Hardin, MM2c, USN
WRIGHT, Dennis Edman, GM2c, USN
ZIMMERMAN, Leonard, S2c, USN

Prisoners of War

ABRUZZINO, Thomas Joseph, AM2c, USN
BECKETT, Franklin Clark, FC3c, USN
BOWLING, Clifford Melvin, Pvt., USMC
BRAGG, Lorel Jonas, Pvt., USMC
BROTHERS, Frank Wheeler, S1c, USN
BYRNSIDE, Fred Lincoln, Cox., USN
CORLEY, John Kenneth, Field Music, USMC
DINGESS, Naaman, AM1c, USN
DORSEY, James Lovell, F2c, USN
EBBERT, Daniel Arch, S1c, USN
EXUM, Wilburn Irvin, RM2c, USN
GIRKIN, Farrell Cyrus, EM2c, USN
GODWIN, Luther Hartzell, PhM3c, USN
HALL, James Walter, Sgt., USMC
HANSON, Jess Willard, S1c, USN
HELMICK, Raymond Arnett, Corp., USMCR
HENDERSON, Clifford M., Pvt., USMC
HIETT, Herman Wesley, S1c, USN
MABRY, Lonnie Green, RM2c, USN

MERRELLS, Robert Dorsey, AMM3c, USN
MILLS, Lee George, Gunner, USN
PERKINS, Elbert Samuel, Pvt., USMC
PICKERING, Ray Wood, QM Sgt., USMC
PRICE, Thomas, S2c, USN
RICHARDS, Elmer Lee, S2c, USN

RINGER, Morris Edward, AM3c, USN
SHELTON, Archie H., PFC, USMC
SIMS, Terrance Abner, S1c, USN
THOMPSON, Carl Robert, S2c, USN
WALKER, Truman Everett, EM3c, USN
WINDON, Gordon Clark, RM3c, USN

WISCONSIN

Dead

BAILKEY, Harold, GM3c, USNR
BANNEN, William John, Bkr1c, USN
BARBER, Leroy Kenneth, F1c, USN
BARBER, Malcolm John, F1c, USN
BARBER, Randolph Harold, F2c, USN
BELONGA, Robert Joseph, S2c, USN
BERNARDY, Donald L., PFC, USMC
BLESSMAN, Lt. Edward Martin, USN
BOVIALL, Walter Robert, AMM2c, USN
BOXRUCKER, Lawrence Anton, F2c, USN
BRUESEWITZ, William Gustave, S1c, USN
CONNOLLY, Keefe Richard, HA1c, USN
COOK, George Edward, SF3c, USN
CURTIS, Lyle Carl, RM2c, USN
DIECKHOFF, Douglas Raymond, SM1c, USN
DOERNENBURG, Kenneth Edward, F1c USN
DULL, Burl William, CM3c, USN
DURAWA, Gregory Joseph, ARM3c, USN
EHLERT, Casper, SM3c, USN
ENGLEHART, Virgil Francis, S1c, USN
FAUCETT, Walter John, F2c, USN
FENSKE, Roger Harold, S1c, USN
FIDLER, Charles Eugene, S2c, USN
FISCHER, Leslie Henry, S1c, USN
FONTAINE, Gordon Raphual, SK2c, USN
GAIDO, Brune Peter, AMM1c, USN
GAZECKI, Ens. Philip R., USNR
GEISE, Marvin Fredrick, S1c, USN
GREGORIC, Charles August, S2c, USN
GROSS, Francis Henry, F1c, USN
HANSEN, Harold M., PFC, USMC
HANSEN, Harvey Ralph, S1c, USN
HANSON, Ens. Burton Roaklvam, USN
HANSON, Helmer Ansel, S2c, USN
HATHAWAY, Albert Edward, CQM, USN
HEATH, Alfred Grant, S1c, USN
HELMS, Philip H., Sgt., USMC
HILT, Fred Albert, MM1c, USN
HOGAJ, Paul George, F2c, USN
HOLDEN, Glen Lester, ARM2c, USN
JENSEN, Donald Charles, SK3c, USN
JOHNSON, Allen Howard, S2c, USN

JONES, Robert O., PFC, USMC
KARABON, Joseph Nicholas, F1c, USN
KEILER, John R., PFC, USMC
KOWALCZEWSKI, Victor, F2c, USN
KRAMER, Harry Wellington, F1c, USN
KREMPLE, William Raymond, GM3c, USN
LEWISON, Neil Stanley, FC3c, USN
LUND, Robert Thomas, F1c, USN
MATHISON, Charles Harris, S1c, USN
MAYER, Edward Frederick, S1c, USN
MEALY, James Irwin, S1c, USN
MEHLTRETTER, John William, EM3c, USN
MILLER, Stephen Joseph, SF2c, USN
MOLTHEN, Victor Roy, F2c, USN
MUHOFSKI, Joseph Alexander, RM3c, USN
NAEGLE, George Eugene, S1c, USN
NEWMAN, Laxton Gail, AMM3c, USN
NICOLES, Frank Edward, F1c, USN
NUSSER, Raymond Alfred, GM3c, USN
OLSON, Errett Blaine, F1c, USN
PARFITT, Francis James, RM2c, USN
PECHACEK, Ermin Joseph, SM2c, USN
PLATT, Paul Franklin, S1c, USN
PROKASH, Clarence H., PFC, USMC
PRZYBYSZ, Alexsandor John, Prtr2c, USN
QUINLAN, Edward F., PFC, USMC
RILEY, David Joseph, S2c, USN
RUDE, Julius, F3c, USN
RUDE, Milton Darwin, Torp. 3c, USN
ST. JOHN, Lewis Fletcher, MM2c, USNR
SANKEY, George W., Corp., USMC
SCHLUESSEL, Marvin B., PFC, USMCR
SCHULTZ, Clarence Emil, Y3c, USNR
SCRIBNER, James Malcolm, S1c, USN
SIMPSON, Percy Henry, SF1c, USN
SMITH, Ens. Frederick Andrew, USNR
SZURGOT, Edward Frank, SK3c, USN
TAYLOR, Ens. Howard Wendall, USNR
THINNES, Arthur Ray, S2c, USN
TILLS, Ens. Robert George, USN
TREDEAU, Alphonse Bernard, M2c, USNR
TRYBA, Richard Frank, S2c, USN

TUTTLE, Ralph Egbert, F2c, USN
UHRENHOLDT, Ens. Andrew, USNR
VAN BUREN, Lt. (jg) John James, USN
VANDER MOLEN, Leo Jacob, F3c, USN
WALKOWIAK, Robert Nicholas, F3c, USN
WALLACE, James Frank, S1c, USN
WALLEN, Earl D., PFC, USMC
WINTERLING, Joe N., Corp., USMC
WINTERS, Victor Junior, SF1c, USN
WOITKIELEVICZ, Adam, AS, USNR
ZAMIATOWSKI, Jerome Anthony, S1c, USN
ZEROZ, Leo Vincent, S1c, USNR

Wounded

BEKKEN, Ray Norman, SF3c, USN
BOURGINGNON, Ivan Arthur, S1c, USN
CATTANACH, Robert Earl, EM3c, USN
COMPTON, Robert Lloyd, PhM2c, USN
DARROW, Dean Grant, FC3c, USN
FISCHER, Howard Gregory, S1c, USN
HIRSCH, Raymond R., Y3c, USCG
KLUG, Russell Kenneth, AM3c, USN
KRAUS, Robert Ambrose, Cox., USN
STENE, Laurence Millard, GM2c, USN
WARRINER, Russell Walter, S1c, USN
WATSON, Lt. (jg) Robert J., USNR
WOLF, Howard F., S1c, USCG

Missing

AMUNDSON, Leo D., PFC, USMC
ANDERSON, Ralph Herman, S2c, USN
ARNESON, Raymond, AMM3c, USN
AUSTIN, John H., PFC, USMC
BLYTON, Otto Merle, Cox., USN
CRIST, Daniel, EM3c, USN
DICKIE, James Clayton, Ptr2c, USN
DREFAHL, Elmer E., Corp., USMC
ERMIS, Robert Louis, CSK, USN
FLEMING, Donald Elwood, F3c, USN
GERKE, Arthur Vernon, Jr., HA2c, USN
GESTNER, Donald Wilbur, F2c, USN
GUSTIN, Ens. John W., USNR
HAVEY, Maurice Charles, S1c, USN
HERRICK, Paul E., Pvt., USMC
HOGAN, Ens. James Joseph, USNR
HOUGLAND, Marte E., PFC, USMC
JELLISON, Norman Bruce, S1c, USN
JENSEN, Werner F., Corp., USMC
JOHNSON, Norman Erving, S1c, USN
JOHNSON, William Arthur, S1c, USN
KARBOWSKI, Adelbert Leonard, S2c, USN
KIESLING, George Lewis, PhM1c, USN
KLEE, Earl Irwin, F2c, USN
KNAUF, Fred, Corp., USMCR

KOHN, Frank, PhM1c, USN
KONDZELA, Lawrence Francis, S1c, USN
KOSKI, George Paul, RM3c, USN
KULIBERT, Ira Robert, S1c, USN
LAIDLAN, Robert John, F2c, USN
LEVCHENKO, Walter, S1c, USN
MAKRIS, Peter, F2c, USN
MARIN, Frederick Klaus, WT1c, USN
MICHALOWSKE, Frank John, S1c, USN
MIZER, Merle Sidney, F1c, USN
MODROW, Donald Martin, RM3c, USN
NELSON, Emery Jennings, S1c, USN
O'TOOLE, Douglas John, RM3c, USN
PEGG, George Edgar, RM1c, USN
REIDER, John Joseph, MM2c, USN
ROCQUE, George Truman, S1c, USN
RUZEK, Lester C., PFC, USMC
SCHROEDER, Walter T., Pvt., USMC
SODEN, William James, Jr., SC3c, USN
STEINBERG, Barry James, S2c, USN
TUTAS, James Leslie, S1c, USN
VILLWOCK, Harvey Henry, EM3c, USN
VOLKMAN, Walter August, S1c, USN
WALDSCHMIDT, Albert Howard, Jr., MM1c, USN
WARGOWSKY, Lawrence Richard, EM2c, USN
WEBER, Emery Martin, S2c, USN
ZIDAR, Joseph F., PFC, USMC

Prisoners of War

ANDERSEN, Frank Raymond, PFC, USMC
AUGUSTINE, Harold Cyril, S1c, USN
BABLER, Edmond J., PFC, USMC
BAREIKA, Stanley P., PFC, USMC
BARTELME, Herbert Emil, PFC, USMC
BEAUCHAMP, Allen, PFC, USMC
BEAVER, Darrell Laverne, Pvt., USMC
BOGDONOVICH, Edward Mitchell, PFC, USMC
BRETTHAUER, Wenzel Christopher, BM1c, USNR
BRILL, Whitton, S1c, USN
BROSKI, Xavier U., Sgt., USMC
BUNN, Evan F., PFC, USMC
BURGLUND, Andrew Lee, Elect., USN
CALKINS, Joseph Valten, S2c, USN
CAREY, Jerry Dalton, PhM3c, USN
CLARE, Ervin Harry, CBM, USNR
CLOUGH, Clarence S., PFC, USMC
COSTELLO, Richard J., Corp., USMC
DAHLSTEDT, Arthur Benedict, F1c, USN
DENNIS, Harold S., Corp., USMC
ELDAL, Oscar M., PFC, USMC
ELLIOTT, Norman Douglas, Pvt., USMC

FERGUSON, Lt. George Theodore, (MC), USN
FORTUNA, Stephen, Sgt., USMC
GEMMEKE, Edward T., Corp., USMC
GILLES, Walter N., PFC, USMC
GOEBEL, Daniel William, PFC, USMC
GOODE, William B., PFC, USMC
HAVLENA, James J., PFC, USMC
HEILIGER, Howard B., PFC, USMC
HODACH, Frank J., PFC, USMC
HOFFMAN, Harold Arnold, Corp., USMC
HUDDELSON, Capt. Clyde R., USMC
JAKUBZAK, Chester M., Pvt., USMC
KARWOSKI, Harry Edwin, S2c, USN
KELNHOFER, Guy James, Corp., USMC
KOHLIN, Alfred Torsten, Corp., USMC
KUKEC, Charles, PFC, USMC
KULIBERT, Chester Leroy, S1c, USN
LAMOVEC, Philip C., PFC, USMC
LU MAYE, Donald R., PFC, USMC
LYPEK, Clemence J., Pvt., USMC
MARTWICK, Philip Walter, S1c, USN
MEAD, Grant Leroy, CSK, USN
MERCER, Harris Lee, PFC, USMC
MIKLAS, Joseph R., PFC, USMC
MOE, Lt. Cdr. Tilden Iver, USN
MUCCIACCIARO, John David, PFC, USMC
MUELLER, John Allison, PFC, USMC
OLSON, Kenneth Morris, GM3c, USN
ORR, Herbert James, PFC, USMC
PAYNE, Harold Keysar, Aer3c, USN
PERLMAN, Jarome, PFC, USMC
PETERSEN, Melvin W., PFC, USMC
PLOG, Francis Louis, PFC, USMC
PODLESNY, John Raymond, Corp., USMC

RENZ, Paul J., PFC, USMC
RETZKE, Harold Ignatius, Corp., USMC
RICHARDSON, Bernard Elliot, Corp., USMC
RINGERSMA, Charles, Jr., PFC, USMC
ROGOWSKI, Arthur Clemense, Prtr2c, USN
RYBICKI, Clarence John, Corp., USMC
SCHADE, 1st Lt. Lester A., USMC
SCHULTZ, Edward J., PFC, USMC
SNOW, Rex Winton, RM3c, USN
SOMMERS, Stanley George, Ptr2c, USN
SORRELL, Jesse Dell, Corp., USMC
SOUSEK, Merlyn Joseph, PFC, USMC
STEFANSKI, Edward, PFC, USMC
STEIGERWALD, Warren Gerald, F2c, USN
STONE, Edward Lyman, PFC, USMC
STUMPGES, Frederick John, Jr., Field Mus. Corp., USMC
SWINCONOS, Peter Paul, Ptr2c, USN
TAYLOR, James F., PFC, USMC
TIMPANY, David Alexander, Corp., USMC
VOGT, Laverne William, S2c, USN
WAGNER, Harry Albert, AMM3c, USN
WALISH, Ens. Robert Charles, USNR
WALKER, Lawrence James, S1c, USN
WELTER, Sylvester Harold, SK3c, USN
WOROZDINAC, Paul, Pvt., USMC
WOZNIAK, Leroy, PFC, USMC
ZABLER, Wallace Ernest, EM1c, USN
ZELLAY, George Paul, PFC, USMC
ZERGMAN, Walter Edward, F1c, USN
ZIVKO, Stephen Martin, PFC, USMC

WYOMING

Dead

BANDEMER, Harold William, S1c, USN
CHRISTENSEN, Elmer Emil, MM2c, USN
DUPES, Frank L., Corp., USMC
FISHER, Delbert Ray, S1c, USN
HANSON, George, MM1c, USN
JONES, Charles William, M1c, USN
LANE, Edward Wallace, Cox., USN
LINTON, George Edward, F2c, USN
MILLER, Fred James, AS, USN
MORGAREIDGE, James Orries, F2c, USN
OSBORN, Arthur Raymond, RM2c, USN
SCHMIDT, Herman, GM3c, USN
STEIN, Walter Claud, S1c, USN
STETZ, Frank Charles, AS, USNR

WALLENSTEIN, Richard Henry, S1c, USN
WOLNEY, George James, Cox., USN

Wounded

DAVIS, Clenroe Willard, S1c, USN
NICHOLS, Frank Wilson, EM3c, USN
SMITH, Arthur Loran, Jr., RM1c, USN
STEWART, Jesse L., Tech. Sgt., USMC

Missing

CORSBERG, Howard C., PFC, USMC
CUSACK, Ralph Roger, RM3c, USN
DAVIS, Howard Earl, Y2c, USN
DICKESON, Truman M., PFC, USMC

LAWSON, Raymond Paul, Chief Mach., USN
NEBEL, Alma Rex, Corp., USMC
OELKE, Clayton Lavelle, MM2c, USN
PIASECKI, Alexander L., Corp., USMC
ROBERTSON, Robert Nehls, F1c, USN
SMITH, Raymond E., Mess Sgt., USMC
VORPAHL, Lt. Arthur Henry, USN
WALKER, Harry Orville, Cox., USN
WHITEHEAD, Wallace Albert, SK2c, USN

Prisoners of War

BISSETT, Everett A., Pvt., USMC
CHRISTENSEN, Alfred Bennet, PFC, USMC
CLARK, Jesse Neilson, BM1c, USN
CRICHTON, Clint Millard, PFC, USMC
DILLMAN, Frank H., Corp., USMC

FROST, Lynn William, PFC, USMC
GUNNERSON, Carl Fredrick, F2c, USN
HENETZ, Michael, PFC, USMC
KIRKPATRICK, Edward Lewis, PFC, USMC
LINDSEY, Kenneth C., PFC, USMC
MARIETTE, Maxwell Albert, PhM2c, USN
McCoy, Clarence William, BM1c, USN
McVay, William A., PFC, USMC
MONTGOMERY, Robert Allen, RM1c, USN
MURPHY, Robert Bruce, PFC, USMC
REED, Clifton Milton, PFC, USMC
SALSBURY, Richard Leroy, PhM3c, USN
SOHN, Rosser E., Field Mus. Corp., USMC
STEWART, Jesse L., Tech. Sgt., USMC
WINTERHOLLER, 1st Lt. John, USMC
WOLLAM, J. P., Pvt., USMC

DISTRICT OF COLUMBIA

Dead

BARON, Lt. Cdr. Richard Swan, USN
BASINGER, Glenn William, BM1c, USN
BENSON, Maj. William W., USMC
BOOTH, Ens. Robert S., Jr., USNR
BRANNON, Kenneth Hugh, PhM1c, USN
CASTLE, Capt. Noel Oker, USMC
CROCKETT, Marshall Gordon, S1c, USN
DARBY, Ens. Marshall Eugene, Jr., USN
DECKELMAN, Lt. Daniel Bernard, USN
DENBY, Lt. Edwin, Jr., USN
DILLEN, Lt. Roscoe Franklin, Jr., USN
FONES, George Everett, FC3c, USN
HENSHAW, John Sylvester, S1c, USNR
HICKOX, Lt. Cdr. Ralph, USN
HOOPER, Granville L., Mach., USN
IRWIN, Warren Hamilton, AS, USNR
JOHNSON, Harlan Wayne, S1c, USN
KEENE, Thomas Bradley, GM1c, USNR
KELLY, Julian Alvin, AS, USNR
KING, Eugene Jordan, S2c, USN
LEWIS, Clifford Alton, Cox., USN
LINDSAY, Clifford Alexander, F1c, USCG
LYNCH, Emmett Isaac, Mus2c, USN
LYNCH, Patrick, SC1c, USN
MARSHALL, Lt. Cdr. Thomas Worth, Jr., USN
MASON, Henri Clay, 1st Mus., USNR
PIERCE, Ens. Beach, USNR
RANDALL, Lt. (jg) Gardner Durfee, USNR
RUSSETT, Arthur William, PhM1c, USN

TISDALE, Cdr. Ryland Dillard, USN (Ret.)
WHITE, Eugene Adam, S2c, USN

Wounded

MEYERS, Robert Konold, S2c, USN

Missing

CHANDLER, Ens. Barron Wallace, USNR
FAIRBANKS, Lt. John Francis, Jr., USN
GALLAGHER, William Joseph, Jr., RM3c, USNR
JENSEN, Lt. Milton Howard, Supply Corps, USN
SHELDON, Robert Thomas, S1c, USN
WARD, Elmer, S1c, USN
WOODRUFF, Lt. (jg) John Ford, USN

Prisoners of War

BARNINGER, Maj. Clarence Andrew, USMC
BENNETT, Ens. Wilmurt Addison, Jr., USNR
BEST, John S., PFC, USMC
BROMEYER, Capt. James R., USMC
BROWN, Maj. Luther A., USMC
COOK, Walter John, Aer1c, USN
CROSS, Lt. Cdr. Cornelius Tunnecliff, USNR
DECK, Vernon Melvin, F1c, USN
DIAL, Lt. Nathaniel Minter, USN

DUDLEY, Floyd J., Jr., Corp., USMC
FREE, Edward Gorman, PFC, USMC
FULTON, Lt. Robert Burwell, II, USN
HEIL, Maj. John Joseph, USMC
HOEFFEL, Capt. Kenneth Mortimer, USN
LEHMANN, Lt. Cdr. Harold Ruppert, Supply Corps, USN
McCRACKEN, Cdr. Alan Reed, USN
NEWMAN, Lt. Cdr. Samuel Arthur, USNR
O'ROURKE, Lt. James Stephen, USN
OSTROM, Jack C., PFC, USMC
PASZKIEWICZ, Andrew J., Tech. Sgt., USMC

PHIFER, Jim Bob, GM1c, USN
PORTZ, Cdr. Warner Philip, USN
ROBINTON, Capt. Roy, USMC
ROGERS, Lt. (jg) Leon William, USN
SEALES, Hollis Macgewin, WT1c, USN
SPEARS, Lt. (jg) William Oscar, Jr., USN
THYSON, Cdr. Leo Cromwell, USN
TINKER, Charles Richard, S2c, USN
WELLS, James Harold, Bkr1c, USN
WHITNEY, Lt. Cdr. Rintoul Thomas, USN
WOLFSHEIMER, Ens. Frank, USNR

ALASKA

Dead

SIMPSON, Ens. Edward, USNR
THOMPSON, Ens. Irvin Andrew Rubin, USN

Missing

SIMPSON, John Earl, RM2c, USN

Wounded

None

Prisoners of War

None

CANAL ZONE

Dead

LORENZANA, Alfredo, OC2c, USN

Wounded

None

Missing

APAS, Felix, SC1c, USNR

Prisoners of War

GILBERT, Ross Henry, F1c, USN

HAWAII

Dead

ALLEN, Lt. Edward Henry, USN
BLANCHARD, Walter Raleigh, Chief Torp., USN
CORUM, Lawrence Ray, CMM, USN
CROFT, Theodore Wheeler, AOM1c, USN
DO COSTA, Thomas, Pvt., USMC
GINN, Lt. (jg) James B., USN
GRENAT, Charles Tilden, ACRM, USN
GRIFFEN, Daniel Thornburg, AMM1c, USN
HARBIN, Earl Charles, CMM, USN
HENDERSON, Lt. Frank Hurst, Jr., USN
HIMEL, Ernest Pier, CBM, USN
ISHAM, Orville Adalbert, CGM, USN

JAMIESON, Glenn Albert, AMM1c, USN
MARZE, Andrew Michael, GM1c, USN
MORRIS, Fred Joseph, SM1c, USN
PETTIE, Robert Lee, RM1c, USN
SARMIENTO, Eusebio, OS2c, USN
SCHMITZ, Andrew James, F1c, USN
SHEECK, George, ACMM, USN
THOMAS, Lt. (jg) Lloyd, USN
WATSON, Raphael August, AMM1c, USN
WEST, Ens. William Price, USNR

Wounded

BARBOUR, William A., Platoon Sgt., USMC
CARMAN, John, CSK, USN
FINN, John William, ACOM, USN

FREY, Morton Neil, AOM1c, USN
LYONS, Dale Shope, AMM1c, USN
MORTON, Amasa Benjamin, ACMM, USN

Missing

FERNANDEZ, Paciano, MA1c, USNR
HEGERFELDT, Paul William, RM1c, USN
MALIT, Roman, OS3c, USNR
NELSON, Claud Luther, RM1c, USN
RISNER, Clifford Odice, EM1c, USN
SMITH, Lt. Cdr. Sidney Layton, USN
WEBB, James Francis, QM1c, USN

Prisoners of War

AGAR, Paul Raymond, 1st Sgt., USMC
BECK, William D., Platoon Sgt., USMC
BOEHM, Lucien Charles, Jr., MM2c, USN
BOLSTER, Richard Lovell, PhM1c, USN
BROUSSARD, Luke Henry, CRM, USN
CAMPBELL, Rodman Y., CMM, USN

FREEL, Edward Elmer, CCStd, USN
GRAHAM, Turner, CGM, USN
HAMLIN, Lt. (jg) Harold Sherwin, Jr., USN
HENSHAW, Ens. George Herbert, USNR
JOHNS, Bruce Eldon, CMM, USN
KETNER, Bernard Oprey, Platoon Sgt., USMC
MALKOWSKI, Harry Leo, CMM, USN
MAIZE, Thomas Woodrow, SC2c, USN
MILLER, Frank, 1st Sgt., USMC
MONTSCH, Henry Joseph, AM1c, USN
NAONE, Daniel Lanikuli, F1c, USN
PIERCE, Don Emerson, MM2c, USN
POTTER, Maj. George Hubbard, USMC
QUINN, Lt. David Long, Chaplain Corps, USN
RUSH, Dave James, Platoon Sgt., USMC
SCOTT, Irving Thomas, CWT, USN
STOCKDALE, Earl Henry, EM1c, USN
THARIN, Capt. Frank Cunningham, USMC

PUERTO RICO

Dead

BESHORE, Edward Arthur, AM2c, USN

CANADA

Dead

BERGIN, Roger Joseph, F2c, USN
ELLIS, Francis Arnold, Jr., EM3c, USN
LANG, Earl Willard, RM2c, USN

JAVA SEA CITATIONS—*continued*

Medal of Honor

ROOKS, Capt. Albert Harold
Born: 12/29/91, Colton, Wash.

For extraordinary heroism, outstanding courage, gallantry in action and distinguished service in the line of his profession as commanding officer of the USS HOUSTON during the period February 4–27, 1942, while in action with superior Japanese enemy aerial and surface forces. While proceeding to attack an enemy amphibious expedition, as a unit in a mixed force, the HOUSTON was heavily attacked by bombers; after evading four attacks she was heavily hit in a fifth attack, lost sixty killed and had one turret wholly disabled. Captain Rooks made his ship again seaworthy and sailed within three days to escort an important reinforcing convoy from Darwin to Koepang, Timor, Netherlands East Indies. While so engaged, another powerful air attack developed which by the HOUSTON's marked efficiency was fought off without much damage to the convoy. The Commanding General of all forces in the area thereupon cancelled the movement and Captain Rooks escorted the convoy back to Darwin. Later, while in a considerable American-British-Dutch force engaged with an overwhelming force of Japanese surface ships, HOUSTON with HMS EXETER carried the brunt of the battle and her fire alone heavily damaged one and possibly two heavy cruisers. Although heavily damaged in the actions, Captain Rooks succeeded in disengaging his ship when the flag officer commanding broke off the action and got her safely away from the vicinity, whereas one half of the cruise was lost.

UNIT CITATION

The President of the United States takes pleasure in presenting the PRESIDENTIAL UNIT CITATION to the UNITED STATES SHIP HOUSTON for service as set forth in the following CITATION:

"For outstanding performance against enemy Japanese forces in the Southwest Pacific from December 7, 1941 to February 28, 1942. At sea almost constantly, often damaged but self-maintaining, the HOUSTON kept the sea. She maneuvered superbly and with deadly anti-aircraft fire repulsed the nine-plane Japanese Bombing Squadrons attacking a troop convoy under her escort. Later, in company with other Allied ships, she engaged a powerful enemy force, carried the brunt of the action with her two remaining 8″ turrets and aided in damaging and routing two enemy heavy cruisers from the line of battle. On February 28, the HOUSTON went down, gallantly fighting to the last against overwhelming odds. She leaves behind her an inspiring record of valiant and distinguished service."

For the President
/s/ JAMES FORRESTAL
Secretary of the Navy

Index

Index

* P=Plates.